# Communication

## The Widening Circle

Estelle Zannes
**UNIVERSITY OF NEW MEXICO**

**ADDISON-WESLEY PUBLISHING COMPANY**
Reading, Massachusetts ■ Menlo Park, California
London ■ Amsterdam ■ Don Mills, Ontario ■ Sydney

The photographs on pages 70 and 82 are used by courtesy of Congressman Charles Wilson of
    Texas
The photographs on pages 75 and 100 were taken by Peter Manchester.
The photograph on page 162 is used by courtesy of Joe Murray.
The photograph on page 206 is used by courtesy of Mary Jean Thomas.
All other photographs in this book were taken by Tom Zannes.


**Library of Congress Cataloging in Publication Data**

Zannes, Estelle.
    Communication.

    Bibliography: p.
    Includes index.
    1. Communication.   I. Title.
P90.Z3        001.51        80-15150
ISBN 0-201-08997-1

ISBN 0-201-08997-1
ABCDEFGHIJ-DO-8987654321

# preface

The purpose of this book is threefold:

1. To acquaint the reader with everyday communication situations and to suggest ways to make those situations more effective.

2. To propose that from the time we get up in the morning until the time we retire at night our communication is evolving and dynamic, extending further and influencing others more than we are capable of imagining. Not only does our communication extend outward and embrace others, but with the use of communication technology the world comes to us.

3. To make specific suggestions about how to improve communication skills as well as how to acquire certain skills directly relevant to our modern information society.

The prologue "Up in the Morning" introduces an American family, Dora and Bert Marroquin and their children, Larry, Gary, and Jerry Lee. These people, as well as some of their acquaintences and friends, reappear in chapters throughout the book. Although during the course of a day Dora and her family speak to many people, I have chosen to mention only a few so as not to confuse the reader with too many names and incidents.

The Prologue depicts a single day in Dora's life from the time she wakes up in the morning. During the day, Dora, Bert, and others communicate in a variety of situations. Identification of those situations appears in the margins.

The reader will note that Dora starts her day with a message from the radio. She then communicates *intra*personally, that is, with herself. Many of us arise and attach meaning to some behavior, thus communicating internally or with self. Dora then moves on to a casual conversation with a person at the pool where she swims, communicating *inter*personally, that is, with another person in a face-to-face encounter. Later on she has a *dialogue* with a friend. I have chosen to distinguish the *casual conversation* from the *dialogue* although the situations may be very similar. The *dialogue*, however, suggests that the two persons are acquainted with each other and that there is a possibility they will continue the same or other conversations at a later date. There is a very fine line between the two types of communication situations, it is true.

When Dora becomes part of a *group* she continues to communicate *interpersonally*, but the situation changes and her circle of influence widens. It widens further when she engages in a *public speaking event*, which, though still interpersonal, is more structured and formal.

The impact of technology upon Dora's life and upon the lives of the others mentioned in this prologue is noted by the many media messages they receive.

All the communication situations are identified in the margins and these situations reappear throughout the book. The prologue is designed to acquaint the reader with the fact that during a *very* average day in anyone's life every possible type of communication situation is handled as a matter of course.

This book further acknowledges that no matter which profession we select, communication plays a major role, and, therefore, we need to acquire effective communication skills.

Chapter 1, "The Individual and the Widening Circle," explores the individual, and the reader is introduced to many communication concepts that will reappear throughout the book. The influences of environment, heredity, and personality are discussed, along with an explanation of needs which propel us all to communicate for satisfaction of those needs. What affects our perception and how we attach meaning to behaviors and events is explored. A section on how we as individuals extend our circle through the *serial transmission* of messages is a unique feature which continues to be a part of the book as it develops in other chapters.

Chapter 2 widens the circle and introduces "The Individual Plus One," continuing where Chapter 1 left off. This chapter begins with one of those who was introduced in the first chapter—Emma, the police officer. Situations involving two people are discussed: the *interview*, *the argument*, the *dialogue*, and the *casual conversation*. How we listen actively, how to build a supportive atmosphere, and the effects of nonverbal communication are highlighted in this chapter.

In Chapter 3, "The Group," we continue to gather others into our circle as it extends to a group. A definition of what constitutes a group, of formal and informal groups, of private and public groups, and suggestions of how to conduct oneself in groups begins the chapter. Methods of problem-solving, how to deal with conflict, and a look at crisis management make this chapter highly diversified, yet specific to groups.

Chapter 4, "Persuasion and the Widening Circle," suggests that most of our communication situations deal with acts of persuading others to believe and feel as we do or persuading others to modify their behaviors with regard to beliefs, values, or attitudes. This chapter suggests that we seek to find a common ground in all of our communication encounters in order to encourage discussion, strengthen freedom of choice, and acquire an understanding of human behavior. How to use argument as a tool for persuasion and different theories proposed through the ages makes this chapter the link between informal communication situations and formal public statements. Theories discussed in this chapter are *applied* realistically to our everyday experiences as well as to large public gatherings.

"The Big Arena: The Audience," brings us into the larger circle. Chapter 5 centers around the suggestion that, as we gather many people around us, we must turn our attention to *their needs* and speak to please, inform, or persuade them by finding a local or common ground.

Still keeping the audience in mind, we move on to Chapter 6, "The Big Arena: Organizing the Speech." A "how-to" approach includes pointers on how to prepare the outline, research the topic, select appropriate language, organize ideas, use emotional and logical proofs, and in general get ready for that public speaking event. Also included in the chapter are suggestions for preparing visual aids and selecting clothing for media messages as well as for "live" audiences. In this chapter the focus is on the *audience*.

In Chapter 7 the spotlight revolves and highlights the speaker: "The Big Arena: The Speaker." Included in this chapter are tips on packaging your image, dealing with anxiety, and actually delivering the speech. What the audience sees and what the audience hears are thoroughly analyzed.

In Chapter 8 we move from "The Big Arena" into the "Global Information Society" as we discuss humans and hardware in the Widening Circle. In this chapter we acknowledge that communication technology affects our lives on a daily basis. A discussion of all the most recent advances in telecommunication systems and their impact on our lives makes this chapter not only unique but necessary reading for the young person about to embark on a career in which communication plays a major role.

Thus the circle which started with a small voice inside us reaches out to include voices from outside our world. Some of us, like Dora, start with an outside message, internalize it, and then send it out until it becomes a social force affecting the lives of others, returning to us in new thought, which we, in turn, send out again.

Finally, the Epilogue states that our circle is ever growing, changing, widening. We are never static; what we say today affects us tomorrow. We can see our past; the future is unknown. But as our inner world turns slowly to face the future, the excitement of communicatng with others makes that world an adventurous and ever-changing one.

Albuquerque, New Mexico                                    E.Z.
May 1981

# author's note

All the people mentioned in this book are real; no names have been changed. On occasion a person might be identified by the role he or she plays, such as the driver, the sergeant, etc., particularly when a real-name identification might cause embarrassment.

All events related in this book actually happened. In some instances some of the details have been omitted or condensed for the sake of brevity.

You will meet the people mentioned in the prologue in many of the other chapters. Some incidents are continued from chapter to chapter until they are either resolved or changed. In this way we can follow the evolution of one idea: the widening of a circle of people and of influence.

When applicable, new faces and events are introduced in later chapters for the sake of variety.

I did not go out and search for my main character, Dora. I merely walked out of my front door, turned right, and met my neighbor. Had I turned left, I would have run into Em and Hopi and their two children. Their circle extends into the Navajo nation. But that's another story. . . .

# acknowledgments

To Timothy Peter Zannes for the prologue,

To Maria Zannes for the stories about Washington,

To Tom Zannes for the great pictures,

To Dora, Bert, Jerry Lee, Larry, and Gary Marroquin for allowing me to look into their lives,

To Bill Hungate for his cooperation at the Hair Shoppe,

To Mayor David Rusk for access to city hall,

To Congressman Charles Wilson for his input,

To Emma Gonzales for being such a good officer,

To Vici Taus for the clever illustrations,

To Peter Manchester for helping out with photographs,

To Sam Soleyn for his research on arguments,

To Joe Murray for his inspired speech,

To Mary Jean Thomas for her wise counsel,

And to the many other people mentioned in this book:

Many thanks for widening the circle of friendship to embrace us all from one end of the country to the other.

# contents

2

3

7

8

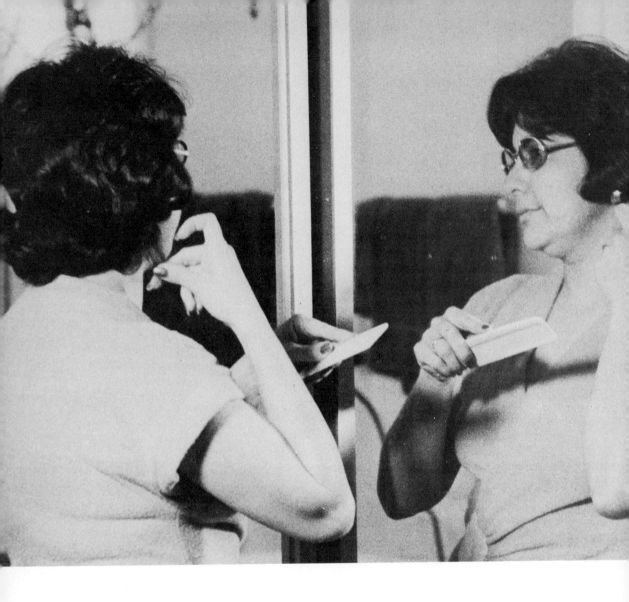

prologue:
up in the morning

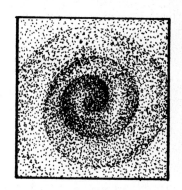

The music stops but Dora keeps on humming. The clock radio displays exactly 6:00 A.M. Dora presses the OFF button, then moves to the center of the room where she dresses quietly in front of the soft vanity light. Bert sleeps on.

Once down the carpeted stairs, away from her sleeping husband and children, she flips on the kitchen radio as she prepares her breakfast: grapefruit, decaffeinated coffee, and whole-wheat toast. The song "Send in the Clowns" is playing. It is one of Bert's favorites, and Dora smiles.

At 7:05 she hurries to the door, coffee cup in hand. She finishes her coffee in the car, and at 7:15 she plunges smoothly into the water at the Los Altos Swim-Club pool. One hour and one mile later, she is out of the pool.

"How's the water?" a swimmer asks.

"Great." She smiles at the swimmer who dives in, splashing her feet. "Great," she repeats inside her head, moving her shoulders. The soreness under her arm and in her right breast is gone; only the scars remind her, momentarily, of the pain. "Great!" This time the word is audible.

Resuming the drive to school, Dora listens to the news on the car radio.

A teachers' meeting is underway when she arrives, and she apologizes briefly.

"Sorry I'm late."

"That's okay, Dora. I was just stating my feelings about our disciplinary program and the sad shape it's in. I don't think that kids should be allowed to bring books into the room they're being disci-

## BEGINNING HUMAN RELATIONSHIPS IN THE WIDENING CIRCLE

*Intrapersonal communication: Dora smiles to herself.*

*Interpersonal communication: casual conversation.*

*Intrapersonal communication: Dora communicates with self.*

*Mass communication medium: radio.*

*Interpersonal communication: group problem-solving session.*

plined in. That isn't a form of punishment." The speaker is a sixth-grade history teacher.

*Interpersonal group: argument.*

The vice-principal, a young woman, interrupts the speaker. "Having the child sit in a room and just get further and further behind in school work is not the answer to the disciplinary problems at our middle school. The ones that get disciplined are usually behind in their studies, and making them get more behind in their work is not the answer."

"Making it a vacation isn't the answer either," states the history teacher.

Dora interrupts before the vice-principal can answer: "It does make sense to look for ways to help the kids who get the low test scores, and it does seem they're the ones who end up also needing discipline."

*Interpersonal group: conclusion.*

A loud ringing noise puts an abrupt end to the discussion.

"We'll take this up again," says the vice-principal as the group scatters. She and Dora walk out of the room together.

*Interpersonal dialogue.*

"I think he's running for School Board again," she whispers. Dora laughs.

At 8:50 Dora stands in front of her first class of eight-grade boys and girls.

*Public speaking: introduction; Dora starts her lesson, which will include visual aids.*

"Okay class, settle down. Today I'm going to try to go over the first page of the handout, which has a lot of nutritional information . . ."

Dora begins her first lesson in a room filled with stoves and sewing machines.

At 7:30 A.M. Jerry Lee jumps on Bert's bed and shakes his father. "Wake up, Dad!" he yells.

*Interpersonal communication: dialogue.*

Bert opens one eye and looks at the clock. "Go away; it's not 7:30 yet."

Fully dressed, Jerry Lee stands in front of his mother's vanity and combs his hair for seven minutes, watching the clock.

*Nonverbal communication: Jerry Lee combs hair and waits.*

"7:30 Dad!" he yells.

Bert leaps out of bed and starts dressing, snatching his clothes from the chair.

"Larry and Gary up?" he asks the question as he draws on his shirt, moving to the adjoining bedroom. Larry rushes by him toward the bathroom.

*Interpersonal communication: dialogue that occurs almost daily.*

Kneeling beside Gary, he imitates a child's sing-song voice and chides his son. "Wake up Gary. It's 7:30, wake up."

*Interpersonal: imitating.*

In ten minutes Bert is downstairs, happy that he showers in the evening. He turns on the television, moves to the kitchen area. Jerry Lee has already started making his breakfast. The twins race downstairs, pour their cereal, eat, and are outside before Jerry Lee is finished. Jerry Lee yells and runs after them. Bert turns off the television and is outside thirty seconds later.

*Mass communication medium: television.*

*Interpersonal: argument.*

The twins are writing on the frosted windows of the station wagon. Although the temperature dropped during the night, the day would be sunny as usual.

"You spelled your middle name wrong, Gary," says Larry.

"Jerry Lee said that was how to spell it," retorts Gary.

As Bert approaches the car, Leonard, the physical-education teacher, drives up, parks his car, and joins Bert in scraping the windows. The boys jump out and help.

*Interpersonal group: problem-solving, action.*

Finally everyone is back in the car, and four minutes later the twins are dropped off at their school. Bert yells "good-bye" to them but they don't seem to hear. He laughs and says, "Brush your teeth." But they have melted into the playground scene.

Jerry Lee is next. After he departs, the drive to work will take about twelve minutes. Bert and Leonard, who both moonlight on weekends and some nights at the Broadway Department Store in the Winrock Shopping Center, talk about the job.

*Interpersonal: dialogue.*

"I told them I would miss yesterday and that I was sick and would not be back for a little while unless I got rid of this cold." Bert laughs and produces a cough.

"They're crazy. If you take one day off, they don't give you the day off with pay, but if you take two off, they give you one of the days off with pay. And all the people in the department always take only one day off and don't get paid for it," Leonard observes.

*Technology: copy machine*

At school Bert's first stop is the office, where he picks up some mimeograph master copies and heads for the mimeograph machine across the hall.

*Nonverbal communication: Bert dances.*

Bert puts the sheets into the machine and starts to run off the copies. Two fourth-graders pass him, and he begins to dance to the beat of the mimeograph machine as it drumrolls sheet after sheet across the master copy.

"Weird," says one child.

*Interpersonal group: children greet Bert.*

Three first-graders crowd around the machine. They are his students.

"Hi, teacher." A six-year-old Chicano boy looks up from behind a woolen sailor's cap.

"Hi, Augie." Bert says hello to each child.

"I brought a story from the newspaper," says Augie.

"Good. I'll read it in class."

*Nonverbal communication: children and Bert walk happily together.*

Like the pied piper, Bert leads the children into the classroom.

At 8:45 AM Bert and his class pledge allegiance to the flag with words that all stick together: "Ipledgelegencetodaflagof . . ."

*Public speaking.*

"Close the door, and turn off the lights. It's time for *Electric Company*." Augie is already climbing the stand to turn on the television. It is his Friday morning ritual. No one officially gave him the job. He just did it one day.

*Mass communication medium: television.*

"See how many words you can remember from the show today. Five minutes' free time for the one who writes the most words."

Angela runs up and hugs and kisses Bert, but no one is paying attention because Angela always hugs and kisses her teacher in the morning. Everyone else is watching the show.

*Public speaking: Bert gives instructions.*
*Nonverbal communication: Angela hugs her teacher.*

Dora walks as she lectures: "Some of you last semester said that you were having candy bars and potato chips with Coke for lunch, eating no breakfast, and having several snacks of junk food before dinner."

*Public speaking: introduction*

*Feedback: audience response.*

*Feedback: negative response.*

*Public speaking: attention-getting device.*

*Audience participation.*

*Conclusion to public address: giving instructions and visual aids.*

*Interpersonal (channel, wire): telephone conversation: Bill is listening then speaks.*

*Mass communication medium: radio.*
*Interpersonal: casual conversation.*

The students laugh, heads nodding.

"Then you have to realize that your bodies are at the stage where they need the most nutrition of their lives."

She stops midway in the room, looks for a moment at two girls, one of whom is busy combing the other's hair.

"Martha," she says, calling attention to the event. "You know better than that."

The girl stops combing and smiles apologetically.

Dora continues to move around the room, talking about vitamin A. Suddenly she stops. She is in front of the light switch. She flicks it off.

The students are attentive.

As the students "ohh" and "ahh," she tells them to watch one another's eyes carefully as the lights go back on, and to notice how the pupils change with the light. The students now relate vitamin A to the enlargement of the pupils. Dora continues to tell them about vitamins. When she finishes, she picks up a sheaf of papers and says, "Remember I'm going to give a test on this on Friday, so you should write that down. You'll be getting five papers between now and Thursday, and they will cover nutrition. When you finish the papers that are take-home work, put them in the tray marked Ungraded Papers." She hands out the papers.

As she stands at the front of the room watching papers move from hand to hand, her own hand moves up to her hair, and she starts twirling a strand, thinking to herself that she needs a good cut.

Martha is combing her friend's hair again. She stops for a moment, then raises her hand, the comb still clutched in it: "Are we going to cook Christmas dinner again?"

Bill Hungate holds the telephone to his ear, resting it on his shoulder as he deftly moves the dryer in one hand while his other hand moves a brush through his customer's hair.

"Okay Dora, Saturday morning, quarter to eight."

His receptionist takes the phone from his ear.

"Put Dora Marroquin down for a cut at 7:45 tomorrow."

The radio is on, and the strains of "Ain't Misbehavin' " fill the little alcove.

"Boy, that's an oldie," he says.

His customer nods. "Everything comes back if you live long enough."

Bill smiles and with a flourish removes the towel from her neck; they look critically at her hair. Satisfied, his customer rises and places a bill on the shelf below his mirror. As she turns to leave, a short middle-aged gentleman comes into the store.

*Nonverbal communication: Bill and customer view hair.*

"Turn down the lights, people, and stand by—because *I'm on!*"

Bill waves to the departing customer, who raises her eyebrows and smiles. He then turns to his next customer, Howie Lane, a local little-theater actor whose daytime job is that of candy-store proprietor. "Center stage, Howie!" he says.

*Public speaking: Howie makes an entrance.*

After calling Bill and making her appointment, Dora moves to the teacher's lounge. She muses that she really hates starting a new unit because she must lecture for a whole period. She prefers cooking the food to talking about it, prefers sewing the garment than talking about how to sew it. Her students like making things, too—rather than listening—she decides.

*Intrapersonal communication: Dora thinks about her day.*

In the teacher's lounge Dora sees her friend and colleague, Mary Ann, and asks how her marriage is coming along. The answer is a long sigh, and Dora laughs. "Come on," she says, "I'll buy you a cup of coffee."

*Interpersonal: dialogue.*

"No, no," says Mary Ann, "it's my turn. You bought last time."

"No," replys Dora, "I've already got it." She puts the quarters into the machine.

"I have a letter from Maria," says Dora. She takes the letter from her notebook and laughs, "I asked her what she does all day, and listen to this:

*Medium: print; Dora has letter from friend.*

*Dear Dora: I must speak with about fifty people each day. I'm concerned and interested when talking to constituents; I listen and ask questions of lobbyists and sometimes debate. I trade information with other staff people. I'm "official" when requesting information from the administration or agencies, I advise other members of the office in addition to listening to advice. I discuss the merits of various political moves with the Congressman and the media and the administrative assistant. I laugh and joke with friends and staff members and then I call my mother because I want sympathy, love and advice about life.*

"And then she has a great story about the congressman and what he said when Carter fired his cabinet." Dora chuckles and hands the letter to her friend. Reading the story, Mary Ann laughs and says, "He's right on about the monkeys."

*Using technology: communicating by telephone.*

Dora adds, "She called me from Washington the other day. She has a WATS line."

"That's what I need. Next time she calls, tell her to say hello to the President for me."

*Interpersonal group: conflict.*

At 4:00 Jerry Lee stands by as Robbie pounds his fist into Doug's face. He follows sympathetically as Doug runs home crying. Jerry Lee waits outside, keeping an eye on his brothers, who are playing down the street.

*Interpersonal: nonverbal communication: Jerry Lee and his friend wait.*

One of his friends comes up and stands with him, and they watch a car come speeding down the street. Doug's father jumps out of the car and strides into the house. Five minutes later a police car arrives and stops in front of the house.

The drama builds for Jerry Lee as the officer emerges from the police car.

*Interpersonal: nonverbal communication: Emma gestures.*

Officer Emma Gonzales, sunglasses perched atop her head, hooks her thumb into her belt, and says "Hi, boys." Encouraged, Jerry Lee and his friend approach the car to talk to her.

"Are you going to Doug's house? He got beat up."

Emma nods, walks toward the house, and tells the boys to wait outside. She knocks on the door and enters at a command. She sees a young boy, a man, and a woman. The boy has a huge bruise under his eye. His cheeks are discolored and swollen.

*Interpersonal: interview session.*

"Who hit you??" she asks.

"Robbie."

"I don't allow my boy to fight," interjects the mother. "I'd better take him to the hospital."

Emma nods. "Take care of your son. Those bruises look like they need attention. I can get the information from your husband and the witnesses. I'll come back if I need your statements."

Relieved, the mother departs with her son.

"Won't you sit down?" says the father.

Emma complies, commenting, "Those bruises look pretty bad. I must tell you, though, that this is a civil action. I will make out a report, and it'll be on file if you decide to press charges."

"I do. I'm going to put an end to this. This isn't the first time that kid beat someone up." The father is determined.

"Did you see the incident?"

"No, my wife called me after Doug came home. I was here in five minutes."

*Interpersonal: interview using open and closed questions.*

"Do you mind if I call in the boys who are outside, so they can answer some questions?" The father nods, and Emma goes to the door.

The curious boys are still there. When Emma calls them, they eagerly come forward and enter the house.

"Anyone see the fight?"

They both nod.

"You did not," says Jerry Lee to his friend.

"What happened?" Emma asks Jerry Lee.

*Interpersonal: interview, information giving.*

"Well, we passed by Robbie's little brother, and I don't know what but somebody said something to him, and he ran home, and then Robbie came out and started beating up Doug."

"How big is Robbie?"

The father interjects, "He's taller than Doug and has muscles."

"Doug didn't do nothin. I saw it." says Jerry Lee.

"Thanks, boys," says Emma. She asks a few more questions of the father and then tells him she hopes his boy will be all right.

"I'm going to put a stop to this," he says firmly. "Those boys are forming gangs."

As Emma returns to her car, Jerry Lee runs after her.

*Interpersonal: interview, information gathering.*

"Where do you live?" she asks.

"Just down the street."

"What's your address?"

"4150 Los Trachos." Then Jerry Lee adds, "Is Robbie going to jail? Are you going to arrest him?"

"No," says Emma, "I'm just going to file a report. Now you be good."

Jerry Lee nods vigorously.

At home after school, Dora is in the laundry room sorting clothes. The twins come in, bringing more laundry.

"Is this everything?" she asks. Gary nods.

"Where are my clothes and Daddy's?" she asks.

*Interpersonal: small-group argument.*

Larry groans, "Do we hafta?"

"You're supposed to pick up *all* the laundry," reminds Dora.

"But that's *your* clothes," protests Gary.

"Hey, don't I cook for you as well as for myself?"

"But that's *easy* work. We hafta do the *hard* work." This is from Larry.

As Dora turns to put soap in the machine, Gary yells 'We picked up ours!' Then the twins race outside, jump on their bicycles and are down the street before she can protest.

*Intrapersonal: Dora talks to self.*

"So *I* get the easy job," Dora says to herself. "Well, we'll see about that."

Jerry Lee comes in breathless: "Robbie beat up Doug, and the policeman came, and she asked *me* the questions!"

"You weren't fighting?"

"Noooooo!"

"Tell me about it at dinner, and go call Daddy. He has to work tonight."

"What about Larry and Gary?"

"They're cooking their own meals for a while," says Dora, moving into the kitchen and toward the microwave oven.

"Ha, all they know how to do is scramble eggs," says Jerry Lee disdainfully.

"I know," smiles Dora. "I *know*."

"Hey Ma, did I tell you that policeman was a police*woman*?"

*Interpersonal: dialogue.*

The street light comes on as Emma pulls into the closed gas station. In a few seconds a second police car drives alongside, facing the opposite direction.

"Hi," says Emma.

The officer nods. For a few minutes they just sit in silence.

"I had this accident, and the people told different stories. I mean they really conflicted. I'm going to check the witness myself." She states the information almost as a question.

The older officer nods. "That's okay. Hey—hear the story about the sergeant?"

*Interpersonal: dialogue including nonverbal signals and gestures.*

*Interpersonal communication: detailed illustration.*

"No."

"He put his hands right on the camera. Pushed Norm, the *Tribune* photographer. Now I don't like reporters or photographers, but Norm's not a bad guy. He printed one of me at that suicide."

"Well, sometimes those guys get out of hand. Remember the TV photographer at that stake-out? I know how the sarge feels."

The male officer nods, then sits silent for a moment. "Hey, speaking about that suicide. Did I ever tell you what happened when the lieutenant walks in? This guy has just shot his brains out, and he's on the couch, and we come in, and we're trying to settle the family down and wait for the ambulance. You know, we're soothing the wife, and everyone is crying but sorta quieting down when the lieutenant comes in and says, right off, '*Where's the stiff?*' Everyone starts wailing again. Then he walks around like a pompadour and says, 'Got a cigarette?' And I say, 'No, I don't smoke.' Everyone else is looking at him, but no one offers him a cigarette. Then he spots the guy on the couch, and you know there's blood all over the shirt, but outlined in the shirt pocket is a pack of filter kings. The lieutenant bends over and grabs the guy by the knee and shakes him. 'Hey, mind if I have a cigarette?' he says and reaches into the pocket, takes out the pack, takes a cigarette, puts the pack back, and lights up."

"No," gasps Emma, "I don't believe it! The suicide?"

"Yeh, the guy's dead on the couch."

The story is so macabre that they both laugh.

*Technology: radio, plus serial transmission of message.*

The radio in Emma's car starts buzzing: "403."

Emma picks up the radio and flicks the switch, "403, Adam."

As she pulls away from the gas station, and the companionship of her fellow officer, a slight drizzle hits the car windshield. She drives a few blocks and turns into a residential area, grazing the curb with her right front tire. A slow hissing noise is audible. "Oh no," she groans. "Oh *no*."

*Mass communication medium: television.*

After working two jobs Bert relaxes in front of the television set while Dora reads. Since it's Friday night, the twins and Jerry Lee are sprawled on the floor in front of the set waiting for the ten o'clock news and a glimpse of their neighbor, Loren, who anchors the news on weekends. A bowl of popcorn is on the floor.

*Mass communication medium: television, persuasive messages.*

At two minutes before ten, three commercials come on in succession:

"Why tuck her in with pink sheets when you can tuck her in with pretty pink sheets that have a great April-fresh smell?"

"To kill germs and odors, I use Lysol Spray every day . . . Have you used your Lysol Spray today?" (To which Bert replies, "No I haven't used my Lysol Spray today.")

"I thought I had everything perfect for my sister's bridal shower . . . then I noticed the spotty glasses . . . get the Cascade look . . . virtually spotless."

(Bert continues to mumble: "*I* had everything *perfect* for *my* sister's bridal shower.")

*Interpersonal: conversation.*

"What sister!" It is an exclamation—not a question—from Dora.

Lively music is on, and the attention turns to the television set and the evening news with Loren Nancarrow.

The twins are fast asleep, and Dora is dozing; Jerry Lee notes this, and even though he considers himself a "big boy," he climbs up on Bert's lap.

*Interpersonal group: nonverbal and verbal communication.*

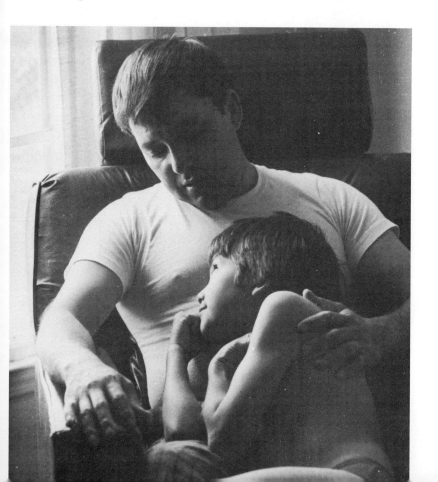

# 1 the individual and the widening circle

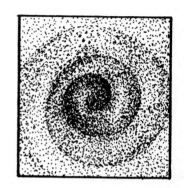

We arise, perched precariously on a point in time. What we say, how we feel at that moment of awareness, puts our world in motion.

Dora wakes up in the morning, pauses at her vanity to reflect upon her image, moves silenty down the stairs, flips on the radio, listens, and smiles. As she begins her day, she becomes a central part of a living system that moves outward to involve others, widening her circle of influence as the day unfolds. Dora herself unfolds slowly, like a flower, as she moves smoothly through the cool waters, submerged in her thoughts. Dora and her friend, Maria, though miles apart, begin their days alike, preferring to communicate *intrapersonally*, that is, with self, before meeting the day's challenges.

Bert bounces out of bed laughing, chiding his children into action, hurrying them into the car, moving quickly into his professional world, and continuing to display that energy as he dances at the mimeograph machine. Bill Hungate is energized in the morning by the loud music from his radio, which, he claims, helps propel him into a world where he spends much of his time listening.

What determines the individual ways in which we behave? Why does Dora swim, Bert dance, and Bill listen?

Of course there are hereditary influences. Certainly, especially of late, people seem to be aware of their roots and interested in genetics.

Another *major* influence on human behavior is the environment in which a person has grown up and lives.

## ENVIRONMENT

What is environment? Environmentalists say it is that which nature has provided—air, water, climate, forests, mountains, minerals, plants, and animals—and that which humans have added or subtracted with their intelligence, ingenuity, greed, and carelessness.

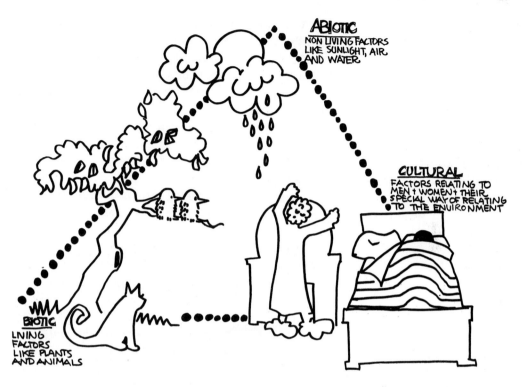

In that sense it is everything around us. Environment is also every*one* around us: our families, the people in our neighborhoods, the people we work with, the people we pass throughout the day, and even the expressions of their faces. Environment is also the *feeling* we have when we get up in the morning facing a new day and the degree of satisfaction we realize when we go to bed at the end of that day. Feelings come from our *inner* environment, which is greatly influenced by our *outer* environment. We are, in fact, parts of an environmental triangle.

Every part of our triangle greets us as we awaken: the sun coming in through the shutters; the tree that we planted in front of our window to replace the one bulldozed for our new subdivision; the thumping of our dog's tail against our bedroom door; the way we arranged our furniture so that our television set is within reach when we awaken.

Photographer and painter Edward Steichen said that one day he looked out of his living room window and noticed for the first time a tree he had planted long before. "I've had a love affair with that tree

*Environment is everything and everyone around us.*

ever since," he told a young reporter. And for years he photographed the little shadblow tree as it became part of his living environment.

An old Indian philosophy claims people are part of a delicately balanced universe in which all components, all life forms and elements, interrelate and interact so that no part is more or less important than another, and only people can upset the balance. As part of an environmental triangle, we may be a part of that delicately balanced universe—if so, our behavior has widespread influence not only on ourselves and those nearby, but also on a great many others.

*Our environment allows us to look inward as well as outward.*

Our environment allows us to look inward as well as outward. Dora begins her day looking inward, turning her eyes toward herself. She closes them as she swims, feeling refreshed, stronger with every stroke. She says to herself, "I am doing something good for myself." As Dora's self-image is strengthened by the harmony of her inner environment, the people and things that surround her are affected.

Dora's environmental triangle is a part of a larger living system that becomes a family, a neighborhood, a city, a nation, a world. But in that total environment she has her own physical and emotional inner environment, an environment that revolves about her. *"Cada cabeza es un mundo,"* she says. "Each head is a world." She comes to her family, her school, her friends, carrying with her her own environment—just as we all do.

Though we have touched only lightly on hereditary influences, we accept that they exist. Our hereditary influences and our environmental influences greatly affect our personalities. Heredity and environment combine to produce the personality that people "see."

Most of us think about personality as what we can observe in someone from "outside." We might talk about an individual and his or her personality as a set of *behavioral characteristics*: "Dora is so *warm* and *sensitive*," observes Maria, her good friend. "He is certainly *outgoing*," Bill's customers say of him.

## PERSONALITY

HOWARD IS SHY

EFFIE IS LIVELY

JOHN IS DULL

HENRY IS ANGRY

ANNE BOLEYN IS WORRIED

How do others decide that a person is "warm" or "friendly" or has a "great personality"? In most instances our friends or enemies obtain clues to our personality by observing something we do or say. Alport and Cantril (1934) studied the extent to which the natural voice is a valid indicator of personality; they concluded that the voice definitely conveys correct information concerning inner and outer characteristics. Later, Addington (1963) found that speakers using greater varieties of pitch were perceived as dynamic and extroverted. He also found that people react negatively to nasal voices and other vocal indicators. This would seem to indicate that we could change our personalities by simply changing our ways of speaking. At least others would perceive us differently if such changes were effected.

Is personality something over which we have ultimate control, or are we born with certain characteristics? Further, is personality what others perceive about us, or is it what we feel about ourselves?

*We believe personality is in fact a balance of how we perceive ourselves and how others perceive us.*

This book will not set forth a definitive answer, because we believe personality is fashioned by *both* the inner and outer environment, and is in fact a balance of how we perceive ourselves and how others perceive us.

What are we born with? The genetic "information" of an organism is embodied in the precise sequence of the four kinds of nucleotide base—adenine, guanine, thymine and cytosin—in the DNA molecules of the nuclei of its cellular constituency. Cells communicate and exchange genetic information and give rise to offspring of mixed parentage. Genetic communication, namely sex, occurs when two gametes (cell types specialized for just such intercourse) meet and pool their entire complement of DNA. Each parent contributes an equal amount of information. Some of that information determines physical characteristics: the color of our hair, eyes, skin; our basic body structures; certain strengths or weaknesses that will affect development.

Our physical well-being often influences our self-concept. Philosophers in ancient Greece held that the three most important parts of a person were the emotions (spiritual), the body (physical), and the mind (rational). Only when there was harmony among the three did true beauty exist. While these philosophers agreed that reason should control the other parts, they also stressed the idea that a person's well-being depended on a combination of a strong body, spiritual or ethical consideration, and the ability to engage in some mental gymnastics.

## Self-concept

*Self-concept can be influenced by others around us.*

We often behave in ways consistent with our self-concepts; that is, we live up to our own image. Sometimes this is referred to as a self-fulfilling prophecy. If we perceive ourselves as being "quiet," we may not speak up at meetings. But self-concept can be influenced by others around us. For example if we finally do stand up and speak, and our audience applauds us warmly, we may change our self-concept in that area. However, people tend to perceive messages selectively and respond only to those consistent with their self-concepts. If we really believe something about ourselves, we try to find evidence to support that belief. We create a personal identity, accept a social identity, and show others our paper identity. In a highly technological world we deal with such tools as credit cards and social-security numbers. When Emma stops a car, she does an NCIC (national computer check). What's on paper or in the machine identifies us and categorizes us. At times we become part of a "group image" and then we communicate with the image instead of the person as she or he actually is.

Certainly our *heredity*, all that internal information transmitted by our parents and stored in our brains, plus our *environment*, which contains our self-concept and how others perceive us and the influence of everything and everyone around us, combine to produce a personality that is then evaluated by everyone in our circle. Our personality includes those instincts and impulses that make us love and hate; it includes our bodies, which attract others to us, and our ability to deal intelligently and rationally with reality. Our personality can give us a clue to how we define our needs and what motivates us to secure those needs.

*Our heredity and our environment combine to produce a personality that is then evaluated by others.*

## NEEDS

*Needs are requirements of life, things we feel we lack.*

We interract with our environment in order to satisfy certian needs. Needs are requirements of life, things we feel we lack. Needs are not necessarily essentials: they may range anywhere on the scale from that which is vital to physical survival to the most outrageously flippant luxury imaginable. Dora needs a cup of coffee every morning, and she also felt she "needed" the diamond ring Bert bought for her at a forty-percent discount (a discount, incidentally, which he felt *he* "needed").

Needs fall into categories, and all people want to satisfy these needs. Because of our personalities, our individual priorities differ. Sometimes our professions are indicators of the positioning in which we order our needs. Dora seems to place self-fulfillment high on the ladder and is also very interested in the fulfillment of others. Emma, a police officer, places safety high on her list.

Needs fall into the following categories but not necessarily in the following order for everyone: that depends upon heredity, environment, and personality; we are members of a very variable species—no two of us are exactly alike.

**A Further Note on Needs**

Since so many have studied so long to acquaint us with how our basic human needs motivate us to perform certain acts, we should understand that opinions—like individuals—vary greatly in this area.

Abraham Maslow (1943) defined a sequential hierarchy of needs. His categories are:

1. Physiological well-being
2. Safety
3. Acceptance
4. Esteem
5. Self-actualization

According to Maslow, human beings must satisfy basic physiological needs, such as hunger and thirst, before becoming concerned with the higher-order needs of safety, acceptance, esteem, self-actualization.

Herzberg, Mausner, and Snyderman (1959) attempted to determine what motivates people to become more productive and more satisfied with jobs and working conditions. Their results indicate that some kinds of work are more satisfying than others and that work experiences associated with positive feelings include achievement, recognition, work itself, responsibility, and advancement. Work experiences that cause dissatisfaction include poor interpersonal relationships with peers and superiors, poor supervision, and unfair salary practices, company policy, or administration. None of these findings is astonishing.

*Physiological*: These are needs such as air and sleep, that usually take care of themselves. Dora and Bert feel the children will not get enough sleep unless they go to bed early. Many parents are more conscious of these needs in their children than in themselves. We all, however, feel cold or heat, hunger or pain, and will instinctively strive to become more comfortable by taking care of these needs.

*Safety*: Safety is freedom from danger, designed to keep the body intact from external threat. This need is high on some people's lists. To be safe, some people will forego the quest for status or even, at times, the need for food. When Emma first joined the police force, her husband, a deputy fire chief, feared for her safety. She had to convince him as well as the male officers that she was secure in her position and able to secure the safety of others.

*Ego*: We fight for psychological life. We need to know that our colleagues regard us favorably. Some of us need status, recognition, and prestige more than we need safety. A psychological profile of executives in national television indicated that status was more important than money, for example. Through the mass media, Tom, our reporter/photographer, recognizes this need when he points the camera at a politician, a businessperson, or a prominent citizen. Because of technological advances in media, society may be evolving so that fulfillment of this need is within easy reach of those who seek it.

*Self-fulfillment*: The need to develop ourselves, to become a complete individual, to mature and become aware of others is primary for some people. As an educator, Bert recognizes this need in young people and assists them in achieving it at a very early age.

Dora wakes up in the morning and feels thirsty. She drinks a cup of coffee and satisfies that need. It is not, however, that easy to satisfy all our needs. Many patterns of behavior in our lives today end in frustration. When Emma was a clerk at city hall, she felt the need to be more fulfilled in her job. Although she worked hard at her job, she was not satisfied that she was maturing and learning. She finally felt that her clerk's position would never satisfy her self-fulfillment need. Because of a change in her environment (i.e., women were moving into jobs generally reserved for men), she applied for police work. Her goals were not easily obtainable but she persevered and eventually satisfied her need for job fulfillment. Sometimes, when we cannot satisfy a

need, we select an alternative activity (as Emma did) that can replace the initial need.

However, at times the alternative activity is not socially acceptable and leads us to trouble. Emma daily deals with people who are frustrated and who sometimes indulge in highly antisocial behavior. She must understand this behavior and be equipped to deal with it. Since she spends most of her time in interpersonal situations, she must be aware of those things that influence behavior.

Like Emma, we all must try to understand why people act as they do and how they interact with their environment. We have seen that we interact because we must satisfy those needs important to us. Now we shall discover that this satisfaction is gained most often by means of communication with ourselves and with others.

The very essence of being human is communication, and our lives depend upon it in more ways than we can name.

---

**COMMUNICATION**

*Internal Communication*: We have a backlog of genetic messages, and without these messages we would not know who we are; without our internal communication system we could not live.

Our internal communications are handled by a network consisting of nervous and metabolic subsystems. John R. Pierce (1972) says: "Nerve impulses are like telephone calls that are switched to a particular recipient and heard nowhere else. Hormones are like messages addressed to individuals or groups but sent out *broadcast*: only those concerned need respond."

Living cells communicate by means of hormones and nerve fibers and information is found in the molecules of nucleic acid. Our bodies tell us things. We cannot live without internal communication.

We can live without *external* communication but few of us do or would wish to. Even hermits communicate with nature.

*External Communication*: When Dora steps out of the water she enjoys exchanging a few words, however casual, with the next swimmer. "Water's great this morning!" The swimmer smiles, nods, and plunges in. Dora has shared a message.

Recently, Emma the police officer came upon a pair of very young boys shooting craps against a grafitti-decorated wall.

"Hey," she said, "what're you doing?"

"Nothin," said one of the boys. The other looked up at the officer who stood, legs slightly apart, hands resting on her hips.

"Nothin," echoed the other boy from his squatting position, his eyes widening at the sight of the female officer.

"Well do it somewhere else, boys," said Emma.

The boys scrambled.

A simple example of a communication situation, yet both the officer and the boys were engaged in some pretty complex mental gymnastics that involved perception, experience with language, a backlog of experience in understanding behavior, and some application of practical communication skills. Without that backlog, the simple question-and-answer exchange would have no meaning at all.

We communicate externally when meaning is assigned to a message.

Human beings actively seek to make a situation meaningful, and this effort toward meaning influences the way in which a person produces and reproduces information. Barnlund (1968) defined the phenomenon of communication as an effort to find meaning: "A creative act initiated by man in which he seeks to discriminate and organize cues

*We cannot live without internal communication.*

## Meaning

*Human beings seek to make a situation meaningful.*

so as to orient himself in his environment and satisfy his changing needs." The search for meaning, therefore, is directed by attitudes, interests, and affects.

But practically speaking, what *do* we mean when we say "Don't do it here"? What did the boys mean when they said "Nothin"? Certainly they were doing *somethin.*

Many scholars believe that communication is the *sharing of meaning,* that is an understandable statement only if more than one person is involved. However, we have seen that communication can occur with just one person involved, but only if that person assigns meaning to a message. The message can be any behavior, person, activity, word, sound, or physical object—indeed, anything to which meaning can be assigned. So every behavior actually has the potential of being assigned meaning.

Dora creates meaning from the activity (swimming). In a sense she is communicating the message intrapersonally (with self) that the activity is good for her. If Dora creates meaning inside her head (which is her world), then she has had an individual experience that she can describe as communicating with herself. Since each person assigns a meaning to what is observed, the term "communication," used in a strictly technical sense, refers exclusively to one person's assigning meaning to some experience (Pace, 1979).

However, if two people are involved, and each one assigns a meaning to the event, then each person can send the message and receive it simultaneously.

Let's take an ideal situation: Dora and her friend, Susan, are drinking coffee. They smile, sigh, and clink cups: "Now that's coffee!" they both remark and laugh. Each of them has assigned meaning to an activity. In this instance they expressed the same thought in identical words, a rare occurrence. But they have obviously shared a previous experience, have transacted a message, and have influenced each other. In their backlog of experience they remember a similar moment, and "Now that's coffee!" is blurted out by both parties. The actual words "that's coffee" can mean a variety of things to a variety of people, but to Dora and Susan the meaning is special and specific to them.

In communication situations each person in the transaction assigns a meaning to a message. It is when the meaning is similar that effective communication takes place. This, however, is extremely hard to achieve since our experiences are never exactly the same, although they may approach a degree of similarity. Shared experiences or the understanding of one another's environment are most conducive to effective communication taking place.

Meaning is greatly affected by our *perception*. That is because while we live in a world of many levels, we experience only one. What we "see" is not the thing itself but the reflection of it. Beneath the surface of things is a layer of events that can be seen with special instruments, like X-rays and microscopes. Beyond the X-ray level is another made up of the interaction of electrical and magnetic forces in constant motion. Still, though we see only patterns of colors and corners of things, the world outside has a tremendous effect on us. But we can react only to a very small part of all that goes on.

**Perception**

Very much depends on how we view ourselves, on our ability to accept others and their opinions and feelings, and on our empathy and sensitivity to others: in other words how we accept our inner and outer environment.

In this environment no two experiences can ever be identical. For example, when we see something, the light rays emitted or reflected from the outside events we have chosen to look at are focused on a tiny 3/8-inch spot on the back wall of the eye. They change into electrical impulses, which set off a chain of electrical and chemical events in our nervous system. Those light rays that enter Dora's eyes do not enter Bert's eyes, and his experience and her experience are individual and unique to him and to her. Yet their fields of experience can *overlap* (as did Dora's and Susan's) when there are similarities both persons can identify. When we find that which is "common," there is chance for greater understanding. We can indeed discover what is common in a succession of our experiences.

*No two perceptions can be identical.*

Before 1900, psychologists assumed that the image on the retina of an observer's eye was an accurate picture of the thing the observer was looking at. Furthermore, they also assumed that the perception—that is, the idea transmitted to the observer's mind—was a fairly accurate copy of the image on the retina. Those early psychologists called the eye the camera, and the retina the film which recorded the light patterns that fell upon it. Modern scientists have challenged that assumption; and most believe that what we observe is determined only partly by the image on the retina of the eye and largely by conditions in the observer's mind. This is the internal environment.

We often err in our perception of things: first, by failing to see something that is there; second, by distorting that which is there so that we see it as different from what it is; and third, by adding things we imagine we see, but which are not actually there at all. As we continue our observation of Dora's and Bert's family we shall see how these things happen quite normally and without malice.

*We select that part of the world we wish to experience.*

All people select that part of their world they wish to experience, and various factors influence their selectivity. One is *intensity*. Emma perceives the intense rather than the weak: A scream of terror gets her attention quicker than a well-modulated greeting. Emotional rhetoric, signs, and slogans influence our perceptions. We are quicker to respond to *contrast*. In other words, we add our own meaning to the data provided by our senses. And for that reason it is easy to confuse observation with inference, to let our perception cloud our observations.

When we add to our own meaning, it is not always due to some learning process in our past. There is evidence that certain innate perceptions require no previous experience with the object. Studies conducted with congenitally blind persons whose sight has been surgically restored revealed that immediately after gaining their sight these individuals perceive figure-ground relationships in much the same manner as do subjects with normal vision. The perception of such geometric forms as circles, squares, and triangles is poor following surgery, suggesting that these perceptions must be *learned*.

Prejudice falls into the "learned" category. As the song from *South Pacific* goes, "You've got to be taught before its too late, before you are six or seven or eight . . . to hate all the people your relatives hate . . . you've got to be carefully taught."

*Prejudice greatly affects our perception.*

Derived from the Latin noun *praejudicium*, prejudice means a judgment based on previous decisions and experiences. Culture (part of our environment) and personality greatly affect prejudice, and prejudice greatly affects perception. If we are predisposed to see something, if we practice selective perception which in turn has been governed by exposure to members of different races under hostile circumstances, we become extremely sensitive to certain communication messages. And whether they evoke our positive or negative response to an individual or a group, our perceptions affect our self-concepts.

We can conclude, then, that we select and choose what we perceive and that we organize sensory stimulations and interpret them into a meaningful picture of the world.

Our selection is affected by:

1. *Physiological factors.* We cannot hear sounds below 20 cycles per second or above 20,000 cycles per second. We cannot see ultraviolet rays. In fact, we see a mere 1/70 of the total light spectrum. Well-built though we may be, we may have other limitations.

2. *Position in space.* One of Emma's colleagues sees his zone as "Lots of cars. No one feeds the meters. Store owners always complain when I give tickets to their customres. I tell them it only takes a dime." Another officer recently assigned to foot patrol says, "Lots of children here. I thought there were only a couple of schools, but did you know we have eight right around this area?"

3. *Psychological factors.* Everyone has interests. Three people looking at the same movie may come out with three impressions. Tom the photographer, Emma the officer, and Bert the schoolteacher all watched the television special, *Scared Straight.* Tom was impressed with how it was photographed; Emma's concern focused on the juvenile problem; Bert experienced a sense of relief that the children weren't his.

4. *Past experiences and learning.* Though we may make mistakes and move too quickly to evaluate, our past experiences are our most valuable assets. In an emergency we must depend greatly on them.

The *organization* of what we perceive is affected by:

1. *Specific designs we anticipate.* We see the round balls on top of the pawnbroker's shop for so many years that when we see partial curves we complete them in our minds. We recall designs.

2. *Our desire to form a whole picture as opposed to something else.* We do not like to leave things half done. Try the ink-blot test—you will see a whole bird, an airplane, a street, or whatever.

Our *interpretation* is affected by:

1. *The ambiguity of the stimuli.* A study in Emma's police department concluded that more stress is felt by the officer on calls which occur less frequently or that give a limited amount of information.

2. *The context.* Every communicative act takes place somewhere. Somewhere means in some environment, and environment means everything and everyone around us at that moment. Since we bring our environment with us, we cannot ignore our inner environment as well as our outer environment.

Given the subjectivity in forming perceptions, it becomes apparent that some method(s) must be available for checking them. The following four are the most common:

1. Consensual—checking with other people.
2. Repetitive—checking with ourselves by repeating the observations.
3. Multisensory—checking with ourselves by using other senses.
4. Comparative—checking with ourselves and our past experiences with similar but not necessarily identical perceptions.

So we have come full cycle: We can say that communication takes place somewhere and with someone—one person, two people, a group. There is a message and someone assigns meaning to it; meaning is affected by perception, and perceived meaning is transacted to one or more others in some context (environment).

## Communication: A Process, Model, and Theory.

Human beings can be notoriously bad communicators. We are taught no formal communication skills early in our lives. As infants, we reach a stage of development at which we learn to speak in order to communicate on a reciprocal basis. It is then taken for granted by many of us that the ability to talk solves the communication issue once and for all.

Emma's neighbor takes her child for a ride in a stroller. A little dog, a cocker spaniel, comes by and the mother says to her baby, "See the dog."

Encouraged by her mother, one day the child sees the cocker spaniel and says "dog," or something close to that sound. Later on if someone says "dog," a mental picture of an animal comes to the child's mind, probably in the shape and size of the cocker spaniel. Thus we begin to store some experiences in our brain. But one dog is not all dogs. When Nick, who works with Emma, says "Boy, was I out with a *dog* last night," Emma retorts, "So what else does a *wolf* deserve?"

Our experiences help us assign meaning. Emma sees the boys shooting craps. She is then the source. She thinks about what she sees. Perhaps in her mind she is thinking, "These boys are too young to gamble," so she decides to send them a message. She encodes the thought and transmits the message through molecules of air (her channel). The boys at the same time are looking up at Emma. Before she even speaks, they are receiving nonverbal messages (visual): Emma's blue uniform, her hands on her hips. Then they hear the oral message: "What are you doing?" One boy receives the verbal and nonverbal clues, encodes, assigns meaning to the message, and replies, "Nothin." He is the receiver and the ultimate destination in this case.

R. Wayne Pace (1979), in his book *Techniques for Effective Communication*, states that people in a dyadic (two-person) communication situation should be considered *transceivers* (transmitters/receivers) rather than communicator and communicatee. Each person simultaneously influences and is influenced by the other. We can also refer to those involved in this type of communication as both speaker/listener and listener/speaker, because although the communication is going on simultaneously, one person usually initiates the contact.

Emma's exchange with the boys, while it contains an enormous backlog of experiences from each participant, is nonetheless a fairly simple communicative exchange—at least simple in terms of today's technological world.

Now let's look at another daily communication exchange in Emma's professional life.

## FROM SIMPLICITY TO SERIALITY

Here is an actual exchange on her portable walkie-talkie.

(Dispatcher) 403, a 10-11 corner of Indian, School, and Pennsylvania.

(Emma) 403, 10-4.

(Another officer) 403, this is 406, am on the freeway proceeding north. I'll take the 10-11.

(Sergeant) Dispatch, did you read 406? That's 403 call. 403, report please.

(Emma) 403, 10-4.

Taking that message from its inception, before Emma received the call on the radio, we find that an accident has occurred and one of the motorists involved, after a heated exchange with the other motorist (dyad, conflict) called the police by dialing 911 (telephone, 2 persons, dyad, interview). The motorist reports the accident (background noise in the channel). Operator obtains information according to information-gathering interview format and types messsage into terminal (computer language). Message is relayed and dispatcher accesses the message, reading the print on the display terminal. Dispatcher then activates (turns on) the microphone, selects a frequency (channel), and converts the message to another language (code, in this instance).

Emma receives the accident report over her radio and is dispatched to the scene. The accident is not in her regular area, but in that of an officer who has been summoned to testify in night court. Stationed in an adjacent area, Emma is his cover. As she heads toward the scene, she hears the officer for whom she is covering call in and say that he is on the freeway and will take the call. Although she is almost at the scene and has priority because she was asked to cover the accident, she doesn't argue over the radio. However, the district sergeant is monitoring the calls, hears the message, and calls in to say that Emma should be the one who answers the call.

The entire exchange on the radio deals with a few simple numbers and a very few words. Behind the scene, so to speak, the sergeant has decided to override the officer. Authority, politics, and personality, plus a backlog of experiences, are all involved in the transaction.

But the message still hasn't reached its destination or conclusion: Emma, at the scene, becomes part of a triad (three people) in a problem-solving situation. Later in the book we shall trace this entire transaction to its completion and see that Emma is part of a serial transmission of a message that goes through this process.

## SERIAL TRANSMISSION

*Every message has widespread social impact.*

Emma's situation is not unusual in today's world. In such professions as teacher, food-checker, airline-ticket official, market analyst, politician (and many, many more), messages are serially transmitted; that is, messages are relayed through humans and hardware many times and the effects of any one message have widespread social impact.

In a matter of minutes, Emma's communication encounters widen her circle of communication: the initial message took 2½ minutes to reach her, went through many changes to accommodate humans and hardware, and will go through many more before ultimately concluded.

Technology has become so much a part of our lives, its influence and sometimes its control so broad, that we have come to accept it as a natural part of our day. As we awaken each morning, the world comes to us via radio and television, and we sometimes relay messages from Egypt as a natural course of events. Dora hears the news of a cold war in Asia on her radio, says "That's terrible," and later repeats part of the news to her students. Bert turns on the television like a ritual and seemingly pays little attention to it, but subliminally he is receiving messages he will relay. In effect, we all relay messages. Some processes are just a bit more complicated, that's all.

Emma's messages involve more sets of senders-receivers. At least three persons are involved in every sequence and in many instances there are a number of sequences involved in a single message. There is always the person who originates the message, the intermediary or relay, and the person who terminates the sequence. For example: the citizen who calls for help, the operator who relays the message (sometimes several operators relay the message), and the officer in the patrol car who receives the message: a multiple set of transceivers. In Emma's situation each person is part of a chain, but the key person or persons are the relayers because that is where error can most easily occur.

Smith (1973) describes four functions of "relay" links that differ from the person who originates the message and the person who terminates it. They (1) link (and potentially unlink) parts of the system; (2) store messages (and potentially preserve them); (3) stretch (and potentially distort) meanings; and (4) control (and potentially own and manage) the system.

In relaying messages, some of us are story-tellers. Some of us definitely tend to highlight certain details of a message, even changing them to conform with interest and feelings. Some people tend to omit portions and make messages more concise. We contribute to the change of a message based upon our environmental predispositions, emotional or physical. Some of us modify a message to be consistent with a theme, modify a message to complete something that is incomplete and is more coherent to us. Others adjust some little detail to accommodate their own linguistic habits, modify details to reflect personal concerns or occupational roles, even to reflect biases.

When the relayed message includes hardware as well as humans, changes occur because of the technology: The telephone, radio, and computer have their own characteristics. We accept restrictions as a matter of course. We now rarely shout into a telephone or a microphone. We've learned to write within the blocks of a computer card. We adjust.

At the heart of both Emma's and Dora's communication network, of their widening circles, is the serial transmission of messages and the serial reproduction of messages.

In that way their lives, and ours, are almost like an organization, a network of connecting people who disseminate information by means of successive dyadic encounters that often grow into groups and sometimes into public-speaking situations.

Elements in serial transmission of messages include remembering, reporting, and rumoring. In a broad sense, everyone of us is a relayer of messages, and many times these messages are defined as rumors. Allport and Postman (1947) defined rumor as "a specific or topical proposition for belief, passed along from person to person, usually by word of mouth, without secure standards of evidence being present." During our daily conversations we do not pay too much attention to "secure standards of evidence." We just pass the word along.

We pass it along to a friend. But just as messages change and become complex, so do our relationships change and grow to include more people.

The simple act of having lunch with a dear friend, at which time you planned to share confidences, can easily become a triad as the waitress appears, or as friends wave to you from across the room. Consider the accident report: The relationships include *dyad* (dialogue between two motorists, *dyad* (motorist and operator), *dyad* (operator and dispatcher), *triad* (Emma and two motorists), *group* (Emma and family), *public speaking* (Emma, participants, and judge).

## RELATIONSHIPS

*Dyadic communication*: In external communication situations, the dyad is the smallest unit of interpersonal communication that can be analyzed. Wilmot (1975) states, "a dyad cannot be subdivided." In most instances, we start the morning alone, move quickly to a two-person relationship. Two people get together and pay attention to each other, agreeing to influence and be influenced. The level of intimacy, seriousness, or purposiveness changes depending upon our intent, our environment and our personality. For example, when Dora is having a friendly talk with the woman at the pool, she is having a conversation. Her intent is not serious, she just wishes to be friendly. However, she has a *dialogue* with her friend Susan and with Maria (on the WATS line). She knows them and their relationships are sustained, more intimate, and sometimes extremely serious. Emma moves more often into a interview relationship, saving dialogue for recurring relationships (her family). The interview has purpose, is serious, and may or may not be intimate (depending upon the type of interview).

*The Triad*  Three people can be called a small group. Three people can get together and solve a problem, engage in a conflict, or have a casual conversation. The uniqueness of the triangle is that conflict occurs

often in this relationship. We know about the "eternal" triangle; equally volatile are three-cornered domestic situations, and two children playing compatibly until a third one comes along.

More attention has been paid to small group relationships during the past two or three decades. Thirty years ago, Admiral Rickover wrote about the decline of the individual and attributed it to the emergence of group discussions and group problem-solving. There are now many forms of small group communication, both public and private. Public groups include councils, panels, symposiums, conferences—in fact, any small group that is open to public scrutiny. Private groups can also be conferences, boards, social clubs, and so on—any group that is in effect its own audience. People gather in groups mainly to solve problems and pursue common interests. Bill Hungate's morning group session with his employees (which will be discussed in

*The Group*

depth in the chapter on groups) is a "discussion" type of group where problems are aired and solutions are quickly reached. Emma's small group "discussion" is led by herself, an authoritative figure who handles the discussion. Questions of leadership are paramount when studying small groups.

*Speaker-Audience*

Of all the relationships so far mentioned, the speaker-audience relationship demands more from those involved. The speaker who engages often in formal presentation of issues must be prepared to research the issue, deliver the statement or speech, and attempt to

make the audience feel and believe as he or she does. The audience, on the other hand, needs to develop good listening habits and generally be prepared to try to understand the speaker's point of view. Though public speaking is considered more formal than the other relationships mentioned, we engage in it much more than we realize. A public speech can be delivered to any size audience from one to one million, via the mass media. A public speech can be a prayer, an oral report at school, a briefing in the military, a sales pitch, a sermon, a political promise, a eulogy, in fact any time we are asked to stand up and speak out we are giving a public speech. Dora gives a public speech when she lectures, Bill Hungate gives a public speech at the hairdressers' convention. Maria gives a speech when she makes a press statement for the Congressman when the news media gather for a briefing. The basic difference between the audience in a public-speaking situation and the "receiver" of a message in a dyadic situation is that the audience spends a greater time listening to a monologue. The audience makes the speaker the object of attention and is prepared to be influenced. However, speaker-audience situations can evolve into interview situations, dialogues between the speaker and a member of the audience, or conflict situations.

All communication relationships share the elements mentioned in the communication model: source, transmitter, message, receiver.* All communication relationships are constantly evolving and require an understanding of ourselves, how and why we behave as we do and an understanding of others who share our environment.

## ETHICS

*Ethics and communication.*

***Ethics involves image.***

All communication relationships also involve ethics, which means that we *choose* to act and speak as we do and that our image is involved in that choice.

Bert is challenged daily by his little students. He chides them, dances with them, and plays word games with them. "Why is school like spaghetti?" he asks.

"It's loose and sloppy," a child replies, playing the game.

Is Bert choosing to mislead the children? Is he examining all sides, weighing his audience's beliefs, considering the evidence, the validity of the source, the vital information about the subject of

*Note: A more complex model, which includes the transmitter, destination, and feedback, is discussed in Chapter 8.

school? In strict ethical terms laid down by Aristotle, Bert may not be playing the game by the rules. But Bert's intent is truly honorable: to motivate children to learn.

*Communication is often intentional.*

Communication is, in most instances, intentional. We definitely wish to influence others. We have something specific in mind and we create a message with some objective in mind.

*Ethics deals with freedom of choice.*

The question of ethics, however, deals not only with our freedom to speak but also with our listener's freedom of choice. We must satisfy two criteria: Does the person we are seeking to influence have the freedom to choose to believe our case? And does that person have the freedom to explore other alternatives? The answer in most cases should be yes.

However, when Emma points a gun at a robbery suspect in a Circle-K store, she is not giving that person freedom to do anything but what she tells that person to do; the gun becomes a powerful persuader. Emma can argue that sometimes, perhaps on rare occasions, the ultimate good for many will be served by removing "freedom of choice" from a few.

The question of ethics in communication is debatable; indeed, we shall explore it further in other chapters. However, when we speak of ethics in communication we are mainly concerned with the ethics we employ when we persuade others. Most of our communicative messages, whether in conversation, dialogue, interview, small group, or speaker-audience situations are in fact messages of persuasion.

Whatever our intent . . . from the time we get up in the morning our world is evolving and widening. Actually we do not even start afresh each morning. Our feelings as we open our eyes could be hangovers from the previous days' good or bad experiences. Our beliefs could be carryovers from a previous experience, and our communication could be a continuation of a dialogue engaged in on the previous day.

We may repeat a similar activity: Dora may swim every morning. But Dora is not the same every morning, nor are her surroundings the same. Perhaps she doesn't meet the same people, or the previous day's events have influenced her in some way, or her body is altered by a cold, or a million other things. She can predict that the water will be "good" only because it has remained the same temperature for days.

*Communication is in a constant, dynamic state.*

But it is possible that the heater broke down during the night, or her body temperature went up for some reason, and then the water is not good. We are in a constant dynamic state and our communication is in a constant dynamic state.

We are ever perched precariously on that point, part of that delicate balance, striving for harmony in a society that changes before our eyes.

There have been so many technological changes in our environment that human beings are hard pressed to adjust rationally. Still we have a brain that adapts—and fortunately it is possible to know the various physical and chemical processes that exist. In fact, someone built the tools—the telephone, the radio, computer; if necessary, someone can be found to make the tools work. Understanding the human being remains the difficult assignment.

*Understanding the human being remains the difficult assignment.*

As professionals, Dora, Emma, Bill, Bert, and all the others in Dora's environment have to manage their resources, which consist of things technical, things economic, and things human. When we encounter technical decisions, we don't mind facing up to the problem. The reason is that a pretty fair degree of predictability can be attached to things technical. Given a number of technical resources and a known process, we have a reasonably good idea as to what the technical output will be.

For example, Bert puts a sheet of paper in the mimeograph machine and he's pretty sure he'll get a duplicate paper out of it. If the machine breaks down, he calls the operator who understands the process. Bert even knows the process for making paper; he knows where to buy the paper; he knows how to read the direction to feed the paper into the machine, and he can predict the output.

Bert also knows that if he works hard at his two jobs, he and Dora and the children will be able to afford the camper and the vacations. He can add up the money, figure out how long he must work, and even compute his own taxes. Economics can be pretty predictable for Bert.

Human beings are less predictable. We humans are a variable species, subject to change, able to adapt, altered constantly by our environment, possessing unique personalities, different perceptions, and so on.

It's important that we look at ourselves and some of the human problems we get ourselves into whenever we become involved with another human being, a group, or a mass audience. Only then will we realize how important is communication if we are to survive—and thrive.

What it all boils down to is finding out and practicing those skills of talking, of getting the other person to respond, and of making it all mean something.

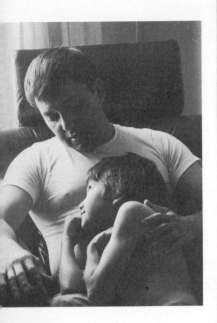

**SUMMARY** Communication relationships are constantly evolving. They require an understanding of ourselves, how and why we behave as we do, and an understanding of others who share our environment. Communication relationships involve sources, transmitters, channels, and receivers, and are usually aimed at persuading someone to do something in some environment. Furthermore, the very act of communicating involves behaving in certain and special ways and behavior is a result of heredity, environment, and personality.

At the very base of being human is the ability to change, to adapt, to learn, to acquire new skills, and to recognize that if something doesn't work, we can fix it.

The question we shall try to confront in this book is this: *How do we fix it?*

Can we really teach people to become more effective communicators by explaining and practicing certain tehcniques?

History tells us we can. The teaching of communicative skills has a long and honorable history. At its roots is one of the oldest disciplines in Western civilization: *Rhetoric.* (Rhetoric, as defined by Aristotle, means finding—or discovering—all the available means of persuasion in a given case. We shall discuss this term in more depth in a later chapter.)

Environment is everything around us and everybody around us, as well as the feeling we have when we face a new day. Our inner environment greatly influences our outer environment and vice-versa. Our environment, our hereditary influences greatly affect our personality which is what people "see." We create a personal identity, accept a social identity, and show others our paper identity.

We interract with our environment to satisfy certain needs. Needs fall into categories of physiological, safety, acceptance, esteem, self-actualization. We attempt to satisfy these needs; when we cannot, we sometimes select an alternative activity that can replace the initial needs.

We interact with others to satisfy our needs, and communication becomes the essence of being human. We communicate internally and externally. We do so externally by assigning a meaning to a message. Meaning is greatly affected by our perception. We select and choose what we perceive and our selection is affected by physiological factors, our position in space, psychological factors, past experiences, and learning. The organization of what we perceive is affected by specific designs we anticipate, and our desire to form a whole picture as opposed to something else. Our interpretation is affected by the ambiguity of the stimuli and the context.

We often communicate in a serial manner, that is, our messages are relayed through humans and hardware many times and the effects of any one message have widespread social impact.

As our messages change and become more dynamic, so do our relationships change at any moment in time. We may start to speak in a dyadic (two-person) environment and move on to a group or a public-speaking event. In each relationship ethics is a dominant factor. We *choose* to speak and we *wish* to influence others. At all times, however, we are *in a constant dynamic state and our communication is in a constant dynamic state.* We are constantly moving outward, seeing our circle grow; our words are like pebbles tossed into a pond, disturbing the surface, moving every living thing in their path.

---

**KEY TERMS**

abiotic
biotic
cultural
dyadic
ego
environment
ethics
external communication
group
heredity
inner environment
internal communication
intrapersonal
listener/speaker
meaning
outer environment
perception
personality
physiological
receiver
relationships
relay links
safety
self-concept
self-fulfillment
serial transmission
speaker/audience
speaker/listener
technology
transmitter
triad

---

**EXERCISES**

1.  Select a typical day in your life and record your contacts for that day. Start with yourself in the center of your circle of communication and widen that circle as your day proceeds until you retire in the evening.

What were your first inner thoughts? Your first contacts with people, your group experiences? How many communication situations did you take part in? How many messages did you pass along? How many media messages did you receive?

2. Select an activity you engage in every day and change the environment of that activity (if you play tennis, choose another court; if you read, sit in another room). What influence did the environment have on the activity? On your feelings?

3. Form a circle in your classroom and play the old "rumor" game: Start with a message and "relay" it to the person next to you. At every point, write down what you relayed. Did you enlarge, condense, distort? What kind of relayer do you think you are?

## CIRCLING BACK

Answers to these questions are found in the text; start with the pages closest to you right now.

1. Do you believe most of our messages are persuasive? Explain.
2. Which is the smallest unit of interpersonal communication in external communication situations?
3. Explain the four functions of relay links. Which link comes closest to describing your behavior?
4. Various factors influence our perception. Name some.
5. Explain the following: Every behavior actually has the potential of having meaning assigned to it.
6. You communicate externally when meaning is assigned to the message. Is that true?
7. Why do you select alternative needs?
8. Name your needs. Do they fit into Maslow's hierarchy?
9. Do you believe self-concept can be influenced by others around you? How?
10. What fashions your personality? What are you born with?
11. What constitutes your environmental triangle?

## REFERENCES

Addington, D.W. "The Relationship of Certain Vocal Characteristics with Perceived Speaker Characteristics." Ph.D. dissertation, University of Iowa, 1963, p. 151.

Allport, G.W., and H. Cantril. "Judging Personality from Voice." *Journal of Social Psychology* **5** (1934):49.

Allport, G.W., and L.J. Postman, *The Psychology of Rumor.* New York: Holt, Rinehart and Winston, 1947.

Barnlund, Dean C. *Interpersonal Communication: Survey and Studies.* Boston: Houghton Mifflin, 1968, pp. 4-8.

Herzbert, Frederick, Bernard Mausner, and Barbara Synderman. *The Motivation to Work.* New York: John Wiley and Sons, 1959.

Maslow, A. "A Theory of Human Motivation." *Psychology Review* **50** (1943):370-396.

Pace, R. Wayne, Brent D. Peterson, and M. Dallas Burnett. *Techniques for Effective Communication.* Reading, Mass.: Addison-Wesley, 1979, p. 196.

Pierce, John R. "Communication." *Scientific American.* San Francisco: W.H. Freeman, 1972. (A special unnumbered edition.)

Smith, A.G. "The Ethic of the Relay Men." In *Communication: Ethical and Moral Issues,* edited by L. Thayer. London: Gordon and Breach, 1973, pp. 313-324.

Wilmot, W.W. *Dyadic Communication.* Reading, Mass.: Addison-Wesley, 1975.

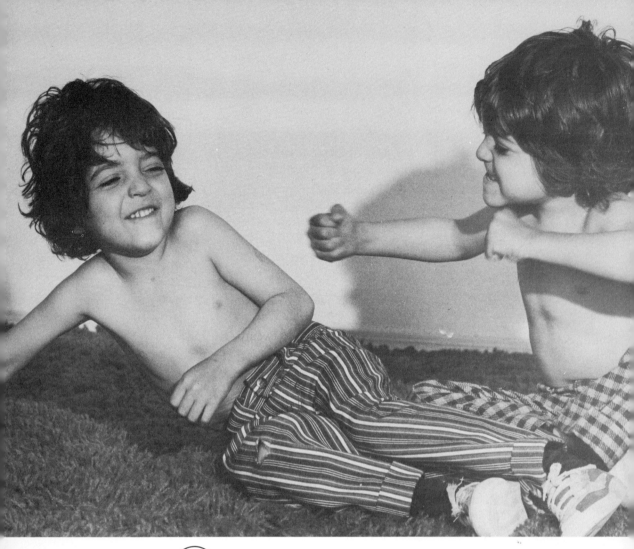

# 2 the circle widens: the individual plus one

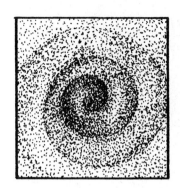

Emma arrives at the scene of the accident approximately twenty-five minutes after it has occurred. The two cars have been moved out of the intersection into a parking lot. A number of persons have gathered around the cars; some are discussing the accident itself, while others are talking about the relative cost of fixing cars.

"Could I have the drivers of the two cars please?" Emma moves into the center of the group.

"We've been waiting for a half an hour. All my witnesses left, but I got their numbers," answers a young man.

"Could I see your license please?"

He hands over his license.

"Which car were you driving?"

"The Cougar, green."

"Can you tell me what happened?" Emma motions the young man to step aside with her. As they move away from the group, the young woman who was driving the other car hands Emma license. Emma takes the license and turns to the young man.

"I started up at a green light, and she ran the red light and broadsided me," he explains.

"In which direction were you proceeding?"

"I was going west on Indian School."

"And the light was green when you started?"

"Yes, and I was stopped at the light. She would have hit one of the witnesses too, but my car blocked him off from her."

"Where was she coming from?"

"She was coming from the south on Pennsylvania. She ran the light."

"Do you have the numbers of the people you have for witnesses?"

"Yes, here they are." The young man hands Emma a couple of business cards, and she takes down the numbers.

"Where were these people in relation to the accident?"

"One guy was in the white van that I blocked from the car that hit me, and the other was in the car behind me."

"Okay. Stick around. Your car is not drivable is it?"

"No."

"Well, wait here and we'll radio for a tow truck. Do you have a preference?"

"Yes, Knettles."

"Okay."

Emma turns to the young woman, who is standing a short distance behind her.

"I guess it was my fault," the young woman says. "I'll pay for the car."

"What exactly happened?" asks Emma.

"I thought I went through a yellow light, but I guess it was red."

"When did it turn red?"

"I don't know. I don't remember. I don't think I saw it turn red."

Emma then repeats the questions she asked the young man and asks Ann (the young woman) if she has any witnesses.

"Just the girls that were in the car."

"You didn't stop anyone?"

"No."

"Come over to my car with me."

When they are seated in the police car, Emma explains that if the light was yellow when Ann went through it, she is not guilty. "It was probably red, then," says the woman. Emma then radios in to have the cars towed. Ann's father is contacted by telephone, and he informs them that there is no insurance on her car. The young man insists the young woman must pay for the damage. Emma explains that it is now a civil matter and that the discussion should end.

"I'm not going to cite anybody until I talk to the witnesses," she explains. "Ann, I'll be at your apartment a little later tonight, after I've talked to the witnesses, and then I'll tell you whether or not you'll be cited."

The preceding situation included some casual conversation as the officer approached the scene; ongoing dialogue among the passengers in the young woman's car; an argument over the incident by the young man and some observers; the information-gathering interviews; and finally some public speaking, when Emma directed everyone to end the discussion and go on their separate ways.

We move so quickly from one relationship to the next that we hardly have time to realize the ways in which we must relate to one another and how we change as we go. We are sometimes unaware of how wide our circle becomes and how far-reaching our influence is.

*We move quickly from one relationship to the next.*

In Chapter 1, we spoke about the individual and his or her needs, environment, personality, communication, and motivation. Central to our discussion was the involvement of human relations—that is, the way people relate to one another or "interact." We noted that individuals were "unpredictable" and that this unpredictability can carry over into their dealings with one another.

In the accident scenario, people moved from one relationship to the next very easily, but the major part of the communication took place between TWO people. Most of our daily communications begin that way, and usually we wish those relationships to be effective *and* happy—two conditions that are not necessarily synonymous.

If being happy means feeling good, and if communicating effectively means finding common ground, then there are techniques for achieving these conditions through the act of communicating.

## WHEN TWO PEOPLE TALK

*Communication can be constructive, acceptable, or destructive.*

Our remarks can be classified generally as:

**Constructive**  (also considered supportive)

**Acceptable**

**Destructive**  (also termed *un*acceptable in a milder  form)

Let us look again at the accident scene to which Emma responded.

1. A *destructive* remark by Emma might have been, "Why did you idiots move the cars? Don't you know I can't make a judgment now?"

2. An *acceptable* remark might have been a simple factual description of what happened: "My bumper was damaged upon impact."

3. A *constructive* approach might have involved the exchange of information—that is, a description of what occurred and an attempt to reach a logical conclusion acceptable to both parties. However, we shall see that this is a difficult procedure at times and takes a careful discovery of the truth.

For the sake of example, let's reconstruct the situation with the motorists. Suppose Emma (the officer) and the young man involved in the accident were involved in this kind of exchange. The "relations" just might break down:

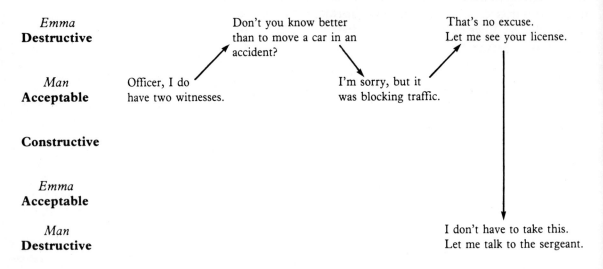

*Emma*
**Destructive**

*Man*
**Acceptable**

**Constructive**

*Emma*
**Acceptable**

*Man*
**Destructive**

Don't you know better than to move a car in an accident?

That's no excuse. Let me see your license.

Officer, I do have two witnesses.

I'm sorry, but it was blocking traffic.

I don't have to take this. Let me talk to the sergeant.

On the other hand, suppose Emma decides to put people at ease in this emotional situation. The man might respond thus:

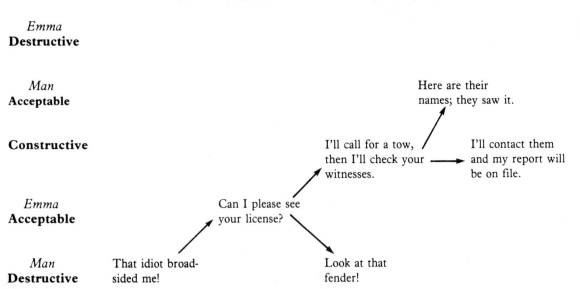

*Emma*
**Destructive**

*Man*
**Acceptable**

**Constructive**

*Emma*
**Acceptable**

*Man*
**Destructive**

Here are their names; they saw it.

I'll call for a tow, then I'll check your witnesses.

I'll contact them and my report will be on file.

Can I please see your license?

That idiot broadsided me!

Look at that fender!

We see that arriving at a common ground and feeling good about an encounter *takes two people*. In other words *either party* in any given situation *has the ability* to create a *destructive* relationship, a *constructive* relationship, or an *acceptable* relationship.

There are times, after all, when we decide to live with or accept a situation; times when we say, "I can take it or leave it," or "I can live with that." Most of the time, however, we prefer a *constructive* relationship.

In order to thrive and not just survive in our human encounters, we should understand those elements involved in building *supportive* (or *constructive*) atmospheres and those elements involved in building *defensive* (or *destructive*) atmospheres.

Keep in mind that while we continually advocate finding a common ground and building a better and more constructive relationship, we fully appreciate that there are times when we must put an end to a relationship, either changing it or destroying it completely. When we do so, we accept the heartache that follows.

Jack R. Gibb (1961) outlined the elements of supportive and defensive atmospheres, and we have adopted them as follows.

A supportive atmosphere . . .

1. *Encourages descriptive language*: "What happened?" "You say the car was green?"

2. *Is problem-oriented*: "I will speak with all the witnesses and attempt to solve the problem."

3. *Features empathy*: "I will listen to everyone and give my undivided attention to you." (Consider the fact that Emma drew each participant aside and was nonthreatening. On some occasions we might talk about having been in the same circumstance ourselves.)

4. *Seeks to establish equality*: This is difficult if you are in a position viewed as authoritative. However, Emma often talks about "service" and being a "public servant" instead of being on the police "force" and has accomplished that feeling of equality.

5. *Recognizes provisionalism*: The sender investigates; he or she does not pontificate.

6. *Allows spontaneity*: The sender reacts as a real person responding to the ever-changing and dynamic communication situation.

## Supportive and Defensive Atmospheres

*Building a Supportive Atmosphere*

*Building a Defensive Atmosphere*

A defensive atmosphere . . .

1. *Emposes evaluation* or *judgment*: One of Dora's students wrote an essay about people in her environment: "While I was in grade school, my father gave this speech to the family as he went through my report card. He read my grades like this: 'A, B+, B, A−, C+, C−, D [a frown] next stop, Los Lunas home for retarded kids.'"

2. *Attempts control*: The sender tries in an obvious manner to change the receiver. "Don't come to me with those papers again. Its time you learned how to figure the totals yourself!" Control is a difficult theme to discuss, as some of us must assume control at times.

3. *Employs strategy*: Defensiveness occurs when the strategy is viewed as ambiguous and self-serving in its motivation. "We'll all meet at the restaurant near my house because I have an appointment right after lunch . . . I think."

4. *Affects neutrality*: The sender indicates an utter lack of concern . . . regards the other person as an object. One nonverbal example is making someone stand at your office door and appearing unconcerned about his or her welfare or message.

5. *Implies superiority*: The sender indicates he or she is superior in wealth, position, power, or intelligence. "The suit is $750.00 more than you can afford, boy."

6. *Stresses certainty*: The sender has all the answers and all the right information. "About 77 percent in 1979 J.B.? Look again—it's 73.15 percent in 1979."

While Gibb's initial elements of *defensive* and *supportive* behaviors make sense, they are not entirely realistic in our changing world. There are times when we must take control, particularly in *interview* situations. There are times when we are in a position of acknowledged authority, which carries with it additional power or wealth. And certainly there are many times when we must make justified judgments. At these times we should always consider the ethics of the situation.

*We should always consider the ethics of the situation*

We must clearly analyze our intent when we set about employing some of the elements mentioned in defensive rhetoric. In effect, the father who made the remark about retarded children clearly meant to intimidate his child. If he had merely commented that the "D" on the report card was not up to the child's potential and that he knew she could do better, the atmosphere might possibly have remained supportive.

The one-on-one or person-to-person relationship (whether it be conversation, dialogue, interview, or debate) is our most important and most common form of oral communication. It progresses through three stages: an *opening*, a *body*, and a *conclusion.* These stages apply to a casual conversation, a dialogue, an argument, or an interview. (Later in this book we shall see that the same three stages are found in groups and in public-speaking situations.)

**Three Stages of a Communication**

Basically, stage one involves the presentation of a good image and establishment of rapport. Your image is best presented as that of an honest and intelligent person. Rapport is established by listening and showing concern.

*Stage One: The Opening*

   In a short conversation, such as a brief encounter in an elevator, you may simply say, "Hi Tony, how's it goin'?" Openings in these situations usually employ a combination of nonverbal communicators (smile, handshake, or nod) and verbal messages about state of health, morning news, or weather. First encounters include observing body shape, clothing, and dialects. We sometimes get "good vibes" and react emotionally to someone, taking an instant like or dislike to the person, usually because of something in our inner environment. Sometimes we can do little about our image because the other person has some prior perception: Emma, for example, finds that some people harbor an inner hatred of "cops," and she tries to accept that if the encounter is a brief one .

   *Dialogue, debate, and interview* are relationships that have more purpose and involve definite topics. The sergeant may say, "Emma, let's sit down and talk about next week's shift changes." Bill may ask a customer, "What do you think of the President's energy program?" In the dialogue, the debate, and (sometimes) in the interview, an image has already been established, and most of these encounters are ongoing relationships. We can establish our credibility further, however, by establishing a supportive climate, and we can build rapport (again!) by listening.

This is the stage at which the two individuals, together by mutual arrangement, seek to be stimulated by their contact. The purpose of a brief conversation simply may be to feel better after contact; thus the

*Stage Two: The Body*

body of such an encounter may be an exchange of a joke, a fact about a coworker, or an agreement about the weather. A dialogue, argument, or interview may go further and solve a problem, exchange information, or make a judgment that affects further contact.

Once again we find that listening is vital if the purpose of the one-on-one encounter is to be achieved.

*Stage Three: The Conclusion*

Brief or lengthy, the encounter either concludes or changes into a new relationship (e.g., another person joins the twosome, a group gathers, a mob erupts).

In concluding a short conversation one might just say, "See you around," "We'll go into that further tomorrow" (implying a continuing relationship), or "Pleased to have met you." In concluding an interview, however, we may wish to summarize or to offer some psychological support, such as, "Have faith, you'll pass the examination." In any event, the manner in which we either take our leave or move into another situation crucially affects our continuing relationships with people in our environment. Since a number of people remain in our environment for some length of time (unless we are constantly moving) it behooves us to consider the importance of leave-taking.

Listening helps us bridge the time so that our next encounter will be even more constructive.

## LISTENING

In all three stages of the person-to-person encounter we place special emphasis on *listening*. While listening is an important element in public speaking and in groups, effective one-on-one communication simply cannot exist without it. You will reach some of the people in groups and part of your audience in public speaking—but in one-on-one relationships you *must* reach that other person! If no one is listening, then it is questionable that any communication takes place.

The problem is this: Immediately after he or she listens to someone talk, the average person remembers only about one-half of what was said. In fact, people tend to forget one-third of what they hear within eight hours, and two months later they remember only about 25 percent. Why, then, bother to listen?

The fact is that few of us really *do* bother to listen at all. We hear a great many things, but we rarely listen. In the Spring of 1958 Dr. Warren Guthrie addressed the members of the Thirteenth Tecnifac Seminar Workshop in Visual Communication at Holyoke, Massachusetts with this startling comment: "At the risk of being rude, I am going to suggest that most of us never listen to anything at all. We hear about a quantity of things, but we never listen."

He went on to say that there are four levels of hearing: However, he said listening really occurs only at the highest level.

1. I can hear.
2. I hear and can repeat back.
3. I hear; I can repeat back; and I obey.
4. I hear, and I participate in the communication process.

*I can hear.*

Emma hears a great many things: the sirens, the police calls, the crickets, the radio buzzing. Bill hears the air conditioner, the blow dryer, the music. Unless these sounds interfere with their work, they do not respond to them. Dr. Guthrie complains that some people will answer the phone and simultaneously talk to a person present in the room, thereby *listening* to neither speaker. Hearing is not listening.

*. . . and can repeat back.*

The second level at which we hear enables us to repeat the message. A teacher says, "Repeat after me, two and two equal four." The class repeats, without analysing or judging whether the teacher is right or wrong. This is another level that may be practical but still is not *listening*.

*. . . and I obey.*

The third level is one that Emma, our police officer, encounters frequently: I hear; I repeat; and I obey. This level occurs often in military organizations, where obedience is necessary for the sake of getting things done quickly and uniformly. However, it tends to make us mentally lazy and automatic in our responses.

*I hear, and I participate.*

As a member of the person-to-person team, you are at once a speaker and a listener. This means you must participate in the highest level of hearing—that is, *listening*—at all times. You should maintain involvement in the process and availability for analysis and decision-making.

**Helping Others to Listen**

Now let's turn our attention to the needs of those who listen to us. How do we make it easier for them to not only hear our words, but also *listen* to them? We know that others listen when we manage to put them in a listening frame of mind. And how do we do that?

**Step one:** We begin by building a supportive atmosphere. If someone walks into our home or office and we start shouting, the chances are good that he or she will react angrily and think only of his or her own responses. But

*Make your listeners comfortable.*

if we make our listeners comfortable (put the heat on if it's cold, the air-conditioner if it's hot, or bring in some coffee if it's midmorning), they will be in a frame of mind to listen. Thus our first step is to create an environment conducive to listening.

**Step two:** Present a message that will benefit the listener. Ask yourself, "Why should he or she listen to me? What am

I offering?" Even if it's a short message, you must obtain the listener's attention and immediately indicate that he or she stands to gain something from your message.

*Indicate the benefits of your message.*

**Step three:** If your message is going to be a long one, or a public speech, think of the presentation in terms of how you can *assist* the audience in its listening role. If you and your audience are ready for an emotional appeal to get a fund drive going, for example, or to raise money for a sick friend, then emphasizing generalities that tend to arouse feelings will assist listening. But if your speech is more rational, that is, if you are presenting many arguments to support a point, then pay more attention to clarifying the issue by paraphrasing it, repeating it, and finally underscoring the important points. In other words, what did *you* have to do to internalize that issue? You certainly read about it, recorded it, wrote it out somewhere, then remembered it. It really isn't rational to expect your audience to get involved in that same issue unless you give them a chance to become well-informed, to go over it, and to ask questions about it.

*Inform your listeners and encourage feedback.*

Listening must be a two-way street. You cannot expect your audience to listen if you don't listen; the communicative act is dynamic and constantly evolving.

Sometimes it evolves so quickly that we have little time to worry about whether our audience is well informed—or whether *we* are well informed, for that matter. One officer in Emma's department remarked, "We often don't have time to 'listen.' We have a few seconds to move a crowd or make a decision that others can debate over for the next year." Widely accepted is the belief that police officers are people of action who must make those snap decisions constantly. Yet the bulk of police work involves listening to initially noncriminal complaints. In a recent discussion on patrol, Albert J. Reiss found that only 2.55 percent of the Chicago Police Department's patrol activity actually dealt with criminal matters. Of those criminal matters processed by the patrol division, 93 percent were citizen initiated.

There arises a serious problem for those of us who are in professions where we are *expected* to respond quickly. In these professions we are usually held accountable for our remarks and the remarks of others, plus the decisions made under crisis and stress conditions. The police officer and others in such professions are like the average person—that is they remember only one-half of what they hear, no matter how hard they think they are listening. Two months later, they will remember only 25 percent of what was said.

What happens when the officer, the attorney, the businessperson, the doctor, or anyone involved in a crisis situation goes to court? Writing things down is not a foolproof solution to our quest for accurate data. When a crisis occurs, we rarely have paper and pencil handy; if we do record the data, often it is done at some considerable length of time after the event in question took place. Remembering the actual words spoken, even when our work depends on them, is difficult unless we have trained ourselves to be perceptive and observant. Even then, misunderstandings occur. Is there anyone who can honestly say he or she has been correctly quoted by a print reporter? Between the time the words are spoken and the time we see them in print, some changes occur in our interpretation or perception of the words or the event. We are not the same people the next day, nor are the reporters. Circumstances have changed our circle of influence and environment.

We can make it easier for others to listen to us, as we noted earlier, by *thinking* about their needs—by taking them through what we have gone through to gather and remember the information. First, however, we must be aware of our own need to develop good listening habits, which will help us *gather* that information. In other words *we* must sharpen our own listening habits, using listening responses effectively to encourage clear, accurate communication.

*Listening Responses*

The following material has been adapted from information originally developed by Dr. Don Liebman and Capt. Walter Konar, Crisis Intervention Unit, Santa Clara County Sheriff's Office, California.

**1.** When you are gathering information, remember that most people need some feedback or other indication that their words are being listened to. If you ask a question and then look away or maintain an impassive look, your respondent may become uneasy.

**2.** If you ask too many questions too quickly, your information source may feel you are invading the privacy of his or her inner circle.

**3.** Listening responses should show interest or understanding and are basically neutral expressions. To frown or show disagreement will immediately put the other person on the defensive.

**4.** Encouraging comments, such as "I see" and "Yes, I understand," can help the speaker without intruding on the story. A simple gesture—perhaps a smile or a nod or eye contact that is not a constant stare—often can maintain sufficient rapport with the other person. Neutral phrases ("Tell me more about it." "And what happened next?") are encouraging without being judgmental.

**5.** The use of *Echoes*—that is, the repetition and rephrasing of the speaker's last few words—can be very helpful. Suppose a person says, "I don't know what's the matter with this place. It used to be different." You might repeat in a questioning tone, "It used to be different?" This encourages the person to clarify what he or she is saying without addressing a direct question or otherwise interrupting the flow of the story.

**6.** Listening responses can also be used to maintain control. Paying attention to what a person is saying *increases* the likelihood of his or her continuous talk. The converse is equally true; *not* paying attention tends to decrease that likelihood. If an officer or a reporter is talking to someone who rambles and will not stay on a relevant subject, giving *no* feedback might encourage the speaker to "stay on the subject."

When we listen to someone, we are saying to that person, "You are important to me." Relationships can dissolve quickly when both parties fail to listen on a participatory level. In a casual encounter listening on a high level can aid a person's memory. A high level of listening entails closer observation and attention to the other person's physical appearance and mental gymnastics. Unfortunately, it is in casual conversation that we most often fail at listening. We are so busy with our own thoughts that we must be wary lest we miss that brief encounter destined to change our lives.

Another element found in all three stages of an effective human relationship is *nonverbal communication.* Even before we listen with our ears, we must "listen" with our other senses.

## NONVERBAL COMMUNICATION

In most situations we communicate nonverbally before we utter a single word. We move our bodies, raise our eyebrows, touch each other, dance, gather people close to us, keep them at a distance, wear clothes that express our moods, and engage in a million other nonverbal acts. Recent communication-process research specific to nonverbal communication settings brought forth estimates that nonverbal communication accounts for 65 percent of all our communication activity. Actually it is probably impossible to generalize about how much we communicate nonverbally.

For some professions, such as that of symphony conductor, nonverbal communication is necessary almost 100 percent of the time.

Consider Emma's first communicative acts upon apprehending a speeder: she starts her siren, the blue light whirls and flashes; she pulls alongside the offending car and gestures. After she stops, she gets out of her car. Around her waist hangs a gun, ammunition, a walkie-talkie, handcuffs, a nightstick, and at times some mace. Small wonder she must first adjust her belt before walking in what appears to the speeder to be a swagger.

Early researchers in the area of nonverbal study, Ruesch and Kees (1956) developed three areas of nonverbal communication: sign language, action language, and object language.

**Sign language** includes all those forms of codification in which words, numbers, and punctuation signs have been supplanted by gestures; these vary from the "monosyllabic" gestures of the hitchhiker to such complete systems as the language of the deaf.

**Action language** embraces all movements that are not used exclusively as signals. Walking and drinking, for example, have a dual function: on one hand they serve personal needs, and on the other they constitute statements to those who may perceive them.

**Object language** comprises all intentional and nonintentional displays of such material things as implements, machines, art objects,

architectural structures, and—last but not least—the human body and whatever clothing covers it.

In a more recent classification of nonverbal behavior, Ekman and Friesen (1969) confined their categorization study to body motions and developed a five-point system.

1. *Emblems*: Any nonverbal behaviors that directly substitute for a verbal expression. Examples include the hand sign meaning "peace," motions used by persons who are not within speaking distance of one another, hand waves, gestures when hailing a taxi, and the repertoire of signals given by the police officer directing traffic at a busy intersection.

2. *Illustrators*: Any nonverbal behaviors that accompany verbal behavior and accentuate or illustrate the verbal. The act of pointing to the right as you verbally give directions to a lost pedestrian is an example of an illustrator.

3. *Affect Displays*: Facial expressions that indicate one's feelings and emotions. (A good example of affective behavior is Bert's expression at the mimeograph machine.) These expressions may be in agreement or in conflict with what is being said verbally.

4. *Regulators*: Any nonverbal behaviors that direct (regulate) the verbal interaction between two people. Regulation of conversations (who speaks and when that speaker expects the other party to respond) is accomplished most often through the use of the eyes, head nods, and such verbal expressions as "uh-hum" and "mmm."

5. *Adaptors*: Any nonverbal behaviors concerning the maintenance of bodily functions or the management of emotions that were first learned as a child and subsequently adapted in adult life.

These category systems are also useful in illustrating the interdependence of verbal and nonverbal communication. In the total communication process, nonverbal communication can adopt various roles in relation to verbal communication. The nonverbal signal may, for example, repeat or contradict what is said verbally; it may act as a substitute, modify or elaborate on the verbal message, emphasize particular parts, or regulate the communicative flow of an interaction (Knapp, 1972).

Research in nonverbal communication suggests that nonverbal messages are often a better indication of a person's attitude and emotions than verbal ones.

Let us consider some of the more common nonverbal communicative acts in which we engage.

## Proxemics

Proxemics is the study of social and personal space and a person's perception of it. Proxemics is said to lead to interaction, which in turn leads to development of friendships. Technology, however, is widening the personal space around us: we sit behind a typewriter, we carry a lot of things (e.g., Emma's walkie-talkie). Our personal space is affected by our cultural (environmental) differences—that is, some cultures assign two or three feet for personal space, yet others feel comfortable at one foot. Then there is the aspect of personal "territory" (a basketball team plays better at home). Assumption of proprietory rights toward some geographic area when there is no basis for these rights is called *territoriality*. The territory is defended by a person (or group) against members of its own species. The twins will defend their right to their chairs, their beds, and whatever is perceived as belonging to them. While territory is stationary, personal space can be defined as an invisible shield that a person carries everywhere. This shield regulates the amount of physical space to be placed between

oneself and other persons. The twins (children) actually stand closer together than the adults in their family.

Gestures, are often used by the individual in place of words and represent a more primitive kind of communicative response. Gestural patterns are culturally induced rather than inherited. In other words, when people move out of their ethnic groups and enter into other groups, they demonstrate less gestural behavior identified with their original ethnic group than those who retain their ethnic ties. Children also learn by imitating gestures of their associates.

*Gestures*

Touching was our earliest means of making contact. It was and still is essential to our well-being. Research indicates that children who are not touched are highly susceptible to a disease called *marasmus* ("wasting away"). Children in orphanages often die from this ailment.

Our professions lead us to touch in different ways. Bill touches his customer's head, which indicates that a great deal of trust is afforded him. Emma touches by "frisking" an offender—seldom an affectionate gesture. When she touches, it is often an invasion rather than a pat or a stroke, which are the types of supportive touching used by teachers Dora and Bert. Many cultures avoid touching certain parts of the body, and some people touch totally only in the lovemaking situation.

*Touch*

Clothing identifies periods of history, social status, and the roles people assume. Clothing seems to be in a state of constant change, al-

*Clothing*

though male business executives apparently have preferred the dark pinstripe suit for ages. Emma pushes her sunglasses atop her head, seldom wears her hat. Compare her picture to the movie stereotype of helmeted officers who wear sunglasses and barely move their lips. Obviously Emma wishes to project a different image.

*Facial Expressions*

Facial expressions tell people how we feel. The muscles in our faces are capable of assuming 20,000 different expressions! We sometimes try to control our expressions because of societal demands. Some theorists claim that we often adopt the expressions of the people around us, especially those we tend to admire.

Emma says she can read *fear* in a person's eyes; Dora claims she knows when a student is telling a "fib." The Profile of Nonverbal Sensitivity Test (PONS) discriminates among personalities, and shows that high scorers (those who are more accurate in interpreting nonverbal clues) function better socially and intellectually; they have fewer friends but enjoy warmer, more honest and satisfying same-sex relationships than low scorers do.

While we are affected by all nonverbal signs, signals, and actions, we must learn to avoid making hasty evaluations of people on nonverbal clues alone. It is important that we consider the context of the setting, the overall behavior of the person, and, if that person is speaking, that we listen to his or her words.

Remember: Nonverbal communication can emphasize, contradict, or regulate verbal messages. In perceiving emotions and attitudes it is a better indicator than verbal. And when verbal and nonverbal communications contradict, the nonverbal channel is considered the most reliable.

Generally speaking, most encounters involve talking. We may use a lot of nonverbal signals, and certainly some of them are persuasive, but the body of the message usually involves words. Stage two in our communication, whether the encounter is a casual conversation, dialogue, debate, or interview, seldom deals in silence.

## VERBAL COMMUNICATION

### We Use a Word . . . or a Group of Words

In Chapter One, we touched briefly on the idea that words have no meanings and that meanings are found in the people involved in the communicative act. That statement is somewhat misleading; individuals do assign denotative definitions as well as connotative conceptions to their vocabularies.

An area known as General Semantics was developed by Alfred Korzybski and further analyzed by scholars Irving Lee, S.I. Hayakawa and I.A. Richards. Korzybski felt that intended messages and received messages are often misinterpreted by the participants in the communication act.

According to these scholars the problem is that we seem to live in two worlds, the real world and the word world. We try to talk about the world of things, but we have a limited number of words with which to talk about a limit*less* number of things. Reality hits us when we discover that for the 500 most commonly used words in our language, there are 14,070 dictionary definitions; and although a single word like *run* or *fast* rigidly adheres to a unique left-to-right pattern, meanings change with speakers, regions, contexts, and time.

Korzybski postulated a symbolic-empirical continuum to help listeners fit their language more effectively into their own perception of reality as well as into the speakers' framework or perception.

1. Dating
2. Indexing
3. Etcetera
4. Quotes
5. Hyphens (Polarization)

### Dating

*People and events are in a state of constant change.*

Mentally we use dates to indicate our awareness that people and situations change with time. As we constantly point out, and will continue to reiterate throughout this text, people and events are always in process. Therefore the listener must adjust his or her thinking to this premise. Just as a reporter keeps track of a story and updates it, so, for example, should Dora realize that the twins will be different in some way after their incident with the dirty clothes.

### Indexing

Semanticists hold that we should look for differences within some assumed similarity. Things that look alike on the surface are often very different. We tend to acknowledge the similarities between situations and ignore the differences. Emma is a police officer, but she is not *every* police officer: Police Officer A (Emma) is not Police Officer B (the sergeant).

### Etcetera

In our ever-changing world, and particularly in our developing and widening circle, no person can say *all* there is to say about any one thing. According to the scholars we must leave ourselves options or "room" to indicate an infinite amount of information on any given subject matter. An apple, for example, is round and red and delicious; but to some it may represent applesauce, or the planting of a tree . . . *et cetera.*

### Quotes

We use words personally and their uses do not cover all possible meanings. Many times authors put highly abstract words in quotation marks because they are giving specialized meaning to those words; the quotation technique lets the reader (listener) know that the implied definition may vary from the reader's (listener's) definition. To Americans "capitalism" may mean a way to achieve a high standard of living, but to Russians the word may suggest an exploitative tactic.

Definitions both *connotative* (applying to the *ideas* associated with a term, sometimes as a result of personal experience) and *denotative* (definitive meaning of a term, the class of things that it names) can change over time and space. People's perceptions of situations can also change the meaning of words. Inherent in the use of quotes is the realization that words are but symbols representing a real or imagined situation— and, as the situation changes, so do the images that the symbols represent.

*Definitions too, can change over time.*

The hyphen device implies that words we use divide our environment into two distinct opposites. When our vocabulary is not appropriate for the situation, we tend to see only two sides: good-bad, rich-poor, tall-short, and so on. We can avoid polarization and become more open minded by considering that most individuals are average in height and neither rich nor poor, and the variations between good and bad are countless.

*Polarization: or Hyphens*

In our later discussion of public speaking, we shall delve further into such aspects of language as the difference between oral and written usages, the various styles we adapt for different audiences, and the manner in which we actually deliver our words (dialects and accents). On a formal basis we are most conscious of those elements of talking, while informally we worry about how others perceive us and understand us.

Perhaps if we change our focus of attention away from ourselves and toward our audience (whether it is one person or many), our language may be an aid instead of a hindrance in the establishment of better human relationships. For example, suppose we focus on the behavior of a person—that is, on what he or she *does* and not on what you imagine he or she *is*. You would use adverbs (which relate to actions) and not adjectives (which relate to qualities). You might say, "Dora paced the floor waiting for the children," instead of "Dora is fit to be tied." In another situation we might focus our attention on giving the other person the information he or she can use instead of on satisfying our own need to talk. We shall explore further the concept of placing the audience in our spotlight in a later chapter on Public Speaking which includes material on audiences.

*Focus on your audience, not yourself.*

"Where are you going?" "Is it raining?" "What's for dinner?"

We interview on an information-gathering basis all day long, and although we associate the interview with two people, a group-

**WHEN TWO PEOPLE ASK QUESTIONS: INTERVIEWING**

*Information-gathering is*
*interviewing*

interview session is possible. We are constantly seeking and giving information, accepting counsel, or solving problems. According to communication scholars, an interview can be *directive* or *nondirective*, that is, we maintain control of a situation or we (willingly or unwillingly) relinquish control.

In real-life situations things are not always so clear-cut; we may move easily from "control" to "no-control" (from directive to nondirective) and back again, still managing to conduct a decent interview and accomplish our purpose. Dora's friend, Maria, works as press secretary to a Member of Congress. In this capacity she is required to conduct and participate in many interviews such as the following one. Study its structure closely.

## An Interview in Process

Maria studies the congressman's back across a wide oblong desk, waiting patiently for him to finish his phone conversation with a *Washington Post* reporter. She knows she has to be prepared and will have only a few minutes of his time. Brevity is the key because of his busy schedule. (The interview will last seven minutes.)

"Well—and you can quote me on this—" says the congressman into the receiver with all the seriousness he can muster, "I think those people in the State Department are a bunch of adolescent anarchists bent on promoting their own ideologies at the expense of losing our closest allies!"

Maria smiles as the congressman wheels his chair around to face her, raises his eyebrows, and smirks with satisfaction at the chance to sock it to the State Department once again.

Every Tuesday morning Maria reviews with the congressman the questions for Thursday's radio show. The broadcast is taped and 25 audio copies are mailed to radio stations throughout his district.

The congressman hangs up the telephone.

"Well, what's next?" (This is his attempt to control.)

"Congressman, here are the questions for Thursday's radio show. We're going to start with inflation. I'll ask you if there's anything Congress can do to fight inflation this year." (Maria assumes control.)

"All right, let's run through it."

"Here goes: recent public-opinion polls pinpoint inflation as the number-one concern of the American people. You've stated that you'll be making inflation your number-one legislative priority. Is there anything Congress can do to stop the inflationary spiral?"

The congressman listens, pauses, and his eyes narrow.

"No," he replies bluntly.

"*No?*" exclaims Maria. Almost immediately she laughs, and so does he.

"Well," he sighs, "all right, let's try it again." (In this brief exchange the congressman has seized control and then relinquished it to Maria.)

Maria then asks the question again, and the congressman answers with a discussion about a proposed Constitutional amendment that would require a balanced budget.

"Next question, about the draft . . ."

The briefing for the interview, which of course is an interview in its own right, continues. During the session the congressman also asks questions of Maria, who supplies him with details of current rumors concerning upcoming legislation.

Finally he says, "Ookay . . .," drawing out the "O" to emphasize that he has heard enough to make a decision.

A gentle knock on the office door signals the appearance of the congressman's personal secretary.

"George is on the line for you," she says. "Do you wish to take the call?"

"Yeah . . . Maria, anything else?" he asks.

"It can wait." Maria knows that this interview is over.

As she rises, the congressman hands her a column she has written for him.

"It's okay, kid. Next week do one on defense spending. Just say we're in favor of the President's budget this year and that we intend to ask for more money for the Navy. Get hold of the Defense Subcommittee on Appropriations and ask for some figures to back up the conclusions."

With this he waves her away.

## Categorizing and Planning Interviews

*Interviews can be dual- or multi-purpose.*

*In a formal interview prepare constructive questions.*

Maria's interview with the congressman clearly contained an opening, a body, and a conclusion. It included nonverbal messages, language, some principles of argument, and a shift of control. Implicit was a continuing relationship and sharing of experiences. There was also a purpose for meeting.

Besides being directive and nondirective, an interview can have one or more specific purposes. Both Maria and the congressman were giving and gathering information. Some counseling occurred as did some gentle persuasion.

Interviews can fall into specific categories or contain elements of a number of categories and purposes. *Information-giving* interviews are used in training, instruction, coaching, and job-related instructions. *Information-gathering* interviews include surveys and polls, investigations, and medical histories, and are the types of interviews conducted by researchers and journalists. *Selection* interviews are used in screening and hiring and placement. *Problems of interviewee's behavior* are interviews conducted in disciplinary situations, counseling, and evaluative sessions. *Problems of interviewer's behavior* are interviews involving the receipt of complaints and grievances. *Problem-solving* interviews deal with mutually shared problems. *Persuasion* interviews involve selling of services and products.

While many interviews shift in emphasis and purpose, some can indeed be narrowed down to one purpose, such as is done with the Neilson poll. We take our own polls daily, for example, when we ask, "Who wants to go to lunch with me?"

All interviewing, whether formal or informal, is a process of dyadic (two-person) communication. In a formal setting it has a predetermined and serious purpose. When we plan the interview, we are most conscious of the value of understanding the types of questions we use.

Some determinants of good questions are:

1. *Language level.* Questions should *not* contain words above the respondent's level of usage. Sometimes a person may give an answer even though he or she does not understand the question (we hate to appear stupid). By the same token if the level of language is *below* a respondent's usage, he or she may feel insulted and end the interview (or remain silent).

2. *Information level.* We should be aware of how much and what level of information the respondent can manage.

3. *Frame of reference.* As interviewers, we should be aware of a respondent's attitude toward place, person, or thing, based upon his or her own experiences. This works both ways; the person being interviewed can benefit by knowing something about the interviewer. Remember: The aim of the interview is to share language.

4. *Relevance.* Stick to the subject. Respondents dislike wasted time when they have been asked to come and talk to someone about a specific topic.

5. *Simplicity.* Novice interviewers tend to ask very complex questions—that is, multiple-stage questions, which amount to several at once. Try to get your answers one at a time.

There are basically two types of questions: open-ended and closed. Open-ended questions are very broad in nature and allow the respondent considerable freedom to determine the information he or she will give.

*Questions are of two types: open-ended and closed.*

*What is your name?* (closed)

*Tell me about your life. Was it full?* (open-ended)

Both are necessary at times, although the closed questions are more often used to save time and obtain specific information. A highly controlled closed question is the bipolar or yes-no question, such as, "Is the man dead?" The *leading* question is somewhat highly controlled and likely to bias the answer that is received. For example, "Does the man have a gun?" can be bipolar and leading, but "Is this where the creep that is making all the noise lives?" is a *loaded* question. Loaded questions tend to be highly emotional and judgmental.

*Questions can be of primary or secondary priority.*

We further put questions into two categories of priority: primary and secondary. The *primary* question introduces a topic or issue, while the *secondary* question flushes it out or probes it more deeply.

*What about the President's energy program?* (primary)

*What are some of its merits?* (secondary)

Unless you establish rapport with your interviewee, no interview will get underway successfully. And when you are being interviewed, it is just as important for you to understand your questioner's position. As the interviewer, how you make contact is an important matter. Under consideration must be (a) what you actually say, (b) the way in which you say it, (c) your nonverbal signals and whether they tie in with (a) and (b), and (d) your physical position in relation to the interviewee.

Most interviews, even when planned, do not fall into neat patterns. Even journalists, whose main job is to gather information, do not adhere to a strict pattern of just so many closed or open-ended questions in a given situation. We seem to have our own methods of obtaining information. The police officer must gather information quickly on the scene; the television reporter needs a short answer to accommodate the medium in which he or she works, the hairdresser must assess a customer's mood before giving information on hair care.

Consider Loren Nancarrow, a television reporter, and friend of Dora's family. Loren jotted down the manner in which he followed an assignment after he covered the news conference at City Hall. Loren deals in interview situations daily on a regular basis.

8:30:  *Given assignment to cover city government environmental planning committee special interest to developmental project across from Winrock shopping center. Sent alone as photographer will shoot for Ann and then join me later. Also assigned to follow up on the Spruce area barricades (street barricaded at request of residents).*

9:00:  *Arrived at meeting. The committee was hearing arguments on another matter, so spent time planning the followup story on barricades. Meeting over, no story.*

12:00:   Go to lunch.

12:30:   Go to Winrock and shoot Park Square (cover film).

1:30:   Arrived Roma Street to talk (about barricade story) to Maxine Bushman, who has a deaf child. Child not home. So will do a sour grapes story. Mrs. Bushman bitching because she lost and barricades will go up. Let her talk. Interesting "soup bite" (visual of subject eating) in which she says some old folks will ignore barricades. Shot "stand up" and decided there is not enough time allotted for story to include another interview.

3:30:   Arrived at station and wrote story to include sound bites on different aspects of the story. Producer says "keep it short" so the second sound bite goes . . . .!

6:00:   Producer runs wrong cart cut. Whole day's work goes down the tubes. Oh well.

Due to technology beyond his control, Loren Nancarrow's story was a combination of closed and open-ended questions: He allowed the lady to talk, which put her in the mood for controversy, and then narrowed the issue to a closed question so that he could get a short "sound bite." His news story generally has an opening shot (establishing the story), the body of the message (which usually means an interview), and a conclusion with Loren standing up and summarizing the event.

## WHEN TWO PEOPLE ARGUE

*Argument is found wherever people are found.*

When that casual conversation or that interview moves on to an argument, we sharpen our listening skills automatically because we use more past experiences and knowledge to conduct the communication exchange, and we become aware of nonverbal acts. We also talk a lot.

In the chapter on persuasion we deal more extensively with the question of argument and proofs. We will see that one theory claims that argument is found wherever people are found and knows no one setting. It is especially prevalent when two people get together. Argument can evolve from casual conversation or ongoing dialogue with people who are friends, enemies, or just chance acquaintances. We argue in normal everyday settings, and we often act as arbiters to settle other people's arguments.

For example, when Larry and Gary refused to pick up the clothes in Dora's room (see Prologue), they were arguing with her on a very simple scale. However, their argument followed a pattern which we will discuss further in the chapter on Persuasion. Simply stated they did the following:

**1.** They took an *inferential leap*. That is, they "figured" it was probably true that picking up clothes was harder than cooking. They really had no hard logic to support their *inference*.

**2.** They had *perceived* Dora's cooking every day and cooking didn't seem so hard to them. They knew how to cook scrambled eggs, after all, and that was fun. At least they wanted Dora to consider what they said. Gathering a heavy load of clothes was hard. So there existed a *perceived rationale.*

**3.** They felt they had a right to choose between picking up the clothes and cooking; at the very least, they felt they had the right to consider which was harder. Having *considered* and *inferred* that picking up clothes was harder, they made the comparison: This was their *right to choose.*

**4.** Of course a regulation of *uncertainty* existed, because neither one had tried that argument before or had, in fact, done a lot of cooking.

**5.** They were willing to risk confrontation with their mother. *Risk* is always a consideration in an argument.

**6.** Both Dora and the twins knew how to cook and how to pick up clothes (maybe not to the same degree!), so they *shared a frame of reference.*

Of course, Larry and Gary did not realize that they had *challenged* Dora, thus challenging the existing state of affairs, and would have to *prove* they were right and show reason for change. Dora gave them that opportunity, but after cooking scrambled eggs for three meals they decided picking up clothes was easier.

There are other things involved in formal debate. If we search, we discover that those things are found in our everyday lives, too. For example, Emma must plead her case to a judge while the defendant argues that he/she is innocent. The judge is the arbiter, listening to both, being fair and objective (hopefully), and coming to a decision based upon the facts in the case. In much the same way a mother listens to two (or more) of her arguing children and decides the issue. It may be argued that the mother finds it difficult to be entirely objective, or even fair, because of her emotional involvement with her children. A father is in the same position, but that doesn't stop either parent from deciding the case.

## SUMMARY

Two individuals who wish to find a common ground of understanding employ language that builds a supportive atmosphere. Descriptive language, empathy, and spontaneity are more constructive than attempts to control and evaluate. Each communicative encounter has an opening, a body, and a closing, and listening is important in every stage of the communication situation. Active listening requires full participation in the event. Besides striving to be more observant, we should make it easier for others to listen to us. We do this by building a supportive atmosphere, offering our audience something of value to them, helping them become well informed about the subject, and encouraging feedback.

Good listening habits include learning how to use listening responses effectively. Listening responses include showing interest and understanding, making encouraging comments, using echoes. Being aware of nonverbal communication, in fact "listening" to silent symbols and gestures, aids communication. Nonverbal communication includes sign, action, and object language. Ekman and Friesen developed a five-point system of classification of nonverbal behavior that included emblems, illustrators, affect displays, regulators, and adaptors. Some of the common nonverbal acts with which we communicate are the gestures we employ in place of words, our facial expressions, and how we dress and touch others.

As a general rule, though, most encounters involve speaking. The area of General Semantics, as developed by Alfred Korzybski, helped the communicator fit language into his or her perception of reality.

When people talk, they find themselves in a variety of situations including interviewing. We interview on an information-gathering basis all day. Interviews can be directive or nondirective and include closed and open-ended questions. An interview has an opening, a body, and a conclusion, and can fall into one specific category or contain elements of a variety of categories.

Any communication situation between two people has the possibility of moving into an argument. Argument is found wherever people are found and can evolve from casual conversation, interview, or dialogue. Many times we find ourselves serving as arbiters.

In our daily lives we move in and out of interpersonal situations and most of the time in those relationships we wish to be effective and happy. The fact that we have reached out to another person clearly means that we *intend* to be heard, that we have attempted to widen our circle of influence. In most instances we wish to influence others in some manner. Perhaps we merely wish to please others, or to reach, or to persuade. Whatever the intent, we have begun the expansion process and possibly may never really know how far we reach nor how many people we touch.

| | | |
|---|---|---|
| acceptable | emblems | nondirective |
| action language | etcetera | nonverbal |
| adaptors | facial expressions | opening |
| affect displays | gestures | proxemics |
| body | hyphens | quotes |
| clothing | illustrations | regulators |
| conclusion | indexing | selection |
| constructive | inferential leap | sign language |
| dating | information-gathering | supportive |
| debate | information-giving | atmosphere |
| defensive atmosphere | interviewing | touch |
| destructive | listening | verbal |
| directive | listening responses | communication |

**1.** *Student:* Make a list of questions that you can give to an interviewer so that he or she will get an accurate picture of you. Then find a partner, and exchange the questions. After you have read the questions, interview your partner using the questions he or she has given to you. As an interviewer, did you feel comfortable with questions you did not originally construct?

Follow this session with an interview session in which you construct your own questions and interview your partner. Then let your partner interview you.

How did the construction of the questions differ? In what session were more open-ended questions used? More closed questions? Leading questions?

**2.** *Instructor:* Divide the class into groups of five or six. The instructor will present a situation possessing the potential of conflict. Any daily local news incident found in the media can be used. After the explanation further divide the group into twos and assign each twosome the task of conducting a destructive, a constructive, or an acceptable discussion. Note voice levels, length of argument, attempts at rational thinking, settlement of conflict.

**3.** *Class:* We have all played charades; now lets play *double* charades: The sender of the message must use nonverbal signals and the *recipient* must respond with nonverbal communication (either symbols or actions).

Discuss the problems you faced in communicating without words. Which signals were easiest to understand? Where any body movements particularly oriented to certain professions?

---

**CIRCLING BACK**  Answers are found in the chapter; start with the pages closest to you.

1. If you keep the interviewee in mind when you devise your questions, what should you consider?
2. Explain directive and nondirective interviews.
3. Korzybski talks about dating, indexing, etcetera, quotes, and hyphens. Can you?
4. What are the three areas of nonverbal communication developed by Ruesch and Kees? What is the five-point system by Ekman and Friesen?
5. How does environment aid the listening process?
6. Name the four levels of listening.
7. How would you attempt to build a supportive atmosphere? A defensive atmosphere?
8. Explain how remarks can be constructive, acceptable, and destructive.

---

**REFERENCES**  Ekman, P., and W.K. Friesen. "The Repertoire of Nonverbal Behavior—Categories, Usage, and Coding." *Semiotica* **1** (1969): 49-98.

Gibb, Jack R. "Defensive Communication," *The Journal of Communication* **2** (1961):1414-1418.

Hayakawa, S.I. *Language in Thought and Action*, 2nd ed. New York: Harcourt, Brace and World, 1965.

Knapp, M.L. *Nonverbal Communication in Human Interaction*. New York: Holt, Rinehart and Winston, 1972.

Korzybski, Alfred. *Science and Sanity*, 2nd ed. Lakeville, Conn.: International Non-Aristotalian Library Publishing Co. 1947.

Lee, Irving J. *How to Talk with People*. New York: Harper and Row, 1952.

Ogden, C.K., and I.A. Richards, *The Meaning of Meaning*. New York: Harcourt Brace Jovanovich, 1925.

Reusch, J., and W. Kees. *Nonverbal Communication*. Berkeley: University of California Press, 1956.

# 3 the group (further expansion)

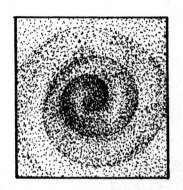

In Chapter 2, we observed the communication procedures of Officer Emma Gonzales as she responded to the scene of an automobile accident. Now let's check in on her followup activities.

Emma has telephoned the witnesses of the accident and from them has received sufficient information to warrant writing a ticket for the young woman. Both witnesses have stated that the young man was stopped at the light, that he proceeded on green, and that the young woman ran a red light. Apparently the young woman proceeded into the intersection *after* the light was completely red and the cars next to her were stopped.

Emma now goes to the young woman's apartment and rings the bell. The door is opened by the young woman's father. After introductions, the father calls his daughter and the *three of them* sit down to discuss the situation.

The discussion follows this line:

Emma:   I've talked to the witnesses and on the basis of their statements I am going to issue a citation for running a red light.

Ann:   All right. But I've been thinking, and I'm sure the light was yellow when I went through the intersection.

Father:   You see, Ann is honest and she doesn't realize the rest of the world isn't. She hasn't been around long enough.

Emma:   (Seeming to disregard the father's comment) May I see your license again please? (Ann hands her the license and Emma begins to write the ticket.)

Father:   Who were the two witnesses that testified for this guy?

Emma: Sir, there has been no testimony. They have made statements that bear out his story of the accident and so I am writing your daughter a ticket which she may fight in court if she feels that she is not guilty.

Father: Could I see the names of those witnesses?

Emma: Sure, here are the cards. (The father takes down the names and Emma continues to write the ticket.)

Father: She just doesn't realize that the world isn't full of people that wouldn't lie.

Emma: (Explaining the ticket to the young woman) You can sign here to admit that you have received the ticket. It is *not* an admission of guilt; it just says that you received the ticket. That's all.

Ann: I really don't think that I went through the red light.

Emma: You told me in the car that you probably did. (They are all silent.)

Father: How did the guy get the witnesses? They are his witnesses, aren't they?

Emma: He got the witnesses at the scene of the accident. They were gone by the time I got to the scene. They were directly behind his car and next to his car and they saw the whole accident.

Father: They are his witnesses.

Emma: They are witnesses that were at the scene of the accident. They didn't know him before the accident and they volunteered their information. They did not collaborate with each other. Is that what you're trying to say?

Father: No . . .

Emma: Call the number at the bottom of the ticket if you have any questions. They will also tell you when the court date will be set. Oh, and sir, did you have any insurance on the car?

Father: No, there was no insurance on the car. It was in her name and not mine. I had just changed it.

**A person assumes different roles in different groups.**

As a police officer, Emma is a part of many different kinds of *groups* in which she assumes very different roles. At times she acts as *counselor* in domestic altercations, at others as *leader* in situations of conflict. She may learn something, share information, or help *solve* the problems of others. As witnessed above, she did all these: *relayed information* (the witnesses' confirmation of the young man's story), *learned something* of the woman's home situation and her relationship with her father (he is protective), and *solved the problem* of who was at fault in the accident (she gathered and presented evidence). On many other days, she is part of an information-gathering team which eventually may link up with state and federal teams. Like many other professionals, Emma's modern workaday world has the capability of expanding and reaching international proportions. Incidents of international cooperation between police agencies have doubled in the last ten years.

Like Emma, we all spend some time each day as part of a team effort or group gathering. We gather in groups to learn something, to share information, or to solve problems.

In our daily lives we move easily in and out of groups. In fact we move from one type of communication situation to another much as an actor moves from one scene to the next. Emma, Dora, and Bill move from small family groups, to professional groups, to social groups. Bill conducts early-morning discussion sessions with his employees, then moves easily to one-to-one relationships with his customers. Loren Nancarrow, our newscaster, finds himself interviewing the mayor of a city, then listening to a news briefing, then moving into the small group which comprises his news crew.

Essential for our sojourn into groups are all the same skills necessary for effective communication between two people. Everything we've discussed in Chapters 1 and 2 applies also to group situations. The only difference is that we're communicating with more people at one time. Our circle widens to include more members.

At this point you may justifiably ask why we bother to study group communication separately, if the necessary skills are so similar to those of one-to-one communication. The reason is this: Despite the many similarities, there are differences in the *structure* of those relationships.

*We gather in groups to learn something, to share information, or to solve problems.*

*Group relationships differ in structure from one-to-one exchanges.*

## WHAT IS A GROUP?

Cartwright and Zander (1968) define a group as "a collection of individuals who have relationships to one another that make them interdependent to some significant degree." Others have offered the opinion that a group shares a relationship in which change in one part produces change in the others, that the group process takes place over time, that the interaction is dynamic and the relationships among component parts in constant flux. Like other communication situations, a group is never static.

*A group is never static.*

But if, as Cartwright and Zander state, a group is a collection of people who have a relationship with one another, how can we distinguish the "collection" from the "group"? For example, do people waiting in line for a bus comprise a group, or are they just a collection of people? Are students gathered in the classroom a collection or a group?

Every day the mayor of Albuquerque waits for the bus a block from his home. He is joined by a collection of people at the bus stop. When he first started riding the bus, he just stood in the line; being an open and receptive individual, however, he soon began to greet people, and discussions on the state of the city ensued. Soon the collection of people came to be known as "the mayor's bus group." On the mayor's birthday they had a party on the bus.

When did they cease to be a *collection of people* and become a *group*? The answer might be, "When they felt a sense of belonging to that particular collection." In other words, the key is *identification*. In Emma's group of three, each person identified the role he or she was assuming in that relationship, became aware of the procedures for functioning effectively, and recognized that there was a task to be performed.

In the mayor's group the goal is primarily social and the discussions are based on current topics. The identifier is the meeting place.

On the other hand, every week Bill Hungate holds a group-discussion meeting, and he says there are five elements present: (1) He plans the session in advance, so that everyone is aware of the time and place. (2) He creates a permissive informal atmosphere by gathering people in a circle and seeing that everyone has coffee. (3) He encourages everyone to speak to his or her fullest capacity. (4) He states his purpose; for example, "We're going to talk about cutting." (5) He exercises some leadership by opening the meeting and keeping it going.

*A group exists because it satisfies some need.*

Bill holds these meetings every week because he and his staff feel a need to get together. A group exists because it satisfies some need: the need may be interpersonal (mayor's group) or the need to accomplish some task for which a group effort is necessary (Emma's group). Bill and his employees remain in the group as long as the need is satisfied. If Bill could handle all the problems of the establishment himself, he probably would not get together with his employees. If the employees felt they were wasting their time, they might be unresponsive to the meetings. Needs of groups vary; us-

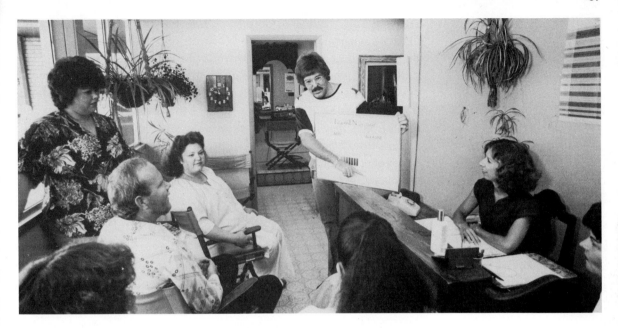

ually the main need is to accomplish some goal that is either task- or socially oriented.

Groups operate along two lines: the *procedural*—that is, its framework (emotional, logical, rules, regulations, etc.) and the *relational* (who likes whom, how people get along, what roles they assume, and so on). Contributing to both lines of operation is the atmosphere, the "climate" in which the group works. The climate may be formal or informal.

What determines the formality or informality of a group? There are no set rules. Much depends on the composition of the members, the personalities involved, and the procedures under which they choose to operate.

## TYPES OF GROUPS

Small groups take many forms, including committees, teams, panels, conferences, boards, commissions, and councils. In most instances such groups are formed to solve problems. This can be done formally or informally through oral or written reports; many groups arrive at consensus simply by "talking it over."

Groups normally perceived as "formal" may operate in an informal atmosphere. A Cable Advisory Committee formed by a southwestern city consisted of members headed by a young woman who stated simply, "We are going to be informal, no gavel pounding, no 'Madam Chairman' talk." The following year a new chairman was appointed, and he adhered strictly to *Robert's Rules of Order*. Such committees can choose to be formal or informal. City councils, on the other hand, and the wide spectrum of public boards and commissions that perform ongoing functions (such as the passing of ordinances and resolutions) usually have a set agenda and employ some rules of parliamentary procedure.

Robert F. Bales states that every group goes through three phases of development:

1. *Orientation*, when members arrive at common definition of the situation or the problem that must be solved.
2. *Evaluation*, when the group establishes the values that will guide them.
3. *Control*, when a status hierarchy is established to deal with the problem of who controls whom.

These phases of development apply to public and private groups alike. By definition, a public group opens its meetings to people other than those involved in the discussion, while a private group does not have this second audience and is open only to those who are involved in the discussion. Thus Congress is a public group, but when Dora, Bert, and the boys sit down to discuss their vacation plans, they comprise a private group.

## Public Groups

**The symposium** Members of a symposium make individual presentations. Sometimes there is one main subject and it is divided into segments, with each member addressing a particular area. Very often the audience will become part of the discussion in a question-and-answer period after the initial subject presentation is over.

**The panel discussion** Participants in a panel discussion seem more spontaneous, although often they are very well prepared and have been chosen because of their intellectual pursuits in a particular field. An agenda is usually planned and problem-solving can occur. Panel discussions can also evolve into participation from a community audience and may focus on issues that do not necessarily involve problem-solving.

## Private Groups

**Small-group and private discussion** Most small groups are private discussion groups that come together to solve problems. There is no audience other than those in the group and this type of group includes workshops, study groups, reading clubs, and training sessions. Private closed discussions are sometimes conducted by committees, boards, councils, and conferences that at most times are public.

**Radio and television discussion groups**  Though held in "closed" sets at times, these radio and television groups can be both public and private—that is, they may or may not have a "live" audience. Of course they have a mass audience, and in this sense they do not fall conveniently within the limits of either definition. The audience that is stimulated by the discussion usually does not have the opportunity for immediate feedback. However, with the recent advent of cable and computer polling, some viewing audiences can make immediate (albeit limited) responses on a push-button terminal attached to their set.

**Public and Private Groups**

Let's look in on one of Bill Hungate's recent meetings with his staff.

As usual, Bill has made certain that no early appointments will interfere with the discussion, and he has arranged comfortable seating so that each employee may face all of the others.

"Everyone have coffee?"

Bill opens the discussion when everyone appears settled. "Everyone have coffee?" he asks. "Well, I'd like to start with Jane and give her a critique of what she's been doing. First off, Jane, keep your station clean. I can't stress that enough."

At this point Jane interrupts with a shy smile and a soft "Yes."

**An Informal Group in Action**

*The discussion has an opening, . . .*

INFORMAL GROUP

The tension in the room disappears as Bill becomes apologetic: "Well, everyone knows I have a kind of fetish with that, but the reason is self-evident. We have always been a clean shop."

*. . . a body,*

Bill continues by telling Carol how well she does nails. Then he shifts the emphasis to an area of general interest by asking, "Who has read one of the journals pertaining to the new trends and styles?"

A discussion about new trends goes on for some minutes, followed by the introduction of other topics. Several problems are aired.

"Sometimes the waiting room looks awfully crowded," comments one employee.

The solution to this problem is a consensus about "not sitting around between customers" and "looking at scheduling again."

*. . . and a closing.*

The group is in deep discussion about the scheduling problem, when someone knocks at the door. Jane says, "That's my customer!" and the meeting is informally adjourned.

In this very simple and informal gathering the elements originally mentioned by Bill are apparent:

1. Advance planning
2. Informal atmosphere
3. Everyone encouraged to speak
4. Purpose stated
5. Leadership present (can shift during meeting)

## The Anatomy of a Formal Group

*In formal groups more attention is paid to the language and form of the opening, the body, and the closing.*

What makes a group formal?

In the preceding account of an informal group we saw an *opening* (Bill said, "Everyone have coffee?" thus calling the meeting to order). We observed the *body* or message (several topics were discussed and

the purpose of the meeting was aired). And finally, it wasn't hard to identify the *closing* ("That's my customer!" was a signal for adjournment).

As in simple two-way conversation, there is generally an opening, a body, and a closing to *all* communication situations. In formal groups, more attention is paid to the language and form of these three elements.

Recently the women in Albuquerque's city government held a series of meetings to plan a conference. At each meeting a prepared agenda was distributed to all who attended.

*Sample Agenda*

Call to Order (welcome by the presiding officer)

Reading and Approval of the Minutes

Treasurer's Report

Reports of Club Officers (president first)

Recommendations from the Board or Executive Committee

Reports of Standing Committees

Reports of Special Committees

Special Orders

Unfinished Business

New Business

Announcements

Adjournment

*Procedure*

In many formal groups the call to order is followed by religious or patriotic exercises. Invocation and prayer always precede the pledge of allegiance. Sometimes a roll call is taken either orally or silently to confirm that a quorum (at least 50 percent of the membership) is present.

The secretary stands to read the minutes and the chair handles the approval of the minutes. If there are corrections, they are usually handled by general consent. The treasurer's report is never adopted (the *auditor's* report is adopted) but is placed on file.

When committee reports are presented, the president (or chairman) introduces them. However, if an officer makes a recommendation in his or her report, he or she does not move that it be adopted; another member makes the motion. The president usually checks in advance and calls on only those who have reports to make.

Unfinished business is that which was recorded as unfinished in the minutes of the previous meeting. New business requiring action is read by the secretary, who makes the necessary motions. Bills are read by the treasurer, who makes the necessary motions.

Sometimes a program is presented. (The program can be presented either before or after the business meeting.) The chair calls on the program chairman, who introduces the program.

Additional business is permissible following the program. Finally, the chair makes announcements and asks for any pertinent announcements from the membership. The meeting may be adjourned by general consent, or by a motion and vote of the assembly.

*Variations are the norm.*

Variations of procedure happen in nearly every meeting. The most widely accepted rules in small formal groups are those set down by *Robert's Rules of Order.* Some city and state public groups follow those rules, while others create their own or use older, more traditional legislative procedures.

For most of us, though, a general knowledge of Robert's rules will suffice. The following is a very brief description of the types of motions made in parliamentary procedures and some guidelines on how to present a motion. Whether we preside or are members of a group, we will at some time make a motion to act in some way.

*Four Types of Motions*

1. *Main motions*: This motion introduces the subject to the assembly for consideration. A main motion cannot be made when another motion is before the assembly. Main motions yield to privileges, subsidiary, and incidental motions.
   Example: "I move that we buy the tape recorder."

2. *Subsidiary motions*: These motions change or affect how a main motion is handled and must be voted before the main motion.
   Example: "I move that we amend the purchase of 24 new buses by adding the stipulation that they must be equipped with lifts for the handicapped as proposed by federal regulations."

3. *Privileged motions*: These are most urgent and concern special or important matters not related to pending business.
   Example: "I move that we adjourn because I smell smoke."

4. *Incidental motions*: These are questions of procedure that arise out of other motions and must be considered before the other motion.
   Example: "I move that we suspend the rules for the purpose of wishing Joe a happy birthday."

When you make a motion, you should ask yourself:

1. *Is it in order?* Does it relate to the business at hand and are you presenting it at the right time? Does it conform with the by-laws?

2. *Should I interrupt the speaker?* If your motion is very important, the speaker may be interrupted. After the interruption has been attended to, that speaker will automatically regain the floor.

3. *Do I need a second?* Usually yes, unless it is a privileged motion. A second indicates that some other member will consider your motion. This prevents motions of interest to only one person from reaching the floor.

4. *Is my motion debatable?* Most motions are debatable because parliamentary procedure guards that right to free and full debate. However, some privileged and incidental motions are not debatable.

5. *Can my motion be amended?* Some motions can be altered by striking out, inserting, or doing both. Amendments must relate to subject as presented in main motion.

6. *What vote is needed?* Most motions require only a majority vote, but motions concerning the rights of the assembly, its members, or its constituency need a two-thirds vote to be adopted.

7. *Can my motion be reconsidered?* Some motions can be redebated to give members a chance to change their minds. The move to reconsider must come from the winning side. Following debate, if reconsideration is favored by two-thirds of the assembly, the motion may be revoted.

As a member of a formal group it behooves you to learn the procedures used by the group so that you can be an active member. Later we shall discuss the leadership role in groups, particularly the process of conducting a meeting. Meanwhile the following information is especially important for the active member. Now that you know how to make up an agenda and what a motion is, here is how you go about moving the group to action.

When you wish to be heard at a meeting, always wait until the last speaker is finished. Then rise and address the chairman. Say: "Mr. [Madam] Chairman," or "Madame [Mr.] President." In council or large groups the person asking for the floor will state his or her name and affiliation, so that the chairman can recognize him or her: "Jack Zorabedian, Precinct Seven."

*Be affirmative.*     Now that you've obtained the floor, *make your motion.* Always state your motion affirmatively. After all, you requested the floor and it's important to you. Say, "I move that we *do* . . . ," not "I move that we *forget* it." Avoid personalities and stay on the subject. This rule is sometimes ignored, however, in state legislatures (as well as in Congress), where the most humorous moments often involve references to other members of the body—but they're always made with respect.

After you have made your motion, *wait for someone to second it.* Usually another member will say, "I second the motion," or the chairman will call for a second. Remember that if there is no second, your motion is lost. This seldom happens, as there is usually someone who will second a motion as a matter of courtesy.

After your motion has been seconded, *the chairman should restate your motion.*

The chairman must say, "It has been moved and seconded that we. . . ." After this happens, debate can occur. Your motion is now the property of the assembly and you cannot change it unless the members consent to the change.

After you hear your motion stated, you may wish to *expand on your motion.*

You are allowed to speak first. When you do, you must direct all comments to the chairman and keep within the time limit as stated by your organization's bylaws (these vary). You may speak again after all the others who wish to speak have spoken; you may speak a third time, if a motion to suspend the rules is passed with a two-thirds vote. (Anything can be done with a two-thirds vote!)

After debate and discussion have been completed, *the chairman will put your question to the members.* He or she asks, "Are you ready for the motion?" If there is no more discussion, a vote is taken or a motion for a previous question may be adopted.

Knowledge of how to open and adjourn a meeting, obtain the floor, and make a motion is beneficial to any member of a small formal group. Most large formal groups include a recognized parliamentarian, who is called upon when rules need to be clarified. However, in the political arena (city councils, state legislatures, and Congress) most members find it essential to study carefully the rules and regulations governing their group sessions. To function effectively without this knowledge is virtually impossible.

If you intend to move into a leadership position, a knowledge of how to conduct a formal meeting is requisite. According to Robert's rules, everything in parliamentary procedure is based on order (one thing at a time), courtesy, justice, rights of the minority and will of the majority.

An attempt to divide rigidly the roles of the leadership and membership within most groups is not only difficult, but also impractical. Realistically we move quite smoothly from one role to another depending on the situation at hand. For the purpose of defining responsibility, however, let's examine them separately.

## ROLES IN GROUPS

### Leaders

"Take me to your leader."

Those five words have served as the caption of many cartoons featuring space-craft landings. If some creatures from outer space landed in *your* front yard and asked *you* that question, where would you take them? To the President? To the mayor? To the chairman of the Downtown Renovation Committee? To the head of your household?

On a planetary basis, we would have a hard time identifying a single leader in the 1980s. Governments change: they also rise and fall pretty fast nowadays. In history books the leaders, at least those to whom we point with pride, are easy to identify. They had *ethos*—that is, a moral character which was the source of the ability to persuade; they had *pathos*, the ability to touch feelings and to move people emotionally; and they had *logos*, the ability to give solid reasons for their actions and to inspire people intellectually. History's great leaders, in retrospect, also seemed to possess a vision of success. Pericles, Alexander the Great, Julius Caesar, Thomas Jefferson, and Franklin D. Roosevelt left a legacy of words devoted to uplifting their people with

visions of a better future. Other leaders gave spiritual guidance, while some prepared their people for war.

*Leadership is difficult to define.*

Today leadership on a day-to-day basis, from heads of state to heads of households, is more difficult to define. Actually it is very elusive. Defining all parts would be an impossible task. Consider the words of French critic Henri Peyre (1974):

*Leadership can be but a broad ideal proposed by the culture of a country, instilled into the young through the schools but also through the family, the intellectual atmosphere, the literature, the history, the ethical teaching of that country. Willpower, sensitivity to the age, clear thinking rather than profound thinking, the ability to experience the emotions of a group and to voice their aspirations, joined with control over those emotions in oneself, a sense of the dramatic . . . are among the ingredients of the power to lead men.*

*Leaders may be charismatic or functional.*

Though we have many different opinions about how to define leaders, we seem to place them into the categories of charismatic or commonplace (sometimes called the romantic and the functional, or the socioemotional leader and the task leader). What do these titles imply? Let us examine two broad definitions.

1. *Charismatic.* Those leaders who possess certain traits such as vision, individualism, courage, and sheer physical stamina. Charismatic leaders inspire others to follow them.

2. *Functional.* Those leaders who facilitate the interaction of people and move the group forward toward the completion of the task. Functional leaders are more pragmatic in their approach to problems.

From charismatic to functional takes in the visionaries who hypnotize and inspire their followers to worship and blind obedience, as well as the pragmatists who are hardly visible in a group of laborers all pulling equally at a task.

The leadership of Aristotle's time had its roots in the Age of Reason and focused on harmony between the emotional, spiritual, and rational, giving priority to the rational being.

During the Age of Reason, the individual was an integrated part of the society and every person became a potential leader. In the United States we support this point of view when we insist that every child can grow up to be President, that leadership can rise from every rank of the society. Opponents of this view declare that democracy mandates mediocrity, that somewhere in the upper echelons of society there should be a training ground for leaders. In the United States only the military provides formal leadership training. The business management courses do so to a limited extent, but they rely heavily on case studies and experience.

Whether a leader provides a function—that is, performs actions that assist the group in achieving its goal—or is so greatly admired that others are inspired to give peak performance, one thing is certain: All leaders need followers. To follow is not a passive position. John Gardner (1974) says: "Leadership in the U.S. is not a matter of scores of key individuals. It is a matter of tens of thousands, even hundreds of thousands, of influential men and women [who] create the climate in which public opinion is formed."

On a practical level, for Bill and Bert and Dora and Emma and all of us who for some reason, at some time, assume the leadership role, the following rules might serve to guide our behavior. They are based upon the democratic point of view that everyone is a potential leader and upon the principles of the Age of Reason, which held that leaders should possess ethos, pathos, and logos.

1. Leaders should know how to create a supportive climate. In other words, break the ice at the opening of the meeting— serve coffee, tell a joke, or sympathize with a member.

2. Leaders should study the task and the problem in depth. If possible, they should do this before the meeting convenes. If not, they should explore it in depth at the meeting.

3. Leaders should encourage participation, help those who are hesitant, and guide those who are overzealous.

4. Leaders should encourge new thought and critical analysis.

5. Leaders should pitch in and help solve the problem.

6. Leaders should understand the objectives and procedures under which the group wishes to operate; they should respect both.

7. Leaders should assume responsibility during a crisis and, if necessary, be willing to take command in a more autocratic manner in order to make the most efficient use of time.

The qualities necessary to use this guide effectively are intelligence and judgment, dependability and aggressiveness, knowledge, cooperation, and a sense of humor.

## Members

Leaders are not excluded from assuming the following roles, just as group members are not excluded from assuming leadership at various times. As we noted earlier, individuals often move smoothly from one role to the other (and sometimes back again) depending upon the situation.

## Task Roles

1. *Initiating*: Defining the problem, setting the rules and contributing ideas. Example: "There is a real energy problem in this city. We need to look seriously at the money allocated to the bus system. Let's go over that budget carefully."

2. *Information giving and seeking*: Asking for or giving opinions about a member's (or the group's) attitude toward a suggestion: Example: "I think we need the budget figures from the transit manager."

3. *Elaborating and clarifying*: Providing additional information about a particular suggestion or idea. Example: "Bill (the transit manager) is really upset over that cut in transit's advertising budget, so we should keep that in mind when we look at the figures."

4. *Orienting and summarizing*: Reviewing the significant points covered when guiding the direction of the discussion. Example: "Well, I think we understand the budget problems here, including why we cut the advertising, so let's move on to finding out what federal funds are available."

5. *Consensus taking*: Checking to see if the group is ready to make a decision. Example: "Sounds like we all want to get those matching funds from Washington, right?"

## Maintenance Roles

We behave in different ways according to our perception, the environment and the situation.

1. *Harmonizing*: Resolving differences and reducing tension, sometimes with the use of humor. Example: "Hey Bill, what's a little budget cut? Now you don't have to put up with that cute reporter!"

2. *Compromising*: Offering a compromise or a change in position. Example: "I'd like to take the federal money, but can we do so and still retain our independence?"

3. *Supporting and encouraging*: Praising and accepting contributions of others. Example: "I think Councillor Baca's idea about complying with the federal regulations and installing the lifts is great!"

4. *Gate-keeping*: Facilitating interaction with all members. Example: "Councillor Hoover, you've been silent. What do you think of those federal regulations?"

5. *Standard setting and testing*: Checking out the group's progress and the group's feelings. Example: "I'm not really sure everyone here is in accord about the budget yet. Is that so?"

In addition to task and maintenance roles, group members at times have individual problems and assume roles that will facilitate the solution of these individual, or self-centered problems. These roles often conflict with the group goals.

*Individual Roles*

1. *Blocking*: Refusing to cooperate by rejecting all ideas. Example: "For crying out loud, why should we go along with *any* government regulations? They always screw us up!"

2. *Withdrawing*: Remaining indifferent, avoiding the topic. Example: "Forget it. Let's just do it our own way."

3. *Dominating*: Interrupting, monopolizing the conversation. Example: "Now hold it a moment, I have something to say about that. . . !"

4. *Being aggressive*: Boasting, criticizing, fighting. Example: "Oh come on now, do you honestly think we're dumb enough to swallow that idea. . . ?"

We agree that people meet in groups to learn something, share information, and solve problems, but seldom do all these things happen within a single session. Remember, groups are never static. In real-life situations, the people in the groups move in and out of other communication environments and carry with them their worlds, their opinions, and their beliefs about the group and its problem. Often one issue goes through many types of communication situations. While it

**HOW GROUPS EVOLVE AND WIDEN**

*Often one issue goes through many types of communication situations.*

### The Ditch-Fence Story: the Widening Circle

may seem that one group has solved a problem, the reality is quite different.

Take, for example, the citizen's group comprised of Dora and her neighbors, who felt very good about the fact that they had "*solved the problem of ditch drownings by getting the city to build fences around the ditches.*" Their statement is accurate—to a point. They really didn't do it alone.

*On May 3, 1978, the prediction of the local Albuquerque radio station ("With summer coming, we can expect some ditch drownings") unfortunately came true when a two-year-old boy drowned in a drainage and irrigation ditch.*

*During the past 10 years, 58 drownings had occurred in unfenced drainage and irrigation ditches. And while much rhetoric had been spent on the issue, the 1978 drowning was the catalyst for a community meeting in an elementary school cafeteria. On May 4, 1978, an angry group of citizens with a common interest gathered and spoke about the problem and came quickly to a solution by shouting out suggestions. The city must fence the ditches! On May 8, a radio station polled 100 randomly selected residents, asking if they favored some form of fencing along the ditches. "Yes," said 57 percent; they did indeed favor fencing for ditch safety. (On May 17, a letter from Officer Gonzales appeared in the newspaper.)*

## Give Children Top Priority

ONCE AGAIN the City of Albuquerque, County of Bernalillo and State of New Mexico have lost a precious child's life to a drainage ditch in the valley.

The questions now are: What can we do? What are the Answers? As public servants, we can stand up and be heard and somehow strive to seek a positive solution to prevent these tragedies.

As a city police officer, assigned to the valley areas for the past two years, I am well aware of the grave dangers of these irrigation ditches. I see kids who are fascinated by water, as most kids are as they grow up. I am constantly getting out of my patrol car to "rap" with them and remind them of the dangers if they fall in. Granted, we have reached many elementary school-age children with our talks and presentations; but, what about the toddlers, like Antonio Tapia, who are too young to understand?

Many times a parent in the valley has approached me and asked, "Where do the priorities lie with the city, county and state? How do thousands of dollars appear to be easily allocated for housing and care of stray animals, renovation of old buildings and freeways that have miles and miles of chain link fences, etc."

These people feel their children's lives should have top priority. They realize that fencing the ditches is not a total solution to the problem; however, it would be a beginning and would ease the minds of the citizens who have to live with the fear that this tragedy could happen to them.

They would like to see the city, county and state unite to amend this problem, not only in Albuquerque, but all over the state.

EMMA EVA GONZALES
Albuquerque

*A second group meeting was held and several people were chosen to meet with Mayor David Rusk and present their proposal. Mayor Rusk agreed to pursue the issue and went to Santa Fe to convince Governor Gerry Apodaca that the state should ap-*

*propriate money for this project. Governor Apodaca responded favorably and granted the city $100,000 of federal funds (which the state had authority to disperse) for the purpose of fencing the most critical drainage ditches. On May 25 the Albuquerque City Council in a formal session supported the mayor and appropriated $62,500 (funds necessary to obtain the federal grant) for the "immediate construction of fencing." Thus, within two weeks, an ad hoc community-action group had obtained financial support to undertake the fencing.*

*But seldom is a public problem solved so easily or implemented so readily. In June an aerial view of the drains revealed that some of the residential property along the drainage ditches had encroached upon the right-of-way of the Middle Rio Grande Conservancy District. The District was under the jurisdiction of the county and governed by a board of elected officials. Within its right-of-way, the Conservancy District maintained a legal right to clean and service the drains without interference. The District knew nothing about the encroachment by new residents because it had last performed a land survey in the late 1920s. The implications of the encroachment situation were obvious: Since the property lines had invaded District territory, the city would have to consult the District on any fencing of the drain.*

*Communication by letter between City officials and County officials was not effective. The Mayor attended a meeting to plead his case. Finally the District agreed to allow the City to build the fences provided the fences conformed to the maintenance requirements of the District and provided the City would handle the maintenance and liability costs. In order to conform to the District's demands, however, the City would be putting up fences on private property through gardens and, in one instance, through a portion of a house.*

*The Mayor countered the District proposal with another plan which he felt was logical and practical. The County disagreed. Negotiations went on while the summer passed quickly and September gave way to October. The issue was kept alive by the press but negotiations broke down. The Mayor finally said that he considered the situation "unfortunate and the pursuit fruitless" and he dropped all negotiations.*

*Then, on March 5, 1979, the Mayor revived the issue and made the decision to begin fencing the ditches* without District approval. *The Mayor made the decision himself, knowing that the most dangerous time, summer, was approaching and that if he did not act soon he would lose the federal money.*

*The Mayor held a news conference and announced his decision. The District responded and said they would send bulldozers to tear down the fences if they were constructed.*

*Nonetheless, fences started to go up and within three days the District sent in a compromise plan. The City in essence had given the District two choices: It could bulldoze the fences and face the wrath of the citizens, or it could compromise.*

*The District offered a compromise plan which the City Council and Mayor accepted.*

*The fences were built.*

*Looking at this "group" problem-solving situation, we note that many other communication situations were involved, not the least of which concerned the mass media.*

*When the City gave the District two choices (bulldoze the fences and face hostility, or offer a compromise), the media covered the event in depth.*

*After the issue was finally settled, one member of the District said that he would have compromised earlier, but did not think that the "mood" for compromise existed at the early stages. In essence, the District member was a victim of his own environment: He had to support the norms of the group, which considered itself insulated from public opinion. The Mayor, on the other hand, recognized that he had to respond to public opinion immediately. The media helped change the mood in the ditch-fencing story.*

Retracing the ditch-fence problem, we note that the following communication situations evolved.

*Communication Situations (Major Meetings)*

1. *Large group*: Identified problem; brainstormed for solution; came quickly to consensus. (Problem, drownings; solution, fences—radio interview.)

2. *Mass media*: Radio interview (survey, random sampling); agreement about solution.

3. *Small group*: Information-giving group presented solutions to mayor. Initial effort to implement.
   *Action Group*: Agreement about problem and solution; implementation step.

4. *Dyad*: Mayor-governor; further agreement after discussion and presentation of evidence. Implementation, money.

5. *Group*: City Council agreed problem existed, solution viable, more money needed. (Summary: Within two weeks of the drowning, city action had obtained the financial support to undertake the fencing.) Problem of encroachment on Conservancy District arises.

6. *Media*: Mayor sent print message to District; messages did not solve anything.

7. *Group*: Mayor and governor attended Conservancy District board meeting to "plead" for the use of District land. City made some concessions. Public presentation, persuasion with evidence.

8. *Media, print*: Series of letters regarding plans and problems (based mainly on District's fear that position of fences might allow inadequate space for maintaining and cleaning ditches). Position and height of fences in constant negotiation as portions of the fencing were studied.

9. *Media, print*: On January 12, 1979, mayor wrote to District, "This unfortunate situation has caused the city to reconsider pursuit of this fruitless effort," and dropped negotiations. City could see no way to proceed without board approval, and board had made no effort to reinstitute discussions.

10. *Intrapersonal*: On March 5, 1979, Mayor Rusk made the decision to begin fencing without District approval, basing decision on (1) money from state would be lost, and (2) summer was coming.

11. *News briefing*: March 7, 1979; fences going up; Mayor gave Conservancy District two alternatives: they could bulldoze fences or move quickly toward a compromise.

12. *Group*: Conservancy District met March 13 and devised a compromise plan; Mayor accepted plan.

13. *Group*: City council met March 19 and approved compromise. Finally the solution had been reached; the fencing began, legally.

## Media Influence

Public group meetings in the latter part of the twentieth century are quite likely to attract media coverage. Years ago town meetings were held, or people gathered 'round the cracker barrel in the general store to discuss issues. The stories of what went on were relayed to the neighbors over fences. Today even the smallest town has a newspaper, if not a radio or television station.

As we observed in our ditch-fence story, media involvement and political climate are highly significant in any group problem-solving situation where a public issue is at stake. Knowledge of how the media work and familiarity with the political situation are necessary for the success of such a group effort.

For years people have been "putting in their two cents' worth." Brainstorming not only makes it *acceptable* to do so, but restricts anyone from saying, "Who asked you?"

Brainstorming was developed by Alex F. Osborn (1963). In his book, *Applied Imagination,* Osborn says that to brainstorm means to use the *brain* to *storm* a creative problem ". . . in commando fashion, with each stormer audaciously attacking the same problem."

To brainstorm effectively, persons in a group must amass all ideas spontaneously.

Below are some suggestions for setting up a brainstorming session. There are several accepted variations of technique, and our approach adopts a few of them.

It is imperative that someone in the group assumes the role of leader and explain that brainstorming is a cooperative effort to solve a problem. He or she encourages seemingly wild ideas, stresses the importance of positive thinking, and sets rules.

## SOLVING PROBLEMS IN GROUPS

### What is Brainstorming?

*To brainstorm effectively, persons in the group must amass all ideas spontaneously.*

| | |
|---|---|
| *Step One—Orient the Group* | 1. Set up a specific problem (don't start off trying to solve the war of the worlds).<br>2. Approach the problem noncritically. Each person (which means every brainstormer) cannot stop to analyze or evaluate his or her own ideas. Just think and talk. |
| *Step Two—Audaciously Attack* | 1. At the word "Go" all brainstormers spill out their ideas. Every suggestion is recorded.<br>2. If a member objects to a suggestion, the timekeeper (or leader) blows a whistle or yells "out of order!"<br>3. Set a time limit on the attack period. Five to ten minutes is usually enough. |
| *Step Three—Regroup* | Relax and discuss the ideas and re-examine the problem. Is it still too broad? Can you build on some of the ideas? |
| *Step Four—Second Assault on the Target* | Recharge! (Repeat step two.) |
| *Step Five—Record the Ideas* | All ideas are recorded (all names eliminated, so that it is truly a group effort). The person(s) who originated the problem are then given the suggestions and it is their job to sift the solutions and evaluate them. |
| *Step Six* | Don't let the solutions gather dust. Talk about how to put the suggestions into action. |

## What is Reflective Thinking?

*Reflective thinking is associated with the attempt to discover a solution to a problem.*

When the scarecrow in *The Wizard of Oz* finally got a brain, he put his forefinger to his head and reflected on the problem of the triangle.

Reflective thinking is associated with the attempt to discover a solution to a problem. It is sometimes called *constructive thinking or reasoning,* in contrast to intentional reasoning, which is associated with advocacy or persuasion. Reflective thinking is thought in process, or discovery. John Dewey prescribed a pattern for reflective thinking, which we have adapted below:

1. *Definition and delimitation of the problem.*
   All reflective thinking starts with a situation that is perplexing. The first task to locate the problem: the reason for the uneasy feel-

ing. We should ask ourselves, "What is the problem? What are its limits? What is the meaning of the terms used to state the problem?"

2. *Analysis of the Problem.*

After a problem has been located and limited in scope, we attempt to find out what is wrong and what is the cause of the trouble. Here we discover the relationship between *cause* and *effect*. Within this process of analysis we must determine what is expected of any proposed solution. In other words, what are the purposes and motives of the persons who are concerned? How will we measure the proposed hypotheses or solutions?

At this point we might ask ourselves:

**a)** What are the symptoms of the problem?

**b)** What are the manifestations of the problem?

**c)** What are the effects that can be observed?

**d)** What is the status quo concerning the problem?

**e)** What are the causes of the problem?

During our analysis we should discover the criteria or standards of value we wish to abide by. We could ask:

**f)** What are the purposes or motives or desires of the persons attempting to solve the problem?

**g)** What are the criteria by which the hypotheses or solutions are to be measured?

**h)** What are the values that are operating?

3. Suggest a solution.

The third logical step in reflective thinking is the suggestion of hypotheses or solutions. By a solution or hypothesis, we mean a proposal that is offered tentatively by some member of a discussion group (or is conceived by a solitary thinker) as a possible explanation or way out of the difficulty. The following questions suggest the nature of this step:

**a)** What are the possible hypotheses ("preliminary guesses at the truth . . . which are to be subjected to rigid tests")?

**b)** What are the possible solutions?

**c)** What is the exact nature of each hypothesis or solution—at least as tentatively conceived?

**4.** *Think through the suggested hypotheses or solutions.*
Ask the following questions:

**a)** What will be the consequences of the adoption of each hypothesis or solution?

**b)** To what extent will each hypothesis or solution answer the basic question or "solve the problem"?

**c)** What is the relation of each hypothesis or solution to the criteria or values?

**d)** What are the advantages and disadvantages of each hypothesis or solution?

**e)** What are the relative merits of each hypothesis or solution?

**5.** *Verify.*
The final step is that of verifying, if possible, the hypothesis or solution concluded to be the best. In problems of policy, this final step may also include consideration of the means of putting the solution into action. Such questions as the following may be raised in connection with this final step:

**a)** What can be done to test (verify) the hypothesis or solution concluded to be the best?

**b)** What "practice situation" can be devised to test the hypothesis or solution concluded to be the best?

**c)** In the case of a question of policy, what steps would need to be taken to put the hypothesis or solution into operation?

## THE PROPOSAL

*A proposal is a claim that must be substantiated by evidence.*

Let's look at what a group faces after it has identified the problem and recommended a solution.

Any proposal, no matter to whom or for what purpose it is submitted, is basically a claim that what is proposed will solve or alleviate a problem. Any claim must be substantiated by evidence. Furthermore, it must be shown that the evidence really supports the claim being made.

*This basically is what constitutes an argument.*

We have mentioned argument in our discussion of individual and one-to-one communication. The same methods are used in groups. An argument in the prosposal must prove at least three things:

**1.** That the problem does exist and should be solved.

**2.** That the solution you are proposing not only solves the problem, but also is the most advantageous way to solve the problem (that is, better than any alternative solutions).

3. That the solution you are proposing is *practicable*. Given the resources you already have, you must ensure that the solution could be put into effect if you acquire the resources requested.

This last condition is most important in our workaday lives. If you can prove each of these claims to the satisfaction of your audience, you will be in a good position to prove your ultimate claim: *It is in the best interests of all concerned that this proposal be approved so that we may implement the solution.*

In the previous discussion on problem-solving, there are a number of questions that must be answered if we are to prove our claim. What is the exact nature of the problem? How did it come to be? What is the present status? Whom does it affect? How serious or extensive is it? We must research that problem and find information that will support our claim. Then we must evaluate the information to judge whether it is really *relevant* and whether it is *reliable*.

*We must research the problem and find information that will support our claim.*

## Testing Reliability

1. Does the source of the information have any reason to falsify evidence? Is the source biased?
2. Is the source in a position to know the facts?
3. Does the source have the capacity (mentally and physically) to report the facts reliably?
4. Is the evidence confirmed by another source?
5. Does the evidence square with the known facts?

Now let's suppose all evidence is gathered and checked for reliability. How do we show that it is *relevant*.

Dora: "Now that summer's coming, one of the kids is going to drown in the ditches." (claim)

Neighbor: "How do you know?"

Dora: "The possibility was discussed on the radio." (evidence or data)

Neighbor: "Aw, come on—do you believe the stuff on the radio?"

Dora: "Well, this station does a lot of research and predicted that the crime rate was going to go up and it did." (warrant)

Neighbor: "Come on, that was a lucky guess. You mean to say you believe they're right about everything?"

Dora: "I wouldn't say they're right about *everything*, but I will say they have a good research staff and they've made sev-

eral predictions that were accurate that I know of."
(backing)

Neighbor: "Then if you're not certain that they're right about everything, you can't be certain that someone is going to drown in those ditches."

Dora: "No, but they've been pretty reliable, and besides, based on my experience—and I've lived here a long time—I've heard of kids drowning every summer in those ditches. I think there is a better-than-even chance that it will happen again this year." (qualification of claim)

Neighbor: "So what you are really saying is that there *probably* will be a drowning this summer because your source predicts that there will be and your source is usually right."

**Note:** It's much tougher to win an argument when you use terms like *everybody, none, always,* and *never,* or make a very *definite* statement. People will ask you to back up the claim. Dora said ". . . one of the kids is *going* to drown," not "*probably* will drown," and she needed stronger evidence to support that claim. If someone says, "That's a dumb kid because he is walking near the ditches, and anybody who walks near the ditches drowns," someone else is going to demand proof that there are absolutely no exceptions to that rule. If the speaker admits to an exception, then he or she has to prove that the dumb kid is not one of the exceptions or change the original claim. If he or she can prove that "most" kids who walk near the ditch will "probably" drown, then the challenger might be willing to accept that.

*Be careful not to overstate your claim!* Unless you can be sure that the only reason for someone drowning is walking near the ditches, you are not warranted—you have no right—to make the claim that anybody who walks near the ditches *will* drown.

You can test the strength of your argument by using self-questioning. In other words, try it out on yourself, anticipate such questions as, "So what?" "Are there any exceptions?"

When gathering evidence, you should make sure it's reliable. When using evidence to support your claim, you must make sure it's sufficient and relevant.

Remember: Submitting the proposal means that you have supported your claim (1) that a problem of the nature you describe does exist; (2) that because of its nature and existence, you—or others involved with you—are suffering in a particular way; (3) that you have established your criteria for an effective solution; (4) that your solution is more advantageous than the available alternatives; and (5) that your solution is practical.

Here the group would submit as evidence the resources, the qualifications of the people who would carry out the project, the availability of necessary materials, property, or personnel, plus costs, timetables, and so on.

Your proposal is actually a chain of arguments leading to a single conclusion: THIS PROPOSAL OUGHT TO BE ACCEPTED. But proposals are not always accepted as quickly as Mayor Rusk accepted the ad hoc citizens' group's proposal to build fences. The proposal instantly satisfied the needs of the citizens' group and the mayor could understand those needs as they were consistent with his own. The county did not accept the city's proposal so quickly. The proposal was not intentionally designed to meet the needs of the county. Thus the conflict.

As evidenced in the ditch-fence controversy, conficts in groups are inevitable mainly because people and groups of people are unique and have different needs and goals.

## CONFLICT AND GROUPS

A *simple conflict* arises when two people or two groups of people know one another's goals but neither can attain its own without preventing that of the other. For example, the county's personal desires were to protect their traditions and territory. These traditions (in the form of set guidelines on the amount of space necessary to clean the ditches) were in conflict with the city's desires to build the fences on the specified land.

A *pseudo conflict* arose through lack of understanding between the two groups. For example, certain letters inaccurately defined the territorial limits of each. When the aerial view was studied, these inaccuracies were eliminated. Sometimes a pseudo conflict arises simply because people do not share a common experience and cannot understand the language. Clarifying the language and the experience often results in erasing the conflict.

*Clarifying the language and the experience often results in erasing the conflict.*

The *ego conflict* is the conflict that arises most often in all communication situations. Throughout the ages "saving face" has been of prime importance, especially in political negotiations. Ego conflict occurs when people become so emotionally involved that there exists (in their minds) a threat to their egos. Focusing on the personalities within the group rather than on the issue encourages an ultimate conflict between two individuals.

Ego conflict can also arise between two groups, such as the "city" and the "county." Simple conflicts can develop into ego conflicts when members move from discussing relevant matters and topics to talking about the *people*, particularly the leaders, involved in the events. Soon they are making judgments about the characters of the individuals.

Is conflict really inevitable? While all groups do not ultimately end in conflict, there is always an element of conflict in even the mildest argument or proposal. Sometimes a degree of conflict is necessary for learning to take place; such conflict is not necessarily destructive if handled with honesty and respect. A simple conflict can find resolution through negotiation and can be resolved ultimately so that both parties win. A pseudo conflict, through clarification, can actually bring a simple conflict under control. The ego conflict is the most difficult to resolve; even if dampened, it can result in dissolved relationships and the ultimate suffering of human beings.

> *There is always an element of conflict in even the mildest argument or proposal.*

## Dealing with Conflict

There are various methods of dealing with conflict, each of which must be looked at in relation to the type of group, the occasion, the people involved, the history of the problem, and the effect of the conflict and its resolution on the widening circle of each of those variables. We can sometimes ignore the conflict in the hopes that it will eventually ease and go away. Waiting does work in some situations, where further involvement or added rhetoric would only serve to stoke the fire. Dampening the embers of conflict by avoiding the heat is not always the coward's way out.

It is always important to verify that a conflict exists—a few well-chosen words may clarify the issue for everyone. When faced with a conflict situation, consider the following procedure:

> *It is always important to verify that a conflict exists.*

1. Clarify the source.
2. Identify the causes that are easily seen (for example, position of fences).
3. Identify underlying causes that are not so easily seen.
4. Identify any hostility between those involved in conflict (whether within your group or in the other camp, as hostility anywhere can delay the resolution of conflict).

**5.** When arriving at solutions, make sure they lie somewhere between possible and acceptable.

There is no one sure way of resolving conflict. A number of people have devised their own methods of dealing with the issue in conflict.

Dr. Joan Harley, for example, teaches supervisors of one of the largest steel companies in America to resolve conflict by negotiation until the situation is "win-win." In fact she teaches these supervisors to deal with their own daily conflict situations. In one session two supervisors needed five trucks on the following day to do a certain job. The company had only five trucks available. Normally one supervisor would "pull rank" or get to the trucks first, and the other supervisor would be out of luck. Joan kept the two supervisors at the negotiation table until they worked out a plan wherein both supervisors would have access to the trucks by adjusting the times when they used the trucks and by pooling their resources (human and hardware) in a joint effort. In the "win-win" exercise Joan made the men (1) clarify their positions; (2) stay at the discussion table as long as necessary; (3) refrain from reaching for the rhetoric of justification too quickly—that is, from saying "I need them more than you do," or "I'm right about this and you're wrong."

Conflicts can also be avoided when the people involved *listen* to each other. Avoiding conflict by changing your mind simply to avoid conflict may create an impossible situation. Differences of opinion are not always detrimental.

*Conflicts can be avoided when people listen to each other.*

Settling conflict through *negotiation*, as Dr. Harley does, may seem a very commonsense approach and easily attainable solution. In crisis situations, however, negotiation requires much skill and planning.

It is not inconceivable that Emma's chances of confronting a serious crisis incident, such as hostage-taking, are increasing daily. She may be the first officer on the scene where hostages have already been taken, or she could even be taken hostage herself.

Today, crisis situations involving hostages are increasing. The problem of providing protection for officials and business executives is real, and training for "crisis teams" is emerging.

Years ago, overpowering the offender with force or attempting to lure the offender out into the open and thus within range of a police marksman was the way to settle such a crisis. Today, however, nego-

**CRISIS**

*In crisis situations negotiation requires much skill and planning.*

tiation is the first step in dealing with serious crisis situations. To negotiate means "to treat with another or others in order to come to terms or reach an agreement."

What skills should the negotiator possess?

The New York City Police Department uses detectives, because they are effective in *verbal* communication.

Richard J. Gallagher, a leading administrator of the Federal Bureau of Investigation, says, "The ideal negotiator is an actor, salesman, and good psychologist." According to Gallagher (1978), the FBI program lists the following traits as those of a good negotiator:

1. An experienced officer usually of lower rank than a chief or captain.
2. An *effective communicator*.
3. One who enjoys the challenge of helping someone in crisis.
4. One who is sincere, patient, and a good *listener*.
5. One who relates well to a *team approach*.
6. One who is honest and flexible.

The good negotiator depends upon his or her strategy and talent for persuasion. They must defuse situations, calm emotions, and reassure offenders that they will not come to harm. The negotiator must always be conscious of both verbal and nonverbal behavior and alert to changes in voice tones. A good negotiator listens actively, speaks more softly and slowly than the offender, and adapts conversation to the offender's level of vocabulary.

Of course a negotiator must have other skills, not the least of which is an ability to work with a *team*. Not all crisis situations are as drastic as hostage-taking, but the same skills apply in semiserious and very serious crisis situations. The basic premise of crisis management is that organized response to crisis is effective, and it requires policies, resources, analyses, *communications*, and decision-making. The overriding philosophy is to do everything possible *before* the event occurs, thus minimizing the difficulty of managing during the crisis. There is a pre-event phase in which all members of a team have a checklist of preparations necessary to their function.

Many companies are looking very seriously at different ways of preparing to deal with conflict and are training their own executives and personnel for the time when a crisis occurs. The possibility of crisis today is increasing at an alarming rate, especially those situations that involve kidnapping, hostage-taking or some other terrorist activity.

Attacks against corporations occur very frequently but are less publicized than attacks against governments. Singer and Reber (1977)

*"The ideal negotiator is an actor, salesman, and good psychologist."*

*The good negotiator depends upon his or her strategy and talent for persuasion.*

report that in 1976 the CIA claimed that 36 of the 61 incidents of aggression against Americans outside the United States were directed against business. Over 1100 executives have been killed since 1968.

Executives involved in crisis situations face challenges outside their field of experience—life-or-death encounters, irrational behavior, no control over negotiations, and grave pressures. Too many individuals in these situations have miscommunicated information and behaved irrationally themselves.

*A Security System for Business*

Motorola Teleprograms, Inc., a security firm, has set up some programs providing for business a system in which *existing* management skills are used to manage crisis (Singer and Reber, 1977). They suggest an approach that involves setting up *crisis management teams* to study all aspects of terrorist and crisis situations. These aspects include legal, leadership, financial, security, personnel/medical, public-relations, adversary communications and crisis counsel. In recomending who should be on a company's team, the MTI president suggests people who are or have been acquainted with some failure over which they had no control.

During the development of a team, the history of the company is explored, and a selection of six to eight persons is made. Simulation training is built into the program, and evaluation, followup training, and ongoing threat-assessment takes place.

In the pre-event stage, each team member must study the aspect of crisis to which he or she has been assigned (that is, legal, financial) and come up with *proposals* on how to handle that section.

Knowledge of the area is important. If someone on the team is responsible for the legal aspects, he or she must be knowledgeable about ransom, emergency funds in the company, and how to handle such funds.

According to the MTI program, the missing ingredient in most corporate protection programs is not planning but *process*. Process is the way in which an organization responds to threats, the manner in which it analyzes them and develops strategies. In order to focus on process, the crisis team uses simulation training. Certain elements imposed in the training include:

- Emotional strain due to the responsibility for human life.
- Insufficient data for making important decisions.

■ Limited time for making decisions.

■ The need to consider implications of seemingly mundane elements of the crisis.

■ The realization of being confined.

In a simulation training session, the team may be given a kidnapping situation. Along the way, members may receive further information that complicates the situation: knowledge that the victim has heart trouble, for example.

Simulation training has been used in many other types of situations. In Cincinnati a group of police operators and dispatchers were given a crisis situation in which a plane was supposed to have crashed on a crowded highway. The team's task was to communicate the information to all responsible agencies and control the situation by becoming a command station for fire, police, and hospitals. Even though the operators and dispatchers knew the situation was not real, they became very involved in every aspect of it. Later one member said he even went to the supermarket that was supposed to have burned down just to make sure it was still intact. "I knew I was acting silly," he said, "but it seemed so real at the time."

We noted earlier that the composition of a group varies. The crisis team is a group that must function to the highest degree of efficiency and effectiveness. For that reason, such a group cannot afford to have a single member not doing exactly the task assigned to him or her. Each member must completely comprehend his or her task. In order to provide organized response to all conditions that arise, the team must have *leadership* which is in touch with the management of the corporation and can guide the team. Security must be knowledgeable about the company's adversaries and have experience in protection; the legal member of the team must guide the team on legal strategies; the finance member must develop a monetary base for the team's operations. Since there is also a risk to personnel's assets, information about personnel in the company must be readily available in order to analyze the adversary's affect on people's assets.

*A crisis team cannot afford to have a single member not doing his or her exact task.*

Though most companies prefer a low profile in these situations, the need for good public-relations skills is paramount. Someone must recognize the impact of the crisis and be able to respond through the media to all appropriate audiences.

Most important to the team is the member (or members) who must deal with adversary communications—that is, exchange information with the terrorists, who may be completely irrational and may reject any communication with the enemy.

Finally, there should be a crisis counsel who advises on terrorist groups and their techniques. In other words, there should be someone who identifies with the opposition and views the team's responses through the eyes of the terrorists.

People selected for such teams already possess certain strengths, knowledge, and skills, although this does not preclude acquiring additional skills. The team goes through a pre-event stage in which procedures are activated and policies applied. After the training there is a post-event stage; here debriefing, evaluation, and refinement of procedures and policy take place.

*The success of the group effort depends on the skill and cooperation of everyone involved.*

In relating the procedures suggested for building crisis teams, it should be noted that the success of such a group effort depends on the skill and cooperation of every member, upon the cooperation of the corporation, and the dedication to preparedness.

Of all the group work mentioned in this chapter, the crisis team requires the utmost in teamwork, the tightest degree of organization, and the greatest reliance on members to acquire very specific skills. It also contains the greatest amount of unpredictability.

As in all communication situations, the possibility of change is ever present.

## SUMMARY

We gather in groups to learn something, to share information and to solve problems. A group is a collection of people who have a relationship with one another. A group exists because it satisfies a need. Groups operate under relational and procedural lines. There are no set rules to determine the formality or informality of groups. Each group goes through its own orientation, evaluation, and control stages.

Public and private groups exist. Formal groups often use *Robert's Rules of Order*, which are based on courtesy, justice, the rights of the minority, and the will of the majority.

Leadership in groups falls into categories of the commonplace and the charismatic. All leaders, however, need followers. Leaders should create supportive climates, study the task and problems, encourage participation, help solve problems, understand the objectives and procedures of the group, and assume responsibility in a crisis.

Members of groups often assume task and/or maintenance roles. Groups evolve, widen, and take on new tasks. Most public groups are quite likely to attract media coverage.

Methods of problem-solving in groups include brainstorming and reflecting thinking. In brainstorming, group members amass ideas spontaneously. Reflective thinking is associated with the attempt to discover a solution to a problem.

Group proposals, like all proposals, are basically claims that what is proposed will solve or alleviate a problem. Submitting a proposal means you have supported your claim. The proposal is actually a chain of arguments leading to a single conclusion: This proposal ought to be accepted.

Conflicts in groups arise because groups have different needs and goals. There are simple conflicts, pseudo conflicts and ego conflicts. Settling conflict through negotiation takes skill and planning. Corporations are forming management crisis teams to combat the growing threat of terrorist activities. The success of such teams depends on the skill and cooperation of every member.

In every group effort, the possibility of change and growth is ever present.

## KEY TERMS

| | | |
|---|---|---|
| agenda | incidental motions | proposal |
| brainstorming | leaders | pseudo conflict |
| charismatic/ | logos | public groups |
| commonplace | main motions | reflective thinking |
| conflict | maintenance roles | reliability |
| crisis | motions | roles |
| ego conflict | panel | simple conflict |
| ethos | pathos | subsidiary motions |
| functional/romantic | private groups | symposium |
| group | privileged motions | task roles |

## EXERCISES

*Instructor*

**1.** Divide your class into small groups of four to six students. Have each group meet several times. Each time: (1) rearrange the seating; (2) assign each member a new role, such as task, maintenance, or leadership; (3) Discuss *the same topic* at every session. The final session should analyze the preceding ones.

*Students*

**2.** Keep a journal of all the group activities in which you are active. Record them as to (1) formality, (2) informality, (3) size, (4) content. After several weeks (the longer the better) note any changes in the people involved and in yourself. How many groups did not change?

**3.** Conduct a class according to parliamentary procedure. (General students may be assigned this task.)

**4.** Review your role in your groups at home and in your groups at school or work. In what environment do you make the greatest number of decisions?

## CIRCLING BACK

Answers found in the text: start with the pages closest to you right now.

**1.** What elements go into establishing a crisis-management team?
**2.** What kinds of conflict exist?
**3.** An argument in a proposal has to prove which three things?
**4.** What is reflective thinking?
**5.** What is brainstorming?
**6.** Can you name the maintenance roles in a group?
**7.** What about the task roles?
**8.** In which two broad categories do we place our leaders?
**9.** Name the types of motions you could make in a formal group.
**10.** How do public groups differ from private groups?
**11.** What five elements are present in most groups?
**12.** What is a group?

## REFERENCES

Bales, R.F. "A set of Categories for the Analysis of Small Group Interaction." *American Sociological Review* **15** (1950):181-187.

Cartwright, D., and A. Zander, editors. *Group Dynamics: Research and Theory.* New York: Harper and Row, 1968.

Dewey, John, *How We Think.* Boston: D.C. Heath, 1933.

Gallagher, Richard, "Techniques of Hostage Negotiation." *International Security Review*, October, 1978.

Gardner, John. *Time*, July 15, 1974, 35.

Osborn, Alex F. *Applied Imagination* "Gracy Brainstorming," (3rd ed.) New York: Scribners, 1963, pp. 151-196.

Singer, Lloyd, and Jan Reber. "A Crisis Management System." *Security Management*, September, 1977 (American Society for Industrial Security).

Peyre, Henri. *Time*, July 15, 1974, 23.

4 widening the circle
of influence
through persuasion

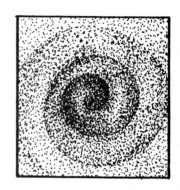

When Dora told the twins to "pick up all the clothes," when the history teacher in Dora's small group protested that the disciplinary system was not working, when Bert told the class to write down the words they recognized in *Electric Company*, some very gentle persuasion was being employed in every instance. The fact is, the moment we reach out, the moment we widen that circle to include another person, we deal with persuasive messages.

On a daily basis we do not plan our persuasive messages in a formal manner. We do not sit down at the desk and formally map out strategies for using our common sense and our emotional and logical arguments. Nor is our audience formally advised that we intend to influence them, to modify their behavior, and to encourage them to act in some manner. We do not *warn* them ahead of time as we do in a formal public-speaking situation.

*From the time we get up in the morning to the time we retire at night, we deal in persuasion.*

We just talk . . . and sometimes we even talk to ourselves. From the time we get up in the morning to the time we retire at night, we deal in persuasion. Dora gets up in the morning and persuades herself that she must face another day; Bill says he sometimes has a dialogue with himself about the merits of holding a staff meeting; Maria has to talk herself into jogging to the pool at six in the morning.

But it is when Dora, Bill, and Maria face someone else in a communication situation that most of their persuading takes place, and this holds true for all of us.

Because the act of persuasion is found throughout our day and is not confined to one communication situation—that is, to the interview, the group, or the public-speaking event—it is important that it be discussed here, in a separate chapter. In Chapter 2, people employ persuasion on a private level, on a professional level, and on a social and political level. Throughout the rest of the text we will continue to examine the methods through which we apply persuasive tactics to our various communication experiences.

Because of our involvement with technology we receive more persuasive messages than we send. According to the latest surveys by media critics, Bert has already seen more than 250,000 commercials on television—and that figure is probably low, considering the fact that Bert loves to watch the tube.

*We deal with persuasion every day.*

We persuade others in groups and in many private situations. When we "go public," we are apt to become more formal and structure our arguments. But in both informal communication situations and public statements we deal daily with persuasion.

When we try to persuade someone to modify his or her behavior with regard to beliefs, values, or attitudes, our intentions are usually pretty honorable. For example, Dora insists that the boys share the household chores so that they will acquire good values (helping their mother and one another, sharing the load, and being responsible). We do not generally persuade without regard to the ethics of the situation. We seek to understand our audience and cooperate with them to establish a common ground; each party benefits equally from the act. When we employ persuasion in this responsible manner, we are exercising the concept of *rhetoric* recorded by the Greek philosophers—that is, the study of persuasion as an instrument of democracy.

*Rhetoric encourages discussion.*

Rhetoric, which in the Greek sense means "discovering all the available means of persuasion in a given case," was conceived to encourage discussion, to strengthen freedom of choice, and to acquire an understanding of human behavior.

In our history books, as well as in our daily lives, we have seen people employ persuasion to further their own gains at the expense of others; we have seen people manipulate others without warning them; and we have seen people persuade others with force, allowing them no alternatives. For these reasons we tend to shy away from the very word "persuasion," valuing instead the concepts of "education," "information," and "discussion." We shall see, though, that in reality we do indeed speak to *persuade* others to (1) believe and feel as we do and (2) modify their behavior with regard to beliefs, values, or attitudes.

However, we do our persuading according to the ethics of those ancient Greek philosophers, by attempting to find a *common ground* and to identify with our audiences. In this text, we shall focus on the concept of rhetoric as set down by Aristotle because we feel that in our private and public daily lives this type of communication (often called the *rhetoric of identification*) is superior and more practical. We believe that if the people involved with persuasion are ethical, their persuasion becomes more ethical.

There exists a *rhetoric of division* as well, which aims at increasing the distances between people, and which accuses, belittles, and vilifies. We accept the fact that in certain situations this type of persuasion may serve some purpose, but our goal is to develop skills that help us *get along* with our daily companions. Because this is of uppermost importance, we shall concentrate on the common-ground concept.

*The common-ground concept (rhetoric of identification) is superior and more practical in helping us to get along with others.*

Let's take the "common ground" concept a step farther. Maria (Dora's friend) and her friend Wendy shared many experiences, including some near tragedies. Wendy, a Native American, was working on a proposal to fund a Native-American art school in Santa Fe, and she needed political support. Wendy called Maria in Washington, who in turn asked her congressman to talk to the chairperson of the subcommittee, who then voted for the appropriation.

Several factors were present in that simple phone call that Wendy made to Maria.

1. *Persuasion occurs when you trust someone.* Maria trusted Wendy's judgment on the merits of the proposal. Before going to Washington, Maria had worked with Wendy on several Native-American projects. Maria had confidence in Wendy's intelligence and in her character.

2. The congressman liked Maria. He thought she had a great personality and was the smartest press secretary he had ever had. He too came from the Southwest, and it was in his best interest to pay attention to the needs of the Native Americans. Maria's proposal thus supported an attitude he possessed.

3. When the congressman spoke to the chairperson of the subcommittee, the chair had been looking at the proposal but hadn't quite made a decision. However, the congressman was not asking for a 180-degree shift in attitude. Voting *for* the funds was something the chair could do without sacrificing any strong beliefs. Persuasion is more effective if you don't ask for too much.

*Persuasion is more effective if you don't ask for too much.*

4. When the chairperson read the proposal, it sounded logical. Wendy had done her homework and set down sound arguments for funding the school. Even though government was cutting budgets for ethnic and minority projects, her school opened on

schedule. Persuasion occurs when you can show logical reasons for your proposal. (But it all started because someone liked and trusted someone else.)

When attempting to persuade, however, it is best not to limit yourself to just one means of proof. In other words, while *trust* is of the utmost importance, the message will be stronger if you also establish a *rapport* with your audience and present your proposal in a *rational* manner. It is through the interlocking of these three elements that you present your strongest case.

## PERSUASION AND OUR EMOTIONS

*Image or credibility assumes some ethical responsibilities.*

"Trust" and "honesty" never seem to go out of style. These words invariably add to a person's credibility: Maria trusts Wendy's judgment, Dora trusts Bill's ability to cut her hair. A person's image skyrockets when she or he is perceived as honest. In ancient times ethos (image) and ethics were interchangeable. As we shall learn in our subsequent discussion on arguments, modern theorists often separate the two. Aristotle, however, suggested that the three constituents of what he called "ethical proof" are character, sagacity, and goodwill. He felt audiences were persuaded by ethical proof of what a speaker chooses to do; he explored the sources of credibility and analyzed the ways in which a person achieved that intangible quality. It was Aristotle's conclusion that a speaker who seeks to build his or her image or credibility assumes some ethical responsibilities. It is difficult today to set one standard of ethics. Individual standards are based upon such variables as personal experience, ethic culture, and religion. Similar standards can be found among a wide number of cultures, however. Aristotle believed that similarities existed because the concept of the "common ground" implied that a speaker and a listener came to some *common* understanding about opinions and beliefs—in other words, a sharing of standards.

Some standards that have been shared and accepted throughout the ages by most cultures include the following:

1. Be responsible for what you say.
2. Examine all sides of an issue.
3. Try not to mislead others out of ignorance.
4. Do not suppress vital information.
5. Weigh and test the validity of your sources.

When Wendy asked Maria to do her a favor, she did so believing in her own cause and not misleading Maria as to the intent of her proposal. She did not suppress vital information and later, when Maria discussed the proposal (after it was funded), she found that Wendy had been truthful about each and every source.

If Maria had found out later on that Native Americans would not benefit from the proposal, or something else that would have embarrassed the congressman, Wendy's image might have suffered.

If building a good image is important, then retaining it is equally important. Most relationships last over a period of time. Prior ethos (how people perceive you prior to the communication event) is valuable in the persuasive situations. However, the image you project during the communication, plus your prior image, combine to actively influence people's perception of you after the event and for days and years to come. Just as our circle widens daily, so does your image (which includes ethics) grow and reach others. Good or bad, news of it travels fast.

*Retaining a good image is important.*

Some of the methods used to establish credibility can be found in very traditional rules set down by Aristotle centuries ago:

**CREDIBILITY/ IMAGE**

### Improving your character:

Associate yourself with that which is virtuous and elevated.

With proper humility, praise yourself, your cause, or your client.

Remove or minimize unfavorable impressions of yourself or your cause that have been previously established by either your opponent or well-meaning but misguided individuals.

**Improving your judgment:**

Use common sense.

Act with tact and moderation.

Display a good sense of taste.

Be familiar with your environment.

**Developing goodwill:**

Identify yourself with your audience and their problems; be straightforward and considerate; be a messenger of truth.

## PERSUASION AND ARGUMENT

*Argument is a tool for persuasion, a method of proving a point.*

While we are swayed by our emotions more than we like to admit, we prefer to believe that we ourselves and those who make up our audiences are rational human beings. Give us a good argument, we like to say, and whether we admire the speaker or not, we'll listen to reason. While Aristotle sincerely believed that a speaker's credibility was important, he, too, preferred to believe that people could be swayed by reason. Therefore he saw argument as a tool for persuasion, a method of proving a point. Plato used argument in his pursuit of absolute truth. Our modern theorists see argument in various lights: as a way of discovering truth and advancing good (Weaver), as a method of analyzing arguments (Toulmin), as a concept of audience (Perelman), and as an entirely human phenomenon (Brockriede).

Argument has been regarded as both an analytical tool and a method of constructing speeches. But whether we are interested in the discovery of truth or in the understanding of how human minds work, we cannot speak of persuasion without discussing argument because, like Aristotle, we believe that it is the logical tool for persuasion.

To understand how to use this tool, we should be aware of how it was fashioned and of its evolution. Primitive beings fashioned the club to hunt for food and protect themselves. We can say that the club has evolved into the rifle, which is more effective in modern society. (Whether it is better or worse is another argument.) By the same token, we can see how argument has evolved. Whether we have made it more effective or more relative to our modern society is for all of us to judge.

In the beginning was Plato, primarily interested in the discovery of truth. He systematically redefined and divided existing ideas until he arrived at the point where further subdivision was impossible. At such a point a universal truth is discovered, he said. Plato called this process *dialectic*. The precise tool at the core of the dialectical process is a form of argument called the *syllogism*.

The syllogism begins with a general statement about reality and then moves to a more specific premise. The conclusion is a natural consequence that stems from the major and minor premises. The conclusion has the same degree of acceptability as the preceding premise. The syllogism is a form of deductive logic that reasons from existing truths to the discovery of new truths.

The most familiar of all deductive syllogisms is:

General truth (major premise): All men are mortal.

Specific truth (minor premise): Socrates is a man.

Specific conclusion: Socrates is mortal.

Notice that Plato used the word *all*, which allowed the premise to include every person. The truth is then absolute. The fact that all people are mortal is unquestioned; the establishment of probability is unnecessary. Of course Plato did not see this method of obtaining truth taking the form of public discourse. Plato himself argued that only philosophers can discover the truth, and truth stands on its own merit, so no one need become an advocate of truth. Dialectic to him was the only valid rhetorical theory.

Then along came Aristotle, a pupil of Plato's, who did not deny the existence of some absolute truth but believed that such truth is unknowable and cannot usefully be pursued! He did believe in local truth, or truth that audiences can perceive. To Aristotle, the speaker didn't have to be a philosopher but could be anyone with a thought or an idea that he or she wished to communicate. (Aristotle didn't use "she"; that is a modern inclusion.) Aristotle took argument away from the single spotlight into which Plato put it and flooded the entire stage with the audience, the occasion, the speaker, and the speech. Argument then became a bit player, merely a component of the speech. But unlike Plato, whose lone emphasis was on the discovery of truth, Aristotle switched to *persuasion*. Because of the local nature of truth, persuading the audience to adopt the truth is the central aspect of the rhetorical act. Argumentation switches, then, from the mind of the philosopher to the joint property of the speaker and audience.

Aristotle then fashioned his tool—the *enthymeme*. It was similar in form to the syllogism but with one important difference. While all the

*The precise tool at the core of the dialectical process is a form of argument called syllogism.*

*The enthymeme has a missing premise.*

lines of argument in the syllogism were clearly drawn, and there was no room for an inferential leap (we'll describe this fully later on), the enthymeme had a missing premise. This missing line of the argument was assumed to be filled in by the audience and not necessarily mentioned by the speaker. This type of argument allowed the audience to supply the missing premise and thereby make the inferential leap.

Aristotle explained it:

*Accordingly, the enthymeme . . . must deal with matters, which as a rule are variable; and the links in the chain must be a few . . . seldom as many as the links in a normal chain of deductions. Thus if one of the premises is a matter of common knowledge the speaker must not mention it, since the hearer will himself supply the link. For example in showing that Dorieus was a victor in a contest, in which the prize was a chaplet, it is enough to say, "He has won a victory at the Olympic games." The speaker need not add that the prize was a chaplet, for everyone knows it.*

Thus the audience is allowed to fill the gaps in the argument, and the argument itself seeks to arrive at a common place with the audience.

After Aristotle, little was said of the argument until the middle ages when such theorists as St. Augustine saw the use of argument as being largely in association with presenting Biblical truth. Unlike the platonic notion of absolute truth, the truth for Augustine was contained entirely in the Bible.

Moving quickly to modern times, four theorists share our arena: Stephen Toulmin, Chaim Perelman, Robert Weaver, and Wayne Brockriede. Stephen Toulmin (1958) sees argument as a compound structure comprised of several interlocking components. He starts with the conclusion of the argument. This he calls the *claim*. All evidence offered in support of this claim he calls the data. The inferential leap (what we infer based on our experiences) between the data and the claim it supports is called the *warrant*. Whenever the inferential leap is not clearly established, he adds the step called *backing*. The backing provides additional support for the warrant. Sometimes there are various degrees of force with which the speaker may wish to assert the claim, so Toulmin proposes a qualifier which serves to regulate the force of the claim. On the other hand, there are instances in which the claim would be definitely false and the speaker would not like to be responsible for making a sweeping generalization. By using a *reservation*, this pitfall can be readily avoided.

*Toulmin sees argument as a compound structure comprised of several interlocking components.*

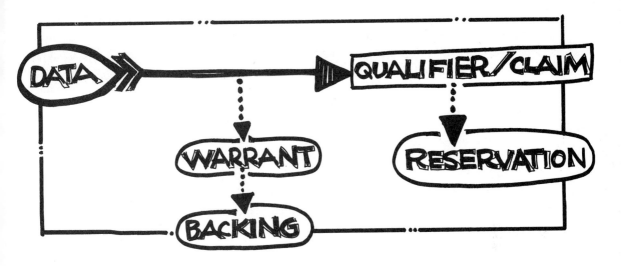

Chaim Perelman (1971), when presenting his theory on argumentation, focuses on the audience and sees the locus (central point) of argument in audience analysis. Both reality and proof, he says, are what the audience says they are. He establishes three categories of audiences:

1. Intrapersonal (the speaker's own internal state). The speaker's argument must first pass his or her own psychological state.

2. Interpersonal (the audience at hand). Any proof acceptable to the audience is to be used. This does not exclude prejudices, biases, or even non-sequitur arguments—in other words, every available argument.

3. Universal (essentially hypothetical and comprised of people who represent all aspects of a given area of specialization). For example, a universal audience of lawyers would be comprised of lawyers who are experts in all areas of the law.

*Perelman's theory focuses on the audience.*

One of the differences between Perelman and Aristotle is the question of *ethics*. Aristotle assumes integrity and morality on the part of the speaker, but Perelman has no such preoccupation. For him the ethics are dictated by the *demands* of the situation.

On the other hand, Robert Weaver (1953) sees argument existing for the presenting of the good. He defines rhetoric as "something which creates an informed appetite for the good." He believes in the existence of absolute truth and evaluates argument in terms of its rela-

*For Perelman, the ethics are dictated by the demands of the situation.*

*Weaver's theory is based on a hierarchy of arguments.*

tion to this truth. His theory of argument is based on a hierarchy of arguments. If the morality of the speaker can be determined by the types of argument he or she consistently uses, then there must be a universal ranking of arguments.

At the top of this chain of argument, Weaver puts argument by *definition* (1). He says, "If the real progress of man is toward the knowledge of the ideal truth, it follows that this is an appeal to his highest capacity—the capacity to understand what exists absolutely."

Next he lists argument from *analogy* (2). He states that analogy is reasoning from something we know to something we do not know in one step.

Argument from *generalization* (3) is the natural next step, because, he says, ". . . behind every analogy lurks the possibility of a general term. . . ."

Argument from *cause and effect* (4) follows. Weaver believes that we are all historical beings.

Next-to-last is argument based on the *appeal to circumstances* (5). He tolerates circumstantial argument as a source only when we know of nothing else to plead.

At the bottom of Weaver's hierarchy is argument based on *testimony and authority* (6). He says, "Today there is a notion that all authority is presumptuous consequently it is held to be improper to try to influence anyone by the prestige of great names of sanctioned pronouncements."

Weaver's concept of truth is platonic (that is, he, too, is interested in the discovery of truth), but his concept of argument is not syllogistical (he ranks *six* types of arguments, none of which is analytical).

The final theorist we shall look at is Wayne Brockriede (1968), who takes a very practical approach to argumentation: "Arguments are not in statements, but in people. Hence a clue to the whereabouts of arguments: People will find arguments in the vicinity of people."

*Brockriede claims that the form of argument has little value, but the character of argument is all important.*

Brockriede claims that the form of the argument has little value, but the character of argument is all important. In discussing the characteristics of argument, he gives six conditions that are necessary before argument can occur; they are:

1. *A reasonable inferential leap.* If there is too little, the conclusion is obvious and the argument is syllogistical. If there is too much, however, one is no longer dealing in the realm of that which is ascertainable.

2. *A perceived rationale* to support that leap.

3. *A choice between two or more competing options.* If there is no choice, then there can be no argument. The same thing holds true if there is too much choice.

4. *A regulation of uncertainty.* If there is no uncertainty associated with a claim, then persons making that claim can be dogmatic. If there is too much uncertainty, then a resolvable argument is impossible. There must be reasonable doubt in order for argument to occur.

5. *A willingness to risk confrontation with peers.* Again, the willingness must be neither too slight nor too great. Little can be resolved by arguing with someone who is only too eager to argue with you. Likewise, nothing is gained by attempting to argue with someone who is always accommodating.

6. *A shared frame of reference.* For example, if two persons do not share a common language then argument is impossible.

All six of these characteristics must be present at once in order for argument to occur, and Brockriede thinks that the list is exhaustive. He does not concern himself with logical sequences and other forms of argument; he maintains that people can and do indeed argue successfully without being aware of these critical tools. Obviously Dora and the twins were not thinking of Brockriede's list of conditions when they argued about the dirty clothes; nonetheless, their argument fitted nicely into his pattern.

From Plato to Brockriede, argument has persisted as a tool for persuasion. In its various twists and turns through the historical course of rhetorical theory, it has persisted, adapted, and survived.

Plato reserved argument for the trained philosophical mind. Brockriede, at the other extreme, reveled in its humanistic appeal. In between we have Aristotle, from whom most of the modern theorists sought adaptation, Augustine, Toulmin, Perelman, and Weaver. These are but a few of the many scholars who have studied and written about rhetorical theory and criticism.

## SYSTEMS OF LOGIC

The fundamental tools of argument are systems of reasoning that have developed over a period of time; these include the theories of argument discussed in the preceding pages. One step beyond argument, however, we find three essential logic systems: inductive reasoning, deductive reasoning, and causal reasoning.

We can implement these systems in every communication situation, no matter how simple or how involved.

## Inductive Reasoning

When Dora decided to start her unit on nutrition, she gathered information from textbooks, from personal experiences, and from other nutritionists. One by one she spoke of the values of certain vitamins, explaining the specific benefits of each and finally concluding that vitamins are good for us. She drew a conclusion about a *general class of objects* (vitamins) by studying certain members of that class (vitamins A, B, C, and so on).

*We employ inductive reasoning to predict the probability of either negative or positive consequences*

To prove her reasoning was sound, she had to (1) use enough examples to support her conclusion, (2) choose the examples fairly, (3) ensure that no outstanding exceptions were unaccounted for. This line of reasoning, which goes from specific (or specifics) to general, seems a very natural system. As children we learn, for example, that stoves burn us when we touch the heating elements. (Larry and Gary learned to cook eggs but touched only the frying pan. Larry touched the stove once, and that was enough.) One bad experience usually helps us the next time around. We employ inductive reasoning to predict the probability of either negative or positive consequences.

Sometimes, however, one experience is not enough. If we buy a dozen eggs and the first three are bad, that may be sufficient evidence for us to take the whole carton back. Someone else may go through at least one-half dozen before concluding that the half dozen is bad. We also gather evidence of specific materials that merely establish the extent and significance of a problem.

## Deductive Reasoning

Deductive reasoning is exactly the opposite of inductive reasoning. When reasoning deductively, we progress *from the general to the specific*. Inductive reasoning requires gathering enough specifics to establish a probable general truth; thus the data must be sufficient and representative enough to establish that probability, at least in the minds of our audiences. In deductive reasoning we assume a general truth and support it with some specific cases. Remember that famous syllogism that connects the truth of mortality to the specific case of Socrates? Bert says, "All of my class members are great dancers. If you don't believe me, just look at Josie."

*We require that our major premises be accepted truths.*

We do not adhere to the absolute truths today; rather, we accept Aristotle's method of deductive reasoning by requiring that our general or major premises be accepted truths. For that we have three forms of deductive reasoning: the categorical syllogism, the hypothetical syllogism, and the disjunctive syllogism.

In the *categorical deduction* (or syllogism) we start with a major premise followed by a minor premise and conclude with a statement connecting the minor to the major premise.

| | | |
|---|---|---|
| General truth: | *All* A's are B. | All humans are mortal. |
| Specific: | C is an A. | Socrates is human. |
| Specific conclusion: | C is B. | Socrates is mortal. |

In the *hypothetical syllogism* (or deduction) the same pattern is followed, but we slip in an "if" clause. The function of the minor premise, then, is to deny or confirm the hypothetical premise. We aren't certain that our general truth is 100-percent absolute. So we say:

| | | |
|---|---|---|
| Major premise: | If A's are B, | If humans are mortal, |
| Minor premise: | and C is an A, | and Socrates is human, |
| Conclusion: | therefore C is B. | then Socrates is mortal. |

(But we make no promises.)

In the *disjunctive syllogism* we not only refuse to stick our neck out, but also offer our listeners an alternative. The purpose is to allow the audience to establish the connection. The alternatives are opposites; therefore the negation or affirmation of one alternative affects the other. For example:

| | |
|---|---|
| Major premise: | Either humans are mortal or they are immortal. |
| Minor premise: | Well I've never seen a 300-year-old human. |
| Conclusion: | Then men must be mortal. |

Inherent in all reasoning is some form of cause and effect. The purpose of causal reasoning is to establish causation. In argument we continually trace our solutions back to one of several causes: When we say, "Smoking is hazardous to your health,"—for example, the *cause* is smoking and the *effect* is ill health. While causal reasoning appears in other forms of reasoning, it is not always structured as cause and effect. Therefore we need to recognize the causal pattern. Let's look at some examples from among Bert's students:

Annette, one of Bert's students, had a toothache and was sent to the nurse. We might say that one of the effects of Annette's infection is pain, stating, "Annette's tooth is sore because it is infected." The *cause* is infection, the *effect* is pain.

We might list a number of circumstances that lead to a predictable effect or set of effects, and say: "Josie, another of Bert's students, watched the television show *Sesame Street* and he saw how they made the letter 'Z'. So Josie practiced making the letter 'Z'. Josie held his pencil right and pressed hard on the paper. Therefore Josie made a good letter 'Z'." Those are the facts: He watched the show; he practiced; he was moved to action; he produced the desired effect. The purpose of casual reasoning is also to analyze and present the causes and effects of a certain problem so that you can focus on the solutions and therefore eliminate the problem.

We must test the validity of our causal reasoning by asking ourselves questions: In Annette's case, for example, we might ask, "Is the cause significant enough to produce the effect?" (Is the infection really so bad that it causes pain?) Or, "Is the cause the actual cause of the effect, or are there other more significant causes?" (Maybe Annette has another tooth that is infected and it, too, is causing pain.)

Reasoning from sign also includes causal relationship but is the reverse of reasoning from cause. Annette has pain because she has an infection, but the pain did not cause the infection.

## Reasoning from Comparison or Analogy

When Bert says that all his students dance like animals in the zoo (he might say that to Dora), he is comparing unlike objects. When the officer told Emma that the sergeant "came in like a pompadour," he, too, was comparing unlike objects—making a *figurative* comparison. A figurative comparison mixes two images and the audience is doubly aroused or amused. A *literal* comparison, such as "My class is on the same level as your class in our study of vitamin deficiencies," is comparing like objects or ideas. Literal comparison serves as a form of reasoning, of logical proof. Figurative comparison is much more emotional.

When reasoning from comparison, we do better when the similarity between the two examples is greater and more significant than the dissimilarity.

When we reason from analogy, another form of comparison, we show that similar circumstances produce similar conclusions. For example, Dora might consider giving the same information to her seventh-grade students as to her sixth-grade students because the sixth-graders did well when tested on the information. She then concludes that the seventh-graders, given the same information, will do well on their test.

## MAKING CLAIMS

In order to apply some form of reasoning, of course, you must have a reason for doing so! Generally we wish to persuade someone because we really feel something should or should not be done, or we believe

*We generally make a claim of policy, a claim of fact, or a claim of value.*

something is good for us (or for our audience) or not good for us (or our audience). So we go about stating a claim (that is, making a point and trying to prove it).

We generally make a claim of policy, a claim of fact, or a claim of value.

*Claim of policy:* This type of claim recommends that some course of action should or should not be followed. Example: Emma says to Doug's father, "I think you should take action against the boy's parents and file a complaint." She is advising Doug's father to follow what she believes to be the best course of action because (1) there is a need for such action; (2) the course of action will work (it may stop Robbie from beating other boys); (3) strong neighborhood approval will minimize disadvantages; (4) it is a course of action that the neighbors think is the *best* course of action.

*Claim of fact:* Let's say Emma does not wish to persuade Doug's father to file a complaint against the parents of the boy because she feels it is not her job to do so. If this is the case, she may just make a statement of fact, such as, "That bruise is swelling." That is *her* observation. She is not suggesting a change or any action, but merely stating something. Propositions of fact can affirm or deny

1. The existence of things. ("There is some swelling.")
2. The occurrence of acts. ("Robbie beat up Doug.")
3. The classification of objects. ("The students are all little boys.")
4. The connection of events. ("The music started and the dance began.")

*Claims of value:* Claims of value really imply a value judgment: "Annette is a beautiful little girl." "Bert works effectively with children." "Emma always conducts a thorough investigation."

We make these claims or propositions of policy, fact, and value every day of our lives, and we are aware we are doing so. In later chapters, we shall delve further into the mechanics of *how to* formulate propositions—indeed, how to propose something and make it happen.

## PERSUASION AND MULTI-JUDGMENTS

When we make a claim—that is, when we say, "America is beautiful," or "We ought to elect a new mayor," or "That bruise is swelling"—we are making a judgment about something. Persuasion deals with judgments, inferences, suggestions, or interpretations. In our daily lives we ask for and give opinions much more often than we make descriptive statements. We say, "Hey Bert, what did you think of the movie, *The China Syndrome*? Wasn't it great?" And Bert answers, "I haven't seen it yet. You liked it?"

Tom (Maria's brother) is a reporter-photographer who works at a television station. He likes to think that reporting is "objective," but he deals with judgments in every step of putting together a story. Every time he selects a lead sentence, takes a picture from a particular angle, or arranges the various shots, he is making a judgment. He is not dealing with "pure" information. For example, consider what Tom says about the story on the bank robbery:

*This morning Norm Bergsma came into the station. The police radio was blaring, and I was loading my camera. The first thing I do in the morning is check the equipment, get the technology straightened out. Bergsma works for the afternoon paper. He comes from Cleveland too, and we talk about the Browns a lot. Well, he was talking about a bank robbery that happened an hour before and we completely blew it—our assignment editor hadn't been listening to the police radio.*

*Anyway, Norm says to me, "Let me tell you what this cop did. I was taking pictures of one of the suspects being put into a car, and I was standing there, and this cop says, 'Who the hell are you. Get of here before you blow the case.' I pull out my I.D. and show it to him and he walks off. So I keep shooting, and he says, 'Get the hell out of here,' and comes back, asks for my I.D. again, waving his arms, blocking my shot, and then pushing my camera against my chest. He says, 'let me see your I.D.,' and this time he takes it away from me and says, 'I'll deal with you later.'"*

*Well, I ask Norm whether the cop still has his I.D., and Norm says, "Yes."*

*So I say, "What the hell is he hasslin' you for?" And Norm says, "I don't know. I have a right to be there."*

*Well, I checked out the story and figured since the robbery already took place, we could do a story on Norm. I spent the rest of the day doing a catch-up (on the robbery). First I went to the bank, which was sealed. I asked whether the sergeant was in the bank, and the answer was "No," but I looked through the window and saw an officer there. I waited until he came out and started shooting film of him. Then I went to the officer who was standing by and said,*

*When we make a claim, we are making a judgment about something.*

*"What's that officer's name?" She said, "Why do you want to know?" I said, "Why don't you want to tell me? What are you afraid of? Is that the sergeant?" She answered, "Yes," and looked at me nervously and got into the car.*

*Well, I got some film later when they apprehended another suspect, but the station decided not to go with the angle on Norm because they said it was "their" fight not ours. This irritated me because several weeks ago one of our reporters was hassled by the police, and the* Tribune *(Norm's paper) was the only paper to support our rights. We should have supported their photographer.*

In one reporter's short account of the bank-robbery story, a number of persuasive messages flew back and forth: Tom tried to persuade his editor to use a certain story; an officer tried to persuade a photographer to move; the photographer tried to persuade the officer to let him stay; Tom used persuasion to learn the officer's identity. Finally, a judgment-based media message was created. A wide variety of techniques was used, and both emotion and logic were employed. But the message was altered by a news editor who decided on an angle different from that of the reporter.

In our modern world we sometimes make claims or judgments that are either dictated by the characteristics of our technology or altered by someone in the serial transmission of the message.

## PERSUASION AND MEDIATED MESSAGES

*Distortions occur in the relay of messages because a number of persons have access to the messages.*

In the preceding example, Tom, our reporter-photographer made a number of judgments and tried to persuade his news director to present the story as he (Tom) perceived it. The public was not treated to a message created entirely by the person who witnessed the event. The distortions, alterations, or revisions in newscasts are not necessarily (and probably not usually) deliberate, but that is irrelevant. They occur in the relay of messages and because a number of persons have access to the messages. Consider this example: The live audience (reporters, staff, concerned citizens) present at the mayor's ten-to twenty-minute news briefing can pick up many cues from the context and the totality of the speaker's presentation. The audience can select certain factors about the man and his ideas from the total experience. But the totality of the briefing as a communicative event will be mediated first by the individual reporter's or camera-person's choice of what is significant at the time and later by a news editor's choice of what is significant enough to be shown. Further mediation will result from the reporter's verbal interpretation, probably limited to a hundred words or less.

By its very nature, television mediates reality. One can see no more than the camera's angle of view permits; thus the more magnified any one object in the environment becomes as a result of a camera manipulation, the less information about the total reality of the event is transmitted to the viewer. When this natural limitation of television is increased by the interposition of value judgments of one or more persons, the chances for distortion are also increased.

**By its very nature, television mediates reality.**

We receive messages that have been relayed, or serially transmitted; when these messages are based on judgments about an event or a person, we should be aware of the process which brings that judgment (or claim) to us. In the live serial transmissions which we receive daily, we usually recognize that a large percentage of message content is hearsay. We ask, "Who told you?" We may even inquire, "Who *told* Jean to tell you?"

With television, we sometimes automatically respond to the ethos or image of the anchor-person (who may have had nothing to do with the formulation of the message). Sometimes we prefer one station to another because of its network affiliation. Sometimes we listen to news only because we're waiting for the program which follows. The persuasive message, however, has passed through many humans and much hardware before it reaches us. At each relay point the person involved (1) adjusts to the characteristics of the hardware (i.e., time, color visualization, type of equipment) in fashioning arguments, and (2) adjusts to the human process, which includes the many people involved (i.e., camera-person, field reporter, studio director, news editor), and to the policies of station, network, and possibly sponsor. The result is increased generalization and simpler terms because a common ground has to be established for the sake of expediency—the show must go on the air. We are thus treated to the Corporate Image on many occasions.

**The persuasive message passes through many humans and much hardware before it reaches us.**

Now that we understand the mediation of news messages, we should be doubly aware of other types of persuasive messages which we receive from the media. Commercials on television are primarily fashioned from arguments that ask the audience to participate in the conclusion. When a certain commercial shows a glamorous model sweeping into a nightclub where a famous singer is singing about a certain perfume, the audience makes that inferential leap and supplies the missing premise: If I wear X perfume, I, too, will be glamorous and surrounded by admiring glances. Advertising messages on television are visualized through pictures, while radio visualizes its messages through sound. Both are effective.

The best examples of persuasion and visualization come from the advertising field. P.T. Barnum is credited with beginning the concept of the advertising campaign with his widely publicized freaks. John Wanamaker, the merchant prince who was also a superb campaigner, scattered six-inch posters reading "W & B" all over the city of Philadelphia. This became the main topic of conversation around town. A few days later a second set of posters was circulated, stating that Wanamaker and Brown were selling clothes at Oak Hall. Later, great 100-foot signs proclaimed the same thing. Then he sent up balloons, announcing that whoever brought back one of them would receive a new suit of clothes.

Today we are literally bombarded every day of our lives by mediated persuasive messages. Knowledge of how to persuade, how to frame our arguments, how to find a common group so that others will trust and listen to us helps us to recognize the ethical and logical arguments that we receive. In a later chapter, we shall go more deeply into the public-speaking presentation, which also involves projecting an honest image, establishing a rapport with others, and motivating others to some new thought or action. We shall *apply* some of the theories related in this chapter. Later also, we shall discuss our role in a technological society more fully.

## SUMMARY

Persuasion deals with reinforcing a belief, changing a belief, or moving an audience to action. We persuade formally and informally throughout the day by proposing ideas and thoughts and telling another person what we want him or her to believe or do. Success depends partially on whether we're meeting a need or supporting an attitude our audience has. Persuasion is more effective if we use both emotional and logical proofs and if we don't ask for too much. We motivate through our language.

Argument is a tool for persuasion, a method of proving a point. Plato used argument in his pursuit of absolute truth. Weaver saw argument as a way of discovering truth and advancing good, Perelman as a concept of audience, Brockriede as an entirely human phenomenon; Toulmin was interested in analyzing argument. Argument has been regarded both as an analytical tool and as a method of constructing speeches.

The best ways to build arguments are systems of reasoning which include inductive reasoning, deductive reasoning, causal reasoning, and reasoning from analogy or comparison. We generally begin by trying to prove a point and we make a claim of policy, of fact, or of value. We make these claims every day of our lives.

Persuasion deals with judgments, inferences, suggestions, or interpretations. Besides preparing persuasive messages, we are daily confronted with many mediated persuasive messages.

Thus, as our circle widens to include another person or persons, we automatically widen our impact through persuasion by reaching out and making a statement. Our ideas have the opportunity to be carried into another circle, into someone else's world.

## KEY TERMS

analogy
argument
Aristotle
Brockriede
causal reasoning
cause and effect
character
circumstances
claim
comparison
credibility
data
deductive reasoning
emotions
enthymeme
ethics
ethos
fact generalization
goodwill
inductive reasoning
inferential leap

logic
mediated messages
multi-judgments
perceived rationale
Perelman
persuasion
Plato
policy
qualifier
reservation
rhetoric of division
rhetoric of
  identification
sagacity
syllogism
testimony
Toulmin
value
warrant
Weaver

## EXERCISES

Student

**1.** Give a speech that uses inductive reasoning. Give the same speech using the deductive pattern of reasoning. Did one form of reasoning lend itself better to the topic you chose? Can you give a speech explaining why this occurred?

**2.** Watch at least six television commercials and record the type of reasoning used in each. Did one type of reasoning predominate? Did the reasoning have anything to do with the product? With the personalities involved?

Instructor

**3.** Explain the difference between Aristotle's and Plato's theories of argument by dividing the class into two groups and allowing each group to persuade the other of the merits of one man's theory.

**CIRCLING BACK**     The answers to these questions are found in the text. Begin at the end of the chapter and work back.

1. Because of the characteristics of television, messages often mediate reality. Explain how this happens.
2. Compare literal and figurative comparisons. Which are more logical? More emotional?
3. Is it true that in inductive reasoning we gather up specific items to establish a probability about some general truth? If you believe that statement is true, give an example to support your claim.
4. Who said, "People will find arguments in the vicinity of people"?
5. Which theorist focused on audience?
6. Aristotle assumes integrity and morality on the part of the speaker. Do any of the other theorists share his point of view?
7. Define the enthymeme.
8. Plato was interested in the discovery of truth. What is the tool he used to arrive at truth?
9. Which three elements are essential for a strong persuasive message to be effective?

**REFERENCES**     Aristotle. *The Rhetoric,* translated by Lane Cooper. Englewood Cliffs, N.J.: Prentice-Hall, 1960, p. 12.

Brockreide, Wayne. "Rhetorical Criticism As Argument." *Quarterly Journal of Speech* **60** (1974):165-174.

Perelman, Chaim, and L. Olbrechts-Tyteca. *The New Rhetoric.* Notre Dame, Ind.: Notre Dame University Press, 1971.

Toulmin, Stephen. *The Uses of Argument.* Cambridge: Cambridge University Press, 1958.

Weaver, R. *Ethics of Rhetoric.* R. Henry Regency Co. 1953.

# 5 the big arena: the audience

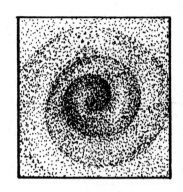

On May 15, 1979, Emma Gonzales was part of an audience gathered for the specific purpose of learning how to prepare for the time when they would widen their circle of influence by engaging in a public-speaking event. Among those present were transit bus operators, fire-fighters, and several other police officers.

Dr. Mary Jean Thomas, Dean of the College of Communication at Little Rock, Arkansas, stood in front of these Albuquerque city employees and said:

*Well, I'm going to ask you to forget about yourself for a moment. Forget about what* you *want to say, how* you *feel about an issue, and pretend you are preparing yourself for an evening with your lover or mate. How would you start planning for the evening? Would you ask yourself: How shall I satisfy his or her needs? How shall I make him or her more comfortable? As the evening progresses, would you constantly look for clues to tell you whether he or she is enjoying the conversation? The evening? Would you adjust your speech, your actions, as you go along? If it rains, would you both find shelter or both decide you love to walk in the rain? Of course you would do all those things and ask yourself all those questions because what you really want is to* end the evening on a mutually satisfying note, *don't you?*

*So why not start planning a public speech that way—by changing the focus of attention, by putting the audience in your spotlight. By thinking first about* their *needs.*

*Ancient theory of public communication had it that there are only three general purposes: to teach, to persuade, and to please.*

**Put your audience in the spotlight.**

*Corresponding responses would be understanding, belief, and delight. However, setting general purposes and responses is what gets most speakers in trouble and keeps them there.*

*From the very beginning, start to think of some very* specific *responses you want from your audience. Unless our communication attempts are to be merely therapeutic for ourselves, we must humbly recognize that all effort is directed to and done for the sake of our audience. You may want glory and acclaim for your efforts, but you won't get either unless you have satisfied the need and desires of your audience. Now, let's start preparing our speeches!*

Emma and the others then began preparing the speeches they would eventually present—first to this small group of coworkers and later to a larger community group. Emma ultimately delivered her speech to school assemblies and groups of citizens interested in police protection measures.

## THE AUDIENCE

Who is the audience? What do its members *need* to know? What do they *already* know?

If you are to put the audience first, then you must discover who they are and what they expect of you. Your invitation to speak on a certain subject will usually come from someone who feels you are the right person to present the information, please the particular audience, or persuade that audience to act in some manner. In all likelihood, the individual who invited you will be a part of your audience.

For example, if you are a hairdresser (as Bill is), a large cosmetic company may ask you to address their sales representatives on the kinds of shampoos hairdressers prefer. In your lifetime, no matter how young you are, you have either given some kind of presentation or listened to someone giving a presentation. Most of your one-on-one presentations require little advance planning beyond what's already in your head. Public speaking, however, requires formal planning, even if your message is exactly the same one you've expressed countless times to your friends and colleagues. The main difference between talking to a few people and making a public statement is advance notice and preparation.

*Public speaking requires formal planning.*

Obviously you know something about the subject or you wouldn't have been asked to speak. Realistically you probably know more than the audience. Your challenge is to put it all together neatly and in an exciting manner, then take just a few minutes to deliver it instead of sitting around for hours discussing it. When you sit around for hours, you may eventually find out what your audience already knows and what it needs to know. When preparing for a public speech, you must find that out ahead of time.

And how do you do that?

Each audience is different. Having stated that, we must move on to those ways of identifying what is common in audiences, both as individuals and members of groups who come together because of similar interests, for there is no way of stating all the differences in each audience (although we shall give it a try later on). We have already stated in earlier chapters that no two people have identical experiences, but they may have overlapping experiences or find some common ground upon which to communicate.

People like to listen to what they already have interest in, because they enjoy hearing facts that confirm their beliefs. One reason for this is that change is so traumatic. Some philosophers believe that change is an ordeal for everyone. Yet we are constantly in a state of change and our reason for speaking nearly always involves change. Chances are good that we will be giving our audience new facts and new ideas so *they* will change in some manner.

*You must find out ahead of time what your audience already knows and needs to know.*

**Audiences at a Glance**

*People enjoy hearing about their own interests.*

*Similarities*

*Audiences are alike physiologically.* That is, they are subject to the same laws of physics for getting light into the retinas and sound into the inner ears. People can tolerate just so much intensity and can process just so much information.

*Audiences are alike psychologically.* That is, they have certain needs such as love, pride, and social worth. Collectively they may create an atmosphere that tells us we must face hostility, indifference, friendliness, or chaos.

*Audiences have similar backgrounds.* We look at an audience and we can see identification of audible and visible signs and symbols of a culture. Then we can plan to use those words to which that culture will respond and to avoid taboo words.

*Differences*

*Audiences gather in different ways.* Some stand around a statue in the downtown plaza, others sit in the grass in front of a museum, and some sit primly in chairs facing the speaker.

*Audiences have strong and weak members.* In the audience Maria gathers for the congressman's news briefing, the reporter from the *Washington Post* is a strong member, while the reporter from the small-town paper in Texas is comparatively weak. Some people in audiences are more interested in the topic than others are.

*Audiences meet at different times.* Early-morning audiences are different from late-evening audiences, and both are different from luncheon audiences.

*Audiences know little or much about a subject.* Even when the audience has chosen the subject, the people in the audience may have varying degrees of prior information about it.

*Audiences view speakers differently.* Five Democrats may come to hear the President speak and each one of the five may have a different perception of the man based on some prior knowledge.

Being aware that there are similarities and differences in audiences gets us in the mood to think about audiences in general, but we still don't know much about our *specific* audience.

So the next step is to ask yourself a few questions based on three key areas.

1. *Logistics:* How large is the audience? (This information will help you in several ways; e.g., larger audiences seem more formal at times and need more amplification of sound.)

2. *Demographics:* What are the social characteristics of the audience? (Sex, religion, occupation, socioeconomic status, and so on.)

3. *Attitudes:* How do the people feel about you? What is the occasion, purpose? Are they hostile, friendly? (You can make many decisions here. If they're hostile, try to find some points of agreement and insert humor. If they're neutral, try to be objective and open minded. If they are friendly, you can even bring in some emotion; but if they're apathetic, you'll need to arouse them—tell a few good stories.)

To find out these specific things about your audience, it's advisable to ask the person who asked you to speak. He or she will be part of that audience, remember? If by chance you initiate the contact because you have a burning desire to address a particular audience, then ask friends about the audience or go to the library and look up the organization and its members.

Even if you have no clues beforehand, don't give up. Listen to the audience prior to your speech (look around on that walk to the podium), observe their nonverbal clues as you speak, and stick around afterwards and ask some members how they liked your speech.

Closely related to the audience is the occasion—that is, the purpose for the gathering. The event may be a luncheon, a police briefing, or a lecture in school. The audience may be compelled to attend, or may have assembled voluntarily.

**Effect of Occasion on Audience**

The time of the occasion is often crucial. You may have no control over it, so you must adjust. However, it's tough speaking to an audience at 8:00 AM. Mid-morning is much better. Lunch is no time for long-winded orations, although a few pleasant words may be welcome. Directly after lunch is not as good as early evening. Speeches in the late evening call for extra-special attention.

*Time*

Days of the week influence an audience. In the business world, Monday is considered a tough day because people are returning to work after a weekend and have a lot to do. It's difficult to change the biorhythms of an audience, although a successful attempt can be great fun. It's easier when you know whether the audience is composed of officers who work the swing shift (speaking to them at 8 AM would be fruitless) or people who work from 8 to 5 and like to relax on Saturday and Sunday.

## Identifying Needs

*What do you want to give the audience, and why does the audience need it?*

What do you want to give the audience, and why does the audience need it? Knowing the logistics, demographics, and attitude plus the day, time, and occasion, will help you get a general feeling for your audience. But remember, you still need to be aware of what that audience already knows and what its members need to know. You can learn these things only if you remember that you are dealing with special or local truth in audiences and that special situations should be considered.

Let's follow Bill, who is planning to address the hairdressers' convention.

Knowing who makes up the audience (a group of hairdressers), what the occasion is (a local convention), what day and time the event occurs (Bill is scheduled to speak on Wednesday morning at 10:30) gives him a great many clues as to what the audience already knows. The audience is comprised of people who have shampooed many heads of hair and used many different types of shampoo. They are at a convention and anxious to exchange information and learn new things about their profession. Since he's been asked to address them, they obviously want his opinion about methods and products. Bill has a lot of information about his audience, so his next step is to decide what responses he wants from that audience.

Dr. Thomas gave the following advice to the Albuquerque city employees who gathered to learn how to give a public speech:

*Have a clear idea of the responses you want from your audience.*

*If you do not have a clear idea from the beginning about the responses you want from your audience, how can you gear your effort toward getting it? Here are some desired audience responses. I'm sure the list is not exhaustive, but it does cover most of the categories.*

*I know something I did not know.*

*I understand something better than I did.*

*I see something from a new perspective.*

*I believe what I had disbelieved.*

*I believe more firmly than I did.*

*I have doubts about what I believed.*

*I am interested in something to which I was indifferent.*

*I am more interested in something than before.*

*I am favorably disposed to something.*

*I am more favorably disposed to something than before.*

*I am hostile to something.*

*I am more hostile to something than I was.*

*I now consider something important that I did not.*

*I consider something more important than I did.*

*I consider something trivial.*

*I consider something less important than I did.*

*I am ambivalent toward the subject.*

With the audience clearly in mind, knowing what they already know and determining what they need to know, Bill can now formulate a purpose sentence:

"*I want this audience to be more interested in the benefits of a pH-balanced shampoo.*"

When Bill formulated his purpose sentence, his *central idea* was right there—narrowed and easily recognized and specific enough to get him going. When you finally determine your central idea, you, like Bill, should be able to state *in one sentence* what your speech is about. If someone at the hairdressers' convention was asked, "What did Bill talk about?" that person should be able to make a statement that resembles Bill's central idea.

Below are statements of central ideas obtainable from the topic of shampoo.

## CENTRAL IDEA

*You should be able to state in one sentence what your speech is about.*

1. This is how to shampoo hair.
2. This is how to shampoo Rosie's short hair.
3. Shampoo is a good/bad thing.
4. Shampoo, as we know it now, evolved through many forms, starting with lard.
5. There should be more shampooing done in early life.
6. This is how to train your employees to shampoo.
7. Shampoo can injure hair if it contains poor ingredients.
8. This is how the hairdressers' association regards shampoo.
9. This is how shampoo affected the hands of one hairdresser.

Which central ideas would demand statistics? Testimony of experts? Examples? Comparisons? Definitions? Which central ideas indicate you are going to be dealing with value systems instead of (or in addition to) cognitive abilities? Which central ideas almost mandate that materials be presented in a particular order?

When you are sure in your mind that you know about the audience and what you want from them, and when you have formulated your purpose sentence, be certain that you know why the audience really needs to have the information you are about to impart. In other words, consider interest and don't forget that both you and they should care.

*Both you and your audience should care about the information.*

Is putting the audience first really realistic? Consider the public speeches given by some of the people mentioned in this book so far.

Dora speaks about nutrition because that's her job. She speaks specifically about vitamins because she wants her students to know something they didn't know before. She has already analyzed her audience as to age, sex, and attitudes because she sees them on a daily basis and she knows that she must motivate them constantly. She knows all this before she starts her research.

Bill, on the other hand, may not know everyone in his audience at the hairdressers' convention, but he does know their interests; he knows they want information about techniques and products. Perhaps he concludes, like Perelman (see Chapter 4), that the locus of argument lies in audience analysis. He analyzes (1) his own internal state (he likes a certain kind of pH-balanced shampoo), (2) the audience at hand (he knows that most hairdressers are always looking for new products and better ways to make hair look great), and (3) the universal audience of all hairdressers (if he can reach the immediate audience, he will really reach experts in all areas of the business).

Bert gives a public speech daily as he cajoles, informs, and tries to please his first-graders. Rarely does Bert start the day thinking, "Now what is it I want those kids to know?" Rather, he asks himself, "How much do my kids know about their alphabet, and what do they need to practice today?" If he moved ahead without regard to their needs, he might go too quickly or too slowly and end up with some frustrated first-graders.

When Emma goes to court to present her testimony in an accident case, she knows that the judge is expecting facts. She thinks about what will help the judge make the right decision.

*Putting the audience first does not mean that the selection and narrowing of the topic is not left up to us.*

Putting the audience first does not mean that the selection and narrowing of the topic is not left up to us. At times, speakers are scheduled because of their credibility as human beings and not because of their knowledge about specific subjects. Knowing the audience is important in those instances, as it helps us to decide how to arrange our topic.

If you have been asked to speak, and the subject of the speech is left strictly up to you, a little brainstorming on your own (with yourself) might help you out. In our discussion of groups we noted that brainstorming must be vigorous, nonevaluative, and fun. So just for fun, try stepping outside your door and looking up and down the street. The simplest observations may lead to a number of intriguing topics. For example:

1. *Observation:* Someone is watering the lawn.
   *Topic:* Is water conservation really working in this city?
2. *Observation:* Street lights just went on.
   *Topic:* Computers and traffic lights.
3. *Observation:* The empty lot across the street.
   *Topic:* How will infill affect the growth of this city?
4. *Observation:* Newspaper on the street.
   *Topic:* What's wrong with the news? It isn't "new" enough.

Whether your speech topic finds you or you find your speech topic, *preparation* is the next step.

## In Search of a Topic

Because she keeps her audience in mind, Dora constantly updates her speech on nutrition for each new session. If she happens across an article in a magazine about a certain vitamin, she cuts it out and puts it in her file. Gathering information to add to her already vast store of knowledge about nutrition is known as "doing research."

We all have a store of valuable information inside our heads. It comes from personal experiences, memories, and educational training. In any research process we should first determine the extent of our own knowledge, and then rummage through our own personal files. Over the years many of us collect books and other items about our favorite topics. Look around your house and you will find many bits of information that tell the casual observer something about the information in your head.

## RESEARCH

*Gathering information to add to your own vast store of knowledge is known as "doing research."*

**Step 1.** *Assess your knowledge.* Find out its limitations, look at the materials you've collected to aid you in that memory search. If you feel you have enough materials and memories to put a speech together, do so. However, keep in mind that new materials emerge daily and your audience has access to them.

**Step 2.** *Seek additional data.* Move on to step two only if you have determined that your materials are inadequate for that particular audience at that particular time. Seek additional data by (1) interviewing others who have knowledge of the subject; (2) reading more about the subject; (3) observing more; (4) checking libraries and doing computer searches.

**Step 3.** *Organize the information.* Get all the materials laid out where you can see them. It doesn't help to have materials stored in boxes or scrawled on the backs of envelopes that you have misplaced. Rearrange those materials until you think you perceive a simple organization plan. Check materials for stories, humor, details. Check to see if all materials relate to audience, to what they need to know and what you think they already know.

*Improve your memory skills by becoming a better observer.*

**Research Comes From. . .**

*Ourselves*

Plato said, "Knowledge is to remember."

Dora's grandmother said, "Get an education. No one can take that away from you!"

Everything you have experienced, everything you have assigned meaning to, is somewhere in your brain. Remembering is the key that opens the door to the knowledge you have already acquired. Our brains are somewhat like computers—a key word will set them to clicking away. You will improve your memory skills if you become a better observer and improve your perceptual skills. You will have memories if you are adventurous enough to accept the challenges life puts in your path.

When Dora first met Bert, she told him of her desire to go to college. Bert said he would work and send her to school first, then, when she got her degree, she could go to work and send him to school for his degree. She agreed, even though she wasn't sure at the time just how their relationship would grow. Equally unsure, but ready for a challenge, Emma walked away from her job as a clerk, took the police exam, and embarked on new adventures. By increasing your world of experiences, you store more knowledge. By attaching meaning to every experience you will be able to recall that experience for later use.

Every day, as our circle widens and we let more people into our world, we have access to more information. Talking to others and discussing our ideas helps to build on them. When you cannot see or talk to someone, you can write a letter or make a phone call. Dial seven digits and you can talk to anyone in the world. By video telephone you can talk *and* see someone. Most people are available if they are approached in the right way. Like any other audience establishing a rapport, finding a common ground is necessary. Most people enjoy talking about what they know, enjoy helping others. In our complex and fast-paced world, however, awareness of people's time constraints and workloads is very important. By knowing your audience, you can select the best ways to approach them. Since you wish something from them, their needs come first.

*Others*

*As our circle widens, we have access to more information.*

You can

1. *Have a short discussion in an elevator.* ("Hey Joe, how's the project coming?") Information will be limited.

2. *Arrange an interview.* (See interview techniques, Chapter 3.) Information will be more detailed.

3. *Write a letter.* (Allow for the time factor; mail can be slow. Letter should be addressed to specific person and ask for specific information.) Information should be detailed.

4. *Make a telephone call.* (Could be too casual unless questions are written out ahead of time. You should call at an appropriate time, state your mission clearly, repeat if necessary to avoid misinterpretation, and be courteous.) Information will depend on how well you make your inquiry.

The information you gather from yourself and from your personal contacts with others is considered *primary* research. You do it yourself.

*Secondary* research is research others have compiled. It can be found in books, periodicals, newspapers, government documents; it may be stored in computers, on microfilm, on electronic media. It's all out there for you to tap. Some research is easier to get than others.

*Don't overlook libraries!* If you know your alphabet, chances are you can find a book in the library. Fortunately for all of us, we have the opportunity to visit libraries from early childhood, when we first learn our alphabet.

*Written Material*

*Don't overlook libraries!*

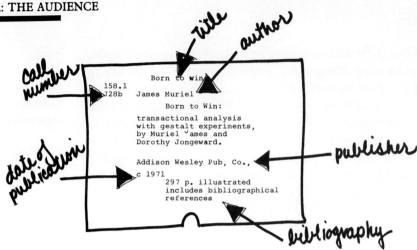

Card catalogs for books, tapes, periodicals, and microfilm archives are prepared according to author, title, and subject. The cards for author and title are in one catalog and those for subject are in another. All cards are filed alphabetically, and each contains the following information: author's name, title of book (and edition), place and date of publication, name of publisher, number of pages, illustrations, portraits, diagrams, maps, size of book, presence of bibliography, related subjects (for cross reference).

*Bibliographies will suggest other books in your subject area.*

One good book leads to another. Once you have a book on the subject, you merely turn to the bibliography and a list of other books in your subject area is available to you.

Most libraries carry popular and scholarly periodicals and journals. They also carry newpaper publications and indexes, government documents and atlases. They even have a bibliography on bibliographies (the *Bibliographic Index*).

Because the volume of information has become so massive, today's libraries have information on microfilm, microfiche, microprint, and microcards. (*Micro* simply means "small.") Libraries have special readers that project these small images at a size that you can easily read.

Many libraries can perform computer searches for you. If yours cannot, you should ask the librarian about the possibility of acquiring computer search facilities.

*Initiate a computer search for additional data.*

To initiate a computer search, you must first make a list of *descriptor words* which you think will appear in the titles or headings of books, articles, or documents. Submit your list to the librarian, who will access a major computer bank such as DOD (Department of Defense) or *New York Times* Index. You then collect a computer printout which lists bibliographic data for entries all keyed to your description. Finally, you find the books on the list.

When *recording* your data, keep in mind that you are gathering the information because you wish to report your findings to an audience. If you develop a basic format according to the guidelines below, your research should be simpler and more productive.

1. *Objective.* What are you trying to find out?
2. *Scope.* Define your area of investigation, the material used, the people contacted, etc.
3. *To be sure you understand what you are trying to explain or prove, write it down.* Elaborate on it here. Introduce the subject to yourself again.
4. *Background information.* Discuss with yourself and whoever knows the industry (or subject) any problems that might come up in such areas as special terminology. Do this while you are researching and while you are recording your research. If others can't understand the special terminology of your project, start making a glossary of terms.
5. *Look at the recorded information.* Study it and start making some assumptions here. Look at the information for size, style, and usefulness of graphs. (Are they useful only to you, or to your audience as well?)
6. *Come to a conclusion.* Do you have enough material? Should you abandon your research or acquire more? If it's sufficient, what seems to emerge? Make a list of questions you think are still unanswered. Make up an appendix for future reference.
7. *Start your preparation with your conclusions.*
8. *Communicate intrapersonally.* Talk with yourself about the speech.

Now that you have a good idea of who your audience is and what you think they need from you, and now that you have researched the subject pretty thoroughly, you are ready to develop some of those great ideas you have been mulling over for several days. In essence you have been "precomposing" your speech since the day you accepted the in-

**PRECOMPOSING THE SPEECH**

*Do some "pre-speaking" to yourself and others.*

vitation. If your speech has a far-off deadline and you don't feel like actually putting it together right away, then don't put it together. But *do* rough-out your ideas, do go over the research and start internalizing it, do mull it over while you are shaving, or putting on makeup, or even driving to work. Do some "pre-speaking" both to yourself and to others.

In that manner you will have started developing your speech before you actually outline your main points. In the precomposing stage, you want to consider what kind of emotional and logical proofs are necessary for your particular audience; you want to think of what kind of image you will project and how you can establish some rapport with the listeners.

No matter what your purpose is, you will want to ask yourself the following questions:

Am I being logical?

Have I considered all the important elements?

What proof do I offer?

Are there other alternatives and consequences?

Do I credit others properly?

Am I prepared for rebuttal?

*You can always choose your line of reasoning.*

How you go about being logical or proving your point depends upon the type of reasoning you select. As we indicated in chapter 4, you have the choice of reasoning inductively, deductively, or causally. You are aware that audiences respond to emotional appeals, which include your own credibility and the way in which you relate to your audience. Up to this point in preparing for your speaking engagement you have been in the preproduction stage—that is, you have been gathering materials, thinking a lot, mulling things over in your mind, and discovering important information about your audience.

The time has come to get organized. Of course it won't hurt to make one more stab at the research, to read or listen to a finished product before you put your own words down on paper or outline that speech.

It always helps to see a film before you produce one, to read a poem before you write one, and to listen to a speech before you give one. Why wait until you have given a speech before you sit down to analyze a speech? Why not find out what goes into a speech you *really* like before you put one together?

You may wish to listen to a speaker someone has recommended to you or read a speech that has survived the ages.

Instead of selecting a famous speech as an example at this point, let's read a speech that motivated one of the people in this book to make a major change in her career.

When Maria first heard Joe Murray, editor of the *Lufkin News*, speak about journalism, she was extremely impressed. After a year of working in Washington for Congressman Wilson (and during the writing of this book), Maria decided to leave her position and interview for a job with that small newspaper in the congressman's home territory. As press secretary for the congressman, she dealt daily with the press, wrote columns for the congressman, prepared radio shows, and relayed information about the congressman's position on national and local matters. But Maria decided that it was time to do what she had gone to school to learn to do—report the news.

One reason why Maria chose to seek a position with the *Lufkin News* was because she liked the way its editor, Joe Murray, spoke about the honesty and integrity of the press. His manner was old-fashioned enough to appeal to a young, eager journalist. Besides, the *Lufkin News*, the smallest newspaper in a big group, had won the Pulitzer Prize. Joe Murray spoke before a number of groups after his paper won that prize, and after interviewing Maria he actually delivered his speech to her, *an audience of one*. Before you read it, we think you'll enjoy a little background information.

Joe Murray, 38, is a native of Lufkin and the editor and publisher of the *Lufkin News*. The highlight of his career came in 1977 when the *Lufkin News* won the Pulitzer Prize for meritorious service for articles written by Murray and reporter Ken Herman on the recruitment and death of a Lufkin Marine. In the fall of 1977 the *Lufkin News* received the national Associated Press Managing Editors Freedom of Information Award for its achievement in bringing about reform of Texas nursing-home laws as a result of stories by reporter Lynn Dunlap. The *News* also received a 1977 National Headliners Award for the Marine stories.

On the following pages you'll find Joe Murray's impressive speech, along with our marginal notes identifying those elements that we've been discussing throughout this text. Murray uses a conversational style. He employs many personal pronouns, examples, and detailed illustrations. Study the marginal explanations and then continue on to Chapter 6 for further explanation of how to prepare *your* materials.

*JOE MURRAY*
*WALKING IN*
*THE FRONT DOOR*

**Introduction: establishes his credibility.** *I grew up in Lufkin, Texas, and except for a three-year stint with* the Houston Chronicle, *the only paper I've ever worked on is the* Lufkin News. *Every once in a while I wonder if I've somehow short-changed myself—that maybe if I'd gotten to the* Washington Post *or the* New York Times, *I could have amounted to something: I could have gotten the really big story.*

*Well, Ken Herman was born in New York, and he had to come to Lufkin, Texas, to get the big story.*

**Establishes rapport with audience.** *Don't worry so much about whether you're on a big newspaper or a small one, an independent newspaper or a group-owned one. Ours is the smallest newspaper of a big group: Cox Newspapers. But that doesn't matter. What matters is finding a newspaper with integrity and then sticking with it.*

**Central theme.** *People are always asking me, "How do you get a story that wins a Pulitzer Prize?"*

*When I'm talking to student groups, I get nervous. I tell them it takes patience. Then I see all the kids in the audience writing down* **Refers to audience again.** *"patience," and underlining it.*

*I have to add that all I did was sit in my office for seven years, and the story finally walked in the front door. Then I look out and* **Uses conversational style.** *see them writing, "Sit in office for seven years; story will walk in front door."*

*But that's exactly what happened. It was a Monday. It was* **Narrative.** *supposed to be my day off, and, for whatever reason, I hadn't done* *what I needed to do to have a day off. So I had to come down to the office.*

*I walked in, and across the newsroom I saw this fellow I knew from the community. I knew right away that he probably was waiting for me.*

*You may or may not know what it's like on a small newspaper, but let me tell you. Regardless of what goes wrong, they always go to the editor.*

*I figured we had probably run his ad upside down in Sunday's paper, and he wanted me to do something about it.*

*Well, I walked right by him and said, "How y'all doin?" and went on into my office. He followed me in and sat down and started telling me this story.*

*It was about a young man named Lynn McClure, who was about 20 years old, and he was dead. The man talking to me was Lynn McClure's great uncle.*

*Lynn McClure had dropped out of high school when he was in the tenth grade. Had he stayed in school, we learned from school authorities later on, he probably would have been put in special education for people with learning disabilities. He was what you might call a borderline retardate.*

*The kid had been unable to hold down even the most menial jobs. In addition, he had been in trouble with the law from time to time, though mainly it was just misdemeanor scrapes.*

*What his great uncle was telling me, though, was that somehow—the family couldn't understand how—he managed to join the Marine Corps. And somehow—the family couldn't understand why or how—he had managed to get himself killed.*

*The Marines were saying it was just one of those things. It was a tragic accident, but there wasn't anything that anyone could have done to make it any different.*

*Lynn McClure had gone off, joined the Marines, and, as the posters say, had become one of those "few good men." And he came home in a box. And the family wanted to know why. And they had questions. And they had no way of getting answers. They didn't have any power or influence, and they didn't have anybody to turn to—except their newspaper.*

*Well, that was just part of the story. We would find out other things later, including that, for a short time, Lynn McClure had even been in a state mental hospital.*

*Transition: internal summary and review.*

But at that moment, as the man sat there and told me the story, my reaction was perhaps like something you've had either professionally or personally.

Somebody comes to you and they tell you about something that's wrong, something that ought to be changed, something we ought to do something about. And you sit there, you listen, and you think to yourself, "This is wrong. There ought to be something done about it. It ought to be changed."

But then you have to ask yourself, or you find yourself asking yourself, "But what can I do? I'm just one person. Can one person make any difference?"

*Hypothetical illustration.*

Sometimes you think to yourself, "Well, maybe if I just listen to him. Maybe if I just let him talk himself out, maybe that'll do some good. But, after all, that's about all I can do, because I'm just one person."

I guess that's what I was doing. I was sympathizing, and I was shaking my head, and I was telling him how sad it was. And at the same time, I was probably wondering, "Well, I wonder how long he's going to take because, after all, I have other things to do."

*Startling statement: attention-getting device.*

But he made this statement, and it made all the difference in the world. He said, "They beat that boy's brains out—literally."

When he said that, he made a cold chill go down my spine. And as many times as I've made this talk around the country, I'm telling you the truth when I tell you, even today, to say it now, it makes a cold chill go down my spine, because we found out they beat that boy's brains out—literally.

*End of introduction.*

*Transition to body of speech; review of speech in a nutshell.*

And so it was at that point I decided—I didn't know what one person, one newspaper could do—but if they had questions, we were going to at least ask them. If there were answers, we were going to get them.

It was also then that I recognized the importance of the story, because I assigned no less than one-third of my reporting staff to cover it. His name was Ken Herman.

*Supportive material: examples.*

Ken's perhaps one of the most remarkable young men I've ever known. He had been with us six months or so, and yet had already proven that he had the perseverance to get on a story and stay on it until he got it.

*Style: comparison.*

You know, some guys—sometimes they're students, people just out of college, or even seasoned professionals who ought to know bet-

*ter*—*they think when they bring you a story it's not written on paper, it's chiseled in stone. They think they're bringing it down from the mountain top and, if you should dare to change even one word, why, you're tampering with their very being.*

*Well, it ought not be that way, and Ken wasn't that way. When he brought me a story, if I told him he had missed the lead, he didn't have enough quotes, this, that, or the other, should be higher up in the story, all he ever asked was, "What do I have to do to make it right?" I like that about him.*

*You know, sometimes I wonder if IRE might stand for Investigative Reporters' Egos.*

*Some think you have to be hard-nosed to be a good reporter. I've seen reporters who call up a news source and ask them a series of insulting questions, to the point that the news source finally hangs up on them. Then they turn around and write their story and say so and so "refused to comment." They think they've done a number on him. Well, they haven't done anything, because they haven't gotten the story. Get the story, get the story: That's what we did down in Lufkin.*

*Ken started out that first day making the basic checks: we checked the police department and found out that the boy had a minor misdemeanor police record. That should have kept him out of the Marines, or at least should have made them look twice at him.*

*Then we checked the school and found out what a poor student Lynn McClure was, the learning difficulties he had. That in itself, if not keeping him out of the Marines, should have made them take another long, hard look at him.*

*Then we checked with somebody else who the Marines hadn't bothered to talk to: their own recruiter in Lufkin.*

*You see, Lynn McClure didn't join the Marines in Lufkin. He tried, but he couldn't get in. He took the test and failed miserably— so miserably that he was a washout. There was nothing the recruiter could do for him. So the boy went halfway across the state to the San Antonio-Austin area and tried it again.*

*That time, he did so good on the test, and he impressed the Marines so much, they actually put him in charge of his recruit detail when it went out to San Diego.*

*Now it never could be proved, either by us or by Congress or any other investigators, who gave Lynn McClure the answers to*

*Repetition.*

*Supportive materials: many examples.*

*Supportive materials: examples of research methods.*

*that test, but this much is obvious: someone took that test for him, or someone gave him the answers in advance. There's no way that young man could have qualified for the U.S. Marines.*

*When Ken went to talk to the recruiter, he didn't start out by asking a bunch of insulting questions. He sat down and started talking to him in a nice, respectful way.*

**Reestablishing rapport with continued use of personal pronouns.**

*Now, sometimes you have to be tough. And sometimes you have to be determined. But don't ever forget that sometimes you just have to be nice. And that's the way Ken started out.*

**Description: use of simile.**

*This recruiter was a big guy. Ken said he looked like a giant fire hydrant and, with all his medals, one that had been decorated for the bicentennial.*

**Continued illustration.**

*Ken had his notebook out, asking the guy questions and writing down answers. Eventually, the guy figured out that Ken was going to put something in the paper. So, he got up and said, "You ain't gonna quote me in no damn newspaper!" He started around his desk to Ken.*

*Well there comes a time when a man's gotta do what a man's gotta do. When the recruiter came around the desk to Ken, Ken went out the door.*

*This is the point: Ken already had the story by the time the fellow got mad at him. He was able to come back to the office and write it any way he wanted to.*

**Use of repetition for effect.**

*Get the story, get the story, get the story.*

*The first day, the story was pretty much the one that would be written time and again through the course of the next year as various news gathering agencies became interested in it. The story was about a young man who wanted to prove himself. He went off to the Marines, and he came back in a box. The question was "Why?"*

**Introduces new point and supports it with examples.**

*If getting the story the first day wasn't so much of a problem, getting it out of Lufkin was. We knew from the start that if anything was going to come of this, it was going to have to be read in places other than Lufkin, Texas.*

*That's why we decided from the start that we would share whatever information we had with whomever was interested. In fact, we encouraged other news-gathering agencies to get interested in the story.*

**Continued detailed illustration.**

*The first thing we did was call on the AP for help. They sent the story all over the country, and it attracted some attention, but not really what we had hoped for.*

*The one exception, from the first, was the* Washington Post. *Within a week or ten days, they had the story on the front page. We were so tickled, we did a story on the fact that the* Washington Post *had done a story.*

*People ask us about what kind of pressure and criticism we were under. It wasn't as bad as you might think, but it certainly was not comfortable.*

*The day after the first story ran, one fellow called me and said, "How come you're making fun of a dead boy?" He said, "Sure this kid didn't have what it took, but he tried. Why do you want to dig all this up now? Why don't you just let it be?"*

*Another fellow called and said, "What are you trying to do, make fun of the military? That's not the way we think around this part of the country. We support our military. What are you trying to do?"*

*I tried to explain to them that we were trying to get answers for the family. I tried to tell them that there are no stupid questions, just stupid answers. I think some of them thought* that *was a stupid answer.*

*Maybe there was some misunderstanding or confusion about what we had in mind. I don't think even we knew what we had in mind.*

*But before it was all over, there would be congressional investigations and hearings and inquiries by the President of the United States. The Secretary of the Navy would get involved personally. There would be courts martial and there would be trials.*

*Most importantly, there would be reforms. Before it was over, no less than the Commandant of the Marine Corps would say that 1976 was a year of change for the U.S. Marines, because of Lynn McClure. And because of that, the Marine Corps was getting well. So I guess, in the best sense, that was what it was about: finding something was wrong and doing something to change it.*

*Let me give you this advice: never depend on anybody or any group to investigate themselves. That's a mistake we made. Because once we laid the story out—once the Congress got interested in it, once the other newspapers got interested in it, and once we got the attention of the Marine Corps—the Corps announced that by golly they were going to have a full, fair, and impartial investigation. Like fools, we believed them.*

*One day I was sitting there feeling that all was right in the world, when the AP wire jangled and a story came out of Washington. They had finished their full, fair, and impartial investigation.*

*They decided the recruitment of Lynn McClure was all the fault of the red-necked law-enforcement agencies in Lufkin, Texas.*

*Story-telling.*

*Transition: internal summary.*

*Direct audience appeal: use of pronouns; rapport.*

*Parallel structure.*

*Introduces new point: example.*

*Supportive material:
explains primary
research methods.*

*Continued use of
pronouns, conversational
style, and detailed
illustrations.*

*They said their records showed their recruiters had contacted the police and sheriff's department in Lufkin before the boy had been recruited and had been told he had a clean record. Had they known about these run-ins with the law, they said, they never would have recruited him—he'd be alive today, and everybody would be living happily ever after. Amen.*

*Well, I was feeling like the ground had been cut out from under me. And Ken was off that day, so that made it a double problem.*

*But the more I read that story, the more I got to thinking. I had a question. Maybe it was a stupid question, but if their records showed they had called, maybe they also showed who they had talked with.*

*So I got on the phone and called various numbers around the country that we had for the Marine Corps. I started in Texas, worked my way up to Washington and back down to New Orleans, which was the original headquarters for this investigation.*

*I called all Friday afternoon, into Friday night, and then started again Saturday morning. I finally got a Marine captain, I think he was, in New Orleans.*

*If it were up to me, I'd make him a general. I called him at home. He was out mowing his yard, and, when he came to the phone, I was able to talk him into going downtown to New Orleans to open the files and tell me who they talked to in Lufkin.*

*He did that and called me back. He told me it was a Johnson and a Ms. Walker. Well, all I had to do then was call the police department and the sheriff's department. I found out there was no Johnson, and there was no Ms. Walker working at either place.*

*So what we found out that day was that the Marines' own files contained fictitious names. It opened up the possibility of a cover-up. We ran that story, copyrighted, the next day. It was carried on the wires all over the country.*

*Now, there's a good example of what not to do in any investigation. Those Marines started out, I suppose, with the idea that they hadn't done anything wrong. The first time someone told them what they wanted to hear, they stopped asking questions and announced they had cleared it all up.*

*How much better it would have been for the Marine Corps had they done that one more check—called the police department and the sheriff's department and said, "Our records show this. What do you say about it?"*

*They would have found out those names were fictitious, and they really could have had a full, fair, and impartial investigation. They could have impressed the public with how concerned they were about making the Marine Corps what it ought to be.*

*Ask questions; ask questions; ask questions.*

**Repetition.**

*Don't stop when somebody tells you what you want to hear. The more people you talk to, the better story it's going to be.*

*This story really had two parts. One was the recruitment of Lynn McClure, which should never have happened. For whatever the reason, the Marines had taken this man with almost no questions asked.*

**Transition: internal summary.**

*The other part, perhaps the more important part, was how he died. The Marines said it was an accident, that it couldn't be helped.*

*Well, what we found out by working with some private detectives who were on the case in the San Diego area, was that Lynn McClure, from almost the first day he hit boot camp, knew he was in the wrong place. He tried to go AWOL, and they put him in something called the "motivational platoon."*

**Detailed illustration: evidence from primary research.**

*They don't have those anymore. They did away with them because of the reforms that came out of this case. But the way it worked was, they took all the oddballs—the Gomer Pyles, the guys who just couldn't make it under the rigid requirements of the Marine Corps—and they put them into this special motivational platoon.*

*There they'd make the requirements even more rigid. The idea was, I guess, that if they pushed somebody to the brink, maybe even a little over it, some of them would respond and could be salvaged. But it didn't work that way because, without exception, every man in the motivational platoon eventually had to be discharged from Marines—they simply weren't Marine material.*

*Lynn McClure's death came in something called pugil-stick exercises—simulated bayonet fighting. They use large, padded sticks and wear protective gear.*

*Lynn McClure was small. He was just a little guy—a runt, I guess you would say, and he wasn't a fighter.*

**Description.**

*They formed a circle and had him in middle of it. The drill instructor was screaming, "Kill, kill, kill!" Lynn was being forced to fight by this guy who was much bigger than he was. At one point, he was trying to crawl away, and he was crying. He was saying, "Oh God help me. Oh God, why is this happening to me?" He was forced to fight and fight and fight until he was beaten into unconsciousness.*

*This was the story given us by some of the men who were there. There was one man who said he can still hear that boy's screams in his nightmares.*

*Well, they took Lynn to the infirmary, and we would later talk to a doctor who described his injuries this way:*

*Hypothetical illustration.*

*"Imagine a wooden box—a small wooden box. Say you fill it most of the way with water and, on the water, you put a network of string. On the string you put a mass of gelatin."*

*Comparison.*

*The box, of course, represents the skull. The water represents the protective fluid. The string represents the nervous system. And the gelatin represents the brain.*

*He said, "Suppose you gave that box a pretty good lick, with your fist or whatever. What would happen inside? Well, the water could be sloshed around a bit, but if you opened up the box, you'd say that everything came back to rest pretty much as it had been."*

*"Now, suppose you opened the box, and everything inside had been mixed up. Imagine what kind of blows it would have taken to do that."*

*There's something I always try to stress, particularly when I'm talking to students. Regardless of what your religious beliefs are, you don't have to set them aside when you sit down at the typewriter.*

*Alliteration.*

*Speaking seriously, and speaking personally, prayer meant a lot to me when we were working on the Lynn McClure story. I guess because I'm Christian and Ken's Jewish, we had all the bases covered.*

*Conclusion: summary of basic points.*

*Good writing—that's something else I've tried to stress to college groups.*

*Most of us of a generation ago got into journalism because, first and foremost, we wanted to be writers. Our heroes where Ring Lardner, Scott Fitzgerald, and Hemingway. Nowadays, the heroes seem to be Robert Redford and Dustin Hoffman. The young folks want to be journalists because they want to save the world from a sea of sin and corruption.*

*Well, there's nothing wrong with that, but before you go splashing out there to rescue the world, you'd better first learn how to swim. Use the good tools and the good rules of your trade, and that means good writing.*

---

| **KEY TERMS** | attitudes | audiences/differences | brainstorming |
|---|---|---|---|
| | audiences | audiences/similarities | central idea |

| | | |
|---|---|---|
| data | libraries | rapport |
| demographics | logistics | research |
| descriptor words | objective | scope |
| general purpose | occasion | specific purpose |
| image | precomposing | time |
| knowledge | | |

## EXERCISES

Student

**1.** Keep a diary for a week and mark the times you are a member of an audience. Keep a record of the size, age, sex, and other logistics as well as the demographics of the audience. Are you part of an audience similar in background to your own? How often do you display many dissimilarities?

**2.** See how many topics you can generate each morning, five minutes after you awaken. How many are a result of the environment?

**3.** Select a topic, visit the library, and use any technology available, such as microfiche or computer search. Is it easier going to a catalog? Explain.

**4.** Record the number of public speeches you hear during the course of one week. Count every public presentation, no matter what the size of the audience. Analyze your results.

## CIRCLING BACK

Starting at the end of this chapter, answer the following questions by working your way back.

1. In the precomposing stage of your speech, what should you consider in the way of proofs?
2. What is a good format for recording your research data?
3. When researching, what is the first step, the second step, the third step?
4. What are some ways of putting the audience first?
5. What is the purpose of the central idea?
6. What elements in the occasion can affect the audience?
7. What is the difference between logistics and demographics?
8. Explain how audiences are alike. Explain how they differ.

# 6 the big arena: the speech

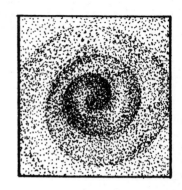

As Dr. Thomas observed in her speech to Emma's group, ancient theorists determined that people speak to teach, to persuade, or to please. We know that these general purposes are not always mutually exclusive—you may be informing, persuading, and entertaining all at the same time. In addition, you will have a specific goal in mind. Bill, for example, wished to persuade his audience to use a particular type of shampoo. Joe Murray wanted to explain how his paper won the Pulitzer Prize. Dora's goal was to inform her students about nutrition.

In choosing your method of reasoning, you will consider both general and specific purposes. But no matter what system of reasoning you select, you must prove your point. To do so, you need support.

When Dora gives her nutrition lecture, she has the facts. When she tells her students which vitamins help build strong bones, she has the facts about calcium and vitamin D. No matter what her line of reasoning, she knows she must support her point of view with strong materials. Dora usually likes to use handouts, but occasionally she brings in pictures of fresh vegetables, which she holds up to the class to support her point that vegetables are necessary for good nutrition. She supports her message verbally and visually whenever possible, because her audience has come to see as well as to hear. If possible, Dora supports every point she makes with an example. She finds students remember examples best of all. They particularly like stories.

Aristotle believed that a good way to support a statement was by example. He was probably brought up hearing the stories of Homer, just as many of us were centuries later.

*Your speech will have a general purpose and a specific goal.*

## SUPPORTIVE MATERIALS

*Support your message verbally and visually whenever possible*

## Illustrations

The words "illustration" and "example" are used interchangeably and both refer to the narration of an incident that helps to clear up the point you wish your audience to understand or consider. There are three types of illustrations: detailed; short (or the example); and hypothetical.

If you feel your audience needs convincing and you have the time, you may wish to use a detailed illustration. Joe Murray took his time and kept in every little detail of the Marine's death.

You may wish to tell several short stories and take less time to make a point. Short examples can be simple statements like "Don't forget the lesson of the Viet Nam war when many protest movements began."

Hypothetical illustrations are used when you do not have a suitable factual example at your disposal or where you wish to adapt a particular moment to the specific audience. They can also be used to explain a complicated process.

Each type of illustration can be effective and can create interest, clarify a point, and supply persuasive evidence. Most important of all, illustrations add life to your speech.

Joe Murray used many illustrations in his speech. Here's a vivid example that brought every audience to attention:

*Lynn McClure's death came in something called pugil-stick exercises—simulated bayonet fighting. They use large, padded sticks and wear protective gear.*

*Lynn McClure was small. He was just a little guy—a runt, I guess you would say, and he wasn't a fighter.*

*They formed a circle and had him in the middle of it. The drill instructor was screaming, "Kill, kill, kill!" Lynn was being forced to fight by this guy who was much bigger than he was. At one point, he was trying to crawl away and he was crying. He was saying, "Oh God help me. Oh God, why is this happening to me?" He was forced to fight and fight and fight until he was beaten into unconsciousness.*

*This was the story given us by some of the men who were here. There was one man who said he can still hear that boy's screams in his nightmares.*

*Well, they took Lynn to the infirmary, and we would later talk to a doctor who described his injuries this way:*

*"Imagine a wooden box—a small wooden box. Say you fill it most of the way with water and, on the water, you put a network of string. On the string you put a mass of gelatin."*

*The box, of course, represents the skull. The water represents the protective fluid. The string represents the nervous system. And the gelatin represents the brain.*

*He said, "Suppose you gave that box a pretty good lick, with your fist or whatever. What would happen inside? Well, the water could be sloshed around a bit, but if you opened up the box, you'd say that everything came back to rest pretty much as it had been.*

*"Now, suppose you opened the box, and everything inside had been mixed up. Imagine what kind of blows it would have taken to do that."*

In that one short segment of Joe Murray's speech he related the incident in narrative style, giving a detailed illustration of Lynn Mc-Clure's death and quoting the testimony of the doctor, who, himself, offered a hypothetical illustration.

Illustrations support your point of view when:

1. *They are relevant.* Both Joe Murray and the doctor were talking about a story relevant to Joe Murray's overall theme.
2. *The order of relationship is clear.* Order of relationship in this short segment could be (1) Lynn McClure's death, (2) doctor's view of Lynn McClure's death.
3. *Details are used, but the point is not crowded with frills.* Although the language was vivid, it was a tight story.
4. *The story is developed in orderly fashion.* Later in the chapter we shall see that Joe Murray's entire speech made sense, with each point following in order.
5. *The example is accurate.* People like to repeat stories. If the example is hypothetical, be sure to tell your audience.
6. *A number and variety of illustrations are used.* As you can see if you read Joe Murray's entire speech, he used many illustrations and they all worked well.

## Statistics

Murray didn't use a lot of statistics. He inferred that he made a lot of telephone calls before reaching the Marine captain who opened up some files for him. Thus we assume that out of many calls, only one was profitable. All speeches aren't filled with numbers, but sometimes this type of statistical data works.

Emma usually has available the latest crime statistics. Every month the chief likes to call a news conference and talk about how crime went up or down that month. At one time, figures from the chief or from the FBI were readily accepted as truth. Recently, however, the credibility of the highest government offices as well as such agencies as the CIA and the FBI has come under close scrutiny. Now it is necessary for anyone who quotes these figures to substantiate his or her position, showing how the figures were computed and what they mean. Merely quoting a few statistics doesn't persuade people.

If you plan to use statistics in a speech, consider these rules:

1. When using statistics in comparisons, make sure each item has the same base. Know the sample size upon which the percentages are based; otherwise the comparisons using statistics are invalid.

Let's look at an example of this: You are comparing Dora's school (school X) with Bert's school (school Y), and you say Dora's school increased participation in sports by 100%, but Bert's school increased participation by only 25%. It looks like Dora's school did better than Bert's. But numerically, Dora's school went from 25 to 50, while Bert's school went from 4000 to 5000. So is school Y doing better than school X? It depends upon the point you are making.

2. Comparative statistics must maintain the same units of measurement. In distances and speeds, for example, 100 miles and 100 kilometers aren't even nearly the same.

3. Statistics should support the point they are intended to reinforce, not something else.

4. If exact figures are relevant to your point, then go ahead and say "It cost the taxpayer $718.92." The audience will remember it as "over $700."

5. Use statistics that are easy for the mind to grasp, but be accurate.

6. Always attribute the statistics to a reliable source.

7. Be prepared to defend your statistics.

## Authority and Testimony

We are constantly giving testimonials. Every day of our lives we tell someone that we really like a certain restaurant, shop, book, record, person, or philosophy. Testimony is easy to obtain but it doesn't prove much. It can be effective, however, if it is relevant, appropriate, and accurate, and if the meaning is not altered when the testimony is taken out of context.

When giving a speech, you may wish to quote a famous person who is admired by the audience. Or, like Joe Murray, you may wish to support your point by quoting a reliable source. (Joe quoted the Marine captain and the doctor.) That works if the quote is short enough to follow and long enough to make sense. You may paraphrase someone else's words, but please inform your audience whenever you do so.

Whether you are using illustrations, statistics, or testimony (or all three) in a speech, the important thing is to present those specific materials that are persuasive to that particular audience. Using a number and variety of materials strengthens your position.

*Use a number and variety of materials to prove your point.*

## Supporting the message Visually

The widespread use of visual aids is a modern-day phenomenon. In private and public sectors and before small groups and large audiences alike, speakers rarely make their presentations without some form of supportive visual aid. One good reason is that when so much information must be absorbed, visual aids help the eyes and enhance the understanding of the audience. Visual aids are primarily exhibits, one purpose of which in our everyday lives is to reduce required reading matter to a minimum. For a public speaker they should supplement rather than supplant, contribute to rather than conflict with, and support rather than substitute for words.

Remember, visual aids are not designed to help *you* understand the subject; as a speaker, you use them to help your audience understand. Therefore you must keep that audience in mind throughout the production of the graphics.

*Visual aids are designed to help your audience understand the message.*

Here are some hints for effective production, and the following pages show the types of visual aids that may be available to a speaker.

USE . . .
Several simple graphics, rather than one complex graphic
No more than 25 words to explain any one visual
Only topics covered in speech

CONSIDER . . .
Time it takes to prepare
The audience and select medium aimed at their comfort
Size, lighting equipment, facilities at your disposal

ALWAYS . . .
Weigh investment of time and money against possible return
Consider what is available
Consider what is convenient
Know visual function

# Make Visual Aids Work for You and Your Audience

### ADVANTAGES AND DISADVANTAGES

Informal: If handled well can hold audience interest as idea unfolds. Easy, front-viewing. Sometimes unacceptable from back of room. Not portable nor colorful. Wastes time unless done earlier. Can look like lack of preparation.

Easy to prepare. Not so easy to change. Poor for large, formal groups. Hard to carry about and can look sloppy unless well done.

## ADVANTAGES AND DISADVANTAGES

Should be prepared by skilled hand letterers and illustrators. Can use press-type or Letraset. Involves time and cost but it is very good for small, informal groups. Poor for large groups and difficult to carry about.

Used with overhead projector. Transparent projectuals can be hand-made, copier-made or regular photos. Good for small informal groups. Too often overcrowded with information. Slows down presentation.

### ADVANTAGES AND DISADVANTAGES

Standard medium for some technical societies. Project farther, sharper, larger than 35mm slides but equipment not always available. Slower than 35mm (no tray loading). Be sure of availability of equipment before making decision.

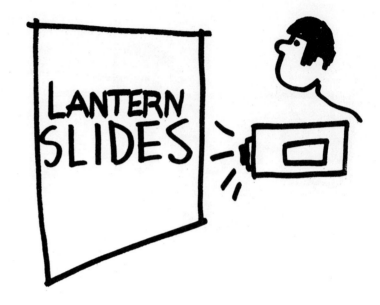

Advance planning needed to be sure equipment is available, photos taken. Can be seen up front, difficult in back. Formal or informal, depending upon material. Can be colorful, but slows presentation.

### ADVANTAGES AND DISADVANTAGES

Combines sight and sound. Permits prerecording, professional narration, sound effects. Not practical for single showing as presentation involves expense. Good for fixed exhibits, multiple showings. Should have professional preparation for best effect.

Good if story requires extra dimension. Poor for large groups. Can be expensive. May be distracting when not being discussed.

*Producing your Graphic*    If you are going to produce your own graphic, you must be able to answer the following questions:

1. What is your message or product? Your layout must represent that message.
2. Is your audience specialized or general?
3. Is your product or topic concrete or abstract? Is the graphic for one specific audience? Is it part of a campaign? Is it meant to inform, to educate, or to sell?

Once you determine these factors, you can set to work on the actual project.

4. Gather your graphic elements—paper, pencil, pen, photo, whatever you plan to use.
5. Arrange your material in a shape that has logical sequence, proper emphasis.
6. Add a creative touch, if possible.
7. Delete anything that complicates or interferes with your message. You can feature a picture, some numbers, or copy—but if you try to feature them all, then you feature none.
8. Pay special attention to the composition. It should encourage the viewer's eye to move easily from one part to the next.

COLOR   Become familiar with the color wheel. There are some principles to consider, one of which is simultaneous contrast: A color is directly affected by its background and adjacent colors. A change of color background will visually change hue, chroma, and value, which will affect your graphic.

*Legibility:* Color harmony and legibility are interrelated. The most legible color combinations are black on yellow, black on orange, yellow-orange on navy blue, green on white, bright red on white, black on white, and navy blue on white. Lowest on the list, and so least desirable where legibility is concerned, are such combinations as bright red on navy, purple on green, yellow on white.

*Color psychology:* Color preference is highly personal. Happy or disagreeable experiences directly affect one's taste for color. While it is easy to find basis for believing that certain colors provoke definite reactions, it is also easy to find contradictions. Americans, for example, wear black as a symbol of mourning, while Japanese wear white.

However, there are some traditional color reactions:

- Red has strong vibrations and warmth, and it is the universal color for danger; but it also suggests Valentines and Christmas decorations.

- Orange suggests harvest, Halloween, warmth, and vitality.

- Yellow suggests sunshine, spring, and new life. (It is also associated with cowardice and deceit.)

- Green suggests the freshness and tranquility of foliage. Pale shades of green are favorites for hospital rooms supposedly giving psychological relief from fever. Green is also the safe color, as opposed to dangerous red.

- Blue is cool, crisp, refreshing. Its range of shades and tones is wider than that of any other color.

- Purple's deep, rich values associated it with royalty, the mysterious, the profound. (In its reddish hues, used profusely, it becomes cheap and garish.)

Don't be arbitrary about color!

LETTERING   Lettering also conjures images. Lettering in itself can become the logo or the design. It's best not to interchange styles. Letters should be chosen for *size* (take into consideration the viewer's distance from the letter as well as the letter's actual size), *form, shape,* and *dimensions,* including the character style, simplicity, shading, amount of space that surrounds the outline, the aspect ratio, and the stroke width. Use upper and lower case for readability.

SYMBOLS   We live in a world of symbols. A symbol becomes a common language between artist and spectator (e.g., cross, swastika, cigarette). Repetition of symbols or words generates an emotional force. People like a feeling of order, and repetition aids this. Consider whether you wish to involve the audience, or simply make sure they understand.

PRINTING   Two basic methods of printing are letterpress and offset. Letterpress goes into the principles of the woodcut, and lithography works on the principle that grease and water don't mix. Go to a printer! A printer will reduce photos, set type. Speed presses can do photo-ready copy, but they have limitations.

*Planning Television Graphics*

Visual aids used for the public speech are not necessarily adaptable to television. If you are going to be on television, rethink your graphics.

Key considerations for the television graphic are (1) picture ratio, (2) system limitations (black and white or color), (3) major types of visuals, and (4) basic lettering systems.

PICTURE RATIO   The ratio of the television picture is three units in height by four units in width. The size of the television image is called the *camera field*. The picture you see on your monitor is smaller than the camera field. Unless a picture is prepared correctly for television, some of the outer edges may be lost on the screen. In the television graphic your pertinent material must appear in what is called the critical area.

When considering the television graphic several factors come to mind:

Is it legible? A graphic must be capable of being read or deciphered. Pictures must be legible in terms of elements which are recognizable and readable.

Is it the right size? Think in terms of the angle the graphics subtend at the eye—in other words, the area that a visual target (object) covers on the eye's retina. This takes into account the distance the viewer is from the object as well as the object's inherent size. For example, a symbol having a height of one inch will measure (subtend) a visual angle of 30 minutes of arc at the eye of a viewer positioned ten feet away.

For television display of standard broadcast quality, an alphanumeric symbol should subtend a minimum visual angle of 10 feet for individual viewing, 12 feet for group viewing in a narrow viewing sector, and 15 feet for wide-angle viewing. You can determine a symbol size by dividing the viewing distance by a number that is a function of the desired viewing angle.

When making a graphic, most people will just guess at how large or small the numbers should be. It's important to remember that shape, form, and dimensions affects the ability of the audience to recognize and read the graphic. When in doubt, consult a graphic artist about the character style, simplicity, shading, amount of space surrounding any outline, aspect ratio, and stroke width.

## ORGANIZING

Let's assume you have evaluated your audience and made note of the occasion, prepared yourself to relate to both, researched your topic, and gathered your material. All the while you have been thinking about that special day when you will stand up and speak out. Now the time has come to get down to business and outline that particular speech.

Time is important. Plan around it. If you have to speak for five minutes, plan for five minutes. If it's one hour, plan for one hour. Your audience expects you to respect their schedule. Think in terms of being a guest in the house (an honored guest, to be sure) and remember that it is a matter of courtesy to respect your host.

*Time is important, so plan around it.*

When Dean Rusk was Secretary of State, he made it a point to leave early from social affairs because he knew that it was impolite for anyone to leave before the honored guest. Most audiences respect their guests enough to stay until they have finished speaking. Don't place the added burden of time on the audience.

After you have planned for time, try to get your ideas grouped under two, three, or four main headings. Your listeners can retain no more than five, so try to stop at four. Make each main heading a clear, logical subordinate of the speech purpose, and be sure that all the main headings fit into some logical organizational pattern, such as time, space, cause-effect, problem solution.

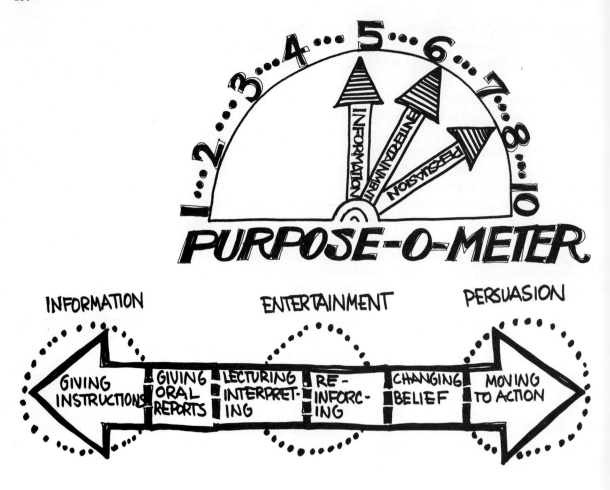

These models originated by Paula Michal and adapted for this text may help in determining the type of outline pattern you wish to use.

*What pattern of organization will be crystal clear to the audience?* This is the very first question you should ask yourself as you begin to organize your speech. Next, perhaps, you'll ask: Will the audience be able to follow the levels of development that support the general thesis?

By gathering your materials, you have already accomplished the first step toward organization. The next step is to put your ideas into a logical order. Finally, you will prepare a preliminary draft of the outline that you can use in rehearsing your speech.

To help determine an appropriate pattern into which you'll arrange your main points, Paula Michal's model may come in handy. She suggests that a problem-solution pattern may be appropriate if it's your mission to persuade the audience to change.

## Arrange your Main Points in an Appropriate Pattern

Of course, before you can arrange your main points, you need to know what they are. Remember, a speech is a system whose parts all affect the whole and one another—so whatever your thoughts are, they should affect the total presentation. Sometimes just putting those initial thoughts or ideas down is difficult. Somerset Maugham said he got his thoughts down on paper by just sitting down with a fountain pen and paper ". . . and the story pours out. However lousy the section is, I let it go. I write to the end. Then subconscious mind has done what it can. . . . The rest is simple effort."

If you sit down to unplug your thoughts and nothing comes out, you can try one or more of these psychological techniques:

1. Pick the time when you feel the sharpest and loosest, and start there.
2. Pretend you are taking an examination and must get something down on paper before your time runs out.
3. Go over your research and pretend a friend has asked you to explain each piece of material.

No matter what technique you select, organization is imperative. After you have selected those main points consider the following patterns.

The chronological pattern of arrangement focuses on the concept of time. Let's look in on Dora's classroom for an example:

*Chronological*

After finishing the unit on nutrition, Dora turns to teaching her students how to cook lentil soup, a highly nutritious dish. She explains:

"First you melt some butter and a little olive oil in a saucepan, then cut up an onion, very fine, the way I showed you last week.

"Let the onion sauté in the butter and olive oil. Add a finely chopped stalk of celery. Then add one-half can of tomato sauce. We can use fresh tomatoes, too, if we have them.

"Let that simmer while you clean the lentils by washing them three or four times. Add the lentils, salt, and pepper, then cook for about one-half hour!"

Dora's speech followed a chronological pattern, that is a sequencing of events.

1. Melt butter and olive oil.
2. Add onions and sauté.
3. Add celery and tomato sauce.
4. Add lentils and cook.
5. You get soup.

*Causal*

In presenting material according to a causal pattern, the speaker lists causes and effects. Let's observe Bert this time:

Bert watches his students dilly-dallying over their work. Two of them put their heads down on their desks. Nothing is getting done. Finally he raps his ruler on the desk and says:

"Okay you kids, you are all just fooling around. Nobody is going to finish their sentences at this rate. If you keep this up, no one will finish the first book, which we are supposed to get through this week. And if you don't finish the first one, we won't be able to get our new readers next week!" The little heads snap up and the pencils start to move.

Bert showed them the relationship between not working and not getting a new book. He pointed out that the effect of their continued dallying might be their failure to get a brand new reader.

The causal pattern is used to show how one thing leads to another. In most speeches, speakers list the causes first, then the effects. For example:

1. The downtown neighborhood association is losing its membership very quickly.
2. The result may be that it will have to disband.

*Problem—Solution*

In the problem-solution pattern, the speaker identifies a problem, presents its consequences, and offers a possible solution.

When Emma finally faced the judge, she was delivering a speech that had been building ever since she decided that Ann, the problem motorist, had run a red light and the solution was to give her a ticket.

When the citizens in Albuquerque got together and met with the mayor, they presented the problem of ditch-fence drownings and offered their solution, which was to fence the ditches.

1. A two-year-old boy drowned in the ditch in May.
   a) His drowning is the first of the season.
   b) Others have drowned in past years.

**2.** Our children are not safe near the ditches.

   **a)** The children have easy access to the ditches.

   **b)** It is difficult to keep children away.

   **c)** Children are attracted by water and mud.

**3.** Only fences will keep the children away from the ditches.

   **a)** Little children will not be able to climb over the fences.

   **b)** Fences will act as a deterrent to older children.

*Topical*

The topical pattern of arrangement approaches the subject on the basis of categories, groups, parts, or reasons.

   When Maria was researching the energy bill for her congressman, she looked at reactions to the President's bill from Congress, the Senate, the White-House staff, the Cabinet, and Washington reporters. In essence she was approaching a subject on the basis of parts—that is, exploring how each section of the government felt about the energy situation. She looked also at the bill itself and its parts—the amendments and various sections. Her topical approach provided a pattern similar to this:

**1.** President Carter's energy bill had a difficult time in the Senate.

**2.** The House of Representatives argued the merits of the bill for eighteen months.

**3.** The President had to summon all his political know-how to persuade Congress to pass the bill.

**4.** The bill was passed, but it bore no resemblance to the first draft.

*Spatial*

Spatial patterns focus on geography, space, or direction.

   Maria could have studied that same bill with regard to the direction it took, its geographical effect (that is, how various parts of the country received it), or she could have examined it from top to bottom. For example:

**1.** The introduction to the bill is unclear.

**2.** Pages 10 through 20 need reevaluation.

**3.** The Senator from Texas will never agree to Section 3.

**4.** There are already five amendments to the bill.

**5.** It should go back to the drafting table.

## Present Your Supporting Points Strategically

*If you face a hostile audience, you may want to begin with a point of agreement.*

*Always keep the audience in mind when organizing your arguments.*

After you have decided what type of organizational pattern best suits you and your audience, your next decision is where to place your supporting points. Aristotle felt the speaker should always start with his or her strongest argument and end with a strong one. He felt the middle of a speech was its weakest point.

Much, however, depends upon your audience. If you are facing a hostile audience, you may wish to begin your message by making a point with which they might agree or at least be willing to consider. You may wish to build to a strong statement only after you feel you have their support, and save your main argument for last. If your audience is supportive, however, you may wish to start with a strong point.

Much depends upon your purpose and your analysis of the audience. It is possible and sometimes necessary to lock yourself into a pattern. For example, if you are giving a recipe, it is hardly advisable to use anything but a chronological pattern.

Finally, you should follow the rules of coordination and subordination for your main and supporting points.

*Coordination* means that the points at a certain level, main or supporting, are equal in importance to one another. All main points should share some common element.

1. Morning lessions include reading, writing, and spelling.
2. Afternoon sessions should be devoted to television and dancing.

If we added

3. Children can participate only if they work hard,

that point would not be chronologically consistent with the first two and not of equal importance. It might, however, support the other two or serve as a main point.

*Subordination* means that one point in a classification can belong to a lower order than another. All ideas are not of equal importance. One can support the other, elaborate upon something, or be of lesser scope.

1. Council will not pass the mayor's budget without alterations.
   a) Council will cut appropriations for the parks.
   b) Salary increases for council staff will be increased.

Let's summarize this short section.

After getting your thoughts together, arrange your main points in an appropriate pattern, remaining always aware of the needs of your audience. Then determine the best order for your main and supporting points and follow the rules of coordination and subordination. However, before you do so, take the time to reexamine your main headings and supporting materials for audience adaptation. Look for the comparisons between your ideas and facts and what you think the audience is already familiar with.

It's like the seventh-inning stretch.

Sometimes to get from one point to another you need to build a bridge. A transition is a verbal bridge, and should be provided clearly and directly to link two points. Otherwise your audience will pass over it, without realizing the connection, like people groping their way in a fog, unaware they have crossed to a greener pasture. You don't have to make the crossing so difficult they feel there's a troll blocking their passage to understanding, or so important that they forget the points and concentrate on the connection. There are artful and functional ways of making a transition, and there are various kinds of transitions. One kind is a preview that alerts the audience to things to come. A blatant and not very artful transition is, "We have finished with point one and now move on to point two."

Joe Murray moved from one point to the next with the words

*Well, that was just part of the story. We would find out other things later, including that, for a short time, Lynn McClure had even been in a state mental hospital.*

Not only did he move the audience along, but he peaked their interest with a preview of coming examples.

Another kind of transition is the internal-summary type. The internal summary works well midway through a speech, when the audience needs a reminder of where they've been in relationship to where they're heading. Observe Joe, midway through his speech:

*But before it was all over, there would be congressional investigations and hearings and inquiries by the President of the United States. The Secretary of the Navy would get involved personally. There would be courts martial, and there would be trials.*

*Most importantly there would be reforms. Before it was over no less than the commandant of the Marine Corps would say that 1976*

## Transitions

*Transitions can be previews or summaries, short phrases or questions.*

*was a year of change for the U.S. Marines, because of Lynn Mc-Clure. And because of that the Marine Corps was getting well. So I guess in the best sense that was what it was about: Finding something that was wrong and doing something to change it.*

Having crossed the bridge and repeated the central theme, Joe Murray then took the audience further down the road.

Transitions need not be long sentences or paragraphs. They can be single words or short phrases, such as:

In addition to . . .

Neither . . . nor

Either . . . or

Similar to . . .

In contrast to . . .

Not only . . . , but also

Transitions can also be in a form of a question. Joe Murray asked,

*But what can I do? I'm just one person. Can one person make any difference?*

And, of course, he found that one person could make all the difference in the world.

**OUTLINING**

Outlines can be helpful in testing the soundness of your reasoning. State the thesis you intend to establish and see if the basic divisions of your speech logically support it. Let's look at an outline of Joe Murray's speech and see whether his reasoning is sound.

*WALKING IN THE FRONT DOOR*
*Joe Murray*

*Introduction*

I. *Introductory technique.*
   A. Joe Murray establishes credibility by describing himself as a journalist and saying, "I grew up in Lufkin."
   B. He establishes rapport with the audience by addressing their desires to be reporters.
II. *Central theme*: How do you get a story that wins the Pulitzer Prize?

**A.** Murray establishes central theme in the introduction by saying that people always ask him that question.

**I.** *Main point*: Murray starts by saying that first you have to recognize the story when it walks in the front door.

*Body*

**A.** *Subordinate point*: After you recognize a story, you have to make a decision to find out what's happened.

   **1.** *Major supporting point*: Murray assigned a reporter to the story.

   **2.** *Major supporting point*: He assigned a *good* reporter to the story.

      **a)** Each point supported further by examples of what a good reporter is and how a good reporter works plus stories of good interviewing techniques.

(Transition)

**II.** *Main point*: Murray restates his initial point adding that after you recognize the story and put a good reporter on it, you have to make sure the story is read.

**A.** *Subordinate point*: (Disseminate the message.) Murray gave the story to the Washington Post and the Associated Press Wire Service for broader circulation.

   **1.** Examples.

(Transition)

**III.** *Main point*: Recap—after you recognize the story, get a good reporter to cover it and get a lot of people to read it. Don't buckle under the pressure!

**A.** *Subordinate point*: Never let anyone investigate themselves. (Murray explains how he wavered and let the Marines take over the investigation.)

**B.** *Subordinate Point*: Ask questions. (Murray explains how he took over the investigation and refused to be intimidated.)

**IV.** *Main Point*: Tell the story. (Murray saves the best for last. By a long example he actually tells the story that won the Pulitzer Prize and he tells it well.)

**A.** *Subordinate point*: Good writing.

*Conclusion*

**I.** *Summary of main points*: Murray says, "The young folks want to be journalists because they want to save the world from a sea of sin and corruption. Well, there's nothing wrong with that—but before you go splashing out there to rescue the world, you'd better first learn how to swim. Use the good tools and the good rules of your trade, and that means good writing."

Was Murray's speech logical? According to the outline, he started by asking a question and ended by answering it. In the body of the speech he illustrated those techniques of good reporting that lead to good writing. In essence, he said you win a Pulitzer Prize with good writing, and good writing means using the tools of the trade—recognizing the story, investigating it, using good interviewing techniques, not abandoning ethics, and, finally, writing it in an unforgettable way.

## MOTIVATING PROCESS

Murray used a lot of examples and several organizational patterns; the most apparent was his chronological narrative of the story. His arrangement is considered to be a *motivating process*. For years books describing the process of selling merchandise and motivating an audience used functional terms such as attention, interest, desire, and action. In 1929, Mr. John A. McGee of Purdue published a book containing the well-used approach designed to stimulate an audience to action.

1. *Securing attention*: Joe Murray certainly got the audience's attention when he stated that Lynn McClure had been beaten to death—"literally." The audience immediately wanted to know how and why.

2. *Stating a problem*: Joe Murray gave the audience a problem to solve: How to write a prize-winning story.

3. *Offering a solution*: (Satisfaction) Murray detailed the solution by explaining the necessary skills a reporter needs.

4. *Visualization*: Murray visualized the image of the reporter in a positive situation to show how much better it would be if his audience were also crusaders.

5. *Inviting definite action*: By demonstrating how his paper told the story and won the Pulitzer Prize, Joe Murray was encouraging the would-be journalists to be courageous and do likewise. He convinced them that one person can make a difference, especially one person with a reporter's pad.

Outlining is a way of gathering your ideas together and determining whether your speech is reasonable. It is the final standardized step before the selection of words and actual delivery that will make your speech unique. Some speakers find it easy to write complete-sentence outlines and then actually speak from the outline.

I.  In outlining, use symbols and be consistent as to level of importance.

   A.  The speech has a central idea and statement of intended change.

   B.  The speech has three divisions: introduction, body, and conclusion.

II. Outlining principles are

   A.  Each point should begin with a capital letter.

   B.  Only one idea to one point.

   C.  A point can be stated in a phrase, complete sentence, or very short paragraph.

   D.  Subpoints can help to

      1.  Break down main points.

      2.  Support main points.

   E.  Main points that have been subdivided can further be subdivided (two or more subpoints).

   F.  The outline should develop the central idea.

Murray didn't sit down and write out an outline before delivering the speech. Perhaps for that reason, the speech doesn't lend itself to the "perfect" outline, an example of which follows at the end of this section. Murray gave that speech many times before he sat down one day and dictated it into a tape recorder because someone wanted a copy and he had never actually written it out. But Murray knew the story and he knew his audience and what they needed. Since he was a writer and had been an editor for many years, it wasn't difficult for him to speak in journalistic style . . . but with an added "oral" quality. If he had written the speech instead of talked it into a recorder, it might not have had that easy conversational (oral) style that is so pleasing to the ear.

". . . But it is with words we govern man."

Thus remarks Disraeli in one of his novels, as he addresses the difficulty of identifying ideas.

**WORDS**

*With words we govern . . . or stumble.*

As Mayor David Rusk discovers at a press conference, it is *words* that separate man from beast (although the orangutan stole the show). James Kilpatrick, who engages in weekly verbal battles with Shana Alexander on the television program *60 Minutes*, denounces the way government misinforms with words: "Regrettably there is no way to bite into the nickel words to see if they are made of lead," he says, being of conservative mind and finding change traumatic. Government is good at stumbling over words, he continues: "Federal funds are really tax funds—ours. . . . Freedom fighters. . . . Liberation Forces are filled with men who do brutal acts."

Throughout the ages, writers and speakers have consistently deplored the way men and women use words. Herbert Gold, a contemporary writer, called the word "that ambiguous tool and blessing."

Call it what we may, speakers can seldom do without it! We start our speech with words, the body of our speech contains words, and the conclusion of our speech contains words. Of course, we also communicate visually, but it is really with words that we stumble . . . or speak out.

Technically we start communicating with the walk to the podium, but realistically we start our speech with the introductory words.

## Starting with Words

*A speaker came out with his face bandaged and launched into a lengthy speech, saying "I must apologize. This morning while I was shaving I was thinking about my speech, and I cut my face." When he was through a man came over and said, "Listen, next time think about your face and cut the speech."*

That story was told by comedian Mickey Freeman as he opened an after-dinner speech. Freeman started with humor (being a comedian, he probably continued with humor and ended with humor).

Ray Baumel begins his speech and takes his time getting down to his real mission—to entertain. Five minutes into his speech his audience is convinced he is a crashing bore, when suddenly he says, "And so I can point to one factor that makes the funeral business more lucrative in my part of the country—guns!"

Baumel is a professional comedian who spends his life going to business conventions and passing himself off as an expert in the field. He has spoken to 500 major corporations in 12 years. He says, "They throw me into meetings to wake them up."

*Your introduction should gain interest, provide background, and establish a good climate.*

His introductions include humor and startling statements.

For most of us, however, humor is difficult to handle, especially in the introduction; so we settle for other means of introducing ourselves and our topics. The introduction, no matter how it is delivered, has three specific purposes:

1. To gain the attention and maintain the interest of the audience.
2. To provide the audience with the necessary background about the speaker and the topic.
3. To establish a good climate (pathos) and establish the speaker as a credible person.

Sometimes it's difficult to accomplish all three purposes in a short introduction, but the speaker should try.

### Gaining Attention

*If we think of the audience first, we are off and speaking.*

Getting started is the toughest part for most of us. Speaking that first word, hearing the commotion subside and the rustling stop, and then feeling all eyes upon us can be a traumatic experience. But it need not be. If we return to the opening statement of this chapter and forget about ourselves, if we start thinking of that audience, acknowledging them first, we are easily off and running. In casual conversation, when we see people we know and immediately think of them, that smile and "hello" in our eyes puts them in a nice frame of mind. Immediately we have caught their attention and established a rapport. In a brief encounter the smile, nod, or "hello" is usually sufficient, but in a formal situation the opening of the speech needs to go a little further. The walk to the podium and the visual acknowledgment of the audience should be followed immediately by a rationale for why they should listen to what you have in store for them. The stories, humorous quotations, statistics, and comparisons you begin with must appeal to their interests and their curiosity.

### Orientation

*Give your audience a preview of coming attractions.*

Once you have their interest, you must inform them of your topic, thus reassuring them that you do not intend to waste their time. Give them a little preview of coming attractions. (We love the teasers on television.) Tell them how much you intend to tell them, so that they will not leave thinking they were swindled. Naturally, how much or how little you inform them of the topic and its background depends solely upon your analysis of the audience. You can simply say, "I'm here to tell you how to become a tennis pro in fifteen months," or you can spend one-fifth of your allotted time introducing the topic and giving a detailed history of it. There are no rules.

*Climate and Credibility*

For most of us, credibility is something we take for granted. When Bert stands up to address his first-graders, he is a trusted teacher. If Bill is asked to address the hairdressers' convention, the audience assumes he knows the business. Most of us are asked to speak formally because someone believes in us. This initial trust should be considered so important to use that we carefully guard it and do nothing during the speech to lose our credibility. There are times, of course, when we will face a hostile audience; those times are the difficult ones, when we'll need to build trust by giving the audience something of value.

*We should guard carefully the trust an audience gives us.*

There are various ways of starting a speech. One is humor, which we have already discussed. Now let's look at some examples of the others: reference, story, comparison-contrast, startling statement, question, quotation, statistics.

*I do not think it entirely inappropriate to introduce myself to this audience. I am the man who accompanied Jacqueline Kennedy to Paris, and I have enjoyed it.* John F. Kennedy in Paris.

**Reference**

*I grew up in Lufkin, Texas, and except for a three-year stint with the* Houston Chronicle, *the only paper I've ever worked on is the* Lufkin News. *Every once in a while I wonder if I've somehow short-changed myself—that maybe if I'd gotten on the* Washington Post *or the* New York Times, *I could have amounted to something; I could have gotten the really big story. Well Ken Herman was born in New York, and he had to come to Lufkin, Texas, to get the big story.* Joe Murray, Texas.

**Story**

*You may not think that eating a candy bar for lunch is so bad, but think of that candy bar as three toothaches a year and you might switch to celery.* Dora Marraquin, opening a lecture on nutrition.

**Comparison–contrast**

*But he made this statement, and it made all the difference in the world. He said, "They beat that boy's brains out—literally."* Joe Murray, Texas.

**Startling statement**

*Well, kids, how many words did you count in* Sesame Street *today?* Bert Marraquin to his first-grade class.

**Question**

*In the words of John Donne, who worked the precincts of seventeenth century England: "Our two souls, therefore, which are one,/ Though I must go, endure not yet/A breach, but an expansion. . ."* Dennis Kucinich, ex-mayor of Cleveland, who loves to quote poets or Robert F. Kennedy when opening a speech.

**Quotation**

*This month's crime statistics indicate a small percentage of increase in the areas of burglaries and homicides. Burglaries are up*

**Statistics**

*4.5 percent and homicides 1.5 percent.* Elroy "Whitey" Hansen, Chief of the Albuquerque Police Department, addressing his officers and members of the press.

Since there is no magic formula that tells you when to use statistics or when to start with a story, the best rule is to follow common sense, relevancy to the subject, and audience analysis.

## Words in the Body

The techniques with which you set the audience at ease and gain attention in the opening moments of a speech are techniques that involve language intelligible to the ear. Oral language or the spoken word differs from written language in that it cannot be replayed immediately by the live audience. That is, the audience cannot move their eyes back over a sentence and reread it. While the written word encourages readers to take themselves on an adventure, the oral word gives speakers an opportunity to take their audience along with them. It's more of a group excursion.

For that reason, oral style is much more conversational, contains more personal pronouns and a variety of sentences, as well as sentence fragments. There's more repetition of phrases and more familiar words. Oral style should be clear, accurate, and appropriate to the audience.

*Oral style should be clear, accurate, and appropriate to the audience.*

All speakers use words, and words have multiple meanings. Often in our search for meaning we look into someone else's eyes; if there is no mirror reflection of our thoughts there, we adjust our words in order to reach some understanding. Words are tools, used wisely or unwisely—we either tighten the screw or ease the tension. We use words for a great number of reasons: We assure ourselves that we are important by giving importance to our words. We use them to establish values such as "good" and "bad" by allotting certain standards to words. We express our emotions by using words that stimulate emotional responses. We use words to create abstract impressions by talking about "love" and "hate," or to give logical explanations and assure others that we are rational human beings.

However we use words, we rely upon them to carry our message to our audience. The concept that words have multiple meanings and the meanings reside primarily in the receiver of the message has been discussed earlier in this book.

For the specific purpose of public speaking, the use of words to add liveliness and the human touch to our message is paramount.

Understanding the way writers and speakers use words for greater effect can aid the novice speaker to achieve oral quality, add excitement, and keep the audience listening.

Here are some points to remember when selecting words and composing sentences:

1. *Use action verbs.* Verbs such as love, hate, caress, sting, leap, catapult, roar, sparkle, and massacre are of the active rather than the passive voice. An action verb makes the noun the subject in the sentence, while the passive verb makes the noun the object. It is more exciting to say, "She cringed!" than "She was cringing."

2. *Use adjectives.* Adjectives modify, clarify, excite. However, the good speaker uses caution in the selection. An adjective can smother the noun, be opinionated, nonspecific, or misleading. Used correctly and specifically (such as, "the cringing girl," rather than "the hesitant girl"), adjectives can create very vivid images.

3. *Listeners love alliteration.* Alliteration helps the rhythm of the speech, makes the sound more pleasing to the ear. Alliteration is the art of designing a sentence so it has several words that start with the same sound. For example, "The dilapidated dog dragged its tail," or, "The curious cat kicked the cheese."

4. *Use personalization* A conversational atmosphere is best created by using personal pronouns and bringing the audience closer to you. If you talk about how "we can do it," and "you and I feel the same way," the audience is gathered in your circle. If you must speak in the third person name names, get personal.

5. *Why not personification?* For example, give your clock some human qualities. Let the "old Dutch clock put its hands before its face," and if "time marches on," well, the image will be sharper. Personification is the practice of endowing ideas and objects with human traits.

6. *Definitely use similes and metaphors!* Images are best created with similes and metaphors. Both can be used to clarify by definition. A simile uses words "as" and "like" while a metaphor *implies* those words. Both state a comparison between two *unlike* things that have something in common. For example, "Dora's sister's temper is mild, like an enchilada without chili," is a simile, while the phrase "Life's but a walking shadow" is an implied metaphor.

7. *Parallelism can be effective.* Parallelism indicates a similarity of structure in sentences or phrases. Bert uses parallel structure when he tells his students: "You'd better study your alphabet, study the way you write the letters, study the cursive way to make them, so you can be a better student." When you present ideas in a parallel structure, it is easier for the audience to follow them.

8. *Try antithesis.* Another type of parallelism is antithesis, which also has a balanced structure but expresses opposing ideas. John F. Kennedy used anthithesis when he said, "Let us never negotiate out of fear. But let us never fear to negotiate."

9. *Consider the rhetorical question.* No one really expects an answer to the rhetorical question. When Dora says, "What kind of a mother do you think I am?" the twins don't respond. When Bert cries, "Where will this rise in prices end?" the family just nods sympathetically. The rhetorical question is good for getting attention, then the audience expects you to move along.

10. *Quotations help the hesitant.* Quotations, like testimony, add vitality and imagery but do not necessarily prove anything. However, when someone else has already said something you like, quoting a passage not only gives you a variety in style but also expresses your preference to the audience. There is a limitless store of quotations ready for the plucking: After all, "All the world's a stage, and all the men and women merely players!" So put a little drama into your speech and quote someone else.

11. *Finally, restate and repeat.* Joe Murray said, "Get the story. Get the story. Get the story," thus emphasizing his main theme and adding a little rhythm to his speech. Repetition uses identical phrasing; important names and dates can be repeated. Restatement, however, is used to clarify and emphasize; it says the same thing over again but in a different way.

*Most important is the concept of simplicity and appropriateness.*

Most important for the speaker in selecting words to flush out his or her ideas and finally deliver the message is the concept of simplicity and appropriateness. While you select your words to suit your personality, it is wise to remember that simplicity can be beautiful if it is used to clarify, if the words are familiar, and if the message is appropriate.

Appropriateness and good taste go hand in hand. Implied in the concept of appropriateness is ethical consideration of the audience. On an informal conversational level, Dora will not use words the twins do not understand when communicating with them, nor will she insult them or use language she has forbidden them to use. In other words, she has their welfare at heart first. Later, in a formal presentation to her students, she is careful not to mislead them out of ignorance, or make statements she knows they do not understand but are hesitant to ask her to clarify. She wants them to do well; she has no desire to show them how incompetent they are. Appropriateness is a very intangible concept and comes from the speaker's desire to consider the audience's point of view in selection of words.

## Words in Your Conclusion

Getting on the stage and getting off are two occasions when you know you have the attention of the audience. Don't play down the importance of both. Conclusions can be logical—that is, you can summarize your speech for the audience so that they are once again aware of your central theme and what it implies. You can leave them laughing, hoping, crying, or, in the other words, your conclusion can be psychological. All the techniques employed in constructing the introduction and the body can be used in the conclusion—that is, you can end with a quote, a story, a question, a restatement, a metaphor, and so on. Once again, the audience will give you your clue. Listen for it. Look for it. If the audience is waiting for you to stop, stop! If they want an encore, oblige. But it's not a bad idea to leave them wanting you to come back.

In conclusion of this section, let us summarize and use the logical conclusion. You, the speaker, have analyzed your audience, researched your topic, and developed your message by selecting your line of reasoning. You have gathered supporting materials, outlined your speech by organizing it into an appropriate pattern, and finally have found the appropriate words that will add imagery and liveliness to your speech.

You're ready.

So start walking to that podium. You have spotlighted that audience; now its time for the spotlight to revolve, to come full circle and focus on *you*.

## SUMMARY

Since your main exercise for this chapter is to prepare and deliver, let's summarize with an orderly rundown of what you must do. Before stepping in front of that audience to deliver your speech, it won't hurt to check the following list one more time:

**Step 1.** Are you clear in your own mind as to what the audience already knows and what the audience needs to know? If so, write down your purpose sentence or central idea.

**Step 2.** Have you decided who the audience is and why that audience needs to know about your particular subject or information? If so, write down how you actually intend to motivate them.

**Step 3.** Are you sure you have all your facts, explanatory details, and stories either in your mind or down on paper. If so, get those materials together and spread them out before you so you can see them. Are they in a logical pattern? Do they look organized to you? Are they narrowed in scope, grouped according to separate ideas and main headings? How do you like your introduction and conclusion? Is it flexible enough in case the audience changes?

**Step 4.** Reexamine those headings and supportive materials for the particular audience as you know them just before you stride to that platform. Can you draw some instant comparisons between your facts and what the audience already knows? Don't be afraid to think on your feet—if it is *relevant*.

**Step 5.** Have you written out your conclusion and introduction? How does it grab you now? Review your conclusion: Are all your highlights summarized very briefly? Are you going to conclude with a story? Does it produce in you the feeling that you wish to produce in your audience? Review that introduction: Does it state very early exactly what you propose to do? Have you planned to tell that audience immediately of your main points?

**Step 6.** Can you reduce your speech to a few brief notes? Do your notes seem logical? Can you read them and understand how they fit into the whole of the speech?

**Step 7.** Rehearse the speech mentally and orally.

# KEY TERMS

| | | | |
|---|---|---|---|
| action | alliteration | attention | causal |
| action verb | antithesis | audience | chronological |
| adjective | appropriateness | authority | climate |

| comparison-contrast | parallelism | repetition | statistics |
| credibility | personalization | restatement | subordination |
| humor | personification | rhetorical question | symbol |
| hypothetical | picture ratio | satisfaction | testimony |
| illustration | problem-solution | simile | topical |
| metaphor | question | simplicity | transition |
| organizing | quotation | spatial | visual aids |
| orientation | reference | startling statement | visualization |
| outline | | | |

---

Now—*deliver that speech*!

**EXERCISE**

---

**CIRCLING BACK**

Working from the end of the chapter towards the beginning, answer the following questions.

1. What elements appear in oral language?
2. What is the purpose of the introduction?
3. Explain motivated sequence.
4. Describe the internal-summary type of transition.
5. Name several types of organizational patterns.
6. What steps help when organizing a speech?
7. What are the key considerations when planning television graphics?
8. Name a few types of visual aids.
9. What specific purpose can visual aids serve?
10. Name three rules which should be considered when using statistics.
11. To be effective, illustrations must be relevant—and what else?
12. Name the three types of illustrations.

---

**REFERENCES**

Bernstein, Paul. "A Phony Thing Happened on the Way to the Annual Meeting." *TWA Ambassador*, November 1978, 68.

Kilpatrick, James, J., "With Words We Govern and Stumble." *Albuquerque Journal*, October 23, 1978.

McGee, John A. *Minimum Essentials of Persuasive Speaking.* New York: Charles Scribner's Sons, 1929.

Monroe, Alan, and Ehninger, Douglas, *Principles and Types of Speech* (6th ed.). Chicago: Scott, Foresman, 1967.

# 7 the big arena: the speaker

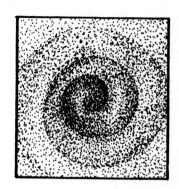

Ever since you began to prepare for your public-speaking event, you have made the audience your center of focus. When you finally walk toward that audience, the reality is that they begin sending *you* messages: they may applaud, smile, or even grow impatient. But they are waiting for you, and you are now *their* center of attention. The circle has revolved, and you are in the spotlight. When you researched them, when you made discoveries and asked questions, very few members of that audience knew they were being spotlighted. But when they focus on you, you are right there before them.

At that moment of awareness when you are the center of attention, your research will make you confident. Preparation and rehearsal will add to that confidence.

At that moment the most important consideration is your IMAGE. The image you project during the first few minutes of your presentation will affect your speech and possibly your entire career.

*During the first few minutes your projected image is most important.*

## IMAGE

In other chapters we have discussed the concept of ethos. The modern word for ethos is *image*. Ethos in Aristotle's time meant to establish your goodwill and intelligence, to be credible to your audience. Earlier we mentioned some guidelines for assuming ethical responsibilities for your speech and actions. To the scholars of Aristotle's time, ethos and ethics were very much intertwined in the formation of a good image.

Now lets talk about image on the practical level of a platform. Your whole personality follows you up to that platform where that podium stands. Your image for that audience is how you walk, talk, and behave. Your image communicates your profession, your attitude, your expertise, and your knowledge.

*Your image is how you walk, talk, and behave.*

In interpersonal situations, time is on your side. You may meet a friend on a day when your hair is not quite brushed or your trousers are torn; you may be depressed, strident—not yourself. Your friend understands because that audience of one does not judge you on a single meeting. That friend has seen you in many roles at many times.

It may be true that some large audiences see you many times, but the reality is that even if the same people are a part of the audience, the audience has changed, the time has changed, and so have you.

On the public-speaking platform you must package that combined image of yours and use the very best ingredients. Consider the fate of Vice-President Andrew Johnson: While giving his inaugural address, Johnson was quite ill. He had come from Tennesee with a fever. Shaking and chilled, he had been given two shots of a sweet brandy (he never drank brandy). Although his message was thoughtful, his speech was slurred. After the occasion, Lincoln held his head in his hands and said, "Andy made a mistake but he ain't no drunkard." The press was not so kind, nor was history. Even when the *London Times* did a thorough research of Johnson's life and found no evidence to support the drunkard charge, the public remained unconvinced.

When you are practicing that speech in front of a mirror, analyze yourself as well as your speech. Is that reflected image the one you wish to project? Are you satisfied with what you see? There is no set of rules or checklist you can follow to assure yourself of the right image. Knowing yourself, being in touch with your body and with your feelings is important. Then honestly ask yourself what others are seeing in you. Usually people are not cruel. Your friends will not say, "What have you done to yourself? You look simply awful!" They may say, "You look a little tired."

If someone you have met at least ten times still can't remember your name, you're not even an image to him or her. Perhaps you are president of Student Council, or hold an important job in your company, yet people see you and exclaim, "*You're* so and so! You're not what I expected!" If these kinds of things happen to you, look at yourself again. You might reanalyze your image.

*Prepare yourself as well as your speech.*

What people usually expect from a speaker is preparation and that means preparation of *self* and *speech*. Take a good look at your clothing, your makeup (if you are a woman), your hairstyle, your walk, *and* your talk. The combination is the image. Look upon the occasion as a whole; don't worry about one little place, worry about them all.

Here are some simple tips:

1. Wear shoes that will allow you to walk briskly and stand firmly. Be sure those shoes complement the rest of your clothing.

2. Don't play with pencils, notes, jewelry, keys. Do look at your audience, but don't stare. Walk around, if walking adds to and does not distract from the message.

3. Your hair must be clean. Remember you will be talking, and the eyes of the audience will rest mainly on your face. Don't be afraid to change your hair style for a real lift.

4. Stand straight but *don't* throw back your shoulders and tense up. Concentrating on pulling in your stomach will affect your voice. Think about your stomach earlier at the gym.

5. If you are a professional, dress like one. Forget about the fact you were once a high-school cheerleader or an athlete.

6. Consider: If you were a press agent, how would you package you?

7. Remember, you have three to five minutes at the most to establish that image. Stand up, speak out, and wait for that first round of applause.

Realistically, let's not rule out the possibility that you may experience a little anxiety. When you do, remember you have already done much to cope with that anxiety. Being prepared and establishing the right image is half the battle. If you practiced in front of that mirror, or before a group of friends, you have given your speech once. Naturally it was not exactly the same as the one you are about to make because the audience, the environment, and the occasion are new. The information remains the same, however.

As the audience looks at you, look back at them. Are they as you pictured them? Did you think (or were you told) that the audience would number nearly 300 people, yet you see only around 50? Were you expecting a balanced audience, yet find only males are facing you?

It is best to check the actual audience and gather information from your host when you arrive. If there isn't time, do a quick scan as you walk to that podium. Mentally adjust your speech to the size and type of audience. Of course, the audience will be taking this opportunity to form an impression of you. They may have heard of you and may even have a "prior image" of you in their minds, just as you have of them. See if you can read any messages in their actions.

**ANXIETY**

*See if you can read any messages in the audience's actions.*

That prior image generally is positive (after all, they have invited you), so you need only reinforce it by looking your best and giving a good speech.

There is no fail-safe way to avoid *all* anxiety, but the following steps may guide your actions:

1. Know your audience while you are preparing your speech.
2. Adjust that knowledge to include the audience you actually see.
3. Take a few deep breaths on the way to the podium.
4. Don't overeat before taking that walk.
5. While you are speaking, be aware of your actions and the audience's responses. Make a mental note as to when they applaud, when they laugh, and what questions they ask afterward. (If possible, arrange to record the speech for later evaluation.)
6. If you really think you've bombed, be a champion. Go over your moves and begin to correct your weaknesses. Make a comeback. Remember, each speech will have a new audience and a new you.

## DELIVERY: WHAT THE AUDIENCE SEES

Successful delivery of any message to a live audience (and before the television camera) always involves a combination of what the audience *sees* and what the audience *hears*. Some speakers or performers rely very heavily on sight. An orchestra conductor, for example, has two audiences—the patrons and the musicians themselves. A conductor may introduce a musical selection with words, but his or her main means of communicating is through a system of signals, a language starting with a simple raised baton or "upbeat" and transcending to a most involved set of signals that have sharp and frequent changes.

### Your Walk

That walk to the podium tells the audience more about us than we care to admit. That walk is a personality indicator. When we straighten up our walk, we straighten out our speech. Audiences react to different kinds of walks.

*Audiences react to different kinds of walks.*

Kinesiologist Maurita Kobarge (she studies how the body moves) feels that walking style evolves from body structure and reflects the influence of family and peer groups as well as our own personalities.

We are unique in the way we walk. As a species, only humanoids stride out for long periods with the bipedal walk as their normal gait. Think about it. This is your locomotion, your means of transportation, and no other species on earth has this unique feature. Most of your 650 muscles are involved in walking. You can saunter as though

you have all the time in the world to get going on your speech; you can slump with your hips forced down and out because your weight has sunk on either side; or you can do a model's walk and place one foot directly in front of the other, emphasizing the pelvic sway. You can be brisk, bouncy, sexy, or sauntering.

Tom's friend Bruce, a mime, loves to demonstrate various walks.

But the first impression that audience has of you is based on that walk to the podium.

Is there a right way to walk? Probably not. However, there is a healthy way to walk. Stand straight but don't become a ramrod. Straighten up and relax, but not too much. When you walk, hold your chest high, stretch your spine, and don't relax those buttocks or stomach—hold them in, but don't tense them.

Start out with vigor. Your pace and your stride should be normal for you. The average pace is about two steps per second or three miles an hour. (And it burns up 300 calories an hour, too. Perhaps a walk to the podium could be doubly rewarding.)

Senator Ted Kennedy came to Albuquerque in 1974 to help some of the Democratic candidates there. The television reporters and cameramen followed his long walk to the podium: He started at the

door of the Civic Auditorium and moved through crowds, smiling and striding down through the long auditorium and up to the podium. Jesse Jackson came to Cleveland when Maria was there; he entered through the front door of the Olivet Baptist Church, striding down the aisle and leaping up to the podium, exuding an image of energy.

**Your Gestures**

Dora and Bert attend performances of the Albuquerque Symphony Orchestra, where the conductor, after his brisk walk to the podium, bows and turns his back to one audience, then taps the podium and addresses the other.

His communication begins with that brisk walk to the podium. In conducting, his system of signals reaches a highly sophisticated level. Concentration and involvement are so intense at times that only eyes and hands communicate with an entire section of the orchestra. If those 100 individuals in front of the conductor don't understand, respond to, or believe in him, neither will those hundreds or thousands in back of him respond, believe, or understand. The conductor in this sense is part of a relay team, widening his circle with the simple gesture of a raised hand.

When the mass media are involved, that walk, those gestures, that love and understanding is spread to a third audience, who is watching the mediated message. The late Arthur Fiedler's 1976 Fourth-of-July concert vibrated from one end of America to the other. His body movements, gestures, and facial expressions were all part of the total message.

*When the mass media are involved, our gestures reach another audience.*

There are no guidelines for how we should move. Movements are unique to the individual and specific to the audience. (Obviously small audiences are best served by less expansive gestures. The size of the room influences your walk, your talk.) However, there is some information about how some observers "feel" about body movements and facial expressions. This information can help us understand the general impressions audiences have of us.

1. *Force.* When two parts of the body move together from opposite directions, an expression of force is perceived. Example: hitting your fist into your hand; clicking your heels together.

2. *Decorative.* When two parts of the body move in the same direction the impression is decorative but weak. Example: moving the head and hand in the same direction; bowing.

3. *Exuberance.* When a movement passes through the entire body in a wave-like motion (e.g., when eyes light up, chest rises, and feet move), the impression the audience receives is one of excitement and enthusiasm.

4. *Fear.* When a gesture is behind us, or when we walk away from the audience, the impression is one of fear, shyness, and reticence.

Our bodies are capable of a wide variety of gestures, just as our faces are capable of 20,000 different expressions. According to Francois Delsarte, 19th Century ballet master and speech teacher, *gesture is the persuasive agent of the heart*; speech is the letter, but gesture is the spirit. He classifies gestures of the head as intellectual, gestures of the torso as emotional, and gestures of the legs and feet as physical.

Each profession sets up its own set of symbols or gestures. In baseball, for example, the communication between catcher and pitcher is intricate and special to the particular team. For maximum effectivess we must learn to implement the specific gestures each audience can understand and relate to.

WOMEN  Today, more and more women are addressing large audiences. More and more women are speaking from positions of

**What to Wear at the Podium**

authority, conducting seminars, and appearing on television. Their numbers will continue to increase.

When Maria holds a news briefing or attends a Congressional hearing, she leaves her dungarees in the closet and takes out a tailored blouse and skirt. When she went to the University in Albuquerque, she was comfortable wearing T-shirts and jeans, but in Washington she had to adjust her choice of clothing to her position.

There is no single "right" look; clothing is certainly as individual as its wearer wishes it to be. From the time of the early Greeks, however, clothing has been identified not only with periods in history, but also with social status and the roles people assume. A distinguished feature of clothing is its constant state of change; yet many styles seem "circularized"—that is, they always seem to "come back."

The look that always seems to be with us revolves around simplicity. *Classic* is the word. Frank N. Magid and Associates, a major U.S. media consultant, suggests that women who speak in public should dress to appear feminine but not sexy, tailored and authoritative, but not rigid. Magid suggests that women avoid distracting prints and accessories for television, and that same advice is good for the live audience. Solid colors and soft fabrics with color accents in scarves always work well.

*"Women should dress to appear feminine and authoritative."*

MEN In *Dress for Success*, John T. Molloy suggests that men are most likely to be liked when wearing suits of light grey or solid blue. He also finds that dark-blue solids give men the highest credibility among the widest range of people. Molloy further states that the choice of tie directly affects impressions of status, credibility, personality, and ability. These hints are very general, but they may be of help if you do not know your audience, or your audience does not know you.

Regional custom frequently indicates an acceptable departure from the traditional mode of dress. In the Southwest, for example, men who wear string ties with "bolos" are not necessarily viewed as lacking credibility. When the former Governor of New Mexico started his grass-roots campaign, he wore leisure suits and open shirts. After he took office, however, his clothing began to change; the leisure suits disappeared and solid grey suits took over. By the end of his four-year term, Governor Apodaca was wearing the type of clothes that John Molloy identifies with the best-dressed executive.

Realistically, people respond to clothing just as they do to your tone of voice, your dialect, and your physical appearance. The line, the color, and the material combine to present a picture that illustrates some part of your personality and environment. It is important that you are aware of the effect your clothes have upon the audience.

At one police briefing, Emma tossed off the Spanish word *entradida* in explaining how she handled a certain situation. Only three of the four people in her group knew what she was talking about. Officer Bakas didn't. He was raised in Greece, schooled in the East, and had moved recently to the Southwest. Like Emma, we all forget at times that our audience may not have heard even the sound of some word that we toss off easily. Emma was talking about her "little entrance" at a domestic situation. She dramatized the word by showing the other officers how she approached the door of the house.

This combination of sight and sound helped understanding. When we deliver a message, effective use of *both* visible and audible codes make the message more palatable. But we should keep in mind that a formal audience has come to hear a speech. Making the sounds familiar to them is the first step; choosing words to which they can attach meaning is next.

# DELIVERY: WHAT THE AUDIENCE HEARS

## Speech

Let's start with the first step.

What is speech? Speech is not a natural phenomenon, as we have obviously *learned* how to speak.

A baby emerges from the womb, takes his or her first breath and makes a sound, perhaps utters a loud cry. Everyone present at the birth utters a sigh of relief—the baby is alive. In order to make that sound, the baby had to take a breath. The baby did not speak, but merely made a sound. The first step on the road to speech is breathing. The purpose of breathing is to supply our body with oxygen (when we inhale) and rid it of excess carbon dioxide (when we exhale). The respiratory cycle—inhalation and exhalation—is automatic and repeated every three to five seconds. It speeds up during moments of excitement or exertion and slows down when we sleep or rest.

When we inhale, the diaphragm contracts and draws downward, and the ribs and sternum raise and move outward. The effect of these actions is to increase the size of the chest cavity, and outside air is drawn in through the respiratory tract (that is, nose, trachea, and lungs), to fill that space. When we exhale, the muscles used in respiration relax and the diaphragm, ribs, and sternum return to their original positions.

*Pronunciation is the way we choose to make a sound.*

In the windpipe, which is part way up the respiratory tract, are the vocal cords or vocal folds. When the vocal cords are tightened by some muscular tension, the passage of air through them makes them vibrate and produce sound. Although breathing itself is automatic, we can control the *way* we breathe. We can let out just a little air, tighten our vocal cords just a mite, and utter a small sound; or we can expel a lot of air and let out a cry. We can utter an amazing variety of sounds simply by controlling the amount of air that comes in and goes out.

The sounds become speech when we start modifying them. We start articulating—that is, we start clarifying the way we make a given sound. Then we move on to pronunciation, which is the way we choose to make the sound. For example, we can articulate by placing our tongue in various positions and then choose to pronounce a certain word according to a habit we've acquired. Our pronunciation is affected by our social conditions, residual habits, and organic or physical impediments, such as overbite.

The further elements that affect our speech are phonation, resonance, pitch, rate, volume, quality of voice, mood, accent, and dialect. We shall address them one at a time, not necessarily in the order of their importance. (The audience has to make that decision.)

These terms are often confused to the point where most of us use them interchangeably. It is generally accepted that those to whom American English is not a native language speak with *accents*, while regional influences on what we consider standard American speech produce *dialects*. We can illustrate this by saying that when Egyptian President Anwar Sadat delivers a speech in English, he speaks with an accent; but when President Jimmy Carter and Senator Ted Kennedy take the podium, we hear the unmistakable traces of their regional dialects.

*Accents and Dialects*

However, the difference is really arbitrary; most regional dialects have evolved from the speech of people from other lands. It is difficult today to find sounds that are "purely" English.

If you have an accent—that is, if English is not your native language—and you feel that your audience may have trouble understanding you, you may wish to speak rather slowly. Audiences also react to dialects according to their home regions. Noam Chomsky, in his book *Syntactic Structures*, reports that a sentence is considered grammatical if it is acceptable to the "native speaker." Audiences will reject a sentence if it doesn't make sense to them, and what makes sense to them is a sentence that is familiar.

Understanding what is familiar and what will make sense to your audience is important, but this does not necessarily mean they will reject everything that is not native to them. Much depends on your image. If you project credibility and establish rapport with your audience, chances are good that they will continue to listen even when the sounds reaching their ears are somewhat unfamiliar. A good speaker respects the regional differences in the speech of an audience and attempts to adjust so that understanding occurs.

*A good speaker respects the regional differences in the speech of his or her audience.*

The mass media have adopted a so-called standard American speech in order to reach their broad audience. Programs that originate from the networks generally adhere closely to this standard pattern of pronunciation. Commercials, on the other hand, are often produced exclusively for certain regions. Bert sees many commercials enacted by performers who speak with Southern dialects, because his geographic region is considered a Southern market. In the Northeast, similar scenarios are shown, but the performers speak differently.

*Phonation*

No matter whether you say "tomahto" and I say "tomatoe," we both start the same way.

Simply stated, we breathe. Our exhaled air passes through the bronchi into the trache (windpipe) and then into the larynx. The larynx, or voice box, contains the vocal folds or vocal cords, and the vibration of the vocal cords produces sound. The aperture between the vocal folds, which is known as the glottis, is regulated by muscles.

Air is pushed up from the lungs by the muscles used in breathing. When pressure below the vocal cords is greater than that above them, the cords (or folds) open upward and sideward, producing a sound wave that moves up through the pharynx. As the process is repeated, vibration occurs. This vibration determines the frequency and pitch of the sound produced. The sound waves generated by the vocal cords change as they reach the cavities of the throat, mouth, and nose.

*Resonance*

The vocal cords produce a tone that is regulated by their size and length. Bert's tone is different from Dora's because his vocal cords are thicker and longer. As the tone passes through the throat, mouth, and nose, the overtones are amplified or dampened. The exact degree of amplification depends on the configuration or condition of these passages, which can be affected by tension. Proper balance between oral and nasal resonance produces good voice.

*Pitch*

**Pitch refers to highness and lowness of tone.**

Once it has passed through the vocal cords, the air makes its way into the cavities of the mouth, and we hear a sound that has a certain pitch. Pitch refers to the highness and lowness of the tone. Thick vocal cords produce low-pitched tones, and thin, short, or tense cords produce high-pitched tones. Optimum pitch depends on the structure of the larynx and the amount of breath used. Your voice is most pleasant at 25 to 33 percent above its lowest level of range. Modal pitch is the pitch you use most of the time. You strain your voice when you reach too often to the lowest or highest levels of our range. Some individuals have wide ranges, others narrow. Range is the number of notes you use in speaking from highest to lowest. A limited range can produce a limited tone.

*Rate*

If your range is insufficiently wide, you can sometimes add life to your speech by varying its rate. The rate of your delivery can be varied by speaking quickly, dragging your syllables, cutting them off short, or using pauses for emphasis. While it's fun and possibly exciting to the audience to hear many changes in rate of speech, you must be wary of speaking so rapidly that your words are distorted or so slowly that your audience falls asleep.

You can control the intensity of the sound you produce. If you have lots of energy, you can amplify oral resonance. You can enter a room and immediately adjust to noise levels. Sometimes our emotions dictate the volume of our speech. We get husky and soft in a romantic setting, we shout in anger, grow clipped and tense in anxious moments. Davitz and Davitz (1959) found that we convey our *active* feelings by using a loud voice, high pitch, blaring timbre, and fast rate. Our *passive* feelings are conveyed with a quiet voice, low pitch, resonant timbre, and a slow rate.

*Volume*

Quality is arbitrary. Ethel Merman's voice may be loud and brassy when compared with the smooth-sweet tones of Ella Fitzgerald, but they are both quality voices and quality women.

*Quality*

As a general rule, we react negatively to hard sounds, to voices that sound strained, or to nasality, a quality that makes the speaker sound as though he or she has a stuffy nose. According to Dale G. Leaders (1976), in *Nonverbal Communication Systems*, "Recent research indicates that a communicator's credibility drops with (1) decreases in vocal variety, (2) the presense of nasality tenseness and throatiness, and (3) faulty articulation."

When listeners describe voices they enjoy, they usually mention words like ". . . a great quality, *warm* and *rich*," or ". . . she surely sounds *happy*." Such terms are ambiguous and subjective, but they do suggest an acceptance by the listener of the speaker.

We've already observed that tones change as emotions change. Obviously, tension will produce harsh sounds, and any great change in our emotional well-being will produce abnormal sounds. Telling people to avoid tension and to take care of themselves is far too simplistic. Mood depends upon your inner and outer environments, upon understanding yourself and those around you, and upon your own unique personality traits. Being aware of the dynamics of a situation and alert to the fact that you are in a constantly evolving state are two positive steps toward putting yourself in the right mood at the right time.

*Mood*

There are four well-known styles of delivery: (1) impromptu, (2) manuscript, (3) memorization, and (4) extemporaneous. There are no hard and fast rules that force a speaker to select one style and stay doggedly

**Styles of Delivery**

with it; many speakers use a combination of styles. With a great deal of knowledge in his or her memory, a speaker can quote exact phrases and hold on to notes at the same time. A knowledge of the basic styles is helpful, however.

## Impromptu

At a recent meeting in the community, Mayor David Rusk was explaining to a group of citizens the need for supporting the bond issue. Suddenly he saw one of the city engineers walk into the meeting. The engineer lived in the community. Mayor Rusk interrupted himself by exclaiming, "I see that John is here. John, why don't you come on down here and tell the folks about the sewer project planned for this area!"

John quickly sized up the situation, noted that a lot of his friends were in the audience, and strode up to the podium. He was actually playing two roles: city engineer and member of community. John's impromptu speech was noteworthy because (1) his delivery was casual; (2) his knowledge of the subject was good and perceived as good, so his credibility was easily established; (3) he was brief.

An impromptu speech is not formally prepared, but that does not mean that it will be sloppy. Most people who are called upon by the audience to speak on a subject are perceived as knowledgeable about that subject. If by chance the audience has been misinformed about a speaker, it is best for the speaker to say simply, "I'm not really up on the latest information on that subject, so I'd better pass."

## Manuscript

The manuscript speech is the opposite of the impromptu speech: It is not only prepared in advance, but written out to the letter.

The manuscript speech has been a question of much controversy among speech teachers, who are quick to cite the disadvantages of reading a speech. However, many politicians, directors of large corporations, and people involved in serious controversies have no other choice. First, they must be extremely careful of what they say because they will be quoted; second, the message undoubtedly will be mediated by several broadcast and print reporters; and third, they are speaking for large bodies of people and may not have written the speeches themselves.

The advantages of manuscript delivery are found in the areas of time and language. You can time your speech to the second (and sometimes in the broadcast medium you must). You can pay more attention to specific language, precisely defining your point without fear of being misunderstood.

Today, most manuscript speeches are read easily with the aid of a teleprompter. Even on a podium before a large audience it is simple to set up an eye-level prompter that rolls the written word before the speaker's eyes. The ability to read well is important. For this reason manuscript speeches should be marked for pauses and emphasis, and must definitely be rehearsed a lot. The professional readers (television anchorpersons, for example) learn by doing—every day.

Very few students now memorize speeches for oratorical contests. There is no royal road to speedy memorization. Some people memorize easily, while others must labor for long periods of time. There is evidence, however, that one's memory can be improved. If this is true, we offer a few hints on how to memorize a speech:

*Memorization*

1. Avoid desultory reading. That is, don't skim over the words; instead, read more intensively and slowly.

2. Select a topic of interest: It is difficult to concentrate on a subject if you have no interest in it. A casual interest will not produce an attitude conducive to attentiveness.

3. Seek out the environment that will help you concentrate. Don't try to learn a speech while the television is blaring unless you can really shut out all distractions. Sit out on the patio instead. Memorizing while doing tasks that do not demand concentration might work.

4. Exercise your will. After all is said and done, the only way to concentrate is to concentrate. You have the will to do it, so do it. Don't let your mind wander. Be a stern taskmaster unto yourself.

Most speakers prepare their speeches, use outlines and partially memorize certain passages. The speech may appear spontaneous, but in reality it has been carefully planned and outlined. Most of the material in this book is aimed at the extemporaneous speaker who knows what he or she is talking about, has researched the subject, and has prepared for a smooth presentation.

*Extemporaneous*

To speak extemporaneously means that you neither completely read your speech nor completely memorize it. It does not mean that the speech is completely unprepared. An extemporaneous speech contains elements of the other three types of delivery—some memorization, some impromptu, and some manuscript. In other words, an extemporaneous speech may include a passage that is read (such as a quote or statistics), a few phrases you clearly know by heart, and a measure of impromptu commentary, perhaps in response to a spontaneous remark from the audience or a desire to adjust to that specific audience.

An extemporaneous speaker is organized yet flexible, speaking with the full knowledge that communication between speaker and audience is a dynamic and constantly changing phenomenon, but knowing, too, that every audience deserves the best possible attention and preparation. The very best extemporaneous speakers use a delivery that is appropriate to the audience, is conversational yet varied, and they are fully in command of the material to be disseminated.

Effective extemporaneous speaking also means you remember a lot of things and take care to rehearse your presentation.

## REMEMBERING AND REHEARSING

All types of presentations involve remembering. Whether you must remember long or short passages, it is better to remember by thoughts and ideas rather than by lines and sentences, then move on to remembering these thoughts and ideas by repeating them to yourself or to others. We all do this naturally when we talk to our friends about certain events or how we feel about something. The ideas should be mastered long before you put them into words. After all, it is the ideas that first impressed you, and your goal is to impress them upon the minds of your listeners. Words are medium for expressing the ideas; in the effort to get the words that will sway your audience, there is nothing more important than repetition.

## WRITING A SPEECH FOR SOMEONE ELSE

At some time you may be called upon to write a speech for someone besides yourself. From the days of the Sophists people have sought help in speechwriting. Business and professional people frequently seek aid, especially when their work is so demanding that they cannot find the time or when they feel they lack the talent. Politicians hire speech writers all the time. The last President to sit down at the typewriter and compose his own speeches was Woodrow Wilson; it is well-known that Presidents hire a stable of writers. Now the practice has filtered down to members of congress, senators, governors, state legislators, and even mayors and city-council members. Skills in public speaking are essential to the campaigns of all who seek (and seek to retain) public office.

How do you write for someone else and manage to retain the essence of that person? In 1967, Carl Stokes and Seth Taft opposed each

other for the mayor's seat in Cleveland. Carl Stokes was the great-grandson of a slave; Seth Taft was the great-grandson of a President. Seth Taft was practicing law; Carl Stokes was a state representative. Stokes's style was rambling, vivid, and at times ungrammatical (according to standard English); Taft was ponderous, dry, and literate.

Stokes described his campaign strategy this way:

*We started out with Al Ostrow [ex-journalist] writing the general structure of the campaign. Then we met in a group, defined, agreed upon the general structure, agreed upon the number of issues we were going to enunciate, and then we began implementing. Ostrow took all the old speeches I had done, and for a month he just followed me on the campaign trail while I was speaking extemporaneously—taking notes—and then he started writing the speeches.*

Ostrow and Stokes made a good combination that year, resulting in the election of the first black mayor of a major American city.

When writing for someone else, be sure that attention is paid to the natural style of the speaker, the integrity of his or her ideas, and the situation that requires the speech. And if someone writes a speech for you, be sure that the same measures are taken.

The chances are good that your speech or the speech you write for a political or business figure will reach beyond the live audience for which you prepare it Andy Warhol points out that with the appeal of communication technology, every person will be famous for at least 15 minutes of his or her lifetime.

## TELEVISION DELIVERY

Delivering a message on television envelopes all the styles thus far discussed. When an anchorperson reads a message from the teleprompter, often the words have been written by someone else. The same anchorperson may *ad lib* to the sportscaster or weatherperson, thus giving an impromptu delivery. A reporter in the field will often memorize a short stand-up piece, often shown as the concluding remarks before the camera. He or she may *read* most of the copy when the final edit is done (or the film is edited to the copy).

.    On public-service talk shows, the reporter or anchorperson may speak extemporaneously from notes or an outline, giving introductions and conclusions and conducting interviews.

The ability to speak well and project a believable image is most important. Speaking before a television camera is different from addressing a live audience in one critical area: The life situation allows you to adjust to changes in audience's attitude and behavior. You can control a live audience much more easily than you can control an unseen audience that needs merely to flick a switch or push a button to turn you off. Before a televised audience you must work with a crew, and the presentation is essentially in the hands of producers and directors.

If television is to be your career, you will, of course, train yourself to read well, speak well extemporaneously, memorize well, and interview well. As a private citizen who seldom appears on television, you may nevertheless have opportunities to be on talk shows or in the news. In most of these instances you will be interviewed. The best on-the-spot advice should come from your host or interviewer, who will tell you where to sit or stand and whether to look into the camera lens or not.

Keep in mind that television audiences see only what the camera chooses to show them. Think of that camera as a channel with your audience at the other end. Look at your audience, relax, be conversational, and most of all, try to be as natural as possible. Here are some helpful hints:

■  If timing is important and you are giving a one-minute editorial, *read* it from the teleprompter. Rehearse it many times. Effective reading is not easy.

■  Hold your gestures and movements down to a minimum so that the camera can follow you easily.

■  Look into the camera if you are delivering a message directly to the public. If you are being interviewed, you may be told to ignore the camera and pay attention to your host.

■ Remember—today's audiences love personalities, and yours may be just the one they wish to see. So speak up, be lively, and enjoy yourself.

## RADIO DELIVERY

If you are participating in a radio broadcast, no one outside the studio will see you—but that doesn't mean you need to sport a poker face. Putting your whole self into that radio speech will help you be more lively. Radio audiences enjoy conversational speech, and all the elements of oral language apply to radio performances.

Before you go on the air, the producer or director will ask you to speak a few words in order to get a volume check. Throughout the program it will be wise to maintain the same volume at which you speak in that audition. Your voice carries the message, and your message is important. Don't waste time; long pauses encourage listeners to turn the dial. There is no question, however, that both radio and television are just the beginning of an era that will put the world in touch with you. Communication technology can extend that public-speaking event until the speaker's circle of influence stretches beyond imagination.

## SUMMARY

As a speaker you become the center of attention and at that moment your image is of prime importance. On a practical level you must consider how you walk, talk, and behave on that platform. Preparation and self-analysis is half the battle. You can control your anxiety by knowing your audience, being physically and emotionally fit for the occasion, and understanding that a speech is a dynamic event.

Delivery is a combination of sight and sound. Some speakers, such as conductors of orchestras, rely heavily on sight. All speakers start with that walk to the podium and each person's walk is unique. Audiences react to body movements; some movements are forceful, some decorative, some display exuberance, and some reveal fear. There are many gestures and as many as 20,000 facial expressions.

Clothing is important, as audiences react to the way a speaker dresses. Classic lines for women and conservative colors for men are preferred in the business, professional, and political world.

Effective use of sight and sound helps understanding. Speech is a learned process. We can utter an amazing variety of sounds by simply controlling the amount of air that comes in and goes out. Elements that affect our speech are phonation, resonance, pitch, rate, volume, quality of voice, mood, accent, and dialect.

There are four styles of delivery: impromptu, manuscript, memorization, and extemporaneous. Most speakers use the extemporaneous method, which is a combination of the others. All variations involve remembering. The television delivery also involves all types of styles. Radio involves the use of voice alone but the voice can produce mental images of you. Radio and television begin the era that puts you in touch with the world.

## KEY TERMS

| | | |
|---|---|---|
| accent | force | quality |
| ad lib | image | radio |
| anxiety | impromptu | rate |
| clothing | manuscript | rehearsing |
| decorative | memorization | resonance |
| delivery | mood | television delivery |
| extemporaneous | phonation | voice |
| exuberance | pitch | volume |
| fear | | |

## EXERCISES

*Students*

**1.** Give yourself an image quiz: Devise ten questions that you as a press agent would ask (yourself) a client, starting with, "What kind of climate do you create when you walk into a room?" Devise a questionnaire to fit your home life, your office life, your social life. Are the answers different? The same? Are the images confusing?

**2.** Practice daily voice exercises by breathing in and making sounds as you expel the air. See how much copy you can read on one breath. Practice with a tape recorder. Analyze your speech as to pitch, mood, and quality. Read your speech slowly, gradually increase the rate, then read it very quickly. Ask your friends to react to the different speeds. Use these exercises to learn something about yourself and your voice. Then decide on the image you wish to project.

**3.** Analyze your wardrobe. Look into that closet and describe the person to fit the clothes. Is it you?

## CIRCLING BACK

Starting at the end of the chapter, work your way backward to find the answers.

**1.** Describe some body movements and typical reactions to them.

**2.** What kind of preparation can you make for a television appearance?

**3.** Describe the manuscript speech.

**4.** Name the four styles of delivery.

**5.** How do we control the intensity of sound?

**6.** What is the difference between articulation and pronunciation?

**7.** How do you cope with anxiety? What steps are possible to follow?

**REFERENCES**

Chomsky, Noam. *Syntactic Structures*. Elmsford, N.Y.: Mouton, 1957.

Davitz, J.C., and L.J. Davitz. "The Communication of Feeling by Content-Free Speech." *Journal of Communication* **9** (1959):9.

Kobarge, Maurita. "Your Image." *Working Woman*, October 1979.

Leathers, Dale G. *Nonverbal Communication Systems*. Boston: Allyn and Bacon, 1976, pp. 132-133.

Molloy, J.T. *Dress for Success*. New York: Warner Books, 1976, pp. 37-91.

Shawn, Ted. *Every Little Movement*. Published by the author, 1954.

# 8 the global information society

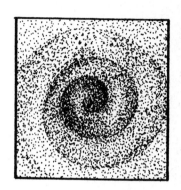

When Bert gets up in the morning and turns on his television set, he becomes part of a vast international circle of people all sharing the same message.

Bert is addicted to television. He readily admits that the first voice he hears in the morning and the last voice he hears at night often come from somewhere in space.

Because Bert has cable television, this remark is no exaggeration—the first voice he hears in the morning *does* come from space; at least it has been bouncing around in space for a while.

The very first voice from space was the "beep-beep" of Russia's Sputnik in 1957. In 1960 the first U.S. communication satellite, orbiting 1000 miles up, sent picture and voice bouncing between the United States and Europe. In 1972 NASA launched AT&T's Telstar, the first active communications satellite. It did more than reflect signals from one earth station to another; before relaying them, it utilized solar power cells to *amplify* the signals it received.

In 1963 a satellite placed 22,300 miles above the earth traveled around the globe at the same speed of earth, making continuous coverage possible.

Comsat (the Communication Satellite Corporation) launched the first commercial global communication satellite, Early Bird, in 1965. In 1974 Western Union sent up Estar to handle 7200 channels or 12 television broadcasts. RCA's Satcom in 1973 boasted 24,000 voice channels. In 1979 there were over 30 Comsats in orbit.

As we move toward the 21st century, as receivers get lighter and more efficient, direct home reception of satellite television transmissions is on the horizon. Soon Bert may be able to pick up a program originating in a small Ohio town, for example, with the simple attachment of a small antenna to his own home—the transmission will not require an earth station.

## WHAT DOES COMMUNICATION TECHNOLOGY OFFER THE INDIVIDUAL?

What do these advances in communication technology mean to Bert, to Dora, to Maria, or to Emma? What do they mean to all of us? Technology is not something for us to think about in terms of a distant future—the future starts today. When Bert gets up and turns on the television, he is immediately in touch with the world.

While satellite transmission certainly brings us more quickly in touch with the world, it is not the only example of how today's communication technology directly influences our lives. Let's take a look at some of the advancements that play a direct part in the lives of the people we've met in this book.

*Maria*

Maria uses a computer to send printed messages to the congressman's district office. This facsimile process is also known as electronic mail. Through the use of telephone lines, it transmits anything printed on paper—letters, photographs, drawings, contracts, and graphics. It's like having a long-distance copying machine.

Maria sets the device near her phone and plugs it into a socket. She inserts the letter, dials the district's number, puts the telephone in an attached cradle, and starts the machine. Her machine then "talks" to the machine at the other end, breaking the written words into dots, translating the dots into electronic sounds, and transmitting the sounds over the telephone line. At the other end the receiving machine reverses the process, translating the sounds back to dots, then to written words or pictures.

This concept was actually discovered in 1842 by Alexander Bain but wasn't widely used until the Associated Press sent out its first wirephoto in 1934. Not until 1968, when the FCC (Federal Communications Commission) allowed outside firms to hook into telephone lines, did the process become part of our growing technological society. Now, with the availability of inexpensive machines, its use is expanding.

The mail carrier, who always rings twice and is never deterred by rain, sleet, or snow, may have stiff competition in the future from another electronic mail system, which requires a network of FM stations. If placed in 50 strategically located U.S. cities, this system could handle from 85 to 90 percent of the country's business correspondence. Its technology includes a data-entry terminal, a computer that converts the message into digital format, and a terminal specified in the computer-coded data transmission. A letter can be sent and received in less than a minute.

Maria works with a constant awareness of time in her daily dealings with the news media. She must make sure that the congressman's points of view find their way to television, radio, and the press. Television and radio stations and networks sell time—it's their only product. Private and public individuals, groups, and corporations buy the time and prepare messages to inform, please, or persuade.

*An awareness of time and media characteristics are essential in dispensing news releases.*

Advertisers buy time to promote their products. Their campaigns are designed to (1) initate a product, (2) compete with other products, (3) reinforce an established image. Advertising is communicating something to somone.

Maria must help "sell" the congressman; in order to do so she must understand the characteristics of the medium, whether it is television, radio, or print. So Maria knows that 3:00 P.M. is a good time for a news briefing, if she wants the television cameras there. She also knows that in order to get headlines in the afternoon papers she has to release the news before 10:00 A.M. Maria understands what the press needs in a press release and how and when to "feed" the stories to the wire services. She understands that reporters aren't responsible for headlines and that photographers can't control what is actually broadcast.

Emma picks up the radio in her car as a matter of course. She doesn't remember the day when officers made their rounds and reported in to the station house every hour, or even when they got their assignments via the telephone. In the short span of a few years, technology has changed the world of the police force.

*Emma*

Consider this: In the year 1845, when the New York Police Department was first established, the average citizen could run and find a policeman on the block or walk to the nearest precinct, where the telegraph connected all precinct station houses directly to central headquarters. Two years after Alexander Graham Bell developed the telephone, the NYPD installed five phones. When the automobile came along, police officers could be found parked at police telephone booths along the streets. In 1922 William (Silver Bill) Rutledge, known as "the father of police radio," predicted, "I can imagine the time when every patrolman on his beat will have an individual receiving apparatus by which he can ascertain wherever he is just what has happened in the city."

Four years after the automobile had been put in use in Detroit, Commissioner Rutledge purchased a Western Electric 1-A 500s broadcast transmitter and installed it in police headquarters. For over six years he and his men tried to develop a practical system to provide satisfactory voice communication in moving cars. But it wasn't until a motorcycle officer named Kenneth Cox became part of the team that the first car radio was installed. Cox pioneered the car radio. On April 7, 1928 (years before Emma was born) station WSFS went on the air, transmitting to a new receiver in cruiser no. 5.

That single act was responsible for Emma's present-day environment: Emma rides in an air-conditioned vehicle, taking orders from a voice on the radio. In some cities officers ride for eight hours, receiving orders from the computer and hearing only the click of the terminal in the car. We shall discuss the implications of technology and its effect on the officer as we continue in this chapter. Dramatic technology changes occurred in U.S. police departments following the establishment of the Law Enforcement Assistance Administration (LEAA) on June 20, 1968. After nearly forty years of living in a technological vacuum, the meagerly equipped and underfunded police were allowed to visit the marketplace of the future. A product of the President's Commission on Law Enforcement and Administration of Justice, LEAA opened the doors, not only paying the price of admission, but also filling the outstretched hands with tickets. The officers

were like kids at a carnival, ripe for the con artists, dazzled by the pretty lights of status boards (equipment installed in communications divisions), and confused by the rhetoric.

Congress appropriated over two billion dollars in the first five years of the program. Crime was the nation's number-one problem. The solution in many cases was identified rather simplistically as faster response time, so a great deal of money was put into communications equipment.

The officers in the communications centers and on the street had little or no input in the design of the systems or the hardware assigned them. There was no Captain Rutledge or Officer Cox available to invent a new kind of computer or redesign the walkie-talkie to suit the officers' needs. The world had become too complex, too technical.

The police, Emma, and all of us, long ago accepted the premise of industrialization. Building a communications center based on technological progress was not out of line. We could adjust to the radio, the television, the computer, and never ask whether the endless economic expansion was irrelevant to the question of truly satisfying work.

Like Emma, most of us still believe life is better because of inventions and technology.

Emma would not be without her portable radio—it's like having a "buddy," she says. At the flick of a switch she can get help and be in contact with other services in the area.

So far, the disadvantages do not overshadow the advantages. However, some of Emma's fellow officers complain that the machines are telling them what to do, that instead of controlling the machines the officers are now tending them.

In St. Louis the *Automatic Vehicle Locator System*, recently installed in police cars, locates the cars by computer and automatically dispatches the nearest car to the scene of the crime. Formerly the dispatchers were police officers; now they have been replaced with civilians, who do not command as much money. Technology affects all aspects of our lives.

The *mobile radio*, because of limited frequencies, is used mainly for community services. However, the mobile *telephone* is available to citizens. Bell currently supplies 40,000 subscribers with mobile telephones. New technology will eliminate the high power transmitters usually located in the center of a city and replace them with a "cellular" approach (service area subdivided into a grid of smaller coverage zones) will make the mobile telephone available to all cars. "Calling all cars" will truly mean "Calling all cars"!

**Loren**

Loren, the television reporter, has a *beeper*. In fact many of Dora's friends and acquaintances have beepers: her doctor, her principal, her neighbor (Steve), who is a pilot, and another one of the neighbor's children. It would be safe to bet that at least one person in anyone's inner circle of friends has a beeper. Whole industries are supplying their employees with beepers: London's call girls have beepers.

Each receiver (beeper) is programmed to respond to its own unique number. When that number is called, a computer accepts the call and converts it into a tone burst of five sharp notes. The coded impulses are transmitted to beepers within a 75-mile radius. (As many as 300 different tone bursts can be handled each minute). All beepers receive all signals, but each *responds* only to the particular signal that its circuit recognizes and decodes. The subscriber then calls the service for the message. Advances in beeper technology will include different tone signals to signify different types of messages.

**Jerry Lee**

Jerry Lee's friend, Donald, has some sophisticated equipment in his garage. "What's for dinner?" Donald's father asks as he approaches Albuquerque. Jerry Lee is fascinated by the fact that Donald can communicate with his father while his father is driving a truck on Highway I-40. Donald himself installed the base station.

> *It operates from a regular wall socket and I leave it on for hours each day. The receiver monitors any channel I choose and I adjust this squelch control so that there's no noise on the station until the calls comes in on the monitored channel. See, Daddy and I agree to call on this channel and I know he's close to home when he comes in loud and clear.* (Albuquerque Tribune, Feb. 17, 1979, TV 17.)

Donald subsequently built a device that allows him to dial a telephone number and patch it in to the mobile unit, enabling the mobile and the third party to converse.

Citizen-band radios are so commonplace that we no longer feel especially excited about the idea of conversing with strangers. The relatively low price of CB units has made them widely available, and they are used for practical as well as social purposes.

Bert is an acknowledged television addict, because he chooses to be. The technology of television provides him with information, amusement, and relaxation.

*Bert*

In his part-time job in the department store, however, Bert encounters communications technology that is not of his choosing. Bert works with the latest in POS (*point-of-sale*) terminal systems and electronic cash registers (ECRs). The manual and electromechanical machines are rapidly disappearing from the checkout scene. Recently Bert heard the clicking of the terminal and looked at a message that read, "Take your sales slips. . ."

The message was incomplete, so Bert returned to his customer, only to hear the clicking continue. He went back to the terminal and read, ". . . to the south door."

Both Bert and his customer laughed about it, but at 6:00 Bert took his sales slips to the south door.

Point-of-sales systems supply reports on daily, weekly, and monthly sales, daily stock replenishment, and other information that helps store management control inventories and keep merchandise moving. These terminals also supply *training* for new employees. Bert is not the only one of our small circle who is trained by machines. Bert uses television to help train his students, just as Dora uses visual aids to train hers. Emma watches a weekly video presentation produced by the police department to inform the officers of new policies and procedures. Emma sits in the substation and watches the chief as he talks about promotional exams. She has *seen* the actual chief but once in her career.

With all our main characters, communication technology has become an integral part of the workaday world. Machines are sharing our culture. Those human engineers who are very concerned with designing machines and work environments so that they *match* human capabilities and limitations know that most of us believe machines can eliminate much of our personal struggle. But there is also a concern that some of us become so involved with development that we forget to raise the question of desirability.

Our literature is filled with stories of machines taking over. In *Machine Stops*, by E.M. Foster, we read of a world where people live in complete isolation from one another, hermetically sealed in air-conditioned cubicles. Is this, we say, so far afield from the officer in St. Louis who patrols in an air-conditioned car, receiving orders from the computer, and hearing only the click of the terminal in the car?

Dora and Bill (her hairdresser) are more resistant to technology than the others in our small circle. They will tell whoever will listen that our society already shows a marked advance toward a machine culture. "Empirical studies in the behavioral sciences," says Dora, "show that we can be standardized, our parts interchanged with others in our mechanical march to work." Dora prefers a slower pace.

Bill and Dora, like everyone, however, are consumers of messages. Bill loves music, loves to play the radio all day. It is speculative whether even he would give up the radio in his shop, or turn off his air-conditioner (although he was forced to turn it down). Dora, like Bill, gets up in the morning and has the world available to her—whether she chooses to tune it in is up to her. She is not averse to buying the latest machines for her home (micro-oven, washer-dryer, electric can-opener). These conveniences give her time to read.

But no matter how we feel about living in a changing society, the advancements in communication technology have greatly improved and extended the connections between individuals. More specifically, the advancements in telecommunications have extended the web of urban and rural communication and changed our lives. Telecommunication, defined by the Committee on Telecommunications of the National Academy of Engineering is "any transmission, emission, or reception of signs, signals, written images, and sounds, or intelligence of any nature by wire, radio, visual, or other electromagnetic systems, including any intervening processing and storage."

Combining the computer and the telephone line moved us into the first stages of an information society. With each new stride in com-

munication technology, the potential for change in our way of life grows more certain. Today, with the advent of fiber optics (light piped through strands of glass or plastic as thin as human hair), thousands of conversations and millions of bits of computer data can be transmitted over a single hair-thin fiber. When teamed with a laser, a single fiber can in *one* second transmit 200 books letter by letter. Dr. Charles K. Kao, a pioneer in the field, said, "The stage is set for an enrichment of life like that following the invention of the steam engine, the light bulb, the transistor."*

In a suburb of Osaka, Japan, cables of glass fibers carry computer services to local homes. In Nashville, Tennessee, crosswalk signals containing as many as 160,000 optical fibers send messages to pedestrians. In certain experimenting cities, light-wave communications send and receive newspapers over home telecopiers and control the climate in homes; they allow viewers to shop by television from their homes and to pay bills by automatically charging their credit cards or deducting from their bank accounts.

In this modern technological society attention is paid both to the manner in which the message is transmitted and to the channel. The channel is the medium through which the code or signal is sent (e.g., fiber optics). Of course, a channel can also be the *direction* in which the information flows or the individual through which information flows.

Claude E. Shannon presented a paper, "The Mathematical Theory of Communication," in 1948, setting forth his theory that the channel could be molecules of air, telephone wire, speech, radio, phonograph, tape, television microwave relay system, coaxial cable system, or even the proposed millimeter waveguide system and the (then) hypothetical laser system. To these we add fiber optics. Shannon's model is adaptable to our discussion of *humans and hardware*, because it deals with a universal communication system consisting of an information source, a transmitter, a communication channel, a noise source, a receiver and a message destination.

In this model, the information source and the final destination are usually human beings; for example, Maria decides upon the information that will go into the letter. She may type a message consisting of letters and spaces on a typewriter. Her typewriter may be the teletypewriter that serves as a transmitter that encodes each character

*The channel is the medium through which the code or signal is sent.*

---

*Allen A. Boraiko, Harnessing Light by a Thread, *National Geographic*, October, 1979, p. 516.

as a sequence of electrical pulses, or she may feed the typewriter letter into a computer which does the same thing. The electrical pulses, in any event, are transmitted by a pair of wires to another machine, which acts as the receiver.

Another machine acts as a receiver and prints out the letters and spaces that are, in turn, read by a human being.

Shannon felt that as the pulses travel from one machine (transmitter) to the other (receiver), an intermittent connection or extraneous current may alter or change the pulses, causing the receiver to print out the wrong characters. This interference he calls *noise*. If the noise is greater in power than the power of the signal (original pulse), the message can be distorted. However, if the power of the signal is greater than the power of the noise, the noise will have less effect on the operation of the communication system.

Shannon also gave us a measure of the commodity we try to transmit; he measured the rate of a message source in bits per message or bits per second. He also measured the capacity of the communication channel. We shall not go into his method of measuring, as the average communicator need not deal with bits per second but with simple language that says, "How much information can I send and how fast can I send it?"

To which we might add, ". . . and will anyone understand it?"

In this complex, technological world, can we ever be sure that someone really understands the message we send? When all those millions of bits of information are traveling through all those paper-thin fibers, can we ever be sure that all that work means something to someone? Earlier in this text we spoke of listening and of the necessity of knowing what it is our audience needs from us and what we have to give to our audience. Listening to a specific audience, whether on a one-to-one basis, in a group, or in a public-speaking situation, is the in-

## LISTENING/ FEEDBACK

itial step. *Feedback* is the next step. However, as we have emphasized, communication relationships change and situations evolve so that we are constantly relaying information throughout the day. Listening and feedback are continuous.

Listening in our technical world is not too much different from listening in our slower-paced interpersonal world. However, several pointers might help us to survive the bombardment of thousands of persuasive messages we receive from machines daily.

- Listen for enjoyment and for what is pleasing to both the eye and the ear.

- Listen for information relevant to your interests.

- Listen to make judgments and to evaluate good music, good films, good stories, good people.

- Listen to understand and to remember, so that we can *feed* the information *back* to society.

*In our technical world, feedback monitors, adjusts, and corrects.*

The rationale for feedback in a technical world is to make communication more effective by monitoring, adjusting and correcting. Feedback is important on an interpersonal level and on a telecommunication level, but what is rational for one level is not necessarily rational for the other.

Since we have not discussed feedback earlier in the book, let's look at some of the popular concepts applied to feedback on the person-to-person level.

## Feedback on the Personal Level

On a person-to-person basis we are senders and receivers simultaneously, constantly speaking/listening/feeding back; influences fly back and forth. Communication is two-way. Even when we communicate intrapersonally (with ourselves), communication is circular. Dora gets up in the morning, thinks about swimming, and persuades herself to swim, thus using *internal* feedback. She may even speak out (to herself), thus using internal and *external* feedback. As a public speaker, she may try out her new nutrition lecture on herself and correct or adjust some sentences so that they will sound better—to herself. She speaks so that she can get certain responses from her students, so she tries out certain phrases and sometimes her students respond exactly as she hopes they will. Sometimes they don't respond as she hopes, and the feedback she gets is *negative*. In that event she may alter her speech, may adjust right on the spot. Negative feedback is not necessarily destructive; it may be that Dora has misread the ability of her students to comprehend a message. The beauty of feedback in a live situation is that the speech can be adjusted and to conclude on a mutually satisfying note. Of course *positive* feedback can be more than satisfying; it can give the speaker confidence.

Dora may receive *direct* and *indirect* feedback from her audience. Her students may nod and clap or write down the information, thus giving her direct feedback. On the other hand, her students may write information but all the while be glancing out of the window or nodding their heads sleepily. One gesture can contradict an action, giving Dora some indirect clues as to how her message is going over.

Feedback can also be *immediate* or *delayed*. In face-to-face communication, especially on a one-to-one basis, immediate feedback is always possible.

Two professors, Leavitt and Mueller, tested four variations of feedback and concluded that immediate and free feedback (all verbal and nonverbal messages between sender and receiver) was very effective. They tested (1) no feedback; (2) seeing each other only (receiver not allowed to talk); (3) yes-no by receiver (the sender could check messages by asking questions to which the receiver could answer yes or no); (4) free feedback (all verbal and nonverbal messages between sender and receiver).

In this experience the sender had to describe verbally some pattern or geometric designs, and the receiver had to draw them. The sender could not draw the design, only tell the receiver how to draw it. The results showed that the greater amount of feedback, the *slower* the communication. They also showed that the accuracy of communication increased as feedback increased. They found that with no feedback, accuracy decreased and confusion set in.

Of course, those results are not unusual. If you meet someone in an elevator and say "Hello," and that person stares right through you, you get confused at the lack of response and wonder what you have done to deserve the snub. If later on you meet that person, and she says she had just come from the doctor's and had drops in her eyes and couldn't see a thing, you will be less confused about her behavior.

In person-to-person situations, immediate feedback may be more valuable than delayed feedback. Person-to-person feedback, is generally more constructive than destructive. A strong desire to help the other person so that a common ground can be reached is the overriding theme in this book.

But positive, immediate, and constructive feedback is not necessarily possible or practical in our technological world. Feedback is important there, however.

## FEEDBACK AND TELECOMMUNICATIONS

*Immediate or Delayed?* A Columbus cable-television station asked hundreds of citizens to respond immediately to a speech delivered by President Carter. They were asked specific questions about their reactions to Carter's speech. Generally, their feedback was *positive*. They felt the President had shown a stronger, more positive image, had convinced them there was an energy crisis, and had emerged as a strong leader.

After these results were flashed on the screen, several reporters were asked for their reaction to the President's speech. Generally, *their* feedback was *negative*. One reporter felt the President had really given two speeches, had not addressed the issue squarely, and had come through like a Baptist minister.

The general public, after hearing the speech and the contradicting analyses, then proceeded to talk about the speech with their friends and neighbors. In essence, feedback information about that particular speech came from a variety of sources.

The President, who was the initial sender of the message, received multiple feedback, both immediate and delayed, positive and negative. Which was best? Probably, like all of us, the President most enjoyed the positive feedback. But *all* the feedback he received was important. Instant analysis (or feedback) by reporters has been hotly contested by former vice-presidents; but in more instances than not, immediate feedback is the goal for telecommunications systems. Whenever possible, two-way communication is preferred over one-way.

*Immediate feedback is usually the goal for telecommunications systems*

For that reason, companies ask for feedback by telling customers to write letters, make phone calls, or buy products. When Colgate runs an ad for toothpaste, the company measures feedback by the number of sales for the month the ad runs, or for subsequent months. Effective feedback for the company is both *positive* and *negative*. If the product doesn't sell, they can change the ad. Effective feedback for companies is also more specific than general. They like to see a particular item sell. Effective feedback is also constructive rather than destructive: that is, the toothpaste *really* shines and cleans teeth, and the company does make money. If the needs of the audience are not served, feedback is ineffective.

*All feedback should serve to exchange meaning accurately*

Therefore, on an interpersonal and technological level, feedback should serve to exchange meaning accurately, to influence people and satisfy needs, and to correct, adjust, and monitor messages.

It is not sufficient merely to accept the fact that as individuals and members of a community we are a part of a constantly changing and advancing technological society. Nor is it sufficient merely to speak about and respond to telecommunication messages.

We must constantly question the very existence of our new technology—not to stop its progress, but to understand and learn to control it.

It takes courage to challenge scientific endeavors. Most of us believe life is better because of inventions and technology. Seventy-percent of a group questioned said computers have a beneficial effect on life. However, this writer recently warned the audience at an electronics convention:

> To those of you here today who are having a love affair with your machines, I suggest that the gods on Olympus were not stupid when they chained Prometheus to the rock, and the God Jehovah tested Abraham for no small reason. Remember, you too can build a Sodom and Gommorah where your machines scorn your intelligence and blaspheme your sacred rights.

We must believe that it is *not* heretical to question the beneficence of scientific rationality and technological progress. After all, if the machine becomes our partner, then we must continue to seek that "common ground" of understanding.

Communication technology has created networks that connect us all to the world; we dial fifteen digits, and presto! we're anywhere. Communication technology becomes smaller, faster, cheaper, smarter. Soon the satellite will connect us to the satellite ground station, connecting cables between ground station and home (or just home), and perhaps connecting to transceiver—and there we are with our at-home communication center!

For a moment, close your eyes and picture Emma, our police officer, in a wired city, one similar to the city in Japan. Her sergeant calls her on the videophone about an arrest she has made. They chat. All evidence, testimony depositions and confessions are on videotape. The conference videophone is to avoid a prejudiced jury or one who may be influenced by local press. So she looks at her computer print-out of available jurors around the United States and sees that an attorney has selected a Protestant, 26, female; a Democrat, 35, emotional at weddings; and so on down the list. A market study tells Emma that certain variables produce certain verdicts in given cases. The trial, of course, is videotaped. Emma is on split-screen. The

## ETHICS IN OUR TECHNOLOGICAL CIRCLE

*We must constantly question the very existence of our new technology.*

jurors, when ready, stationed around the United States, proceed to dial-a-trial. Emma knows her next case will be on the docket right away, and she won't even have to appear. She has videotaped her testimony.

McLuhan warns, "Electronics and automation make mandatory that everyone adjust to a vast global environment as if it were his home town."

The networks of communication and transportation have come a long way, faster in the last 50 years than in all the 500,000 years preceding. Exactly when humans first spoke is speculative, but it certainly was not during the first 4,000,000 years. About 500,000 years ago human history began; man and woman spoke and kept a record of those words, first in their minds (memoria, it was called) and later in writing. We are still making records—that's what most of our communication technology is geared for.

Picture Emma once again—today, not tomorrow. She and a citizen have their first meeting. She establishes her ethos, creates a rapport with the citizen (remaining mindful of verbal and nonverbal clues), then moves on to a small group and later a larger group, finally speaking before the judge. During the course of her day she is a communicator, ever mindful that she is a person interested in the orderly search for truth in the interest of justice.

*Are we preparing ourselves to face the communications changes in our professions?*

The question for Emma and for us all today is not whether face-to-face communication is better than mediated messages, not even whether we have a choice between the two, but whether we are preparing ourselves for the changes in our professions and our lives.

Can Emma effectively conduct her search for the truth or enforce the law using a channel other than air? Is Emma prepared for the effect of technology upon herself and upon the entire criminal justice system? Is she prepared for what is happening on the street and in the courtroom?

Let's look for a moment at what *is* happening in the courtroom. CANON 3A of the American Bar Association allows a judge to authorize electronic or photographic means of recording for presenting of evidence, for perpetuating the record, for purposes of judicial administration, and for educational uses by educational institutions.

You and I may be neither police officers nor judges, but the implications of those decisions do affect us. What of the sixth-amendment right of the accused to confront witnesses against him or her? What if we are the witnesses? Is this constitutional right upheld when the defendant is present during the videotaping of witness testimony prior to trial and during its subsequent playback at trial? What about the accused's sixth-amendment right to counsel? Live questions of witnesses at trials may bring up questions that should have been asked of a witness in a previous videotaped deposition.

What of police taping? What of access? Who has the right to order or ask for videotaping and under what circumstances?

Changes in communication technology are not simply mechanical: they raise thoughtful and important issues. It is not only Emma but every member of society who must be prepared to face a more complicated and more technical world.

We have discussed the fact that all of us are part of a world in which communication technology is changing our environment on an individual and community level. We recognize that this technology brings with it responsibilities we cannot ignore. We must continue to question the desirability of change and the effect of change upon our society.

For example, two important issues arise from our communication technology: privacy and access. There is no record system that is absolutely fail-safe. The human element is the weak link in the data-collecting systems, but it is the human element that is concerned with such intangibles as inalienable rights. Recognizing this, Massachusetts created a privacy and review board to screen the information coming into its own system after it discovered that more than 75 state and private agencies and individuals had access to criminal records. Massachusetts officials now refuse to share this information with the FBI until they have screened it. New bills in Congress stress regulation and control. Technology has made it very easy to collect information, but technology does not improve the accuracy of such information.

*Technology has made it easy to collect information, but technology does not ensure its accuracy.*

More and more, however, technology is being cited as the answer to communication problems. More time and energy is being devoted to the videophone, the computer, the satellite, the cable system.

Perhaps the reason for going in that direction is that it is easier to learn the various physical and chemical processes than to understand humans. Somebody built the tools—and somebody can fix them. Machines are not as complicated as humans are.

The time has not arrived when humans can be phased out of communication situations that arise daily in private and public sectors. On the contrary, we are probably communicating more than ever on both the human and the media level—we just need to understand the environment and acquire a few more skills to help us use the new tools ethically and effectively.

## TECHNOLOGY AND SERIAL TRANSMISSION

*Today's communication involves sequences of events and series of transmissions.*

In Maria's work as a press secretary, in the Mayor's discussion with the media, in Emma's job with the police, as well as in Dora's and Bert's work with children, the serial transmission of messages occupies a serious place.

Perhaps the most distinguishing feature of today's communication is that it more often than not involves a sequence of events and a series of transmissions. Most of us act as relay links during the day; if we originate a message, we are a part of a relay team that includes both humans and hardware. Maria uses the facsimile machine, but she is actually writing a letter *for* the congressman. Emma gets a message that started three sequences ago. Because of the combination of humans and hardware, messages get simpler and shorter. When using mass media, messages also become more general, as opposed to more particular or specific.

Much more study is needed in the area of communication technology's far-reaching implications for human being. There are, however, a few commonsense observations that may help the average person become more aware of what's moving rapidly around him or her:

1. In serial transmission, communication is easier if one has a format to follow.
2. There is a need to build in feedback responses in the message.
3. Language must be general enough so several persons at different levels can understand.
4. It is imperative to understand that both machines *and* humans do break down.

## COMMUNICATION SKILLS IN A TECHNOLOGICAL SOCIETY

**Print**

When Maria decided to work for a newspaper, she interviewed for a position as a reporter. Throughout her interview she responded to and asked various questions. She was then conducted to the associate editor's office and was interviewed by two more people. Finally she became part of a discussion group on the question of energy. She had to use all the skills of public speaking mentioned in this book so far: she established her ethos, gained rapport with her audience, was perceptive about them, spoke in language they could understand, listened carefully to what was said, and offered feedback to their questions. Articulating well was important to her and to her interviewers.

However, Maria had to learn an additional skill that afternoon: She was told to cover an opening of a play and write a review. Fortunately she had seen many plays and felt confident about analyzing one. She wrote the review after carefully organizing her thoughts. Because she was using written skills, she followed a journalistic style.

Then she had to learn how to use the new computer.

Fortunately she knew how to type. That helped. Still, she had to learn a set of symbols so that the computer could "read" her copy and set it in type for the evening newspaper.

One skill necessary for the new communication technology is usually learning a new set of symbols. Each new machine has a language. Messages usually have to be redesigned to adjust to the new machinery. In most instances learning the new language is not difficult. Maria, for example, had to learn to place certain symbols before paragraphs.

*New communication skills usually require learning a new set of symbols.*

When Emma was assigned to communications in the police force, however, she had to learn a certain format for putting information in the computer. For example, the machine was programmed to accept an address first, then a name, then a description of the incident. The machine could accept only a given number of characters, so Emma had to enter the message using a limited number of words. Emma's assignment was harder than Maria's, because she was putting into a machine information being fed to her by another person—who, incidentally, knew nothing about the way the machine was programmed.

*Sometimes it is necessary to learn a new format as well.*

When dealing with the new communication technology, we must learn to redesign messages to suit machines and still strive for the greatest level of accuracy.

Designing messages for computers is not as difficult at times as writing messages for radio and television. Writing for radio is much like preparing our speeches—we are writing for the ear. The active voice, action verbs, alliteration, and personification all make our words come alive for our listening audiences. Writing for television, however, requires producing visual messages that are complemented with sound. Thinking visually is a new experience for most of us who learned to write sentences with words instead of drawing pictures in our minds.

As communicators of the future we will use both skills, speaking and writing, interchangeably. Some new machines are "talking" ma-

*As communicators of the future we will use the skills of speaking and writing interchangeably.*

chines. You can now ask a computer a question and the computer will respond, orally. Sometimes you will feed information into a computer and the computer will print out the answer. Our society continues to emerge as one that deals with services that are based on the treatment of information itself. The computer industry today is one of our primary employers. As it evolves, it depends on a high degree of literacy from the people who work in the industry and those who use the services.

The United States now produces information as well as food products for emerging nations. Communication technology allows us to use information as a "resource." (A resource is any commodity that fulfills a need.) We might run out of a certain kind of food or animal, but the human mind has the vision to create a way to preserve both food and animals, to build pollution-free energy sources, to preserve nature's beauty.

Learning new languages, designing messages to fit the peculiarities of a machine, learning to write more precisely, to ask good questions and respond well—all are skills that both the consumer *and* the producer of the message need know.

## Television

The mayor of Albuquerque holds a weekly news briefing. He does not produce the message, but he certainly wishes to have some control over it. So he usually opens the session with a short statement that constitutes his central theme:

"Today I have presented City Council with our fiscal budget, which amounts to 140 million dollars."

He gets right down to business. He gives some specifics about the budget, then recaps and repeats his main theme. If a reporter asks him to summarize, he knows that reporter needs a sound bite, and the mayor may say:

"The balanced budget I turned over to Council reflects two months of careful thought on the part of myself and my staff."

The television reporter gets the sound bite and a cutaway shot (perhaps a shot of the audience or the budget message). If a print reporter asks a specific question, the mayor takes more time to answer it and might ask the reporter to clarify the question so that they understand each other. Since the print reporter will usually do more interpretive reporting, the mayor wants to make sure they are on common ground. For the radio reporter, the mayor livens up his quote and avoids vocal pauses. Throughout the briefing, however, the mayor

caters to the electronic media because he knows the print reporter can catch him anytime for a question. Because news briefings are a phenomenon of the electronic age, more attention is paid to the visual aspect of the briefing.

When Vice-President Walter Mondale came to Albuquerque, the advance person brought Mondale's own "malt" box, carrying it as though it was the most precious of all commodities. The "malt" box is a simple device that allows all electronic media to plug in their equipment for a sound feed—that is, everyone is plugged into the public-address system. With this device, Walter Mondale needed only one microphone in front of him, not twelve. Mondale's press person and the mayor's press person negotiated the positions around a table where the Vice-President would sit to "discuss" the issues of the city and nation.

A round table was used to create the feeling of discussion rather than public speaking. But the round table posed a problem: Where would the live audience sit, and where would the media be stationed? Since the mediated audience was very important, the media were stationed in a position that would put Walter Mondale and the mayor in view. The mayor's press person insisted that the Democrats be in camera view and the Republicans be seated with their backs to the

*How One Vice-Presidential Visit Was Covered*

cameras. (Since the mayor and the Vice-President are Democrats, there was no real argument here.)

Negotiations for a media event are long and detailed. When the final message is produced it is the result of still another group of people:

1. *Photographer's* selection of what is visually exciting.
2. *Reporter's* interpretation of the event.
3. *Editor's* restrictions on time and point of view.
4. *Production crew's* ability to air the piece.
5. *Anchorpersons'* decision on item placement (first, middle, last).

The public, however, had a choice of three television stations, two newspapers, six radio stations and some added network coverage in the case of the Walter Mondale event. In larger cities the coverage would have been even more extensive.

The people who are part of a story need to know about the media. The people who produce the message certainly (or hopefully) must know, and the public who views the message will be in a better position to judge its merits if they know how the message is produced. Fortunately, with such a variety of media from which to choose, the public is offered more of the totality of an event than they could receive from one source. Those viewers who watch only one station, or read only one paper must settle for only part of the story.

## Telephone

Maria already does more with her telephone line than talk to her friend Dora and to her mother. She transmits data, pictures, and voice. She has learned to be professional in her printing, to use graphic materials supplied by an artist, and to organize every message as simply and concisely as possible. By telephone she has access to computer data. Because of digital transmission techniques (reconstructing a signal periodically along its path of movement and finally at its destination), Maria's messages are as clean and discernible at their destination as they are when she initiates them. Bell Telephone is now testing fiber optics so that a system can carry up to 400,000 telephone conversations simultaneously. When Maria wishes to call, she uses a telephone that has a memory of her most often used numbers. She just presses a button.

## Cable

It doesn't take too much skill to select a channel or switch to another. But cable offers more opportunities to you for producing messages for your neighbors and for your city and schools. In Spokane, Washington, community groups, schools, and the local public-broadcasting station are all part of a cable system, producing and using programs for information and educational purposes. The public-access channels in cable have not been used to their capacities. The police department in Emma's city recently built a studio and trained several officers to produce information about the police department for dissemination on cable television. You can become more involved with city government by *responding* via cable to programs and to polls taken by researchers. You can even take courses for college credit; Dora has already taken several.

## Computers

We cannot talk about telephone transmission networks without talking about computers, for it is the telephone networks that have the physical capability of carrying millions of computer dialogues simultaneously. In addition, bursts of data known as *packets* are routed over networks operating in many countries today. Packet-switching can be accomplished by means of radio and satellite transmission and perhaps in the future can be connected to any telephone extension. In this manner we can have access, via our telephone, to a global data communications network!

Commercial computers were introduced in the early 1950s and have advanced faster than any known communication technology. Today by means of large-scale integration circuitry, thousands of components are fabricated on a single chip. Today, a development known as Josephoxson logic gate can make a binary decision in ten trillionths of a second. In other words, 100 times faster than the early computers, which were capable of performing about a million simple mathematical operations in one second. Another advance, called *bubble memory*, is a process of storing binary information on a thin film of magnetic material in areas that are less than five ten-thousandths of an inch in diameter.

Yes, the computer has advanced—and what does that mean to all of us?

Well, it *employs* us. More than one-million persons are employed in U.S. domestic industry. Small businesses use computers, large businesses use computers, individuals use computers. Someday we may be able to access EURONET, a system now operating in Europe for the exchange of scientific and technical information. America already has a system called ARPANET.

The world's data communication network is expanding. The data can be distributed through the medium of television, too. In fact, the British post office now operates a system in which electronic circuits connect a television receiver with the Britsh telephone network. Users have keyboards that permit access to the post-office computer. A system which allows users to enter information for others to use is now possible.

We will, without doubt, have access to much information. If this information gives us knowledge of one another and causes us to communicate with one another more effectively, we will all be neighbors sharing our circles no matter where we live on this planet.

It is not the machines themselves that will make us neighbors, but the manner in which we *use* the information they store. It is our ability to use information that has brought us to this point in our lives. The creative genius in us will determine the future of our new information society.

## SUMMARY

Technology is a part of our lives. We deal daily with communications machines ranging from the familiar telephone to the sophisticated facsimile machine, and including the computer, radio, and television. While accepting that machines can send messages faster and more efficiently, we should nonetheless continue to question both the desirability and implication of communications technology upon our lives.

Technology widens our circle of messages to include the neighborhood, the city, the nation, and the world. We have available to us several networks. They include the developing telephone network that can transmit pictures, voice, and written materials between two points; a network based on existing cable-television systems, which can distribute information from central facilities to offices and homes; a network that involves broadband communications highway systems carrying up to 30 equivalent TV channels in both directions; and a multipurpose city sensing network capable of collecting data.

The new strides in technology include the emergence of fiber optics. By means of fiber optics thousands of conversations and millions of bits of computer data may be transmitted over a single hair-thin fiber. While we now have the capabilities of transmitting more information, we must consider the problems involved with understanding these relayed messages.

Listening in the technological world is not much different from listening in the slower-paced interpersonal world. However, we must listen to understand and to remember, so that we can feed the information back to society. The several types of feedback include external and internal, direct and indirect, positive and negative, and immediate and delayed.

In the technological society we must consider such ethical questions as privacy and access; we must prepare ourselves for the changes that raise thoughtful and important issues and be prepared to face a more complicated world.

In order to do so we should develop skills to understand and use the new hardware, so that we are equipped to deal with a life that constantly expands in influence and in human relationships until it reaches international proportions.

| | | |
|---|---|---|
| **1753** | The "idea" for the electric telegraph appeared in Scots Magazine. | **KEY DATES IN ELECTRONIC COMMUNICATIONS** |
| **1844** | Samuel F.B. Morse sent the first telegraph message. | |
| **1866** | First transatlantic cable linking principal cities of the world. | |
| **1876** | Alexander Graham Bell patented first commercially feasible telephone. (Each paired circuit transmits one message.) | |
| **1901** | Guglielmo Marconi successfully transmitted a wireless morse signal across the Atlantic. (Theoretical work by James Clerk Maxwell in 1873 and experiments by Heinrick Herzin in 1885 made this possible.) | |
| **1918** | Carrier techniques—single wire carries several conversations simultaneously. | |
| **1920s** | Lee deForest broadcast voice of Enrico Caruso over wireless. | |
| | Radio launched in Britain, America, and throughout Europe. | |
| **1930s** | Computers talked about by American researchers. | |
| **1936** | England's BBC initiated commercial transmissions in TV from London. | |
| **1940s** | Coaxial cable can carry large number of voice channels at once. | |

| | |
|---|---|
| **1948** | Invention of transistor responsible for data-processing capabilities. |
| **1950s** | Microwave carriers—dispensed with coaxial cables between switching centers. First commercial computers produced. |
| **1960s** | Crossbar switching machines—eliminated electromechanical switch, increased speed of information from point to point—transmitted computer-generated data over common carrier networks—linked computers and networks remotely. Application of digital technology. |
| **1970s** | Digital transmission and switching systems. Improved transmission quality and operating efficiency. Decreased cost to any home equipped with telephone. Ability to transmit two billion bits per second. Telephone networks can carry millions of computer dialogues simultaneously. |
| **1980s** | Fill in the future yourself. |

**KEY TERMS**

| | | |
|---|---|---|
| beeper | feedback | print media |
| cable | format | radio |
| citizen's-band radio | internal feedback | serial transmission |
| computer | listening | Shannon model |
| Comsat | mobile radio | Sputnik |
| electronic mail | point-of-scale | telephone |
| ethics |   terminal | |
| external feedback | | |

**EXERCISES**  *Students*

1. Keep a diary of all the telecommunications messages you receive during the day. Note also all the messages you *send* through a channel other than molecules of air. Do you receive more than you send? Which channel do you use most often?

2. Visit a television studio and follow a message from the time the reporter/photographer is given the assignment until the event is aired. How many people are involved in the story? What kind of restrictions are imposed by hardware? What kind are human?

3. Note the topics you *relay* during the day. Are they mainly dealing with national, local, or international news? Can you determine where

they originated? After making the determination, compare your findings with others in your class.

**4.** How much information about yourself do you have access to? Where is the information kept? Gather in groups in your class and discuss the question of access.

---

Starting at the end of the chapter, work backwards to find the answers to these questions. **CIRCLING BACK**

1. What makes the media message so complicated to produce?
2. What is the difference between delayed and immediate feedback?
3. Describe the Shannon model.
4. What are the possibilities of fiber optics in the communication field?
5. Describe the functions of a beeper.
6. How does television deal with time?
7. What does a facsimile machine do?
8. Where did the first voice from space originate?

---

Abramson, Martin. "Electronic Mail." *TWA Ambassador*, October 1978, p. 68. **REFERENCES**

Boraiko, Allen A. "Harnessing Light by a Thread." National Geographic, October 1979, p. 516.

Leavitt, H.J., and R. Mueller. "Some Effects of Feedback Communication." *Human Relations* **4**:401-416.

Noble, D.E. "The History of Land-Mobile Radio Communications." *Proc. IRE* **50** (1962):1405-1414.

Shannon, Claude E. "The Mathematical Concept of Communication." *The Bell System Technical Journal*, July/October 1948.

Zannes, Estelle. *Police Communications: Humans and Hardware.* Santa Cruz, Calif.: Davis, 1972.

epilogue

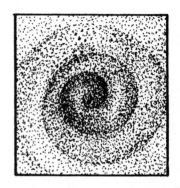

When Dora awakened on Thursday, December 20, she debated with herself as to whether she should spend an hour at the pool. Twelve turkeys, dressing, sweet potatoes, salad, eighty-four pies, and assorted vegetables danced about in her head. She had spent the better part of a month organizing 80 students for the big parent-student Christmas turkey dinner. Every bite of the 450 dinners had been prepared by the students, including the pie that had salt instead of sugar in it. Yesterday one of the girls found the salt pie (she had been tasting bits of crust from the pies), but in the confusion she lost it again.

*Intra-personal communication: inner dialogue.*

The day would be a long one, Dora thought, and so she decided to swim at the pool. "Something for me," she said to herself. "I'm surely going to need it today."

*How in the world had these dinners become so large?* Dora looked back. It was twelve years ago that she first organized the students in one of her classes to cook Christmas dinner for their parents. Overhearing them talk about their parents in uncomplimentary terms, she suddenly decided that a little togetherness might help them all. "Perhaps," she thought then, "if the parents just saw their children doing something for them!"

Well, she mused, as she slipped on her dress, what began as a small group of parents and children soon developed into a massive community gathering. But she was happy that all of her classes had joined in the spirit of Christmas. Not only parents and children were expected; other relatives and friends were coming, too.

By the time that evening was over, Dora's Christmas dinner party would be televised and the entire city would share in the event. New friends would be made at the long, decorated, family-style tables. And

*Media: television.*

*Hint of the future.*

even the student who put salt in the pie would be congratulated for his work in preparing the feast.

That evening the vice-principal of the school would say to Dora, "You surely are a great organizer!"

And Dora would say to Bert, "I've decided to start on my doctorate. I think I'd like administration. How about taking care of the kids for nine weeks this summer?"

Dora widened her circle of influence and of friends on that special evening. Like most of us, Dora doesn't worry about influencing the nation or the world. We don't expect our words to be carried on national television or broadcast in Asia or in some remote corner of the world. But Dora, like the rest of us, knows people whose words do have a chance of reaching the nation. And sometimes those people are not necessarily in high positions.

Of all Dora's friends, Maria has the greatest opportunity of becoming involved, at least, with the messages that are distributed to the widest circle of people. When Dora received the letter from Maria (see Prologue), she read the congressman's remarks about "cutting down the trees and leaving the monkey," and she laughed. Later that same day, Dora read that remark in her daily newspaper. Where did that remark start . . . and how did it travel?

Maria's boss was on the floor of the House of Representatives voting on legislation when news came of the President's intention to fire Secretary of the Treasury Michael Blumenthal and H.E.W. Secretary Joseph Califano.

"My God," said Wilson of Texas, "they're cutting down the biggest trees and leaving the monkeys!" Those members of congress within earshot roared with laughter. — *Public statement.*

"Good ol' Charlie," said one southern colleague. "He gets right to the heart of the matter." — *Relay teams.*

"Did you hear Charlie Wilson's comment?" said another Democrat to a reporter seeking House comment on the firings. The story was related and again the listener roared.

"Can I use it?" asked the reporter.

"Ask Charlie," replied the congressman.

Maria was working on a press release when her boss walked briskly into the inner office. "Folks," he said to his staff, "looks like they're cutting down the trees and leaving the monkeys!" — *Repetition of remark.*

The staff laughed, then went on to discuss the President's cabinet shakeup. It wasn't long until Maria's phone rang.

"I'm from the New York Times," said the reporter on the other end. "I'd like to confirm a statement your boss is reported as saying." — *Relaying via telephone, radio, print, and television.*

All in all Maria, must have received more than 20 phone calls on the subject of monkeys. By late afternoon Charlie's spontaneous comment was on every major newswire in the country. Many reporters called the congressman for a different angle on his comment.

The story calmed by the second day; by the end of the week the media were focusing on the administration's plans for Cabinet members, not House reaction.

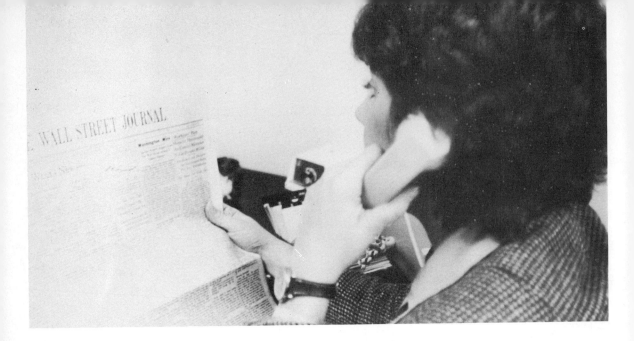

**Letters: print.**    Leslie Marks, Charlie's receptionist, was sorting mail when the letter from the Chicago woman caught her eye. "Maria," she said, "do you want to read all the letters to Charlie about the monkeys or should I give them to Charlie directly?"

"If they're from the district, put them in his box," said Maria, and then added, "and if they're clever."

The Chicago letter was clever.

Charlie walked past his secretary's desk several minutes later, picking up the notes and letters in the "in" box. He began to read through several, when suddenly he roared—much as his listeners had done several days earlier when they heard the monkey comment.

**Relaying.**    "Listen to this," he said to his staff, and read aloud:

*Dear Representative Wilson:*

**Public statement: relaying.**    *As a monkey lover, I take offense at your wont to equate monkeys with certain White House staffers. Monkeys and other primates are known to display great social adaptability and can even demonstrate wondrous political acumen and sophistication. Since these abilities are noticeably absent in top White House personnel, your "monkey" reference is quite incongruous, inappropriate, and insulting to a much beloved species.*

*I am certain that your insult to monkeys was inadvertent. However, in case there are a great number of primate fanciers in your district,*

*I strongly suggest that you issue a public apology geared towards dispelling notions about any contempt you may feel towards monkeys.*

*Most sincerely,*

*Brenda Greenstone*

"Charlie," said Maria after her boss had read the letter, "Can I give that to the AP?"

He nodded approval. "And tell the AP I apologize if I offended any primate fanciers," he said, tongue planted firmly in cheek.

Maria called the AP reporter for Texas.

*Media: relaying.*

"John," said Maria in a solemn tone, "Charlie wants to apologize for his statement equating White-House staffers with monkeys."

"What for?" asked John, "Is he getting heat from the White House?"

"No, just a well-written letter from a Chicago woman pointing out the errors of his ways." She laughed. "Listen to this," she said and read the letter to him.

*Everyone is famous for a few minutes.*

"That's funny," said John. "We'll put it on the wire."

And so a homemaker from Chicago was quoted in the *New York Times*, the *Washington Star*, and assorted other newspapers, as well as on the electronic media. She shared the space and air time with a congressman from Texas.

Dora got to know Emma a little better after Emma experienced the flat tire. (If you recall, Emma was driving to answer a call when her car hit a curb and the tire flattened. Darkness and the curve in the street made it impossible for her to see the curb.) As Emma got out of the car, several people came out of nearby houses and converged upon her.

"Well, we're glad it's a police car," said one woman. "Now maybe we can get the attention of someone at city hall. We've been trying to get the city to paint that curb for months."

*Group communication: advocacy.*

Another person told Emma that he had witnessed numerous accidents at that curb. "They hit it at least twice a night."

One man offered to help Emma change the tire. Even when she assured him she could handle it, he went right ahead and helped her anyway.

As she and the man were changing the tire, the others related their frustrations with the city for ignoring them. "The original plans

*Group communication: problem-solving.*

for this street did not include a through street. This used to be a cul-de-sac and they just came in and cut it through without so much as a by-your-leave or a meeting. That's why the street is so poorly engineered."

Emma told the neighbors gathered that she would have to report her flat tire to her sergeant and said she'd appreciate it if they would support her claim that it was not her fault. They all promised to write letters about the dangers of that curb.

"Listen," said one, "That curb is unsafe at any speed."

*Panel: review board.*

Emma was anxious that the incident not mar her record. She wanted to continue taking her police car home, so she went before the review board armed with letters and a scale drawing of the street. The members of the review board hardly looked at her evidence and found her guilty of negligent driving.

Emma was furious!

One fellow officer said, "Aw, come on Emma, it's no big deal. We've all been through it."

But to Emma it was a matter of justice, and she decided to appeal. The Chairman informed her that she could *not* appeal an Accident Review Board ruling. After she heard that she was placed under one year's probation, she said to herself, "We'll see about that," and she began her series of calls to the office of the Chief of Police.

*Community group: problem-solving.*

When the citizens learned that Emma had been found guilty by the review board, they were very upset. They invited her to a community meeting, where it was agreed that they were involved in a common problem and could help one another. Since the repeated calls by the citizens to the street-maintenance department had proven fruitless, Emma said she would call a friend of hers at city hall. The friend was a consultant to the mayor. Soon after Emma spoke with her friend, a call was made from the mayor's office to the maintenance department.

*Relaying.*

Meanwhile, Emma kept waiting for an appointment with the Chief. She was getting nowhere until she told a member of her union about her problem. The union decided to support her case. Recently an ordinance had been passed allowing officers with good driving records to take home their cars. The union wished to support that ordinance to the fullest degree.

*Group communication: decision-making.*

Several weeks later, Emma, the chairman of the Accident Review Board, and a member of the union hierarchy met with the Chief of Police. Emma had 20 letters from the citizens of the area, her drawings, and an admission from the maintenance department that they had indeed promised to look into the situation. After personally inspecting the area, the Chief of Police reversed the board's decision: an unprecedented move.

Soon after, the street-maintenance crew painted the curb with fluorescent paint and later put up reflector lights. The speed limit on that street was lowered to fifteen miles per hour.

*Solution.*

The months of meetings were contributing factors to the improved police-citizen relationships in that community. Emma got to know a number of the people she was assigned to protect from 3:00 to 11:00 P.M. five days a week. She discovered that she and Dora had children in the same school. She became knowledgeable about the types of jobs the women and men had, the make of cars they drove, and the pets they owned. All the information assisted her in her job.

*The circle widens.*

Weeks after the incident was resolved, Emma was called to assist in a domestic incident. A tall, heavy-set young man was threatening his aged parents. The officer on the scene had grabbed the young man's arm and was threatening to subdue him physically. Emma knew that the young man was retarded and that his parents had had trouble handling him before. She also felt he needed medical attention, not incarceration. When she arrived, she spoke to him quietly. The young man listened and allowed himself to be taken to the hospital, looking all the while toward Emma for approval. She had met the parents and the son during the many meetings devoted to the curve in the road.

*Another circle begins.*

We can never tell how far-reaching the single incident or a short phrase can be. Indeed, we can never tell where any one encounter will lead us, or where it will end. We cannot easily write "finis" to any word or act in our lives, so long as we are still alive. Nor can we always predict the outcome of any act. But we can learn from it.

When Bert was a little child, his mother would call him to come in from play and if he did not respond, she would warn him in Spanish about the old witch who was out there in the dark waiting to steal the little children. He grew up thinking it was a story his mother had made up to get him into the house at night.

*Remembering.*

When Augie, Bert's student, brought a newspaper to class for Bert to read (see Prologue), Bert was astonished to find that the newspaper contained a story about the origin of his mother's witch tale, a tale he discovered was based on ancient Mexican folklore.

*Print: story-telling.*

Bert told his class that Augie had brought in a story about a witch and anyone who was afraid of witches could go outside while he read the story. Of course, no one wanted to leave the room. The children giggled and their eyes widened as he read the story about a woman who had two children, whom she dearly loved. One day the children disappeared and were never found. The woman searched the world for her children, and became so deranged that now she will steal any children she finds outside at night.

For Bert, that story brought back remembrances of times past. He always encourages his students to bring in stories, to try to read the newspaper or have someone read it to them. He wants his students to be aware of all the information available to them in every medium.

*Result of relaying: a new thought.*

Three days after he read the witch story, Bert received a very strongly worded letter from a parent who said she did not wish to have her child frightened by old Mexican myths. Bert called the woman and explained the incident. He said there was no attempt to single out any one race or ethnic group when reading stories, and that he read stories from *all* cultures. Indeed, he encouraged the children to learn about various cultures.

But he had to promise not to "scare" the children again.

*A new awareness.*

Bert didn't stop reading stories. The incident did make him aware of the various perceptions of his *extended* audience—that is, the parents of the children he taught.

Dora, Bert, Emma, Maria, the congressman, the mayor, and all the other people mentioned in this book spend a great portion of their days dealing with a product called *information.* The process by which information is disseminated and the manner in which it is produced grows more and more complicated. Yet even when it involves only oneself or just two persons, even when the channel is air and the destination only a few inches from the sender, the process is not simple.

We have seen throughout this book that perception, intricacies of language, channels, and many, many other elements are involved every time a single thought enters our minds. We can predict the outcome for only a limited time; we can never know everything there is to know about everyone or every incident. Nor can we know exactly how the incident will evolve or where it will lead.

The *human connection* in the widening circle, the manner in which human beings connect with one another and start a chain of thought that extends through generations of time and space, is the spark that illuminates the world and sets men and women apart from all other species.

The connection was always there, from the time men and women ventured forth from the cave to meet their neighbors. Their rate of change and growth in their small circle of acquaintences was slow. It was during the fifteenth century, when the printed word and the sharing of information on a large scale began, that the circle was first mass produced.

At that time also began the gathering and storing of information. Minds leaped to examine, to explore, to create. New thought leaped from old. Books led to the Industrial Revolution, to steampower, the railway, the machine-tool industry. Mass production led to the interchangeability of mass-produced parts.

Without a doubt, the most significant change today deals with communication technology. Modern systems of communication will affect every major future accomplishment. However, it is not the machine, but the *use* of it; not the word but the *meaning* of it; not the incident but *where it leads us* as our circle widens that will determine how future generations benefit from our knowledge and experiences.

# PHYSICAL CHEMISTRY
## An Advanced Treatise

Volume VIA / Kinetics of Gas Reactions

**PHYSICAL CHEMISTRY**

**An Advanced Treatise**

Edited by

HENRY EYRING
*Departments of Chemistry*
*and Metallurgy*
*University of Utah*
*Salt Lake City, Utah*

DOUGLAS HENDERSON
*IBM Research Laboratories*
*San Jose, California*

WILHELM JOST
*Institut für Physikalische*
*Chemie der Universität*
*Göttingen*
*Göttingen, Germany*

# PHYSICAL CHEMISTRY
## An Advanced Treatise

Volume VIA / Kinetics of Gas Reactions

Edited by

WILHELM JOST

*Institut für Physikalische
Chemie der Universität
Göttingen
Göttingen, Germany*

 1974

ACADEMIC PRESS    NEW YORK / LONDON

*A Subsidiary of Harcourt Brace Jovanovich Publishers*

ACADEMIC PRESS, INC.
111 Fifth Avenue, New York, New York 10003


*United Kingdom Edition published by*
ACADEMIC PRESS, INC. (LONDON) LTD.
24/28 Oval Road, London NW1


**Library of Congress Cataloging in Publication Data**

Jost, Wihelm, Date
    Kinetics of gas reactions.

    (Physical chemistry, v. 6 A)
    Caption title.
    Includes bibliographies.
    1.    Chemical reaction, Rate of.    2.    Gases, Kinetic
theory of.    I.    Title.
QD453.P55 vol. 6A      [QD502]        541'.3'08s        [541'.39]
ISBN 0−12−245606−8        74-1282

# Contents

## Chapter 1 / Formal Kinetics

*W. Jost*

## Chapter 2 / Survey of Kinetic Theory

*C. F. Curtiss*

# Chapter 6 / The Dynamics of Bimolecular Reactions

*J. C. Polanyi and J. L. Schreiber*

# List of Contributors

*Numbers in parentheses indicate the pages on which the authors' contributions begin.*

**C. F. Curtiss,** Theoretical Chemistry Institute, University of Wisconsin, Madison, Wisconsin (77)

**H. Eyring,** Department of Chemistry and Metallurgy, University of Utah, Salt Lake City, Utah (121)

**W. Jost,** Institut für Physikalische Chemie der Universität Göttingen, Göttingen, Germany (1)

**S. H. Lin,** Department of Chemistry, Arizona State University, Tempe, Arizona (121)

**E. E. Nikitin,** Institute of Chemical Physics, Academy of Sciences of the U.S.S.R., Moscow (187)

**J. C. Polanyi,** Department of Chemistry, University of Toronto, Toronto, Ontario, Canada (383)

**J. L. Schreiber,** Department of Chemistry, University of Toronto, Toronto, Ontario, Canada (383)

**J. Peter Toennies,** Max-Planck-Institut für Strömungsforschung, Göttingen, Germany (227)

## Foreword

In recent years there has been a tremendous expansion in the development of the techniques and principles of physical chemistry. As a result most physical chemists find it difficult to maintain an understanding of the entire field.

The purpose of this treatise is to present a comprehensive treatment of physical chemistry for advanced students and investigators in a reasonably small number of volumes. We have attempted to include all important topics in physical chemistry together with borderline subjects which are of particular interest and importance. The treatment is at an advanced level. However, elementary theory and facts have not been excluded but are presented in a concise form with emphasis on laws which have general importance. No attempt has been made to be encyclopedic. However, the reader should be able to find helpful references to uncommon facts or theories in the index and bibliographies.

Since no single physical chemist could write authoritatively in all the areas of physical chemistry, distinguished investigators have been invited to contribute chapters in the field of their special competence.

If these volumes are even partially successful in meeting these goals we will feel rewarded for our efforts.

We would like to thank the authors for their contributions and to thank the staff of Academic Press for their assistance.

HENRY EYRING
DOUGLAS HENDERSON
WILHELM JOST

# Preface

Reaction Kinetics began with the formal treatment of overall reactions (Wilhelmy, 1850; Guldberg and Waage, 1864), followed by attempts to understand the reaction mechanism (van't Hoff, Arrhenius, Boltzmann). The present aim in theory and practice is to gain a detailed understanding single reaction steps, i.e. of transformations of atoms and molecules in specified velocities, impact parameters, and inner states into products of specified states. This line developed roughly within the last 50 years, with outstanding experimental success during the last decade. Formal kinetics, at the beginning of this century, dealt with comparatively trivial problems. At that time, however, it was discovered that periodic reactions are feasible, unless a restriction holds, corresponding to what we now call the principle of microscopic reversibility. Explicit application of classical thermodynamics and of thermodynamics of irreversible processes led to more insights, allowed of certain statements on the formal behavior of reaction systems, especially near equilibrium and near stationary states, e.g. in open systems. In the first chapter an attempt has been made to cover the domain between the almost trivial and the not-at-all trivial in formal kinetics, where there are rapid new developments.

The second chapter, by C. F. Curtiss, gives a modern survey of kinetic theory, as one of the bases of reaction kinetics. II. Eyring and S. H. Lin, in a critical review, deal with potential energy surfaces of reacting systems, while Chapter 4 by E. E. Nikitin is devoted to the theory of energy transfer in molecular collisions, considering the several possible types of energy exchange (translational–rotational, translational–vibrational, rotational–vibrational, etc.).

Molecular beam technique has contributed much to our knowledge of elementary scattering processes, elastic, inelastic, and reactive. In Chapter 5 J. P. Toennies covers this field giving sufficient details of experimental methods, as necessary for an understanding of the results.

Chapter 6 by J. C. Polanyi deals with the dynamics of bimolecular reactions. Reaction dynamics is defined as the details of a reaction event at the molecular level. One of the aims of this chapter is to establish the connection between bulk properties and microscopic details, while in further sections detailed models and simple models are treated, which essentially contribute to understanding.

WILHELM JOST

*July, 1974*

# Contents of Previous and Future Volumes

Chapter 1

# Formal Kinetics

## W. JOST

## I. Introductory Remarks

In order to bridge the gap between textbooks and this treatise, we start with a cursory critical survey of classical reaction kinetics. From a formal point of view the status of reaction kinetics at the beginning of this century might be characterized as follows. There was reliable experimental material giving qualitative and quantitative evidence as to

1

the dependence of reaction rate* $r$ on concentrations and temperature. In addition, it had been shown that a rate expression

$$r = f(\ldots c_i, \ldots, T, \ldots), \qquad (1.3)$$

depending on concentrations $c_1, c_2, \ldots c_i, \ldots$, and temperature, could be factorized

$$r = f_c(\ldots c_i, \ldots) f_T(T), \qquad (1.4)$$

the function $f_c$ depending on concentrations only,[†] $f_T$ only on temperature. A purist, writing today, might feel inclined to state: This idea of separation of temperature and concentration influences has proved completely wrong during the last 50 years, beginning roughly with F. A. Lindemann. What formerly had been introduced as a rate constant, or better, a rate coefficient, is actually a function of both temperature and concentrations. Only in limiting cases, and near equilibrium, can it be considered a function of temperature only.

Criticizing this extreme view one could say: Most difficulties are avoided if we may consider our reaction system immersed in a heat bath, as is usually very well achieved by having the reactants in solution. Consequently, when considering reactions in solution—which actually are excluded in this volume—a separation of temperature and concentration influences in most cases is justified, and easily done.

It was known that the dependence on concentration of the rate of a simple reaction could be expressed by

$$\partial r/\partial c_i = k' g(c_j) c_i^{n-1}, \qquad j \neq i, \qquad (1.5)$$

if we consider a reaction of $n$th order with respect to $c_i$, if $g(c_j)$ is a func-

---

* We adopt the convention of defining a reaction rate $r$, referring to a stoichiometric reaction equation (insofar as this exists)

$$\sum_i \nu_i B_i = 0. \qquad (1.1)$$

Here the $B_i$ are reactants and products, the stoichiometric numbers $\nu_i$ being positive or negative, depending on whether we consider an appearing or a disappearing species. The rate

$$r = (1/\nu_i)\, d[B_i]/dt = (1/\nu_i)\, dc_i/dt \qquad (1.2)$$

is independent of the reference species chosen, both with respect to sign and amount.

† Where care is to be taken that an additional temperature dependence due to concentrations be avoided by an appropriate definition of concentrations, i.e., unless stated otherwise, we suppose reaction at constant volume.

tion of all concentrations $c_j$, $j \neq i$, and $k'$ will depend on temperature only. When consequently carried through, this gave a rate expression

$$r = kc_i^n \cdots \qquad (1.6)$$

and $k$ differs from $k'$ only on account of factors appearing upon integration. It is remarkable that already Wilhelmy's results (1850) for the hydrolysis (inversion) of sucrose in the presence of nitric acid led to an expression

$$r = k[HNO_3][\text{sucrose}], \qquad (1.7)$$

i.e., Wilhelmy implicitly* had the correct rate expression for a homogeneous catalysis, $HNO_3$ not appearing in the stoichiometric reaction equation. With respect to temperature it was known to hold

$$(1/T)\, \partial r / \partial T = Q/RT^2, \qquad (1.8)$$

where $Q$ was called energy of activation.† In either case, whether we infer from Eq. (1.8) that there is a reactive isomeric compound in equilibrium with the bulk of one species (active isomer of sucrose, according to Arrhenius) or we assume only particles carrying an excess of kinetic or potential energy, or both, we are led to the conclusion that these "active species," in a generalized sense, are present in equilibrium. In stating this, we follow an old practice of physics, introducing the approximation of a "quasi-steady" or stationary state.

Again, taking the point of view of the extreme purist, one must admit that in a reacting system equilibrium concentration and energy distributions will be more or less affected, and in the literal sense it would be wrong to apply equilibrium concentrations or energy distributions to a reacting system.

Consider a black body with a small hole. Without the hole

$$I_{\text{em}} = I_{\text{abs}}, \qquad (1.9)$$

where the radiation emitted from the walls equals that absorbed, there is equilibrium at temperature $T$, with the equilibrium condition

$$I_{\text{em}} - I_{\text{abs}} = 0. \qquad (1.10)$$

---

* He gave explicitly the correct dependence on sucrose concentration. The influence of pH, expressed by $[HNO_3]$, is implicit in his rate constants.

† This leaves open an arbitrary temperature dependence of $Q$, and consequently the true temperature dependence need not be given simply by an exponential; for example, it may be of the form $T^n \exp[-Q'/RT]$, $Q' \neq Q$.

If now we bore a hole into the hollow body, a small part of the radiation escapes, and we may agree to write instead of Eq. (1.10)

$$I_{\text{em}} - I_{\text{abs}} \approx 0, \tag{1.11}$$

which put into a more rigorous shape states*

$$\{I_{\text{em}} - I_{\text{abs}}\}/\{I_{\text{em}} + I_{\text{abs}}\} \ll 1. \tag{1.12}$$

The rigorous prescription, obviously, would be to observe with holes of varying diameter and to extrapolate the results to the hole area zero. Normally, one will state: Provided the hole is sufficiently small (compared to the inner area of the black body) the emitted radiation will be close enough to that of a truly black body in equilibrium.

Another example is that of diffusion measurements, as carried out in classical experiments by Fick (1855). Two containers, one filled with a solution of concentration $c$ the other filled with the pure solvent are connected by a narrow tube, of cross section area $q$, of moderate length $l$. The rate of diffusion is measured by observing the slow change of concentration in one of the containers[†] after a "steady state" had been established. If the concentrations in the containers were time-independent, the steady state would be characterized by a linear concentration profile in the tube (provided the diffusion coefficient $D$ is independent of concentration, $dD/dc = 0$, within the range of observation), and one has within the tube

$$\partial c/\partial x = (0 - c)/l, \tag{1.13}$$

if $x$ is measured vertically, and the diffusion current $J$ ($J$ = flux times area) will be

$$J = Dqc/l, \tag{1.14}$$

i.e., in the $x$ direction, upward. Since actually the concentrations in the containers change slowly, also the concentration in the connecting tube must change, and since a local concentration change occurs only for nonvanishing $\partial^2 c/\partial x^2$, the concentration in the tube can no longer vary

---

* Since we know that $I_{\text{em}} > I_{\text{abs}}$, and $I_{\text{em}}, I_{\text{abs}} > 0$, it is unnecessary to denote in the numerator the absolute amount. In kinetics we shall have to use similar relations where $I_1$ and $I_2$ have different, but arbitrary, signs. Then it will be safe to write:

$$||I_1| - |I_2||/\{|I_1| + |I_2|\} \ll 1.$$

† Which are considered well stirred, accomplished by proper geometrical arrangement.

linearly with height. Though this process could be treated rigorously, the "steady state" approximation gives easily results of sufficient accuracy. The formulation for the actual state would be ($J_l$ and $J_0$ upward flows at $x = l$ and $x = 0$)

$$||J_l| - |J_0||/\{|J_l| + |J_0|\} \ll 1. \tag{1.15}$$

The assumption of a steady state, as characterized by equations like (1.10) or (1.15), is neither necessary nor exact. However, if this approximation is permissible, it allows of a marked simplification of calculations.

## II. Rate and Thermodynamics

Near equilibrium, of course, one has the relation for forward ($\rightarrow$) and backward ($\leftarrow$) reactions

$$\vec{k}/\overleftarrow{k} = K,$$

where $K$ is the equilibrium constant. This equation, by using van't Hoff's equation, taking logarithmic derivatives on either side, suggests the relation (1.8). It does not follow from this argument that far from equilibrium these rate constants have the same values and the above equation still holds. But one can generally predict that, when approaching equilibrium, this equation must hold and all deviations from equilibrium distributions must disappear.*

We try to formulate rigorously the situation as sketched above. Writing with Guldberg and Waage (1864) the kinetic mass action law for a reaction,

$$A + B \rightleftarrows C + D, \tag{2.1}$$

$$\vec{r} = \vec{k}[A][B]; \qquad \overleftarrow{r} = \overleftarrow{k}[C][D]; \tag{2.2}$$

in equilibrium ($t \rightarrow \infty$),

$$r = \vec{r} - \overleftarrow{r} = \vec{k}[A][B] - \overleftarrow{k}[C][D] = 0, \tag{2.3}$$

$$K = \vec{k}/\overleftarrow{k}, \tag{2.4}$$

where $K$ is the equilibrium constant.

---

* For a discussion see especially: Light *et al.* (1969). The above formulation does not exclude the validity far from equilibrium, it only states that additional considerations are required.

Reversing the argument, one could state: With Eq. (2.4) and (2.3) a formulation for the rate is compatible:

$$\vec{r} = \vec{\varkappa}[A][B]\, f\{[A],\, [B],\, [C],\, [D],\, [M],\, T\},$$
$$\bar{r} = \bar{\varkappa}[C][D]\, f\{[A],\, [B],\, [C],\, [D],\, [M],\, T\},$$

$$(2.5)$$

where $f$ is an arbitrary function of concentrations and temperature, and where $\vec{\varkappa}$ and $\bar{\varkappa}$ are also functions of temperature, [M] denoting that the rate might also depend on species not appearing in the stoichiometric equation. Experience showed that in most cases $f$ apparently could be equalled to a constant.

Again, taking logarithmic derivatives, and using van't Hoff's law, one obtains from Eq. (2.4)

$$\Delta H/RT^2 = d \ln \vec{k}/dT - d \ln \bar{k}/dT = [\vec{Q} - \bar{Q}]/RT^2,$$

$$(2.6)$$

which suggests a relation for the $\varkappa$:

$$\vec{\varkappa} = \vec{\varkappa}_0 \exp[-\vec{Q}/RT]\varphi\{\ldots c_i,\, \ldots,\, T\},$$
$$\bar{\varkappa} = \bar{\varkappa}_0 \exp[-\bar{Q}/RT]\varphi\{\ldots c_i,\, \ldots,\, T\}.$$

$$(2.7)$$

Here experience suggested that often the function $\varphi$ might be independent of concentrations and only weakly dependent on temperature. Thus the relations obtained from thermodynamics are rather weak, and, in addition, without further discussion, rigorously valid only at or near equilibrium.

We conclude this with an unusual example for conditions near equilibrium. The experimentally determined rate expression for formation far from equilibrium is [see Eq. (4.1), Section IV]

$$d[HBr]/dt = +\vec{k}[H_2]\sqrt{[Br_2]}\Big/\{1 + m[HBr]/[Br_2]\},$$

$$(2.8)$$

which may be rewritten

$$d[HBr]/dt = +\vec{k}[H_2][Br_2]\Big/\sqrt{[Br_2]}\,\{1 + m[HBr]/[Br_2]\}.$$

$$(2.9)$$

From the mechanism, discussed in Section IV, it follows for the reverse reaction far from equilibrium,

$$d[HBr]/dt = -\bar{k}[HBr]^2\Big/\sqrt{[Br_2]}\,\{1 + m[HBr]/[Br_2]\},$$

$$(2.10)$$

which exactly corresponds to the formulation of Eq. (2.5).* One may object that Eqs. (2.8), (2.9), and (2.10) refer to a composite reaction, which ought to be excluded from a discussion in this connection.

But then let us choose another example. At sufficiently high pressures we may describe the rate of the reaction (Troe 1968, 1969)

$$I_2 \rightleftarrows 2I \tag{2.11}$$

by

$$d[I]/dt = \vec{k}[I_2] - \overleftarrow{k}[I]^2, \tag{2.12}$$

in accordance with the equilibrium condition

$$[I]^2/[I_2] = K = \vec{k}/\overleftarrow{k}. \tag{2.13}$$

At ordinary pressures, and still more at reduced pressures, this description is insufficient and ought to be replaced at least by

$$d[I]/dt = \sum_i \vec{k}_i[M_i][I_2] - \sum_i \overleftarrow{k}_i[M_i][I]^2, \tag{2.14}$$

where all species present are to be considered as $M_i$. It might even be necessary to still further refine this expression by considering in detail all activation and deactivation processes.

Before mentioning thermodynamics of irreversible processes, we make a few more remarks with respect to classical thermodynamics. Clausius states that for an adiabatically isolated system entropy can only increase. Generally, there is

$$dS \geqq dQ/T, \tag{2.15}$$

where $S$ is the entropy, $Q$ is the heat supplied to the system, and $T$ is the absolute temperature. The equality sign holds for reversibility, i.e., for a succession of equilibrium states. Meixner (1964 and later) claims (see also Hofelich, 1969; Keller, 1969) that the inequality sign for irreversible processes is without motivation and foundation in Clausius' work, and he applies the same criticism to the so-called Clausius–Duhem inequality

$$\varrho\, ds/dt - \operatorname{div}(q/T) \geqq 0, \tag{2.16}$$

where $\varrho$ is density, $s$ the specific nonequilibrium entropy, and $q$ the vector

---

* Here a factorizing into a concentration dependent and a temperature dependent factor is no longer possible, because $m$, the ratio of two rate constants, is a temperature function, though only a weak one.

of heat flux. There is no objection to this equation when referring to equilibrium entropy. The arguments are essentially: Clausius seems to surmise that all states reached in irreversible processes are also accessible in reversible processes, and consequently have a well-defined entropy. Since, however, it must be admitted that for an arbitrary irreversible process the final state may not have an unambiguously defined, or even not at all definable, entropy, these inequalities need not always hold. We do not follow up Meixner's arguments, but we must remember that in all cases, to be treated here, either only states are admitted that could also be reached reversibly, and whose entropy is uniquely defined by measurable macroscopic variables, or one might have relations that under extreme conditions will become meaningless.

We may safely assume that in most cases of interest to the chemist the simple relations will hold, but for extreme cases the above quoted papers ought to be consulted.

The monotonic increase of entropy in a closed adiabatic system precludes the occurrence of true periodic reactions (see however, Section V,C) in static systems. This holds no longer for open systems, as a flow reactor, and needs specification for closed systems. Thermodynamics of irreversible processes (see Section VI) permits statements concerning the number of possible extrema of single reactants in composite reactions. Consequently, it is not quite unexpected if in cool flames in closed systems a finite number of oscillations is observed (though even in a closed, stationary system flow phenomena may be involved). We refer here to a discussion by Perche et al. (1970), who were able to derive a finite number of oscillations from simplified reaction schemes of cool flames; compare, also, Gray and Yang (1969), who prove that a Lotka scheme for a closed system cannot yield oscillations, and Frank-Kamenetskii (1955).

## III. Some Elementary Formal Relations

The formal treatment of chemical reactions is well known since Guldberg and Waage (1864) and good comprehensive reviews are available.*

We can guess some general, though rather elementary, relations by considering extreme, or limiting expressions for simple reactions. We

---

* Compare, for example, Z. G. Szabo.

start with a bimolecular reaction, with bimolecular reverse reaction, and equilibrium at finite concentrations of reactants and products.*

We write the equation in the form

$$B_1 + B_2 \underset{\overleftarrow{k}}{\overset{\overrightarrow{k}}{\rightleftharpoons}} B_3 + B_4 \tag{3.1}$$

with a rate expression according to this stoichiometric equation[†]

$$r = \dot{b}_1 = -\overrightarrow{k}b_1b_2 + \overleftarrow{k}b_3b_4 \tag{3.2}$$

and

$$r_e = \dot{b}_{1e} = 0 = -\overrightarrow{k}b_{1e}b_{2e} + \overleftarrow{k}b_{3e}b_{4e}, \quad b_{3e}b_{4e}/b_{1e}b_{2e} = \overrightarrow{k}/\overleftarrow{k} = K. \tag{3.3}$$

In the limit $t \to \infty$ we have the mass action law of thermodynamics (3.3) with $K$ equilibrium constant and the subscript $e$ referring to equilibrium. Subtracting Eq. (3.3) from Eq. (3.2), using $b_1 = b_{1e} + \delta$, etc., neglecting terms in $\delta^2$, we find near equilibrium[‡]

$$\dot{\delta} = -\lambda\delta = -\delta/\tau, \quad \lambda = 1/\tau = \overrightarrow{k}b_{1e}b_{2e} \times \sum_{i=1}^{4} 1/b_{ie}. \tag{3.4}$$

Thus: the rate expression is linearized to a "relaxation process" with rate constant $\lambda$ or a "relaxation time" $\tau$. For systems of reactions the situation is more complicated; we obtain a "relaxation spectrum." If we can disturb a system in equilibrium the process of relaxation to equilibrium provides an experimental method for the determination of rate constants (see Section VI). Here we mention only that expressions of the type (3.4) near equilibrium also follow from thermodynamics of irreversible processes (see Section VII). The above argument, of course, is not restricted to bimolecular reactions.

Where the molecularity of a rate expression does not coincide with that of the stoichiometric equation, we discern "order of the reaction," that is, the exponent of the concentration or concentrations in the formal rate expression, and "molecularity," this referring to the stoichiometric equation as given by the true mechanism.

* If in a reaction such as Eq. (3.1) equilibrium is shifted to negligible concentrations of the reactants, then it is often said: the reaction is irreversible. This, however, is not the meaning of irreversibility in thermodynamics. Therefore, we avoid the term reversible or irreversible in this connection.

† It is sometimes convenient to write the rate coefficients and concentrations in the above way, though this is not always the most rational way (cf. Section VI).

‡ For $\lambda$ also holds: $\lambda = \overleftarrow{k}b_{3e}b_{4e} \times \sum_{i=1}^{4} 1/b_{ie}.$

Again, only as an example among many conceivable ones, we consider a simple bimolecular reaction far from equilibrium,

$$B_1 + B_2 \xrightarrow{k} \cdots, \tag{3.5}$$

where the nature of the products does not matter. Usually two types of solutions are given for the rate expression (a) $b_{10} = b_{20}$, the subscript 0 referring to the initial state,

$$(b_{10} - b_1)/b_{10}b_1 = kt, \tag{3.6}$$

and (b) $b_{10} \neq b_{20}$, $b_1 = b_{10} - x$, $b_2 = b_{20} - x$,

$$\{1/[b_{20} - b_{10}]\}\{\ln[b_{10}/(b_{10} - x)] - \ln[b_{20}/(b_{20} - x)]\} = kt, \tag{3.7}$$

with several obvious variants. In practical experiments one often may have the case $b_{20} \neq b_{10}$, but $\mid b_{20} - b_{10} \mid/(b_{20} + b_{10}) \ll 1$, all coefficients and concentrations being positive, by definition. In this case Eq. (3.7) may become useless. As a possible way out we rewrite Eq. (3.7) setting $b_{20} - b_{10} = \delta$,

$$(1/\delta)\{\ln[(b_{10} - x + \delta)/(b_{10} - x)] - \ln[(b_{10} + \delta)/b_{10}]\} = kt \tag{3.8}$$

or

$$kt = 1/(b_{10} - x) - 1/b_{10} - (\delta/2)[1/(b_{10} - x)^2 - 1/b_{10}^2] \pm \cdots . \tag{3.9}$$

In the limit $\delta \to 0$ this passes into the former solution (3.6), with $b_{10} - x = b_1$. For small values of $\delta$ one uses Eq. (3.9). Considering that, due to finite errors in setting up an experiment, one almost never will have exactly $b_{10} = b_{20}$, it often may be necessary to use Eq. (3.9) or similar approximations, at least for late stages of a run.

A naive treatment of the simplest system of consecutive reactions

$$X_1 \xrightarrow{k_1} X_2 \xrightarrow{k_2} X_3$$

(which could correspond to a sequence of radioactive decay), gives

$$\dot{x}_1 = -k_1 x_1, \qquad \dot{x}_2 = k_1 x_1 - k_2 x_2, \qquad \dot{x}_3 = k_2 x_2 \tag{3.10}$$

with $x_1 = x_{10}$, $x_2 = x_{20} = 0 = x_{30} = x_3$ for $t = 0$. Of course, only two of these reactions are independent. Conservation of matter requires, and this follows from Eq. (3.10), too, that

$$x_1 + x_2 + x_3 = x_{10}, \qquad \sum_{i=1}^{3} \dot{x}_i = 0. \tag{3.11}$$

The first equation yields at once

$$x_1 = x_{10} \exp(-k_1 t). \tag{3.12}$$

Straightforward calculation gives

$$x_2 = [x_{10}k_1/(k_2 - k_1)][\exp(-k_1 t) - \exp(-k_2 t)]. \tag{3.13}$$

Again we can pass to the limit $k_2 \to k_1$, setting $k_2 = k_1 + \delta$,

$$x_2 = [x_{10}k_1/\delta] \exp(-k_1 t)[1 - \exp(-\delta t)] \tag{3.14}$$

or

$$x_2 = x_{10}k_1 t \exp(-k_1 t)[1 - \delta t/2 \pm \cdots] \tag{3.15}$$

for $\delta$ small, and in the limit $\delta \to 0$,

$$x_2 = x_{10}k_1 t \exp(-k_1 t). \tag{3.16}$$

Now we look at the simple reaction

$$X_1 \underset{\overleftarrow{k}}{\overset{\overrightarrow{k}}{\rightleftharpoons}} X_2, \qquad x_1 = x_{10} \quad \text{for} \quad t = 0, \quad x_{20} = 0;$$
$$\dot{x}_1 = -\overrightarrow{k}x_1 + \overleftarrow{k}x_2, \qquad \lim_{t \to \infty} \dot{x} = 0, \qquad x_{2e}/x_{1e} = \overrightarrow{k}/\overleftarrow{k} = K. \tag{3.17}$$

We are interested in the approach to equilibrium. Dividing both sides of Eq. (3.17) by $x_1 + x_2 = x_{10}$, we have one independent equation,

$$\dot{N}_1 = -\overrightarrow{k}N_1 + \overleftarrow{k}N_2, \qquad N_1 = 1 - N_2 = x_1/(x_1 + x_2). \tag{3.18}$$

The last equation (3.17) gives

$$N_{2e} = KN_{1e} = N_{1e}\overrightarrow{k}/\overleftarrow{k}. \tag{3.19}$$

From Eq. (3.18) we have

$$\dot{N}_1 = -N_1[\overrightarrow{k} + \overleftarrow{k}] + \overleftarrow{k} = -[\overrightarrow{k} + \overleftarrow{k}][N_1 - \overleftarrow{k}/(\overrightarrow{k} + \overleftarrow{k})] \tag{3.20}$$

and

$$\ln\{[N_1 - \overleftarrow{k}/(\overrightarrow{k} + \overleftarrow{k})]/[1 - \overleftarrow{k}/(\overrightarrow{k} + \overleftarrow{k})] = -(\overrightarrow{k} + \overleftarrow{k})t \tag{3.21}$$

(implying $N_1 = 1$ for $= t = 0$).
   Thus

$$N_1 = \overleftarrow{k}/(\overrightarrow{k} + \overleftarrow{k}) + [\overrightarrow{k}/(\overrightarrow{k} + \overleftarrow{k})] \exp[-(\overrightarrow{k} + \overleftarrow{k})t], \tag{3.22}$$

and the time for relaxation to equilibrium for $N_1$ is

$$\tau = 1/\lambda = 1/(\overrightarrow{k} + \overleftarrow{k}). \tag{3.23}$$

Equilibrium is enhanced by the reverse reaction. It seems worthwile to deal with this well-known aspect of general validity. We see from Eq. (3.23) that the relaxation time $\tau$ is largest for $\overleftarrow{k} = 0$. That $\tau$ decreases from its maximum value, $\tau_{10} = 1/\overleftarrow{k}$, has two reasons: first, $N_{1e}$ is shifted upwards with increasing $\overleftarrow{k}$; second, $N_1$ decreases, both by a decrease of $x_1$ and by an increase in $x_2$ (see Fig. 1).

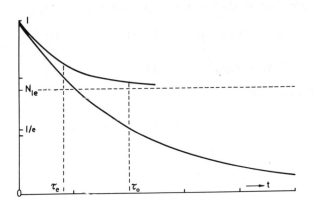

FIG. 1.   Mole fraction of component 1, $N_1$ versus time. $\tau_0$ relaxation time for simple reaction $1 \rightarrow 2$; $\tau_e$ relaxation time for equilibration according to Eq. (3.19).

Thus we are led to ask: Do analogous times also appear in other cases? We return to the example of this Section, the scheme

$$X_1 \xrightarrow{k_1} X_2 \longrightarrow X_3.$$

We found

$$x_1 = x_{10} \exp(-k_1 t); \quad \text{thus} \quad \tau_1 = 1/\lambda_1 = 1/k_1. \qquad (3.24)$$

The expression Eq. (3.14) for $x_2$,

$$x_2 = [k_1 x_{10}/(k_2 - k_1)][\exp(-k_1 t) - \exp(-k_2 t)], \qquad (3.25)$$

is not of this type. But in analogy with classical mechanics we may try to introduce "normal coordinates" of the type (this will be treated in a more general context; see Section VI,A):

$$\begin{aligned}
\text{(a)} \quad & \dot{\xi}_1 = -\lambda_1 \xi_1, \\
\text{(b)} \quad & \dot{\xi}_2 = -\lambda_2 \xi_2,
\end{aligned} \qquad (3.26)$$

to which, in this case, we might add for symmetry a third (dependent) variable

$$\text{(c)} \quad \dot{\xi}_3 = -\lambda_3 \xi_3 \tag{3.27}$$

with $\lambda_3 = 0$, $\xi_3 = x_1 + x_2 + x_3$, stating the conservation of mass. Obviously, we can identify $\xi_1$ with $x_1$ of the above Eq. (3.25),

$$\dot{\xi}_1 = \dot{x}_1 = -\lambda \xi_1, \qquad \lambda_1 = k_1, \qquad \xi_1 = x_{10} \exp(-k_1 t). \tag{3.28}$$

In order to find $\xi_2$ we must choose the appropriate linear combination of $x_1$ and $x_2$ that is easily found to be

$$\xi_2 = x_1 k_1/(k_2 - k_1) - x_2 = x_{10}[k_1/(k_2 - k_1)] \exp(-k_2 t) \tag{3.29}$$

and $\lambda_2$ in this case must be

$$\lambda_2 = k_2. \tag{3.30}$$

Thus, merely by guessing, we have found: in a system with two independent first-order reactions there exist two normal coordinates, that is, linear expressions of the concentrations, which depend on time according to simple exponentials. This is a very general result for systems of first-order reactions; however, the relaxation times will, in general, not be given simply by the rate constants. For non-first-order systems the same holds in the neighborhood of equilibrium (see Sections VII and VIII).

The question whether periodic reactions are possible arose already in early chemical kinetics (see Section VI,A). In complex, heterogeneous reaction systems periodic processes definitely are known that lie outside the domain of this chapter. We ask: Are periodic reactions possible in homogeneous gas reactions? For sufficiently restricted systems near equilibrium the answer is definitely no. For an early discussion, compare Lotka (1912), Rakowski (1906), and Skrabal (1941).

Formally, it is possible to obtain periodic solutions from rate expressions similar to those occuring in reaction kinetics, that is, keeping only the most relevant terms,

$$\begin{aligned} \dot{x}_1 &= \cdots - k_{12} x_2 \cdots, \\ \dot{x}_2 &= +k_{21} x_1 \cdots, \qquad k_{12}, k_{21} > 0, \end{aligned} \tag{3.31}$$

which give

$$\ddot{x}_1 = -k_{12} k_{21} x_1 \cdots, \qquad x_1 \propto \exp(i\varrho t) \tag{3.32}$$

with $\varrho = \sqrt{k_{12} k_{21}}$, that is, a purely harmonic change of $x_1$ with time.

Necessary is the different sign in Eqs. (3.31). The essential terms in a generalized system could lead to a skew (antisymmetric) matrix of the coefficients that is the opposite of what thermodynamics of irreversible processes suggests, at least for systems close to equilibrium (Onsager, 1931; Meixner, 1949; Jost, 1947). Consequently, it will be necessary to deal with this problem in connection with thermodynamics of irreversible processes, which gives an answer for unimolecular systems close to equilibrium (Onsager, 1931, ternary systems), for arbitrary reactions close to equilibrium (Meixner, 1949), for unimolecular systems in general (Jost, 1947) (see Sections VII and VIII).

For questions relating to general features of reaction systems it will be necessary to consider both normal thermodynamics and thermodynamics of irreversible processes. Here, first, it will be necessary to specify the general conditions imposed upon a reacting system. If one writes the usual formal equations for reactions, with rate coefficients taken as constants, this obviously implies a system at constant temperature. The condition of constant temperature, to a certain extent, implies a statement of stability, for even in systems with branching chains the final, sometimes dangerous, rise in reaction rate is coupled with a disturbance of thermal equilibrium.

Therefore, we can deal with two simple limiting conditions: systems of constant temperature or adiabatic systems. For isothermal systems thermodynamics requires that the Helmholtz or Gibbs energies $A$ or $G$ decrease monotonically with time, depending on the additional limiting conditions of constant volume or constant pressure. For an adiabatic system thermodynamics requires a monotonic increase of entropy. When dealing with questions of practical stability, obviously intermediate conditions are the most important ones, that is, a finite rate of heat transfer. For all nonstable systems one usually tries to find limiting conditions for an infinite rise of temperature, or of reaction rate, or of both. It should be emphasized that in all conceivable cases an infinite increase is possible only in the limit $t \to \infty$, and in addition for infinite systems only.* Consequently, the mathematically simplest expressions for instability need not always be the best applicable to practical problems.

From the above it follows that we ought to give due consideration to the implications of thermodynamics of irreversible processes (see also

_____

* One can formally write equations that seem to contradict this statement. Then, usually, in addition to other possible simplifications, the decrease of initial concentrations of reactants with time has been neglected.

Meixner, 1949, 1959; Ono, 1961; Bak, 1961, 1963). We consider once more a sequence of reactions

$$B_1 \xrightarrow{k_1} B_2 \xrightarrow{k_2} B_3,$$

in Christiansen's terminology an "open sequence" because the final product is different from the initial product (which in a sequence of unimolecular steps, of course, is always the case). In the following figures we visualize several special cases.

(a) The direct reaction $B_1 \xrightarrow{k_1} B_3$, Fig. 2. We have symmetry with respect to the horizontal at $b_1 = b_{10}/2$. The first increase of $b_3$ is linear in time, which is trivial, and follows both from the differential equation and from the integral, after expansion of the exponential for small values of $t$.

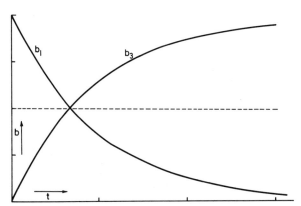

FIG. 2.   Concentrations $b_1$ (falling) and $b_3$ (rising) versus time for direct reaction $B_1 \rightarrow B_3$.

(b) The general case is shown in Fig. 3. The curve for $b_3$ of Fig. 2 is drawn as dashed line. The figure shows a few obvious relations. In the limit $t \rightarrow \infty$ the actual curve for $b_3$ must approach the dashed line. Curve $b_2$ now starts proportional to $t$, then passes through a maximum to reach a state of almost exponential decay. We note that the maximum will be reached the later, the smaller $k_2$. There are obvious relations among the sums of $b_1$, $b_2$, and $b_3$.

(c) Figure 4 gives a limiting case, with $k_2 \gg k_1$. Now at very low concentrations $b_2$ will pass through its maximum and then slowly decrease, $b_2$ being very small compared to $b_1$, and even for a considerable time

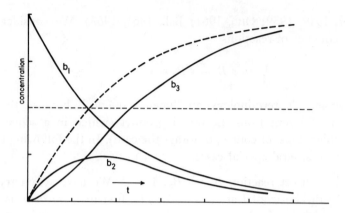

FIG. 3.  Concentrations $b_1$ falling, $b_2$ (with maximum), $b_3$ rising monotonically, for reactions $B_1 \to B_2 \to B_3$, versus time. Dashed curve corresponds to $b_3$ of Fig. 2.

$\ll b_3$, $t \gg \tau$, $\tau$ being a relaxation time for establishment of the "quasi-steady" state.

This method of the "quasi-steady" state is very useful, but has been, and often is being misunderstood* (see Sections I and II). The essence of the method is seen in Fig. 4. We may call $B_2$, in this case, an unstable (short-lived) intermediate, because the very small concentration is due

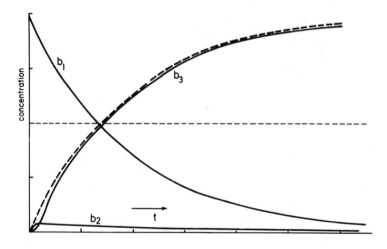

FIG. 4.  Corresponds to Fig. 3, but with $k_2 \gg k_1$, which shifts maximum of $b_2$ to shorter times and smaller amounts.

* Compare M. Bodenstein (1913, 1927).

to the rapid reaction of $B_2$. With the above differential equation the approximation of a steady state may be formulated

$$\dot{b}_2 = k_1 b_1 - k_2 b_2 \approx 0, \tag{3.33}$$

which, for purists, may be rewritten (all concentrations and coefficients are always positive)

$$| k_1 b_1 - k_2 b_2 | \ll k_1 b_1 \tag{3.34}$$

(which implies $| k_1 b_1 - k_2 b_2 | \ll k_2 b_2$). The consequence of Eq. (3.33),

$$b_2 = k_1 b_1 / k_2, \tag{3.35}$$

does *not* imply $\dot{b}_2 \equiv 0$; on the contrary, $b_2$ is proportional to $b_1$, which itself is time dependent. Inspection of the equations, or of Fig. 4 reveals that $0 = \dot{b}_2$ can hold exactly only for $t = t_1$ if $t_1$ corresponds to the maximum of $b_2$. For $t < t_1$, Eq. (3.33) is not applicable. We can, however, easily compute either $t_1$, or $\tau$, the relaxation time for the quasi-steady state. We have

$$t_1 = \ln(k_2/k_1)/(k_2 - k_1) \tag{3.36}$$

or

$$t_1 \approx \ln(k_2/k_1)/k_2 \tag{3.37}$$

because we had to surmise $k_2 \gg k_1$. The necessary assumption (3.33) for the steady state, of course, is valid for $k_2 \gg k_1$. In other cases, where we have no explicit solution for $b_2$, at least in the beginning, one may question the validity of (3.33). The answer is: The necessary assumption (3.34) $| \dot{b}_2 | \ll | \dot{b}_1 |$ is not a general mathematical consequence of $b_2 \ll b_1$. But given the physical problem: $b_1, b_2 > 0$; $k_1, k_2 > 0$, and the knowledge, that an intermediate passes through one extremum only (if necessary, this has to be investigated*) and some knowledge about the smoothness of all curves admissible as solutions of our kinetic equations, we may state that, except for $t < t_1$, as defined above, the inequality

$$b_2 \ll b_1 \tag{3.38}$$

has as a consequence

$$\dot{b}_2 \ll \dot{b}_1 \quad \text{for} \quad t > t_1, \quad \text{as defined above.} \tag{3.39}$$

---

* Compare the discussion for systems of first order and for relaxation phenomena, Section VI.

Of course, one may imagine examples, where the condition for a stationary state holds exactly. We assume the system, as above, at time $t_1$, with $\dot{b}_2 = 0$. If, now, we replace continuously all substance $B_1$, disappearing due to chemical reaction, by means of semipermeable walls, keeping $b_1$ constant, and on the other hand withdraw all newly formed $B_3$ by means of another semipermeable wall, keeping $b_3$ constant and having of course the reactor well stirred to avoid any local concentration differences, then $\dot{b}_2 = 0$ holds exactly, simultaneously, of course, $\dot{b}_1 = 0$ and $\dot{b}_3 = 0$.* A more realistic approximation to the same conditions would be a stationary flow system with perfect stirring.

In addition, it is easily seen that a quasi-stationary state may be preceded by several reactions, of which the last one may be written

$$B_0 \xrightarrow{k_0} B_1$$

and followed by other reactions as

$$B_{n-1} \xrightarrow{k_{n-1}} B_n$$

without a change in the formal expression for $\dot{b}_2$, and a number of further generalizations are conceivable. The basic idea might be stressed once more. We have a system of reaction equations, with a corresponding system of differential equations for the reactants, without restrictions. Except for relatively simple cases an analytical integration will not be possible. Then every conceivable and permissible simplification is of great value. If for certain intermediates we may assume a steady state, this implies that the corresponding differential equations pass into algebraic equations, an invaluable simplification for further treatment. The actual calculation will show if such an assumption was correct (i.e., if the error introduced by it is negligible), or if it is an approximation of only moderate accuracy that might be improved by iteration, or must be dropped at all. In dealing with chain reactions we shall meet this problem once more (see Section VI).

The preceding discussion shows that the assumption of a quasi-stationary state for some intermediate might even be compatible with reaction systems, which, on the whole, are not stable; compare also Lodato *et al.* (1969).

---

* Of course, each such expression consists now of two terms, one due to chemical reaction, e.g., if $V$ is the volume of the reactor, $R_{1,\mathrm{ch}} = \dot{b}_{1,\mathrm{ch}} \times V$, which is negative, and a flow term $R_{1,f2} = b_1 \vec{M}$, if $\vec{M}$ is the volume flow per second, and we have $R_{1,\mathrm{ch}} + R_{1,f2} = 0$; $\dot{b}_{1,\mathrm{ch}} = |\, b_1 \vec{M}/V \,|$.

## IV. Open and Closed Reaction Sequences. Establishment of a True or Pseudo-Steady State

### A. THE STEADY STATE

We treat a series of reactions

$$A_1 + B_1 \underset{\overleftarrow{k_1}}{\overset{\overrightarrow{k_1}}{\rightleftharpoons}} C_1 + B_2$$

$$A_2 + B_2 \underset{\overleftarrow{k_2}}{\overset{\overrightarrow{k_2}}{\rightleftharpoons}} C_2 + B_3$$

$$\vdots$$

$$A_n + B_n \underset{\overleftarrow{k_n}}{\overset{\overrightarrow{k_n}}{\rightleftharpoons}} C_n + D_n$$

corresponding to the overall reaction

$$\sum_{i=1}^{n} A_i + B_1 \rightleftharpoons \sum_{i=1}^{n} C_i + D_n.$$

We have to write down the corresponding system of differential equations, consider the auxiliary conditions (e.g., conservation of masses) and try to integrate the system, exactly or approximately.

This question becomes much more interesting if we assume the $B_i$ to be "active species"; compare Christiansen (1941). We then write two different types of sequences (using the last letters $X$, $Y$, etc. for "active species"):

$$A_1 \underset{\overleftarrow{k_1}}{\overset{\overrightarrow{k_1}}{\rightleftharpoons}} C_1 + X_2 \qquad A_1 + X_1 \underset{\overleftarrow{k_1}}{\overset{\overrightarrow{k_1}}{\rightleftharpoons}} C_1 + X_2$$

$$A_2 + X_2 \underset{\overleftarrow{k_2}}{\overset{\overrightarrow{k_2}}{\rightleftharpoons}} C_2 + X_3 \qquad A_2 + X_2 \underset{\overleftarrow{k_2}}{\overset{\overrightarrow{k_2}}{\rightleftharpoons}} C_2 + X_3$$

$$\vdots \qquad\qquad \vdots$$

$$A_n + X_n \underset{\overleftarrow{k_n}}{\overset{\overrightarrow{k_n}}{\rightleftharpoons}} C_n \qquad A_n + X_n \underset{\overleftarrow{k_n}}{\overset{\overrightarrow{k_n}}{\rightleftharpoons}} C_n + X_1$$

$$\overline{\sum_{i=1}^{n} A_i \rightleftharpoons \sum_{i=1}^{n} C_i} \qquad \overline{\sum_{i=1}^{n} A_i \rightleftharpoons \sum_{i=1}^{n} C_i}$$

For the general treatment of reaction sequences we refer to Christiansen

(1941). Here the following notation has been used: substances, denoted by the first letters of the alphabet are normal stable compounds, while the last letters denote "active" intermediates. By "active" we mean that these compounds are highly reactive and react very quickly after they once have been formed, and, consequently, never reach high concentrations unless we are dealing with unstable reactions. These we exclude for the present.

If we assume a stationary state, at once a characteristic difference appears between the left system, called "open system" by Christiansen (1941), and the right system, called "closed system." This type of system turns out to be essentially what we call a "chain reaction." The assumption of a stationary state gives for the left system, for $n = 3$:

$$\dot{x}_2 = \vec{k}_1 a_1 - \vec{k}_1 a_1 x_2 - \vec{k}_2 x_2 a_2 + \vec{k}_2 c_2 x_3 \approx 0,$$
$$\dot{x}_3 = \vec{k}_2 a_2 x_2 - \vec{k}_2 c_2 x_3 - \vec{k}_3 a_3 x_3 + \vec{k}_3 c_3 \approx 0$$

(where the sign $\approx$ is to be understood as in previous examples, see Section I), i.e., two linear, inhomogeneous algebraic equations for $x_2$ and $x_3$ from which these concentrations of the intermediates can be calculated. The corresponding equations for the open system and $n = 3$ are

$$\dot{x}_1 = -\vec{k}_1 a_1 x_1 + \vec{k}_1 c_1 x_2 + \vec{k}_3 x_3 a_3 - \vec{k}_3 c_3 x_1 \approx 0,$$
$$\dot{x}_2 = +\vec{k}_1 a_1 x_1 - \vec{k}_1 c_1 x_2 - \vec{k}_2 a_2 x_2 + \vec{k}_2 c_2 x_3 \approx 0,$$
$$\dot{x}_3 = -\vec{k}_3 a_3 x_3 + \vec{k}_3 c_3 x_1 + \vec{k}_2 a_2 x_2 - \vec{k}_2 c_2 x_3 \approx 0.$$

Here we have three homogeneous, first-order algebraic equations for $x_1$, $x_2$, and $x_3$, which give only the ratios $x_1 : x_2 : x_3$, not the absolute values. The necessary condition for the solvability of the homogeneous equations, that the determinant of the coefficients* vanishes, is always obeyed, because the equations are not independent, the sum $\dot{x}_1 + \dot{x}_2 + \dot{x}_3$ vanishing. This condition remains valid if further equations are added, provided these equations correspond to the above scheme (see the remarks about order of the reactions, below). If we want to characterize the above "closed sequence" which corresponds to a chain reaction, but does not yet represent a complete reaction chain, we may state the following: We have a sequence of reactions, each of the bimolecular type with bimolecular reverse reaction. One active species $X_i$ enters into each of these reactions, and another active species $X_{i+1}$ is formed in each reaction

* These are the products $k_i a_i$, etc.

step, $X_{n+1} = X_1$. The species $n + 1$ is identical with species 1, this being the characteristics of the closed system. This sequence must be written in a definite order, in our notation running from 1 to $n$, the system forming a cycle, in which the last appearing species $X_i$ re-enters into equation 1. Obviously this sequence is invariant towards cyclic permutation of its members.

In the open sequence, there is no permutation possible, because in the last reaction no new active species is being created.

For open sequences we have, in addition, to consider, as already pointed out by Christiansen, that only even radicals or atoms (with even valency) are admitted if a scheme with disappearance (or appearance) of a radical in one step is to be admitted.

In order to understand the additional features of a true chain reaction we simply discuss the first completely analysed chain reaction, the formation of hydrogen bromide. Bodenstein and Lind's (1907) experimental result was

$$d[\mathrm{HBr}]/dt = k[\mathrm{H_2}] \sqrt{[\mathrm{Br_2}]} \Big/ \{1 + [\mathrm{HBr}]/m[\mathrm{Br_2}]\} \qquad (4.1)$$

and they made a first suggestion with respect to a mechanism, involving atoms. The mechanism accepted since Christiansen (1919), Herzfeld (1919), and Polanyi (1920) is, with the traditional numbering of the reactions, as follows:

| | | |
|---|---|---|
| 1. | $\mathrm{Br_2} \rightarrow 2\mathrm{Br}$ | $k_1$, |
| 2. | $\mathrm{Br} + \mathrm{H_2} \rightarrow \mathrm{HBr} + \mathrm{H}$ | $k_2$, |
| 3. | $\mathrm{H} + \mathrm{Br_2} \rightarrow \mathrm{HBr} + \mathrm{Br}$ | $k_3$, |
| 4. | $\mathrm{H} + \mathrm{HBr} \rightarrow \mathrm{H_2} + \mathrm{Br}$ | $k_4$, |
| 6. | $\mathrm{Br} + \mathrm{Br} \rightarrow \mathrm{Br_2}$ | $k_6$. |

The reverse reaction of 3 has been omitted because its influence is negligible.[*] The equations 1 and 6 ought today be written as second- and third-order reactions. This, however, does not appear explicitly in the result of the present calculation, and we may or may not imagine that in $k_1$ and $k_6$ a factor proportional to the total pressure (or better, to the weighted sum of the partial pressures) has been included. In the result this factor does cancel anyway, it becomes relevant if one considers the photochemical reaction. Equations 2 and 3 represent a reaction cycle,

---

[*] But we must introduce it when considering the HBr decomposition; compare Section I.

as introduced above, and consequently a closed sequence; Eq. 4 is an additional parallel reaction for the hydrogen atom. It is seen without actual calculation that in the expressions for $h$ and $b$ (if we denote [H] and [Br] by these abbreviations) every term appears twice, once with positive and once with negative sign. Thus, irrespective of the values of $\dot{h}$ and $\dot{b}$, the sum $\dot{h} + \dot{b}$ will vanish, and consequently the determinant of the resulting scheme of coefficients must vanish.

We might, considering a true simple chain given by Eqs. 2, 3 and 4, characterize the individual reaction by an order with respect to active species, giving each one an order for the direct, and one for the reverse reaction. Then we may state: the members of a reaction chain proper, that is, the above three equations, are of order 1.1. With this notation, obviously, we should have to give Eq. 1 the order 0.2, and Eq. 6, the order 2.0; compare above.

As a matter of routine we write the equations for $\dot{b}$ and $\dot{h}$, as derived from the chain proper

$$\dot{b} = -k_2 b[H_2] + k_3 h[Br_2] + k_4 h[HBr], \tag{4.2}$$

$$\dot{h} = k_2 b[H_2] - k_3 h[Br_2] - k_4 h[HBr] \tag{4.3}$$

with the trivial consequence

$$db/dh = \dot{b}/\dot{h} = -1. \tag{4.4}$$

With $h$ and $b$ given for $t = 0$ we have

$$h + b = h_0 + b_0, \qquad h = h_0 + b_0 - b, \tag{4.5}$$

which we further shall specialize to

$$b = b_0 \quad \text{for} \quad t = 0, \quad h_0 = 0. \tag{4.6}$$

Without specialization and simplification we have for the pure chain, using (5),

$$\dot{b} = -b\{k_2[H_2] + k_3[Br_2] + k_4[HBr] + \{b_0 + h_0\}\{k_3[Br_2] + k_4[HBr]\}, \tag{4.7}$$

which we write

$$\dot{b}/\{b - [b_0 + h_0]\Sigma_2/\Sigma_1\} = -\Sigma_1 \tag{4.8}$$

with the abbreviations

$$\Sigma_1 = k_2[H_2] + k_3[Br_2] + k_4[HBr],$$
$$\Sigma_2 = k_3[Br_2] + k_4[HBr]. \tag{4.9}$$

From Eq. (4.8) we have

$$\ln[\{b - [b_0 + h_0]\Sigma_2/\Sigma_1\}/\{b_0 + [b_0 + h_0]\Sigma_2/\Sigma_1\}] = -\Sigma_1 t. \tag{4.10}$$

If we pass to the limit $t \to \infty$, but assume that for the establishment of a stationary value of $b = b_e$ a time is necessary which still is negligible with respect to changes of concentrations of stable products as $[H_2]$, etc.,* we have

$$b_e = [b_0 + h_0]\Sigma_2/\Sigma_1$$
$$= [b_0 + h_0]\{k_3[Br_2] + k_4[HBr]\}/\{k_2[H_2] + k_3[Br_2] + k_4[HBr]\}, \tag{4.11}$$

for with $t \to \infty$ the right-hand side of Eq. (4.10) tends to $-\infty$; consequently, the numerator to the left must approach zero.† Equation (4.11) is the value of the bromine atom concentration in the quasi-steady state. We test this by putting the expressions (4.2) and (4.3) equal to zero, either equation giving the same result,

$$b/h = \{k_3[Br_2] + k_4[HBr]\}/k_2[H_2] = \Sigma_2/\{\Sigma_1 - \Sigma_2\}. \tag{4.12}$$

Obviously, these equations cannot give more than the ratio $b/h$. But, using our initial condition (4.5), we must have

$$h_e = h_0 + b_0 - b_e, \tag{4.13}$$

$$h_e = [h_0 + b_0]\{(\Sigma_1 - \Sigma_2)/\Sigma_1\}, \tag{4.14}$$

and, of course, the ratio of Eqs. (4.11) and (4.12) gives the expression corresponding to Eq. (4.12):

$$b_e/h_e = \Sigma_2/\{\Sigma_1 - \Sigma_2\}. \tag{4.15}$$

The last expressions would hold for the idealized case of flash photolysis, if instantaneously a finite initial concentration $b_0$ of bromine atoms was created, and if the establishment of the steady state was fast compared to the relaxation of the bromine recombination equilibrium.

---

* That is, the initial values of $[H_2]$ and $[Br_2]$ are practically preserved.
† The denominator does not contain the variables $b$ and $h$.

We want to estimate a realistic half time for Eq. (4.10). We have

$$b = b_0 \quad \text{for} \quad t = 0 \quad \text{and} \quad h_0 = 0. \qquad (4.16)$$

Thus we may set

$$b_{1/2} = (b_0 + b_e)/2 \quad \text{for} \quad t = \tau_{1/2} \qquad (4.17)$$

We find

$$\tau_{1/2} = \ln 2/\Sigma_1. \qquad (4.18)$$

The above complete scheme of the hydrogen bromine reaction is an interesting though specialized case of a chain reaction. The chain proper, Eqs. 2, 3, and 4, gives the ratio of the atom concentrations of bromine and hydrogen. The additional equations 1 and 6 fix the absolute values of these concentrations. One may as well say that it is assumed that thermal equilibrium of the bromine dissociation is established. Skrabal calls such systems appendix systems. The more general case differs from this, as we shall see below. It is, however, unnecessary to postulate that thermal dissociation equilibrium be established.

We have already seen that the sum of the rate expressions, as derived from Eqs. 2, 3, and 4, i.e., Eqs. (4.2) and (4.3), gives

$$\dot{h} + \dot{b} = 0$$

without any further assumptions. Thus, if we write a rate expression for $\dot{b}$, including the contributions of 1 and 6, and adding that for $\dot{h}$, we obtain

$$\dot{b} = 2k_1[Br_2] - 2k_6 b^2. \qquad (4.19)$$

With the assumption of a steady state we find

$$b = \sqrt{k_1[Br_2]/k_6}, \qquad (4.20)$$

that is, establishment of thermal equilibrium. This expression, as is well known, includes the case of the photochemical reaction if we replace $k_1[Br_2]$ by $I_{abs}$, the amount of light absorbed per unit time and volume, expressed in the same units as $k_1[Br_2]$, for example, moles sec$^{-1}$ cm$^{-3}$. Of course, now the exact pressure dependence of $k_6$ must be introduced. For, an eventual pressure dependence no longer cancels between $k_1$ and $k_6$.

We try to calculate a half time of relaxation for the establishment of the dissociation equilibrium, if, as a possible initial state, we assume the gas to be heated instantaneously to the reaction temperature, the initial concentration of bromine atoms $b_0$ having been kept to zero. We rewrite Eq. (4.19),

$$\dot{b} = 2k_1\{[\text{Br}_2] - b^2/K\}, \tag{4.21}$$

with $K = k_1/k_6$ and

$$\dot{b}/\{[\text{Br}_2] - b^2/K\} = 2k_1, \tag{4.22}$$

and upon integration, with $b = b_0 = 0$ for $t = 0$, and with the abbreviation $\sqrt{K[\text{Br}_2]} = b_e$, the atom concentration in equilibrium, this gives

$$[K/4b_e] \ln\{[b_e + b]/[b_e - b]\} = k_1 t. \tag{4.23}$$

Choosing $b = b_e/2$ for $t = \tau_{1/2}$, we find

$$\tau_{1/2} = [K/4b_e k_1] \ln 3 = \ln 3/4b_e k_6. \tag{4.24}$$

We found the following degrees of dissociation, $\alpha$, in the literature:

| $T$ (°K) | 400 | 600 | 800 | 1000 | 1200 |
|---|---|---|---|---|---|
| $\alpha$ (°K) | $7.8 \times 10^{-11}$ | $1.2 \times 10^{-6}$ | $1.6 \times 10^{-4}$ | $3 \times 10^{-3}$ | $2.1 \times 10^{-2}$ |

With bromine of about 1 atm and $k_6 \approx 10^{-2} \times$ collision number (which, for this pressure and our present estimate, considers with sufficient accuracy the number of triple collisions), we find for

$$600\,°\text{K}: \quad \tau_{1/2} \approx 2 \times 10^{-2} \text{ sec}$$

$$1000\,°\text{K}: \quad \tau_{1/2} \approx 1.6 \times 10^{-5} \text{ sec}$$

But for 600°K and 1/100 atm we find $\tau_{1/2} = 2 \times 10^3$ sec. In connection with the steady-state approximation reference is made to Bowen, Acrivos, and Oppenheim.

## B. Reactions outside the Steady State

The establishment of a quasi-steady state requires, as we saw, a certain relaxation time. There are several possibilities for working outside this normal steady state. If we have a photochemical reaction with rate proportional to $I^n$, $n \neq 1$, as is the case with the hydrogen-bromine reaction, there appear pronounced effects if the system is irradiated intermittently. We discuss two cases.*

1.  The irradiation is intermittent, but the time of a single pulse is very long compared to the relaxation time of the steady state. Then the rate during the single pulse is, to a sufficient approximation, still given by the same expression as that for continuous irradiation, but with careful consideration of the light intensity.

If, as it was and often is usual, the light is weakened by means of a rotating sector, letting pass the light only during a fraction $1/v$ of the total time $v > 1$, then for light intensity $I_0$, the rate will be proportional to the effective light intensity only if the rate is proportional to the first power of $I$.

We note the expressions obtained for a rate

$$r = \varkappa I^n \tag{4.25}$$

and compare this to the standard rate $r_0$ with $I = I_0$, when at the same time the intensity is changed by a factor $\mu$

$$r = (1/v)\varkappa(\mu I_0)^n. \tag{4.26}$$

Examples:

$$\mu = v, \qquad r = v^{n-1}\varkappa I_0^n, \tag{4.27}$$

and we have

$$
\begin{array}{llll}
1. & n = 1, & r = r_0, & r_0 = \varkappa I_0, \\
2. & n = 1/2, & \mu = v = 2, & r = r_0/\sqrt{2}, \\
3. & n = 1/2, & v = \mu = 4, & r = r_0/2.
\end{array} \tag{4.28}
$$

2.  If the time of a single pulse, $\vartheta \leq \tau$, $\tau$ relaxation time for establishment of the steady state, the situation is quite different. If $\vartheta \ll \tau$, then the reverse reaction of atom or radical recombination is still negligible, and the atom or radical concentration will be represented by Fig. 5. Here the ordinate shows the concentration of the active species, $x$, the abscissa is the time.

* Compare also Calvert and Pitts (1966).

Under the above assumption $x$ will rise almost linearly with time during the illumination period $\vartheta$, as will the reaction rate. If $\Theta$ is the rotation period of the sector (or the sum of time of illumination and of darkness) then during time $(\Theta - \vartheta)$ the atom concentration will decrease according to the law of destruction of the active species. In our previous

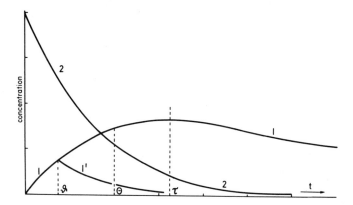

FIG. 5. Concentration of active species versus time during photochemical reaction. Curve 1: rise of concentration during continuous illumination, maximum obtained at $t = \tau$ due to consecutive reactions. Curve 2: concentration due to an instantaneous light source (flash photolysis), at $t = 0$. $1 - 1'$: concentration for intermittent illumination. $\Theta - \vartheta$ relaxation time for disappearance of active species after illumination.

example this will be according to a rate law of the second order with respect to the active species. As mentioned above, the rate constant still will be a function of pressure and composition, because the atom recombination obeys a third-order law, being a three-body collision process. If a $t = \Theta$ the concentration of the active species has declined to almost zero, then the rate will be given by the average within time $\Theta$. If, however, $x$ does not decline sufficiently, then increase and fall of $x$ during the following period $\Theta$ must be calculated once more explicitly, the average rising above that of the first period, and this is to be repeated until a steady rise and fall has been obtained. We now have again a "quasi-steady" state, but with periodically fluctuating concentrations of active species and of reaction rate.

This description includes the case of flash photolysis, curve 2 in Fig. 5, where due to a single pulse a very high concentration of the active species is obtained almost instantaneously, which decreases according to the rate law valid for the process under consideration; compare Norrish, Porter (1949).

We return once more to the general formulation of a chain reaction. We start from a closed sequence (some of the $X_i$ may be identical).

$$X_1 + B_1 \rightleftarrows R_1 + X_2$$
$$\vdots$$
$$X_i + B_i \rightleftarrows R_i + X_{i+1}$$
$$\vdots \tag{4.29}$$
$$X_n + B_n \rightleftarrows R_n + X_1$$

$$\overline{\sum_{i=1}^{n} B_i \rightleftarrows \sum_{i=1}^{n} R_i}$$

where the reactants have been denoted by $B_i$, the products by $R_i$, and the active species by $X_i$. We obtain a series of linear rate expressions (linear in the $x_i$) which we write

$$\dot{x}_1 = L_1 \approx 0$$
$$\vdots$$
$$\dot{x}_i = L_i \approx 0 \tag{4.30}$$
$$\vdots$$
$$\dot{x}_n = L_n \approx 0,$$

where the $L_i$ are the homogeneous linear expressions in $x_i$, and the sign $\approx 0$ is to be written after one has made certain that a quasi-steady state is a reasonable approximation; compare Section I. Because every term in the $L_i$ appears twice, once with a plus sign for an appearing species, once with a minus sign for a disappearing one, we have generally

$$\sum_{i=1}^{n} L_i \equiv 0, \tag{4.31}$$

irrespective of the fact that the single $L_i$ may be zero. To obtain absolute values, to this set of equations of order 1.1 some reactions of order, for example, 0.1 or 0.2 and the reverse, that is, 1.0 or 2.0, must be added. For the hydrogen-bromine reaction we had one term of order 0.2, the formation of two atoms from one bromine molecule, and the reverse reaction, the recombination of two bromine atoms, to form one bromine molecule, that is, of order 2.0. If we denote the contribution of these terms to the rate expression for $x_1$ by $R_1$, we had simply put

$$R_1 = 0.$$

We test the validity of this procedure. Assuming a steady state, we might have set

$$L_1 + R_1 \approx 0,$$
$$L_2 \qquad \approx 0,$$
$$\vdots \qquad \vdots \qquad\qquad (4.32)$$
$$L_n \qquad \approx 0,$$

and if we use Eq. (4.31), stating that $\sum L_i = 0$, irrespective of the existence of a steady state, we see that in this case we automatically obtain a splitting of the first Eq. (4.32) into two expressions,

$$L_1 = 0, \qquad R_1 = 0. \qquad\qquad (4.33)$$

This is, as already mentioned, only a special case of a chain reaction, but it is valid for the hydrogen-bromine reaction, and it explains many characteristic features of other chain reactions. We repeat: the complete chain reaction consists of the following.

(a) A closed sequence of reactions, or a reaction cycle, of order 1.1.

(b) An "appendix," to use Skrabal's terminology for the present purpose. The appendix consists of at least two reactions, one of order, for example, 0.2, generally of order 0, $k$, $k > 0$, and one of order 2.0, generally of order $l, 0, l > 0$, that is, we have introduced at least one reaction by which active particles are created, and one by which this species is destroyed.

Since it is easy to modify this appendix, or to replace it by another appendix, we recognize the source of many specific features of chain reactions. If we add a compound that destroys free atoms or radicals, as NO or propylene in many reactions, or oxygen in the hydrogen-chlorine reaction, we can explain a strong inhibiting effect, sometimes called "negative catalysis," which otherwise would not be understandable. On the other hand, if we add a substance which creates active particles (like $H_2O_2$ or organic peroxides in some reactions), then we may observe a pronounced or strong acceleration of the reaction, or a positive homogeneous catalysis. In the simple appendix systems this is easiest to see, because we can split the rate expressions into two parts, one determining the absolute value of one species.

Conditions are somewhat more involved, if reactions other than those of the closed sequence refer to more than one type of active species, for example, to $x_1$ and $x_2$. Then, in analogy to the preceding, we may write

$$L_1 + R_1 \approx 0$$

$$L_2 + R_2 \approx 0$$

$$\vdots \qquad \vdots \qquad\qquad\qquad\qquad (4.34)$$

$$L_n \qquad \approx 0$$

$$\overline{\sum L_i + R_1 + R_2 \approx 0,} \qquad \sum L_i \equiv 0, \qquad (4.35)$$

$$R_1 + R_2 \approx 0,$$

where the last identity holds as always. Now we can conclude, by adding all equations and making use of (4.35), that

$$R_1 + R_2 \approx 0 \quad \text{and} \quad L_1 + L_2 \approx 0, \qquad (4.36)$$

but it does not follow $L_1 \approx 0$ and $L_2 \approx 0$. Thus, we simply have to solve the inhomogeneous, and generally nonlinear system of algebraic equations (4.34), where the special relations (4.36) may be helpful but do not allow of a simplification analogous to that encountered previously.

We purposely omitted reactions of the type 1.2, or more generally $n$, $k$, $n > 0$, $k > n$, because these reactions may lead to instabilitites, even in isothermal systems, and need a treatment in a distinct section ("branching chain reaction"); compare Section V.

## V. Stability. Thermal and Chain Explosions

### A. General Discussion. Chain Explosions

In the preceding section we omitted steps with active particles participating according to 1.2 mechanisms (this applies to all reactions of type $n$, $k$, with $n > 0$, $k > n$), because these may lead to instabilities.

One first may ask what are the necessary conditions for the exclusion of this type of reaction. There is no easy definition for the simple chain type in contrast to the branching chain. Obviously a sufficient condition

consists in the participation of univalent atoms and radicals only, as in
the typical halogen-hydrogen reactions, the reactions of H and D atoms
with the corresponding molecules, reactions of all these atoms with
organic molecules, provided only univalent radicals are formed, as in

$$Cl + CH_4 \rightarrow HCl + CH_3, \qquad \text{etc.}$$

As soon as divalent atoms or radicals are involved complications may,
but need not, arise, for example, in NO-formation a simple chain is
feasible at sufficiently high temperatures,

$$N + O_2 \rightarrow NO + O,$$

$$O + N_2 \rightarrow NO + N,$$

though representing only part of the actual processes. On the other hand
the chain breaking action of NO, due to its radical character, is well
known and is a valuable tool in testing the chain character of gas reactions.
In order that instabilities may occur, it is usually necessary that the
overall reaction be exothermal. For, in the opposite case, endothermal
reaction, a sufficient increase in reaction rate would always lead to a
disturbance of the thermal equilibrium, in this case connected with a
decrease in temperature. Since almost all chemical reactions, with possible
exceptions for limited temperature ranges only, decrease in rate with
falling temperature, endothermal reactions almost always will be stable.
An exothermal reaction may lead to instabilities, irrespective of the
reaction mechanism. This will be dealt with below. Reactions that are
unstable due to intrinsic instabilities in the mechanism will also finally
lead to thermal instability—unless the amount of reactants is so limited
that its disappearance causes a decrease in reaction rate before thermal
instability is reached. Here we shall deal only with instabilities inherent
in the mechanism. As the oldest formal example one may quote the autocatalytic hydrolysis of an ester by hydrogen ions, with all the characteristics of a branching chain reaction, though it was never formulated
this way before Semenow's discovery of branching chain processes. If
we write, with AH acid, ROH alcohol,

$$AR + H_3O^+ \rightarrow AH + ROH + H^+,$$

$$AH + H^+ + 2H_2O \rightarrow A^- + 2H_3O^+,$$

we may combine these equations for conditions of almost complete dissociation of the acid into

$$AR + H_3O^+ + 2H_2O \xrightarrow{k_1} A^- + 2H_3O^+ + ROH \tag{5.1}$$

from which follows the rate expression

$$[\dot{H_3O^+}] = k_1[AR][H_3O^+], \tag{5.2}$$

$$[H_3O^+] = [H_3O^+]_0 \exp\{[AR]k_1t\}, \tag{5.3}$$

that is, an exponential increase in the rate of hydrolysis as long as the consumption of the ester is negligible and the temperature is being kept constant. If $[H_3O^+]$ was very small compared with $[AR]_0$, there can be a considerable relative increase in rate of hydrolysis before the consumption of the reactant becomes marked.

We can classify Eq. (5.1) as the simplest instance of a 1,2-reaction with $[H_3O^+] = X$, which, with the above simplification, would lead to an instability with exponential increase both in concentration of $H_3O^+$ and in reaction rate, provided $T$ is being kept constant. Since the reaction is not exothermal, there is no explosion. Under the same scheme falls a simplified model of the uranium fission if we write

$$^{235}U + n \rightarrow (1 + k)n + \text{fission products.}$$

Here, in contrast to all other sections, we denote by n the neutron. In either case, formally written without an explicit chain-breaking process, it would be impossible to write an equation of the type

$$\dot{x} = 0$$

and to see if this determines an explosion limit. By explosion we understand an unlimited formal increase of concentration or rate, or of both.

Once more, it ought to be stressed, however, that the type of all our equations allows of no singularity for $t < \infty$. Consequently, the formal condition for instability (explosion) always refers to an extrapolated fictitious process. This is not always quite satisfactory, but it is almost impossible to arrive at another sufficiently general relation, and the meaning of considering only the asymptotic behavior for $t \rightarrow \infty$ will probably never be misunderstood. The last equation, of course, gives an exponential increase in neutrons and in reaction rate. Since in nonstationary reactions very often a tremendous relative increase in rate is obtained, we treat the concentration of the original reactant as slowly varying, compared with that of the active intermediate, here neutrons, that is, as constant to a first approximation. If we imagine a homogeneous reaction of $^{235}U$ and neutrons in the presence of Cd we may write for the rate $r$ (with an arbitrary initial concentration of neutrons)

$$r = \dot{n} = k_1 n - k_2 n, \tag{5.4}$$

where $k_1$ is proportional to the concentration of $^{235}U$, $k_2$ to that of Cd. Inquiring into possible stability, one may try to put

$$r = n(k_1 - k_2) = 0 \quad \text{or} \quad k_1 = k_2, \tag{5.5}$$

that is, we do not obtain a value for the concentration of active particles (in analogy to the system of homogeneous first-order equations for the pure, nonbranching chain) but we obtain a condition for stability (or for a quasi-steady state). Considering that $k_1$ and $k_2$ contain the concentrations of $^{235}U$ and Cd, respectively, we see that this is a true condition, which may be fulfilled. For $k_1 < k_2$, an initially finite neutron concentration would decline exponentially with time, while for $k_1 > k_2$ it would increase exponentially. Equations (5.4) or (5.5) already correspond formally to Semenow's explosion condition for a branching chain reaction. But it gives, as it ought to, no definite answer for the rate, in case of stability. In order to obtain such an expression which then corresponds to Semenow's rate expression, we must introduce a neutron generating reaction of productivity $k_0$. Then we have

$$n = k_0 + k_1 n - k_2 n \tag{5.6}$$

with the steady-state condition

$$n = k_0/(k_2 - k_1), \quad k_2 > k_1, \tag{5.7}$$

while

$$k_2 = k_1 \tag{5.8}$$

gives the explosion limit as above.* Equation (5.6) yields upon integration (initial condition n = 0 at $t = 0$)

$$n = \{k_0/(k_1 - k_2)\}\{\exp(k_1 - k_2)t - 1\}, \quad k_1 > k_2. \tag{5.9}$$

---

* But then Eq. (5.7) is not applicable! Equations (5.7) and (5.8) are mutually exclusive.

From (5.6) or (5.9) we obtain for the initial rate $(\dot{n})_0 = k_0$, that is, concentration of active particles and rate first increase linearly with time, while for $t$ sufficiently large compared to $1/(k_1 - k_2)$ this increase will turn into a further exponential increase with time. It might be pointed out that a chain breaking due to diffusion to the wall, with diffusion rate determining, is always formally a first-order process.* Thus in that case we may expect similar expressions as above, however, we have a rate that is inhomogeneous in space.

Consider reaction in an infinite vessel of parallel plates at $x = \pm d$, with chain destruction at the walls. We may write

$$D \, d^2n/dx^2 + \alpha n + k_0 = \dot{n}, \tag{5.10}$$

where $\alpha = k_1 - k_2$ is the "effective branching coefficient." With boundary condition $n = 0$ for $x = \pm d$, we obtain, upon integration and averaging from $-d$ to $+d$,

$$\bar{n} = [k_0/\alpha]\left\{\tan d \sqrt{\alpha/D} \Big/ d \sqrt{\alpha/D} - 1\right\}, \tag{5.11}$$

with the limiting condition for stability or for explosion depending on the point of view

$$d \sqrt{\alpha/D} = \pi/2, \qquad \alpha = \pi^2 D/4d^2. \tag{5.12}$$

$\alpha$ is formally a first-order rate constant, as is $\pi^2 D/4d^2$, which may be considered the average rate of destruction of active particles at the walls for the above conditions. If, in addition to a first-order chain breaking, we have second-order breaking (as due to combination of two radicals, which, of course, never happens with neutrons) we formally write

$$\dot{n} = k_0 + k_1 n - k_2 n - k_3 n^2. \tag{5.13}$$

It is not by chance, that, so far, we always consider reactions with one type of active particles only. The condition for a stationary state (or stability) gives a quadratic equation for n,

$$n^2 = \{k_0 + k_1 n - k_2 n\}/k_3, \tag{5.14}$$

---

* Compare Jost (1965). Formally the above means: if we want to have a definite value for the concentration of active particles and of the rate, we must introduce an inhomogeneity into the equation.

where all constants and concentrations, as always, are positive. In addition, we may expect critical conditions only for $(k_1 - k_2) > 0$; consequently, (5.14) has always a solution for finite n, and from this point of view, we formally shall never have explosion. For sufficient increase in n the right-hand side of Eq. (5.13) would vanish. However, reactions of this type may lead to reaction rates sufficiently high to disturb the temperature equilibrium of the system. For examples, where the consumption of the reactants also has been considered we refer to Semenow (1935, 1954, 1958, 1959), Frank-Kamenetskii (1955), Jost (1938, 1939, 1941, 1946, 1965), Kondratjew (1958), and von Müffling (1943).

We have to point out two more topics.

1. The case of quadratic branching, formally represented by an equation like

$$B + X + X \to C + (2 + k)X, \qquad k > 0.$$

This case, as to the question of stability, does not introduce essentially new concepts. With initial condition $x = 0$, the question of stability is essentially settled by consideration of the first-order terms. In case of stability, the second-order terms remain negligible, in case of explosion, this will occur a fortiori if positive second-order terms are included, provided no active particles are created from outside.

2. The case of more than one type of active particle, without and with second-order terms.

If we write chains with more than one active species, neglecting reactions of order 0, 1 [or 0, k, with $k > 0$], and reactions of order 1,0 [or $k, 0$ with $k > 0$], but admitting reactions of order 1, 2 [or generally 1, $k$, $k > 1$], we must write (see Jost 1965)

$$X_1 + B_1 \to R_1 + \sum_i \nu_{1i} X_i$$
$$\vdots$$
$$X_j + B_j \to R_j + \sum_i \nu_{ji} X_i \qquad \text{(I)}$$
$$\vdots$$
$$X_n + B_n \to R_n + \nu_{n1} X_1 + \sum_{i=2}^{n} \nu_{ni} X_i.$$

We emphasize: in order to have a closed sequence, one species, $X_1$ must at least once reappear on the right. We wrote this explicitly for the $n$th equation. All reactions are first order with respect to the species $X_i$

entering into the reaction. In order to admit the possibility of instability, at least one equation must be of order 1, $k$, $k > 1$. In our formulation we left all possibilities open. In the complete reaction scheme, in addition, there must be at least one step with order 1, 0, accounting for chain breaking. While in a normal nonbranching chain, with reactions of order 1, 1 only, there was always the identity* $\sum L_i \equiv 0$, such an identity no longer exists, the sum of the above equations will not vanish.

If we now write a scheme of rate equations according to I, we have

$$\dot{x}_i = \sum_j \alpha_{ij} x_j, \qquad i, j = 1, 2, \ldots, m, \quad m \leq n, \qquad (5.15)$$

where the meaning of the $\alpha_{ij}$ follows from the explicit reaction expressions I. The equations (5.15) still remain homogeneous and first order, because the equations I are all of first order to the left. We may attempt at putting (5.15) $= 0$, in order to investigate the possibility of a steady state, or a limiting condition for explosion. One realizes at once that a system of equations, derived from (5.15),

$$\dot{x}_i = \sum_j \alpha_{ij} x_j = 0, \qquad (5.16)$$

has normally only the trivial solution

$$x_i = 0$$

because the determinant of this system, without additional constraints, will not vanish.

Before, we found a relation among "constants" (which usually still contain concentrations of stable compounds) as critical condition, we may now try to set the determinant of the system $\alpha_{ij}$ equal to zero,

$$\det || \alpha_{ij} || = 0, \qquad (5.17)$$

and try if there is a solution. This solution is an equation among rate constants and concentrations of stable compounds (and of temperature, because the rate constants depend on temperature) and it will now represent the critical condition for explosion. Here, further complications must be envisaged: among others the appearance of second-order, positive or negative terms in the concentrations of active species. Again positive terms will not interfere. With negative, second-order terms, however,

---

* Compare Section IV.

the situation differs from that in the case of one type of active species only. Jost and von Müffling (1938) have given an example with one negative term and more than one active species, which still may yield explosion. For these questions we refer to literature and to Chapter 12, Vol. VI,B by Hoyermann of this volume.

## B. THERMAL INSTABILITY

We cannot conclude this section on stability in time* without considering thermal stability. We recall the geometric properties of the function $\exp(-1/\vartheta)$, with $\vartheta = T/\Theta$, $\Theta$ a characteristic temperature, often given by $\Theta = \Delta H_{ac}/R$, $\Delta H_{ac}$ enthalpy of activation, $R$ gas constant. If we compare $\exp x$ with $\exp(-1/\vartheta)$, $0 \leq \vartheta < +\infty$, the following values of the abscissa are corresponding:

$$x = -\infty \quad -1 \quad 0,$$
$$\vartheta = \quad 0 \quad 1 \quad \infty.$$

The exponential $\exp(-1/\vartheta)$ is much more inconvenient in analytical expressions than $\exp x$. If the neighborhood of a definite value $\vartheta_0$ is of interest, it is advisable to expand around $\vartheta_0$ by setting

$$\vartheta = \vartheta_0[1 + (\vartheta - \vartheta_0)/\vartheta_0] = \vartheta_0[1 + \delta], \qquad \delta = (\vartheta - \vartheta_0)/\vartheta_0,$$
$$\exp(-1/\vartheta) = \exp(-1/\vartheta_0)\exp(\delta/\vartheta_0),$$
(5.18)

replacing the exponential of the reciprocal argument by a simple exponential of $\delta$. The exponential of $-1/\vartheta$ has an inflection point for $\vartheta = 1/2$, and approaches asymptotically the value 1, as $\vartheta \to \infty$. If we are dealing with a self-heating system (i.e., an exothermal gas reaction, proceeding in a closed vessel), it is obvious to first try Newton's cooling law for the heat loss of the system, that is, to draw a straight line in Figs. 6 and 7 passing through the point $T_0$ (corresponding to the constant temperature of the reaction vessel).†

The question of stability has already been seen by van't Hoff (1884) and formulated: "It would not be difficult to formulate the preceding

* We refer to Section VIII for the question of stability in space, which we omit here.
† One should not forget that an exponential $\exp(-E/RT)$ in physical formulas usually is only an interpolation for a limited temperature range. Consequently, the quantitative relations obtained for a wide temperature range should not be taken too serious, and extrapolations are uncertain.

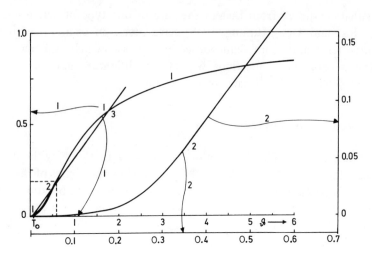

Fig. 6. The function $\exp(-1/\vartheta)$ for $0 < \vartheta < 6$, curve 1 left scale and upper abscissa scale. Curve 2 for $0 < \vartheta < 0.6$, right scale. Abscissa $\times 10$; ordinate $\times 10/1.6$; inflection point at $\vartheta = 0.5$. Except for catalytic reactions (not discussed here) only curve 2, corresponding to the part in the dashed rectangle of curve 1, is of interest.

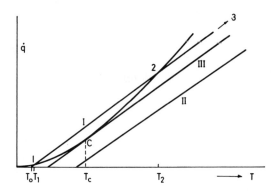

Fig. 7. The curve corresponds to the lower part of Fig. 6, now representing rate of heat production $\dot{q}$, proportional with $r$. Abscissa is temperature, $T_0$ corresponds to the constant temperature of the container. Straight lines I, II, and III correspond to Newton's cooling law, for varying conditions. II: cooling always below heating, explosion. I: stability, between intersections 1 and 2 cooling always above heating, between $T_0$ and $T_1$ (stationary temperature in the container) heating up to, but not above $T_1$. Intersection 2 cannot be reached under the given conditions (temperature of the container being kept constant). For other conditions (i.e., heating by adiabatic compression above 2, $T_2$) instability; this could correspond to ignition by adiabatic compression and to the knocking process in an engine. III: tangent to the curve in point $C$, critical ignition condition as discussed in the text.

mathematically; in the meantime we may review it as follows: Ignition temperature is that temperature, at which the original heat loss (due to conduction, etc.) equals the heat produced by the transformation (Umwandlung)." A qualitative drawing corresponding to Fig. 7 is due to Taffanel and Le Floche (1913).

It is obvious, without calculation, that a stable state can only be obtained if the Newton straight line cuts the exponential curve, Fig. 7; that is, I may, II never can lead to a stable state. A few further remarks are possible. If we write the exponential

$$\exp(-\Theta/T), \qquad \Theta = \Delta H_{ac}/R, \qquad (5.19)$$

then for normal reactions $\Theta$ could hardly be smaller than 10,000, that is, $\vartheta = T/\Theta$ never higher than about 0.2 if we admit the extremely high temperature of 2000 K for the reactor. Since the inflection point of the exponential is situated at $\vartheta = 0.5$, and since the third intersection of the straight line with the curve 3 is always situated above the inflection point, only points 1 and 2 need be considered for a stable state. Now it is seen that point 2 cannot be stable. For, assume that 2 has been reached, and that the heats, produced by chemical reaction and removed by conduction and convection, exactly cancel. Then a slight disturbance may move the representative point by a small amount up or down the reaction curve. Above $T_2$ heat production will always surpass heat removal, and explosion will occur,* while below 2 heat removal will be increased relative to heat production, and the temperature will fall to point 1, where 1 represents stable reaction. The limiting case is the straight line III, tangent to the exponential curve in point B. This is the critical condition for explosion, first treated quantitatively by Semenow 1928.[†] The conditions for

* Obviously the case that point 3 will be reached need not be considered because $T_3$ usually will be above the temperature accessible by adiabatic reaction. If really the temperature should rise considerably above $T_2$, then always much of the original reactants will have been used up, while the discussion about stability usually refers to the very early stages of reaction only. The situation may change completely if we are dealing with a catalytic reaction. Here the effective energy of activation (or more exactly: the formal expression $RT^2 \, d \ln k_{eff}/dT$, where $k_{eff}$ is the effective rate constant) may become rather small, and then the region around and above the inflection point of the corresponding exponential curve may gain importance. However, here we are not dealing with heterogeneous catalysis and with technical reactors, and it may suffice to point out this problem; compare also Chap. 12, by Hoyermann, Vol. VI,B.

[†] Compare also Jost (1939, 1946), Lewis and van Elbe (1961), Frank-Kamenetskii (1938, 1947), Vulis (1961).

the tangent are (Fig. 7) heat removal $\dot{q}_2 = A(T - T_c)$ (Newton), equal to heat production $\dot{q}_1 = VQf \exp(-\Delta H_{ac}/RT)$ (Arrhenius), $A$ constant, $T$ average gas temperature, $T_0$ constant temperature of the container. The total heat production per unit time $\dot{q}_1$ is assumed to be proportional to an Arrhenius expression, where the dependence of $f$ on concentrations and pressure has not been specified, $Q$ is the heat of reaction for unit transformation, $V$ the reaction volume. The condition for $B$, Fig. 7, is

$$\dot{q}_1 = \dot{q}_2, \tag{5.20}$$

$$(\partial/\partial T)\dot{q}_1 = (\partial/\partial T)\dot{q}_2 \quad \text{for} \quad T = T_c. \tag{5.21}$$

This gives

$$QVf \exp(-\Delta H_{ac}/RT_c) = A(T_c - T_0), \tag{5.22}$$

$$(\Delta H_{ac}/RT_c^2)QVf \exp(-\Delta H_{ac}/RT_c) = A. \tag{5.23}$$

Division of Eq. (5.22) by Eq. (5.23) yields

$$RT_c^2/\Delta H_{ac} = T_c - T_0. \tag{5.24}$$

If we knew that $(T_c - T_0)/T_0 \ll 1$, then we could replace, to a first approximation, $T_c$ on the left-hand side of Eq. (5.24) by $T_0$, and obtain

$$T_c \approx T_0 + RT_0^2/\Delta H_{ac}. \tag{5.25}$$

Knowing that $\Delta H_{ac}/RT_0 \approx 20$ to $50$, we have

$$T_c - T_0 \approx T_0/(20 \text{ to } 50), \tag{5.26}$$

or better, as an approximation,

$$0.02 < (T_c - T_0)/T_0 < 0.05, \tag{5.27}$$

which gives a justification to Eq. (5.25). Solving the quadratic equation (5.24) for $T_c$ and expanding the square root up to second-order terms in $T_0/\Delta H_{ac}$, we find

$$T_c - T_0 \approx RT_0^2/\Delta H_{ac} \tag{5.28}$$

in accordance with Eq. (5.25). Setting $f$ proportional to a power of $P$ while leaving $A$ independent of $P$, we gain relations between $\ln P$ and $1/T$, as found similarly for chain explosions; that is, formal criteria, normally, are not sufficient to discern between chain and heat explosions.

We want to point out that one can easily obtain a relation for the ignition (or explosion) condition which does not contain arbitrary factors like $A$ of Newton's law, and which, at the same time, is quite rigorous, at least under the usually valid assumption that the temperature rise up to the critical temperature $T_c$ is only a few percent of the possible maximum reaction temperature.

The procedure, due to Frank-Kamenetskii (1938, 1955), is as follows. We write the expression for heat loss, due to conduction, and heat production, due to chemical reaction, per unit volume:

$$\lambda \, \Delta T + Q\mathrm{r} = \varrho \bar{c}_p \dot{T}, \tag{5.29}$$

where $\Delta$ is the Laplace operator. With the above assumption we look for a possible stationary state, that is, we try to equal Eq. (5.29) to zero. After dividing by $\varrho \bar{c}_p$ we have

$$\varkappa \, \Delta T + Qr/\varrho \bar{c}_p = 0, \tag{5.30}$$

where $\varkappa = \lambda/\varrho \bar{c}_p$ is the thermometric conductivity, $r$ the reaction rate, $\varrho$ density, and $\bar{c}_p$ the average specific heat.* The idea of the further treatment is the following. First we introduce dimensionless coordinates, $\xi = x/a$, where $a$ is a linear dimension, that is, the radius of a sphere or infinite cylinder, or half the thickness of a plane parallel vessel, and

$$\Phi = \Delta H_{ac}\varphi/RT_0{}^2, \tag{5.31}$$

where, as above, $\Delta H_{ac}$ is the enthalpy of activation, $\varphi = T - T_0$, and the following expression has been used for the reaction rate:

$$r = z \exp[-\Delta H_{ac}/RT].$$

In order to get rid of the clumsy exponential of the reciprocal $T$, the exponential is expanded in the neighborhood of $T_0$, as discussed above (see Section V,B).

$$\exp[-\Delta H_{ac}/RT] = \exp[-\Delta H_{ac}/RT_0] \exp[\varphi \, \Delta H_{ac}/RT_0{}^2]. \tag{5.32}$$

---

* For higher precision it would have been necessary to consider the temperature dependence of $\lambda$, replacing $\lambda \Delta T$ by div $\lambda$ grad $T$, which, however, would lead to considerable complication. At the same time it would be necessary to take into consideration local density changes due to temperature differences.

Thus we finally obtain an expression*

$$\Delta_\xi \Phi + \psi \exp \Phi = 0, \tag{5.33}$$

where the dimensionless constant $\psi$ must contain all individual constants. Equation (5.33) is to be solved for the boundary condition $\Phi = 0$ for $\xi = 1$.

With the above assumption $\psi$ has the meaning

$$\psi = \{\Delta H_{ac}/RT_0^2\}\{Q/\lambda\}a^2 z \exp[-\Delta H_{ac}/RT_0]. \tag{5.34}$$

Integration of Eq. (5.33) has been carried out for the three cases (see Fig. 8): infinite plane parallel vessel of thickness $2a$, sphere and infinite cylinder of radius $a$. The critical values of $\psi$ above which a stationary solution is impossible are

| $\psi$ = | 0.88 | 2.00 | 3.32 |
|---|---|---|---|
| maximum temperature rise | 1.2 | 1.37 | $1.62 \times RT_0^2/\Delta H_{ac}$ |
| | infinite plane parallel vessel of thickness $2a$ | infinite cylinder of radius $a$ | sphere of radius $a$ |

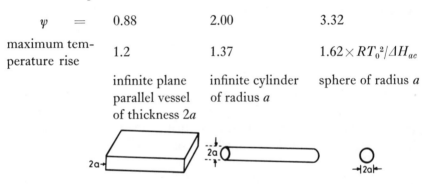

FIG. 8.   Shapes of reaction vessel, discussed according to Eq. (5.33).

A necessary condition for the applicability of the method of a steady state is the assumption that the temperature rise be sufficiently small, compared to $T_0$, and the values above, in connection with former estimates of $RT_0/\Delta H_{ac}$, show that this is justified. It should be emphasized that this treatment presents a tremendous progress beyond Semenow's original method because now there is no arbitrary parameter left in the result, contrary to the factor $A$ of Newton's law.

It is obvious that Frank-Kamenetskii's treatment, too, is an approximation only, though a very convincing one, and it could be further improved. We refer here only to a paper by Gray et al. (1970). Gray and

* $\Delta_\xi$ means the Laplace operator with respect to the dimensionless coordinates $\xi$.

co-workers treat the case of special practical importance that the heating of a reactive, especially a combustible mixture is asymmetrical, while Frank-Kamenetskii considers the symmetrical case only. They deal especially with a hollow sphere, heated at the inner surface. Approximating the exponential near a reference temperature $T_i$ by a fifth power expression (quintic),

$$\exp(-E/RT) \approx \exp(-E/RT_0)(\alpha + \beta\Theta)^5, \qquad (5.35)$$

where $\alpha$ and $\beta$ are constants and $\Theta = E(T - T_0)/RT_0^2$ they obtain an analytically solvable equation.

Gray *et al.* (1970) further investigated thermal effects accompanying spontaneous ignition in gases. In actual experiments, strong deviations from idealized conditions used in theoretical work may occur, as is to be expected. If a gas is admitted to a heated reaction vessel, there may arise considerable temperature differences due to compression of the gas first entering by the following gas. Temperature differences may amount to ~50°C, a quasi-steady state may be attained within some tenths of a second. Further it is confirmed that in low pressure experiments convective heat transfer usually may be neglected. As examples, the slow exothermic and the explosive decomposition of diethyl peroxide were investigated in detail. Boddington *et al.* (1971), treated the thermal theory of spontaneous ignition and the criticality in bodies of arbitrary shape.

## C. STABILITY OF THE STEADY STATE. OSCILLATIONS

Thermodynamics requires that systems near equilibrium approach equilibrium with monotonic change of the appropriately chosen function, for example, decrease of the Gibbs free energy $G$, $P = $ const, $T = $ const. Thermodynamics of irreversible processes, in addition, excludes true oscillations of the concentrations; compare Section VI. Near a *true* steady state outside the equilibrium state these conditions do not hold. Consequently, a steady state, in contrast to real equilibrium, need not be stable. Further, in case of instability, this may lead to explosion, or may lead to true oscillations, both of which are excluded for the vicinity of chemical equilibrium.

It ought to be stressed that here we are dealing with a "true" steady state; that is, we assume for the several reactants and products that

$$\dot{x}_i = 0, \qquad i = 1, 2, \ldots, n \qquad (5.36)$$

holds exactly. To what extent results obtained here might be applicable to certain pseudo-steady states shall not be discussed at present.

The existence of a true steady state implies several physical conditions not encountered in normal homogeneous reactions, or, for a limited time only, as an approximation. Thus there is no contradiction if we consider a formally steady state, and closer inspection may show that this steady state is either unstable or may exhibit oscillations, when slightly disturbed. If a system is to be exactly steady, reactants must be supplied at the same rate as they are used up, and products must be removed correspondingly. This requires at least one flow process. Examples are a stationary burning flame or a flow reactor, appropriately run. But also a living cell may approach conditions of a true steady state. Here, normally, diffusion flow will be more important than convective flow. In either case, the system usually will cease to be homogeneous, and generalized equations for convective and diffusive flow, chemical reaction, and often heat conduction must be applied. Conditions, at least in idealized limiting cases, may be simplified by assuming a very rapid mixing process (e.g., by stirring a reactor, or by assuming diffusion within a living cell to be very fast compared to the diffusion through the cell membrane, etc.). Reaction and diffusion in the living cell have been extensively treated by biophysicists, and have led to problems of stability which are outside the scope of this article; compare Rashewsky (1938, 1960) and Frank-Kamenetskii (1939 and later). It is well known that for steady states far from equilibrium instabilities in space and true oscillations may appear, as in case of "polyhedral" disturbed flames; compare Section VIII and Fig. 9.

In the case of the flame, convective flow and heat flow, in addition to reaction and diffusion, play a role. Rashewsky gave already examples of reactions in a cell leading to true oscillations. On account of its general interest we mention Prigogine's and Lefever's work (1969) on instabilities in biological systems, Chernavskaya and Chernavskii's (1960, 1961; see also Sel'kov 1967, 1968) discussion of periodic phenomena in photosynthesis of plants, starting from the Calvin cycle.

We shall deal briefly with this problem, not on account of the photosynthesis, but because it presents a model for periodic reactions that is not formally constructed ad hoc but starts from a real observed process. In order to treat this mathematically, however, a number of radical simplifications are unavoidable. Thus, finally, two independent differential equations are retained, referring to the formation of a triose $c_3$ and a hexose $c_6$. For us it is irrelevant whether this scheme really applies to

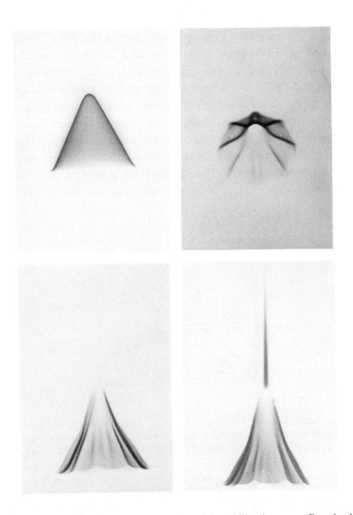

FIG. 9. "Polyhedric" flames, as examples of instability in space. Premixed gas of benzene with air, approaching the burner mouth in laminar flow, and burning above a nozzle, guaranteeing almost constant velocity distribution above the mouth. Flames are protected from perturbation by secondary air with a flame separator (circular or rectangular outer tube, not visible). In case of stability the flames would exhibit a shape very close to a geometrical cone 9a. The pronounced deviations are due to the interaction of mass flow by convection and by specific diffusion, of heat conduction, and of chemical reaction. In this way a stationary burning of lean hydrogen containing mixtures in three or more single "threads" is possible, though for combustion in a homogeneous conical surface the temperature would remain below the minimum required to maintain reaction. Benzene concentration increasing from *a* to *d*.

45

the observed phenomena. The equations are treated\* by Chernavskaya and Chernavskii in two steps. In order to find the limiting conditions for stability, it is sufficient to linearize the differential equations near the steady state and find for this linearized system the steady state condition. The linearization is insufficient for dealing with the unstable case. Here the nonlinearized equations must be discussed. This is possible only after reasonable numerical coefficients have been introduced. Then either the differential equation must be solved numerically, or one may discuss the behavior qualitatively by construction of a field of isoclines in the "characteristic plane" of $c_6 - c_3$ (by dividing the former differential

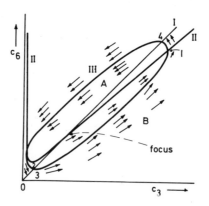

FIG. 10.   "Limit Cycle." The focus at $c_3 = c_6 = 1$ (the numerical values are arbitrarily normalized) is a point of unstable stationarity. Any small perturbation will lead the representative point away from the focus, and it will approach asymptotically the "limit cycle," that is, the ellipse-like curve, according to the arrows of the direction field. The same holds for a representative point outside the "cycle" in the field $B$, where the curve approaches the cycle from the outside. The straight line I is the locus for slope zero, the hyperbola II for slope infinity, in the focus every slope is possible. A system of reaction equations for a triose (concentration $c_3$) and a hexose (concentration $c_6$) from the Calvin cycle has been adapted by Chernavskaya and Chernavskii to give this type of instability.

equations for $c_6$ and $c_3$, an equation for $dc_6/dc_3$ is obtained). This has been done in Fig. 10, taken from Chernavskii and Chernavskaya. The point $c_6 = c_3 = 1$ is singular; here the isoclines may have any direction. The straight line I is the locus of isoclines with slope zero (as seen in point 4), while the hyperbola II is the locus for isoclines of infinite slope

\* The quoted translation contains a number of printing errors, which, however, are rather easily traced. This paper may be consulted for further references.

(see point 1). There exists a closed curve III, called, according to Poincaré, limit cycle. Any integral curve, starting inside the limit cycle, will approach this asymptotically from the inside, while any curve starting from the outside will do the same from the outside. The limit cycle corresponds to a periodic movement; compare Fig. 11.

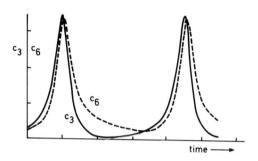

FIG. 11.   Periodicity in time, derived from the reactive system discussed in Fig. 10; compare the text, according to Chernavskii and Chernavskaya.

As a further example Sel'kov has treated mathematically self-oscillations in glycolysis, the phosphofructokinase reaction (Sel'kov, 1967, 1968; both sources contain further references).

Prigogine and Lefever *et al.* (1968, 1969) (see also Prigogine, 1967; Prigogine and Nicolis, 1967) start from the preceding example to show that for unstable steady states instabilities in space may also result (see also Sel'kov, 1968; Darvey and Matlak, 1967; Coleman and Mizel, 1968; Puri, 1967).

We shall now give some details due to Chernavskaya and Chernavskii.

An investigation of the formal consequences of a rather complex reaction mechanism is not feasible unless rather drastic simplifications are introduced, restricting the number of species explicitly appearing to two. This first step will not be discussed here in detail. The authors start from the Calvin cycle for photosynthesis (see the review articles by Rabinovitch, 1951; Calvin *et al.*, 1952; Lumry *et al.*, 1953; Spikes and Mayne, 1960; Robinson, 1964). With reasonable, occasionally rather robust simplification they arrive at two rate expressions for a triose (concentration $c_3$) and a hexose (concentration $c_6$),

$$dc_3/dt = c_3{}^2 - (\alpha_2/\alpha_1)c_3 c_6 + (\alpha_0/\alpha_1),$$

$$dc_6/dt = (\beta_1/\alpha_1)\{c_3{}^2 - (\beta_2/\beta_1)c_6{}^2 - (\beta_3/\beta_1)c_3 c_6\}. \tag{5.37}$$

The simplifications introduced imply the choice of a properly chosen dimensionless time $t$ (by which the first coefficient in the first equation was reduced to unity). In addition, the influence of the light intensity and of the carbon dioxide concentration is not considered explicitly, but is supposed to be taken care of by the numerical values of the rate constants.

Stoichiometric relations and inspection of the relative magnitudes of the several constants lead to the conditions

$$\beta_1/\beta_2 = 7, \qquad \beta_1/\beta_3 = 7/6, \qquad \beta_2/\beta_3 = 1/6,$$
$$\alpha_2/\alpha_1 = 1 + \alpha_0 + \alpha_1 \approx 1. \tag{5.38}$$

For the sake of simplicity the concentrations $c_3$ and $c_6$ in Eq. (5.37) are supposed to be normalized to one for the stationary state, and the behavior near the stationary state is investigated by putting

$$c_3 = 1 + x, \qquad c_6 = 1 + y, \qquad x, y \ll 1. \tag{5.39}$$

Inserting these expressions into Eq. (5.37) and neglecting second-order terms, we have with Eq. (5.38)

$$\dot{x} = [1 - \alpha_0/\alpha_1]x - [1 + \alpha_0/\alpha_1]y,$$
$$\dot{y} = [x - y]8\beta_1/7\alpha_1. \tag{5.40}$$

The characteristic equation for this system of first-order homogeneous differential equations is

$$\begin{vmatrix} 1 - \alpha_0/\alpha_1 - \lambda & -[1 + \alpha_0/\alpha_1] \\ 8\beta_1/7\alpha_1 & -8\beta_1/7\alpha_1 - \lambda \end{vmatrix} = 0 \tag{5.41}$$

with the roots

$$\lambda_{1,2} = -\tfrac{1}{2}[8\beta_1/7\alpha_1 - 1 + \alpha_0/\alpha_1]$$
$$\pm \sqrt{[8\beta_1/7\alpha_1 - 1 + \alpha_0/\alpha_1]^2/4 - 16\alpha_0\beta_1/7\alpha_1^2}. \tag{5.42}$$

The sign of the real part of the two roots determines the stability of the system, for positive sign the solution $\propto \exp(\lambda t)$ will increase with time, that is, be unstable, while for the negative sign it will decrease, that is, after a perturbation return to the stationary state. Generally the solution will be periodical, that is, will be given by a spiral around the stationary point, unless the root in Eq. (5.42) vanishes.

Thus the solution is stable for

$$8\beta_1/7\alpha_1 - 1 + \alpha_0/\alpha_1 > 0 \tag{5.43}$$

and unstable for

$$8\beta_1/7\alpha_1 - 1 + \alpha_0/\alpha_1 < 0, \tag{5.44}$$

the critical condition being

$$8\beta_1/7\alpha_1 - 1 + \alpha_0/\alpha_1 = 0 \tag{5.45}$$

or approximately

$$\beta_1/\alpha_1 = 7(1 - \alpha_0/\alpha_1)/8 \approx 0.87 \tag{5.46}$$

using Eq. (5.38).

With increasing $\alpha_1$ (as, for instance, with increasing light intensity), a stable state may pass into an unstable one.

In order to find out details, the nonlinearized equations (5.37) must be treated. Since an analytical solution is impossible, a geometrical treatment of the time-independent equation, derived by dividing the two equations (5.37), is tried:

$$\frac{dc_6}{dc_3} = \left(\frac{\beta_1}{\alpha_1}\right) \frac{c_3{}^2 - c_6{}^2/7 - 6c_3c_6/7}{c_3{}^2 - 21c_3c_6/20 + 1/20}, \tag{5.47}$$

where reasonable numerical values have been inserted for the rate constants, and $\beta_1/\alpha_1$, in the region of instability but not too far from the critical value 0.87, will be chosen equal to 0.67. We construct the field of isoclines in the $c_3c_6$ plane; see Fig. 10.

The curves

$$c_3{}^2 - c_6{}^2/7 - 6c_3c_6/7 = 0$$

and

$$c_3{}^2 - 21c_3c_6/20 + 1/20 = 0 \tag{5.48}$$

give respectively the loci for $dc_6/dc_3 = 0$ and $\infty$. The first equation corresponds to the straight lines $c_6 = c_3$ and $c_6 = -7c_3$, of which the second is meaningless because negative concentrations are impossible. The second equation

$$(21c_6/20 - c_3)c_3 = 1/20 \tag{5.49}$$

is a hyperbola, which intersects the straight line $c_3 = c_6$ in the point $c_3 = c_6 \simeq 1$, which is singular with all directions for $dc_3/dc_3$ possible; see Fig. 10.

This is shown in Fig. 10 after Chernavskii and Chernavskaya, where in addition to the isoclines determined by Eqs. (5.48) and (5.49) the field of isoclines is inserted, as obtained by choosing pairs of numerical values for $c_3$ and $c_6$ and calculating by means of Eq. (5.47) the corresponding slopes $dc_6/dc_3$. This has been done in Fig. 10 by Chernavskaya and Chernavskii. The focus as point of intersection of straight line I and hyperbola II is situated at 1,1; the ellipse-like curve III is the limit cycle (cf. Poincaré, or a text on differential equations, e.g., Cesari and Hurewicz). This limit cycle separates the regions A and B, a representative point may approach this curve from the outside or the inside on a spiral path asymptotically, but no path can cross the limit cycle. Numerical integration of one of the original differential equations allows of a determination of the time dependence of the process; see Fig. 11.

Prigogine *et al.* (1967, 1969) have discussed these phenomena from the point of view of thermodynamics of irreversible processes, and have, in addition to the instability in time, discussed and observed instabilities in space; compare Section VIII.

Space does not permit to go into details of periodic (oscillating) reactions. Recently Higgins (1967) gave a comprehensive report on this question to which we refer. Most examples are known from biosystems, in heterogeneous systems, and usually in systems consisting primarily of a liquid phase. It is, however, quite simple to obtain periodic reactions in gaseous flow systems, for example, in hydrocarbon–air (or oxygen) mixtures, passing through a reaction tube, heated to 250 to 350°C. The periodic process then may consist in a sequence of cool flames. Here the interaction of chemical reaction, flow, and transport processes is essential. There is one example quoted by Higgins which at least was supposed to occur in a truly homogeneous liquid system: the reactions (as formulated by Bray, 1921)

$$2H_2O_2 + I_2 \rightarrow 2HIO_3 + 4H_2O$$

and

$$5H_2O_2 + 2HIO_3 \rightarrow 5O_2 + I_2 + 6H_2O$$

corresponding to an overall reaction

$$H_2O_2 \rightarrow H_2O + \tfrac{1}{2}O_2.$$

There are doubts whether the reaction is really homogeneous. For the discussion of oscillating reactions we refer, in addition to the above quoted review and to Prigogine's work, to Bak (1959, 1963) and, with respect to the last example to Rice and Reiff (1927).

Since it can be clearly stated that near equilibrium in a truly homogeneous system oscillations do not occur, this theory is less important for stable gas reactions than it is for liquid systems, and especially for living matter and for the growth of interacting populations. For periodic cool flames in gases, compare Sieg (1965).

## VI. Systems of First-Order Reactions. Microscopic Reversibility. Relaxation Systems

### A. GENERAL TREATMENT OF FIRST-ORDER SYSTEMS

Onsager (1931), in his derivation of the reciprocity relations, considered the "triangular" reaction* between compounds I, II, and III:

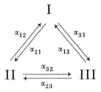

The arrows indicate the mutual transformations, $\alpha_{ij}$ is the constant of the rate of unimolecular transformation, leading from $j$ to $i$. The reason for this choice of the subscripts will be obvious from an inspection of the determinantal equation (6.5). This reaction scheme had received early consideration and it had been recognized, both that it could formally lead to periodic reactions and that it might suggest the formulation of the principle of detailed balancing.[†]

If equilibrium with respect to each binary reaction system is required, this leads to the equations

$$x_{1e} : x_{2e} = \alpha_{12} : \alpha_{21}, \quad x_{2e} : x_{3e} = \alpha_{23} : \alpha_{32}, \quad x_{3e} : x_{1e} = \alpha_{31} : \alpha_{13}, \quad (6.1)$$

where $x_i$ is the concentration of component $i$ ($i =$ I, II, III) and the

---

* Compare also: Hirnjak (1911), Lotka (since 1910), Skrabal (1941), and Volterra (1910).

† Since in a closed system entropy never can decrease, periodicity can mean only sufficiently damped oscillations compatible with thermodynamic requirements. The rigorous formulation is: the characteristic equation (6.5) for $\lambda$ may have complex roots, unless additional restrictions beyond those of equilibrium thermodynamics are imposed.

subscript $e$ refers to equilibrium. This system of equations was later called the principle of detailed balancing. Already in the early papers it was recognized that Eq. (6.1) was sufficient to exclude periodic reactions (by an elementary, though slightly cumbersome inspection of the resulting second-order equation). From Eq. (6.1) follows one relation among the $\alpha_{ij}$:

$$\alpha_{12}\alpha_{23}\alpha_{31} = \alpha_{13}\alpha_{32}\alpha_{21}. \qquad (6.2)$$

The above reaction scheme leads to the system of (dependent) rate expressions,

$$\dot{x}_i = \sum_k \alpha_{ik}x_k, \quad i, k = 1, 2, 3, \qquad (6.3)$$

where, on account of $\sum_i \dot{x}_i = 0$,

$$\sum_i \alpha_{ik} = 0, \quad \text{i.e.,} \quad \alpha_{ii} = -\sum_j{}' \alpha_{ji}, \quad j \neq i. \qquad (6.4)$$

The routine method of solving the system (6.3) leads to the "characteristic equation"

$$\begin{vmatrix} \alpha_{11} - \lambda & \alpha_{12} & \alpha_{13} \\ \alpha_{21} & \alpha_{22} - \lambda & \alpha_{23} \\ \alpha_{31} & \alpha_{32} & \alpha_{33} - \lambda \end{vmatrix} = 0. \qquad (6.5)$$

Due to the condition $\sum \dot{x}_i = 0$ only two roots are nonvanishing, Eq. (6.5) is a quadratic equation for $\lambda$, and the determinant of the $\alpha_{ik}$ vanishes. If one formally writes this as a cubic equation, one obtains $\lambda = 0$, expressing the fact that

$$x_1 + x_2 + x_3 = c \exp(0t).$$

We do not follow Onsager's treatment, which refers to the proximity of equilibrium, but we shall prove (see Jost, 1947, 1950) that Eq. (6.5) can be transformed to a new system with symmetric coefficients, that is, the symmetry of the so-called "secular equation," which has only real roots.

Turning back to a former remark, Eq. (6.1) shows that it was rational to define the $\alpha_{ik}$ in the above sense because this leads to the usual matrix notation in Eq. (6.5). The following proof was first given by the author in 1946. We consider a system of an arbitrary number of compounds I, II, III, etc., with unimolecular transformation between any pair of compounds where, as above, the rate constant for the transformation I → II is given by $\alpha_{21}$, etc. For more than three components, in addition to the former relations (6.1) and (6.2), there arise cycles of four and more, like

$$\alpha_{12}\alpha_{23}\alpha_{34}\alpha_{41} = \alpha_{14}\alpha_{43}\alpha_{32}\alpha_{21}, \quad \text{etc.} \tag{6.6}$$

It is not required that all $\alpha_{ij}$'s be $\neq 0$. In the general case, with a system of equations

$$\dot{x}_i = \sum_k \alpha_{ik}x_k, \qquad i, k = 1, 2, \ldots, n \tag{6.7}$$

the substitution $x \propto \exp(\lambda t)$ leads to the determinantal equation

$$\begin{vmatrix} \alpha_{11} - \lambda & \alpha_{12} & \alpha_{13} & \cdots & \alpha_{1n} \\ \alpha_{21} & \alpha_{22} - \lambda & \alpha_{23} & \cdots & \alpha_{2n} \\ \vdots & \vdots & \vdots & & \vdots \\ \alpha_{n1} & \alpha_{n2} & & \cdots & \alpha_{nn} - \lambda \end{vmatrix} = 0. \tag{6.8}$$

We prove that Eq. (6.8) has only real (negative) roots, by reducing Eq. (6.8) to the "secular equation."* This can be done the following way. The determinant (6.8) is multiplied by a factor

$$1 = \frac{\varrho_1\varrho_2\cdots\varrho_n}{\varrho_1\varrho_2\cdots\varrho_n} \tag{6.9}$$

in such a way that each factor of the numerator multiplies the column of equal number, and each factor of the denominator correspondingly each row. Thus we obtain

$$\begin{vmatrix} \beta_{11} - \lambda & \beta_{12} & \cdots & \beta_{1n} \\ \beta_{21} & \beta_{22} - \lambda & \cdots & \beta_{2n} \\ \vdots & \vdots & & \vdots \\ \beta_{n1} & \beta_{n2} & \cdots & \beta_{nn} - \lambda \end{vmatrix} = 0, \tag{6.10}$$

where

$$\beta_{ij} = \alpha_{ij}\varrho_j/\varrho_i. \tag{6.11}$$

We now require that the so far arbitrary $\varrho_l$ be chosen such that

$$\beta_{ij} = \beta_{ji}, \tag{6.12}$$

---

\* For the secular equation it is sufficient that the matrix be Hermitian. Here the physical problem admits only real coefficients.

that is, we require that

$$\alpha_{ij}\varrho_j/\varrho_i = \alpha_{ji}\varrho_i/\varrho_j \qquad (6.13)$$

or

$$\varrho_j/\varrho_i = \sqrt{\alpha_{ji}/\alpha_{ij}} = \sqrt{x_{je}/x_{ie}} \qquad (6.14)$$

from Eq. (6.1). A possible solution is

$$\varrho_i = \sqrt{x_{je}}. \qquad (6.15)$$

Thus Eq. (6.10) has a symmetrical matrix and all roots are real.

In this proof use has not been made of the condition (6.4). Obviously, the roots will remain real for an arbitrary choice of real coefficients $\alpha_{ii}$. But for actual systems there is a further requirement, that the system be stable, that is, solutions of the type

$$x \propto \exp(\lambda t), \qquad \lambda > 0 \qquad (6.16)$$

must be excluded. In order to prove that all the $\lambda_i \leq 0$, we must make use of the properties of the $\alpha_{ii}$. There exists the following theorem due to Bankwitz (1930). In a determinant

$$\begin{vmatrix} A_1 + \sum_\nu a_{1\nu} & -a_{12} & \cdots & -a_{1m} \\ -a_{21} & A_2 + \sum_\nu a_{2\nu} & \cdots & -a_{2m} \\ \vdots & \vdots & & \vdots \\ -a_{m1} & -a_{m2} & \cdots & A_m + \sum_\nu a_{m\nu} \end{vmatrix} = \Delta_m \qquad (6.17)$$

with $A_\nu, a_{\mu\nu} \geq 0$, every principal minor is $>0$. These determinants of $m$th order differ from those arising in our problem by a factor $(-1)^{n-m}$. In our notation the unknown $\lambda$ appears as factor $(-\lambda)^{n-m}$; consequently, the secular equation reads

$$(-1)^n\lambda^n + b_1\lambda^{n-1}(-1)^n + \cdots + b_n(-1)^n = 0, \qquad (6.18)$$

where all $b_l > 0$ ($b_n$ in the above system of rank $r = n - 1$ vanishes). After dividing by $(-1)^n$ all coefficients are positive, and in this case Descartes' rule for algebraic equations states that all roots are negative, that is, the system of solutions is stable as the physical problem requires.

To repeat: In our proof we made use of the principle of detailed balancing, or of microscopic reversibility, but we did not make use of any further relations following from thermodynamics of irreversible processes.

In retrospect, we may state: We have found that every solution for the concentration $x_i$ of compound $i$ is a linear combination of exponential expressions $\exp(\lambda_i t)$, with $\lambda_j \leq 0$. We may imagine this set of $n - 1$ equations solved with respect to the simple exponentials $\xi_i$:

$$\xi_i = a_i \exp(\lambda_i t), \tag{6.19}$$

then $\xi_i$ is obtained as a linear transformation of the $x_j$

$$\xi_i = \sum_j \gamma_{ij} x_j, \qquad i = 2, 3, \ldots, n, \tag{6.20}$$

and the dependent $\xi_1 = \sum_j x_j$, $j = 1, 2, 3, \ldots, n$ with

$$\dot{\xi}_i = \lambda_i \xi_i, \qquad i = 2, 3, \ldots, n. \tag{6.21}$$

Here the $\xi_i$ play the role of "normal coordinates" as known from oscillations of a system of $n$ degrees of freedom, but for second-order differential equations. To each "normal mode" corresponds a proper value $\lambda_i$ which here, contrary to the problem of vibrations, is real and negative.

Instead of dealing with the natural coordinates $x_i$, we may consider the "normal coordinates" $\xi_i$ of the system that give us a simpler picture of the whole process. For the sake of simplicity we consider the example $n = 3$, with two independent $\lambda$'s and $\xi$'s; if we retain the constant $\xi_1 = x_1 + x_2 + x_3$, we have

$$\xi_1 = \sum_k x_k = a_1, \qquad \dot{\xi}_1 = 0\xi_1, \qquad \xi_1 = a_1 \exp(0t),$$

$$\xi_2 = a_2 \exp(\lambda_2 t), \tag{6.22}$$

$$\xi_3 = a_3 \exp(\lambda_3 t).$$

It is seen that

$$\xi_2^{\lambda_3} \xi_3^{-\lambda_2} = a_2^{\lambda_3} a_3^{-\lambda_2} = \text{const.} \tag{6.23}$$

If we plot $x_1$, $x_2$, and $x_3$ as rectangular coordinates, then the first equation (6.22) restricts the range of these coordinates to the plane

$$x_1 + x_2 + x_3 = a_1.$$

If we agree to set $a_1 = 1$, we see that this reduces to the simplex, triangular coordinates, that is, the equilateral triangle with corners 1,0,0;

0,1,0; 0,0,1, where the equilibrium point $x_{1e}, x_{2e}, x_{3e}$ is situated somewhere in the interior; see Fig. 12.

The $\xi_2$ and $\xi_3$ axes pass through the equilibrium point, and since equilibrium is reached for $t \to \infty$, the point $x_{1e}, x_{2e}, x_{3e}$ corresponds to the
point $\xi_2 = \xi_3 = 0$ (in the plane $\xi_1 = x_1 + x_2 + x_3 = 1$). If a representative point of the system was situated for $t < +\infty$ on one of the $\xi$ axes,

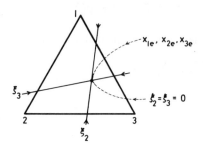

FIG. 12. Ternary system of first order reactions (*two* independent concentrations,
$x_2, x_3; x_1 = a - x_2 - x_3$); equilibrium point $x_{1e}, x_{2e}, x_{3e}$ in the inner of the triangle.
In this point the "normal coordinates" $\xi_2, \xi_3$ vanish. The normal coordinates are the
linear combinations of the natural coordinates which vary according to a simple exponential of the time. One consequence of this is that a representative point on one of
the axes $\xi_2 = 0$ or $\xi_3 = 0$ moves on a straight line according to a simple exponential
time law.

it will always remain on its axis and approach $\xi_2 = \xi_3 = 0$ as

$$\xi_{2,3} \propto \exp(\lambda_{2,3}t).$$

This corresponds to the behavior of a normal mode in a system of harmonic oscillators, where each mode can be excited independently of all
others, and will oscillate indefinitely with its proper frequency. For points
outside the normal axes Eq. (6.23) gives the path of the representative
point, moving in the direction to equilibrium (this follows because
$\lambda < 0$). Curves of this type are well known in mathematics as "W-curves,"
treated by Klein and Lie (1876).

In Fig. 13 W-curves have been drawn schematically. This is the well-
known picture of a nodal point of a differential equation.* In Fig. 13
we have drawn the straight line from the corner 2 to the equilibrium point.
This line is the locus of compositions with $x_1 : x_3 = x_{1e} : x_{3e} = $ const.

---

* Compare Hurewicz (1958), Lefschetz (1957), and Poincaré (1881, 1882, 1885,
1886).

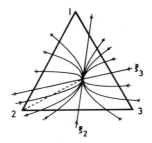

FIG. 13.   The system of W-curves, according to Klein and Lie, that represent the
solution of the system. The point $\xi_2 = \xi_3 = 0$ is a nodal point, approached for $t \to \infty$.
It is seen that a concentration, as function of time, may pass through one extremum.

It is seen that an integral curve may cut this straight line, and this means
that the ratio $x_1 : x_3$ may pass through one extremum (in this case a
minimum). It can be proved generally that an expression $\sum_1^n c_{ik} \exp(\lambda_k t)$,
$\lambda_k < 0$, may have $n - 2$ extrema as a maximum (cf. Jost, 1947). This
is a general property of first-order reactions if the validity of the principle
of microscopic reversibility is admitted.

With the additional assumption that the reaction be restricted to the
neighborhood of equilibrium, the proof has been extended to systems
of first-order and special second-order reactions (Jost, 1947). A general
theory of relaxation phenomena on the basis of Onsager's reciprocity
relations was developed by Meixner (1949, 1959). He shows that the
above results are valid for all relaxation phenomena, that is, processes
restricted to the neighborhood of equilibrium which lead to the establishment of equilibrium.

The above systems were further systematically treated by Wei and
Prater (1962).

Before continuing with a systematic treatment we mention a few
examples of appropriate ternary systems. The isomerization of xylene
in the presence of aluminium chloride in toluene solution was measured
at 50°C. In spite of the catalytic nature of the process the principle of
microscopic reversibility ought to be preserved, the influence of the
catalyst being included in the values of the rate constants $\alpha_{ik}$. If, instead
of the former subscripts, we use the letters $o$, $m$, and $p$ corresponding
to the three isomers, the empirical rate constants are

$$\alpha_{op} = \alpha_{po} = 0, \qquad \alpha_{mo} = 3.6, \qquad \alpha_{om} = 1.0, \qquad \alpha_{mp} = 6, \qquad \alpha_{pm} = 2.1.$$

In accordance with our former custom, we denote by $\alpha_{mo}$ the rate coefficient for the ortho-meta conversion, etc., contrary to the notation of the authors. The rate constants are given in relative values, which for our discussion only is sufficient. In addition, equilibrium values have been obtained that are

$$O_e = 17, \qquad M_e = 62, \qquad P_e = 21,$$

again relative values which may be taken as percentages. That $\alpha_{op} = \alpha_{po} = 0$ does not hurt our argument, though the information available is reduced due to this fact. This, of course, is easily understood from the point of view of reaction mechanism. Since the equilibrium is known from these experiments, though only indirectly established, we also know the ratio of the rate coefficients:

$$\alpha_{po} : \alpha_{op} = P_e : O_e = 21 : 17.$$

In this case one has to imagine that one has passed to the limit $\alpha_{po} \to 0$, $\alpha_{op} \to 0$, maintaining the ratio constant at $21/17$.

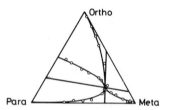

Fig. 14. Isomerisation reaction of xylenes (which for given $AlCl_3$ concentration is first order), values observed by Allen and Yats (1959), reproduced by kind permission of the copyright owner, reprinted from *J. Amer. Chem. Soc.* **81**, 5290. Copyright by the American Chemical Society.

Figure 14, taken from Allen and Yats (1959), reproduces almost exactly the schematic features of our previous argument; see Fig. 13.

As a second example we mention the system butene-1, *cis*-butene, *trans*-butene. As Fig. 15* shows, the equilibrium point is approached, starting from the *cis*-2-butene corner. It is seen how the tangent from this point to the reaction trajectory gives a first approximation to the characteristic straight line (normal coordinate), which may be improved by starting a new experiment from the point 0 of intersection of this tangent with the 1-butene-*cis*-2-butene side, etc.

It is instructive to see that rate constants derived with varying catalysts

---

* Reprinted from Wei and Prater (1962).

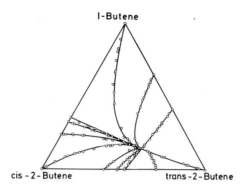

Fig. 15. Isomerisation in the system 1-butene, *cis*-2-butene, *trans*-2-butene, taken from Wei and Prater, 1962 (from *Advan. Catal.* **13**, 256, Academic Press).

(alumina) differ, but their ratios (in this case the ratios $[\alpha_{ik}/\alpha_{kj}]$ are equal to the equilibrium constants) are identical within the limits of error for different catalysts; compare Table I, taken from Jungers (1967).

Faith and Vermeulen (1967) made use of this method for interpreting batch or tubular flow reactor data.

It might be pointed out that the consideration of this section include the proof that a system of first-order reactions leads to an unambiguously given single equilibrium. For a relaxation system, that is, a system of higher-order reactions linearized for the surrounding of an equilibrium site, the same argument allows only of the conclusion that in this environ-

TABLE I

Isomerisation of *n*-Butenes over Alumina

Ratio of equilibrium concentration at 230°C

| $\dfrac{[\text{butene-1}]}{[\textit{cis}\text{-butene}]} = 0.5$ | | $\dfrac{[\textit{cis}\text{-butene}]}{[\textit{trans}\text{-butene}]} = 0.53$ | | $\dfrac{[\textit{trans}\text{-butene}]}{[\text{butene-1}]} = 3.8$ | |
|---|---|---|---|---|---|
| Relative rate constants ($\alpha_{13} \equiv 1$) | | | | | |
| $\alpha_{21}$ | $\alpha_{12}$ | $\alpha_{32}$ | $\alpha_{23}$ | $\alpha_{13}$ | $\alpha_{31}$ |
| Catalyst 1    9.1 | 4.6 | 4.6 | 2.4 | 1 | 3.8 |
| Catalyst 2    16.7 | 8.5 | 8.5 | 4.4 | 1 | 3.8 |
| Catalyst 3    10.344 | 4.623 | 5.616 | 3.371 | 1 | 3.724 |

ment equilibrium is uniquely determined. This argument alone would not exclude the possibility that more than one equilibrium exists.

The question of uniqueness of chemical equilibrium in the general case has been treated by Shear (1968); compare also M. Klein, this treatise Vol. I, p. 501. Shears' proof is entirely kinetic and makes use of Ljapunow's method and of Brouwer's topological fixed-point theorem. Wei (1962) made a first attempt at an axiomatic treatment of chemical reaction systems. This seems the first time general theorems concerning the equilibrium point have been enounced from kinetics and topology. Of course, the uniqueness of chemical equilibrium, under normally valid conditions, ought to be a purely thermodynamic consequence. The question of uniqueness of chemical equilibrium has been shortly mentioned in an earlier review article on calculation of complex chemical equilibria (Zeleznik and Gordon, 1968). A definite answer is possible only for ideal systems. According to Hancock and Motzkin and to Shapiro and Shapley the solution for ideal systems is unique if it exists; compare also Gavalas (1968).

A very detailed discussion of first-order reaction systems along the lines sketched above is due to Prater *et al.* (1967, 1968, 1970). Wei (1965) also gave a first treatment of a more general system of reaction equations. Rather simple results are obtained in exceptional cases, only, as in the system

$$2A \rightleftarrows 2B \rightleftarrows 2C,$$

$$\dot{a} = -a^2 + b^2,$$

$$\dot{b} = \qquad - 2b^2 + c^2,$$

$$\dot{c} = \qquad b^2 - c^2,$$

where all rate constants are set equal to unity. Here straight-line reaction paths, like in first-order reaction systems, are possible.

In this connection we also refer to Frederickson, and to Ishida.

A few papers of general interest will only be mentioned. Ames (1962) formulates a method for reducing nonlinear kinetic differential equations to canonical forms. Aris (1964) treats the algebra of systems of second-order reactions, and in a survey paper of 1969 (Ames, 1969) deals with mathematical aspects of chemical reaction in a very general way, with a rather complete list of references.*

---

* We add a few more references that might occasionally be of value, but cannot be treated here. Ames (1969), Recent developments in the nonlinear equations of transport

## B. Relaxation Processes

Every approach to equilibrium may be considered a relaxation process, provided the system under consideration is sufficiently close to equilibrium. By sufficiently close we mean the difference of the variable under consideration, for example $x$, from its equilibrium value $x_e$, is very small in comparison to $x_e$, that is, $| x - x_e | \ll x_e$. $x$ may approach $x_e$ both from lower and higher values.

Suppose a system of reactions with reactants $x_1, x_2, \ldots, x_n$, reacting according to first-, second-, third-, ... order reactions. We may write a system of rate expressions

$$\dot{x}_i = \sum_k \alpha_{ik} x_k + \sum_{k,j} \beta_{ikj} x_k x_j + \cdots . \qquad (6.24)$$

If equilibrium does exist, it is characterized by

$$0 = \dot{x}_i = \sum_k \alpha_{ik} x_{ke} + \sum_{k,j} \beta_{ikj} x_{ke} x_{je} + \cdots , \qquad (6.25)$$

where the subscript $e$ refers to equilibrium. Subtracting (6.25) from (6.24), and introducing the distance from equilibrium, $\xi_i$, for every variable, we have $(\dot{x}_i = \dot{\xi}_i)$

$$\dot{\xi}_i = \sum_k \alpha_{ik} \xi_k + \sum_{k,j} \beta_{ijk} [(x_{ke} + \xi_k)(x_{je} + \xi_k) - x_{ke} x_{je}] + \cdots \qquad (6.26)$$

---

processes. Arbesman and Kim (1969), Generalized relaxation method in chemical kinetics. Bowen (1968), On the stoichiometry of chemically reacting materials. Aris and Amundson (1958), An analysis of chemical reactor stability and control—I. Aris and Gavalas (1965), On the theory of reactions in continuous mixtures. Aris (1965), Introduction to the analysis of chemical reactors. Bak and Fisher (1967), The concept of diffusion in chemical kinetics. Harris and Lapidus (1967), The identification of non-linear systems. Bowen et al. (1963), Singular perturbation theory refinement to quasi-steady state approximation in chemical kinetics. Coleman (1964), Thermodynamics of materials with memory. Dean and Hinshelwood (1967), Kinetics of cell growth in conditions of phase infection, substrate imbalance and synchronization. Goodrich (1963), Approximate solutions to the pure birth process. Heineken et al. (1967), On the mathematical status of the pseudo-steady state hypothesis of biochemical kinetics. Kittrell et al. (1966), Precise determination of reaction orders. Markus and Amundson (1968), Nonlinear boundary-value problems arising in chemical reactor theory. Mezaki and Kittrell (1967), Parametric sensitivity in fitting non-linear kinetic models. Mikovsky and Wei (1963), A kinetic analysis of the exchange of deuterium with hydrides. Walles and Platt (1967), Autocatalysis analysed.

and neglecting square and higher terms in $\xi$,

$$\dot{\xi}_i = \sum_k \alpha_{ik}\xi_k + \sum_{k,j} \beta_{ijk}[x_{ke}\xi_j + x_{je}\xi_k] + \cdots, \qquad i, j, k = 1, 2, \ldots, n. \tag{6.27}$$

Considering that within a single experiment the equilibrium values are constant, we may include them in the coefficients. We write the result for the special case $k = j$:

$$\dot{\xi}_i = \sum_k \alpha_{ik}\xi_k + 2\sum_{k,j} \beta'_{ikj}\xi_k + \cdots. \tag{6.28}$$

Both (6.27) and (6.28) represent systems of linear, homogeneous first-order differential equations, with constant coefficients that can be solved by standard methods. If there are $n$ independent equations, then the solution will be composed of $n$ exponential terms, $\sum_r c_{ir} \exp(\varrho_r t)$, where without constraints, the $\varrho_r$ may be complex and the real part may be $\gtrless 0$. If we are dealing with a true relaxation process consisting of the first terms of Eq. (6.26), or of the linearized first-order system (6.27), (6.28), it may be proved (see Section VI,A) that all $\varrho_r$ are real and negative (see Jost, 1947, 1950, Meixner, 1949, and Eigen and de Maeyer, 1963, 1968), which implies that each variable $\xi_i$ can pass through a finite number of extrema only; that is, in a system of $n$ independent variables $n - 1$ extrema may occur (see Jost, 1947).

The genuine field for the application of relaxation methods is that of fast reactions in solutions, especially ionic reactions that otherwise are not accessible to measurement (Eigen and de Maeyer, 1963, 1968). There may, however, be applications in gas reactions, for example, freezing out of equilibria in cooled flame gases (see Haase and Jost, 1950). We mention the relaxation method chiefly because of its general interest, neglecting the question of practical applicability and of its limitations. It should be kept in mind that a meaningful analysis of a relaxation spectrum is possible only if there are not too many relaxation frequencies (usually the reciprocal, the relaxation time $\tau$, is used) and if these are sufficiently far apart. On the other hand, if we look at Eq. (6.28) we see that for a given system the relaxation times must be functions of the rate constants $\alpha_{ik}$, etc. Since these still contain the equilibrium concentrations of the second- and higher-order reactions, by varying these concentrations one must obtain relaxation frequencies as functions of concentrations, and it must be possible to evaluate a reaction mechanism from relaxation times.

## VII. Reactions near Equilibrium and close to a Steady State. Reaction Rates and Thermodynamics

We try to deal with a reaction near equilibrium in some detail. For this we refer primarily to Prigogine (1967) and Glansdorf and Prigogine (1971); compare also Sanfeld in this treatise (Vol. I, 1970), de Groot and Mazur (1961), and Haase (1963, 1969). We may start from Gibbs' fundamental equation for entropy,

$$T \, dS = dU + P \, dV - \sum_i \mu_i \, dn_i, \tag{7.1}$$

where the symbols have the usual meaning. $n_i$ is an appropriate variable for the amount of substance, which here will be expressed, for the sake of simplicity, by the number of moles. From (7.1) it is seen that for the chemical potential, in addition to the well-known relations

$$\mu_i = (\partial G/\partial n_i)_{P,T,n_j} = (\partial A/\partial n_i)_{V,T,n_j},$$

(where $G$ is the Gibbs free energy, $A$ is the Helmholtz free energy, and $n_j$ denotes that all $n_j$ except for $j = i$ are to be kept constant) there holds in addition

$$\mu_i = -T(\partial S/\partial n_i)_{U,V,n_j} = -T(\partial S/\partial n_i)_{H,P,n_j}. \tag{7.2}$$

We shall first deal with a single reaction, written

$$\sum_i \nu_i B_i = 0, \tag{7.3}$$

and a reaction rate $r$ defined by

$$r = (1/\nu_i) \, d[B_i]/dt, \tag{7.4}$$

where $B_i$ are reactants or products, depending on whether the stoichiometric numbers $\nu_i$ are negative (reactants) or positive (products). Equation (7.4) is equivalent to writing (for one reaction)

$$dn_i = \nu_i \, d\xi, \tag{7.5}$$

$\xi$ reaction variable (or extent of reaction) of dimension number of moles, if the $\nu_i$ are defined as dimensionless numbers, and

$$r = d\xi/dt = (1/\nu_i) \, dn_i/dt. \tag{7.6}$$

Now we introduce in Eq. (7.1) the affinity $\mathscr{A}$ as defined by de Donder (cf. Chapter 2 of Volume I)

$$\mathscr{A} = -\sum_i \nu_i \mu_i \tag{7.7}$$

(de Groot and Mazur use the opposite sign), giving

$$T\,dS = dU + P\,dV + \mathscr{A}\,d\xi \tag{7.8}$$

and

$$\mathscr{A} = T(\partial S/\partial \xi)_{U,V} \tag{7.9}$$

if we agree to keep $U$ and $V$ constant. We further have

$$dG = -S\,dT + V\,dP - \mathscr{A}\,d\xi, \tag{7.10}$$

$$\mathscr{A} = -(\partial G/\partial \xi)_{T,P}. \tag{7.11}$$

The equilibrium condition is now

$$\mathscr{A} = 0. \tag{7.12}$$

On account of (7.7) we can obtain the mass action law in the usual form for ideal gases or solutions, with

$$\mu_i = \mu_i^{\bullet} + RT\ln(c_i/c^{\bullet}), \tag{7.13}$$

where $c_i = [B_i]$, $\mu_i^{\bullet}$ is the standard value for $c_i = c^{\bullet}$, with $c^{\bullet}$ standard concentration (introduced for dimensional reasons)

$$\mathscr{A} = 0 = -\sum_i \nu_i \mu_i = -\sum_i \nu_i \mu_i^{\bullet} - RT\sum_i \nu_i \ln(c_i/c^{\bullet}) \tag{7.14}$$

or

$$\prod c_{ie}^{\nu_i} \times (c^{\bullet})^{-\nu} = K_c, \qquad \nu = \sum_i \nu_i, \tag{7.15}$$

where $e$ refers to equilibrium and $K_c$, by definition, is dimensionless. If instead by Eq. (8.3) we had defined the reaction by

$$\sum_j \nu_j B_j \underset{\overset{\rightharpoonup}{\kappa}}{\overset{\overset{\rightharpoonup}{\kappa}}{\rightleftharpoons}} \sum_l \nu_l B_l, \tag{7.16}$$

where now both $\nu_j$ and $\nu_l$ are $>0$, we could write for the mass-action law instead of (7.15) the equivalent equation

$$\prod_l c_{le}^{v_l} \Big/ \prod_j c_{je}^{v_j} = K_c(c^\bullet)^v. \tag{7.17}$$

For constant $U$ and $V$ we may write Eq. (7.9)

$$dS = (\mathscr{A}/T)\,d\xi, \tag{7.18}$$

and further

$$dS/dt \equiv \Theta = (1/T)\mathscr{A}\,d\xi/dt, \tag{7.19}$$

where $\Theta$ is the rate of entropy production. This may be generalized for a system of reactions, $\varrho = 1, 2, \ldots, n$,

$$dS/dt \equiv \Theta = (1/T)\sum_\varrho d\xi_\varrho/dt, \tag{7.20}$$

where the rate of the $\varrho$th reaction is

$$r_\varrho = d\xi_\varrho/dt. \tag{7.21}$$

Thermodynamics requires

$$\Theta \geqq 0. \tag{7.22}$$

Instead of $\Theta$ often a function $\Psi$ is used, corresponding to the dissipation function $\Psi$ introduced into hydrodynamics by Rayleigh,

$$\Psi = T\Theta = \sum_\varrho r_\varrho \mathscr{A}_\varrho \geqq 0. \tag{7.23}$$

For equilibrium both the $r_\varrho$ and the $A_\varrho$ must vanish. But Eq. (7.23) does not require that the individual products $r_\varrho A_\varrho$ be $\geqq 0$. If this condition is not obeyed then we talk of coupled reactions. We shall see, however, that near equilibrium it is always possible to transform the variables in such a way that in the new variables all equations are uncoupled; that is, in the new reaction variables $\eta_i$ and affinities $A_i{}'$ not only

$$\sum_i \eta_i \mathscr{A}_i{}' \geqq 0, \tag{7.24}$$

but also individually

$$\eta_i \mathscr{A}_i{}' \geqq 0, \qquad i = 1, 2, \ldots, n, \tag{7.25}$$

The next step is to set with de Donder, near equilibrium

$$r = a\mathscr{A}, \tag{7.26}$$

with $a > 0$. Since $r$ has always the same sign as $A$, the rate of entropy production will be

$$\Theta = (1/T)a\mathscr{A}^2 \geqq 0, \tag{7.27}$$

that is, always $\geqq 0$, and one necessary condition, at least, is obeyed by Eq. (7.26). Prigogine justifies Eq. (7.26) as follows. Let us assume $n+1$ independent reaction variables $x_1, x_2, \ldots, x_n, x_{n+1}$; then we may write for the rate

$$r = r(x_1, x_2, \ldots, x_n, x_{n+1}). \tag{7.28}$$

The affinity will depend on the same set of variables

$$\mathscr{A} = \mathscr{A}(x_1, x_2, \ldots, x_n, x_{n+1}). \tag{7.29}$$

If we assume the variable $x_{n+1}$ eliminated between Eqs. (7.28) and (7.29), we arrive at an expression

$$r = f(x_1, x_2, \ldots, x_n, \mathscr{A}), \tag{7.30}$$

where we know that for equilibrium

$$f(x_1, x_2, \ldots, x_n, \mathscr{A}) = 0, \tag{7.31}$$

since for $\mathscr{A} = 0$ there is equilibrium; in this case the $x_i$ assume their equilibrium values $x_{ie}$. By expanding near equilibrium, that is, near $\mathscr{A} = 0$, we find

$$r = (\partial f/\partial A)_{x_{ie}}\mathscr{A} + \cdots, \tag{7.32}$$

and in Eq. (7.26)

$$a = (\partial f/\partial \mathscr{A})_{x_{ie}}. \tag{7.33}$$

If we assume the ideal mass-action law for the rate of reaction we have

$$r = \vec{\varkappa} \prod_j c_j^{\nu_j} - \overleftarrow{\varkappa} \prod_l c_l^{\nu_l} = \omega\left\{1 - \lambda \prod_k c_k^{\nu_k}\right\}, \tag{7.34}$$

if, as before, in the products over $j$ and $l$ all $\nu_j, \nu_l$ are positive, while in the product over $k$ we have the usual sign convention, and where the rate constants for the direct and reverse reactions $\vec{\varkappa}$ and $\overleftarrow{\varkappa}$ are connected with the new constants $\omega$ and $\lambda$ by

$$\omega = \vec{\varkappa} \prod_j c_j^{\nu_j}, \qquad 1/\lambda = \vec{\varkappa}/\overleftarrow{\varkappa} = K_c c^{\bullet\nu}. \tag{7.35}$$

With our previous conventions and

$$\mathscr{A} = -\sum_k \nu_k \mu_k = RT \ln \frac{K_c c^{\bullet\nu}}{\prod_k c_k^{\nu_k}} \tag{7.36}$$

and

$$v = \sum_k \nu_k, \qquad RT \ln K_c = -\sum_k \nu_k \mu_k^\bullet, \qquad (7.37)$$

we can rewrite Eq. (7.34)

$$r = \omega\{1 - \exp(-\mathscr{A}/RT)\}, \qquad (7.38)$$

which, after expanding the exponential, will lead back to our phenomeno-
logical relation $r = a\mathscr{A}$ and $\omega = \omega_e$, that is, $c_j = c_{je}$ in Eq. (7.35), the
value for equilibrium concentrations. Here, we must justify the use of
the primitive Guldberg–Waage formulation, Eqs. (7.34) and (7.35), with
the ideal mass-action law for rate and equilibrium. We try to correct
this in two steps.

1.  If we retain the ideal mass-action law for equilibrium, we may
write instead of Eqs. (7.34) and (7.35)

$$r = \vec{F}(\dots c_j, \dots, T)\varkappa \prod_j c_j^{\nu_j} - \overleftarrow{F}(\dots c_l, \dots, T)\varkappa \prod_l c_l^{\nu_l}, \quad (7.39)$$

with

$$\omega = \vec{F}\varkappa \prod_j c_j^{\nu_j}, \qquad 1/\lambda = \varkappa\vec{F}/\varkappa\overleftarrow{F}, \qquad (7.40)$$

if only we require that

$$\lim_{\mathscr{A}\to 0} \vec{F} = \lim_{\mathscr{A}\to 0} \overleftarrow{F}, \qquad (7.41)$$

that is, in equilibrium the ideal mass-action law is retained, while the
individual rates near equilibrium and outside equilibrium may deviate
arbitrarily from the ideal values. Thus examples such as the unimolecular
decomposition and bimolecular recombination are included in our treatment

$$AB + M \rightleftharpoons A + B + M$$

near to or far from equilibrium, and over the whole pressure range.

2.  The next step would be to split both $\vec{F}$ and $\overleftarrow{F}$ into two factors,
$\prod_j f_j^{\nu_j}\vec{F}'$ and $\prod_l f_l^{\nu_l}\overleftarrow{F}'$. Then, in the above equations, we have in equilibrium the products of activities $a_k = c_k f_k$ instead of concentrations, and
still the arbitrary functions $\vec{F}'$ and $\overleftarrow{F}'$ take care of a change in mechanism
with distance from equilibrium and other parameters, for example,
pressure.

We stress: for any rate expression, considering nonideality effects and
complex rate laws, we can linearize the rate expression near equilibrium.
We generally have for a single reaction

$$r = d\xi/dt = a\mathscr{A}, \qquad (7.42)$$

with $\xi$ an appropriately defined reaction variable. For the affinity $A$ near equilibrium we can always write the expansion

$$\mathscr{A} = \mathscr{A}_0 + (\partial \mathscr{A}/\partial \xi)_e \xi + \cdots = (\partial \mathscr{A}/\partial \xi)_e \xi + \cdots , \qquad (7.43)$$

where $\mathscr{A}_0$ of course vanishes. The rate depends linearly on the reaction variable, even in nonideal cases.

## VIII. Structure and Stability

"Thermodynamic theory of structure and stability and fluctuations" is the title of a monograph by Glansdorff and Prigogine (1971) with rather far-reaching implications. This monograph, or at least basic work and discussions preceding its publication, is fundamental for Eigen's (1971) comprehensive discussion on "Self-organization of matter and the evolution of biological macromolecules," which is likely to influence permanently our concepts of the origin of life. We can deal only superficially with the specialized principles involved, but we start with an example of a reaction that is very close to "periodical," and was first investigated by Zhaboutinsky (1964, 1967, 1968), Zaikin and Zhaboutinsky (1971). Glansdorff discusses this as an outstanding example for a reaction exhibiting oscillations in time which also can lead to periodicity in space. This is the oxidation of malonic acid by potassium bromate in the presence of cerium sulfate. A typical composition, according to Glansdorff and Prigogine, is: $48\ mM$ malonic acid; $0.12\ mM$ ceric sulfate; $0.60\ mM$ potassium bromate, in $3\ m$ sulphuric acid at $60°C$. The high concentration of malonic acid and the marked excess of potassium bromate over ceric sulfate furnish conditions far from equilibrium, possibly approaching for a certain time a quasi-stationary nonequilibrium state. Thus, after an induction time the reaction rate is almost periodic (though not governed by harmonic oscillations). This behavior is explained by Glansdorff and Prigogine (following Zhaboutinsky and Degn, 1967) by a sequence of, so far not proved, overall reactions.

1.   $CH_2(COOH)_2 + 6Ce^{4+} + 2H_2O \rightarrow 2CO_2 + HCOOH + 6Ce^{3+} + 6H^+$
2.   $10Ce^{3+} + 2HBrO_3 + 10H^+ \rightarrow 10Ce^{4+} + Br_2 + 6H_2O$
3.   $CH_2(COOH)_2 + Br_2 \rightarrow CHBr(COOH)_2 + HBr$

The second reaction is supposed to be autocatalytic, and to compensate during the induction period (e.g., of the order of $100\ sec$) the first reaction, that is, the reactions $Ce^{4+} \rightarrow Ce^{3+}$ and $Ce^{3+} \rightarrow Ce^{4+}$, compensate each other. But due to the supposed liberation of bromine and the formation of bromomalonic acid and di-bromomalonic acid a complex of di-bromomalonic acid and $Ce^{3+}$ is formed, which removes $C^{3+}$, necessary for the autocatalytic reaction 2, and, consequently, this inhibits reaction 2. In this phase the $C^{4+}$ concentration decreases. However, the inhibiting complex decomposes due to the transition di-bromomalonic acid $\rightarrow$ di-bromoacetic acid $+ CO_2$. Then the autocatalytic reaction starts again, and so on, giving the observed periodic behavior, observed by light absorption at 317 *nm*.

The most remarkable phenomenon, in connection with this reaction, is the appearance of periodicity in space (Busse, 1969, Herschkowitz, 1970), as discussed by Glansdorff and Prigogine. These authors reproduce periodic structures, similar to those obtained with periodic precipitations (Liesegang rings), starting from a mixture of equal parts of $4 \times 10^{-3}$ $M$ $Ce_2(SO_4)_3$, $3.5 \times 10^{-1}$ $M$ $KBrO_3$, $1.2$ $M$ $CH_2(COOH)_2$, and $1.5$ $M$ $H_2SO_4$ in the presence of a redox indicator. According to their theory of symmetry breaking instabilities and dissipative space structures, such a behavior could in principle be predicted though concrete examples still usually are too complicated to allow of definite predictions.

The cases of interest to Glansdorff and Prigogine lead to limit cycles, as defined by Poincaré. Without going into details we add a few remarks concerning the singularities of differential equations as met in reaction kinetics; compare also the example treated in Section VI,A.

The type of systems encountered in reaction kinetics is called autonomous,* that is, a system

$$\dot{x}_i = X_i(x_1, \ldots, x_j, \ldots, x_n), \qquad i, j = 1, 2, \ldots, n, \qquad (8.1)$$

where the functions $X_i$ are independent of time (the dot, as usual, indicates the time derivative).

---

* Though this is the usual type of kinetic equations, and all reactions treated in this chapter are of this type, one easily can imagine reaction systems which are not autonomous. Since the functions $X_i$ depend on the concentrations $x_j$, it is only necessary to make one concentration depend explicitly on time, that is, by changing one (or more) concentration(s) arbitrarily with time, for example, by means of semipermeable walls, subjecting at least one concentration to a chosen time program, as a special case make it depend periodically on time. This type of explicit time dependence is excluded for closed systems. Another way would be to make one or more rate coefficients time dependent. Since rate coefficients depend on temperature, this is possible by applying a given time program for temperature. Hence it is advisable to restrict our considerations to closed systems, and, in case of interest, introduce open systems explicitly as separate type.

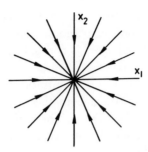

FIG. 16. Degenerate nodal point (cf. the nodal points of Figs. 14 and 15).

1. A special case of a nodal point was encountered in Section VI for first-order reaction systems, or for general reaction systems near equilibrium, the system of parabola-like curves, all tangent to the axis of one of the normal coordinates (Fig. 13) in the same point, the singular point, called nodal point. This nodal point may degenerate into one with a system of straight lines, all passing through this same point (which may be the origin of the coordinate system). If in the just-mentioned example the two "normal coordinates" $y_1$ and $y_2$ have the same relaxation times $\lambda$, then the ratio $y_1/y_2$ is a constant, independent of time. This constant varies with initial conditions, and we obtain a system of straight lines through the origin of the $y_1 - y_2$ system (Fig. 16). The origin is a degenerate nodal point.

2. The so-called Lotka case, of which the main terms and the strictly periodic solutions were mentioned in Section III, leads to a singularity of the type of a vortex point (Fig. 17). We may write the complete differential equations in the form

$$\dot{x}_1 = k_1 a x_1 - k_2 x_1 x_2, \qquad \dot{x}_2 = k_2 x_1 x_2 - k_3 x_2. \qquad (8.2)$$

There exists a degenerate, nonequilibrium but steady state solution

$$x_{10} = k_3/k_2, \qquad x_{20} = a k_1/k_2. \qquad (8.3)$$

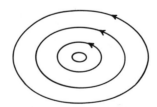

FIG. 17. Vortex point, corresponding to the so called "Lotka case."

In the neighborhood of this point the solution is (with proper choice of scale for the new coordinates $\eta_1$, $\eta_2$)

$$\eta_1 = \alpha \cos \omega t, \qquad \eta_2 = \alpha \sin \omega t, \qquad \eta_1{}^2 + \eta_2{}^2 = \alpha^2, \qquad (8.4)$$

that is, a system of circles, depending on the initial value $\alpha$, around the singular point $\eta_1 = \eta_2 = 0$. With the original coordinates $x_1$ and $x_2$ this system of circles will pass into a system of ellipses, and without restriction to the neighborhood of the singular vortex point $x_{10}$, $x_{20}$ this will change into a general system of closed convex curves.

3. In case 1, the roots of the characteristic equations were real and, in addition, negative, which ensured stability. In case 2, the roots of the characteristic equation (as always, either for a linear system or a system linearized in the neighborhood of the singular point) were imaginary, giving sine or cosine functions for each variable.

If now the roots are complex, but not purely imaginary, the solution for the linear system near the singular focal or spiral point is

$$x_1 = \exp(\alpha t) \cos \beta t, \qquad x_2 = \exp(\alpha t) \sin \beta t, \qquad (8.5)$$

a logarithmic spiral around the singular origin, which only in the limit $t \to \infty$ and $\alpha < 0$ would be approached. Of course there exist an infinite number of such spirals. This refers to a stable state. For $\alpha > 0$ the solution is unstable, tending to infinity for $t \to \infty$.

In this case it is not sufficient to deal with the linear system near the singular point, but the nonlinear system must be treated. Then it may be that in the originally unstable case $\alpha > 0$ the integral curves approach finite limits, Poincaré's limit cycles, as mentioned several times; compare Section VI,A.

There seems, so far, to exist no mechanism, investigated and proved in all details, which conforms to Prigogine's concept of limit cycles near stationary, nonequilibrium points. But the examples treated by Chernavskaya and Chernavskii, and by Sel'kov are very close to experimental facts, and the author of this article shares Prigogine's conviction that his conjecture is of much deeper importance than just presenting one of a number of conceivable models.

For Eigen's (1970, 1971) fundamental attempt at a theoretical understanding of self-organization of matter and the evolution of biological macromolecules, the preceding theoretical concepts form a necessary background.

## References

ALLEN, R. H., and YATS, L. D. (1959). *J. Amer. Chem. Soc.* **81**, 5289–5292.

ALLEN, R. H., ALFREY, T., and YATS, D. (1959). *J. Amer. Chem. Soc.* **81**, 426.

AMES, W. F. (1969). *Ind. Eng. Chem. Fundamentals* **8**, 522.

ARBESMAN, R. W., and KIM, YOUNG GUL (1969). *Ind. Eng. Chem. Fundamentals* **8**, 216.

ARIS, R. (1965). "Introduction to the Analysis of Chemical Reactors." Prentice Hall, Englewood Cliffs, New Jersey.

ARIS, R. (1971). Algebraic Aspects of Formal Chemical Kinetics, *in* "Studies in the Foundation Methodology and Philosophy in Science; Problems in the Foundations of Physics" (Mario Bunge, ed.), Vol. 4, p. 119–129. Springer-Verlag, Berlin and New York.

ARIS, R., and AMUNDSON, N. R. (1958). *Chem. Eng. Sci.* **7**, 121.

ARIS, R., and GAVALAS, G. R. (1965). *Phil. Trans. Roy. Soc. London A* **260**, 351.

BAK, T. A. (1961). *Advan. Chem. Phys.* **3**, 33.

BAK, T. A. (1963). "Contributions to the Theory of Chemical Kinetics. A Study of the Connection Between Thermodynamics and Chemical Rate Processes." Benjamin, New York, Munksgaard, Copenhagen (first printed Munksgaard, Copenhagen, 1959).

BAK, T. A., and FISHER, E. R. (1967). *Ind. Eng. Chem.* **59**, 51.

BANKWITZ, C. (1930). *Math. Ann.* **103**, 145.

BODDINGTON, F., GRAY, P., and HARVEY, D. I. (1971). *Phil. Trans. Roy. Soc. London* **270**, 467–507.

BODENSTEIN, M. (1913). *Z. Phys. Chem.* **85**, 329.

BODENSTEIN, M. (1927). *Ann. Phys.* **82**, 836.

BODENSTEIN, M., and LIND, S. C. (1907). *Z. Phys. Chem.* **57**, 168.

BOWEN, J. R., ACRIVOS, A., and OPPENHEIM, A. K. (1963). *Chem. Eng. Sci.* **18**, 177.

BOWEN, R. M. (1969). *Arch. Rational Mech. Anal.* **19**, 81.

BRAY, W. C. (1921). *J. Amer. Chem. Soc.* **43**, 1262.

BÜSSE, H. (1969). *J. Phys. Chem.* **73**, 750.

CALVERT, J. G., and PITTS, J. N. (1966). "Photochemistry." John Wiley, New York.

CALVIN, M., BASHAM, J. A., BENSON, A. A., and MASSINI, P. (1952). *Ann. Rev. Physical Chem.* **3**, 215.

CESARI, L. (1963). Asymptotic Behavior and Stability Problems in Ordinary Differential Equations, *Erg. Math.* **16**.

CHERNAVSKAYA, N. M., and CHERNAVSKII, D. S. (1960). *Usp. Fiz. Nauk* **72**, 627–652.

CHERNAVSKAYA, N. M., and CHERNAVSKII, D. S. (1961). *Sov. Phys. Usp.* **4**, 850–865.

CHRISTIANSEN, J. A. (1919). *Kgl. Danske Vidensk. Selsk. Math. Fys. Medd.* **1**, 14.

CHRISTIANSEN, J. A. (1941). *Handbuch Katal.* **1**, 244–266. Springer, Wien.

COLEMAN, B. D. (1964). *Arch. Rational Mech. Anal.* **17**, 1.

COLEMAN, B. D., and MIZEL, V. J. (1968). *Arch. Rat. Mech. Anal.* **29**, 105.

DARVEY, I. G., and MATLAK, R. F. (1967). *Bull. Math. Biophys.* **29**, 335.

DEAN, A. C. R., and HINSHELWOOD, SIR CYRIL (1967). *Nature (London)* **214**, 1081.

DEGN, H. (1967). *Nature (London)* **213**, 589.

DEPOY, P. E., and MASON, D. M. (1971). *Combust. Flame* **17**, 108.

EIGEN, M. (1971). *Naturwissenschaften* **58**, 465–523. First presented 1970

EIGEN, M. (1971). Selforganization of matter and the evolution of biological macromolecules, *Naturwiss.* **58**, 465–527 (first presented in lectures, 1970).

EIGEN, M., and DE MAEYER, L. (1963). "Relaxation Methods in Technique of Organic

Chemistry" (L. S. Friess, E. S. Lewis, and A. Weissberger, eds.), Vol. VII, II, Investigation of rates and mechanism of reactions, 2nd ed. Wiley (Interscience), New York.

EIGEN, M., and DE MAEYER, L. (1968). "Kinetik schneller Reaktionen in Lösung und chemische Relaxation, in Chemische Elementarprozesse" (H. Hartmann, M. J. Heidberg, H. Heydtmann and G. H. Kohlmaier, eds.). Springer-Verlag, Heidelberg.

FAITH, L. E., and VERMEULEN, TH. (1967). AIChE J. 13, 936–947.

FICK, A. (1855). Pogg. Ann. 94, 59.

FRANK-KAMENETSKII, D. A. (1939). Acta Physicochim. URSS 10, 365.

FRANK-KAMENETSKII, D. A. (1939a). J. Phys. Chem. 13, 738.

FRANK-KAMENETSKII, D. A. (1939b). Zh. Fiz. Khim. 13, 738.

FRANK-KAMENETSKII, D. A. (1940). Acta Physicochim. URSS 13, 730.

FRANK-KAMENETSKII, D. A. (1945). Acta Physicochim. URSS 20, 729.

FRANK-KAMENETSKII, D. A. (1955). "Diffusion and Heat Exchange in Chemical Kinetics" (transl. by N. Thon). Princeton Univ. Press, Princeton, New Jersey.

FREDERICKSON, A. G. (1966). Stochastic triangular reactions. Chem. Eng. Sci. 21, 587–591.

GAVALAS, G. R. (1968). "Nonlinear Differential Equations of Chemically Reacting Systems." Springer Tracts in Natural Philosophy.

GLANSDORFF, P. and PRIGOGINE, I. (1971). "Thermodynamic Theory of Structure, Stability and Fluctuations," Wiley (Interscience), London.

GOODRICH, F. C. (1963). Nature (London) 198, 220.

GRAY, B. F. (1970). Combust. Flame 14, 273.

GRAY, B. F., and YANG, C. H. (1969). Combust. Flame 13, 20.

GRAY, P., and LEE, P. R. (1966). Studies on temperature profiles in explosive systems and criteria for criticality in thermal explosions. Symp. Combust., 11th, pp. 1123–1132. Combustion Inst., Pittsburgh, Pennsylvania.

GRAY, P., LEE, P. R., and MACDONALD, J. A. (1969). Combust. Flame 13, 461.

GRAY, P., FINE, D. H., and MACKINVEN, R. (1970). Proc. Roy. Soc. London A 316, 223–240, 241–254, 255–268.

DE GROOT, S. R., and MAZUR, P. (1961). "Non-equilibrium Thermodynamics." North-Holland Publ., Amsterdam.

GULDBERG, C. M., and WAAGE, P. (1864), reprinted in German translation in "Ostwalds Klassiker," No. 104. Leipzig, 1899.

HAAG, W. O., and PINES, H. J. (1960). J. Amer. Chem. Soc. 82, 387, 2488.

HAASE, R. (1969). "Thermodynamics of Irreversible Processes." Addison-Wesley, Reading Massachusetts (translated from R. Haase, Thermodynamik der irreversiblen Prozesse, Dr. D. Steinkopff Verlag, Darmstadt, 1963).

HAASE, R., and JOST, W. (1950). Z. Phys. Chem. 196, 215.

HANCOCK, J. H., and MOTZKIN, T. S. (1967). In "Kinetics, Equilibria, and Performance of High Temperature Systems" (G. S. Bahn and E. E. Zukoski, eds.), p. 82. Butterworth, London and Washington, D.C.

HARRIS, G. H., and LAPIDUS, L. (1967). Ind. Eng. Chem. 59, 67.

HEINEKEN, F. G., TSUCHIYA, H. M., and ARIS, R. (1967). Math. Biosci. 1, 95.

HERSCHKOWITZ, M. (1970). C. R. Acad. Sci. Paris 270, C, 1049.

HERZFELD, K. F. (1919a). Ann. Phys. 57, 635.

HERZFELD, K. F. (1919b). Z. Elektrochem. 25, 301.

HIGGINS, J. (1967). Ind. Eng. Chem. 59, 18–62.

HIRNJAK, J. (1911). Z. Phys. Chem. 75, 675.

HOFELICH, F. (1969). Z. Phys. **226**, 395.

VAN'T HOFF, J. H. (1884). "Etudes de dynamique chimique." Amsterdam, revised German edition by Ernst Cohen, Amsterdam (1895). I quote from the German edition.

HUREWICZ, W. (1958). "Lectures on Ordinary Differential Equations." Technol. Press of MIT, Cambridge, Massachusetts and Wiley, New York, 2nd Printing, 1961.

ISHIDA, K. (1966). J. Phys. Chem. **70**, 3806.

JOST, W. (1939). "Explosions- und Verbrennungsvorgänge in Gasen." Springer, Berlin and New York (transl. 1946). McGraw-Hill, New York.

JOST, W. (1941). Handbuch Katalyse **I**, 65–141, 444–480.

JOST, W. (1947). Z. Naturforsch. **2a**, 159–163, from an address delivered December 6, 1946.

JOST, W. (1950). Z. Phys. Chem. **193**, 317.

JOST, W. (1965). "Low Temperature Oxidation." Gordon and Breach, New York.

JOST, W., and von MÜFFLING, L. (1938). Z. Phys. Chem. **183**, 43.

JUNGERS, J. C., and SAJUS, L., avec la collaboration de Aguirre, I., and Decroocq, D. (1967). "L'analyse cinétique de la transformation chimique." Publ. de l'Inst. Français du Pétrole, Paris, Technip.

KELLER, J. (1969). Z. Naturforsch. **24a**, 1989.

KITTRELL, J. R., MEZAKI, R., and WATSON, C. C. (1966). Ind. Eng. Chem. **58**, 50.

KLEIN, F., and LIE, S. (1876). Math. Ann. **4**.

KONDRATJEW, V. N. (1958). "Kinetics of Gas Reactions." Acad. of Sci. of the U.S.S.R., Moscow.

LEFSCHETZ, S. (1949). "Introduction to Topology." Princeton Univ. Press, Princeton, New Jersey.

LEFSCHETZ, S. (1957). "Differential Equations: Geometric Theory." Wiley (Inter-science), New York. 2nd ed., 1963.

LEWIS, B., and VON ELBE, G. (1961). "Combustion, Flames and Explosion of Gases," 2nd ed. Academic Press, New York.

LIGHT, J. C., ROSS, J., and SHULER, K. E. (1969). "Rate Coefficients, Reaction Cross Sections and Microscopic Reversibility in Kinetic Processes in Gases and Plasmas" (A. R. Hochstim, ed.). Academic Press, New York.

LODATO, V. A., MCELWAIN, D. L. S., and PRITCHARD, H. O. (1969). J. Amer. Chem. Soc. **91**, 7688.

LOTKA, A. J. (1910a). J. Phys. Chem. **14**, 271.

LOTKA, A. J. (1910b). Z. Phys. Chem. **72**, 508.

LOTKA, A. J. (1912). Z. Phys. Chem. **80**, 159.

LOTKA, A. J. (1920). J. Amer. Chem. Soc. **42**, 1595.

LOTKA, A. J. (1932). J. Washington Acad. Sci. **22**, 461.

LUMRY, R., SPIKES, J. D., and EYRING, H. (1953). Ann. Rev. Phys. Chem. **4**, 399.

MARKUS, L., and AMUNDSON, N. R. (1968). J. Differential Eq. **4**, 102.

MEIXNER, J. (1949a). Z. Naturforsch. **4a**, 142.

MEIXNER, J. (1949b). Z. Naturforsch. **4a**, 594–600.

MEIXNER, J. (1964). Arch. Rational Mech. Anal. **17**, 278.

MEIXNER, J. (1966). J. Appl. Mech. **33**, Ser. E, 481.

MEIXNER, J. (1968). Rheolog. Acta **7**, 8.

MEIXNER, J. (1969a). Arch. Rational Mech. Anal. **33**, 33.

MEIXNER, J. (1969b). Z. Phys. **219**, 79.

MEIXNER, J., and REIK, H. G. (1959). Handb. Phys. III **2**, 413.

MERZHANOV, A. G., and AVERSON, A. E. (1971). *Combust. Flame* **16**, 89–124.

MEZAKI, R., and KITTRELL, J. R. (1967). *Ind. Eng. Chem.* **59**, 63.

MIKOVSKY, R. J., and WEI, J. (1963). *Chem. Eng. Sci.* **18**, 253.

VON MÜFFLING, L. (1943). *Handb. Katal.* **VI**, 94–131.

VON MÜFFLING, L. (1944). *Z. Phys.* **122**, 787.

NINHAM, B., NOSSAL, R., and ZWANZIG, R. (1969). *J. Chem. Phys.* **51**, 5028.

NORRISH, R. G. W., and PORTER, G. (1949). *Nature (London)* **164**, 658. Cf. also NORRISH, R. G. W., PORTER, G., and THRUSH, B. A. (1953). *Proc. Roy. Soc. A* **216**, 165; (1955) **227**, 423. NORRISH, R. G. W. (1962). "The Study of Energy Transfer in Atoms and Molecules by Photochemical Methods," Inst. Int. Chim., Douzième Conseil de Chimie, Bruxelles; Wiley (Interscience), New York; "Some Fast Reactions in Gases Studied by Flash Photolysis and Kinetic Spectroscopy." Nobel Lecture, 1967.

ONO, S. (1961). *Advan. Chem. Phys.* **3**, 267.

ONSAGER, L. (1931a). *Phys. Rev.* (2) **37**, 405.

ONSAGER, L. (1931b). *Phys. Rev.* **38**, 2265.

PERCHE, A., PEREZ, A., and LUCQUIN, M. (1970). *Combust. Flame* **15**, 89.

POINCARÉ, H. (1880). *C. R. Acad. Sci Paris* **90**, 673–675.

POINCARÉ, H. (1881). *J. Math. Pures Appl.* (3) **7**, 375–422.

POINCARÉ, H. (1882). *J. Math. Pures Appl.* **7**, 251–296.

POINCARÉ, H. (1885). *J. Math. Pures Appl.* (4) **1**, 167–244.

POINCARÉ, H. (1886). *Oeuvres* **1**, 3–84, 90–161, 167–221.

POLANYI, M. (1920). *Z. Elektrochem.* **26**, 50.

PORTER, G. (1950). *Proc. Roy. Soc. (London)* **A 200**, 284; cf. CHRISTIE, M. I., NORRISH, R. G. W., and PORTER, G. (1953). *Proc. Roy. Soc.* **A 216**, 153; (1954) *Discuss. Faraday Soc.* **17**, 107; CHRISTIE, M. I., HARRISON, A. J., NORRISH, R. G. W., and PORTER, G. (1955). *Proc. Roy. Soc.* **A 236**, 446.

PRATER, C. D., SILVESTRI, A. J., and WEI, J. (1967). *Chem. Eng. Sci.* **22**, 1587–1606.

PRIGOGINE, I. (1967). "Introduction to Thermodynamics of Irreversible Processes," 3rd ed. Wiley (Interscience), New York, where earlier work is quoted.

PRIGOGINE, I. (1967). *Nobel Symp. Fast Reactions Primary Processes Chem. Kinet.*, p. 371. Wiley (Interscience), New York.

PRIGOGINE, I., and LEFEVER, R. (1968). *J. Chem. Phys.* **48**, 1695.

PRIGOGINE, I., and NICOLIS, G. (1967). *J. Chem. Phys.* **46**, 3541.

PRIGOGINE, I., LEFEVER, R., GOLDBETER, A., and HERSCHKOWITZ-KAUFMANN, M. (1969). *Nature (London)* **223**, 913–916.

PURI, P. S. (1967). *Math. Biosci.* **1**, 77–94.

RABINOVITCH, E. (1951). *Ann. Rev. Phys. Chem.* **2**, 361.

RAKOWSKI, A. (1906). *Z. Phys. Chem.* **57**, 321.

RASHEWSKY, N. (1960). *Math. Biophys.* **I**, 48ff. (1st ed. 1938).

RICE, F. O., and REIFF, O. M. (1927). *J. Phys. Chem.* **31**, 1352.

ROBINSON, W. G. (1964). *Ann. Rev. Phys. Chem.* **15**, 301.

SANFELD, A. (1971). "Thermodynamics of Irreversible Processes," this treatise, Vol. I, Chapter 2B. Academic Press, New York.

SEL'KOV, E. E. (1967). "Oscillatory Processes in Biological and Chemical Systems" (Russian). Nauka, Moscow.

SEL'KOV, E. E. (1968). *Eur. J. Biochem.* **4**, 79–86.

SEMENOW, N. N. (1935). "Chemical Kinetics and Chain Reactions." Clarendon Press, Oxford.

SEMENOW, N. N. (1954). "Some Problems of Chemical Kinetics and Reactivity." Akad. Nauk, Moscow.

SEMENOW, N. N. (1958/1959). "Some Problems of Chemical Kinetics and Reactivity" (transl. by M. Boudart). Princeton Univ. Press, Princeton, New Jersey.

SHAPIRO, N. Z., and SHAPLEY, L. S. (1965). *J. Soc. Ind. Appl. Math.* **13**, 353.

SHEAR, D. B. (1967). *J. Theor. Biol.* **16**, 212.

SHEAR, D. B. (1968). *J. Chem. Phys.* **48**, 4144.

SIEG, L. (1965). "The Oxidation of Hydrocarbons in: Low Temperature Oxidation" (W. Jost, ed.). Gordon and Breach, New York.

SILVESTRI, A. J., PRATER, CH. D., and WEI, J. (1968). *Chem. Eng. Sci.* **23**, 1191.

SILVESTRI, A. J., PRATER, CH. D., and WEI, J. (1970). *Chem. Eng. Sci.* **25**, 407.

SKRABAL, A. (1930). *Z. Phys. Chem. B* **6**, 382.

SKRABAL, A. (1941). "Homogenkinetik." Steinkopff, Dresden.

SPIKES, J. D., and MAYNE, B. C. (1960). *Ann. Rev. Phys. Chem.* **11**, 501.

SZABO, Z. G. (1969). Kinetic characterization of complex reaction systems, *in* "Comprehensive Chemical Kinetics" (C. H. Bamford and C. F. H. Tipper, eds.), Vol. 2, The Theory of Kinetics, Chapter I. Elsevier, Amsterdam.

TAFFANEL, and LEFLOCHE (1913). *C. R. Acad. Sci. Paris* **156**, 1544; **157**, 496, 714.

TROE, J. (1968). *Ber. Bunsenges. Phys. Chem.* **72**, No. 8, 908–927.

TROE, J. (1969). *Naturwissenschaften* **56**, 553–557.

VOLTERRA, V. (1910). *Rend. Sem. Mat. Milano* **3**, 158.

VULIS, L. A. (1961). "Thermal Regimes of Combustion" (transl. Russian ed. by M. D. Friedmann and G. G. William). McGraw Hill, New York.

WALLES, W. E., and PLATT, A. E. (1967). *Ind. Eng. Chem.* **59**, 41.

WEI, J. (1962). *J. Chem. Phys.* **36**, 1578.

WEI, J., and PRATER, CH. D. (1962). *Advan. Cataly.* **13**, 203–392. For unpublished work of Lago and Haag, cf. also the discussion by J. C. Jungers, and L. Sajus, in collaboration with I. d. Aguirre and D. Decroocq, "l'analyse cinétique de la transformation chimique," Vol. I. Publ. de l'Inst. Français du Pétrole, Editions Techniq, Paris, 1967.

WEI, J., and PRATER, CH. D. (1963). *AIChE J.* **9**, 77.

WEI, J. (1965). *Ind. Eng. Chem. Fundamentals* **4**, 161–167.

WILHELMY, L. (1850). *Pogg. Ann.* **81**, 413–427, 499–526, 527–532; reproduced in Ostwald's Klassiker der Exakten Wissenschaften, Nr. 29, 1891.

ZHABOUTINSKY, A. M. (1967). Symposium on Oscill. Processes in Biological Chemistry. No. 252. Academic Press, Inc., New York.

ZAIKIN, A. N., and ZHABOUTINSKY, A. M. (1971). *J. Phys. Chem. (USSR)* **45**, 147.

ZELEZNIK, F. J., and GORDON, S. (1968). *Ind. Eng. Chem.* **60**, 27.

ZHABOUTINSKY, A. M. (1964). *Biofizika* **2**, 306; (1967). "Oscillations in Biological and Chemical Systems." Acad. Sci. USSR, Moscow (NAUK); (1968). *Russ. J. Phys. Chem.* **42**, 1649; cf. also BELUSOV, B. P. (1958). Sborn referat. radiat. medistinza: "Collection of Abstracts on Radiation Medicine," p. 145. Medgiz, Moscow, 1959.

Chapter 2

# Survey of Kinetic Theory

## C. F. Curtiss

The macroscopic behavior of matter may be interpreted and predicted through a statistical description of the dynamics of the large number of constituent molecules. The statistical behavior of a single system is taken to be the average behavior of the systems in an ensemble of a large number of identical systems. If the dynamics of the molecules is described by classical mechanics, the state of the ensemble may be described by a distribution function in the phase space of a single system. In the quantum mechanical case, the state of the ensemble may be described by the statistical probability density matrix. It is convenient, however, to transform the representation and introduce the Wigner distribution function. This is a function in the phase space that is a direct quantum analog of the classical distribution function.

The time evolution of the distribution function of the system, or the corresponding Wigner distribution function, is described by the classical or quantum mechanical Liouville equation. Most properties of the system, however, may be obtained from a knowledge of the low-order contracted distribution functions. In general, the transport properties depend only on the singlet and pair distribution functions. The Boltzmann equation is an equation for the time evolution of the singlet distribution function. Expressions for the transport properties of a low density gas of spherical molecules may be obtained through the Chapman–Enskog solution of the classical or quantum mechanical Boltzmann equation.

# I. Statistical Concepts

An ensemble is a collection of an infinite number of identical, noninteracting systems. The state of a single system is described by a point in the corresponding phase space, the space of the configuration coordinates and conjugate momenta.

We consider, using classical mechanics, a system consisting of a mixture of several different kinds of molecules with structure. Let $\mathbf{r}_{\alpha i}$ and $\mathbf{p}_{\alpha i}$ be the position and momentum coordinates of the center of mass of molecule $i$ of species $\alpha$, $Q_{\alpha is}$ represent the internal coordinates, relative to the center of mass, and $P_{\alpha is}$ be the conjugate momenta. To simplify the notation, $Q_{\alpha i}$ and $P_{\alpha i}$ are used to represent the full set of internal coordinates and conjugate momenta of molecule $\alpha i$ and $x_{\alpha i}$ to represent the full set of phase space coordinates, that is,

$$Q_{\alpha i} = (Q_{\alpha i1}, Q_{\alpha i2}, Q_{\alpha i3}, \cdots), \tag{1.1}$$

$$P_{\alpha i} = (P_{\alpha i1}, P_{\alpha i2}, P_{\alpha i3}, \cdots), \tag{1.2}$$

$$x_{\alpha i} = (\mathbf{r}_{\alpha i}, Q_{\alpha i}, \mathbf{p}_{\alpha i}, P_{\alpha i}). \tag{1.3}$$

In a similar manner,

$$x = (x_{11}, x_{12}, x_{13}, \cdots, x_{21}, x_{22}, x_{23}, \cdots) \tag{1.4}$$

is used to represent a point in the full phase space of the system.

The statistical behavior of a single system is the average behavior of the members of an ensemble of identical systems. The state of an ensemble is described by the corresponding set of "numbered" points in the phase space. However, the statistical average is determined by the distribution of "un-numbered" points, described by the distribution function $f^{(N)}(x, t)$ in the phase space of a single system. In the present discussion it is convenient to normalize this distribution function so that

$$\int f^{(N)}(x, t)\, dx = \prod_{\alpha} N_{\alpha}!, \tag{1.5}$$

where $N_{\alpha}$ is the number of molecules of species $\alpha$.

Let $G(x)$ represent an arbitrary time-independent dynamical variable, that is, a function defined in the phase space of a single system. Then the average value of the dynamical variable over the systems of the ensemble is

$$\langle G(x) \rangle = \left( \prod_{\alpha} N_{\alpha}! \right)^{-1} \int G(x) f^{(N)}(x, t)\, dx. \tag{1.6}$$

This is the expected or statistical average value of the dynamical variable associated with the system represented by the ensemble.

## A. Contracted Distribution Functions

Many of the dynamical variables of interest are sums of functions each of which depends on only a small subset of the total set of phase space variables. For this reason the contracted distribution functions are of importance. The contracted distribution functions may be obtained from the full distribution function by integrating over most of the phase space variables. In order to retain the symmetry, however, it is more convenient to define the contracted distribution functions as average values of special dynamical variables. The dynamical variable

$$\delta(x_{\alpha i} - x_{\alpha}) = \delta(\mathbf{r}_{\alpha i} - \mathbf{r}_{\alpha})\, \delta(Q_{\alpha i} - Q_{\alpha})\, \delta(\mathbf{p}_{\alpha i} - \mathbf{p}_{\alpha})\, \delta(P_{\alpha i} - P_{\alpha}) \tag{1.7}$$

may be considered a function in the phase space $x$, which depends parametrically on the parameters,

$$x_{\alpha} = (\mathbf{r}_{\alpha}, Q_{\alpha}, \mathbf{p}_{\alpha}, P_{\alpha}). \tag{1.8}$$

The average value of this dynamical variable,

$$\langle \delta(x_{\alpha i} - x_{\alpha}) \rangle, \tag{1.9}$$

is the average over the ensemble of the probability that molecule $i$ of species $\alpha$ is at $\mathbf{r}_\alpha$ with momentum $\mathbf{p}_\alpha$ and in the internal state described by $Q_\alpha$, $P_\alpha$, the other molecules being anywhere. With this interpretation, it follows that

$$f_\alpha(x_\alpha, t) = \sum_i \langle \delta(x_{\alpha i} - x_\alpha) \rangle \qquad (1.10)$$

is the probability density of molecules of kind $\alpha$ at $\mathbf{r}_\alpha$ with momentum $\mathbf{p}_\alpha$ in the internal state $Q_\alpha$, $P_\alpha$. This average value may be considered a function in the phase space of a single molecule of kind $\alpha$ and is a contracted distribution function, the singlet distribution function of molecules of kind $\alpha$.

The higher-order contracted distribution functions are defined and interpreted in a similar manner. In particular the pair distribution functions are defined by

$$f_{\alpha\alpha}(x_\alpha x_\alpha', t) = \sum_i \sum_{j \neq i} \langle \delta(x_{\alpha i} - x_\alpha) \delta(x_{\alpha j} - x_\alpha') \rangle \qquad (1.11)$$

and for $\alpha \neq \beta$

$$f_{\alpha\beta}(x_\alpha x_\beta, t) = \sum_i \sum_j \langle \delta(x_{\alpha i} - x_\alpha) \delta(x_{\beta j} - x_\beta) \rangle. \qquad (1.12)$$

The first function is the joint probability that two molecules of $\alpha$ are simultaneously at $x_\alpha$ and $x_\alpha'$, and the second function is the probability that molecules of kinds $\alpha$ and $\beta$ are simultaneously at $x_\alpha$ and $x_\beta$. As an example, a particular triplet distribution function is defined as

$$f_{\alpha\alpha\beta}(x_\alpha x_\alpha' x_\beta, t) = \sum_i \sum_{j \neq i} \sum_k \langle \delta(x_{\alpha i} - x_\alpha) \delta(x_{\alpha j} - x_\alpha') \delta(x_{\beta k} - x_\beta) \rangle. \quad (1.13)$$

The lower-order contracted distribution functions are, of course, integrals of the higher-order functions. For example, it follows directly from the definitions given above that

$$f_{\alpha\alpha}(x_\alpha x_\alpha', t) = N_\beta^{-1} \int f_{\alpha\alpha\beta}(x_\alpha x_\alpha' x_\beta, t)\, dx_\beta, \qquad (1.14)$$

$$f_{\alpha\beta}(x_\alpha x_\beta, t) = (N_\alpha - 1)^{-1} \int f_{\alpha\alpha\beta}(x_\alpha x_\alpha' x_\beta, t)\, dx_\alpha', \qquad (1.15)$$

and

$$f_\alpha(x_\alpha, t) = (N_\alpha - 1)^{-1} \int f_{\alpha\alpha}(x_\alpha x_\alpha', t)\, dx_\alpha', \qquad (1.16)$$

$$f_\alpha(x_\alpha, t) = N_\beta^{-1} \int f_{\alpha\beta}(x_\alpha x_\beta, t)\, dx_\beta. \qquad (1.17)$$

It is also convenient to define contracted distribution functions or densities in the configuration space. As an example of these functions we introduce the density of molecules in the one molecule configuration space,

$$\tilde{n}_\alpha(\mathbf{r}_\alpha Q_\alpha, t) = \sum_i \langle \delta(\mathbf{r}_{\alpha i} - \mathbf{r}_\alpha) \, \delta(Q_{\alpha i} - Q_\alpha) \rangle, \qquad (1.18)$$

or from Eq. (1.10),

$$\tilde{n}_\alpha(\mathbf{r}_\alpha Q_\alpha, t) = \iint f_\alpha(x_\alpha, t) \, d\mathbf{p}_\alpha \, dP_\alpha. \qquad (1.19)$$

This is the probability density of molecules of kind $\alpha$ at point $\mathbf{r}_\alpha$ with internal configuration coordinates $Q_\alpha$. In a similar manner $(\alpha \neq \beta)$

$$\tilde{n}_{\alpha\beta}(\mathbf{r}_\alpha Q_\alpha \mathbf{r}_\beta Q_\beta, t) =$$
$$\sum_i \sum_j \langle \delta(\mathbf{r}_{\alpha i} - \mathbf{r}_\alpha) \, \delta(Q_{\alpha i} - Q_\alpha) \, \delta(\mathbf{r}_{\beta j} - \mathbf{r}_\beta) \, \delta(Q_{\beta j} - Q_\beta) \rangle, \qquad (1.20)$$

or from Eq. (1.12)

$$\tilde{n}_{\alpha\beta}(\mathbf{r}_\alpha Q_\alpha \mathbf{r}_\beta Q_\beta, t) = \iiiint f_{\alpha\beta}(x_\alpha x_\beta, t) \, d\mathbf{p}_\alpha \, dP_\alpha \, d\mathbf{p}_\beta \, dP_\beta \qquad (1.21)$$

is the probability density that molecules of kinds $\alpha$ and $\beta$ are simultaneously at the indicated point in the two molecule configuration space.

The densities in the translational space are contractions of the densities in the configuration space. For example,

$$n_\alpha(\mathbf{r}_\alpha, t) = \sum_i \langle \delta(\mathbf{r}_{\alpha i} - \mathbf{r}_\alpha) \rangle, \qquad (1.22)$$

or from Eq. (1.18)

$$n_\alpha(\mathbf{r}_\alpha, t) = \int \tilde{n}_\alpha(\mathbf{r}_\alpha Q_\alpha, t) \, dQ_\alpha \qquad (1.23)$$

is the usual density of molecules of kind $\alpha$ at $\mathbf{r}_\alpha$. The corresponding pair density function is [see Eq. (1.20)]

$$n_{\alpha\beta}(\mathbf{r}_\alpha \mathbf{r}_\beta, t) = \sum_i \sum_j \langle \delta(\mathbf{r}_{\alpha i} - \mathbf{r}_\alpha) \, \delta(\mathbf{r}_{\beta j} - \mathbf{r}_\beta) \rangle$$
$$= \iint \tilde{n}_{\alpha\beta}(\mathbf{r}_\alpha Q_\alpha \mathbf{r}_\beta Q_\beta, t) \, dQ_\alpha \, dQ_\beta. \qquad (1.24)$$

This is the joint probability density of molecules of species $\alpha$ and $\beta$ being simultaneously at $\mathbf{r}_\alpha$ and $\mathbf{r}_\beta$.

## B. Equations of Change

The state of an individual system in the ensemble changes with time according to the laws of mechanics. The statistical averages, however, are determined by the state of the ensemble which is described by the distribution function $f^{(N)}(x, t)$. The time evolution of this function is described by the Liouville equation.

The Hamiltonian of the system may be written in the form

$$H = \sum_{\alpha i} \left[ \frac{p_{\alpha i}^2}{2m_\alpha} + H_\alpha(Q_{\alpha i} P_{\alpha i}) \right] + \Phi + \Phi^{(E)}, \tag{1.25}$$

where $\Phi$ is the intermolecular potential, $\Phi^{(E)}$ is the potential associated with an external force, and

$$H_\alpha(Q_{\alpha i} P_{\alpha i}) = \sum_{st} a_{st}^{(\alpha)}(Q_{\alpha i}) P_{\alpha i s} P_{\alpha i t} + \varphi_\alpha(Q_{\alpha i}) \tag{1.26}$$

is the Hamiltonian of an independent molecule in a center-of-mass coordinate system. In the latter expression $\varphi_\alpha(Q_{\alpha i})$ is the intramolecular potential and $a_{st}^{(\alpha)}(Q_{\alpha i})$ is a matrix of coefficients which depends upon the explicit definitions of the internal coordinates, $Q_{\alpha i s}$.

The potential associated with the external forces is taken to be of the form

$$\Phi^{(E)} = \sum_{\alpha i} \varphi_\alpha^{(E)}(\mathbf{r}_{\alpha i} Q_{\alpha i}). \tag{1.27}$$

Often the intermolecular potential is assumed to be of the additive form

$$\Phi = \tfrac{1}{2} \sum_{\alpha\beta ij} \varphi_{\alpha\beta}(\mathbf{r}_{\alpha i} Q_{\alpha i} \mathbf{r}_{\beta j} Q_{\beta j}), \tag{1.28}$$

where a single term describes the interaction of an isolated pair of molecules. This potential is defined so that

$$\varphi_{\alpha\beta}(\mathbf{r}_\alpha Q_\alpha \mathbf{r}_\beta Q_\beta) = \varphi_{\beta\alpha}(\mathbf{r}_\beta Q_\beta \mathbf{r}_\alpha Q_\alpha). \tag{1.29}$$

It is a standard result of classical mechanics that in terms of these quantities the equation for the time evolution of the distribution function or the Liouville equation is

$$\left( \frac{\partial}{\partial t} + \mathscr{L}^{(N)} \right) f^{(N)}(x, t) = 0, \tag{1.30}$$

where $\mathscr{L}^{(N)}$ is the Liouville operator of the system

$$\mathscr{L}^{(N)} = \sum_{\alpha i} \left\{ \frac{1}{m_\alpha} \mathbf{p}_{\alpha i} \cdot \frac{\partial}{\partial \mathbf{r}_{\alpha i}} - \left[ \frac{\partial}{\partial \mathbf{r}_{\alpha i}} (\Phi + \Phi^{(E)}) \right] \cdot \frac{\partial}{\partial \mathbf{p}_{\alpha i}} \right.$$
$$\left. + \mathscr{L}_{\alpha i}^{(int)} - \sum_s \left[ \frac{\partial}{\partial Q_{\alpha i s}} (\Phi + \Phi^{(E)}) \right] \frac{\partial}{\partial P_{\alpha i s}} \right\} \tag{1.31}$$

and

$$\mathscr{L}_{\alpha i}^{(int)} = \sum_s \left( \frac{\partial H_\alpha}{\partial P_{\alpha i s}} \frac{\partial}{\partial Q_{\alpha i s}} - \frac{\partial H_\alpha}{\partial Q_{\alpha i s}} \frac{\partial}{\partial P_{\alpha i s}} \right) \tag{1.32}$$

is the Liouville operator of molecule $\alpha i$ in a center-of-mass coordinate system.

The average value of a dynamical variable changes with time due to the time evolution of the distribution function. It follows directly from the Liouville equation, Eq. (1.30), and the definition of the average value, Eq. (1.6), that

$$\frac{\partial}{\partial t} \langle G(x) \rangle = - \left( \prod_\alpha N_\alpha! \right)^{-1} \int G(x) \mathscr{L}^{(N)} f^{(N)}(x, t) \, dx. \tag{1.33}$$

From this it may be shown that

$$\frac{\partial}{\partial t} \langle G(x) \rangle = \left( \prod_\alpha N_\alpha! \right)^{-1} \int f^{(N)}(x, t) \, \mathscr{L}^{(N)} G(x) \, dx$$
$$= \langle \mathscr{L}^{(N)} G(x) \rangle. \tag{1.34}$$

The "constant" terms that appear in the formal integration are zero since the distribution function approaches zero sufficiently rapidly for large values of those variables which have an infinite range and both $f^{(N)}(x, t)$ and $G(x)$ are periodic in those variables which have a finite range.

## C. BBGKY Equations

In Section I,A, the contracted distribution functions are defined as averages over the ensemble of dynamical variables which are products of $\delta$-functions. Hence the general equation of change may be used to obtain equations for the time evolution of the contracted distribution functions. The resulting equations are the Bogolubov, Born–Green, Kirkwood, Yvon (BBGKY) equations (Bogolubov, 1946; Born and Green, 1946, 1947, 1948; Kirkwood, 1946, Yvon 1935).

To derive the first equation in the hierarchy let us consider the dynamical variable

$$G(x) = \sum_i \delta(x_{\alpha i} - x_\alpha). \tag{1.35}$$

From the definition of the singlet distribution function, Eq. (1.10), it follows directly that

$$\langle G(x) \rangle = f_\alpha(x_\alpha, t) \tag{1.36}$$

and from the form of the Liouville operator, Eq. (1.31), that

$$\mathscr{L}^{(N)} G(x) = -\sum_i \left\{ \frac{1}{m_\alpha} \mathbf{p}_{\alpha i} \cdot \frac{\partial}{\partial \mathbf{r}_\alpha} - \left( \frac{\partial}{\partial \mathbf{r}_{\alpha i}} (\varPhi + \varPhi^{(E)}) \right) \cdot \frac{\partial}{\partial \mathbf{p}_\alpha} \right.$$
$$\left. + \sum_s \left[ \frac{\partial H_\alpha}{\partial P_{\alpha i s}} \frac{\partial}{\partial Q_{\alpha s}} - \left( \frac{\partial}{\partial Q_{\alpha i s}} (H_\alpha + \varPhi + \varPhi^{(E)}) \right) \frac{\partial}{\partial P_{\alpha s}} \right] \right\}$$
$$\times \delta(x_{\alpha i} - x_\alpha). \tag{1.37}$$

Thus

$$\langle \mathscr{L}^{(N)} G(x) \rangle = - \mathscr{L}_\alpha f_\alpha(x_\alpha, t)$$
$$+ \sum_i \left\langle \left( \frac{\partial \varPhi}{\partial \mathbf{r}_{\alpha i}} \cdot \frac{\partial}{\partial \mathbf{p}_\alpha} + \sum_s \frac{\partial \varPhi}{\partial Q_{\alpha i s}} \frac{\partial}{\partial P_{\alpha s}} \right) \right.$$
$$\times \delta(x_{\alpha i} - x_\alpha) \Big\rangle, \tag{1.38}$$

where

$$\mathscr{L}_\alpha = \frac{1}{m_\alpha} \mathbf{p}_\alpha \cdot \frac{\partial}{\partial \mathbf{r}_\alpha} + \mathscr{L}_\alpha^{(int)} - \frac{\partial \varphi_\alpha^{(E)}}{\partial \mathbf{r}_\alpha} \cdot \frac{\partial}{\partial \mathbf{p}_\alpha}$$
$$- \sum_s \frac{\partial \varphi_\alpha^{(E)}}{\partial Q_{\alpha s}} \frac{\partial}{\partial P_{\alpha s}} \tag{1.39}$$

is the Liouville operator of a single molecule of species $\alpha$. In the last expression $\varphi_\alpha^{(E)}$ is the potential associated with the external force on a molecule of species $\alpha$ [see Eq. (1.27)], and

$$\mathscr{L}_\alpha^{(int)} = \sum_s \left( \frac{\partial H_\alpha}{\partial P_{\alpha s}} \frac{\partial}{\partial Q_{\alpha s}} - \frac{\partial H_\alpha}{\partial Q_{\alpha s}} \frac{\partial}{\partial P_{\alpha s}} \right) \tag{1.40}$$

is the Liouville operator in the internal degrees of freedom of a molecule of kind $\alpha$ defined by Eq. (1.32).

If the intermolecular potential is of the additive form of Eq. (1.28), the second term on the right of Eq. (1.38) may be reduced to the form

$$\sum_\beta \int \theta_{\alpha\beta} f_{\alpha\beta}(x_\alpha x_\beta, t) \, dx_\beta, \tag{1.41}$$

where

$$\theta_{\alpha\beta} = \left(\frac{\partial}{\partial \mathbf{r}_\alpha} \varphi_{\alpha\beta}\right) \cdot \frac{\partial}{\partial \mathbf{p}_\alpha} + \sum_s \left(\frac{\partial}{\partial Q_{\alpha s}} \varphi_{\alpha\beta}\right) \frac{\partial}{\partial P_{\alpha s}}. \tag{1.42}$$

It thus follows from the general equation of change, Eq. (1.34), that

$$\left(\frac{\partial}{\partial t} + \mathcal{L}_\alpha\right) f_\alpha(x_\alpha, t) = \sum_\beta \int \theta_{\alpha\beta} f_{\alpha\beta}(x_\alpha x_\beta t) \, dx_\beta. \tag{1.43}$$

This is the first BBGKY equation. The streaming terms on the left describe the time evolution of the distribution function due to the free motion of the independent molecules. The integral on the right describes the effect of the coupling or the interaction with the other molecules of the gas.

Equations for the time evolution of the higher-order distribution functions may also be obtained from the general equation of change. The equation for the time evolution of the pair distribution function and the general equation of the hierarchy are

$$\left(\frac{\partial}{\partial t} + \mathcal{L}_{\alpha\beta}\right) f_{\alpha\beta}(x_\alpha x_\beta, t) = \sum_\eta \int (\theta_{\alpha\eta} + \theta_{\beta\eta}) f_{\alpha\beta\eta}(x_\alpha x_\beta x_\eta, t) \, dx_\eta \tag{1.44}$$

and

$$\left(\frac{\partial}{\partial t} + \mathcal{L}_{\alpha\beta\cdots\mu}\right) f_{\alpha\beta\cdots\mu}(x_\alpha x_\beta \cdots x_\mu, t)$$
$$= \sum_\eta \int (\theta_{\alpha\eta} + \theta_{\beta\eta} + \cdots + \theta_{\mu\eta}) f_{\alpha\beta\cdots\mu\eta}(x_\alpha x_\beta \cdots x_\mu x_\eta, t) \, dx_\eta, \tag{1.45}$$

where

$$\mathcal{L}_{\alpha\beta} = \mathcal{L}_\alpha + \mathcal{L}_\beta - \theta_{\alpha\beta} - \theta_{\beta\alpha} \tag{1.46}$$

and

$$\mathcal{L}_{\alpha\beta\cdots\mu} = \sum_\omega \mathcal{L}_\omega - \sum_\omega \sum_{\lambda \neq \omega} \theta_{\omega\lambda} \tag{1.47}$$

are the Liouville operators of the pair $\alpha$, $\beta$ and the set $\alpha$, $\beta$, $\ldots$, $\mu$. In the sums of Eqs. (1.44) and (1.45), $\eta$ ranges over the various species in the mixture; in the sums of Eq. (1.47), $\omega$ and $\lambda$ range over the set $\alpha, \beta, \ldots, \mu$.

## D. Macroscopic Variables and Conservation Equations

The macroscopic variables of a system are averages over the ensemble of dynamical variables associated with the additive constants of motion. The conservation equations are equations for the time evolution of the corresponding densities. These equations were derived from the general equation of change for a system of particles without structure by Irving and Kirkwood (1950).

An additive constant of motion is a function defined in the phase space which is of the additive form

$$\Psi(x) = \sum_{\alpha i} \psi_\alpha(x_{\alpha i}) \tag{1.48}$$

and has the property that, in the absence of an external force, it is a constant of motion; that is, if $\Phi^{(E)} = 0$,

$$\mathcal{L}^{(N)}\Psi(x) = 0. \tag{1.49}$$

The corresponding macroscopic variable is defined as the average value,

$$\sum_{\alpha i} \langle \psi_\alpha(x_{\alpha i}) \, \delta(\mathbf{r}_{\alpha i} - \mathbf{r}) \rangle$$
$$= \sum_\alpha \iiint \psi_\alpha(\mathbf{r}Q_\alpha\mathbf{p}_\alpha P_\alpha) f_\alpha(\mathbf{r}Q_\alpha\mathbf{p}_\alpha P_\alpha, t) \, dQ_\alpha \, d\mathbf{p}_\alpha \, dP_\alpha. \tag{1.50}$$

If $\psi_\alpha(x_{\alpha i})$ is taken to be simply

$$\psi_\alpha(x_{\alpha i}) = \delta_{\alpha\beta}, \tag{1.51}$$

the corresponding macroscopic variable is

$$n_\beta(\mathbf{r}, t) = \iiint f_\beta(\mathbf{r}Q_\beta\mathbf{p}_\beta P_\beta, t) \, dQ_\beta \, d\mathbf{p}_\beta \, dP_\beta, \tag{1.52}$$

the number density of molecules of species $\beta$, as defined by Eq. (1.22). The corresponding conservation equation, the equation of continuity of molecules of species $\beta$ is a special case of the general equation of change, Eq. (1.34). The equation, however, may be more readily obtained simply by integration of the first BBGKY equation, Eq. (1.43). It follows directly upon integration of both sides of this equation over $Q_\alpha$, $\mathbf{p}_\alpha$, and $P_\alpha$, that

$$\frac{\partial}{\partial t} n_\alpha + \frac{\partial}{\partial \mathbf{r}} \cdot n_\alpha \mathbf{u}_\alpha = 0, \tag{1.53}$$

where

$$n_\alpha \mathbf{u}_\alpha = m_\alpha^{-1} \int\int\int \mathbf{p}_\alpha f_\alpha (\mathbf{r} Q_\alpha \mathbf{p}_\alpha P_\alpha, t)\, dQ_\alpha\, d\mathbf{p}_\alpha\, dP_\alpha \tag{1.54}$$

is interpreted as the (number) flux of molecules of species $\alpha$.

The second macroscopic variable is obtained by taking

$$\psi_\alpha(x_{\alpha i}) = \mathbf{p}_{\alpha i}. \tag{1.55}$$

In this case, the corresponding macroscopic variable is

$$\varrho\mathbf{u} = \sum_\alpha \int\int\int \mathbf{p}_\alpha f_\alpha (\mathbf{r} Q_\alpha \mathbf{p}_\alpha P_\alpha, t)\, dQ_\alpha\, d\mathbf{p}_\alpha\, dP_\alpha, \tag{1.56}$$

the density of linear momentum. The total mass density is

$$\varrho = \sum_\alpha n_\alpha m_\alpha \tag{1.57}$$

and $\mathbf{u}$ is the macroscopic stream velocity of the fluid.

The diffusion velocity of molecules of species $\alpha$ is defined as the difference

$$\mathbf{U}_\alpha = \mathbf{u}_\alpha - \mathbf{u}. \tag{1.58}$$

From this definition and Eqs. (1.54), (1.56), and (1.57) it readily follows that

$$\sum_\alpha n_\alpha m_\alpha \mathbf{U}_\alpha = 0. \tag{1.59}$$

The detailed equations of continuity, Eqs. (1.53), may be written in terms of the stream velocity and the diffusion velocities in the form

$$\frac{\partial}{\partial t} n_\alpha + \frac{\partial}{\partial \mathbf{r}} \cdot n_\alpha \mathbf{u} = -\frac{\partial}{\partial \mathbf{r}} \cdot n_\alpha \mathbf{U}_\alpha. \tag{1.60}$$

The overall equation of continuity is obtained from this equation by multiplying each equation by $m_\alpha$, summing on $\alpha$, and using Eqs. (1.57) and (1.59). The result is

$$\frac{\partial}{\partial t} \varrho + \frac{\partial}{\partial \mathbf{r}} \cdot \varrho\mathbf{u} = 0. \tag{1.61}$$

The equation of conservation of linear momentum, or the equation of motion, is also a special case of the general equation of change, (1.34). The equation may, however, also be derived more directly from the first BBGKY equation, Eq. (1.43), by first multiplying by $\mathbf{p}_\alpha$, then integrating over $Q_\alpha$, $\mathbf{p}_\alpha$, and $P_\alpha$ and summing on $\alpha$. After rather lengthy manipulations the resulting equation may be written in the form

$$\varrho\left(\frac{\partial}{\partial t} + \mathbf{u} \cdot \frac{\partial}{\partial \mathbf{r}}\right)\mathbf{u} = -\frac{\partial}{\partial \mathbf{r}} \cdot \mathbf{p} + \sum_\alpha n_\alpha \mathbf{F}_\alpha^{(E)}, \qquad (1.62)$$

where $\mathbf{F}_\alpha^{(E)}$ is the average external force on molecules of species $\alpha$ defined by

$$n_\alpha \mathbf{F}_\alpha^{(E)} = -\int \left(\frac{\partial}{\partial \mathbf{r}} \varphi_\alpha^{(E)}\right)\tilde{n}_\alpha(\mathbf{r}Q_\alpha, t) \, dQ_\alpha \qquad (1.63)$$

and $\mathbf{p}$ is the pressure tensor, the sum of a kinetic contribution $\mathbf{p}^{(K)}$, and a collisional transfer contribution $\mathbf{p}^{(\phi)}$,

$$\mathbf{p} = \mathbf{p}^{(K)} + \mathbf{p}^{(\phi)}. \qquad (1.64)$$

The kinetic contribution to the pressure tensor is an integral of the singlet distribution function

$$\mathbf{p}^{(K)} = \sum_\alpha m_\alpha \iiint \mathbf{V}_\alpha \mathbf{V}_\alpha f_\alpha(\mathbf{r}Q_\alpha \mathbf{p}_\alpha P_\alpha, t) \, dQ_\alpha \, d\mathbf{p}_\alpha \, dP_\alpha, \qquad (1.65)$$

where

$$\mathbf{V}_\alpha = m_\alpha^{-1}\mathbf{p}_\alpha - \mathbf{u} \qquad (1.66)$$

is the "Brownian velocity" of a molecule, that is, the velocity relative to the stream velocity $\mathbf{u}$. If the intermolecular potential is of the additive form, Eq. (1.28), the collisional transfer contribution to the pressure tensor is

$$\mathbf{p}^{(\phi)} = -\tfrac{1}{2}\sum_{\alpha\beta} \iiint \int_0^1 \tilde{n}_{\alpha\beta}(\mathbf{r} - \mu\mathbf{r}_{\beta\alpha}, Q_\alpha, \mathbf{r} + (1-\mu)\mathbf{r}_{\beta\alpha}, Q_\beta, t)$$

$$\times \mathbf{r}_{\beta\alpha} \frac{\partial}{\partial \mathbf{r}_{\beta\alpha}} \varphi_{\alpha\beta}(\mathbf{r}_{\beta\alpha}Q_\alpha Q_\beta) \, d\mu \, d\mathbf{r}_{\beta\alpha} \, dQ_\alpha \, dQ_\beta, \qquad (1.67)$$

where $\tilde{n}_{\alpha\beta}(\mathbf{r}_\alpha Q_\alpha \mathbf{r}_\beta Q_\beta, t)$ is the density of molecules in the pair configuration space, Eq. (1.21), and

$$\varphi_{\alpha\beta}(\mathbf{r}_\beta - \mathbf{r}_\alpha, Q_\alpha Q_\beta) = \varphi_{\alpha\beta}(\mathbf{r}_\alpha Q_\alpha \mathbf{r}_\beta Q_\beta) \qquad (1.68)$$

is the potential of interaction of a pair of molecules. It may be shown that $p^{(K)}$ is the contribution to the flux of linear momentum, relative to the stream velocity $\mathbf{u}$ associated with the flow of molecules, and $p^{(\phi)}$ is the contribution associated with the direct effects of the intermolecular potential.

The total energy of the system is only approximately additive and represents a somewhat special case. If the intermolecular potential energy is of the additive form of Eq. (1.28), it is a "two molecule" property. In order to "localize" the energy and obtain an essentially additive property one-half of the potential energy of interaction is taken to be associated with each of the two interacting molecules. If the intermolecular potential energy is of sufficiently short range this localization introduces no conceptual problem. The equation of conservation of energy may be derived in a manner similar to that discussed above in connection with the equation of motion. The result of such a derivation may be written in the form

$$\frac{\partial}{\partial t} nU + \frac{\partial}{\partial \mathbf{r}} \cdot nU\mathbf{u} = -\frac{\partial}{\partial \mathbf{r}} \cdot \mathbf{q} - p^{\dagger} : \frac{\partial}{\partial \mathbf{r}} \mathbf{u} + \sum_{\alpha} n_{\alpha} Q_{\alpha}^{(E)}, \quad (1.69)$$

where $U$ is the thermodynamic internal energy density of the fluid, excluding both the kinetic energy associated with the macroscopic stream velocity $\mathbf{u}$ and the potential energy associated with the external forces. In the last equation, $Q_{\alpha}^{(E)}$ is a work term associated with the external forces. If the molecules have no structure this term is simply

$$Q_{\alpha}^{(E)} = -\mathbf{U}_{\alpha} \cdot \frac{\partial}{\partial \mathbf{r}} \varphi_{\alpha}^{(E)}. \quad (1.70)$$

In addition, $p^{\dagger}$ is the transpose of the pressure tensor given by Eq. (1.64), and $\mathbf{q}$ is the energy flux relative to the stream velocity. In general there are a number of contributions to the energy flux. In the limiting case of a gas of spherical molecules at low density the flux is simply

$$\mathbf{q} = \tfrac{1}{2} \sum_{\alpha} m_{\alpha} \int V_{\alpha}^{2} V_{\alpha} f_{\alpha}(\mathbf{r}\mathbf{p}_{\alpha}, t) \, d\mathbf{p}_{\alpha}. \quad (1.71)$$

More general expressions are given elsewhere (Irving and Kirkwood, 1950; Hoffman and Curtiss, 1965).

In general the total angular momentum of the system is another additive constant of motion, which leads to another macroscopic variable, which is seldom recognized. In a gas of spherical molecules the additional variable is simply the vorticity; in the treatment of a gas of nonspherical molecules the additional variable may be of some interest because of the exchange of angular momentum between the intrinsic angular momentum of the molecules and the angular momentum associated with the macroscopic flow. An equation of conservation of angular momentum may be derived by methods similar to those discussed above (Curtiss, 1956).

## II. Quantum Formulation

A classical description of the statistical behavior of fluids is discussed in the preceding section. In the present section, an analogous quantum mechanical treatment is presented. To simplify the notation, let

$$\xi_{\alpha i} = (\mathbf{r}_{\alpha i}, Q_{\alpha i}) \tag{2.1}$$

represent the full set of configuration coordinates of a single molecule, including any required spin coordinates. In addition let

$$\xi = (\xi_{11}, \xi_{12}, \xi_{13}, \ldots, \xi_{21}\xi_{22}\xi_{23}, \ldots) \tag{2.2}$$

represent the full set of configuration coordinates of the gas.

The quantum mechanical state of a system may be described by a wave function $\psi(\xi)$, a function in the full configuration space. Let $\mathscr{G}(\xi)$ be an operator associated with a dynamical variable. Then the quantum mechanical expectation value of the dynamical variable in the state characterized by the wave function $\psi(\xi)$ is

$$\bar{G} = \int \psi^*(\xi)\mathscr{G}(\xi)\psi(\xi)\,d\xi, \tag{2.3}$$

where $d\xi$ indicates an integration over the entire configuration space.

The expectation value may also be written in terms of the probability density matrix

$$\varrho(\xi; \xi') = \psi^*(\xi')\psi(\xi). \tag{2.4}$$

In terms of this matrix, the expectation value, Eq. (2.3), is

$$\bar{G} = \mathrm{Tr}\,\mathscr{G}\varrho$$

$$= \int \mathscr{G}(\xi'; \xi)\varrho(\xi; \xi')\,d\xi\,d\xi', \tag{2.5}$$

where the matrix $\mathscr{G}(\xi'; \xi)$ in the coordinate representation may be written formally in the form

$$\mathscr{G}(\xi'; \xi) = \delta(\xi' - \xi)\mathscr{G}(\xi). \tag{2.6}$$

Next let us consider an ensemble of systems. The state of a particular system $k$ in the ensemble may be characterized by a probability density matrix $\varrho_k$. The state of the ensemble then determines the statistical probability density matrix $\mathscr{P}$, which is defined as the average over the systems $k$ of the $\varrho_k$. It then follows from the linear form of the expression given by Eq. (2.5) for the quantum mechanical expectation value $\bar{G}$ that the average over the ensemble of the $\bar{G}$ is simply

$$\langle G \rangle = \mathrm{Tr}\ \mathscr{G}\mathscr{P}. \tag{2.7}$$

This is the statistical average value of the dynamical variable associated with the ensemble.

## A. Wigner Distribution Functions

The statistical probability density matrix may, of course, be expressed in various representations. Let us consider, in particular, a representation based on the energy eigenfunctions of the independent molecules.
Let

$$\chi_\alpha(j_{\alpha i}; Q_{\alpha i}) \tag{2.8}$$

be an energy eigenfunction of molecule $\alpha i$ in a center of mass coordinate system, with $j_{\alpha i}$ representing the full set of quantum numbers necessary to specify the state. A product of functions of this type associated with each of the molecules in the system defines a unitary matrix. If one neglects the statistics effects of the Pauli principle, one may use this matrix to transform the statistical probability matrix to a new basis. The result of the transformation is the matrix

$$\mathscr{P}(\mathbf{r}j; \mathbf{r}'j'), \tag{2.9}$$

where $\mathbf{r}$ and $\mathbf{r}'$ represent continuous coordinates,

$$\mathbf{r} = (\mathbf{r}_{11}, \mathbf{r}_{12}, \mathbf{r}_{13}, \ldots, \mathbf{r}_{21}, \mathbf{r}_{22}, \mathbf{r}_{23}, \ldots), \tag{2.10}$$

and $j$ and $j'$ represent discrete indices,

$$j = (j_{11}, j_{12}, j_{13}, \ldots, j_{21}, j_{22}, j_{23}, \ldots). \tag{2.11}$$

The Wigner distribution function may be defined in terms of the density matrix in this representation by

$$f^{(N)}(jj';\mathbf{rp},t)$$

$$= (2/h)^{3N}\left(\prod_\alpha N_\alpha!\right)\int\left[\exp-\frac{2i}{\hbar}\,\mathbf{s}\cdot\mathbf{p}\right]\mathscr{P}(\mathbf{r}+\mathbf{s}\,j;\mathbf{r}-\mathbf{s}\,j')\,d\mathbf{s}. \quad (2.12)$$

That is, the function is a type of Fourier transform in the space of the translational motion of the molecules, but is a matrix in the internal space.
Let

$$G(jj';\mathbf{rp}) \qquad\qquad (2.13)$$

be a function in the same space as the Wigner distribution function, that is, a function in the space of $\mathbf{r}$ and $\mathbf{p}$ and a matrix in the space of $j$. Then we define the "Wigner average" as

$$\langle G\rangle_W = \left(\prod_\alpha N_\alpha!\right)^{-1}\sum_{jj'}\int G(jj';\mathbf{rp})f^{(N)}(j'j;\mathbf{rp},t)\,d\mathbf{r}\,d\mathbf{p}, \quad (2.14)$$

or using matrix notation

$$\langle G\rangle_W = \left(\prod_\alpha N_\alpha!\right)^{-1}\mathrm{Tr}\int G(\mathbf{rp})f^{(N)}(\mathbf{rp},t)\,d\mathbf{r}\,d\mathbf{p}. \quad (2.15)$$

This expression is formally quite similar to the classical average over an ensemble given by Eq. (1.6). It is easily shown that if $G$ is a function of $\mathbf{r}$ only, the Wigner average given by the last expression is identical with the statistical average given by Eq. (2.7). This identity is also true under somewhat more general conditions; however, in spite of numerous statements in the literature, it is not the basis of a general correspondence principal.

In the present development it is convenient to introduce contracted distribution functions in a manner analogous to that used in the previous section in the classical treatment. In analogy with the classical definition, Eq. (1.10), the singlet Wigner distribution function is defined as

$$f_\alpha(j_\alpha j_\alpha';\mathbf{r}_\alpha\mathbf{p}_\alpha,t) = f_\alpha(\mathbf{r}_\alpha\mathbf{p}_\alpha,t)$$

$$= \sum_i \langle\delta(j_{\alpha i}j_{\alpha i}';j_\alpha j_\alpha')\,\delta_{\alpha i}(j;j')\,\delta(\mathbf{r}_{\alpha i}-\mathbf{r}_\alpha)\,\delta(\mathbf{p}_{\alpha i}-\mathbf{p}_\alpha)\rangle_W, \quad (2.16)$$

where the second factor in the braces is the product of Kronecker deltas in the quantum numbers of all the molecules except molecule $\alpha i$. Higher-order contracted distribution functions may also be defined as in the classical treatment. For example, in analogy with Eq. (1.12), the pair distribution function $(\alpha \neq \beta)$ is

$$f_{\alpha\beta}(j_\alpha j_\beta j_\alpha' j_\beta'; \mathbf{r}_\alpha \mathbf{r}_\beta \mathbf{p}_\alpha \mathbf{p}_\beta, t) = f_{\alpha\beta}(\mathbf{r}_\alpha \mathbf{r}_\beta \mathbf{p}_\alpha \mathbf{p}_\beta, t)$$

$$= \sum_{ij} \langle \delta(j_{\alpha i} j_{\beta j} j_{\alpha i}' j_{\beta j}'; j_\alpha j_\beta j_\alpha' j_\beta') \, \delta_{\alpha i \beta j}(j; j') \, \delta(\mathbf{r}_{\alpha i} - \mathbf{r}_\alpha)$$

$$\times \delta(\mathbf{r}_{\beta j} - \mathbf{r}_\beta) \, \delta(\mathbf{p}_{\alpha i} - \mathbf{p}_\alpha) \, \delta(\mathbf{p}_{\beta j} - \mathbf{p}_\beta) \rangle_W . \tag{2.17}$$

These contracted distribution functions are also related as in the classical case. From these definitions, it readily follows that in analogy with Eq. (1.17)

$$f_\alpha(\mathbf{r}_\alpha \mathbf{p}_\alpha, t) = N_\beta^{-1} \sum_{j\beta} \int\int f_{\alpha\beta}(j_\alpha j_\beta j_\alpha' j_\beta; \mathbf{r}_\alpha \mathbf{r}_\beta \mathbf{p}_\alpha \mathbf{p}_\beta, t) \, d\mathbf{r}_\beta \, d\mathbf{p}_\beta$$

$$= N_\beta^{-1} \operatorname*{Tr}_{(\beta)} \int\int f_{\alpha\beta}(\mathbf{r}_\alpha \mathbf{r}_\beta \mathbf{p}_\alpha \mathbf{p}_\beta, t) \, d\mathbf{r}_\beta \, d\mathbf{p}_\beta . \tag{2.18}$$

Thus the Wigner distribution functions play a role in the quantum development analogous to the ordinary distribution functions of the classical treatment.

## B. Quantum Mechanical Liouville Equation

The time evolution of the state of a single system as characterized by the wave function $\psi(\xi)$ is described by the Schroedinger equation

$$\frac{\partial}{\partial t} \psi = -\frac{i}{\hbar} \mathscr{H} \psi, \tag{2.19}$$

where $\mathscr{H}$ is the Hamiltonian operator. It follows directly from this relation and the definition of the probability density matrix $\varrho$, Eq. (2.4), that the time evolution of $\varrho$ is described by the Heisenberg equation of motion

$$\frac{\partial}{\partial t} \varrho = \frac{i}{\hbar} (\varrho \mathscr{H} - \mathscr{H} \varrho). \tag{2.20}$$

It then follows from the linearity of this relation and the definition of the statistical probability density matrix $\mathscr{P}$ that the time evolution of $\mathscr{P}$ is described by essentially the same equation,

$$\frac{\partial}{\partial t} \mathscr{P} = \frac{i}{\hbar} (\mathscr{P} \mathscr{H} - \mathscr{H} \mathscr{P}). \tag{2.21}$$

The Hamiltonian of the system is the quantum analog of the classical Hamiltonian given by Eq. (1.25). This is

$$\mathscr{H} = \mathscr{K} + \Phi + \Phi^{(E)} + \sum_{\alpha i} \mathscr{H}_\alpha(\alpha i), \qquad (2.22)$$

where $\mathscr{K}$ is the operator associated with the kinetic energy of the centers of mass of the molecules, $\Phi$ is the intermolecular potential energy, $\phi^{(E)}$ is the potential energy associated with the external forces, and $\mathscr{H}_\alpha$ is the Hamiltonian of an individual molecule of kind $\alpha$ in a center-of-mass coordinate system. In a representation based on the energy eigenfunctions of the independent molecules, Eq. (2.8), the $\mathscr{H}_\alpha$ are diagonal and are

$$\mathscr{H}_\alpha(\alpha i) = \delta(j; j') E_\alpha(j_{\alpha i}), \qquad (2.23)$$

where the $E_\alpha(j_{\alpha i})$ are the energy eigenvalues of the molecule.

The quantum mechanical Liouville equation, Eq. (2.21), may be transformed into an equation for the time evolution of the Wigner distribution function. After rather lengthy manipulations it may be shown that the resulting equation is

$$\left(\frac{\partial}{\partial t} + \sum_{\alpha i} \frac{1}{m_\alpha} \mathbf{p}_{\alpha i} \cdot \frac{\partial}{\partial \mathbf{r}_{\alpha i}}\right) f^{(N)}(\mathbf{r}, \mathbf{p}, t)$$

$$+ \frac{i}{\hbar} \sum_{\alpha i} [\mathscr{H}_\alpha(\alpha i) f^{(N)}(\mathbf{r}\mathbf{p}, t) - f^{(N)}(\mathbf{r}\mathbf{p}, t) \mathscr{H}_\alpha(\alpha i)]$$

$$= \int \left[\exp -\frac{2i}{\hbar} \mathbf{p}' \cdot \mathbf{r}\right]$$

$$\times [\chi(\mathbf{p}') f^{(N)}(\mathbf{r}, \mathbf{p} + \mathbf{p}', t) - f^{(N)}(\mathbf{r}, \mathbf{p} - \mathbf{p}', t) \chi(\mathbf{p}')] \, d\mathbf{p}', \qquad (2.24)$$

where $\chi(\mathbf{p}')$ is a Fourier transform of the potential,

$$\chi(\mathbf{p}) = -\frac{i}{\hbar} \left(\frac{2}{h}\right)^{3N} \int \left[\exp \frac{2i}{\hbar} \mathbf{p} \cdot \mathbf{r}\right][\Phi(\mathbf{r}) + \Phi^{(E)}(\mathbf{r})] \, d\mathbf{r}. \qquad (2.25)$$

This equation may be written formally as

$$\left(\frac{\partial}{\partial t} + \mathscr{L}^{(N)}\right) f^{(N)}(\mathbf{r}\mathbf{p}, t) = 0, \qquad (2.26)$$

where the "superoperator" $\mathscr{L}^{(N)}$ is then the quantum analog of the classical operator defined by Eq. (1.31).

It follows in a straightward manner from the last equation and the definition of the Wigner average, Eq. (2.15), that the time derivative is given by an equation analogous to the classical equation, Eq. (1.34),

$$\frac{\partial}{\partial t} \langle G \rangle_W = \langle \mathscr{L}^{(N)} G \rangle_W. \tag{2.27}$$

This is the quantum mechanical general equation of change.

## C. BBGKY Equations

The quantum mechanical BBGKY equations are equations analogous to the classical equations discussed in Section I,C, which may be considered as special cases of the general equation of change, Eq. (2.27). In particular the first quantum mechanical BBGKY equation is obtained by taking the quantity $G$ to be

$$G = \sum_i \delta(j_{\alpha i} j'_{\alpha i}; j_\alpha j'_\alpha) \, \delta_{\alpha i}(j; j') \, \delta(\mathbf{r}_{\alpha i} - \mathbf{r}_\alpha) \, \delta(\mathbf{p}_{\alpha i} - \mathbf{p}_\alpha). \tag{2.28}$$

With this choice, if the intermolecular potential is of the additive form of Eq. (1.28), the general equation of change, Eq. (2.27), becomes, in particular,

$$\left( \frac{\partial}{\partial t} + \frac{1}{m_\alpha} \mathbf{p}_\alpha \cdot \frac{\partial}{\partial \mathbf{r}_\alpha} \right) f_\alpha(\mathbf{r}_\alpha \mathbf{p}_\alpha, t)$$

$$+ \frac{i}{\hbar} [\mathscr{H}_\alpha f_\alpha(\mathbf{r}_\alpha \mathbf{p}_\alpha, t) - f_\alpha(\mathbf{r}_\alpha \mathbf{p}_\alpha, t) \mathscr{H}_\alpha] - \int \left[ \exp - \frac{2i}{\hbar} \mathbf{p}'_\alpha \cdot \mathbf{r}_\alpha \right]$$

$$\times [\chi_\alpha^{(E)}(\mathbf{p}'_\alpha) f_\alpha(\mathbf{r}_\alpha, \mathbf{p}_\alpha + \mathbf{p}'_\alpha, t) - f_\alpha(\mathbf{r}_\alpha, \mathbf{p}_\alpha - \mathbf{p}'_\alpha, t) \chi_\alpha^{(E)}(\mathbf{p}'_\alpha)] \, d\mathbf{p}'_\alpha$$

$$= \operatorname*{Tr}_{(\beta)} \iint \left[ \exp - \frac{2i}{\hbar} (\mathbf{p}'_\alpha \cdot \mathbf{r}_\alpha + \mathbf{p}'_\beta \cdot \mathbf{r}_\beta) \right]$$

$$\times [\chi_{\alpha\beta}(\mathbf{p}'_\alpha \mathbf{p}'_\beta) f_{\alpha\beta}(\mathbf{r}_\alpha \mathbf{r}_\beta, \mathbf{p}_\alpha + \mathbf{p}'_\alpha, \mathbf{p}_\beta, t)$$

$$- f_{\alpha\beta}(\mathbf{r}_\alpha \mathbf{r}_\beta, \mathbf{p}_\alpha - \mathbf{p}'_\alpha, \mathbf{p}_\beta, t) \chi_{\alpha\beta}(\mathbf{p}'_\alpha \mathbf{p}'_\beta)] \, d\mathbf{r}_\beta \, d\mathbf{p}_\beta \, d\mathbf{p}'_\alpha \, d\mathbf{p}'_\beta, \tag{2.29}$$

where

$$\chi_\alpha^{(E)}(\mathbf{p}_\alpha) = -\frac{i}{\hbar} \left( \frac{2}{h} \right)^3 \int \left[ \exp \frac{2i}{\hbar} \mathbf{p}_\alpha \cdot \mathbf{r}_\alpha \right] \varphi_\alpha^{(E)}(\mathbf{r}_\alpha) \, d\mathbf{r}_\alpha \tag{2.30}$$

and

$$\chi_{\alpha\beta}(\mathbf{p}_\alpha \mathbf{p}_\beta) = -\frac{i}{\hbar} \left( \frac{2}{h} \right)^6 \iint \left[ \exp \frac{2i}{\hbar} (\mathbf{p}_\alpha \cdot \mathbf{r}_\alpha + \mathbf{p}_\beta \cdot \mathbf{r}_\beta) \right]$$

$$\times \varphi_{\alpha\beta}(\mathbf{r}_\alpha \mathbf{r}_\beta) \, d\mathbf{r}_\alpha \, d\mathbf{r}_\beta. \tag{2.31}$$

The higher-order BBGKY equations may be derived in a similar manner.

## D. Equations of Change

The equations of change of the macroscopic variables may be derived in a manner similar to the classical development of the previous section. From the usual interpretation of the wave function it follows that the diagonal elements of the probability density matrix are probability distributions in the configuration space. Hence, the integral over the $\mathbf{r}_{\alpha i}$ of all of the molecules except one, of the trace of the statistical probability density matrix over the indices associated with the internal coordinates, is the probability of finding the molecule at this point. The average over all molecules of this species is then the corresponding number density. It is readily shown from the definitions that this quantity is

$$n_\alpha(\mathbf{r},\, t) = \mathrm{Tr} \int f_\alpha(\mathbf{r}\mathbf{p}_\alpha,\, t)\, d\mathbf{p}_\alpha. \tag{2.32}$$

Next, let us integrate the first BBGKY equation, Eq. (2.29), over the momentum $\mathbf{p}_\alpha$ and take the trace over the indices associated with the internal degrees of freedom. The resulting equation is

$$\frac{\partial}{\partial t}\, n_\alpha + \frac{\partial}{\partial \mathbf{r}} \cdot n_\alpha \mathbf{u}_\alpha = 0, \tag{2.33}$$

where

$$n_\alpha \mathbf{u}_\alpha = \frac{1}{m_\alpha}\, \mathrm{Tr} \int \mathbf{p}_\alpha f_\alpha(\mathbf{r}\mathbf{p}_\alpha,\, t)\, d\mathbf{p}_\alpha. \tag{2.34}$$

This equation is identical in form with the classical detailed equations of continuity, Eqs. (1.53). Hence $\mathbf{u}_\alpha$ as defined above may be interpreted as the average velocity of molecules of species $\alpha$.

The overall mass density $\varrho$ and stream velocity $\mathbf{u}$ are defined by

$$\varrho = \sum_\alpha n_\alpha m_\alpha, \tag{2.35}$$

$$\mathbf{u} = (1/\varrho) \sum_\alpha n_\alpha m_\alpha \mathbf{u}_\alpha. \tag{2.36}$$

It follows from these definitions and Eq. (2.33) that

$$\frac{\partial}{\partial t}\, \varrho + \frac{\partial}{\partial \mathbf{r}} \cdot \varrho \mathbf{u} = 0. \tag{2.37}$$

This is the usual overall equation of continuity.

The equation of motion is an equation for the time evolution of the stream velocity. To derive this equation we multiply the first BBGKY equation, Eq. (2.29), by $\mathbf{p}_\alpha$, and then integrate on $\mathbf{p}_\alpha$, take the trace $\alpha$ and sum on $\alpha$. The result is an equation identical in form with the classical equation, Eq. (1.62), but with modified definitions of the pressure tensor and external force terms (see Imam-Rahajoe and Curtiss, 1967). The quantum mechanical equations of conservation of energy and angular momentum may also be derived in a similar manner.

## III. Boltzmann Equation

In this section, we consider first the classic Boltzmann (1872) development of the basic equation of the kinetic theory of gases at low density. Later in this section, we discuss a more recent, more rigorous development of a more general equation based on the BBGKY hierarchy of Section I,C. The present discussion is restricted to a classical gas of structureless particles. An analogous quantum development has been considered by Hoffman, Mueller, and Curtiss (1965) and the effects of internal structure, particularly rotational degrees of freedom have been considered classically (Curtiss, 1956; Curtiss and Dahler, 1963) and quantum mechanically (Waldmann, 1957, 1958; Snider, 1960).

### A. Boltzmann Development

The four basic limitations of the Boltzmann equation are (a) that classical mechanics applies, (b) that the molecules are spherical, that is, without structure, (c) that the gas is sufficiently dilute that only binary collisions occur, and (d) that the intermolecular potentials are of short range. The essential idea of the development is that the collisions between the molecules are binary collisions and are essentially instantaneous, that is, that the time between collisions of a particular molecule is long compared to the duration of a single collision.

In the Boltzmann development, the singlet distribution function $f_\alpha(\mathbf{r}\mathbf{p}_\alpha, t)$ is interpreted in a manner different from that implied by the definition of Eq. (1.10). In the Boltzmann development the singlet distribution function is interpreted as describing the distribution function of molecules of a single vessel of gas in the one molecule phase space. That is,

$$f_\alpha(\mathbf{r}\mathbf{p}_\alpha, t)\, d\mathbf{r}\, d\mathbf{p}_\alpha \tag{3.1}$$

is the number of molecules of species $\alpha$ in the vessel of gas whose coordinates and momenta lie in the volume element about $\mathbf{r}, \mathbf{p}_\alpha$. Of course, it is implicitly assumed that the number of molecules in the volume element is sufficiently large that this distribution is essentially continuous. In more rigorous developments, this problem is avoided by "time-smoothing" or averaging over an ensemble.

To develop the Boltzmann equation, let us consider an arbitrary volume in the phase space of a single molecule. The integral over this volume,

$$\iint f_\alpha(\mathbf{r}\mathbf{p}_\alpha, t) \, d\mathbf{r} \, d\mathbf{p}_\alpha, \tag{3.2}$$

is the total number of molecules whose coordinates and momenta lie in this volume. This number changes in time due to the free flow of the molecules along straight lines with constant momentum and due to binary collisions. It is assumed that the collisions are essentially instantaneous, and discontinuously change the momentum, but occur at a point in the position space. It is shown later in this section that these assumptions lead to equations which are valid in the limit of low density. With these assumptions then the time rate of change of the number of molecules in the arbitrary volume is

$$\frac{d}{dt} \iint f_\alpha(\mathbf{r}\mathbf{p}_\alpha, t) \, d\mathbf{r} \, d\mathbf{p}_\alpha$$
$$= -\int (\mathbf{n}_1 \cdot \dot{\mathbf{r}} + \mathbf{n}_2 \cdot \dot{\mathbf{p}}_\alpha) f_\alpha(\mathbf{r}\mathbf{p}_\alpha, t) \, d\Sigma + \iint J_\alpha \, d\mathbf{r} \, d\mathbf{p}_\alpha, \tag{3.3}$$

where $d\Sigma$ indicates an integration over the surface in the six dimensional phase space and $\mathbf{n}_1$ and $\mathbf{n}_2$ are the $\mathbf{r}$ and $\mathbf{p}_\alpha$ components of the unit vector in the direction of the outward normal. The first term on the right is thus an integration over the surface of the flux of points through the surface. In the second term on the right, $J_\alpha$, is a net source (or sink) term due to collisions.

It follows from Gauss's theorem that the surface integral on the right of the last equation may be changed to a volume integral and hence

$$\iint \left( \frac{\partial}{\partial t} f_\alpha + \frac{\partial}{\partial \mathbf{r}} \cdot \dot{\mathbf{r}} f_\alpha + \frac{\partial}{\partial \mathbf{p}_\alpha} \cdot \dot{\mathbf{p}}_\alpha f_\alpha - J_\alpha \right) d\mathbf{r} \, d\mathbf{p}_\alpha = 0. \tag{3.4}$$

Since this result is valid for an arbitrary volume the integrand above is identically zero. Furthermore,

$$\dot{\mathbf{r}} = \mathbf{p}_\alpha / m_\alpha \tag{3.5}$$

and

$$\dot{\mathbf{p}}_\alpha = - \frac{\partial}{\partial \mathbf{r}} \, \varphi_\alpha^{(E)}, \tag{3.6}$$

where $\varphi_\alpha^{(E)}$ is the potential associated with the external force on molecules of species $\alpha$. Thus

$$\left( \frac{\partial}{\partial t} + \mathscr{L}_\alpha \right) f_\alpha(\mathbf{r}\mathbf{p}_\alpha, t) = J_\alpha, \tag{3.7}$$

where

$$\mathscr{L}_\alpha = \frac{1}{m_\alpha} \, \mathbf{p}_\alpha \cdot \frac{\partial}{\partial \mathbf{r}} - \frac{\partial \varphi_\alpha^{(E)}}{\partial \mathbf{r}} \cdot \frac{\partial}{\partial \mathbf{p}_\alpha} \tag{3.8}$$

is a special case of the Liouville operator of a single molecule defined by Eq. (1.39). Thus the streaming terms on the left of Eq. (3.7) are a special case of the streaming terms on the left of the first BBGKY equation, Eq. (1.43). These terms simply describe the time evolution of the distribution function due to the free motion of the molecules.

## B. Collision Integral

The collision integral $J_\alpha$ may be considered as the difference of a source term $J_\alpha^{(+)}$ and a sink term $J_\alpha^{(-)}$,

$$J_\alpha = J_\alpha^{(+)} - J_\alpha^{(-)}. \tag{3.9}$$

We consider the sink term $J_\alpha^{(-)}$ first. It is assumed that every collision instantaneously changes the momentum by a finite amount. Hence $J_\alpha^{(-)} \, d\mathbf{r} \, d\mathbf{p}_\alpha \, dt$ is simply the total number of collisions molecules of species $\alpha$ in the volume element $d\mathbf{r} \, d\mathbf{p}_\alpha$ about $\mathbf{r}, \mathbf{p}_\alpha$ make during the time interval $dt$. Since the collisions are binary collisions

$$J_\alpha^{(-)} = \sum_\beta J_{\alpha\beta}^{(-)}, \tag{3.10}$$

where $J_{\alpha\beta}^{(-)}$ is the effect of collisions between molecules of kinds $\alpha$ and $\beta$.

### 1. Loss Term

To evaluate $J_{\alpha\beta}^{(-)}$, let us consider a pair of molecules with momenta $\mathbf{p}_\alpha$ and $\mathbf{p}_\beta$. The velocity of molecule $\beta$ with respect to molecule $\alpha$ is

$$\mathbf{g} = \frac{1}{m_\beta} \, \mathbf{p}_\beta - \frac{1}{m_\alpha} \, \mathbf{p}_\alpha, \tag{3.11}$$

and until the collision begins this is constant. Let us introduce a coordinate system moving with the center of mass of the pair and with
the z axis in the $-\mathbf{g}$ direction. In this coordinate system, until the collision begins both molecules move with constant velocity parallel to the
z axis. We now consider projections of these lines which cross the xy
plane, the plane through the origin (or center of mass) normal to the
z axis. The distance between the points of intersection is the impact
parameter b and direction of the line between the points defines an
azimuthal angle $\epsilon$. The origin of the angle $\epsilon$ may be chosen in any
manner.

In the time interval $dt$, molecule $\beta$ moves a distance $g\,dt$ relative to $\alpha$
if no collision occurs. Hence, if $dt$ is long compared to the duration of a
collision, a collision will occur if at the beginning of the time interval $\beta$
is within a distance $g\,dt$ of $\alpha$ and the impact parameter $b$ is small enough.
Thus the total number of collisions is the total number of molecules in
the required initial configuration. This is

$$[f_\alpha(\mathbf{r}\mathbf{p}_\alpha, t)\, d\mathbf{r}\, d\mathbf{p}_\alpha][f_\beta(\mathbf{r}\mathbf{p}_\beta, t)b\, db\, d\epsilon\, g\, dt\, d\mathbf{p}_\beta]$$
$$= f_\alpha f_\beta g b\, db\, d\epsilon\, d\mathbf{p}_\beta\, d\mathbf{r}\, d\mathbf{p}_\alpha\, dt. \qquad (3.12)$$

The total number of collisions of molecules of kind $\alpha$ in $d\mathbf{r}\, d\mathbf{p}_\alpha$ during the
time interval $dt$ with molecules of kind $\beta$ is thus

$$\left(\int\int f_\alpha f_\beta g b\, db\, d\epsilon\, d\mathbf{p}_\beta\right) d\mathbf{r}\, d\mathbf{p}_\alpha\, dt, \qquad (3.13)$$

where the integral is over all momenta $\mathbf{p}_\beta$ of the colliding molecules, all
values of $\epsilon$, and over the range of the impact parameter $b$, which leads
to "collisions." Thus

$$J_{\alpha\beta}^{(-)} = \int\int f_\alpha f_\beta g b\, db\, d\epsilon\, d\mathbf{p}_\beta \qquad (3.14)$$

is the loss (or sink) term in the collision integral arising from collisions
of molecules of kind $\alpha$ and kind $\beta$.

Let us consider the trajectory of a collision. Let $\mathbf{k}$ be a unit vector in
the direction of the apse line, the line from $\alpha$ to $\beta$ at the time of closest
approach. Since the molecules are spherical the entire trajectory of $\beta$,
in the center-of-mass coordinate system, lies in the plane determined by
$\mathbf{k}$ and $\mathbf{g}$. We define the angle $\theta$ by

$$\mathbf{k} \cdot \mathbf{g} = -g \cos \theta, \qquad (3.15)$$

noting that from the definitions

$$\mathbf{k} \cdot \mathbf{g} < 0 \quad \text{or} \quad 0 < \theta < \pi/2. \tag{3.16}$$

The direction angles of $\mathbf{k}$ are $\theta$ and $\epsilon$ and the angle $\theta$ is a function of $b$ and $g$. Thus in the integral of Eq. (3.14) we may change the integration variable from $b$ to $\theta$ and write

$$J_{\alpha\beta}^{(-)} = \iint f_\alpha f_\beta g Q \, d\mathbf{k} \, d\mathbf{p}_\beta, \quad (\mathbf{k} \cdot \mathbf{g} < 0) \tag{3.17}$$

where

$$Q = b \left( \sin\theta \left| \frac{\partial\theta}{\partial b} \right| \right)^{-1} \tag{3.18}$$

and

$$d\mathbf{k} = \sin\theta \, d\theta \, d\epsilon \tag{3.19}$$

indicates an element of integration over the surface of a unit sphere. Because of the restriction of Eq. (3.16) the integration is restricted to the hemisphere indicated. It should be noted, however, that although $\theta$ is a function of $b$ it is not always a single valued function. Particularly if the intermolecular potential has an attractive portion it is necessary under some conditions to integrate over the several branches of the function $Q$. The function $Q$ has the dimensions of area and may be referred to as a differential cross section. The usual differential cross section, however, is defined in terms of the angle of deflection, rather than the angle $\theta$ used here.

## 2. Collision Dynamics

Let $\mathbf{g}'$ be the relative velocity of the pair of colliding molecules after the collision and define

$$\boldsymbol{\varkappa} = \mu(\mathbf{g}' - \mathbf{g}), \tag{3.20}$$

where

$$\mu = m_\alpha m_\beta / (m_\alpha + m_\beta) \tag{3.21}$$

is the reduced mass of the pair of molecules. It follows directly from the conservation of energy that

$$(g')^2 = g^2. \tag{3.22}$$

From this condition it follows that $\boldsymbol{\varkappa}$ is of the form

$$\boldsymbol{\varkappa} = -2\mu(\mathbf{k} \cdot \mathbf{g})\mathbf{k}, \tag{3.23}$$

where **k** is a unit vector. Thus **g**′ and **g** are vectors of the same magnitude and **k** is a unit vector in the direction, **g**′ − **g**. Hence **k** bisects the angle between **g**′ and −**g** as indicated in Fig. 1. It may be shown that a trajectory is symmetric about the distance of closest approach. Thus the vector **k** introduced in the last equation is identical with the vector **k** introduced earlier as the direction of the apse line.

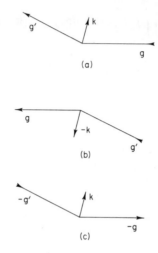

Fɪɢ. 1.   (a) Direct, (b) inverse, and (c) reverse collisions.

From Eqs. (3.20) and (3.23) it follows that

$$\mathbf{g}' = \mathbf{g} - 2(\mathbf{k} \cdot \mathbf{g})\mathbf{k} \tag{3.24}$$

and thus

$$\mathbf{k} \cdot \mathbf{g}' = -\mathbf{k} \cdot \mathbf{g}. \tag{3.25}$$

From these relations it follows that

$$\mathbf{g} = \mathbf{g}' - 2(\mathbf{k} \cdot \mathbf{g}')\mathbf{k}. \tag{3.26}$$

Thus associated with a collision in which the relative velocity changes from **g** to **g**′ with apse line **k** there exists an inverse collision in which the relative velocity changes from **g**′ to **g** with the apse line −**k**. The relation between a collision and its inverse is illustrated in Fig. 1. This relation is to be distinguished from the existence of reverse collisions which follows directly from time reversibility and which are also illustrated in the figure.

The relative velocity after a collision $\mathbf{g}'$ is given in terms of the velocity before the collision $\mathbf{g}$ and the direction of the apse line $\mathbf{k}$ by Eq. (3.24) and the inverse relation is given by Eq. (3.26). From these relations it follows that the Jacobians are

$$\left|\frac{\partial}{\partial \mathbf{g}}\,\mathbf{g}'\right| = \left|\frac{\partial}{\partial \mathbf{g}'}\,\mathbf{g}\right| = |\,\mathbf{U} - 2\mathbf{kk}\,|, \qquad (3.27)$$

where $U$ is the unit tensor. Since one Jacobian is the inverse of the other, they must both be absolute value unity; it follows directly from the last equation that

$$\left|\frac{\partial}{\partial \mathbf{g}}\,\mathbf{g}'\right| = \left|\frac{\partial}{\partial \mathbf{g}'}\,\mathbf{g}\right| = -1. \qquad (3.28)$$

## 3. Source Term

Let us consider collisions between molecules of species $\alpha$ and $\beta$ with momenta $\mathbf{p}_\alpha'$ and $\mathbf{p}_\beta'$ and apse line $-\mathbf{k}$, such that after the collision the momenta are $\mathbf{p}_\alpha$ and $\mathbf{p}_\beta$. From conservation of energy the magnitude of the relative velocity $g$ of the collision and its inverse are equal and from conservation of angular momentum this is also true of the impact parameter $b$. Thus since the cross section $Q$ is a function of only $g$ and $b$, the cross section for the collision and its inverse are equal.

It then follows from the previous arguments that the probable number of such collisions in $d\mathbf{r}$ during $dt$ is

$$f_\alpha' f_\beta' gQ \, d\mathbf{k} \, d\mathbf{p}_\alpha' \, d\mathbf{p}_\beta' \, d\mathbf{r} \, dt; \ -\mathbf{k} \cdot \mathbf{g}' < 0, \qquad (3.29)$$

where to shorten the notation

$$f_\alpha' = f_\alpha(\mathbf{r}\mathbf{p}_\alpha', t). \qquad (3.30)$$

Let us now consider a change of integration variables from $\mathbf{p}_\alpha'$ and $\mathbf{p}_\beta'$ to the velocity of the center of mass and the relative velocity $\mathbf{g}'$. Then secondly from velocities associated with the inverse collision to the velocities associated with the direct collision. Since the velocity of the center of mass of the collision and its inverse are the same, this portion of the Jacobian is unity. According to Eq. (3.28) the absolute value of the Jacobian of the transformation from $\mathbf{g}'$ to $\mathbf{g}$ is unity. Finally we transform back to the momenta $\mathbf{p}_\alpha$ and $\mathbf{p}_\beta$. Thus the last expression becomes

$$f_\alpha' f_\beta' gQ \, d\mathbf{k} \, d\mathbf{p}_\alpha \, d\mathbf{p}_\beta \, d\mathbf{r} \, dt; \quad \mathbf{k} \cdot \mathbf{g} < 0. \qquad (3.31)$$

From this it follows that the total number of collisions in $d\mathbf{r}$ during $dt$ between molecules of kinds $\alpha$ and $\beta$ that lead to a molecule of kind $\alpha$ with momentum $\mathbf{p}_\alpha$ is

$$J_{\alpha\beta}^{(+)} \, d\mathbf{p}_\alpha \, d\mathbf{r} \, dt, \tag{3.32}$$

where

$$J_{\alpha\beta}^{(+)} = \int\!\!\int f_\alpha' f_\beta' g Q \, d\mathbf{k} \, d\mathbf{p}_\beta, \qquad (\mathbf{k} \cdot \mathbf{g} < 0). \tag{3.33}$$

The total source term $J_\alpha^{(+)}$ is then the sum over all species

$$J_\alpha^{(+)} = \sum_\beta J_{\alpha\beta}^{(+)}. \tag{3.34}$$

Combining Eqs. (3.9), (3.10), (3.14), (3.33), and (3.34) we obtain an expression for the collision integral on the right of the Boltzmann equation, Eq. (3.7),

$$J_\alpha = \sum_\beta J_{\alpha\beta}, \tag{3.35}$$

where

$$J_{\alpha\beta} = \int\!\!\int (f_\alpha' f_\beta' - f_\alpha f_\beta) g Q \, d\mathbf{k} \, d\mathbf{p}_\beta, \qquad (\mathbf{k} \cdot \mathbf{g} < 0). \tag{3.36}$$

In these integrals, the integration over $\mathbf{k}$ may be transformed back to an integration over $b$ and $\epsilon$ by use of Eqs. (3.18) and (3.19). In the resulting form it is clear that the integrals over $f_\alpha' f_\beta'$ and $f_\alpha f_\beta$ are separately divergent. This is associated with the idea mentioned earlier that from the physical arguments the integration over $b$ should be restricted to those values which lead to significant changes in the momenta. It may be shown, however, that if, at large separation distances, the potential goes to zero more rapidly than $r^{-1}$, the integration over $b$ of the difference converges. Hence, in practice, the range of integration on the impact parameter $b$ is not restricted. With this expression for the collision integrals, the set of Boltzmann equations, Eqs. (3.7), becomes a closed set of equations for the singlet distribution functions $f_\alpha(\mathbf{r}\mathbf{p}_\alpha, t)$.

## C. FLUXES

Geometrical arguments may also be used to obtain expressions for the kinetic contributions to the fluxes, identical with those discussed in Section I,D.

We first consider the frequency of collisions of molecules with a wall. Let $ds$ be an element of surface of the wall and $\mathbf{n}$ be a unit vector in the direction of the outward normal to the wall. Consider a molecule of species $\alpha$ near the surface with momentum in the range $d\mathbf{p}_\alpha$ about $\mathbf{p}_\alpha$. Such a molecule will collide with the wall in the time interval $dt$ if at the beginning of the interval it lies inside a cylinder with base $ds$ and generators $(1/m_\alpha)\mathbf{p}_\alpha\,dt$. The volume of this cylinder is

$$(1/m_\alpha)\,|\,\mathbf{p}_\alpha \cdot \mathbf{n}\,|\,ds\,dt \qquad (3.37)$$

and the number of such molecules is

$$(1/m_\alpha)f_\alpha\,|\,\mathbf{p}_\alpha \cdot \mathbf{n}\,|\,d\mathbf{p}_\alpha\,ds\,dt. \qquad (3.38)$$

Thus the flux to the wall of molecules of species $\alpha$ of momentum $\mathbf{p}_\alpha$ is

$$(1/m_\alpha)\mathbf{p}_\alpha f_\alpha\,d\mathbf{p}_\alpha \qquad (3.39)$$

and the total flux of molecules of kind $\alpha$ is

$$(1/m_\alpha)\int \mathbf{p}_\alpha f_\alpha\,d\mathbf{p}_\alpha, \qquad (\mathbf{p}_\alpha \cdot \mathbf{n} < 0). \qquad (3.40)$$

At equilibrium in a stationary system the distribution function is isotropic in $\mathbf{p}_\alpha$. It may readily be shown from the last expression that for an isotropic distribution the flux to the wall is normal to the wall and the magnitude of the flux is $n_\alpha \bar{p}_\alpha/4m_\alpha$, where $\bar{p}_\alpha$ is the average over the distribution of the magnitude of the momentum.

Next let us consider the net flux of molecules across a surface in the gas moving with the stream velocity $\mathbf{u}$. Let $ds$ be an element of this surface and $\mathbf{n}$ be a unit vector normal to the surface. The direction of this unit vector defines the positive and negative sides of the surface element. Next consider a molecule of species $\alpha$ of momentum $\mathbf{p}_\alpha$. The velocity of this molecule relative to the surface is the Brownian velocity

$$\mathbf{V}_\alpha = (1/m_\alpha)\mathbf{p}_\alpha - \mathbf{u}. \qquad (3.41)$$

Such a molecule will cross the surface in the time interval $dt$ if at the beginning of the interval it lies inside the cylinder with base $ds$ and generators $\mathbf{V}_\alpha\,dt$ on the approach side of the surface. The volume of this cylinder is

$$|\,\mathbf{V}_\alpha \cdot \mathbf{n}\,|\,ds\,dt \qquad (3.42)$$

and the number of molecules in the cylinder is

$$f_\alpha \mid \mathbf{V}_\alpha \cdot \mathbf{n} \mid d\mathbf{p}_\alpha \, ds \, dt. \tag{3.43}$$

If $\mathbf{V}_\alpha \cdot \mathbf{n} > 0$, the molecules cross the surface from the negative to the positive side, that is, in the positive direction; if $\mathbf{V}_\alpha \cdot \mathbf{n} < 0$ the molecules cross in the negative direction. Thus in either case the flux of molecules of species $\alpha$ of momentum $\mathbf{p}_\alpha$ across a surface in the gas moving with the stream velocity $\mathbf{u}$ is

$$\mathbf{V}_\alpha f_\alpha \, d\mathbf{p}_\alpha \tag{3.44}$$

and the flux of molecules of species $\alpha$ across this surface is

$$n_\alpha \mathbf{U}_\alpha = \int \mathbf{V}_\alpha f_\alpha \, d\mathbf{p}_\alpha, \tag{3.45}$$

where $\mathbf{U}_\alpha$ is the diffusion velocity. This expression is a special case of the definition of Eq. (1.58).

The pressure tensor describes the flux of momentum relative to the surface. The momentum of a molecule relative to the surface is $\mathbf{p}_\alpha - m_\alpha \mathbf{u} = m_\alpha \mathbf{V}_\alpha$, and since each molecule carries its momentum as it crosses the surface, the net flux of this momentum across the surface due to the flow of molecules of species $\alpha$ is

$$\mathsf{p}_\alpha^{(K)} = m_\alpha \int \mathbf{V}_\alpha \mathbf{V}_\alpha f_\alpha \, d\mathbf{p}_\alpha. \tag{3.46}$$

The total flux of momentum, relative to the surface, due to the flow of molecules across the surface is the kinetic contribution to the pressure tensor

$$\mathsf{p}^{(K)} = \sum_\alpha \mathsf{p}_\alpha^{(K)}. \tag{3.47}$$

This result is a special case of Eq. (1.65).

The energy flux $\mathbf{q}$ is the flux of energy relative to the stream velocity. The kinetic energy of a molecule relative to a surface moving with the stream velocity $\mathbf{u}$ is $\tfrac{1}{2} m_\alpha V_\alpha^2$ and since each molecule carries this kinetic energy with it as it crosses the surface, the net flux of this kinetic energy across the surface due to the flow of molecules of species $\alpha$ is

$$\mathbf{q}_\alpha^{(K)} = \tfrac{1}{2} m_\alpha \int V_\alpha^2 \mathbf{V}_\alpha f_\alpha \, d\mathbf{p}_\alpha. \tag{3.48}$$

The total flux of kinetic energy is then the kinetic contribution to $\mathbf{q}$,

$$\mathbf{q}^{(K)} = \sum_{\alpha} \mathbf{q}_{\alpha}^{(K)}. \tag{3.49}$$

This result is the special case given by Eq. (1.71).

The kinetic contributions to the flux of momentum and energy are the principle contributions in low density gases. At higher densities the collisional transfer contributions associated with the direct effect of collisions becomes more important.

## D. BOGOLUBOV–HOLLINGER SERIES

The Boltzmann form of the collision integral may also be obtained from considerations of the Liouville equation and the BBGKY hierarchy. In this section, we discuss a series approximation to the term on the right of the first BBGKY equation first proposed by Bogolubov (1946). The derivation of this series which is presented, however, is one proposed by Hollinger and Curtiss (1960). Although the derivation and some of the arguments differ from those of Bogolubov, the resulting series are identical.

The development is based on the BBGKY hierarchy as developed in Section I,C. A formal solution of the Liouville equation may readily be written in the form

$$f^{(N)}(x, t + \tau) = (\exp - \tau \mathscr{L}^{(N)}) f^{(N)}(x, t). \tag{3.50}$$

In a similar fashion, one may write a formal solution of the general non-homogeneous BBGKY equation, Eq. (1.45), in the form

$$f_{\alpha\beta\dots\mu}(x_\alpha x_\beta \cdots x_\mu, t + \tau)$$

$$= (\exp - \tau \mathscr{L}_{\alpha\beta\dots\mu}) \Big[ f_{\alpha\beta\dots\mu}(x_\alpha x_\beta \cdots x_\mu, t) + \int_0^\tau d\tau_1 (\exp \tau_1 \mathscr{L}_{\alpha\beta\dots\mu})$$

$$\times \sum_\eta \int dx_\eta (\theta_{\alpha\eta} + \theta_{\beta\eta} + \cdots + \theta_{\mu\eta}) f_{\alpha\beta\dots\mu\eta}(x_\alpha x_\beta \cdots x_\mu x_\eta, t + \tau_1) \Big]. \tag{3.51}$$

By an iterative process one may thus develop an expression for any contracted distribution function at time $t + \tau$ in terms of the same function and all higher-order distribution functions at time $t$.

To develop the Boltzmann equation, one must obtain an expression for the functional dependence of the pair distribution functions in the collision integral on the right of the first BBGKY equation on the singlet distribution functions. For this purpose, we consider the pair distribution functions as examples of the iterative solution,

$$
\begin{aligned}
f_{\alpha\beta}(x_\alpha x_\beta,\, t + \tau) = (\exp - \tau \mathscr{L}_{\alpha\beta}) \Big[ & f_{\alpha\beta}(x_\alpha x_\beta,\, t) \\
& + \int_0^\tau d\tau_1 (\exp \tau_1 \mathscr{L}_{\alpha\beta}) \sum_\eta \int dx_\eta (\theta_{\alpha\eta} + \theta_{\beta\eta}) \\
& \times (\exp - \tau_1 \mathscr{L}_{\alpha\beta\eta}) f_{\alpha\beta\eta}(x_\alpha x_\beta x_\eta,\, t) + \cdots \Big]. \quad (3.52)
\end{aligned}
$$

From the properties of the operator $\theta_{\alpha\beta}$ appearing in the collision integral on the right of the first BBGKY equation, Eq. (1.43), it may easily be shown that contributions to the integral arise only from that region of the two molecule phase space which is associated with collision configurations. Thus, we are interested in the pair distribution functions only in this region of phase space. If $x_\alpha x_\beta$ corresponds to a collision configuration and $\tau$ is sufficiently large the phase space transformation operators on the right of the last equation, in general, transform the phase space coordinates to precollision configurations. If the interaction potentials are purely repulsive and go to zero sufficiently rapidly, it is always possible to take $\tau$ sufficiently large. On the other hand, if the potential has an attractive portion some regions of phase space describe bound pairs of molecules which are not separated by transformations back along two molecule trajectories. We thus restrict the present disscussion to purely repulsive potentials.

The essential assumption of the development of the Boltzmann equation, the assumption which introduces irreversibility, is the statement of molecular chaos or the boundary condition on the distribution functions. This is the statement that at sufficiently large separations on the approach side of a trajectory the distribution functions factor into products of singlet distribution functions. Thus we rewrite the last equation replacing the distribution functions on the right by products of singlet distribution functions, and also formally replacing $t$ by $t - \tau$,

$$
f_{\alpha\beta}(x_\alpha x_\beta,\, t) = (\exp - \tau \mathscr{L}_{\alpha\beta}) f_\alpha(x_\alpha,\, t - \tau) f_\beta(x_\beta,\, t - \tau) + \cdots . \quad (3.53)
$$

It is necessary, however, to express the pair distribution functions in terms of the singlet distribution functions at the same time. Hence we write an equation for the singlet function analogous to Eq. (3.52), with

$\tau$ replaced by $-\tau$,

$$f_\alpha(x_\alpha, t - \tau) = (\exp \tau \mathscr{L}_\alpha) f_\alpha(x_\alpha, t) + \cdots . \qquad (3.54)$$

If this expression is used on the right of Eq. (3.53) one obtains a functional relation expressing the pair distribution functions in terms of the singlet functions,

$$f_{\alpha\beta}(x_\alpha x_\beta, t) = \mathscr{S}_{\alpha\beta}^{(2)} f_\alpha(x_\alpha, t) f_\beta(x_\beta, t) + \cdots , \qquad (3.55)$$

where since the boundary condition or the molecular chaos assumption applies in the limit $\tau \to \infty$,

$$\mathscr{S}_{\alpha\beta}^{(2)} = \lim_{\tau \to \infty} (\exp - \tau \mathscr{L}_{\alpha\beta})(\exp \tau \mathscr{L}_\alpha)(\exp \tau \mathscr{L}_\beta). \qquad (3.56)$$

In general the limit exists. In two important cases, however, it does not exist. As mentioned above, if the intermolecular potential has an attractive portion bound pairs exist. In the corresponding regions of phase space the transformation back along two particle trajectories does not lead to separated molecules and hence the operator $\mathscr{S}_{\alpha\beta}^{(2)}$, defined as the limit, does not exist. The second important exception arises in the case of a long range potential such as the coulomb interaction between charged particles. The limit exists only if the potential goes to zero for large separation faster than $r^{-1}$.

The terms in Eq. (3.55) are ordered according to the order of the integrand in the singlet distribution functions. When these expressions for the pair distribution functions are used in the integral on the right of the first BBGKY equation, Eq. (1.43), one obtains a closed set of equations for the singlet distribution functions

$$\left(\frac{\partial}{\partial t} + \mathscr{L}_\alpha\right) f_\alpha(x_\alpha, t) = J_\alpha, \qquad (3.57)$$

where to lowest order

$$J_\alpha = \sum_\beta \int \theta_{\alpha\beta} \mathscr{S}_{\alpha\beta}^{(2)} f_\alpha(x_\alpha, t) f_\beta(x_\beta, t) \, dx_\beta. \qquad (3.58)$$

This expression for the collision integral describes, fully, the effects of binary collisions; the higher terms, which have been omitted in this expression, describe the effects of three body, and higher-order, collisions.

From the definition, Eq. (3.56), it follows that the operator $\mathscr{S}_{\alpha\beta}^{(2)}$ is a phase space transformation operator. This operator transforms the phase space coordinates back along a trajectory associated with a binary collision until the molecules are no longer interacting and then forward the same length of time, along trajectories associated with noninteracting molecules. The effect of this transformation is to transform the momenta to "precollision" momenta, which we denote as $\mathbf{p}_\alpha^{(0)}$ and $\mathbf{p}_\beta^{(0)}$, and to transform the position coordinates to the points $\mathbf{r}_\alpha^{(0)}$ and $\mathbf{r}_\beta^{(0)}$, which may be described as the positions at which the molecules would have arrived if they had not interacted. As an approximation, we assume that the distribution functions are slowly varying functions of the position coordinates and neglect the differences $\mathbf{r}_\alpha^{(0)} - \mathbf{r}_\alpha$ and $\mathbf{r}_\beta^{(0)} - \mathbf{r}_\alpha$, that is, we take

$$\mathscr{S}_{\alpha\beta}^{(2)} f_\alpha(x_\alpha, t) f_\beta(x_\beta, t) = f_\alpha(\mathbf{r}_\alpha \mathbf{p}_\alpha^{(0)}, t) f_\beta(\mathbf{r}_\alpha \mathbf{p}_\beta^{(0)}, t). \tag{3.59}$$

The effects of the correction terms, which are neglected in this expression, are referred to as collisional transfer effects. It may be shown (Hoffman and Curtiss, 1964, 1965) that these terms lead to density corrections to the transport coefficients that are of the same order as those which arise from the three-body collision terms which were neglected in the expression given by Eq. (3.58).

With the approximation given by the last expression, the integrand of Eq. (3.58) becomes

$$\theta_{\alpha\beta} f_\alpha(\mathbf{r}_\alpha \mathbf{p}_\alpha^{(0)}, t) f_\beta(\mathbf{r}_\alpha \mathbf{p}_\beta^{(0)}, t). \tag{3.60}$$

From the definition, Eq. (1.42), it is seen that $\theta_{\alpha\beta}$ is a differential operator that, for spherical molecules, involves the derivative with respect to the momentum $\mathbf{p}_\alpha$. In the last expression, the function upon which $\theta_{\alpha\beta}$ operates depends on $\mathbf{p}_\alpha$ only through the precollision momenta $\mathbf{p}_\alpha^{(0)}$ and $\mathbf{p}_\beta^{(0)}$. On the other hand, these precollision momenta are clearly constants of motion which are functions of the momenta $\mathbf{p}_\alpha$ and $\mathbf{p}_\beta$ and the relative position

$$\mathbf{r}_{\beta\alpha} = \mathbf{r}_\beta - \mathbf{r}_\alpha. \tag{3.61}$$

Thus the last expression is

$$\left( \mathbf{g} \cdot \frac{\partial}{\partial \mathbf{r}_{\beta\alpha}} - \theta_{\beta\alpha} \right) f_\alpha(\mathbf{r}_\alpha \mathbf{p}_\alpha^{(0)}, t) f_\beta(\mathbf{r}_\alpha \mathbf{p}_\beta^{(0)}, t), \tag{3.62}$$

where

$$\mathbf{g} = \frac{1}{m_\beta} \mathbf{p}_\beta - \frac{1}{m_\alpha} \mathbf{p}_\alpha \tag{3.63}$$

is the relative velocity. When this expression is used for the integrand in Eq. (3.58), it is clear that the second term does not contribute to the integral. To evaluate the integral of the first term, we transform the integral over $\mathbf{r}_\beta$ to an integral over $\mathbf{r}_{\beta\alpha}$ and write the integral of the divergence as the surface integral

$$J_\alpha = \sum_\beta \iint f_\alpha(\mathbf{r}_\alpha \mathbf{p}_\alpha^{(0)}, t) f_\beta(\mathbf{r}_\alpha \mathbf{p}_\beta^{(0)}, t) \mathbf{g} \cdot \mathbf{n} \, d\sigma \, d\mathbf{p}_\beta, \qquad (3.64)$$

where $d\sigma$ indicates the surface integral and $\mathbf{n}$ is the direction of the outward normal.

Since the integration over $\mathbf{r}_{\beta\alpha}$ was over the entire space one must consider the last integral in the limit that the bounding surface goes to infinity. For this purpose we take the bounding surface to be a right circular cylinder with its axis in the $-\mathbf{g}$ direction. With this choice of bounding surface it is clear that there is no contribution to the integral from the integration over the curved surface. If the cylinder is sufficiently large, on the top end the molecules have not yet started to interact and $\mathbf{p}_\alpha^{(0)} = \mathbf{p}_\alpha$ and $\mathbf{p}_\beta^{(0)} = \mathbf{p}_\beta$. Thus the integral over this surface contributes

$$-\sum_\beta \iint f_\alpha(\mathbf{r}_\alpha \mathbf{p}_\alpha, t) f_\beta(\mathbf{r}_\alpha \mathbf{p}_\alpha, t) gb \, db \, d\epsilon \, d\mathbf{p}_\beta, \qquad (3.65)$$

where $b$ and $\epsilon$ are the radial and azimuthal coordinates of a cylindrical coordinate system. On the other hand, if the cylinder is sufficiently large, on the bottom end the molecules have completed the collision and $\mathbf{p}_\alpha^{(0)}$ and $\mathbf{p}_\beta^{(0)}$ are the precollision momenta $\mathbf{p}_\alpha'$ and $\mathbf{p}_\beta'$ as functions of the post-collision momenta $\mathbf{p}_\alpha$ and $\mathbf{p}_\beta$. The integral over this surface then contributes

$$\sum_\beta \iint f_\alpha(\mathbf{r}_\alpha \mathbf{p}_\alpha', t) f_\beta(\mathbf{r}_\alpha \mathbf{p}_\beta', t) gb \, db \, d\epsilon \, d\mathbf{p}_\beta. \qquad (3.66)$$

Combining these two contributions and using the notation of Eq. (3.30), one then finds that

$$J_\alpha = \sum_\beta \iint (f_\alpha' f_\beta' - f_\alpha f_\beta) gb \, db \, d\epsilon \, d\mathbf{p}_\beta. \qquad (3.67)$$

If the integration over $b$ and $\epsilon$ is transformed to an integration over $\mathbf{k}$ using Eqs. (3.18) and (3.19), this expression for the collision integral becomes identical with that given by Eq. (3.36) and derived by the physical arguments of Boltzmann.

## IV. Transport Properties

In Sections I and II, expressions are derived for the various fluxes as integrals of the distribution functions. In general, the flux is the sum of a kinetic contribution that is expressed as an integral of the singlet distribution function and a collisional transfer contribution that is an integral of the pair distribution function. It may be shown that at low density the collisional transfer contribution is negligible with respect to the kinetic contribution. Thus to evaluate the transport coefficients at low density it is sufficient to evaluate the singlet distribution function. The Boltzmann equation which is discussed in the previous section is the low density equation for the time evolution of the singlet distribution function. In this section, we discuss the explicit expressions for the transport coefficients which have been obtained through the Chapman–Enskog perturbation solution of the Boltzmann equation.

### A. EQUILIBRIUM

It may be shown that the Boltzmann equation, in contrast to the Liouville equation, is irreversible in time. The H theorem of Boltzmann is a proof that the quantity H, which is proportional to the negative of the entropy, never increases with time. Furthermore, H is constant in time only if the distribution is of the Maxwellian form. For a stationary system, this is

$$f_\alpha = n_\alpha (2\pi m_\alpha kT)^{-3/2} \exp(-p_\alpha^2/2m_\alpha kT). \tag{4.1}$$

Since the velocities are simply related to the momenta, the distribution in molecular velocities is simply $m_\alpha^2 f_\alpha$. Clearly the equilibrium function is isotropic and thus the distribution function in the magnitude of the velocity is obtained by integrating over the angles. This is

$$4\pi m_\alpha^3 f_\alpha = 4\pi n_\alpha (m_\alpha/2\pi kT)^{3/2} v_\alpha^2 \exp(-m_\alpha v_\alpha^2/2kT). \tag{4.2}$$

The distribution $f_\alpha$ is Maxwellian or Gaussian in each of the components of the momentum or velocity of the molecules. That is, the most probable velocity, $\mathbf{v}_\alpha$, of a molecule in a stationary gas at equilibrium is zero. On the other hand, the distribution in the magnitude of the velocity, as given by the last equation, is zero at the origin and has a maximum at

$$v_{\alpha m} = (2kT/m_\alpha)^{1/2}. \tag{4.3}$$

This is the most probable magnitude of the velocity of a molecule in the gas. Two other measures of the molecular velocities are the average of the magnitude

$$\bar{v}_\alpha = (8kT/\pi m_\alpha)^{1/2} \tag{4.4}$$

and the square root of the average of the square,

$$(\overline{v_\alpha{}^2})^{1/2} = \tfrac{3}{2}(2kT/m_\alpha)^{1/2}. \tag{4.5}$$

B. COLLISIONS

According to the arguments of Section III,B,1, the frequency of collisions per unit volume between molecules of $\alpha$ with momentum in the range $\mathbf{p}_\alpha$, $d\mathbf{p}_\alpha$ with any molecule of kind $\beta$ is $J_{\alpha\beta}^{(-)}$, Eq. (3.17). Thus if $\alpha \neq \beta$ the total number of collisions between molecules of these species per unit time per unit volume is

$$Z_{\alpha\beta} = \int J_{\alpha\beta}^{(-)} \, d\mathbf{p}_\alpha$$

$$= \iiint f_\alpha f_\beta g Q \, d\mathbf{k} \, d\mathbf{p}_\alpha \, d\mathbf{p}_\beta, \qquad (\mathbf{k} \cdot \mathbf{g} < 0). \tag{4.6}$$

(For collisions between like molecules one must divide by two to avoid counting all collisions twice.) From the defining expression of the classical cross section, Eq. (3.18), it follows that the integration over $\mathbf{k}$ in the last expression is

$$Q_{\alpha\beta}^{(0)} = \int Q \, d\mathbf{k}$$

$$= \iint b \, db \, d\epsilon = \pi R_{\alpha\beta}^2, \qquad (\mathbf{k} \cdot \mathbf{g} < 0), \tag{4.7}$$

where $R_{\alpha\beta}$ is the largest value of the impact parameter $b$, which leads to a collision. In terms of this quantity the frequency of collisions is

$$Z_{\alpha\beta} = n_\alpha n_\beta \bar{g}_{\alpha\beta} Q_{\alpha\beta}^{(0)}, \tag{4.8}$$

where

$$\bar{g}_{\alpha\beta} = (n_\alpha n_\beta)^{-1} \iint f_\alpha f_\beta g \, d\mathbf{p}_\alpha \, d\mathbf{p}_\beta \tag{4.9}$$

is the average relative velocity. The evaluation of this integral may be carried out in a straightforward manner. The result is

$$\bar{g}_{\alpha\beta} = (8kT/\pi\mu_{\alpha\beta})^{1/2}, \tag{4.10}$$

where

$$\mu_{\alpha\beta} = m_\alpha m_\beta/(m_\alpha + m_\beta) \tag{4.11}$$

is the usual reduced mass of the pair of molecules. This is simply the average of the magnitude of the velocity, Eq. (4.4), for a system of molecules with the reduced mass $\mu_{\alpha\beta}$.

The quantity $Q_{\alpha\beta}^{(0)}$ is the total cross section. Clearly, for the rigid sphere model

$$Q_{\alpha\beta}^{(0)} = \pi\sigma_{\alpha\beta}^2, \tag{4.12}$$

where $\sigma_{\alpha\beta}$ is the distance between the centers at contact, and for any potential of infinite range $Q_{\alpha\beta}^{(0)}$ is infinite. This is characteristic of the classical total cross section in contrast with the quantum expression which is finite. It should be noted, however, that $Z_{\alpha\beta}$ may be interpreted as the frequency of collisions in which the impact parameter $b$ is less than any arbitrarily assigned value $R_{\alpha\beta}$. If $R_{\alpha\beta}$ is sufficiently large so that the limiting trajectory is a straight line, this is simply the frequency of collisions in which the distance of closest approach is less than $R_{\alpha\beta}$.

The mean free path of a molecule in a gas is an ill-defined quantity. From the above considerations of the frequency of collisions it follows directly that in a single component system the mean time between collisions of single molecule is

$$(2^{1/2}n\bar{v}Q^{(0)})^{-1}. \tag{4.13}$$

A mean free path may be defined as the product of this time and the average of the magnitude of the velocity of a molecule. This is

$$l = (2^{1/2}nQ^{(0)})^{-1} \tag{4.14}$$

or, for a gas of rigid spheres of diameter $\sigma$,

$$l = (2^{1/2}n\pi\sigma^2)^{-1}. \tag{4.15}$$

The mean free path is thus inversely proportional to the density of the gas.

C. Cross Sections

The Chapman–Enskog (Chapman and Cowling, 1939; Hirschfelder *et al.*, 1954) perturbation solution of the Boltzmann equation leads to expressions for the perturbations that are linear in the gradients of the macroscopic variables. When these expressions are used in expressions for the kinetic contributions to the fluxes discussed in Section I one obtains expressions for the fluxes in the Navier–Stokes form,

$$\mathbf{U}_\alpha = (n^2/n_\alpha\varrho) \sum_\beta m_\beta D_{\alpha\beta}\mathbf{d}_\beta - (D_\alpha^T/n_\alpha m_\alpha)\, \partial \ln T/\partial\mathbf{r}, \tag{4.16}$$

$$\mathsf{p} = p\mathsf{U} - 2\eta\mathsf{S}, \tag{4.17}$$

$$\mathbf{q} = -\lambda' \frac{\partial T}{\partial\mathbf{r}} - nkT \sum_\alpha \frac{D_\alpha^T}{n_\alpha m_\alpha}\, \mathbf{d}_\alpha. \tag{4.18}$$

The "forces" in these expressions are the "diffusion force"

$$\mathbf{d}_\alpha = \frac{\partial}{\partial\mathbf{r}}\left(\frac{n_\alpha}{n}\right) + \left(\frac{n_\alpha}{n} - \frac{n_\alpha m_\alpha}{\varrho}\right)\frac{\partial}{\partial\mathbf{r}} p$$
$$- \frac{1}{p}\left(n_\alpha\mathbf{F}_\alpha - \frac{n_\alpha m_\alpha}{\varrho}\sum_\beta n_\beta\mathbf{F}_\beta\right), \tag{4.19}$$

the rate of shear tensor

$$\mathsf{S} = \frac{1}{2}\left(\frac{\partial}{\partial\mathbf{r}}\mathbf{u}\right) + \frac{1}{2}\left(\frac{\partial}{\partial\mathbf{r}}\mathbf{u}\right)^\dagger - \frac{1}{3}\left(\frac{\partial}{\partial\mathbf{r}}\cdot\mathbf{u}\right)\mathsf{U}, \tag{4.20}$$

and the temperature gradient. The various coefficients are the transport coefficients: the diffusion coefficients $D_{\alpha\beta}$; the shear viscosity $\eta$; the thermal conductivity $\lambda'$; and the cross terms, the coefficients of thermal diffusion $D_\alpha^T$. The resulting expressions for the transport coefficients involve integrals of the cross section. In a multicomponent system, two definitions of the thermal conductivity are possible. The coefficient defined here is the thermal conductivity of a chemically uniform system. Equations (4.16) and (4.18) may be combined to obtain an equation for the energy flux in terms of the temperature gradient and the diffusion velocities. The coefficient, $\lambda$, of the temperature gradient in such an expression is the thermal conductivity of a stationary system with concentration gradients resulting from thermal diffusion.

The various moments of the cross section are defined by

$$Q^{(l)} = \int (1 - \cos^l \chi)Q\, d\mathbf{k}, \qquad (\mathbf{k}\cdot\mathbf{g} < 0), \tag{4.21}$$

where $\chi$ is the angle of deflection in the collision. From the definition of the cross section, Eq. (3.18), it readily follows that

$$Q^{(l)} = 2\pi \int (1 - \cos^l \chi) b \, db. \tag{4.22}$$

The angle of deflection $\chi$ is a function of the impact parameter $b$ and the initial relative velocity of the colliding molecules $g$, which depends on the intermolecular potential energy function $\varphi(r)$. From the dynamics of the collision process it may be shown that

$$\chi = \pi - 2b \int_{r_0}^{\infty} \left[ 1 - \frac{2\varphi}{\mu g^2} - \frac{b^2}{r^2} \right]^{-1/2} r^{-2} \, dr, \tag{4.23}$$

where $r_0$ is the distance of closest approach, the largest root of the denominator of the integrand, and $\mu$ is the reduced mass of the colliding molecules.

The moments of the cross section are functions of the relative velocity. The temperature dependent cross sections are defined as averages of $Q^{(l)}$ involving weight factors that are functions of the temperature. These are

$$Q^{(ls)} = \frac{2}{(s+1)!} \left( \frac{\mu}{2kT} \right)^{s+2} \int Q^{(l)} g^{2s+3} [\exp(-\mu g^2/2kT)] \, dg. \tag{4.24}$$

The transport coefficients may be written in terms of these cross sections.

The solutions of the integral equations that arise in the Chapman–Enskog solution of the Boltzmann equation are obtained by a variational method based on trial functions which are finite sums of Sonine polynomials. In most cases the lowest approximation leads to expressions for the transport coefficients that are good to a few percent. These are the results that are given here. Expressions for the correction terms are given elsewhere (see Hirschfelder et al., 1954). In the lowest approximation the coefficients of viscosity and thermal conductivity of a single component system are

$$\eta = \frac{5(\pi m k T)^{1/2}}{24 Q^{(22)}}, \tag{4.25}$$

$$\lambda = \frac{25k}{32 Q^{(22)}} \left( \frac{\pi k T}{m} \right)^{1/2}, \tag{4.26}$$

and in a binary mixture the coefficient of diffusion is

$$D_{\alpha\beta} = \frac{3(2\pi \mu k T)^{1/2}}{8 \varrho Q^{(11)}}. \tag{4.27}$$

Expressions applicable to multicomponent mixtures and expressions for the thermal diffusion coefficients are given elsewhere (see Hirschfelder *et al.*, 1954).

It is readily shown that for the rigid sphere model

$$Q^{(1s)} = Q^{(1)} = \pi\sigma^2, \tag{4.28}$$

$$Q^{(2s)} = Q^{(2)} = \tfrac{2}{3}\pi\sigma^2. \tag{4.29}$$

It may be shown from dimensional considerations that for any two constant empirical form of the intermolecular potential function

$$Q^{(1s)} = \pi\sigma^2 Q^{(1s)*}, \tag{4.30}$$

$$Q^{(2s)} = \tfrac{2}{3}\pi\sigma^2 Q^{(2s)*}, \tag{4.31}$$

where $\sigma$ is a constant of the potential of the dimensions of length and $Q^{(ls)*}$ is a function of

$$T^* = kT/\epsilon, \tag{4.32}$$

where $\epsilon$ is a constant of the potential of the dimensions of energy. The functional dependence of $Q^{(ls)*}$ on $T^*$ depends on the empirical form of the potential. In terms of these functions

$$\eta = \frac{5(\pi m k T)^{1/2}}{16\pi\sigma^2 Q^{(22)*}}, \tag{4.33}$$

$$\lambda = \frac{75k}{64\pi\sigma^2 Q^{(22)*}} \left( \frac{\pi k T}{m} \right)^{1/2}, \tag{4.34}$$

$$D_{\alpha\beta} = \frac{3(2\pi\mu k T)^{1/2}}{8\varrho\pi\sigma^2 Q^{(11)*}}. \tag{4.35}$$

The functions $Q^{(ls)*}$ (which are usually denoted $\Omega^{(ls)*}$) have been tabulated, elsewhere, for a number of empirical forms of the intermolecular potential (see, for example, Monchick and Mason, 1961).

## D. GENERALIZATIONS

Expressions for the transport coefficients have been obtained which are valid under more general conditions than the expressions given above. The results described above may be readily generalized to obtain the quantum formulation. The introduction of the effects of internal degrees of freedom or the effects of higher density is more difficult.

## 1. Quantum Considerations

The quantum mechanical Boltzmann equation of a system of structureless particles has been developed from the quantum mechanical BBGKY equations discussed in Sections II,C in manner similar to the classical development of Section III,D (Hoffman et al., 1965). If terms associated with density corrections are again neglected the resulting Boltzmann equation is identical with the classical equation except that the cross section is replaced by the quantum cross section. Thus the formalism of the Chapman–Enskog solution of the Boltzmann equation applies to the quantum treatment as well as to the classical treatment.

The resulting quantum mechanical expressions for the transport properties are identical with the classical expressions given above except that the moments of cross section, as defined by Eq. (4.21), are replaced by the moments of quantum cross section. In the quantum treatment the cross sections are usually expressed in terms of the angle of deflection $\chi$. Thus the quantum expression for the moments of the cross section is

$$Q^{(l)} = 2\pi \int (1 - \cos^l x)I \sin \chi \, d\chi. \tag{4.36}$$

The quantum mechanical differential cross section $I$ may be expressed simply in terms of the phase shifts, $\eta_l$. Using this expression and neglecting statistics effects, one obtains the following explicit expressions for the moments of the cross section,

$$Q^{(1)} = \frac{4\pi}{\varkappa^2} \sum_l (l + 1) \sin^2(\eta_{l+1} - \eta_l), \tag{4.37}$$

$$Q^{(2)} = \frac{4\pi}{\varkappa^2} \sum_l \frac{(l + 1)(l + 2)}{2l + 3} \sin^2(\eta_{l+2} - \eta_l), \tag{4.38}$$

where $\varkappa$ is the quantum mechanical wave number

$$\varkappa = (\mu/2)^{1/2}\hbar^{-1}g. \tag{4.39}$$

Dimensional considerations show that when the quantum expressions for the cross sections are used in the expressions for the transport coefficients the dimensionless cross sections $Q^{(ls)*}$ become functions of two dimensionless groups, the reduced temperature $T^*$, and the (modified) de Boer parameter

$$\hbar = \frac{\hbar}{\sigma(m\epsilon)^{1/2}}. \tag{4.40}$$

It may be shown, as is to be expected, that in the limit as $\hbar \to 0$ the quantum expressions approach the classical expressions. Numerical calculations of the quantum mechanical transport coefficients have been carried out using both the WBK, semiclassical expansion (see Wood and Curtiss, 1964) and direct summation over the partial waves as indicated by Eqs. (4.37) and (4.38) (Iman-Rahajoe et al., 1965).

## 2. Internal Degrees of Freedom

A Boltzmann equation for a system of molecules with structure may be obtained from either the classical first BBGKY equation, Eq. (1.43) or the quantum equation, Eq. (2.29). The classical development has been, to a large extent, restricted to a model in which the molecules are idealized as rigid nonspherical bodies, that is, rigid ovaloids. Explicit expressions for the transport properties of a gas of rigid ovaloids have been obtained. Numerical values have been obtained for a number of models (see Curtiss and Dahler, 1963). A quantum mechanical Boltzmann equation for a gas of molecules with structure was proposed by Wang-Chang et al., (1964). The development of the equation from the first BBGKY equation was described by Waldmann (1958) and Snider (1960). The essential problem in the application of these equations is a knowledge of the scattering cross sections.

## 3. Density Effects

A description of the effects of density on the transport coefficients may be based on the Bogolubov–Hollinger series approximation to the collision integral on the right of the first BBGKY equation as described in Section III,D. Two types of terms lead to the first density corrections to the transport coefficients, that is to terms of order $n$. Terms associated with the effect of three-body collisions arise from the first correction term neglected in the expression for the collision integral given by Eq. (3.58). Terms associated with collisional transfer effects arise from the first correction term in the expansion which leads to Eq. (3.59). The terms associated with collisional transfer effects were first obtained by Born and Green (1946, 1947, 1948). Their effect on the transport coefficients was discussed by Snider and Curtiss (1958). Later Hoffman and Curtiss (1964, 1965) considered an approximation to the effect of three-body collisions to obtain expressions for the first density correction to the transport coefficients. The resulting numerical values are in good agreement with experiment at high temperatures. At low temperatures the approximation breaks down due to the effect of bound pairs of molecules. This treatment of the first density correction has been extended to mixtures (Bennett and Curtiss, 1969) and the analogous quantum formulation has been developed (Gibboney, 1969). It has been shown, however, that the term in the series of order $n^2$ is divergent. Resummation methods have been used to obtain a term in the viscosity of order $n^2 \ln n$.

## GENERAL REFERENCES

CHAPMAN, S., and COWLING, T. G. (1939). "The Mathematical Theory of Non-uniform Gases." Cambridge Univ. Press, London and New York.
MAZO, R. M. (1967). "Statistical Mechanical Theories of Transport Process." Pergamon, Oxford.

## SPECIAL REFERENCES

BENNETT, D. E., and CURTISS, C. F. (1969). *J. Chem. Phys.* **51**, 2811.
BOGOLUBOV, N. N. (1946). *J. Phys. (U.S.S.R.)* **10**, 265; see (1962). "Studies in Statistical Mechanics," Vol. I. North-Holland Publ., Amsterdam.
BOLTZMANN, L. (1872). *Wien. Ber.* **66**, 275.
BORN, M., and GREEN, H. S. (1946). *Proc. Roy. Soc.* **A188**, 10; (1947). **A190**, 455; (1947). **A191**, 168; (1948). **A192**; see BORN, M., and GREEN, H. S. (1949). "A General Kinetic Theory of Liquids." Cambridge Univ. Press, London and New York.
CURTISS, C. F. (1956). *J. Chem. Phys.* **24**, 225.
CURTISS, C. F., and DAHLER, J. S. (1963). *J. Chem. Phys.* **38**, 2352.
GIBBONEY, D. (1970). Quantum Theory of Density Corrections to the Gaseous Transport Coefficients. Thesis, Univ. of Wisconsin, Madison.
HIRSCHFELDER, J. O., CURTISS, C. F., and BIRD, R. B. (1954). "Molecular Theory of Gases and Liquids." Wiley, New York.
HOFFMAN, D. K., MUELLER, J. J., and CURTISS, C. F. (1965). *J. Chem. Phys.* **43**, 2878.
HOFFMAN, D. K., and CURTISS, C. F. (1964). *Phys. Fluids* **7**, 1887; (1965). **8**, 667, 890.
HOLLINGER, H. B., and CURTISS, C. F. (1960). *J. Chem. Phys.* **33**, 1386.
IMAN-RAHAJOE, S., and CURTISS, C. F. (1967). *J. Chem. Phys.* **47**, 5269.
IMAN-RAHAJOE, S., CURTISS, C. F., and BERNSTEIN, R. B. (1965). *J. Chem. Phys.* **42**, 530.
IRVING, J. H., and KIRKWOOD, J. G. (1950). *J. Chem. Phys.* **18**, 817.
KIRKWOOD, J. G. (1946). *J. Chem. Phys.* **14**, 180.
MONCHICK, L., and MASON, E. A. (1961). *J. Chem. Phys.* **35**, 1676.
SNIDER, R. F. (1960). *J. Chem. Phys.* **32**, 1051.
SNIDER, R. F., and CURTISS, C. F. (1958). *Phys. Fluids* **1**, 122.
WALDMANN, L. (1957). *Z. Naturforsch.* **12a**, 660; (1958). **13a**, 609.
WANG-CHANG, C. S., UHLENBECK, G., and DE BOER, J. (1964). "Studies in Statistical Mechanics," Vol. II, Part C. Wiley, New York.
WOOD, H. T., and CURTISS, C. F. (1964). *J. Chem. Phys.* **41**, 1167.
YVON, J. (1935). "Actualités scientifiques et industrielles." Hermann et Cie, Paris.

Chapter 3

# Potential Energy Surfaces

## H. Eyring and S. H. Lin*

## I. Introduction

The theoretical approach of the calculation of the rates of most chemical reactions consists of three separate parts: The first of these is concerned with the determination of the potential energy surface (or surfaces)

* John Simon Guggenheim Fellow.

for the interaction species; the second step is the evaluation of the reaction cross section (or reaction probability) as a function of the initial states of the reactants (or reactant) and the final states of the products (or product); and the third part deals with the determination of the reaction rate by carrying out the integration of the reaction cross section (or reaction probability) over the initial state distributions for the reactants (or reactant). In this chapter, we are mainly concerned with the discussion of the theoretical methods used in the construction of the potential energy surface for a chemical reaction and of the properties associated with the potential energy surface. It should be noted that the semiempirical methods and a priori methods that are used in the construction of potential energy surfaces can be applied to other areas like hydrogen bonding, molecular energy transfer, etc.

## II. The Born–Oppenheimer Adiabatic Approximation

Consider a system composed of nuclei and electrons. Let $\hat{T}_n$ denote the kinetic energy operator of the nuclei, and $\hat{T}_e$, that of the electrons. The total potential energy of nuclei and electrons will be represented by $V(\mathbf{r}, \mathbf{R})$. $\mathbf{r} = (\mathbf{r}_i)$ represents the set of electronic coordinates and $\mathbf{R} = (\mathbf{R}_\alpha)$ the set of nuclear coordinates. The potential energy $V(\mathbf{r}, \mathbf{R})$ includes the potential energy of electron–electron, electron–nucleus, and nucleus–nucleus interactions. The total Hamiltonian of the system is then given by

$$\hat{H} = \hat{T}_e + \hat{T}_n + V(\mathbf{r}, \mathbf{R}) \tag{2.1}$$

and the corresponding wave equation is given by

$$\hat{H}\Psi(\mathbf{r}, \mathbf{R}) = E\Psi(\mathbf{r}, \mathbf{R}) \tag{2.2}$$

where $\Psi(r, R)$ and $E$ represent the eigenfunction and eigenvalue of the system. Explicitly, Eq. (2.2) can be written as

$$\left[ -\frac{\hbar^2}{2} \sum_\alpha \frac{1}{M_\alpha} \nabla_\alpha^2 - \frac{\hbar^2}{2m} \sum_i \nabla_i^2 + V(\mathbf{r}, \mathbf{R}) \right] \Psi(\mathbf{r}, \mathbf{R}) = E\Psi(\mathbf{r}, \mathbf{R}), \tag{2.3}$$

where $M_\alpha$ is the mass of the $\alpha$th nucleus, $m$ the mass of electron, $\nabla_\alpha^2$ the Laplace operator in terms of the coordinates of the $\alpha$th nucleus, and $\nabla_i^2$ the same operator for the $i$th electron.

The solution of the wave equation (2.3) for any but the simplest molecule is a very difficult problem. However, the empirical results of molecular spectroscopy show that in many cases the energy values bear a simple relation to one another, such that the energy of a molecule, aside from translational energy of the molecule, can be conveniently considered to be made up of several parts, called the electronic energy, the vibrational energy, and the rotational energy. To discuss the separation of electronic and nuclear motion, Born and Oppenheimer (Born, 1951; Born and Huang, 1956), making use of the fact that the mass of every atomic nucleus is at least a couple of thousand times as great as the mass of an electron, carry out a systematic expansion of the wave functions and other quantities entering in the complete wave equation (2.2) or (2.3) as power series in $(m/M)^{1/4}$ in which $M$ is an average nuclear mass. In the original form the argument of Born and Oppenheimer is long and complicated. Here for simplicity we present the derivation due to Born for discussing the separation of electronic and nuclear motion of the wave equation (2.2) or (2.3) (Born, 1951).

From Eq. (2.1), the Hamiltonian corresponding to fixed nuclei can be written as

$$\hat{H}_e = \hat{T}_e + V(\mathbf{r}, \mathbf{R}). \tag{2.4}$$

Suppose that the wave equation for the electronic motion, with the nuclei in arbitrary fixed positions,

$$\hat{H}_e \phi_n(\mathbf{r}, \mathbf{R}) = U_n(\mathbf{R})\phi_n(\mathbf{r}, \mathbf{R}) \tag{2.5}$$

is solved. In Eq. (2.5), $U_n(\mathbf{R})$ and $\phi_n(\mathbf{r}, \mathbf{R})$ represent the energy and the wave function of the electrons in the state $n$ for a fixed nuclear configuration $\mathbf{R}$ and are regarded as known. The wave equation of the system, Eq. (2.2), is then solved by introducing the expansion

$$\Psi(\mathbf{r}, \mathbf{R}) = \sum_n \Theta_n(\mathbf{R})\phi_n(\mathbf{r}, \mathbf{R}). \tag{2.6}$$

Substituting Eq. (2.6) into Eq. (2.2) or Eq. (2.3), multiplying the result by $\phi_n^*(\mathbf{r}, \mathbf{R})$ and integrating over $\mathbf{r}$, yields

$$[\hat{T}_n + U_n(\mathbf{R}) - E]\Theta_n(\mathbf{R}) + \sum_{n_1} C_{nn_1}(\mathbf{R}, \mathbf{P})\Theta_{n_1}(\mathbf{R}) = 0, \tag{2.7}$$

where

$$C_{nn_1}(\mathbf{R}, \mathbf{P}) = \sum_\alpha \frac{1}{M_\alpha} (\mathbf{A}_{nn_1}^{(\alpha)} \cdot \mathbf{P}_\alpha + B_{nn_1}^{(\alpha)}) \tag{2.8}$$

with $\mathbf{P}_\alpha = -i\hbar\,\mathbf{\nabla}_\alpha \cdot \mathbf{A}_{nn_1}^{(\alpha)}$ and $B_{nn_1}^{(\alpha)}$ in Eq. (2.8) are defined by

$$\mathbf{A}_{nn_1}^{(\alpha)}(\mathbf{R}) = \int \phi_n{}^*(\mathbf{r},\,\mathbf{R})\mathbf{P}_\alpha\phi_{n_1}(\mathbf{r},\,\mathbf{R})\,d\mathbf{r} \qquad (2.9)$$

and

$$B_{nn_1}^{(\alpha)}(\mathbf{R}) = \tfrac{1}{2}\int \phi_n{}^*(\mathbf{r},\,\mathbf{R})\mathbf{P}_\alpha{}^2\phi_{n_1}(\mathbf{r},\,\mathbf{R})\,d\mathbf{r}. \qquad (2.10)$$

Consider the diagonal matrix elements of $\mathbf{A}_{nn_1}^{(\alpha)}$. For stationary states the electronic wave function $\phi_n(\mathbf{r},\,\mathbf{R})$ can be chosen as real functions, thus

$$\mathbf{A}_{nn}^{(\alpha)}(\mathbf{R}) = -\tfrac{1}{2}i\hbar\,\mathbf{\nabla}_\alpha\int \phi_n{}^2(\mathbf{r},\,\mathbf{R})\,d\mathbf{r} = 0 \qquad (2.11)$$

as the wave function $\phi_n(\mathbf{r},\,\mathbf{R})$ can be normalized to the same constant value for all values of $\mathbf{R}$. Hence $C_{nn}$ is independent of the differential operator $\mathbf{P}_\alpha$. We can now write Eq. (2.7) as

$$[\hat{T}_n + U_n^{(c)}(\mathbf{R}) - E]\Theta_n(\mathbf{R}) + \sum_{n_1}{}' C_{nn_1}(\mathbf{R},\,\mathbf{P})\Theta_{n_1}(\mathbf{R}) = 0, \qquad (2.12)$$

where

$$U_n^{(c)}(\mathbf{R}) = U_n(\mathbf{R}) + C_{nn}(\mathbf{R}) = U_n(\mathbf{R}) + \sum_\alpha \frac{1}{M_\alpha}B_{nn}^{(\alpha)}(\mathbf{R}). \qquad (2.13)$$

Thus it is the quantity $U_n^{(c)}(\mathbf{R})$, and not $U_n(\mathbf{R})$, which plays the part of the potential energy of the nuclei when the coupling of different electronic states $C_{nn_1}$ can be neglected. In other words, the wave equation of the nuclear motion for negligible coupling of different electronic states can be expressed as

$$[\hat{T}_n + U_n^{(c)}(\mathbf{R})]\Theta_n(\mathbf{R}) = E\Theta_n(\mathbf{R}). \qquad (2.14)$$

In the adiabatic approximation which neglects the coupling terms in Eq. (2.12), the molecular wave functions reduce to the simple product terms,

$$\Psi_{nr}(\mathbf{r},\,\mathbf{R}) = \phi_n(\mathbf{r},\,\mathbf{R})\Theta_{nr}(\mathbf{R}). \qquad (2.15)$$

The difference between $U_n^{(c)}(\mathbf{R})$ and $U_n(\mathbf{R})$ as given by Eq. (2.13) can be determined when the electronic eigenfunctions for fixed nuclear configurations are known (Kolos, 1970).

The physical argument supporting the foregoing treatment is that on account of the disparity of masses of electrons and nuclei the electrons carry out many cycles of their motion in the time required for the nuclear configuration to change appreciably, and that in consequence it is allowed to quantize their motion for fixed nuclear configurations by solving the electronic wave equation, and then to use the electronic energy functions as potential energy functions (for negligible $C_{nn}$) determining the motion of the nuclei. The question, under what conditions the coupling parameters $C_{nn_1}$ will be small, cannot be answered in general. Even if they are not very small their influence will be negligible if the electronic state $n$ under discussion is separated from all others by a large energy gap, as can be seen from the perturbation theory,

$$A_{nn_1}^{(\alpha)}(\mathbf{R}) = -\frac{i\hbar\langle\phi_{n_1}^0 \mid (\boldsymbol{\nabla}_\alpha V)_0 \mid \phi_n^0\rangle}{U_{n_1}^0 - U_n^0} + \cdots \qquad (2.16)$$

and

$$B_{nn_1}^{(\alpha)}(\mathbf{R}) = -\frac{\hbar^2}{2}\frac{\langle\phi_n^0 \mid (\boldsymbol{\nabla}_\alpha^2 V)_0 \mid \phi_{n_1}^0\rangle}{U_{n_1}^0 - U_n^0}$$

$$- \hbar^2 \sum_m{}' \frac{\langle\phi_n^0 \mid (\boldsymbol{\nabla}_\alpha V)_0 \mid \phi_m^0\rangle \cdot \langle\phi_m^0 \mid (\boldsymbol{\nabla}_\alpha V)_0 \mid \phi_{n_1}^0\rangle}{(U_{n_1}^0 - U_n^0)(U_{n_1}^0 - U_m^0)} + \cdots,$$
$$(2.17)$$

where

$$\langle\phi_{n_1}^0 \mid (\boldsymbol{\nabla}_\alpha V)_0 \mid \phi_n^0\rangle = \int \phi_{n_1}^*(\mathbf{r}, \mathbf{R}_0)(\boldsymbol{\nabla}_\alpha V)_0\phi_n(\mathbf{r}, \mathbf{R}_0)\, d\mathbf{r}, \text{ etc.}$$

This will be the case for the ground state of many molecules and non-conducting metals. In this case, the zero-order approximation is a non-harmonic nuclear vibration with the potential energy $U_n^{(e)}(\mathbf{R})$ and the coupling with higher electronic states can be calculated from Eq. (2.12) by the perturbation method. For metals, however, where the electronic states form a quasi continuum, the sum in Eq. (2.12) cannot be regarded as a small perturbation and will become an integral-differential equation, which expresses the coupling of electronic and nuclear motion in a rigorous way.

Recently, many investigations on the approximation of the Born–Oppenheimer separation have been carried out. Fisk and Kirtman (1964) and Jepsen and Hirschfelder (1960) respectively evaluated the energy corrections to the adiabatic approximation for the $H_2$ and $H_2^+$ molecules. Chiu (1964) discussed the rotation–electronic interactions of diatomic molecules from the nonadiabatic viewpoint of the Born–Oppenheimer approximation. Wu and Bhatia (1956) and Dalgarno and McCorroll (1957) respectively studied the interactions of hydrogen and helium atoms in the ground and excited states, and found that the diagonal terms of the coupling between electronic and nuclear motion are not negligible at large separations. The nonstationary character of the adiabatic approximation has been discussed by Lin (1966, 1967) and the transition rate for the system to oscillate from one electronic state to another accompanied by a change in the quantum states of nuclear motion to conserve energy has been derived. The viewpoint of the breakdown of the adiabatic approximation has been adopted by Lin and Bersohn (Lin, 1966, Lin and Bersohn, 1968), Jortner *et al.* (1969), Robinson and Frosch (1963, 1964) and Siebrand (1967) in discussing the radiationless transitions of molecular luminescence.

As mentioned above, in the case of close lying vibronic states belonging to different electronic configurations, it is expected that the adiabatic approximation will completely fail. This breakdown of the Born–Oppenheimer approximation is well known in the case of a degenerate electronic state—the Jahn–Teller effect (Jahn and Teller, 1937; Moffit and Thorson, 1957), in the case of nearly degenerate states—the pseudo Jahn–Teller effect, and in the case of widely separated electronic states giving rise to vibrationally induced electronic transitions—the Herzberg–Teller effect (Herzberg and Teller, 1933; Albrecht, 1960).

The study of the atomic and molecular collisions leading to chemical reactions requires in general the solution of the Schrödinger equation with the full Hamiltonian of the system, Eq. (2.1). However, for the collision energies of most chemical interest, the nuclear velocities are sufficiently small relative to those of the electrons that the Born–Oppenheimer separation of nuclear and electronic motion is valid. A further simplification applicable to many chemical processes is to treat the motion as adiabatic; that is, a single electronic eigenfunction is used to represent the state of the electrons throughout the reactive encounter. Thus in the Born–Oppenheimer approximation, the determination of a potential energy surface involved in a chemical reaction requires solution of the electronic Schrödinger equation, Eq. (2.5), with the Hamiltonian given by

$$\hat{H}_e = -\frac{\hbar^2}{2m}\sum_i \nabla_i^2 - \sum_i \sum_\alpha \frac{Z_\alpha e^2}{r_{i\alpha}} + \sum_{i<j} \frac{e^2}{r_{ij}} + \sum_\alpha \sum_\beta \frac{Z_\alpha Z_\beta e^2}{R_{\alpha\beta}} \quad (2.18)$$

where the second term on the right-hand side of Eq. (2.18) represents the nucleus–electron interaction, the third term, the electron–electron repulsion, and the last term, the nucleus–nucleus repulsion. For a given system, one can obtain a series of energy surfaces corresponding to the different electronic energy eigenvalues. However, in most cases the potential energy surface corresponding to the lowest eigenvalue of the Hamiltonian (2.18) (or at most a few of the lowest-lying surfaces) is of interest to chemists.

## III. Valence Bond Method

### A. THE LONDON EQUATION

As discussed in the previous section, according to the Born–Oppenheimer adiabatic approximation the potential energy of nuclear motion of a molecule can be obtained by solving the electronic wave equation for any fixed nuclear configurations. In this section, we shall discuss the solution of the electronic wave equation by the valence bond method and for this purpose we use the three-electron systems as an example.

For a system of three atoms, each with one valence electron, we denote the wave functions of the valence orbitals of the atoms by $a(x, y, z)$, $b(x, y, z)$ and $c(x, y, z)$. Let us imagine the three atoms to be divided into pairs $(a, b)$, $(b, c)$, etc. $a$ and $b$ will form a stable bond between them only if the spins of the corresponding electrons are paired. It would seem reasonable to assume that the most stable configuration would be that corresponding to the maximum number of bonds. To the approximation in which spin interactions are neglected, the spin operators $\hat{S}^2$ and $\hat{S}_z$ commute with the Hamiltonian and may be used to reduce the order of the secular determinant. For the eigenvalue of $\hat{S}_z$ to be $\frac{1}{2}$, we have (Eyring $et\ al.$, 1944)

$$
\begin{array}{cccl}
c & b & a & \\
\alpha & \alpha & \beta & \varphi_1 = |\ (a\beta)_1(b\alpha)_2(c\alpha)_3\ | \\
\alpha & \beta & \alpha & \varphi_2 = |\ (a\alpha)_1(b\beta)_2(c\alpha)_3\ | \\
\beta & \alpha & \alpha & \varphi_3 = |\ (a\alpha)_1(b\alpha)_2(c\beta)_3\ |
\end{array}
$$

where $\alpha$ and $\beta$ represent the spin wave functions, and $\varphi_i$ are the Slater determinants,

$$
\varphi_3 = \frac{1}{\sqrt{3!}}
\begin{vmatrix}
(a\alpha)_1 & (b\alpha)_1 & (c\beta)_1 \\
(a\alpha)_2 & (b\alpha)_2 & (c\beta)_2 \\
(a\alpha)_3 & (b\alpha)_3 & (c\beta)_3
\end{vmatrix}
\tag{3.1}
$$

etc.

We will now form a linear combination of the $\varphi_i$'s which corresponds to a bond between $a$ and $b$. This requires $a$ and $b$ to have opposite spins, so that we are limited to the functions $\varphi_1$ and $\varphi_2$. The combination will therefore be of the form

$$\Psi_{ab} = a_1\varphi_1 + a_2\varphi_2. \tag{3.2}$$

If we interchange the spins on $a$ and $b$, the function $\Psi_{ab}$ must change sign, since the spin function associated with a stable bond is antisymmetric in the electrons,

$$\Psi_{ab} = -a_2\varphi_1 - a_1\varphi_2. \tag{3.3}$$

Equations (3.2) and (3.3) are consistent only if $a_2 = -a_1$. We have, therefore, the unnormalized bond eigenfunction representing the bond $a$-$b$ as

$$\Psi_{ab} = \varphi_1 - \varphi_2. \tag{3.4}$$

Similarly, we find the bond eigenfunction for the bond $b$-$c$ as

$$\Psi_{bc} = \varphi_2 - \varphi_3. \tag{3.5}$$

In terms of the two independent canonical structures $\Psi_{ab}$ and $\Psi_{bc}$, the variational wave function can be written as

$$\Psi = A\Psi_{ab} + B\Psi_{bc} \tag{3.6}$$

and the corresponding secular equation is given by

$$\begin{aligned} A(H_{AA} - \zeta_{AA}U) + B(H_{AB} - \zeta_{AB}U) &= 0, \\ A(H_{BA} - \zeta_{BA}U) + B(H_{BB} - \zeta_{BB}U) &= 0, \end{aligned} \tag{3.7}$$

where $H_{AA} = \langle \Psi_{ab} | \hat{H}_e | \Psi_{ab} \rangle$, $H_{AB} = \langle \Psi_{ab} | \hat{H}_e | \Psi_{bc} \rangle$, $H_{BB} = \langle \Psi_{bc} | \hat{H}_e | \Psi_{bc} \rangle$, $\zeta_{AA} = \langle \Psi_{ab} | \Psi_{ab} \rangle$, $\zeta_{AB} = \langle \Psi_{ab} | \Psi_{bc} \rangle$, and $\zeta_{BB} = \langle \Psi_{bc} | \Psi_{bc} \rangle$. Elimination of $A$ and $B$ gives

$$\begin{aligned} U^2(\zeta_{AA}\zeta_{BB} - \zeta_{AB}^2) - U(H_{AA}\zeta_{BB} + H_{BB}\zeta_{AA} - 2H_{AB}\zeta_{AB}) \\ + H_{AA}H_{BB} - H_{AB}^2 = 0. \end{aligned} \tag{3.8}$$

Solution of Eq. (3.8) yields the energy values of the form

$$\begin{aligned} U_\pm = \{(H_{AA}\zeta_{BB} + H_{BB}\zeta_{AA} - 2H_{AB}\zeta_{AB}) \\ \pm [(H_{AA}\zeta_{BB} + H_{BB}\zeta_{AA} - 2H_{AB}\zeta_{AB})^2 \\ -4(H_{AA}H_{BB} - H_{AB}^2)(\zeta_{AA}\zeta_{BB} - \zeta_{AB}^2)]^{1/2}\}/2(\zeta_{BB}\zeta_{AA} - \zeta_{AB}^2). \end{aligned} \tag{3.9}$$

The normalization and overlap matrix elements in Eq. (3.9) can be evaluated as follows:

$$\zeta_{BB} = \langle \varphi_2 - \varphi_3 \mid \varphi_2 - \varphi_3 \rangle = \langle \varphi_2 \mid \varphi_2 \rangle + \langle \varphi_3 \mid \varphi_3 \rangle - 2\langle \varphi_2 \mid \varphi_3 \rangle$$
$$= 2 - \Delta_{ab}^2 - \Delta_{ac}^2 + 2\,\Delta_{bc}^2 - 2\,\Delta_{ab}\,\Delta_{ac}\,\Delta_{bc}, \qquad (3.10)$$

where $\Delta_{ab}$, etc., are defined as $\Delta_{ab} = \langle a \mid b \rangle$, etc. Similarly,

$$\zeta_{AA} = 2 - \Delta_{bc}^2 - \Delta_{ac}^2 + 2\,\Delta_{ab}^2 - 2\,\Delta_{ab}\,\Delta_{bc}\,\Delta_{ac} \qquad (3.11)$$

and

$$\zeta_{AB} \doteq -1 - \Delta_{ab}^2 - \Delta_{bc}^2 + 2\,\Delta_{ac}^2 + \Delta_{ab}\,\Delta_{ac}\,\Delta_{bc}. \qquad (3.12)$$

The Hamiltonian matrix elements in Eq. (3.9) can be evaluated similarly.

$$H_{AA} = \langle \Psi_{ab} \mid \hat{H}_e \mid \Psi_{ab} \rangle$$
$$= \langle \varphi_1 \mid \hat{H}_e \mid \varphi_1 \rangle + \langle \varphi_2 \mid \hat{H}_e \mid \varphi_2 \rangle - 2\langle \varphi_1 \mid \hat{H}_e \mid \varphi_2 \rangle$$
$$= [Q - (bc)] + [Q - (ac)] - 2[-(ab) + (bca)]$$
$$= 2Q - (bc) - (ac) + 2(ab) - 2(bca), \qquad (3.13)$$

where $Q = \langle (a)_1(b)_2(c)_3 \mid \hat{H}_e \mid (a)_1(b)_2(c)_3 \rangle$ the Coulomb integral, $(bc) = \langle (a)_1(b)_2(c)_3 \mid H_e \mid (a)_1(c)_2(b)_3 \rangle$ the exchange integral, etc. $H_{BB}$ and $H_{AB}$ are given by

$$H_{BB} = 2Q - (ab) - (ac) + 2(bc) - 2(bca) \qquad (3.14)$$

and

$$H_{AB} = -Q - (ab) - (bc) + 2(ac) + (bca). \qquad (3.15)$$

So far it is general. Now suppose we remove the electron $c$ to infinity. Then

$$\zeta_{BB} = 2 - \Delta_{ab}^2, \qquad \zeta_{AA} = 2 + 2\Delta_{ab}^2, \qquad \zeta_{AB} = -1 - \Delta_{ab}^2, \qquad (3.16)$$

$$H_{AA} = 2Q + 2(ab), \qquad H_{BB} = 2Q - (ab), \qquad H_{AB} = -Q - (ab). \qquad (3.17)$$

Substituting Eqs. (3.16) and (3.17) into Eq. (3.9), we obtain

$$U_{\pm} = [Q \mp (ab)]/(1 \mp \Delta_{ab}^2). \qquad (3.18)$$

This is the Heitler–London equation for homopolar bonding (Heitler and London, 1927).

Next if we neglect all the overlap integrals $\Delta_{ab}$, etc., or assume that the orbitals $a$, $b$, and $c$ are mutually orthogonal, then we have

$$\zeta_{BB} = -2, \qquad \zeta_{AA} = 2, \qquad \zeta_{AB} = -1, \qquad (3.19)$$

and Eq. (3.19) becomes

$$U_{\pm} = \tfrac{1}{3}(H_{AA} + H_{BB} + H_{AB}) \pm \tfrac{1}{3}\{\tfrac{1}{2}[(H_{AA} - H_{BB})^2 + (H_{AA} + 2H_{AB})^2$$
$$+ (H_{BB} + 2H_{AB})^2]\}^{1/2}. \tag{3.20}$$

From Eqs. (3.13)–(3.15), we obtain

$$H_{AA} + H_{BB} + H_{AB} = 3[Q - (bca)], \tag{3.21}$$

$$H_{AA} - H_{BB} = 3[(ab) - (bc)], \tag{3.22}$$

$$H_{AA} + 2H_{AB} = 3[(ac) - (bc)], \tag{3.23}$$

and

$$H_{BB} + 2H_{AB} = 3[(ac) - (ab)]. \tag{3.24}$$

Substitution of Eqs. (3.22)–(3.24) into Eq. (3.20) yields

$$U_{\pm} = Q \pm [\tfrac{1}{2}([(ab) - (bc)]^2 + [(bc) - (ac)]^2 + [(ac) - (ab)]^2)]^{1/2}$$
$$- (bca). \tag{3.25}$$

Since the double-exchange integral $(bca)$ equals to zero in this case, Eq. (3.25) reduces to the London formula,

$$U_{\pm} = Q \pm [\tfrac{1}{2}(\{(ab) - (bc)\}^2 + \{(bc) - (ac)\}^2 + \{(ac) - (ab)\}^2)]^{1/2}. \tag{3.26}$$

From the above derivation, we can see that the London equation is applicable only for the homopolar compounds with the overlap integrals and the double-exchange integrals neglected. The limitation of the applicability of the London equation has been discussed critically by James and Coolidge (1934) and others (Slater, 1931; Cashion and Herschbach, 1964). Although in the above discussion, we use the three-electron system as an example, the above derivation can be generalized easily for the more complicated systems (Eyring *et al.*, 1940, 1944).

## B. The London–Eyring–Polanyi Method

In the simplest form of the Heitler–London approximation, from Eq. (3.18) the binding energy of a diatomic molecule can be written as

$$U = Q \mp \alpha, \tag{3.27}$$

where $Q$ and $\alpha$ [$\alpha = (ab)$] are the Coulomb and exchange integrals. The lower (positive) signs in Eq. (3.27) or Eq. (3.18) give rise to the lower energies, since the integrals are negative in value, and correspond to the bound state $^1\Sigma$ of the molecule. The upper, negative sign refers to the repulsive state. The Heitler–London equation (3.18) accounts for 66% of the bonding in $H_2$; the experimental binding energy is 109.4 kcal and Eq. (3.18) leads to 72.4 kcal. However, if one uses Eq. (3.27), the calculated binding energy is now $-107.5$ kcal, in much better agreement with the experimental value than that given by Eq. (3.18). There is no justification for neglecting the overlap integral $\Delta_{ab}$, the better agreement being due to a cancellation of errors.

Although the binding energy of a three-electron system can be evaluated from Eq. (3.9) by calculating all of one-, two-, and three-centered integrals, it is not desirable to do so. The main reason for this is that the binding energy obtained thereby would be no more accurate than that resulting from the Heitler–London or Wang (1928) treatment for diatomic molecules. A semiempirical approach is developed by Eyring and Polanyi (1931) based on the London equation (3.26) and it is found that the energy of the three-electron system obtained from this semiempirical approach is fairly accurate because the errors resulting from the calculation partially cancel out.

In obtaining the potential energy formula for a three-electron system, it is required that the correct diatomic limits are approached when one atom is removed to infinity. If the atom $A$ is removed to infinity, there remains the diatomic molecule $B$-$C$, the Coulombic and exchange energies for $B$-$C$ are designated as $Q_{bc}$ and $\alpha_{bc}$ (cf. Fig. 1). Similarly, $Q_{ac}$ and $\alpha_{ac}$,

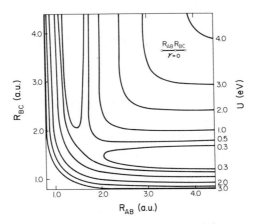

FIG. 1.   Interaction of A, B, and C.

and $Q_{ab}$ and $\alpha_{ab}$ are the Coulombic and exchange integrals for the $A$-$C$ molecule, and the $A$-$B$ molecule, respectively. For the three-electron system, London wrote down the equation without proof (London, 1929),

$$U_{\pm} = Q \pm \tfrac{1}{2}\{[(\alpha_{ab} - \alpha_{bc})^2 + (\alpha_{bc} - \alpha_{ac})^2 + (\alpha_{ac} - \alpha_{ab})^2]\}^{1/2}, \quad (3.28)$$

where $Q = Q_{ab} + Q_{bc} + Q_{ac}$, this equation reduces to Eq. (3.27), if any one of the atoms is removed to infinity. Equation (3.28) should be compared with Eq. (3.26). Actually Eqs. (3.28) and (3.26) are not equivalent. For example, the integrals $Q_{ab}$, $Q_{bc}$, $Q_{ac}$, $\alpha_{ab}$, $\alpha_{bc}$ and $\alpha_{ac}$ used in Eq. (3.28) are assumed to be the same as if the third atom is removed. The more detailed comparison between these two equations will be given later.

The Coulombic and exchange integrals $Q$ and $\alpha$ for the isolated $H_2$ molecule was calculated by Sugiura (1927) as a function of interatomic distance. From an inspection of Sugiura's calculations of the Coulombic and exchange integrals for the $H_2$ molecule, Eyring and Polanyi concluded that over a range of interatomic distances (in particular, for $R > 0.8$ Å) the fraction

$$\varrho = Q/(Q + \alpha) \quad (3.29)$$

is roughly constant at 10 to 15%. For any triatomic configuration it is therefore possible to evaluate for each pair of atoms the Coulombic and exchange energies on the basis of the spectroscopic value for the total energy; $Q_{ab}$, $Q_{bc}$, $Q_{ac}$, $\alpha_{ab}$, $\alpha_{bc}$, and $\alpha_{ac}$ can be readily calculated for the system, and by inserting these quantities into the London equation (3.28) we can obtain the required potential energy for the three-atom system. For the total energy of a diatomic molecule, say, $A$-$B$, as a function of internuclear distance, Eyring and Polanyi use the Morse potential,

$$U_{ab} = D_{ab}[\exp\{-2\beta_{ab}(R_{ab} - R^0_{ab})\} - 2\exp\{-\beta_{ab}(R_{ab} - R^0_{ab})\}], \quad (3.30)$$

where $R^0_{ab}$ is the equilibrium internuclear distance of $A$-$B$, $D_{ab}$, the classical dissociation energy, and $\beta_{ab}$, a spectroscopic constant. The spectroscopic constant $\beta_{ab}$ can be determined by differentiating $U_{ab}$ with respect to $R_{ab}$ twice,

$$\beta_{ab} = \pi c \omega^0_{ab} \sqrt{2\mu_{ab}/D_{ab}}, \quad (3.31)$$

where $\mu_{ab}$ is the reduced mass, and $\omega^0_{ab}$, the ground state vibrational frequency expressed in wave numbers.

The London–Eyring–Polanyi (LEP) method has proved useful in making rough estimates of energies of activation, but is not capable of high accuracy. A reasonable value of $\varrho$ usually succeeds in accounting for the experimental barrier heights. It has been shown that in most cases the LEP method gives rise to a surface that has a basin at the activated state. There are a number of reasons why the London equation cannot give very reliable energies. In the first place, the Heitler–London equation gives for the $H_2$ binding energy an error which is much greater than the activation energy of the $H + H_2$ reaction. The London equation is in fact related not to the original Heitler–London equation (3.18), but to the simplified form (3.27). Admittedly, the latter happens to lead to a better result for $H_2$, but this is clearly fortuitous; a similar cancellation of errors might not happen for triatomic systems. The double-exchange integral has been neglected in the London equation, which has been shown to be quite significant. Furthermore, the integrals $Q_{ab}$, $\alpha_{ab}$, etc., used in the London equation are assumed to be the same as if the third atom is removed to infinity. In spite of these deficiencies the London equation has proved useful in giving the right general form for potential energy surfaces. In dealing with such surfaces one is concerned with the difference between the energy of the triatomic system and that of $A + BC$, and it is possible that by a cancellation of errors this difference would be fairly reliable.

## C. THE LONDON–EYRING–POLANYI–SATO METHOD

Sato (1955a) has proposed an alternative method to calculate the potential energy surface of a triatomic system in which $\varrho$ in Eq. (3.29) is treated as a function of the internuclear distance. He obtains the dependence of $\varrho$ on $R$, the internuclear distance, on the basis of the shape of the repulsive state curve, which is well known for the $H_2$ molecule. In order to determine the analytical expression for the repulsive curve, Sato modifies the Morse potential by changing the sign between the two exponential terms from minus to plus and dividing the resulting expression by 2,

$$U_+ = \tfrac{1}{2}D[\exp\{-2\beta(R - R^0)\} + 2\exp\{-\beta(R - R^0)\}]. \quad (3.32)$$

According to the simplified Heitler–London treatment [of Eq. (3.27)], the potential energy for the repulsive state of a diatomic molecule is given by $U_+ = Q - \alpha$, which can then be set equal to that given by Eq. (3.32),

$$Q - \alpha = \tfrac{1}{2}D[\exp\{-2\beta(R - R^0)\} + 2\exp\{-\beta(R - R^0)\}]. \quad (3.33)$$

Similarly for the ground state, we have

$$Q + \alpha = D[\exp\{-2\beta(R - R^0)\} - 2\exp\{-\beta(R - R^\circ)\}]. \quad (3.34)$$

From Eqs. (3.33) and (3.34), $Q$ and $\alpha$ can be calculated as a function of internuclear distance without the assumption of a constant ratio $\varrho$. Instead of using the original London equation (3.26) for the triatomic system, Sato uses a modified expression with an overlap integral $\zeta$,

$$U_\pm = \frac{1}{1 + \zeta^2}\,(Q \pm \{\tfrac{1}{2}[(\alpha_{ab} - \alpha_{bc})^2 + (\alpha_{bc} - \alpha_{ac})^2 + (\alpha_{ac} - \alpha_{ab})^2]\}^{1/2}). \quad (3.35)$$

Sato concludes on intuitive grounds that this equation would be valid if the overlap integrals for the three diatomic species are equal.

To discuss the validity of the Sato equation, we rewrite Eq. (3.9) as

$$U_\pm = [-C_2 \pm (C_2^2 - C_1C_3)^{1/2}]/C_1, \quad (3.36)$$

where

$$C_1 = \zeta_{BB}\zeta_{AA} - \zeta_{AB}^2,$$
$$C_2 = H_{AB}\zeta_{AB} - \tfrac{1}{2}H_{AA}\zeta_{BB} - \tfrac{1}{2}H_{BB}\zeta_{AA} \quad (3.37)$$
$$C_3 = H_{AA}H_{BB} - H_{AB}^2.$$

It is to be noticed that only $C_1$ and $C_2$ contain the overlap integrals $\Delta_{ab}$, $\Delta_{bc}$, and $\Delta_{ac}$ explicitly. Expanding $C_1$ and $C_2$ in power series of the overlap integrals yields

$$C_1 = 3(1 - 2\Delta_{ab}\Delta_{bc}\Delta_{ac}) + O(\Delta^4) \quad (3.38)$$

and

$$C_2 = C_2^0 + \Delta C_2, \quad (3.39)$$

where

$$C_2^0 = -(H_{AA} + H_{BB} + H_{AA})(1 - \Delta_{ab}\,\Delta_{bc}\,\Delta_{ac})$$
$$= -3(1 - \Delta_{ab}\,\Delta_{bc}\,\Delta_{ac})[Q - (bca)] \quad (3.40)$$

and

$$\Delta C_2 = \Delta_{ab}^2(-H_{AB} + \tfrac{1}{2}H_{AA} - H_{BB}) + \Delta_{bc}^2(-H_{AB} - H_{AA} + \tfrac{1}{2}H_{BB})$$
$$+ \Delta_{ac}^2(2H_{AB} + \tfrac{1}{2}H_{AA} + \tfrac{1}{2}H_{BB})$$
$$= \tfrac{3}{2}\{\Delta_{ab}^2[2(ab) - (bc) - (ac)] + \Delta_{bc}^2[2(bc) - (ab) - (ac)]$$
$$+ \Delta_{ac}^2[2(ac) - (ab) - (bc)]\}. \tag{3.41}$$

Here we have only retained the terms up to the third order with respect to the overlap integrals.

Substituting Eqs. (3.38) and (3.39) into Eq. (3.36) and expanding $U_\pm$ in terms of overlap integrals, we obtain

$$U_\pm = \frac{1}{C_1}\left[-C_2^0 \pm (C_2^{02} - C_1 C_3)^{1/2}\right]$$
$$+ \frac{1}{C_1}\left[-\Delta C_2 \pm \frac{C_2^0 \Delta C_2}{(C_2^{02} - C_1 C_3)^{1/2}}\right], \tag{3.42}$$

which can be written as

$$U_\pm = U_\pm^0\left[1 \mp \frac{\Delta C_2}{(C_2^{02} - C_1 C_3)^{1/2}}\right], \tag{3.43}$$

where

$$U_\pm^0 = \frac{-C_2^0 \pm (C_2^{02} - C_1 C_3)^{1/2}}{C_1}. \tag{3.44}$$

Introducing the expressions for $C_1$, $C_2^0$, and $C_3$ into Eq. (3.44), Eq. (3.44) becomes

$$U_\pm^0 = \frac{(H_{AA} + H_{BB} + H_{AB}) \pm [\tfrac{1}{2}\{(H_{AA} - H_{BB})^2 + (H_{AA} + 2H_{AB})^2 + (H_{BB} + 2H_{AB})^2\}]^{1/2}}{3(1 - \Delta_{ab}\Delta_{bc}\Delta_{ac})}. \tag{3.45}$$

Substituting Eqs. (3.13)–(3.15) into Eq. (3.45), we find

$$U_\pm^0 = \frac{Q - (bca) \pm [\tfrac{1}{2}\{[(ab)-(bc)]^2 + [(bc)-(ac)]^2 + [(ac)-(ab)]^2\}]^{1/2}}{1 - \Delta_{ab}\Delta_{bc}\Delta_{ac}}. \tag{3.46}$$

Equation (3.46) reduces to the London equation when $\Delta_{ab}\Delta_{bc}\Delta_{ac}$ and $(bca)$ are neglected.

If we let

$$\zeta^2 = -\frac{\Delta C_2}{(C_2^{02} - C_1 C_3)^{1/2}}, \tag{3.47}$$

Eq. (3.43) becomes

$$U_{\pm} = U_{\pm}^0(1 \pm \zeta^2) = \frac{U_{\pm}^0}{1 \mp \zeta^2} \tag{3.48}$$

or

$$U_{\pm} = \frac{Q - (bca) \pm [\frac{1}{2}\{[(ab)-(bc)]^2 + [(bc)-(ac)]^2 + [(ac)-(ab)]^2\}]^{1/2}}{1 \mp \zeta^2 - \Delta_{ab}\,\Delta_{bc}\,\Delta_{ac}}. \tag{3.49}$$

Equation (3.49) is valid up to the third order approximation with respect to overlap integrals. To the second-order approximation, $U_{\pm}$ reduces to the Sato equation when the double-exchange integral $(bca)$ is neglected. It should be noticed that $\zeta^2$ in this case does not exactly represent the square of an overlap integral, but is given by

$$\zeta^2 = \frac{\frac{1}{2}\{\Delta_{ab}^2[(bc) + (ac) - 2(ab)] + \Delta_{bc}^2[(ab) + (ac) - 2(bc)] + \Delta_{ac}^2[(ab) + (bc) - 2(ac)]\}}{[\frac{1}{2}\{[(ab) - (bc)]^2 + [(bc) - (ac)]^2 + [(ac) - (ab)]^2\}]^{1/2}}. \tag{3.50}$$

Therefore, it appears that although there is theoretical basis for Eq. (3.35), the validity and applicability of Eq. (3.35) must still be justified empirically.

The LEPS method is preferable to the LEP method in that it leads to surfaces free of basins. In a comparison of the LEP and LEPS methods, Weston (1959) observes that the LEPS method give barriers which are too thin. A consequence of this is that calculations for the LEPS surface lead to considerably more tunneling than is observed experimentally.

## IV. Examples

Excellent reviews on the theoretical calculation of the potential energy surfaces for various systems are available (Laidler, 1969; Karplus, 1969; Conroy, 1969; Laidler and Polanyi, 1965). In this section, we shall discuss some typical examples of the potential energy surfaces in some detail, rather than reviewing all the potential energy surfaces published in the literature.

### A. H + H₂ (Porter and Karplus, 1964)

Instead of using the London equation, Porter and Karplus utilize the complete expression for three-atom systems [cf. Eq. (3.9) or Eq. (3.36)] to obtain the potential energy surface of the reaction $H + H_2$. To parametrize the energy expression, first consider the Coulomb integral $Q$, which can be decomposed into diatomic contributions as follows:

$$Q = \left\langle abc \left| \sum_i^3 \hat{h}_i + \sum_{i>j}^3 \sum^3 \frac{e^2}{r_{ij}} + \sum_{\alpha>\beta} \sum \frac{e^2}{R_{\alpha\beta}} \right| abc \right\rangle$$

$$= \langle a \mid \hat{h}_1 \mid a \rangle + \langle b \mid \hat{h}_2 \mid b \rangle + \langle c \mid \hat{h}_3 \mid c \rangle + \left\langle ab \left| \frac{e^2}{r_{ij}} \right| ab \right\rangle$$

$$+ \left\langle bc \left| \frac{e^2}{r_{ij}} \right| bc \right\rangle + \left\langle ac \left| \frac{e^2}{r_{ij}} \right| ac \right\rangle + \sum_{\alpha>\beta} \sum \frac{e^2}{R_{\alpha\beta}}, \tag{4.1}$$

where $\hat{h}_i = -(\hbar^2/2m) \nabla_i^2 - \sum_\alpha (e^2/r_{\alpha i})$ and

$$\langle a \mid \hat{h}_1 \mid a \rangle = \left\langle a \left| -\frac{\hbar^2}{2m} \nabla_1^2 - \frac{e^2}{r_{a_1}} \right| a \right\rangle - \left\langle a \left| \frac{e^2}{r_{b_1}} \right| a \right\rangle - \left\langle a \left| \frac{e^2}{r_{c_1}} \right| a \right\rangle, \tag{4.2}$$

etc. Choosing the zero energy as that of the separated atoms, $\langle a \mid \hat{h}_1 \mid a \rangle = -\langle a \mid e^2/r_{b_1} \mid a \rangle - \langle a \mid e^2/r_{c_1} \mid a \rangle$ and Eq. (4.1) becomes

$$Q = Q_{ab} + Q_{bc} + Q_{ac}, \tag{4.3}$$

where

$$Q_{ab} = -2\left\langle b \left| \frac{e^2}{r_{ai}} \right| b \right\rangle + \left\langle ab \left| \frac{e^2}{r_{ij}} \right| ab \right\rangle + \frac{e^2}{R_{ab}}, \tag{4.4a}$$

$$Q_{bc} = -2\left\langle c \left| \frac{e^2}{r_{bi}} \right| c \right\rangle + \left\langle bc \left| \frac{e^2}{r_{ij}} \right| bc \right\rangle + \frac{e^2}{R_{bc}}, \tag{4.4b}$$

and

$$Q_{ca} = -2\left\langle a \left| \frac{e^2}{r_{ci}} \right| a \right\rangle + \left\langle ca \left| \frac{e^2}{r_{ij}} \right| ca \right\rangle + \frac{e^2}{R_{ac}}. \tag{4.4c}$$

The diatomic Coulomb integral, say, $Q_{ab}$, represents the Coulomb integral for an $H_2$ molecule with internuclear distance $R_{ab}$. For the single-exchange integrals, we have

$$(ab) = \langle abc \mid \hat{H}_e \mid bac \rangle$$

$$= \Delta_{ab}^2 \sum_{\alpha>\beta} \sum \frac{e^2}{R_{\alpha\beta}} + 2\Delta_{ab} \langle a \mid \hat{h}_i \mid b \rangle + \Delta_{ab}^2 \langle c \mid \hat{h}_i \mid c \rangle$$

$$+ \left\langle ab \left| \frac{e^2}{r_{ij}} \right| ba \right\rangle + 2\Delta_{ab} \left\langle ac \left| \frac{e^2}{r_{ij}} \right| bc \right\rangle. \tag{4.5}$$

Because of the choice of the zero of energy for the separated atoms, Eq. (4.5) reduces to

$$(ab) = \alpha_{ab} + \Delta\alpha_{ab},$$ (4.6)

where

$$\alpha_{ab} = -2\Delta_{ab}\left\langle a\left|\frac{e^2}{r_{ai}}\right|b\right\rangle + \left\langle ab\left|\frac{e^2}{r_{ij}}\right|ba\right\rangle + \Delta_{ab}^2\frac{e^2}{R_{ab}}$$ (4.7a)

and

$$\Delta\alpha_{ab} = 2\Delta_{ab}\left(-\left\langle a\left|\frac{e^2}{r_{ci}}\right|b\right\rangle + \left\langle ac\left|\frac{e^2}{r_{ij}}\right|bc\right\rangle\right)$$

$$+\Delta_{ab}^2\left(-\left\langle c\left|\frac{e^2}{r_{ai}}\right|c\right\rangle - \left\langle c\left|\frac{e^2}{r_{bi}}\right|c\right\rangle + \frac{e^2}{R_{bc}} + \frac{e^2}{R_{ca}}\right).$$ (4.7b)

$\alpha_{ab}$ is the exchange integral of the $A$-$B$ molecule and $\Delta\alpha_{ab}$ represents the residual terms composed of triatomic interactions. Expanding the double-exchange integral $(cab)$ similarly yields

$$(cab) = \langle abc\,|\,\hat{H}_e\,|\,cab\rangle$$

$$= \Delta_{ab}\,\Delta_{bc}\langle a\,|\,\hat{h}_i\,|\,c\rangle + \Delta_{ac}\,\Delta_{bc}\langle b\,|\,\hat{h}_i\,|\,a\rangle$$

$$+\Delta_{ab}\,\Delta_{ac}\langle c\,|\,\hat{h}_i\,|\,b\rangle + \Delta_{ab}\left\langle ac\left|\frac{e^2}{r_{ij}}\right|cb\right\rangle + \Delta_{bc}\left\langle ab\left|\frac{e^2}{r_{ij}}\right|ca\right\rangle$$

$$+\Delta_{ca}\left\langle bc\left|\frac{e^2}{r_{ij}}\right|ab\right\rangle + \Delta_{ab}\,\Delta_{bc}\,\Delta_{ca}\sum_{\alpha>\beta}\sum\frac{e^2}{R_{\alpha\beta}}$$ (4.8)

or

$$(cab) = -\Delta_{ab}\,\Delta_{bc}\left(\left\langle a\left|\frac{e^2}{r_{bi}}\right|c\right\rangle + \left\langle a\left|\frac{e^2}{r_{ai}}\right|c\right\rangle\right)$$

$$-\Delta_{ac}\,\Delta_{bc}\left(\left\langle b\left|\frac{e^2}{r_{ci}}\right|a\right\rangle + \left\langle b\left|\frac{e^2}{r_{bi}}\right|a\right\rangle\right)$$

$$-\Delta_{ab}\,\Delta_{ca}\left(\left\langle c\left|\frac{e^2}{r_{ai}}\right|b\right\rangle + \left\langle c\left|\frac{e^2}{r_{ci}}\right|b\right\rangle\right)$$

$$+\Delta_{ab}\left\langle ac\left|\frac{e^2}{r_{ij}}\right|cb\right\rangle + \Delta_{bc}\left\langle ab\left|\frac{e^2}{r_{ij}}\right|ca\right\rangle$$

$$+\Delta_{ca}\left\langle bc\left|\frac{e^2}{r_{ij}}\right|ab\right\rangle + \Delta_{ab}\,\Delta_{bc}\,\Delta_{ca}\sum_{\alpha>\beta}\sum\frac{e^2}{R_{\alpha\beta}}$$ (4.9)

after using the condition that the zero energy is chosen as that of the separated atoms.

To determine $\alpha_{ab}$ and $Q_{ab}$, etc., Porter and Karplus make use of the Heitler–London equation for the ground state and the triplet excited state, Eq. (3.18), to obtain

$$Q_{ab} = \tfrac{1}{2}[U_{+ab} + U_{-ab} + \Delta^2_{ab}(U_{-ab} - U_{+ab})]$$
$$\alpha_{ab} = \tfrac{1}{2}[U_{-ab} - U_{+ab} + \Delta^2_{ab}(U_{-ab} + U_{+ab})] \qquad (4.10)$$

by solving for $Q_{ab}$ and $\alpha_{ab}$ from $U_+$ and $U_-$ in Eq. (3.18). For the analytical expressions of empirical energies $U_{+ab}$ and $U_{-ab}$, they employ the Morse potential and Sato potential,

$$U_- = {}^1D[\exp\{-2\beta(R - R^0)\} - 2\exp\{-\beta(R - R^0)\}] \qquad (4.11a)$$

and

$$U_+ = {}^3D[\exp\{-2\beta'(R - R^0)\} + 2\exp\{-\beta'(R - R^0)\}]. \qquad (4.11b)$$

The quantities ${}^1D$, ${}^3D$, $\beta$, $\beta'$, and $R^0$ have been determined by fitting Eqs. (4.11a) and (4.11b) to the calculated results of Kolos and Roothaan (1960) for the singlet and triplet states of the $H_2$ molecule, and are given in Table I. The overlap integrals $\Delta_{ab}$, etc., are, however, calculated directly from the $1s$ orbitals of the exponential screening constant,

$$s = 1 + \varkappa \exp(-\lambda R) \qquad (4.12)$$

with $\varkappa$ and $\lambda$ chosen to approximate the Wang results for $H_2$ (Wang, 1928; cf. Table I).

TABLE I

POTENTIAL ENERGY CONSTANTS FOR $H + H_2$

| | | |
|---|---|---|
| ${}^1D = 4.7466$ ev | $\lambda = 0.65$ | $\varkappa = 0.60$ |
| $R^0 = 1.40083$ a.u. | ${}^3D = 1.9668$ ev | $\sigma = 1.12$ |
| $\beta^1 = 1.000122$ a.u. | $\beta = 1.04435$ a.u. | $\varepsilon = -0.616$ |

For the evaluation of $\Delta\alpha_{ab}$, etc., the unscaled $1s$ orbital has been used for simplicity, and the two-center integrals have been evaluated by using the elliptic coordinate systems, that is, for $AB$, $\mu = (1/R_{ab})$

$\times (r_{ai} + r_{bi})$, $v = (1/R_{ab})(r_{ai} - r_{bi})$ and $\varphi$. Thus

$$\left\langle b \left| \frac{e^2}{r_{ai}} \right| b \right\rangle = \int 1s_b(i)^2 \frac{e^2}{r_{ai}} d\tau_i$$

$$= \tfrac{1}{2}\pi e^2 R_{ab}^2 \left( \frac{1}{\pi a_0{}^3} \right) \int_{-1}^{1} dv \int_{1}^{\infty} d\mu(\mu - v) \exp\left[ -\frac{R_{ab}}{a_0}(\mu - v) \right]$$

$$= \frac{e^2}{R_{ab}} \left[ 1 - \left( 1 + \frac{R_{ab}}{a_0} \right) \exp\left( -\frac{2R_{ab}}{a_0} \right) \right], \quad \text{etc.}, \qquad (4.13)$$

and

$$\left\langle a \left| \frac{e^2}{r_{ai}} \right| b \right\rangle = \int 1s_a(i) 1s_b(i) \frac{e^2}{r_{ai}} d\tau_i$$

$$= \tfrac{1}{2}\pi e^2 R_{ab}^2 \left( \frac{1}{\pi a_0{}^3} \right) \int_{-1}^{1} dv \int_{1}^{\infty} d\mu(\mu + v) \exp\left[ -\frac{R_{ab}}{a_0}\mu \right]$$

$$= \frac{e^2}{a_0} \left( 1 + \frac{R_{ab}}{a_0} \right) \exp\left[ -\frac{R_{ab}}{a_0} \right], \quad \text{etc.} \qquad (4.14)$$

For the three-center integral $\langle ac \mid e^2/r_{ij} \mid bc \rangle$, we have

$$\left\langle ac \left| \frac{e^2}{r_{ij}} \right| bc \right\rangle = \iint 1s_a(i) 1s_b(i) \frac{e^2}{r_{ij}} 1s_c(j)^2 \, d\tau_i \, d\tau_j$$

$$= \int 1s_a(i) 1s_b(i) \, d\tau_i \int 1s_c(j)^2 \frac{e^2}{r_{ij}} d\tau_j$$

$$= \int 1s_a(i) 1s_b(i) \frac{e^2}{r_{ci}} \left[ 1 - \left( 1 + \frac{r_{ci}}{a_0} \right) \exp\left( -\frac{2r_{ci}}{a_0} \right) \right] d\tau_i$$

$$= \left\langle a \left| \frac{e^2}{r_{ci}} \right| b \right\rangle - \left\langle a \left| \frac{e^2}{r_{ci}} \left( 1 + \frac{r_{ci}}{a_0} \right) \exp\left( -\frac{2r_{ci}}{a_0} \right) \right| b \right\rangle \quad (4.15)$$

by using Eq. (4.13). Substituting Eqs. (4.13) and (4.15) into Eq. (4.7b) yields, approximately

$$\Delta \alpha_{ab} = \Delta_{ab}^2 \left[ \frac{e^2}{R_{ac}} \left( 1 + \frac{R_{ac}}{a_0} \right) \exp\left( -\frac{2R_{ab}}{a_0} \right) \right.$$

$$\left. + \frac{e^2}{R_{bc}} \left( 1 + \frac{R_{bc}}{a_0} \right) \exp\left( -\frac{2R_{bc}}{a_0} \right) \right]. \qquad (4.16a)$$

In accordance with the use of the experimental $H_2$ curves to evaluate $\alpha_{ab}$, etc., Porter and Karplus introduce a correction factor $\delta$ in Eq. (4.16) which is to be adjusted by the ratio of the empirical values for $\alpha_{ab}$, etc., to the calculated Heitler–London values for $\alpha_{ab}$, etc. Over the significant range of internuclear distances, the average value of the correction factor $\delta$ is found to be 1.12,

$$\Delta\alpha_{ab} = \delta \, \Delta_{ab}^2 \left[ \frac{e^2}{R_{ac}} \left( 1 + \frac{R_{ac}}{a_0} \right) e^{-2R_{ac}/a_0} \right.$$
$$\left. + \frac{e^2}{R_{bc}} \left( 1 + \frac{R_{bc}}{a_0} \right) e^{-2R_{bc}/a_0} \right]. \tag{4.16b}$$

The double-exchange integral $(cab)$ is written as

$$(cab) = \varepsilon \, \Delta_{ab} \, \Delta_{bc} \, \Delta_{ca}. \tag{4.17}$$

Here $\varepsilon$ is assumed to be constant. Actually the ratio $(cab)/\Delta_{ab} \, \Delta_{bc} \, \Delta_{ca}$ has been shown to be nearly constant except for the smaller internuclear distances that are of less importance for the reaction rate problem because of higher energy, and the average value of $\varepsilon$ is found to be $-0.616$. The overlap integral, $\Delta_{ab}$, $\Delta_{bc}$, and $\Delta_{ca}$ are evaluated analytically, for example,

$$\Delta_{ab} = \langle a \mid b \rangle = \int 1s_a(i) 1s_b(i) \, d\tau_i$$
$$= \frac{s^3}{\pi a_0^3} \int \exp\left[ -\frac{s}{a_0} (r_{ai} + r_{bi}) \right] d\tau_i$$
$$= \frac{s^3}{\pi a_0^3} \int_0^{2\pi} \int_{-1}^1 \int_1^\infty \exp\left( -\frac{sR_{ab}}{a_0} \mu \right) \frac{R_{ab}^3}{8} (\mu^2 - \nu^2) \, d\mu \, d\nu \, d\varphi$$
$$= \left( 1 + \frac{sR_{ab}}{a_0} + \frac{1}{3} \frac{s^2 R_{ab}^2}{a_0^2} \right) \exp\left( -\frac{sR_{ab}}{a_0} \right), \quad \text{etc.,} \tag{4.18}$$

where $s$ is defined by Eq. (4.12).

After discussing how to evaluate the matrix elements, one is ready to discuss the calculation of the potential energy surface of $H_3$. For this purpose, we use Eq. (3.36),

$$U_- = \frac{-C_2 - (C_2^2 - C_1 C_3)^{1/2}}{C_1}, \tag{4.19}$$

where $U_-$ is chosen because it corresponds to the lower-energy state in the region of interest. $C_1$, $C_2$, and $C_3$ are defined in Eq. (3.37). Substituting Eqs. (3.10)–(3.12) into Eq. (3.37) yields

$$C_1 = \zeta_{AA}\zeta_{BB} - \zeta_{AB}^2 = 3(1 - \Delta_{ab} \, \Delta_{bc} \, \Delta_{ca})^2 - \tfrac{1}{2}[(\Delta_{bc}^2 + \Delta_{ca}^2 - 2\Delta_{ab}^2)^2$$
$$+ (\Delta_{ab}^2 + \Delta_{ca}^2 - 2\Delta_{bc}^2)^2 + (\Delta_{ab}^2 + \Delta_{bc}^2 - 2\Delta_{ca}^2)^2] \tag{4.20}$$

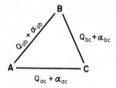

FIG. 2.   Potential energy surface of $H_0$ for $\gamma = 0$.

or, in a more symmetric form,

$$C_1 = 3(1 - \Delta_{ac} \Delta_{bc} \Delta_{ca})^2$$
$$- \tfrac{3}{2}[(\Delta_{ab}^2 - \Delta_{bc}^2)^2 + (\Delta_{bc}^2 - \Delta_{ca}^2)^2 + (\Delta_{ca}^2 - \Delta_{ab}^2)^2]. \quad (4.21)$$

From Eqs. (3.39)–(3.41), we have

$$C_2 = -3[Q - (bca)](1 - \Delta_{ab} \Delta_{bc} \Delta_{ca}) + \tfrac{3}{2}[\Delta_{ab}^2\{2(ab) - (bc) - (ca)\}$$
$$+ \Delta_{bc}^2\{2(bc) - (ab) - (ca)\} + \Delta_{ca}^2\{2(ca) - (ab) - (bc)\}] \quad (4.22)$$

or

$$C_2 = -3[Q - (bca)](1 - \Delta_{ab} \Delta_{bc} \Delta_{ca}) + \tfrac{3}{2}[(\Delta_{ab}^2 - \Delta_{bc}^2)\{(ab) - (bc)\}$$
$$+ (\Delta_{bc}^2 - \Delta_{ca}^2)\{(bc) - (ca)\} + (\Delta_{ca}^2 - \Delta_{ab}^2)\{(ca) - (ab)\}]. \quad (4.23)$$

Similarly, substituting Eqs. (3.13)–(3.15) into Eq. (3.37), we obtain

$$C_3 = 3[Q - (bca)]^2 - \tfrac{1}{2}[\{(ab) + (bc) - 2(ac)\}^2$$
$$+ \{(ca) + (bc) - 2(ab)\}^2 + \{(ab) + (ca) - 2(bc)\}^2] \quad (4.24)$$

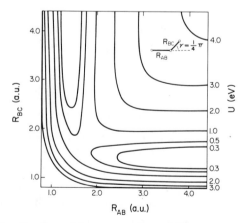

FIG. 3.   Potential energy surface of $H_3$ for $\gamma = \tfrac{1}{4}\pi$.

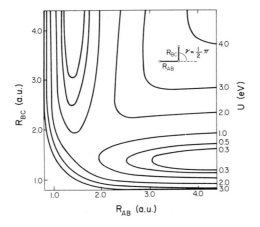

FIG. 4.   Potential energy surface of $H_3$ for $\gamma = \tfrac{1}{2}\pi$.

or, in a more symmetric form,

$$C_3 = 3[Q - (bca)]^2$$
$$- \tfrac{3}{2}[\{(ab)-(bc)\}^2 + \{(bc)-(ca)\}^2 + \{(ca)-(ab)\}^2]. \qquad (4.25)$$

Using Eq. (4.19), the potential energy surfaces for the reaction $H + H_2$ are constructed by Porter and Karplus as a function of the distances $R_{ab}$ and $R_{bc}$ for a fixed bending angle $\gamma$ (Figs. 2–5). As can be seen from these figures, the linear configuration $(\gamma = 0)$ provides the path of

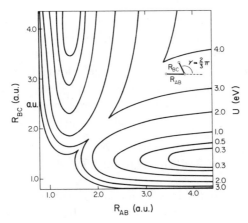

FIG. 5.   Potential energy surface of $H_3$ for $\gamma = \tfrac{2}{3}\pi$.

minimum energy, a single saddle point is present along the line $R_{ab} = R_{bc}$, and the contour maps for various $\gamma$'s are qualitatively similar except for $\gamma = \frac{2}{3}\pi$. However, the increasing energy of these interaction surfaces is clearly evident from displacement of the contour lines. For $\gamma = \frac{2}{3}\pi$, which corresponds to the equilateral triangle configuration along the line $R_{ab} = R_{bc}$, the potential energy surface is significantly different; there exist cusps along the line $R_{ab} = R_{bc}$ which arise from the degeneracy of the equilateral triangle and the resulting Jahn–Teller instability (Karplus, 1970). In Fig. 6 is given the plot of the potential energy along the mini-

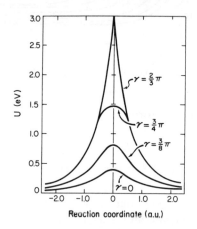

FIG. 6.   Potential energy of $H_3$ along the reaction path of minimum energy.

mum energy path for various $\gamma$'s. The path of linear collision ($\gamma = 0$) can be seen to require the least energy. For $\gamma = \frac{2}{3}\pi$, the potential energy curve along the path of minimum energy is considerably steeper and has a cusp at its maximum corresponding to the equilateral triangle configuration. For $\gamma$ angles other than $\gamma = \frac{2}{3}\pi$, the potential energy curves are well behaved with maxima considerably lower than that of $\gamma = \frac{2}{3}\pi$. In Table II are given the configuration and force constants of the activated complex, and the activation energy of the reaction $H + H_2$ obtained by using various theoretical approaches.

## B.  $H + H_2$ (Cashion and Herschbach, 1964)

The procedure adopted by Cashion and Herschback for the calculation of the potential energy surface for the hydrogen exchange reaction is based on the London equation originally employed by Eyring and Polanyi,

TABLE II

<small>Potential-Energy Surface Properties in Saddle-Point Region</small>

| Surface | $R_{sp}$ (a.u.) | $U_{sp}$ (a.u.)[a] | $\varepsilon_0^{\dagger}$ (kcal)[b] | $K_{11}$ (a.u.) | $K_{22}$ (a.u.) | $K_{33}$ (a.u.) |
|---|---|---|---|---|---|---|
| E[c] | 1.614 | $-1.6565$ | 11.3 | 0.323 | 0.041 | $(+)0.136$ |
| ES | 1.781 | $-1.6497$ | 15.6 | 0.331 | 0.028 | $-0.137$ |
| PK | 1.701 | $-1.6600$ | 9.1 | 0.36 | 0.024 | $-0.124$ |
| BS(1s, 1s′)[d] | 1.779 | $-1.6119$ | 15.4 | 0.29 | 0.023 | $-0.047$ |
| 1s[e] | 1.883 | $-1.6106$ | 23.4 | — | — | — |
| I(1s, 1s′) | 1.788 | $-1.6305$ | 14.0 | 0.30 | — | — |
| II (1s, 1s′, 2p) | 1.764 | $-1.6521$ | 11.0 | 0.31 | 0.024 | $-0.061$ |
| CB | 1.76 | $-1.6621$ | 7.7 | 0.32 | 0.026 | $\sim0.00$ |
| One-center expansion[f] | $\sim1.8$ | $-1.6358$ | — | — | — | — |
| Gaussian set[g] | $\sim1.8$ | $-1.6493$ | 13.5 | — | — | — |

[a] $U_{sp}$ is the total energy at the saddle point.
[b] $\varepsilon_0^{\dagger}$ is the barrier height referred to the corresponding $H_2$, H result (see text).
[c] All results for Surface E refer to the bottom of the well ($R_{AB} = R_{BC}$) and not to its rim.
[d] The Boys and Shavitt calculation used all configurations for the (1s, 1s′) set with the exponentes $\alpha_{1s} = 1.0\lambda$, $\alpha_{1s'} = 1.5\lambda$ for all atoms, where $\lambda$ is a scale factor.
[e] This calculation used the complete set of four configurations and optimized exponents $\alpha_{1sA} = \alpha_{1sC} = 1.058$, $\alpha_{1sB} = 1.202$ (unpublished calculation).
[f] Edmiston and Krauss (1965).
[g] Hayes and Parr (1967).

Eq. (3.28),

$$U_- = Q_{ab} + Q_{bc} + Q_{ca}$$
$$-[\tfrac{1}{2}\{(\alpha_{ab} - \alpha_{bc})^2 + (\alpha_{bc} - \alpha_{ca})^2 + (\alpha_{ca} - \alpha_{ab})^2\}]^{1/2}, \quad (4.26)$$

where $Q_{ab}$ and $\alpha_{ab}$, etc., refer to diatomic integrals. To determine $Q_{ab}$ and $\alpha_{ab}$, etc., they utilize the simplest Heitler–London equation (3.27) for the potential energy curves of the ground electronic state $^1\Sigma_g^+$, and the first repulsive state $^3\Sigma_u^+$, for example,

$$Q_{ab} = \tfrac{1}{2}(U_{-ab} + U_{+ab}), \qquad \alpha_{ab} = \tfrac{1}{2}(U_{-ab} - U_{+ab}). \quad (4.27)$$

For $U_{-ab}$ and $U_{+ab}$, the accurate potential energy curves of the $H_2$ molecule are to be used. This permits the potential energy surface for the

H + $H_2$ reaction to be constructed over a wide range of interactomic distances, without introducing further empirical adjustments. It should be noticed that in order for the potential energy surface obtained by using Eqs. (4.26) and (4.27) to be accurate to within 1 kcal/mole over the range $R_{ab} \geq 0.5$ Å, $R_{bc} \leq 2.5$ Å, the potential energy curves of diatomic molecules should be accurate to within 0.2 kcal/mole over the range $R = 0.5$ to 5 Å. The potential energy curve to such accuracy is available for the $^1\Sigma_g{}^+$ state of $H_2$ but not for the triplet state.

For the $^1\Sigma_g{}^+$ state of $H_2$, the potential energy curve has been derived from the spectroscopic data of Herzberg and Howe (1959) by means of the Rydberg–Klein–Rees (RKR) method (Tobias and Vanderslice, 1961). The classical turning points obtained span the region of $R = 0.411$ to 3.284 Å. The perturbation calculation of Dalgarno and Lynn (Dalgarno and Lynn, 1956), which extends from $R = 2.1$ Å to beyond 6 Å, agrees very closely with the RKR points in the region of their overlap (0.15 kcal/mole disparity at worst). In the calculation of the potential energy surface of H + $H_2$, Cashion and Herschbach use the potential energy curve of the $^1\Sigma_g{}^+$ state of $H_2$ obtained by seventh-order Lagrangian interpolation using the RKR points up to $R = 3.2$ Å and the points given by Dalgarno and Lynn outside this region. They point out that the variational calculation of Kolos and Roothaan (1960) agrees with the RKR results within 0.2 kcal/mole in the range of 0.5 to 1.3 Å, but is found to be high by 2.4 kcal/mole at $R = 2.2$ Å.

For the potential energy curve of the $^3\Sigma_u{}^+$ state of $H_2$, several theoretical calculations have been carried out (Kolos and Roothaan, 1960; Hirschfelder and Linnett, 1950; Dalgarno and Lynn, 1956; Dalgarno, 1961); these results are shown in Fig. 7 for comparison. The potential curves of Kolos and Roothaan, and Hirschfelder and Linnett are obtained by a variational calculation. The perturbation calculation by Dalgarno and Lynn for $R \geq 2.1$ Å seems to be the best in view of the excellent agreement which their procedure gives for the $^1\Sigma_g{}^+$ state as mentioned above. In a later paper, Dalgarno gives an empirical equation for calculating the energy separation of the triplet and singlet states,

$$U_- - U_+ = 7696.8R^2 \exp(-3.730R), \qquad (4.28)$$

where the energy is in kcal/mole and $R$ is in angstroms. Cashion and Herschbach choose the perturbation results of Dalgarno given by Eq. (4.28) for the potential curve of the $^3\Sigma_u{}^+$ state down to $R = 1.4$ Å, and then join it smoothly to the potential curve of Kolos and Roothaan for $R < 1.3$ Å.

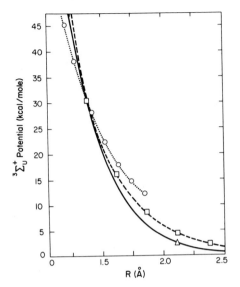

FIG. 7. Calculated potential curves for $^3\Sigma$ of $H_2$: $\cdots\bigcirc\cdots$ Kolos and Roothaan; $-\text{-}\square\text{-}-$ Hirschfelder and Linnett; $-\triangle-$ Dalgarno and Lynn.

Figure 8 shows a contour map of the potential energy surface obtained from Eqs. (4.26) and (4.27) for a linear complex of the hydrogen exchange reaction by Cashion and Herschbach. The force constants, vibrational frequencies, and configuration of the activated complex and the activation energy of the reaction $H + H_2$ obtained by Cashion and Herschbach are

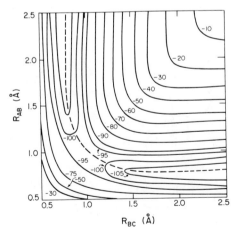

FIG. 8. Potential surface for $H + H_2$. (Energies are in kcal/mole relative to a zero of energy at infinity separation of three atoms.)

given in Table II along with those obtained by other methods. The antisymmetrical stretching frequency in this case appears to be too large (Weston, 1959). Cashion and Herschbach have compared the Coulomb fraction of the binding energy of $H_2$, $\varrho$, defined by Eq. (3.29), as a function of internuclear distance obtained by various methods (cf. Fig. 9). In the LEP method, the $\varrho$ value of 0.14 has often been used for each diatomic pair in the calculation of the potential energy surface with good results in some cases even though the London equation applies only to $s$ electrons and $\varrho$ may become much larger for bonds involving higher orbitals (Fraga and Mulliken, 1960). As can be seen from Fig. 9, for $H_2$, $\varrho = 0.14$ conforms approximately to the ratio calculated from the Heitler–London–Sugiura integrals (Hirschfelder, 1941); near $R = 0.96$ Å, the bond distance of the activated complex, and $R = 1.93$ Å, these curves are fairly close together; and $\varrho$ ($R = 0.96$ Å) and $\varrho$ ($R = 1.93$ Å) differ by more than a factor of 2. This type of variation of $\varrho(R)$ seems to be required if the "washbowl" or "basin" is to be eliminated from the potential surface. It is to be noted that in the LEP method, $\varrho$ has to be less than 0.1 in order for the "washbowl" to disappear from the potential energy surface. Neither Sato's $\varrho(R)$ nor that calculated from the Heitler–London–Sugiura integrals approach the proper limit at large distances where $\varrho(R)$ should approach unity.

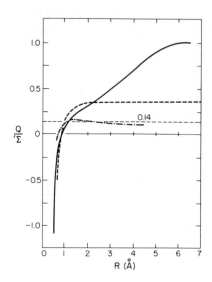

FIG. 9. Coulomb fraction of the binding energy of $H_2$ as a function of internuclear distance: — Cashion and Herschbach; - - - Sato; —·— Heitler–London–Sugiura.

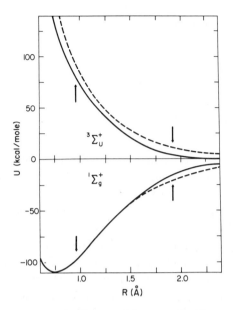

FIG. 10.   Comparison of the "best" potential curves for $H_2$: — "best;" - - - Sato.

Cashion and Herschbach have also compared their $^1\Sigma_g^+$ and $^3\Sigma_u^+$ potentials of $H_2$ with Sato's approximations [cf. Eqs. (3.33) and (3.34)]. The results are shown in Fig. 10. Figure 10 shows that the potential curve of the triplet state given by Sato is too high at $R = 0.96$ Å by 14.6 kcal/mole (a factor of 1.18) and at $R = 1.93$ Å by 6.0 kcal/mole (a factor of 2.35). The slope of Sato's result at $R = 1.93$ Å approximately agrees with that of Cashion and Herschbach, and thus Sato's bending force constant will be expected to be close to that of Cashion and Herschbach.

It is interesting to notice that when the calculations of Porter and Karplus (cf. Section 4,A) have been repeated with the use of the best potential curves of $H_2$ adopted by Cashion and Herschbach, it is found that the classical activation energy is reduced to 4.6 kcal/mole compared with their original value of 9.1 kcal/mole and with 9.7 kcal/mole of Cashion and Herschbach.

## C.  H + H₂ (Shavitt *et al.*, 1968)

Shavitt *et al.* employ the variational method to minimize the energy of the system by writing the wave function of the system $\phi$ as a linear combination of the real configuration $\Phi_r$,

$$\phi = \sum_r C_r \Phi_r. \tag{4.29}$$

It follows that

$$\sum_s (H_{rs} - U \delta_{rs})C_s = 0 \qquad (r = 1, 2, 3, \ldots), \tag{4.30}$$

where $H_{rs} = \langle \Phi_r \mid \hat{H}_e \mid \Phi_s \rangle$ and $\delta_{rs}$ the Kronecker delta. The configurational wave functions $\Phi_r$ consist of sums of Slater determinants constructed from one electron exponential functions centered on the nuclei. Calculations are carried out for optimized exponent basis sets consisting of 6 orbitals (1s, 1s' on each nucleus of $H_3$) and 15 orbitals of 1s, 1s', $2p_x$, $2p_y$, and $2p_z$ on each nucleus of $H_3$. To achieve comparable accuracy for different nuclear geometries (i.e., symmetric and asymmetric, linear and nonlinear), all possible determinants which can be formed from a given basis set are included in the configuration interaction wave function $\phi$ (e.g., for the 15 orbital set, there are 200 configurations for the linear symmetric cases and 402 for the linear assymmetric case). The basis orbitals used to form the configurational determinants $\Phi_r$ are not the atomic orbitals, but arbitrary symmetry orbitals defined as linear combinations of the atomic orbitals. The only restriction on the symmetry orbitals is that they belong to the proper irreducible representations of the symmetry group corresponding to the nuclear geometry. A Schmidt orthogonalization routine is used to convert the symmetry orbitals to an orthogonal set.

To determine the barrier height of the $H_3$ potential energy surface, corresponding results for the $H_2$ molecule are required. Shavitt et al. carry out a full set of calculations for $H_2$ with a 4 orbital basis set (1s, 1s' on each center of $H_2$) and a 10 orbital basis set (1s, 1s', $2p_x$, $2p_y$, and $2p_z$, on each center of $H_2$). They include all configurations in the optimized configuration interaction calculations for $H_2$, 6 configurations for the (1s, 1s') set and 16 configurations for the (1s, 1s', 2p) set. Theoretical results for the equilibrium distance, force constant, and dissociation energy are given in Table III for comparison with experimental values. Table III shows that although the equilibrium distance and force constant obtained with the 10 orbital basis set are satisfactory, the calculated dissociation energy is still 3.0 kcal/mole above the true energy.

The potential energy surfaces of $H_3$ have been obtained from the 6 orbital calculation and from the 15 orbital calculation, and the contour

TABLE III

SOME RESULTS OF OPTIMIZED CI CALCULATIONS FOR $H_2$

| Basis set | $R_e$ (a.u.) | $U(R_e)$ (a.u.) | $D_e$ (kcal) | $K$ (a.u.) | Optimized exponents (in order of basic set) |
|---|---|---|---|---|---|
| 1s | 1.42 | −1.1479 | 93 | 0.43 | 1.193 |
| 1s, 1s′ | 1.4148 | −1.1528 | 96 | 0.35 | 1.122, 1.386 |
| 1s, 1s′, 2p | 1.4018 | −1.16959 | 106 | 0.36 | 1.078, 1.426, 1.800 |
| 1s, 1s′, 2s, 2p | 1.4013 | −1.16696 | 104 | — | 0.965, 1.43, 1.16, 1.87($\sigma$), 1.71($\pi$) |
| Experiment | 1.4008 | −1.17445 | 109 | 0.365 | |

maps of the potential energy surface in the saddle point region of linear $H_3$ are given in Fig. 11. In Fig. 12 are shown the locations of the minimum energy paths as a function of apex angle for comparison. The numerical results of the potential energy surface properties in the saddle point region are tabulated in Table II for comparison. Shevitt *et al.* have also made some calculations for the linear case to test if the correct $H_2 + H$ limit is approached as one H atom is removed to infinity; with the $R_{ab}$ distance equal to the $H_2$ theoretical value and the other atom at distances greater than 11 a.u., full agreement with the separately calculated $H_2$ result is obtained. It is interesting to notice that they find a possible van der Waals minimum at a distance of about 6 a.u. Since the depth of the

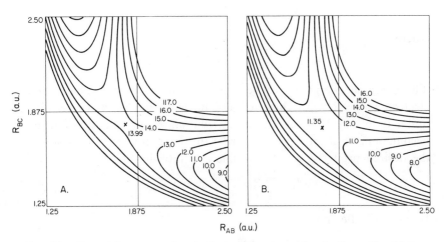

FIG. 11.  Potential energy surface in the saddle-point region for linear $H_3$: (a) from 6-orbital calculation; (b) from 15-orbital calculation.

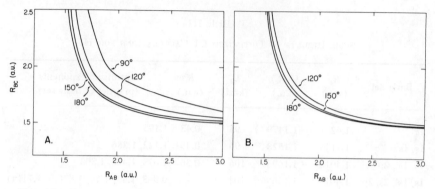

FIG. 12. Position of minimum-energy path as a function of apex angle; (a) from 6-orbital calculation; (b) from 15-orbital calculation.

well is very small (approximately, $4 \times 10^{-4}$ a.u.), considerable effort in terms of exponent optimizations and higher integral accuracy would be required to obtain reliable results.

### D. H + H₂ (Conroy and Bruner, 1967)

To describe the procedure of Conroy and Bruner used in the calculation of the $H_3$ potential energy surface, first consider the one-electron problem (Conroy, 1970). In this case, the Schrödinger equation in atomic unit for a single electron moving in the field of a number of fixed nuclei with charges $Z_a$, $Z_b$, ... is given by

$$\hat{H}_e \phi = -\tfrac{1}{2} \nabla^2 \phi + V\phi = U\phi, \qquad (4.31a)$$

where

$$V = -\sum_\alpha Z_\alpha / r_\alpha. \qquad (4.31b)$$

The potential energy $V$ reaches $-\infty$ whenever the coordinates of the electron coincide with those of any nucleus, and since $U\phi$ is always finite, it follows that for any exact solution $\phi$, the quantity $\nabla^2 \phi$ must become infinite at the nuclei. In order to construct an eigenfunction with the desired property, a new variable $d$ is introduced,

$$\gamma d = \sum_\alpha Z_\alpha r_\alpha, \qquad \gamma = \sum_\alpha Z_\alpha. \qquad (4.32)$$

It can easily be shown that

$$\gamma \, \nabla^2 d = 2 \sum_\alpha Z_\alpha / \gamma_\alpha = -2V. \qquad (4.33)$$

Thus a trial function containing $d$,

$$F_1 = \exp(-\gamma d), \qquad (4.34)$$

will give a complete cancellation of $V$ including the accompanying singularities at the nuclei from Eq. (4.31),

$$-\tfrac{1}{2}\nabla^2 F_1 = -[V + \tfrac{1}{2}\gamma^2(\nabla d)^2]F_1, \qquad F_1^{-1}\hat{H}_e F_1 = -\tfrac{1}{2}\gamma^2(\nabla d)^2. \qquad (4.35)$$

The quantity on the right side of the second equation in (4.35) lies in a numerical value between $-\tfrac{1}{2}\gamma^2$ and 0; it obviously never reaches $\infty$, but neither is it everywhere equal to the eigenvalue $U$. Thus the trial function $F_1$ is only a crude approximation. Choosing the origin of the spherical coordinates $(r, \theta, \phi)$ at the center of nuclear charges, that is, $\sum_\alpha Z_\alpha \mathbf{r}_\alpha = 0$, it can be shown that $\lim_{r\to\infty}(d/r) = 1$, from which it follows that

$$\lim_{r\to\infty} \gamma^2(\nabla d)^2 = \gamma^2(\nabla r)^2 = \gamma^2. \qquad (4.36)$$

The asymptotic behavior at large $r$ is therefore not correctly given by $F_1$ in Eq. (4.34), since usually $-\tfrac{1}{2}\gamma^2 < U$. This can be remedied by using

$$F = \sigma^{-\alpha} \exp[-\gamma d + (\gamma - \varepsilon)\sigma^{-1}], \qquad (4.37)$$

where $\sigma = (\gamma^2 + s^2)^{1/2}$, $\varepsilon = (-2U)^{1/2}$, and $\alpha = \gamma/\varepsilon - 1$. $s$ is a parameter that is chosen as an average radius, specifically as that value of $r$ at which half of the integrated radial density is accumulated. Operationally this procedure for determining $s$ requires cumbersome three-dimensional integrations to be performed. It is found that the utility of $F$ is not critically dependent on $s$, and that the deficiency due to the choice of some nonoptimal value is rather quickly compensated by the radial series expansion. Thus Conroy (1967) introduces

$$F = \sigma_2^{-\alpha} \exp[-\gamma d + (\gamma - \varepsilon)\sigma_1^{-1}], \qquad (4.38)$$

where $\sigma_1 = (r^2 + d_0^2)^{-1/2}$, $\sigma_2 = (r^2 + d_0^2 + \varepsilon^{-2})^{-1/2}$, and $d_0$ is the value of $d$ at the origin. To add flexibility the final form of the one-electron molecular were function is chosen to be a series expansion

$$\phi = \sum_n C_n \chi_n = \sum_n C_n A_n(r, \theta, \varphi) F(r, \theta, \varphi), \qquad (4.39)$$

where $F(r, \theta, \varphi)$ is defined by Eq. (4.38), and the functions $A_n(r, \theta, \varphi)$

are members of a single-center basis set,

$$A_n(r, \theta, \varphi) = r^j \sigma_2^{i-1} Y_j^k(\theta, \varphi) L_{i+j}^{2j+1}(q) \qquad (4.40)$$

with $q = 2\varepsilon(\sigma_1^{-1} - d_0)$. $Y_j^k(\theta, \varphi)$ and $L_{i+j}^{2j+1}(q)$ represent the spherical harmonics and associated Laguerre polynomials, respectively.

Next, consider the two-electron problem. In this case, Conroy writes the wave function as a product of two factors, electron correlation factor $\phi_c$ and a molecular shape factor $\phi_s$,

$$\phi = \phi_c \phi_s. \qquad (4.41)$$

The functional form of the shape factor $\phi_s$ is restricted to a linear super-position of configurations; each configuration is taken as a symmetrized or anti-symmetrized product of one-electron terms,

$$\phi_s = \sum_{nm} C_{nm}[\chi_n(1)\chi_m(2) \pm \chi_n(2)\chi_m(1)], \qquad (4.42)$$

where the positive sign is used for the singlet and the negative sign is used for the triplet spin states. The electron correlation factor $\phi_c$ consists of two parts,

$$\phi_c = a(r_{12})b(r_{12}, \sigma_1, \sigma_2), \qquad (4.43)$$

$a(r_{12})$ is introduced to improve convergence by explicitly taking care of the singularity $1/r_{12}$ in the Hamiltonian and is defined by

$$a(r_{12}) = \sum_{k=0}^{\infty} \frac{1}{k!(k+1)!} \left(\frac{r_{12}}{t}\right)^k, \qquad (4.44)$$

where $t = 1 - (1/\gamma)(-2U/N)^{1/2}$, $N$ being the number of electrons, and $b(r_{12}, \sigma_1, \sigma_2)$ is introduced to provide more flexibility (mostly for angular correlation), and is defined by

$$b(r_{12}, \sigma_1, \sigma_2) = \sum_{ijk} C_{ijk} W_{12}^i \lambda_{12}^j \mu_{12}^k, \qquad (4.45)$$

where $W_{12} = (r_{12}^2 + t^2)^{1/2}$, $\lambda_{12} = \sigma_1^{-1}(1) + \sigma_1^{-1}(2)$, and $\mu_{12} = \sigma_1^{-1}(1) - \sigma_1^{-1}(2)$. This procedure can be expanded to more than two electrons by including all singlet and triplet pair correlations and proper anti-symmetrization (Conroy, 1967).

To find the optimal wave function and energy, Conroy proposes to minimize the energy variance

$$W^2 = \frac{\int (\hat{H}_e \phi - U\phi)^2 \, d\tau}{\int \phi^2 \, d\tau}. \tag{4.46}$$

For example, for $\phi$ given by Eq. (4.39), $W^2$ is given by

$$W^2 = \frac{\sum_n \sum_m (H_{nm} - UV_{nm} + U^2 S_{nm}) C_n C_m}{\sum_n \sum_m C_n C_m S_{nm}}, \tag{4.47}$$

where $H_{nm} = \langle \hat{H}_e \chi_n \mid \hat{H}_e \chi_m \rangle$, $V_{nm} = \langle \chi_n \mid \hat{H}_e \mid \chi_m \rangle + \langle \chi_m \mid \hat{H}_e \mid \chi_n \rangle$, and $S_{nm} = \langle \chi_n \mid \chi_m \rangle$. The best possible $\phi$ is the one which gives the lowest numerical value of $W^2$. Minimization of Eq. (4.47) gives a secular equation of the type

$$\mid H_{nm} - UV_{nm} + (U^2 - W^2) S_{nm} \mid = 0. \tag{4.48}$$

The main advantage of this procedure is the reduced sensitivity of the energy obtained with respect to errors in the matrix elements, and this energy variance calculation permits extrapolation to a more accurate approximation to the true energy than can be obtained solely from a knowledge of the ordinary upper and lower bounds. It is well known that the energy $E$ obtained from the minimization of

$$E = \frac{\langle \phi \mid \hat{H}_e \mid \phi \rangle}{\langle \phi \mid \phi \rangle} \tag{4.49}$$

gives the upper bound to the true lowest energy $U_0$. Temple (1928) derives a formula allowing the simultaneous calculation of a lower bound to $U_0$,

$$U_0 \geq \lambda_T = E - \frac{W^2}{U_1 - E}, \tag{4.50}$$

where $U_1$ is the energy of the first excited state. The quantity $\lambda_T$ is the Temple lower bound to the energy. The range of uncertainty in $U_0$, $E - \lambda_T = W^2 (U_1 - E)^{-1}$ can be made to vanish if the energy variance $W^2$ vanishes. Thus by plotting $E$ vs $W$ obtained from the use of a number of different wave functions and extrapolating to zero $W$, one will obtain the best energy.

The method described above has been applied to $H_3$ by Conroy and Bruner (1967). The energy contour maps for linear and isosceles $H_3$—arrangements are given in Figs. 13 and 14. In agreement with other treatments, the surface of linear configuration lies lower than that of the triangular ones. The saddle point is at $R_{ab} = R_{bc} = 1.76$ a.u. with an activation energy of 7.74 kcal/mole above $H + H_2$. The other properties of the saddle point region are given in Table II for comparison.

The calculated results of the potential energy surface properties of $H_3$ in the saddle point region obtained by using the theoretical approaches described above are summarized in Table II for comparison. To permit a valid comparison, Shavitt *et al.* (1968; Karplus, 1970) have repeated the

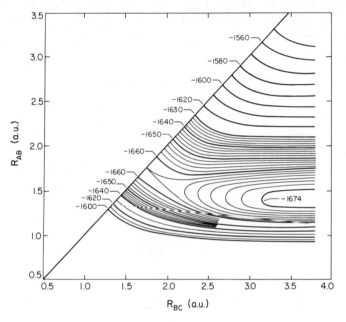

FIG. 13.  Potential energy surface for linear $H_3$.

semiempirical calculations of Cashion and Herschbach and of Eyring and Polanyi by using the potential energy curves of $^1\Sigma_g{}^+$ and $^3\Sigma_u{}^+$ for $H_2$ adopted by Porter and Karplus. All calculations agree that the minimum energy path lies in the linear geometry of $H_3$. The energy profile along the minimum energy path for the linear $H_3$ obtained from various treatments is shown in Fig. 15 and the location of the minimum energy path for various computed linear $H_3$ surfaces is given in Fig. 16. In these figures and Table II, "E" refers to the original version of Eyring and Polanyi, "S," the modification of the Sato type by Cashion and Hersch-

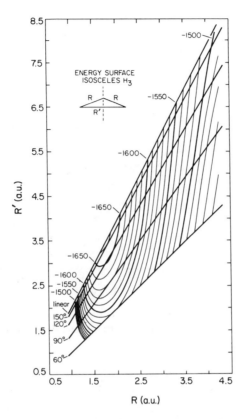

FIG. 14.   Potential energy surface for isosceles $H_3$.

bach, "PK," the semiempirical calculation by Porter and Karplus, "CB," the a priori treatment of Conroy and Bruner, and "I" and "II," the theoretical calculation by Shavitt et al. for the 6 orbital basis set and 15 orbital basis set, respectively. Figure 15 shows that the original LEP method with $\varrho = 0.14$ gives a curve having a very broad and pronounced well, and other semiempirical calculations and a priori treatments show no minimum. The geometry of the minimum energy paths plotted on the linear $H_3$ surface in Fig. 16 shows some interesting differences. All of the semiempirical curves (Eyring–Polanyi, Cashion–Herschbach, Porter–Karplus) have some "kinks" in the saddle point region, in contrast to the a priori curves of Shavitt et al., which are completely smooth; the curve of Conroy and Bruner gives some indication of a slight kink corresponding to that of Cashion and Herschbach. Curves I and II are almost parallel, but they differ from all other curves in approaching the $H_2$ equilibrium

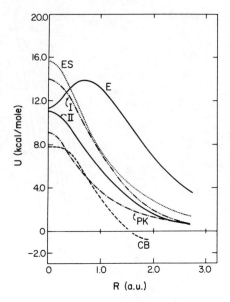

FIG. 15.　Energy profile along the minimum-energy path for linear $H_3$ from various computations: E, Eyring; ES, Eyring–Sato; PK, Porter–Karplus; CB, Conroy–Bruner.

distance much more slowly as the third atom moves away. Curves II and CB are in excellent agreement on the saddle point region, but diverge rapidly in the intermediate region.

The potential energy of $H_3$ as a function of internuclear distance for the linear-symmetric geometry is plotted in Fig. 17 for the surfaces II, CB and PK. The curves represent the potential function for the symmetric

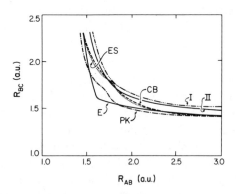

FIG. 16.　Location of the minimum-energy path for linear $H_3$ from various computations.

stretching vibration at the saddle point. Aside from the difference in the height and position of the saddle point, all three curves in Fig. 17 are similar with curves CB and II almost parallel.

Table II gives the saddle point results obtained from various calculations for $H_3$. For the semiempirical surfaces, and the CB surface, the classical activation energies are computed relative to the Kolos–Roothaan energy for the $H_2$ molecule, while in other cases (Boys and Shavitt, 1959) (BS, 1s basis set, I and II), the values of classical activation energies are relative to a $H_2$ energy computed with a wave function constructed from a comparable basis set. Table II shows that Calculation II and the Gaussian calculation (Edmiston and Krauss, 1965) are about 1.9 and 4.4 kcal/mole,

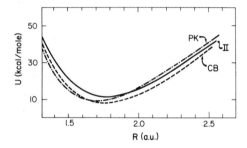

FIG. 17. Potential energy as a function of internuclear distance for linear symmetric $H_3$.

respectively, above the PK result, while the CB value is about 1.4 kcal/mole below. The Calculation II value is certainly somewhat too high, but it does not appear likely to be too high by as much as the 3.3 kcal required to bring it down to the CB result. This is because the method used by Conroy and Bruner includes an extrapolation procedure that does not necessarily yield an upper bound. Also it is to be noted that Fig. 15 shows that the CB energy curve drops to more than 1 kcal/mole below the $H_2 + H$ limit. This somewhat surprising result has been attributed by Conroy and Bruner to the fact that their calculation at any point could be 0.6–1.2 kcal/mole above or below the true value.

Table II indicates that Calculations II and CB for the internuclear distance at the saddle point are in close agreement ($R_0 = 1.765$ a.u.) while the PK value ($R_0 = 1.701$ a.u.) is significantly smaller. The symmetric stretching force constant $K_{11}$ and the bending force constant $K_{22}$ vary only by relatively small amounts among the calculations. The third ofrce constant $K_{33}$ changes more markedly for the different surfaces;

it is positive for Surface E evaluated at the center of the well; $K_{33}$ is significantly larger for the semiempirical surfaces ES and PK than for the a priori surfaces. Thus considerable differences in the tunneling would be predicted from the simple models which fit the barrier to the force constant $K_{33}$.

From comparisons with the earlier a priori studies of the $H_3$ potential surface (Laidler, 1969), it is clear that a significant improvement in accuracy has been achieved by the 15 orbital multiconfiguration calculations by Shavitt et al. and the CB calculation. It is very likely that the general features of the $H_3$ surface are essentially correct, and that in the not too distant future, sufficiently accurate theoretical calculations can be done to reduce the uncertainty in the energy of potential surfaces to the acceptable value of 0.3 kcal/mole.

## E. $Cl + Cl_2$ (Eyring et al., 1970)

The potential energy surfaces of the halogen atom-molecule exchange reactions, $Cl + Cl_2$, $Br + I_2$, and $Cl + Br_2$ have recently been calculated by Eyring et al. using the LEP and LEPS methods. Here only the potential energy surface of the reaction $Cl + Cl_2$ will be discussed. It should be noted that strictly speaking, the London equation in its original form applies only to s orbitals; since the calculation is semiempirical in nature, it is possible that the London equation may be used in general as a tool for an extrapolation of the binding energy between atoms from the diatomic to the polyatomic problem.

In the LEP method, $\varrho$ is chosen as 0.1, 0.14, and 0.2 in the calculation of the $Cl + Cl_2$ surfaces.

Previous analysis of the potential energy for the $Cl_3$ system by means of the LEP method has been done by Rollefson and Eyring (1932). Assuming that the exchange energy of the diatomic molecules constitutes 90% of the diatomic molecule, they found an activation energy of 4.5 kcal for the forward formation of the intermediate and 8.6 kcal for its decomposition. This may be compared to the 4.6 kcal for the formation of the intermediate and 9.2 kcal for its decomposition which results from the present calculations. The differences are attributed to the use of more recent spectroscopic data. Table IV shows that as the value of $\varrho$ is increased, the value of the activation energy for the formation of the intermediate is decreased while that of its decomposition increases. Thus as $\varrho$ increases, the intermediate species has a greater stability. As $\varrho$ increases, the diatomic limits are approached more readily indicating less interaction

TABLE IV

POTENTIAL ENERGY SURFACES OF $Cl + Cl_2$

| The LEP method | | | |
|---|---|---|---|
| Reaction | $\varrho$ | Equilibrium distance (Å) | Activation energy (kcal) |
| $Cl + Cl_2 \rightarrow Cl - Cl - Cl$<br>$Cl - Cl - Cl \rightarrow Cl + Cl_2$ | 0.1 | 2.00 | 4.60<br>9.20 |
| $Cl + Cl_2 \rightarrow Cl - Cl - Cl$<br>$Cl - Cl - Cl \rightarrow Cl + Cl_2$ | 0.14 | 2.00 | 2.95<br>10.58 |
| $Cl + Cl_2 \rightarrow Cl - Cl - Cl$<br>$Cl - Cl - Cl \rightarrow Cl + Cl_2$ | 0.20 | 2.00 | 12.65 |

| The LEPS method | | | |
|---|---|---|---|
| Reaction | $\zeta^2$ | Equilibrium distance (Å) | Activation energy (kcal) |
| $Cl + Cl_2 \rightarrow Cl + Cl_2$ | 0.0 | 2.13 | 6.44 |
| $Cl + Cl_2 \rightarrow Cl - Cl - Cl$<br>$Cl - Cl - Cl \rightarrow Cl + Cl_2$ | 0.1 | 2.13 | 1.61<br>0.46 |
| $Cl + Cl_2 \rightarrow Cl - Cl - Cl$<br>$Cl - Cl - Cl \rightarrow Cl + Cl_2$ | 0.1475 | 2.13 | 0.46<br>1.51 |

between the halogen atom and molecule. In all cases, the basin lies along the axis of the valleys, which means that the intermediate is formed with very little contribution of vibrational motion of the $Cl_2$ molecule. Since the equilibrium internuclear distances of the atoms in the intermediate are about the same as that of the diatomic molecules, the LEP surfaces describe the formation of the intermediate as if a halogen atom were approaching a diatomic molecule. This is similar to the behavior found in ion-molecule reactions. For the LEPS surfaces Table IV indicates that, for $\zeta^2 = 0.1$ and $\zeta^2 = 0.1475$ the $Cl_3$ intermediate is stable. As $\zeta^2$ increases the stability increases.

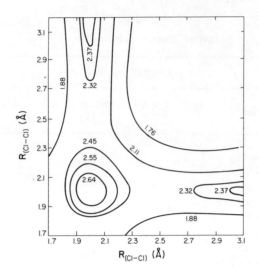

Fig. 18.　Potential energy surface of $Cl_3$ by the Eyring–Polanyi method for $\varrho = 0.1$.

Figures 18–23 are the LEPS and LEP surfaces for the $Cl_3$ system. The scales used are not symmetric so the symmetry of the surfaces is not apparent. In general the activation energy for the formation of the intermediate species is greater in the LEP calculations. The basin is also deeper indicating that the complex is more stable. Both the LEP and LEPS surfaces can only give a qualitative picture of the electronic

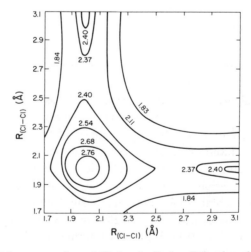

Fig. 19.　Potential energy surface of $Cl_3$ by the Eyring–Polanyi method for $\varrho = 0.14$.

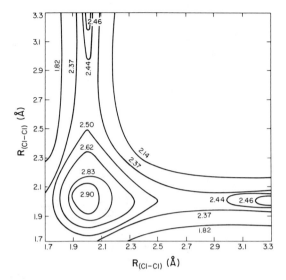

FIG. 20.   Potential energy surface of $Cl_3$ by the Eyring–Polanyi method for $\varrho = 0.2$.

interactions of the systems. Their validity must be determined largely by the experimental results obtained.

## F. K + NaCl (Roach and Child, 1968)

The calculation of the potential energy surface of the reaction $K+NaCl$ carried out by Roach and Child is based on a model in which a single

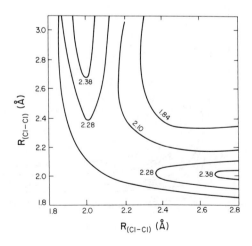

FIG. 21.   Potential energy surface of $Cl_3$ by the Sato method for $\zeta^2 = 0$.

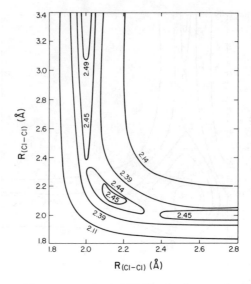

FIG. 22. Potential energy surface of $Cl_3$ by the Sato method for $\zeta^2 = 0.1$.

valence electron moves in the fields of $Na^+$, $K^+$, and $Cl^-$, with the ions retaining their essential structural identity at all configurations of interest, and behaving in their long-range interactions as polarizable charged spheres. Their approach is suggested by Rittner's successful calculations of the potential curves of isolated alkali halide molecules (Rittner, 1959). Rittner's calculation is based on the assumption of classical interactions

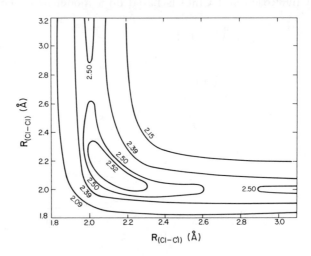

FIG. 23. Potential energy surface of $Cl_3$ by the Sato method for $\zeta^2 = 0.1475$.

between two mutually polarized charged spheres, together with supplementary van der Waals' forces and close range repulsions. If $\mu_+$ and $\mu_-$ are the point dipoles induced at each ion, the potential energy of an isolated alkali halide molecule in atomic unit can be written

$$U(R) = -\frac{1}{R} - \frac{\mu_+ + \mu_-}{R^2} - \frac{2\mu_+\mu_-}{R^3} + \frac{\mu_+^2}{2\alpha_+} + \frac{\mu_-^2}{2\alpha_-} - \frac{C}{R^6}$$
$$+ Ae^{-R/\varrho}, \tag{4.53}$$

where the successive terms represent the charge–charge, charge–dipole, dipole–dipole interactions, the quasielastic energies of dipole formation, the van der Waals energy, and the close range overlap repulsion. $\alpha_+$ and $\alpha_-$ are the ion polarizabilities. Thus the Hamiltonian of the K+NaCl can be written in the form

$$\hat{H}_e = \hat{H}_e^0 + V(\text{core}),$$
$$\hat{H}_e^0 = -\tfrac{1}{2}\nabla^2 + V(\text{Na}^+) + V(\text{K}^+) + V(\text{Cl}^-). \tag{4.54}$$

$\hat{H}_e^0$ includes the potential energy of its interaction with the isolated ions, all polarization terms being neglected. $V(\text{core})$ in Eq. (4.54) is composed mainly of the interactions between the ion cores, a generalization of Eq. (4.53), but contains in addition the contribution of the valence electron to the polarization energy, which is treated as a first-order correction to the electronic energies $U_n^0$ obtained from the Schrödinger equation,

$$\hat{H}_e^0\phi_n = U_n^0\phi_n. \tag{4.55}$$

The valence electron which occupies a K 4s orbital in the ground state of the reactants is transferred in the course of reaction to a Na 3s orbital. Thus Roach and Child expand $\phi_n$ at all configurations as a linear combination of Na and K valence atomic orbitals. The inclusion of the four p-orbitals directed in the plane of the nuclei in addition to Na 3s and K 4s orbitals, is found to contribute substantially to the stability of the ground state potential surface and is necessary in order to obtain the correct form of long-range dipole-induced dipole interactions. Strictly speaking, $\phi_n$ must be orthogonal to all the occupied orbitals of $\text{Na}^+$, $\text{K}^+$, and $\text{Cl}^-$; however, the Na valence orbitals, for instance, while orthogonal to the occupied $\text{Na}^+$ core orbitals, have small nonzero overlaps with the $\text{K}^+$ and $\text{Cl}^-$ core functions. To avoid complete and rigorous orthogonalization of the atomic orbitals to all foreign core orbitals, the problem is treated by using suitably modified expressions for $V(\text{Na}^+)$,

$V(K^+)$ and $V(Cl^-)$ such that their interaction with the undisturbed atomic functions reproduces the energetic effects of orthogonalization (Austin *et al.*, 1962). The expressions adopted by Roach and Child are for $Na^+$ and $K^+$,

$$V(M^+) = \begin{cases} 0, & r < \sigma, \\ -1/r, & r > \sigma, \end{cases} \tag{4.56}$$

where $\sigma$ is the gaseous ionic radius proposed by Rittner, and for $Cl^-$,

$$V(Cl^-) = 1/r. \tag{4.57}$$

In calculating the matrix elements of $\hat{H}_e$, ionization potentials $I$ are used to estimate all one center and kinetic energy integrals. For example,

$$\langle \chi_{Na,s} \mid -\tfrac{1}{2}\nabla^2 + V(Na^+) \mid \chi_{Na,s} \rangle$$
$$= I(Na, s); \langle \chi_{Na,s} \mid -\tfrac{1}{2}\nabla^2 + \tfrac{1}{2}V(Na^+) + \tfrac{1}{2}V(K^+) \mid \chi_{K,p\sigma} \rangle$$
$$= \tfrac{1}{2}[I(Na, s) + I(K, p)]\langle \chi_{Na,s} \mid \chi_{K,p\sigma} \rangle, \tag{4.58}$$

etc. The two-center integrals are calculated analytically in elliptic coordinates and the nine three-center integrals of the type $\langle \chi_{Na} \mid V(Cl^-) \mid \chi_K \rangle$ are evaluated numerically. For this purpose, single term Slater-type orbitals are chosen (Clementi, 1963, 1964),

$$\chi_{Na,s} = N_{Na,s} r^2 e^{-0.85r}, \qquad \chi_{K,s} = N_{K,s} r^3 e^{-0.736r}. \tag{4.59}$$

It is assumed that the radial parts of the corresponding p orbitals are given by the same expressions. The electronic energy also contains the contributions from the term $V(core)$. These interactions include the charge-charge electrostatic energies, the van der Waal's attraction for each pair of ions, the close-range overlap repulsions between the ions, the polarization of ion cores, etc. [cf. Eq. (4.53)]. The calculation of terms involving the electron is simplified to the interaction of point charges and dipoles.

Using the approach described above, Roach and Child carry out the test calculations of potential curves for the ions $N_{a_2}^+$ and $K_2^+$. The calculated results are found to be in very satisfactory agreement with the experimental binding energies, bond lengths and spectroscopic constants. For the reaction between K and NaCl the calculated reaction exothermicity is 6 kcal/mole compared with an experimental value of 4 kcal/mole (Brewer and Brackett, 1961). The ground state potential energy surface is found to be of the attractive type and there is no activation barrier.

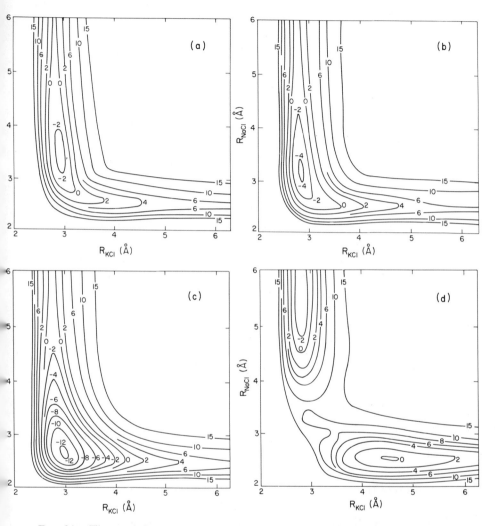

FIG. 24. The ground state potential surface; (a) 180°, (b) 135°, (c) 90°, (d) 45°.

The calculations of Roach and Child predict a potential well with maximum depth, $D_0{}^\circ = 13.5$ kcal/mole, in a triangular configuration $R_{\text{NaCl}}$ = 1.7 Å, $R_{\text{KCl}} = 2.9$ Å, and $<$NaClK $= 75°$. The contour maps of the reaction Na + KCl as a function the angle $\theta = {}<$NaClK are shown in Fig. 24. They conclude that an adiabatic model will adequately describe reactive collisions at thermal energies, but that a nonadiabatic mechanism, yielding electronically excited products, could become important for highly energetic collisions.

# V. Orbital Symmetry in Reaction Kinetics

Chemical reactions consist of the breaking of certain bonds between atoms and the making of new bonds. A reaction has associated with it a reaction coordinate, and any detailed analysis of a reaction mechanism requires a knowledge of how the electron distribution changes for various modes of the system. All MO's of a system correspond to the binding together of certain atoms, the antibonding of other atoms, and the non-bonding of the remaining atoms. Thus in a chemical reaction certain MO's must be vacated of electrons and others must be filled to create the new bonding situation. The most important of these changes is a flow of electrons from the highest occupied MO to the lowest unoccupied MO (Fukui, 1965). Electron movement between two orbitals cannot occur unless the orbitals meet the symmetry requirement (Bader, 1962; Woodward and Hoffmann, 1965a,b,c). The subject of orbital symmetry in reaction kinetics has recently been reviewed by Woodward and Hoffmann (1970) and by Pearson (1971).

## A. General Theory

The chemical reaction may be considered as a perturbation on the reactant system. Any arbitrary small motion of the nuclei away from the original configuration can be analyzed as a sum of displacements corresponding to the normal modes of the system representing the reactants. When the nuclei are displaced from their equilibrium positions the electron distribution relaxes in such a way as to follow the motion of nuclei. By determining which nuclear motion allows for the most favorable relaxation of the electron density, we can in effect determine the reaction coordinate. Now we expand the Hamiltonian of electronic motion in power series of the reaction coordinate $Q$ about the original configuration with Hamiltonian $\hat{H}_e^0$,

$$\hat{H}_e = \hat{H}_e^0 + \left(\frac{\partial V}{\partial Q}\right)_0 Q + \frac{1}{2}\left(\frac{\partial^2 V}{\partial Q^2}\right)_0 Q^2 + \cdots . \qquad (5.1)$$

If the last two terms in Eq. (5.1) are regarded as perturbation, then using the perturbation theory we can solve for the wave functions and energies as

$$\phi^0 = \phi_0^0 + \sum_{\varkappa}{}' \frac{\langle \phi_0^0 \mid (\partial V/\partial Q)_0 \mid \phi_\varkappa^0 \rangle Q}{U_0^0 - U_\varkappa^0} \phi_\varkappa^0 + \cdots \qquad (5.2)$$

and

$$U_0 = U_0^0 + \left\langle \phi_0^0 \left| \left( \frac{\partial V}{\partial Q} \right)_0 \right| \phi_0^0 \right\rangle Q + \frac{Q^2}{2} \left\langle \phi_0^0 \left| \left( \frac{\partial^2 V}{\partial Q^2} \right)_0 \right| \phi_0^0 \right\rangle$$

$$+ Q^2 \sum_{\varkappa}' \frac{|\langle \phi_0^0 | (\partial V/\partial Q)_0 | \phi_\varkappa^0 \rangle|^2}{U_0^0 - U_\varkappa^0} + \cdots . \tag{5.3}$$

Although Eqs. (5.2) and (5.3) are valid only for small $Q$, since we can select any configuration to carry out the expansion Eq. (5.1), Eqs. (5.2) and (5.3) are quite general. Figure 25 shows the usual adiabatic plot of potential energy against reaction coordinate. At any maximum or minimum in the potential energy curve, $\partial U_0 / \partial Q = 0$, and

$$U_0 = U_0^0 + \frac{Q^2}{2} \left\langle \phi_0^0 \left| \left( \frac{\partial^2 V}{\partial Q^2} \right)_0 \right| \phi_0^0 \right\rangle$$

$$+ Q^2 \sum_{\varkappa}' \frac{|\langle \phi_0^0 | (\partial V/\partial Q)_0 | \phi_\varkappa^0 \rangle|^2}{U_0^0 - U_\varkappa^0} + \cdots . \tag{5.4}$$

It is convenient to employ the electron density functions $L_{00} = |\phi_0^0|^2$ and $L_{0\varkappa} = \phi_0^{0*} \phi_\varkappa^0$ in the above integrals. This fact makes it possible to give simple interpretations to $\langle \phi_0^0 | (\partial V/\partial Q)_0 | \phi_0^0 \rangle$ and $\langle \phi_0^0 | (\partial V/\partial Q)_0 | \phi_\varkappa^0 \rangle$. If the undistorted position is chosen to be the equilibrium configuration of the system, then the quantity $L_{00}$ is the electron density for the undistorted system, and the second term of Eq. (5.4) determines the increase in the energy of the system when the nuclei are displaced from their equilibrium positions and the electron distribution is held fixed. From Eq. (5.2), we can see that it is the term $\langle \phi_0^0 | (\partial V/\partial Q)_0 | \phi_\varkappa^0 \rangle$, which allows for a relaxation of the electron distribution. The relaxation is brought about by mixing in with the ground state $\phi_0$ the wave function for an excited state $\phi_\varkappa$. The electron density function $L_{0\varkappa}$ appearing in $\langle \phi_0^0 | (\partial V/\partial Q)_0 | \phi_\varkappa^0 \rangle$ is often termed the transition density (Bader, 1960). It is a measure of the amount of charge which is transferred within the molecule when the nuclei are displaced from their equilibrium positions and represents the correction to the electron density of the undistorted system. As the integral of the transition density over all space is equal to zero, $L_{0\varkappa}$ does not represent any absolute amount of charge but instead gives a three-dimensional representation of the movements of charge density within the system. Thus we may now interpret the matrix element $\langle \phi_0^0 | (\partial V/\partial Q)_0 | \phi_\varkappa^0 \rangle$ as the force (often called the transition force) exerted on the nuclei which are displaced in the mode $Q$ by the displaced charge density, or, alternatively, the matrix element may be regarded as the interaction of the point dipoles centered on the nuclei with the displaced charge distribution.

Next we shall use Eqs. (5.2)–(5.4) to discuss the symmetry rules in chemical reactions (Bader, 1962; Pearson, 1971).

It is evident from the denominator in the expression $U_0$ that the lowering in energy due to the relaxation effect will be greatest for that mode of vibration which allows for an interaction with the lowest excited state. Furthermore, the transition force $\langle \phi_0{}^0 \mid (\partial V/\partial Q)_0 \mid \phi_\varkappa{}^0 \rangle$ will be different from zero only if the transition density $L_{0\varkappa}$ and $Q$ have identical symmetries. We then assume that the most favored motion, the one which leads to the smallest increase in potential energy will be that one whose symmetry allows for an interaction with the lowest excited state. The principal change brought about in the electron distribution for any of the nuclear motions is assumed to be determined by the admixture of the lowest excited state of the proper symmetry. For convenience we shall assume that $\phi_0$ is nondegenerate. At all points in the potential energy curve other than maximum or minimum, $\partial U_0/\partial Q \neq 0$, and the linear term in Eq. (5.3) dominates. In this case, the reaction coordinate belongs to the totally symmetric representation, because the direct product of a nondegenerate symmetric representation with itself is always totally symmetric. That is, since $\phi_0^{02}$ is totally symmetric, $(\partial V/\partial Q)_0$ and also $Q$ must be totally symmetric, otherwise the product of $\phi_0^{02}$ and $(\partial V/\partial Q)_0$ will not be totally symmetric. This means that once a reaction embarks on a particular reaction path it must stay within the same point group until it reaches an energy maximum or minimum.

Equation (5.2) indicates that each excited state wave function is mixed into the ground state wave function and the amount of mixing is shown in Eq. (5.2). The wave function is changed only because the resulting electron distribution $\phi_0^2$ is better suited to the new nuclear positions. Salem (1969) calls the resulting decrease in energy the relaxability of the system along the coordinate $Q$. Now since $(\partial V/\partial Q)_0$ is totally symmetric, we can easily show that only excited state wave functions $\phi_0{}^0$ which have the same symmetry as $\phi_0{}^0$ can mix in and lower the potential barrier. This can be easily verified from Eq. (5.3) or Eq. (5.4), because $U_0$ decreases with increasing $\mid \langle \phi_0{}^0 \mid (\partial V/\partial Q)_0 \mid \phi_\varkappa{}^0 \rangle \mid^2$. The last term in Eq. (5.3) or Eq. (5.4) represents the change in energy that results from changing the electron distribution to one more suited to the new nuclear positions determined by $Q$. Its value is always negative since $U_0{}^0 - U_\varkappa{}^0$ is a negative number. Thus for a reaction to occur with a reasonable activation energy, there must be low-lying excited states of the same symmetry as the ground state. In other words, during the chemical reaction the symmetry of the wave function of the system is preserved (Woodward and Hoffmann). Such a reaction is said to be symmetry-allowed. A symmetry-forbidden reaction is simply one which has a very high activation energy because of the absence of suitable excited states. For practical applications, some other assumptions must be made. One is that LCAO–MO theory will be used in place of the exact wave functions, $\phi_0{}^0$, $\phi_x{}^0$, etc. Since we are concerned only with the symmetry properties, this creates no serious error. MO theory has the great advantage of accurately showing the symmetries of the various electronic states. The second assumption is that we replace the infinite sum of excited states in Eqs. (5.2)–(5.4) by only a few lowest-lying states. It can be shown (Bader, 1962) that the various states contributing to Eqs. (5.2)–(5.4) fall off very rapidly as the difference $| U_0{}^0 - U_x{}^0 |$ becomes large. This is because the matrix element $\langle \phi_0{}^0 | (\partial V/\partial Q)_0 | \phi_x{}^0 \rangle$ decreases very rapidly for two wave functions of quite different energy. In MO theory, the symmetry of $\phi_0{}^0 \phi_x{}^0$ is replaced by $\chi_i \chi_f$, where $\chi_i$ is the occupied MO in the ground state and $\chi_f$ is the MO in the excited state. Since $(\partial V/\partial Q)_0$ is a one-electron operator, the matrix element $\langle \phi_0{}^0 | (\partial V/\partial Q)_0 | \phi_x{}^0 \rangle$ in MO theory reduces to

$$\left\langle \phi_0{}^0 \left| \left( \frac{\partial V}{\partial Q} \right)_0 \right| \phi_x{}^0 \right\rangle = C \left\langle \chi_i \left| \left( \frac{\partial V_j}{\partial Q} \right)_0 \right| \chi_f \right\rangle,$$

where $C$ is a constant. Since excitation of an electron from the highest occupied MO to the lowest unoccupied MO defines the lowest excited state, $\chi_i$ and $\chi_f$ refer to HOMO and LUMO, respectively. From the above discussion, we can see that the orbitals $\chi_i$ and $\chi_f$ are of the same symmetry which implies that they have a nonzero overlap.

## B. Bimolecular Reactions

Suppose that two molecules approach each other with a definite orientation. They have started to interact with each other, but the interaction energy is still small. This means that the MO's of the two separate molecules are still a good starting point for considering the combined system (point A in Fig. 25). Those of the same symmetry will interact more and more strongly as the reaction coordinate is traversed, and at the transition state (point B in Fig. 25) quite different

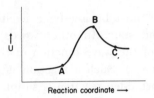

FIG. 25.   Potential energy curve of a chemical reaction.

MO's will be produced. The transition state of a bimolecular reaction represents the configuration of maximum potential energy along the reaction coordinate, and, therefore, as for a stable molecule, the energy is independent of the reaction coordinate to the first order. In this case, we have

$$\frac{|\langle\phi_0{}^0|(\partial V/\partial Q)_0|\phi_\varkappa{}^0\rangle|^2}{U_\varkappa{}^0 - U_0{}^0} > \frac{1}{2}\left\langle\phi_0{}^0\left|\left(\frac{\partial^2 V}{\partial Q^2}\right)_0\right|\phi_0{}^0\right\rangle.$$

Thus, in general, we should expect to find that at least one excited state is relatively low lying for transition-state molecules in order that the above requirement may be met. It is in general the nature of this first excited state that determines the course of reaction. Now we can add an additional requirement on $\chi_i$ and $\chi_f$ using chemical knowledge rather than mathematical or quantum mechanical arguments; $\chi_i$ must represent bonds that are broken and $\chi_f$ bonds that are made during the reaction, for their bonding parts. The reverse statement holds for their antibonding parts. The requirement for a bimolecular reaction is simply that the two have a net overlap. As we know, some atoms are much more electronegative than other atoms. Therefore electrons will move more easily from $\chi_i$ to $\chi_f$ when they move in the direction of the more electronegative atoms. In such cases, $|U_0{}^0 - U_\varkappa{}^0|$ will be small and the stabilizing effect of electron excitation will be large.

To illustrate these principles, we consider one of the simplest chemical reactions,

$$H_2 + D_2 \rightarrow 2HD. \tag{5.5}$$

It will be assumed that the reaction, Eq. (5.5) occurs by a bimolecular mechanism in which $H_2$ and $D_2$ collide broadside, giving rise to a four-center transition state

$$
\begin{array}{c}
\text{H——H} \\
|\quad\ \ | \\
\text{D——D}
\end{array}
\tag{5.6}
$$

The point group of this transition state is $C_{2v}$, and the character table

TABLE V

CHARACTER TABLE FOR C$_2$

| C$_{2v}$ | | E | C$_2$ | $\sigma_v$ | $\sigma_{v'}$ |
|---|---|---|---|---|---|
| $z$ | A$_1$ | 1 | 1 | 1 | 1 |
| | A$_2$ | 1 | 1 | $-1$ | $-1$ |
| $x$ | B$_1$ | 1 | $-1$ | 1 | $-1$ |
| $y$ | B$_2$ | 1 | $-1$ | $-1$ | 1 |

of C$_{2v}$ is given in Table V. The MO's of H$_2$ and D$_2$ can now be classified as A$_1$ for the bonding $\sigma_g$ and B$_1$ for the antibonding $\sigma_u$*. As Fig. 26 shows, there is no empty MO of the same symmetry as any of the filled MO's. Hence the reaction is forbidden by orbital symmetry. The same conclusion can be obtained by using the orbital correlation method due to Woodward and Hoffmann. To prepare a correlation diagram for a chemical reaction, on one side one writes down the approximately known

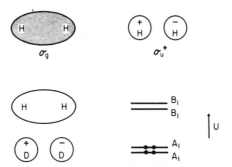

FIG. 26.  Molecular orbitals and energy levels of H$_2$ and D$_2$.

energy levels of the reactants, on the other side those of the product. Assuming a certain geometry of approach one can classify levels on both sides with respect to the symmetry maintained throughout the approach, and then connect levels of like symmetry. Such a molecular correlation diagram yields valuable information about the intermediate region, which represents in a chemical reaction the transition state for the reaction. In this case, we choose the plane occupied by H$_2$ and D$_2$ as the XZ plane (Fig. 27) and use the following notations for the molecular orbitals of

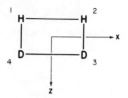

FIG. 27. Interaction between $H_2$ and $D_2$: $C_2(z)$; $\sigma_v(xz)$; $\sigma_v'(yz)$.

reactants and products:

|  | bonding | antibonding |
|---|---|---|
| $H_2(1.2)$ | $\sigma$ | $\sigma^*$ |
| $D_2(3.4)$ | $\sigma'$ | $\sigma'^*$ |
| $HD(1.4)$ | $\sigma_1$ | $\sigma_1^*$ |
| $HD(2.3)$ | $\sigma_2$ | $\sigma_2^*$ |

It can then easily be shown that the characters $\chi(R)$ of the reducible representation resulted from the molecular orbitals of both reactants $(H_2 + D_2)$ and products $(2HD)$ are given by

$$\chi(E) = 4, \qquad \chi(C_2) = 0, \qquad \chi(\sigma_v) = 4, \qquad \chi(\sigma_v') = 0. \qquad (5.7)$$

By using the relation (Eyring et al., 1944)

$$a_i = \frac{1}{h} \sum_R \chi(R)\chi_i(R), \qquad (5.8)$$

we can find the number of times the irreducible representation $\Gamma_i$ occurs in the reducible representation. $h$ in Eq. (5.8) represents the number of elements in the symmetry group. In this case, we obtain $a_{A_1} = 2$, and $a_{B_1} = 2$. In other words, we expect that there will be two MO's belonging to the $A_1$ symmetry and two MO's belonging to the $B_1$ symmetry. The symmetry orbitals can easily be found as

$$\chi_1(A_1) = \sigma, \qquad \chi_2(A_1) = \sigma', \qquad \chi_1(B_1) = \sigma^*, \qquad \chi_2(B_1) = \sigma'^* \qquad (5.9)$$

for reactants and

$$\chi_1'(A_1) = \sigma_1 + \sigma_2, \qquad \chi_2'(A_1) = \sigma_1^* + \sigma_2^*,$$
$$\chi_1'(B_1) = \sigma_1 - \sigma_2, \qquad \chi_2'(B_2) = \sigma_1^* - \sigma_2^*, \qquad (5.10)$$

for products. Based on this information we can prepare a correlation diagram for the reaction Eq. (5.5), as shown in Fig. 28. From this correlation diagram, we can see that if orbital symmetry is to be conserved, there is a very large symmetry-imposed barrier to the reaction under discussion in either direction.

Four-center reactions of diatomic molecules almost always turn out to be forbidden. The statement that the reaction is forbidden, as stated

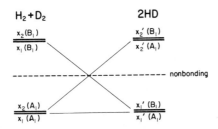

FIG. 28.  Orbital correlation for $H_2 + D_2 \rightarrow 2HD$.

earlier, is simply that of saying that the assumed mechanism has an excessive activation. Indeed, the energy of the transition state in this case can be calculated quite accurately by *ab initio* quantum mechanical methods (Conroy and Malli, 1969). It lies 123 kcal above the energy of the reactants $H_2$ and $D_2$. The mechanism is impossible for all practical purposes. Instead the atom-molecule mechanisms take over for reaction (5.5), because reactions of free atoms and radicals rarely have serious symmetry restrictions and are often found.

To illustrate in some more detail the construction of a molecular correlation diagram (Woodward and Hoffmann, 1970), we choose the maximum-symmetry approach of two ethylene molecules leading to cyclobutane as another example (cf. Fig. 29). As usual in theoretical investigations, maximum insight into the problem is gained by sim-

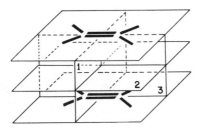

FIG. 29.  Parallel approach of two ethylene molecules: $3 = x - z$; $2 = x - y$; $1 = y - z$.

plifying the case as much as possible, while maintaining the essential physical features. In this case we treat in the correlation diagram only four orbitals, the four $\pi$ orbitals of the two ethylene molecules. In the course of reaction, these four $\pi$ orbitals are transformed into four $\sigma$ orbitals of cyclobutane. We may safely omit the C—H and the C—C $\sigma$ bonds of the ethylene skeleton from the correlation diagram because, while they undergo hybridization changes in the course of reaction, their number, their approximate positions in energy, and, in particular, their symmetry properties are unchanged. The first step in the construction of a correlation diagram involves isolating the essential bonds and placing them at their approximate energy levels in reactants and products; the result is shown for the case under discussion in Fig. 30, in which the dashed horizontal line is the nonbonding level. In the next step the proper molecular orbitals for the reactants and products are written down. Molecular orbitals must be symmetric or antisymmetric with respect to any molecular symmetry element which may be present. For this purpose, for simplicity, we shall deliberately choose $C_{2v}$ as the point group of this system, although we could use the appropriate $D_{2h}$ symmetry. Let $\pi_1$, $\pi_2$, $\pi_1{}^*$, and $\pi_2{}^*$ be the four $\pi$-orbitals of the two ethylene molecules. Then the characters of the reducible representation of these

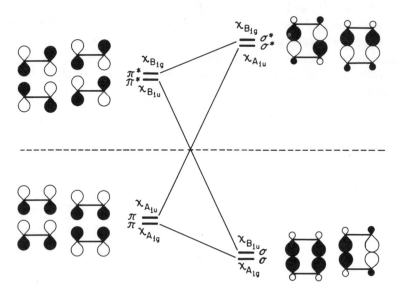

Fig. 30.   Correlation diagram for the formation of cyclobutane from two ethylene molecules.

four $\pi$ orbitals can be shown to be

$$\chi(E) = 4 = \chi(\sigma_v), \qquad \chi(C_2) = \chi(\sigma_v') = 0. \tag{5.11}$$

Thus by using Eq. (5.8), we find $a_{A_1} = 2$ and $a_{B_1} = 2$, that is,

$$A_1 = \pi_1, \pi_2, \qquad B_1 = \pi_1{}^*, \pi_2{}^*. \tag{5.12}$$

Choosing the proper linear combination between $\pi_1$ and $\pi_2$, and between $\pi_1{}^*$ and $\pi_2{}^*$ so that the resulting orbitals will be either symmetric or antisymmetric with respect to inversion, we obtain

$$\chi_{A_{1g}} = \pi_1 + \pi_2, \chi_{A_{1u}} = \pi_1 - \pi_2, \chi_{B_{1g}} = \pi_1{}^* - \pi_2{}^*, \chi_{B_{1u}} = \pi_2{}^* + \pi_2{}^*. \tag{5.13}$$

We must next analyze the situation in cyclobutane in an entirely analogous way. The results are given in the following:

$$\chi'_{A_{1g}} = \sigma_1 + \sigma_2, \chi'_{B_{1u}} = \sigma_1 - \sigma_2, \chi'_{A_{1u}} = \sigma_1{}^* + \sigma_2{}^*, \chi'_{B_{1g}} = \sigma_1{}^* - \sigma_2{}^*, \tag{5.14}$$

where $\sigma_1$, $\sigma_2$, $\sigma_1{}^*$, and $\sigma_2{}^*$ represent the four $\sigma$ orbitals of the cyclobutane molecule. Now we are equipped to examine the correlation of the orbitals of reactants with those of the product (cf. Fig. 30). The direction in which the various levels will move may be obtained without detailed calculation, by examining in each case whether any level is bonding or antibonding along the reaction coordinate. It should be noticed that electrons placed in a bonding orbital bring the nuclei closer together (i.e., $\partial U/\partial R > 0$), while the electrons put into an antibonding orbital push the nuclei apart (i.e., $\partial U/\partial R < 0$). Also, in bonding orbitals, electrons occupying it lie in the region between and are shared by the nuclei, while in antibonding orbitals, there usually exist modes (or a mode) between the nuclei, which isolate electrons populating the orbital in the regions of the individual terminal nuclei.

From Fig. 30, we can see that the lowest level $\chi_{A_{1g}}$ of two ethylenes is bonding in the region of approach of the two molecules to each other and thus will be stabilized by interaction. The $\chi_{A_{1u}}$ level has a node and consequently is antibonding in the region of approach. At large distances the interaction is inconsequential, but as the distance between the reacting molecules diminishes, this orbital is destabilized and moves to higher energy. Similarly, the antibonding $\pi^*\chi_{B_{1u}}$ orbital becomes bonding in the region of approach. It will thus be stabilized as the reaction proceeds, while the antibonding $\pi^*\chi_{B_{1g}}$ orbital will be destabilized. On the cyclobutane side both the $\sigma$ levels are bonding in the region where the cyclobutane is being pulled apart. Thus they resist the motion, that is, they are destabilized along the reaction coordinate. On the other hand, both the $\sigma^*$ levels are antibonding along the reaction coordinate and thus move to lower energy as the cyclobutane is pulled apart. These qualitative conclusions can also be arrived at from a completed correlation diagram in which levels of like symmetry are connected. The most obvious and striking feature of this diagram is the correlation of a bonding reactant level with an antibonding product level, and vice versa. Clearly, if orbital symmetry is to be conserved, two ground state ethylene molecules cannot combine in a concerted reaction to give ground state cyclobutane and vice versa, through a transition state having the geometry assumed here. In other words, there exists a symmetry-imposed barrier to the reaction in both directions. By the same reasoning, there is no such symmetry-imposed barrier to the reaction of one molecule of ethylene with another, if one of these electrons has been promoted, say, by photochemical excitation, to the lowest antibonding orbital (cf. Fig. 31). For these reasons, the reactions of the first type are designated as symmetry-forbidden, and those of the second type as symmetry-allowed.

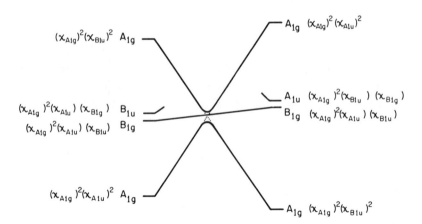

Fig. 31.　Electronic state diagram for the formation of cyclobutane from two ethylene molecules.

The argument may be further illuminated by inspection of the corresponding electronic state correlation diagram for the reaction under discussion (cf. Fig. 31). The ground state electron configuration of two ethylene molecules correlates with a very high-energy doubly excited state of cyclobutane; conversely, the ground state of cyclobutane correlates with a doubly excited state of two ethylenes. Electron interaction will prevent the resulting crossing, and force a correlation of ground state with ground state. But in the actual physical situation, the reaction still must pay the price in the activation energy for the intended but avoided crossing.

The lowest excited state of two ethylenes, the configuration $(\chi_{A_{1g}})^2 \times (\chi_{A_{1u}})^1 (\chi_{B_{1u}})^1$ or $B_1(g)$ correlates directly with the first excited state of cyclobutane. Consequently, there is no symmetry-imposed barrier to this transformation. This represents the course which is followed in many photochemical transformations. However, it should be emphasized that there are ambiguities in excited state reactions which do not exist in their simpler thermal counterparts. Thus it may happen that the chemically reactive excited state is not that reached on initial excitation; radiationless decay may be so efficient that the chemical changes subsequent to irradiation may be those of a vibrationally excited ground state or lower excited electronic state; the formation of a transition state for a given concerted reaction may be competitive with the relaxation of the excited state component to an equilibrium geometry which renders the reaction geometrically impossible. It should be emphasized that none of these punctilios in any way vitiates the consequences of orbital symmetry control. The principle of conservation of orbital symmetry remains applicable, provided that the chemically reactive excited state is identified.

It should be noticed that the conclusions obtained by using the principle of conservation of orbital symmetry for the reaction $2C_2H_4 \rightarrow C_4H_8$ can also be obtained by using Eqs. (5.1)–(5.4).

## C. Unimolecular Reactions

Consider point B in Fig. 25. This point refers to the activated complex and here the term linear in $Q$ in Eq. (5.3) vanishes. The first quadratic term is positive and the second one is negative. Clearly, at a maximum, point B, the second quadratic term is larger than the first, but the magnitude of the first term determines whether we have a high or low potential barrier. Again the existence of low-lying states $\phi_k$ of the correct symmetry to match with $\phi_0$ is important. $\phi_0$, $(\partial V/\partial Q)_0$ and $\phi_k$ are bound by the symmetry requirement that their direct product must contain the totally symmetric representation. In MO theory the product $\phi_0 \phi_k$ is again replaced by $\chi_i \chi_f$, where both the occupied and empty MO's must be in the same molecule. Electron transfer from $\chi_i$ to $\chi_f$ results in a shift in charge density in the molecule. Electron density increases in the regions where they have the same signs. The positively charged nuclei then move in the direction of increased electron density. The motion of the nuclei defines a reaction coordinate. The symmetry of $Q$ is the same as that of the product $\chi_i \chi_f$.

The size of the energy gap between $\chi_i$ and $\chi_f$ is critical. A small gap means an unstable structure, unless no vibrational mode of the right symmetry exists for the molecule capable of changing its structure. A large energy gap between the HOMO and LUMO means a stable molecular structure. Reactions can occur, but only with a high activation energy. For an activated complex there must necessarily be at least one excited state of low energy. The symmetry of this state and the ground state then determines the mode of decomposition of the activated complex (Bader, 1962). Now suppose the unimolecular reaction proceeds from point C to point B in Fig. 25. When a molecule lies in a shallow potential well at point C, the activation energy for unimolecular change is small. In this case, we again expect a low-lying excited state. The symmetry of this state and the ground state will determine the preferred reaction of the unstable molecule. Thus for a series of similar molecules, we expect a correlation between the position of the absorption bands in the visible-uv spectrum and the stability (Pearson, 1971).

As an example, consider the similar molecules, $O_3$ and $SO_2$ (Bader, 1962). The former is blue in color and is highly unstable,

$$O_3 \rightarrow O_2 + O, \qquad SO_2 \rightarrow SO + O. \qquad (5.15)$$

Sulfur dioxide is colorless and is much more stable toward dissociation into SO and O. An *ab initio* calculation (Peyerimhoff and Bruenker, 1967) gives the MO sequence, . . . $(3b_1)^2(4b_1)^2(6a_1)^2(1a_2)^2(2b_2)^0$ for $O_3$, with $SO_2$ probably having the same sequence. Both molecules have an angular structure and the point group is $C_{2v}$. The $a_2$ and $b_2$ orbitals are $\pi$ orbitals, while the $a_1$ and $b_1$ orbitals are $\sigma$ orbitals. The lowest-energy transition is expected to be between the nonbonding $a_2$ orbital and the antibonding $b_2$ orbital. The symmetry of the transition is $a_2 \times b_2 = b_1$, which indicates that $Q$ belongs to $b_1$. The $b_1$ vibration is the unsymmetric stretch in which one O—O bond shortens and the other lengthens. It corresponds to the dissociation of Eq. (5.15). The first absorption bands for $O_3$ are at 1.5 and 2.1 ev, and those for $SO_2$ are at 3.2 and 3.7 ev (Maria *et al.*, 1970). Unfortunately, for the simple interpretation, these correspond to triplet and singlet excitations from the $6a_1$ MO to the $2b_2$ MO. Hence the symmetry of $\chi_i \times \chi_f$ is $b_2$, which does not correspond to any vibration of these molecules. A higher pair of bands at 2.2 and 4.7 ev for $O_3$ and at 3.7 and 5.3 ev for $SO_2$ does correspond to the required $a_2$ to $2b_2$ transition. For most molecules there is still considerable uncertainty in assigning the observed absorption bands to the definite MO transitions.

For molecules that lie in deep potential wells, it may not be the LUMO which is important. The reason is that, since a high activation energy is required, higher lying states may be utilized. It is also difficult to place the higher excited states of a molecule in correct order. Nevertheless, the symmetry rules may still be of great help in selecting the reaction path. Suppose we know that a certain unimolecular reaction occurs, but do not know the detailed mechanism. Certain bonds must be made and broken during the reactions, which can then select $\chi_i$ and $\chi_f$. These MO's in turn will fix the symmetry of the reaction coordinate $Q$. The only requirement is a knowledge of the symmetries of the MO's that relate to the bonds that are affected.

Next let us discuss the application of the principle of the conservation of orbital symmetry to unimolecular reactions. For this purpose we consider electrocyclic reactions and use the conversion of butadiene to cyclobutene as an example (Woodward and Hoffmann, 1970). An electrocyclic reaction is defined as the formation of a single bond between the termini of a linear system containing $k$ $\pi$ electrons, and the converse process, and can be disrotatory or conrotatory (cf. Fig. 32). In the former case the transition state is characterized by a plane of symmetry while in the latter a twofold axis of symmetry is preserved. Consider the essential molecular orbitals in the conversion of cyclobutene to butadiene. These are the four $\pi$ orbitals of the butadiene, the $\pi$ and $\pi^*$ levels of the cyclobutene double bond, and the $\sigma$ and $\sigma^*$ orbitals of the simple bond to be broken (cf. Fig. 33). We shall assume that the system belongs to the point group $C_{2v}$. Let $\pi_{1b}$, $\pi_{2b}$, $\pi_{3a}$, and $\pi_{4a}$ be the four $\pi$ orbitals of butadiene. The characters of the reducible representation of these four $\pi$ orbitals are given by

$$\chi(E) = 4, \qquad \chi(\sigma_v) = -4, \qquad \chi(C_2) = (\sigma_v') = 0. \qquad (5.16)$$

thus $a_{A_2} = 2$ and $a_{B_2} = 2$. In other words, we expect to have two molecular orbitals belonging to $A_2$ and two belonging to $B_2$,

$$\chi_{A_2} = \pi_{2b}, \qquad \chi_{A_2}^* = \pi_{4a}, \qquad \chi_{B_2} = \pi_{1b}, \qquad \chi_{B_2}^* = \pi_{3a}. \qquad (5.17)$$

First let us consider the conrotatory electrocyclic reaction. Carrying out a conrotatory motion of the $\sigma$ orbitals of cyclobutene, the resulting

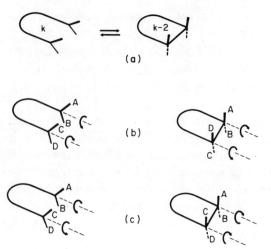

FIG. 32. Diagram for electrocyclic reactions. (a) Electrocyclic reaction, (b) disrotatory, (c) conrotatory.

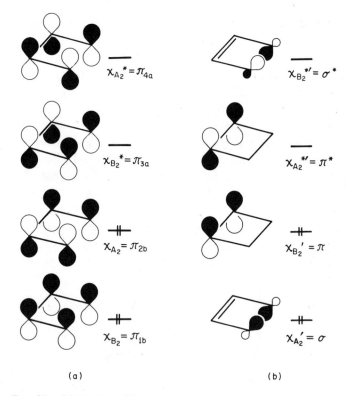

(a)

(b)

FIG. 33. Molecular orbitals of (a) butadiene and (b) cyclobutene.

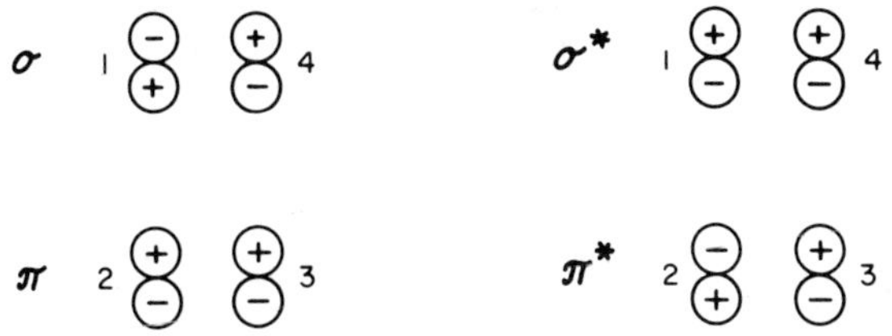

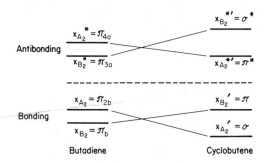

Fig. 34.   Correlation of orbitals.

orbitals are shown in Fig. 34. Thus by using the group theory, we find

$$\chi'_{A_2} = \sigma, \qquad \chi^{*'}_{A_2} = \pi^*, \qquad \chi'_{B_2} = \pi, \qquad \chi^{*'}_{B_2} = \sigma^*. \qquad (5.18)$$

Now we can prepare an orbital correlation diagram by using the principle of conservation of orbital symmetry (cf. Fig. 35). From Fig. 35, we can see that there is no symmetry-imposed barrier to the conrotatory reaction. In other words, the thermal reaction should be a facile one.

Fig. 35.   Correlation diagrams for the conrotatory conversion of cyclobutenes to butadienes.

Next we consider the disrotatory reaction. The $\sigma$ orbitals of cyclobutene after a disrotatory opening are shown in Fig. 36. We find

$$\chi'_{B_2} = \sigma, \qquad \chi''_{B_2} = \pi, \qquad \chi^{*'}_{A_2} = \pi^*, \qquad \chi^{*''}_{A_2} = \sigma^*. \qquad (5.19)$$

The orbital correlation diagram in this case is given in Fig. 36. Conservation of orbital symmetry requires in this case a high-lying transition state and the thermal reaction is symmetry-forbidden. It is clear that in the conrotatory process a twofold rotation axis is maintained at all times; whereas in the disrotatory motion, an invariant plane of symmetry is

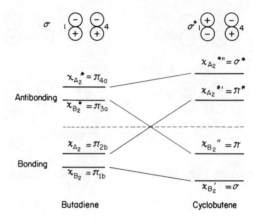

FIG. 36. Correlation diagram for the disrotatory conversion of cyclobutenes to butadienes.

maintained. Obviously the correlation diagram for the conrotatory process is characteristic of a symmetry-allowed reaction, while the pattern for the disrotatory process is that of a symmetry-forbidden reaction.

## ACKNOWLEDGMENTS

The authors wish to thank the National Institutes of Health, Grant GM 12862, National Science Foundation, Grant GP 28631, and Army Research-Durham, Contract DA-ARO-D-31-124-72-G15, for support of this work.

## GENERAL REFERENCES

BORN, M., and HUANG, K. (1954). "Dynamical Theory of Crystal Lattices." Oxford Univ. Press, London and New York.

EYRING, H., WALTER, J., and KIMBALL, G. E. (1944). "Quantum Chemistry." Wiley, New York.

GLASSTONE, S., LAIDLER, K. J., and EYRING, H. (1940). "The Theory of Rate Processes." McGraw-Hill, New York.

LAIDLER, K. J. (1969). "Theories of Chemical Reaction Rates." McGraw-Hill, New York.

LAIDLER, K. J., and POLANYI, J. C. (1965). *Progr. Reaction Kinet.* **3**, 1.

NITKIN, E. E. (1970). *Advan. Quantum Chem.* **5**, 135.

SCHLIER, C. (ed.) (1970). "Molecular Beams and Reaction Kinetics." Academic Press, New York.

WOODWARD, R. B., and HOFFMANN, R. (1970). "The Conservation of Orbital Symmetry." Academic Press, New York.

SPECIAL REFERENCES

ALBRECHT, A. C. (1960). *J. Chem. Phys.* **33**, 156, 169.

AUSTIN, B., HEINE, V., and SHAM, L. J. (1962). *Phys. Rev.* **127**, 276.

BADER, R. F. W. (1960). *Mol. Phys.* **3**, 137.

BADER, R. F. W. (1962). *Can. J. Chem.* **40**, 1164.

BORN, M. (1951). *Gott. Nachr. Math. Phys. Kl.* 1.

BORN, M., and HUANG, K. (1954). "Dynamical Theory of Crystal Lattices." Oxford Univ. Press, London and New York.

BOYS, S. F., and SHAVITT, I. (1959). Univ. of Wisconsin Naval Res. Lab. Tech. Rep. WIS-AF-13.

BREWER, L., and BRACKETT, E. (1961). *Chem. Rev.* **61**, 425.

CASHION, J. K., and HERSCHBACH, D. R. (1964). *J. Chem. Phys.* **40**, 2358.

CHIU, Y. N. (1964). *J. Chem. Phys.* **41**, 3235.

CLEMENTI, E. (1963). *J. Chem. Phys.* **38**, 1001.

CLEMENTI, E. (1964). *J. Chem. Phys.* **41**, 295.

CONROY, H. (1967). *J. Chem. Phys.* **47**, 912.

CONROY, H., and BRUNER, B. L. (1967). *J. Chem. Phys.* **47**, 921.

CONROY, H., and MALLI, G. (1969). *J. Chem. Phys.* **50**, 5049.

CONROY, H. (1970). *In* "Molecular Beams and Reaction Kinetics" (C. H. Schlier, ed.), p. 349. Academic Press, New York.

DALGARNO, A., and McCORROL, R. (1956). *Proc. Roy. Soc. (London)* **237A**, 383.

DALGARNO, A., and LYNN, N. (1956). *Proc. Phys. Soc. (London)* **A69**, 821.

DALGARNO, A., and McCORROL, R. (1957). *Proc. Roy. Soc. (London)* **239A**, 413.

DALGARNO, A. (1961). *Proc. Roy. Soc. (London)* **A262**, 132.

EDMISTON, C., and KRAUSS, M. (1965). *J. Chem. Phys.* **42**, 1119.

EYRING, H., and POLANYI, M. (1931). *Z. Phys. Chem.* **B12**, 279.

EYRING, H., WALTER J., and KIMBALL, G. E. (1944). "Quantum Chemistry." Wiley, New York.

EYRING, H., DALLA RIVA, L., and LIN, S. H. (1970). *In* "Schumacher Volume." *Anales. Asoc. Quím. Argentina* **59**, 133.

FISK, G. A., and KIRTMAN, B. (1964). *J. Chem. Phys.* **41**, 3516.

FRAGA, S., and MULLIKEN, R. S. (1960). *Rev. Mod. Phys.* **32**, 254.

FUKUI, K. (1965). *In* "Modern Quantum Chemistry" (O. Sinanogulu, ed.), p. 49. Academic Press, New York.

GLASSTONE, S., LAIDLER, K. J., and EYRING, H. (1940). "The Theory of Rate Processes." McGraw-Hill, New York.

HAYES, E. F., and PARR, R. G. (1967). *J. Chem. Phys.* **47**, 3961.

HEITLER, W., and LONDON, F. (1927). *Z. Phys.* **44**, 455.

HERZBERG, G., and TELLER, E. (1933). *Z. Phys. Chem. (Leipzig)* **218**, 410.

HERZBERG, G., and HOWE, L. L. (1959). *Can. J. Phys.* **37**, 636.

HIRSCHFELDER, J. O., and LINNETT, J. W. (1941). *J. Chem. Phys.* **9**, 645.

HIRSCHFELDER, J. O., and LINNETT, J. W. (1950). *J. Chem. Phys.* **18**, 130.

JAHN, J. A., and TELLER, A., (1930). *Proc. Roy. Soc. (London)* **161A**, 220.

JAMES, A. S., and COOLIDGE, H. M. (1934). *J. Chem. Phys.* **2**, 811.

JEPSEN, D. W., and HIRSCHFELDER, J. O. (1960). *J. Chem. Phys.* **32**, 1323.

JORTNER, J., RICE, S. A., and HOCHSTRASSER, R. M. (1969). *Advan. Photochem.* **7**, 149.

KARPLUS, M. (1970). *In* "Molecular Beams and Reaction Kinetics" (C. H. Schlier, ed.), p. 320. Academic Press, New York.

KOLOS, W. (1970). *Advan. Quantum Chem.* **5**, 99.

KOLOS, W., and ROOTHAAN, C. C. J. (1960). *Rev. Mod. Phys.* **32**, 219.

LAIDLER, K. J., and POLANYI, J. C. (1965). *Progr. Reaction Kinet.* **3**, 1.

LAIDLER, K. J. (1969). "Theories of Chemical Reaction Rates." McGraw-Hill, New York.

LIN, S. H. (1966). *J. Chem. Phys.* **44**, 3759.

LIN, S. H. (1967). *Theoret. Chim. Acta* **8**, 1.

LIN, S. H., and BERSOHN, R. (1968). *J. Chem. Phys.* **48**, 2732.

LONDON, F. (1929). *Z. Elektrochem.* **35**, 552.

MARIA, H. J., LARSON, P., McCARVILLE, M. E., and McGLYNN, S. P. (1970). *Accounts Chem. Res.* **3**, 368.

MOFFIT, W., and THORSON, W. (1957). *Phys. Rev.* **108**, 1251.

PEARSON, R. G. (1971). *Accounts Chem. Res.* **4**, 152.

PEYERIMHOFF, S. D., and BUENKER, R. J. (1967). *J. Chem. Phys.* **47**, 1953.

PORTER, R. N., and KARPLUS, M. (1964). *J. Chem. Phys.* **40**, 1105.

RITTNER, E. S. (1951). *J. Chem. Phys.* **19**, 1030.

ROACH, A. C., and CHILD, M. S. (1968). *Mol. Phys.* **14**, 1.

ROBINSON, G. W., and FROSCH, R. P. (1963). *J. Chem. Phys.* **38**, 1187.

ROBINSON, G. W., and FROSCH, R. P. (1964). *J. Chem. Phys.* **41**, 357.

ROLLEFSON, G. K., and EYRING, H. (1932). *J. Amer. Chem. Soc.* **54**, 170.

SALEM, L. (1969). *Chem. Phys. Lett.* **3**, 99.

SATO, S. (1955a). *Bull. Chem. Soc. Japan* **28**, 450.

SATO, S. (1955b). *J. Chem. Phys.* **23**, 592.

SATO, S. (1955c). *J. Chem. Phys.* **23**, 2465.

SHAVITT, I., STEVENS, R. M., MINN, F. L., and KARPLUS, M. (1968). *J. Chem. Phys.* **48**, 2700.

SIEBRAND, W. (1967). *J. Chem. Phys.* **46**, 440.

SLATER, J. C. (1931). *Phys. Rev.* **38**, 1109.

SUGIURA, Y. (1927). *Z. Phys.* **45**, 484.

TEMPLE, G. (1928). *Proc. Roy. Soc. (London)* **A119**, 276; cf. FROMAN, A., and HALL, G. G. (1963). *J. Chem. Phys.* **38**, 1104.

TOBIAS, I., and VANDERSLICE, J. T. (1961). *J. Chem. Phys.* **35**, 1852.

WANG, S. C. (1928). *Phys. Rev.* **31**, 579.

WESTON, R. E. (1959). *J. Chem. Phys.* **31**, 892.

WOODWARD, R. B., and HOFFMANN, R. (1965a). *J. Amer. Chem. Soc.* **87**, 395.

WOODWARD, R. B., and HOFFMANN, R. (1965b). *J. Amer. Chem. Soc.* **87**, 2046.

WOODWARD, R. B., and HOFFMANN, R. (1965c). *J. Amer. Chem. Soc.* **87**, 2511.

WOODWARD, R. B., and HOFFMANN, R. (1970). "The Conservation of Orbital Symmetry," Academic Press, New York.

WU, T. Y., and GHATIA, A. B. (1956). *J. Chem. Phys.* **24**, 48.

Chapter 4

# Theory of Energy Transfer in Molecular Collisions*

## E. E. NIKITIN

## I. General Remarks about Binary Molecular Collision

The analysis of energy transfer in molecular collisions in the gas kinetic regime can be divided into two independent stages. This comes about because the duration of a collision between two molecules ($10^{-12}$

* Translated by A. Baratoff, Institut für Festkörperforschung der Kernforschungsanlage Jülich G.m.b.H., Jülich.

to $10^{-13}$ sec) is much shorter than the mean time between successive collisions (about $10^{-9}$ sec under usual conditions). One can therefore choose a time interval that is short compared to the mean time between collisions, but is still long compared to the duration of a single collision. The system consisting of two particular colliding molecules can be considered as isolated from all the remaining molecules over such a time interval. The state of the system can then be described by mechanical equations that only take into account the degrees of freedom of the two molecules under consideration. In this approximation the influence of all the other molecules manifests itself only through initial conditions specifying the states of both molecules before they collide. The first *dynamic stage* of the analysis is completed when the solution of the appropriate (classical or quantum) mechanical problem is obtained. This yields the relevant transition probabilities or inelastic scattering cross sections, that is, the microscopic characteristics of the fundamental collision processes.

In the second stage of the analysis one computes macroscopic quantities, directly accessible to experiment, namely, the rates of different possible relaxation processes. The aim of the theory is then to provide a microscopic interpretation of macroscopic parameters describing reaction kinetics. At this *statistical stage* of the analysis one relies on various types of kinetic equations which govern the temporal evolution (relaxation) of the distribution of molecules among various states which arises as a result of many successive collisions.

This chapter deals only with the first part of the general problem, that is, the discussion is mainly concerned with the transformation and transfer of different kinds of energy in binary molecular collisions. In view of the proliferation of papers concerned with these questions, no attempt is made to systematize all the existing literature. References to recently published books and reviews (Takayanagi, 1965; Stupochenko *et al.*, 1965; Stevens, 1967; Gordon *et al.*, 1968; Rapp and Kassal, 1969; Nikitin, 1970b) are given whenever possible. References to original papers are indicated either in order to illustrate specific questions or in dealing with problems of a general nature that have not yet been adequately reviewed.

The following problem arises when one discusses essentially any physical problem, in particular, energy transfer in collisions: how to correlate different theoretical approaches to a particular problem, and how to decide which one is preferable. In our opinion the simplest and, at the same time, sufficiently informative approximation is the semiclassical one. It enables one to easily go beyond the lowest orders of perturbation theory and to obtain an approximate solution of the quantum mechanical problem based on the presumably known solution of the corresponding classical problem (Miller, 1971; Wong and Marcus, 1971).

The basic idea behind that approximation is that certain degrees of freedom of the system under consideration, that is, the one which in our case consists of two colliding molecules, are described classically, while others are treated quantum mechanically (Nikitin, 1970b). We denote the formes by $Q$, and the latter by $q$. Accordingly, the full Hamiltonian is written in the form

$$H(q, Q) = H_1(q) + H_2(Q) + H_{12}(q, Q), \qquad (1.1)$$

where $H_1(q)$ and $H_2(Q)$ are Hamiltonians corresponding to noninteracting subsystems with coordinates $q$ and $Q$, while $H_{12}(q, Q)$ describes their interaction. The classical solution of the problem governed by the Hamiltonian $H_2(Q)$ yields a family of classical trajectories $Q = Q(t)$ describing the temporal evolution of the $Q$ subsystem, neglecting its interaction with the $q$ subsystem. The remaining part of the Hamiltonian that contains the quantum degrees of freedom is then considered in turn. One looks for the wave function $\Phi(q, t)$ of the corresponding subsystem which describes its evolution under the influence of the interaction $H_{12}(q, Q)$, as a result of the motion of the classical subsystem along a given trajectory $Q(t)$. This wave function obeys the Schrödinger equation

$$i\hbar \frac{\partial \Phi(q, t)}{\partial t} = \{H_1(q) + H_{12}[q, Q(t)]\}\Phi(q, t), \qquad (1.2)$$

which is the semiclassical analog of the full equation

$$H\Psi(q, Q) = E\Psi(q, Q) \qquad (1.3)$$

that should in principle be solved in a complete quantum mechanical approach to the problem. Although a nonstationary quantum mechanical problem is, generally speaking, more difficult than a stationary one, Eq. (1.2) is easier to solve than Eq. (1.3) in practice since it involves fewer degrees of freedom.

One of the necessary conditions for a proper description in terms of a classical trajectory is that changes in the De Broglie wavelength of the appropriate variables be small over the scale determined by the spatial variation of the wave function. This condition is usually obeyed if the

above-mentioned De Broglie wavelength is much smaller than the distance characterizing the spatial dependence of the potential energy. This
requirement is, for instance, satisfied by the interaction potential between
two molecules of average molecular weight at energies corresponding
to room temperature and higher. Another necessary condition for the
validity of such a semiclassical approximation is that the interaction
$H_{12}$, which is neglected in solving the classical problem for the subsystem
described by the Hamiltonian $H_2(Q)$, do not lead to large deviations from
the corresponding trajectories. This requirement is usually satisfied if
the kinetic energy $E_{kin}$ associated with the classical degrees of freedom
is much larger than the total energy shift $\Delta E$ due to their interaction with
the quantum subsystem. If this condition $E_{kin} \gg \Delta E$ is not obeyed, one
must correct the final result obtained within the semiclassical approximation or take into account the influence of the interaction $H_{12}$ in determining the trajectories.

The separation of degrees of freedom into classical and quantum
mechanical ones is not unique; it depends on the approximation(s) made
in solving a particular problem. As the simplest example one might
consider a quantum mechanical description of the electronic states of
two colliding molecules and a classical treatment of the nuclear motion.
Another example is the semiclassical description of the vibrational excitation of molecules; their relative motion is then treated classically,
while internal vibrations are treated quantum mechanically.

A significant simplification of the general problem of inelastic scattering
can be obtained on the basis of the adiabatic principle. According to this
principle, the transition probability from a given quantum state under
the influence of a time-dependent perturbation is small if $\omega\tau \gg 1$
(*adiabatic condition*). This expression, the so-called Massey parameter,
contains the characteristic angular frequency $\omega = \Delta E/\hbar$, corresponding
to a typical transition of the quantum subsystem, and the characteristic
time $\tau$ over which the interaction acts effectively, due to the motion of the
classical subsystem (Landau and Lifshitz, 1963).*

This criterion enables one to introduce into the theory of molecular
collisions the concept of interaction potential between atoms (or molecules) in the ground and excited electronic states. Such potentials are

---

* The adiabatic principle is also significant within the framework of classical mechanics. In this case $\omega$ represents a typical frequency of classical motion, while the so-
called "action variables" are adiabatic invariants, that is, quantities which change
little with time under the condition $\omega\tau \gg 1$ (Landau and Lifshitz, 1958).

conveniently pictured as *potential energy surfaces*. They retain their significance as long as atomic motions are adiabatic, as far as electrons are concerned ($\omega_{el}\tau_{vib} \gg 1$, $\omega_{el}\tau_{rot} \gg 1$, $\omega_{el}\tau_{tr} \gg 1$). We first examine the transformation of translational, rotational, and vibrational energy within this approximation in Sections II to IV. It is often convenient to talk about vibrational ($\omega_{vib}\tau_{tr} \gg 1$) and rotational ($\omega_{rot}\tau_{tr} \gg 1$) adiabatic conditions as well.

Violation of the adiabatic approximation for electronic states leads to transitions between different potential surfaces (so-called *nonadiabatic transitions*). Such processes, which are accompanied by transfer of electronic, vibrational, rotational, and translational energy between molecules, are briefly discussed in Sections VI and VII.

## II. Translational to Rotational Energy Transfer (TR Processes)

The collision of a hard sphere A with a rigid dumbbell BC can serve as the simplest model that provides a qualitative description of the transformation of molecular translational energy into rotational energy. The actual energy transfer depends on the relative positions of all three particles at the time of collision. It is clear that for masses of the same order, a significant fraction of translational energy can on the average be converted to rotational energy since the laws governing the transfer of translational energy in binary collisions between hard spheres (Landau and Lifshitz, 1958) apply at the instant when spheres A and B come into contact. The dumbbell model is just the simplest one among a whole class of models which envisage collisions between rigid bodies of various shapes, such that energy can be transferred when one part comes into contact with another one. Models involving circular cylinders, loaded and rough spheres have thus been considered (Stevens, 1967; Stupochenko *et al.*, 1965). In such models the transformation of translational into rotational energy is completely determined by the conservation laws, and therefore represents an easily soluble problem.

Unfortunately such models fail to take into account the noninstantaneous nature of real collisions, which can be characterized by a finite time $\tau$ that, generally speaking, can either be longer or shorter than the period of rotation $\sim\omega_{rot}^{-1}$. As mentioned in Section I, the magnitude of the parameter $\omega\tau$ has a significant influence on the probability that the state of the system will in fact change from its initial value. In order to build a qualitatively correct theory of translational-rotational energy transfer it is therefore necessary to consider a more realistic model of the relevant collisions.

For the sake of simplicity, consider the collision of an atom A with a diatomic molecule BC—the discussion remaining classical for the time being. This last assumption is valid if the rotational quantum number $j$ of the molecule BC, as well as its change $\Delta j$ in a collision, are both much larger than unity. Note that, for molecules of average molecular weight, typical values of $j$ at room temperature are of order 10.

If one ignores possible vibrations of molecule BC, the intermolecular potential $V(R, \gamma)$ depends on two coordinates: the separation $R$ between atom A and the center of mass of molecule BC, and the angle $\gamma$ between the vector $R$ and the axis of the rotor. Splitting $V(R, \gamma)$ into a spherically symmetric part $V_s(R)$ and an anisotropic part $V_a(R, \gamma)$, one can write the Hamiltonian of the system A + BC under consideration as

$$H = \frac{\mu \dot{R}^2}{2} + \frac{L^2}{2\mu R^2} + V_s(R) + \frac{J^2}{2I} + V_a(R, \gamma). \qquad (2.1)$$

The successive terms in this expression can be identified as the kinetic energies associated with the radial and angular components of the motion of A relative to the center of mass of BC, the spherically symmetric part of the interaction, the rotational energy of molecule BC, and the anisotropic part of the interaction. Let $J = \hbar j$ be the classical angular momentum of the rotor and $L = \hbar l$ be the classical orbital angular momentum of the relative motion. There is a well-known connection between $L$, the relative translational energy $E_{\mathrm{tr}}$, and the corresponding reduced mass $\mu$ and impact parameter $b$ of the colliding molecules, for example, $E_{\mathrm{tr}} b^2 = L^2/2\mu$.

$V_a$ is usually given by an expansion in terms of Legendre polynomials (Hirschfelder *et al.*, 1954),

$$V_a(R, \gamma) = \sum_k V_{ak}(R) P_k(\cos \gamma). \qquad (2.2)$$

Only terms with an even index $k$ are present in this sum in the case of homonuclear molecules, since the interaction potential $V_a$ should not change under a rotation of the molecule which permutes B and C, that is, under the substitution $\gamma \to \pi - \gamma$.

If $V_a$ is sufficiently small, the problem of collisional energy transfer can be solved by means of perturbation theory. Then in zero-order approximation the problem reduces to the elastic scattering of A and BC in the spherically symmetric potential $V_s$, as described by the first three terms in Eq. (2.1), and the free rotation of molecule BC, described by the fourth term in Eq. (2.1). The asymmetric part of the interaction $V_a(R, \gamma)$, evaluated in terms of the zero-order solutions $R(t)$ and $\gamma(t)$, is then considered as a perturbation which produces variations in $J$. Such a calculation for a model in which one retains only the lowest even term in the expression (2.2), that is,

$$V_{a2}(R)P_2(\cos \gamma) = V_{a2}(R)\tfrac{1}{2}(3 \cos^2 \gamma - 1)$$

yields the following expression for the change $\Delta J$ (Cohen and Marcus, 1970):

$$\Delta J = J' - J = 2F_0 \sin^2 \theta \sin 2\psi - (1 - \cos \theta)^2 F_+ \sin(2\psi + 2\phi)$$
$$+ (1 + \cos \theta)^2 F_- \sin(2\psi - 2\phi), \qquad (2.3)$$

where

$$F_0 = \tfrac{3}{8} \int_{-\infty}^{\infty} V_{a2}(R) \cos(2\omega t) \, dt,$$

$$F_\pm = \tfrac{3}{8} \int_{-\infty}^{\infty} V_{a2}(R) \cos\left(2\omega t \pm \int_0^t \frac{L \, dt}{\mu R^2}\right) dt.$$

The quantities $F_0$, $F_+$ and $F_-$ depends on the relative translational energy $E_{tr}$ of the two molecules, their impact parameter $b$, the characteristic collision time $\tau$, and the angular frequency of rotation $\omega_{rot}$ before the collision; $\omega_{rot}$ is related to the initial angular momentum and to the moment of inertia $I$ of the rotor via the standard expression $\omega_{rot} = J/I$. In addition $\Delta J$ also depends on the following three parameters: the polar and azimuthal angles $\theta$ and $\phi$ specifying the relative orientation of the vector $\mathbf{J}$ with respect to $\mathbf{L}$, and the phase $\psi$ of the rotor at the instant of closest approach. These parameters are assumed to be randomly distributed within their respective intervals of definition, $0 \le \theta < \pi$, $0 \le \phi < 2\pi$, $0 \le \psi < 2\pi$ for different collisions with given values of $E_{tr}$, $b$ and $\omega_{rot}$. The spread in allowed values of $\theta$, $\phi$, and $\psi$ leads to a finite allowed range for $\Delta J$. The result is expressed by means of a classical distribution function $f(J, J')$ for the probability density corresponding to a change in orbital momentum of the molecule from $J$ to $J'$ in a single collision. This function is normalized as follows

$$\int f(J, J') \, dJ' = 1. \qquad (2.4)$$

The corresponding quantum distribution function can be obtained from the classical one by replacing $J$ and $J'$ by their quantum analogs $\hbar j$ and $\hbar j'$, at least in the semiclassical limit ($j, j' \gg 1$). If, in addition, one takes $dj' = 1$, then $f(j, j')$ is just the transition probability $P_{jj'}(E_{tr}, b)$ of the rotor between initial and final states with quantum numbers $j$ and $j'$, respectively, while Eq. (2.4) is simply the normalization condition of the probability $P_{jj'}$. The cross section for a $j \to j'$ transition can then be computed from the well-known relation

$$\sigma_{jj'}(E_{tr}) = \int_0^\infty P_{jj'}(E_{tr}, b) 2\pi b \, db. \tag{2.5}$$

The width of the distribution $f(J, J')$ can be characterized by the corresponding mean square change in angular momentum,

$$\langle \Delta J^2 \rangle = \int (\Delta J)^2 f(J, J') \, dJ'. \tag{2.6}$$

A rough estimate of $\langle \Delta j^2 \rangle$ can be obtained from Eq. (2.4) if one sets $F_0 \sim F_+ \sim F_-$ and ignores all factors explicitly depending on $\theta$, $\phi$, and $\psi$,

$$\langle \Delta j^2 \rangle = \frac{\langle \Delta J^2 \rangle}{\hbar^2} \approx \left| \int_{-\infty}^\infty \frac{V_{a2}(R)}{\hbar} \cos(2\omega t) \, dt \right|^2. \tag{2.7}$$

Let us first assume that the molecule BC has no time to rotate during the collision time $\tau = R_0/v$ (the so-called sudden approximation), and that the anisotropic interaction parameter $V_{a2}$ is proportional to $V_s$, that is, $V_{a2} = aV_s$. Substituting $V_s \sim E_{tr}$ into Eq. (2.7) and replacing the cosine factor by unity, one obtains

$$\langle \Delta j^2 \rangle \approx (aE\tau/\hbar)^2 \approx (aR_0/\lambda)^2, \tag{2.8}$$

$\lambda$ being the De Broglie wavelength corresponding to the relative motion of the two molecules.

For typical molecules $\lambda \ll R_0$ at room temperature, whereas the asymmetry parameter $a$ usually varies between 0.1 and 0.4 in magnitude (Cohen and Marcus, 1970). Equation (2.8) therefore implies that transitions involving rotational energy changes of several quanta can be expected in each collision.

The situation changes, however, if $\omega_{rot}\tau \geq 1$. As mentioned in Section I, the transformation of energy is less efficient in this limit. These general arguments are well illustrated by a calculation of the quantities $\Delta j$ in a $K + I_2$ collision for a particular choice of the parameters $b$, $v$, $\theta$, $\phi$, and

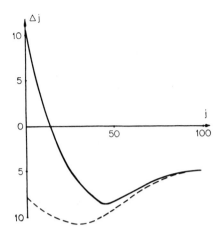

FIG. 1.   Dependence of the change $\Delta j$ in the angular momentum of an $I_2$ molecule on its initial angular momentum $j$ in a collision with a K atom. Dashed curve: classical perturbation theory; full curve: exact classical solution. Both calculations (Cohen and Marcus, 1970) were performed with the same initial conditions.

$\psi$, which assume a Lennard–Jones potential for both $V_s$ and $V_{a2}$ (Cohen and Marcus, 1970). Results are plotted on Fig. 1; the parameter $\omega_{\text{rot}}\tau$ is approximately $j/60$ in the particular case under consideration. The full curve represents the exact solution of the classical problem, while the dashed one is the solution given by Eq. (2.3). It is seen that both curves merge as $\omega_{\text{rot}}\tau$ increases and the condition $\Delta j \ll j$ for the validity of perturbation theory becomes satisfied. Besides $\Delta j$ decreases with increasing $\omega_{\text{rot}}\tau$ when $\omega_{\text{rot}}\tau$ exceeds unity. For small values of $j$, perturbation theory yields negative answers, so that $j'$ itself apparently becomes negative. This incorrect result is obtained because perturbation theory is no longer applicable. The exact calculation always yields positive values of $\Delta j$ for small $j$, as expected, since the rotational energy of an unexcited rotor certainly cannot decrease in a collision.

This example illustrates a situation in which the transformation of translational into rotational energy can be satisfactorily interpreted within the framework of classical mechanics. For even larger values of the Massey parameter $\omega_{\text{rot}}\tau$ or for smaller values of the asymmetry parameter $a$ the change $\Delta j$ computed by classical methods may be smaller than one. Rigorously speaking, one should then solve the appropriate quantum mechanical problem since the necessary condition for a classical description, $\Delta j \gg 1$, is then violated. The classical results can nevertheless be approximately used in such a case: the small change in angular momentum can be interpreted in terms of transitions with probability less than unity between adjacent rotational levels which are allowed according to the relevant quantum selection rules, that is, $\Delta j_{\min} = \pm 1$ for heteronuclear molecules and $\Delta j_{\min} = \pm 2$ for homonuclear ones.

If, in addition to $\Delta j$, the initial angular momentum $j$ is also small, the classical description must be completely replaced by a quantum mechanical or, at least, a semiclassical treatment. The rotational excitation ($j = 0 \rightarrow j = 2$) of $H_2$ molecules by collisions with He atoms is a good example of such a process. The corresponding cross section $\sigma_{02}(E_{tr})$, calculated for an assumed interaction of the form

$$V_s = 470.1 \exp(-3.83R) \text{ eV} \qquad (R \text{ in Å}),$$
$$V_a = 0.375 V_s, \qquad\qquad\qquad\qquad\qquad (2.9)$$

is plotted on Fig. 2. One sees that different results such as the exact quantum mechanical solution (Allison and Dalgarno, 1967), quantum mechanical perturbation theory (Roberts, 1963), and the semiclassical approximation (Lowley and Ross, 1965) are in close agreement with each other. The cross section for rotational excitation $\sigma_{02}$ grows almost linearly with increasing translational energy $E_{tr}$ away from the treshold at 0.045 eV. In the limit $\omega_{rot}\tau \ll 1$ this dependence follows even from a crude estimate of the transition probability that is proportional to the square of the integral in Eq. (2.7). The marked deviation from linearity just above treshold reflects the nearly adiabatic ($\omega_{rot}\gamma > 1$) character of collisions in that range.

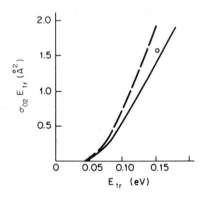

FIG. 2. Energy dependence of the cross section $\sigma_{02}$ for a $j = 0 \rightarrow j = 2$ transition of a $H_2$ molecule colliding with a He atom. Full curve: exact quantum calculation; dashed curve: quantum mechanical perturbation theory; circle: result of semiclassical approximation.

## III. Translational to Vibrational Energy Transfer (TV Processes)

A. General Remarks

The transformation of translational energy into vibrational energy cannot, strictly speaking, be correctly analyzed within the framework of any model that ignores the possible transformation of translational into rotational energy and of rotational into vibrational energy. This is a consequence of the high efficiency of TR processes; the interaction between translational and rotational degrees of freedom cannot be neglected in rigorous discussions of the mechanisms of vibrational molecular excitation. However, in the case of molecules with a small interaction anisotropy, a theory which leaves out interactions involving rotational degrees of freedom nevertheless gives good results for the dependence of the rate of molecular vibrational excitation on the relevant interaction parameters and molecular constants. Since the exact values of these interaction parameters are not known anyway, such a theory is semi-empirical in character, so that errors which arise from the neglected TR processes may be implicitly accounted for via an optimal choice of parameters. In certain cases it is, of course, possible that no reasonable choice of interaction parameters will be able to explain experimental results. One must then explicitly take into account either rotational interaction processes (see Section IV) or nonadiabatic interactions with closely lying electronic levels (see Section VII). In the present section we limit ourselves to a discussion of the simple theory that ignores such interactions.

Such a theory should best apply to the vibrational excitation and deactivation of homonuclear diatomic molecules (least interaction anisotropy) which are in nondegenerate electronic states. In what follows we shall consider, in particular, a collision between atom A in a closed shell ($^1S_0$) electronic state and a symmetric diatomic molecule BC, also assumed to be in an analogous ($^1\Sigma^+$) electronic state. Symbolically

$$A + BC(n) \rightarrow A + BC(n'). \tag{3.1}$$

Molecule BC makes a transition from the $n$th to the $n'$th vibrational level as a result of interactions. The difference $E_n - E_{n'}$ in internal energy is equal to the change in relative kinetic energy of the colliding partners. The theory of such processes has developed in two main directions, namely, the description of transitions between low-lying vibrational levels and that of transitions involving highly excited states. The first type of theory is connected with studies of the vibrational relaxation of molecules, while the second one is connected with investigations of nonequilibrium population distributions in chemical reactions. Perturbation theory can be used in the first case; it enables one to take into account many delicate interaction effects. In the second case one must go beyond the framework of perturbation theory; in practice this can be done with crude models that are only capable of explaining the general physical features of processes involving strong vibrational excitation or large vibrational energy losses of molecules.

### B. Transitions between Low-lying Vibrational Energy Levels

Consider a symmetric diatomic molecule in any of its low-lying vibrational states. The amplitude of nuclear displacements is small compared to the characteristic width of the corresponding potential which we assume to be of the Morse form for the purposes of discussion,

$$U_{BC}(r) = D\{1 - \exp[-\alpha'(r - r_e)]\}^2. \qquad (3.2)$$

Here $D$ is the depth of the potential well, $\alpha'^{-1}$ the characteristic distance over which the potential approaches its asymptotic value, and $r_e$ is the equilibrium internuclear separation in the molecule. In order to estimate the amplitude of vibration corresponding to a given energy $E_{vib}$, the Morse potential can be approximated by a parabola near its minimum. The amplitude $x_0$ is then obtained by requiring the potential energy $U_{BC}$ of the molecule to be equal to the total vibrational energy of the molecule; this yields $x_0 = \alpha'^{-1}(E_{vib}/D)^{1/2}$. Since the ratio $E_{vib}/D$ is small for the lowest levels, one sees that $x_0 \ll \alpha'^{-1}$. Since the intramolecular and intermolecular potentials have characteristics ranges of the same order, $x_0$ must also be small with respect to the characteristic range $l$ of the intermolecular potential $V(R, r, \gamma)$. Let us consider the spherically symmetric part $V_s(R, r)$ alone and keep the lowest two terms in its expansion in powers of $x = r - r_e$, namely, $V_s(R, r) = V_0(R) + V_1(R)x/l$. Since neither $V_0$ nor $V_1$ depend on $\gamma$ in this approximation, it is referred to as the breathing sphere model (Herzfeld and Litovitz, 1959). The Hamiltonian of the A + BC system can then be written as follows:

$$H = \frac{P^2}{2\mu} + V_0(R) + \frac{p^2}{2M} + U_{BC}(r) + V_1(R)\frac{x}{l}. \qquad (3.3)$$

The first two terms are the kinetic energy of the relative motion of A with respect to BC, and the interaction potential between A and BC, respectively, while the third and fourth terms are the kinetic and potential energies associated with the internal degrees of freedom of molecule BC. The last term represents the interaction responsible for the exchange of translational and rotational energy. If $V_1 = 0$ the motion of A relative to BC and the internal motion of BC are completely decoupled. Since $V_1 x/l$ is assumed small, the probability of transitions between given quantum states can be calculated within the framework of semiclassical perturbation theory. In zero-order approximation one considers the collision between A and BC to be elastic, and treats BC as a freely rotating and vibrating molecule. According to the golden rule of perturbation theory

$$P_{nn'}(v, b) = \left| \frac{x_{nn'}}{l} \int \frac{V_1(R)}{\hbar} \exp\left[ \frac{i}{\hbar} (E_n - E_{n'})t \right] dt \right|^2. \qquad (3.4)$$

For $R$ one substitutes the function $R(t)$ describing the appropriate classical elastic collision between A and BC. Some information about the dependence of $P_{nn'}$ on the quantum numbers $n$ and $n'$, and the relative velocity $v$ can be obtained without a detailed knowledge of that function, however. Thus if one makes a harmonic approximation for $U_{BC}$, the selection rules for matrix elements of the displacement allow transitions to adjacent states only; in particular,

$$x_{n,n+1} = \left( \frac{\hbar}{2M\omega} \right)^{1/2} (n + 1)^{1/2},$$

and $| E_{n'} - E_n | = \hbar\omega$. For large values of the Massey parameter $\omega\tau$, $\tau$ being a time characterizing the variation of $V_1$, the main dependence of the integral in Eq. (3.4) on the relative velocity is given by an exponential factor of the form $\exp(-\omega\tau)$ (Landau and Teller, 1936; Nikitin, 1970b). Letting $\tau = l(b)/v$, where $l(b)$ characterizes the range of interaction for trajectories with impact parameter $b$, the above expression for $P_{nn'}$ can be written as follows:

$$P_{n,n+1} = (n + 1)B(v, b) \exp\left[ - \frac{2\omega l(b)}{v} \right], \qquad (3.5)$$

$B$ being a function whose dependence on $v$ and $b$ is slower than exponential. When $\omega l/v \gg 1$, the latter is strongly dependent on $l$. If the intramolecular potential consists of several segments with different steep-

ness, the main contribution to the transition probability will come from
that with the shortest value of $l$. Thus, in constructing models of translational-vibrational energy transfer, one usually takes into account the
short-range part of the potential which represents intramolecular repulsion, while the long-range attraction is treated as a small perturbation,
if at all. The collision cross section is computed according to a formula
analogous to Eq. (2.6), and averaged over a Maxwell velocity distribution;
one thus obtains the rate constant $K_{n,n+1}$ for a particular vibrational
transition. It can be conveniently written as the product of the number
of collisions $\pi R_0^2 (8kT/\pi\mu)^{1/2}$ predicted by kinetic theory, and of the
average transition probability $\langle P_{n,n+1} \rangle$. Detailed calculations give (Herzfeld and Litovitz, 1959; Nikitin, 1970b)

$$\langle P_{n,n+1} \rangle = (n + 1)B(T, \omega) \exp[-3(\omega^2 l_0^2 \mu/2\varkappa T)^{1/3}],$$
$$\langle P_{n,n+m} \rangle = 0, \qquad m > 1,$$
(3.6)

where $B(T, \omega)$ is a slowly varying function compared to the exponential,
and $l_0$ is the characteristic interaction range for a head-on collision.
Equation (3.6), which is known in the literature as the Landau–Teller
formula, describes the following features of the collisional excitation and
deactivation of molecular vibrations:

(a)   Only transitions between adjacent vibrational levels are allowed.

(b)   The transition probability increases linearly with vibrational
quantum number.

(c)   The temperature dependence of the transition probability obeys
the law $\ln P \propto T^{-1/3}$.

Explicit expressions for $B$ and $l_0$ can only be derived when special
assumptions are made about $V_0$ and $V_1$. In the one-dimensional treatment of Landau and Teller (1936), further developed by Schwartz,
Slawski, and Herzfeld in the so-called SSH theory (Herzfeld and Litovitz,
1959), it is assumed that the impinging atom A interacts only with the
closest atom of the molecule, say, B, according to an exponential law.
In that case $V_0$ and $V_1$ are given by

$$V_0 = Ce^{-\alpha R},$$
$$\frac{x}{l} V_1 = x\alpha \frac{m_C}{m_B + m_C} V_0.$$
(3.7)

Equation (3.5) then takes on the following form

$$P_{n,n+1} = (n+1)Z_{\text{vib}}Z_{\text{tr}},$$

$$Z_{\text{vib}} = \frac{\varepsilon_0}{\hbar\omega}\cot\beta_{\text{ABC}} = |\,\alpha x_{01}\,|^2, \tag{3.8}$$

$$Z_{\text{tr}} = \frac{4E_0}{\varepsilon_0}f(\xi), \qquad f(\xi) = \left(\frac{\xi}{\sinh\xi}\right)^2,$$

where $\varepsilon_0 = (\hbar^2\alpha^2/2\mu)$, $\xi = (\pi\omega/\alpha v)$, and $\cot^2\beta_{\text{ABC}} = m_A m_B/m_C(m_A + m_B + m_C)$. It is worth pointing out that $\beta_{\text{ABC}}$ is the angle between the axes of the skewed coordinate system that is often used to describe energy transfer in a linear system $ABC$ in terms of the motion of its representative point on a potential energy surface (Smith, 1959). The function $f(\xi)$ decreases monotonically as $\xi$ increases, for example, from 1 to 0.5 when $\xi$ varies between 0 and 1.5. The approximation $f(\xi) \simeq 4\xi^2 e^{-2\xi}$ is valid for $\xi \gg 1$. In order to obtain quantitative estimates of $Z_{\text{vib}}$ and $Z_{\text{tr}}$, let us assume that all three masses are nearly the same and that $\alpha$ is equal to the constant $\alpha'$ of the Morse potential. Then $\cot^2\beta \sim \frac{1}{3}$, $\varepsilon_0 \sim (\hbar\omega)^2/D$, and

$$Z_{\text{vib}} \approx \hbar\omega/D, \qquad Z_{\text{tr}} \approx [DE_{\text{tr}}/(\hbar\omega)^2]\,f(\xi),$$

$$P_{n,n+1} \approx (n+1)(E_{\text{tr}}/\hbar\omega)\,f(\xi). \tag{3.9}$$

For molecules like $N_2$, $\hbar\omega/D \approx 1/30$, so that $Z_{\text{vib}} \ll 1$, while the first factor in $Z_{\text{tr}}$ is much larger than unity.

The transition from the one-dimensional model to a real three-dimensional situation is possible if the condition $R_0\alpha \gg 1$ is satisfied. Each encounter can then be treated as a head-on collision by introducing an effective radial velocity (Nikitin, 1970b; Takayanagi, 1965), replacing $\cot^2\beta_{\text{ABC}}$ by the average $\frac{1}{2}(\cot^2\beta_{\text{ABC}} + \cot^2\beta_{\text{ACB}})$, and multiplying the result by an additional steric factor $Z_{\text{rot}} \approx \frac{1}{3}$. Further corrections can be made for the attraction between A and BC at large distances and the change in velocity associated with the transformation of part of the translational energy into vibrational energy. Finally, corrections for anharmonicity can also be included. One of them is related to the change in molecular vibration frequency caused by the interaction $V(R,r)$. Since this correction is independent of $n$, it can be lumped together with that accounting for the attraction. The second one is directly related to the nonequidistant nature of the energy levels of the anharmonic oscillator and to selection rules allowing transitions involving several vibrational quanta. Such transitions are not important in the limit $\omega\tau \gg 1$, however, since the corresponding Massey parameters are two, three, etc., times larger than the corresponding parameter for single quantum transitions. The nonequidistance of the levels does have a strong influence on the transition probabilities, however. For a Morse oscillator the frequency associated with a transition between the $n$th and $(n+1)$st levels depends linearly on $n$,

$$\omega_{n,n+1} = \omega_0[1 - (\hbar\omega/2D)n]. \tag{3.10}$$

Taking this into account, one finds that $\langle P_{n,n+1} \rangle$ exhibits a stronger increase than the linear variation with $n$ predicted by Eq. (3.6). The following expression is finally obtained for the probability of a single quantum excitation of molecule BC by atom A:

$$\langle P_{n,n+1} \rangle = (n + 1)\gamma^n \exp(-\Delta E_{n,n+1}/Z\varkappa T)Z_{\text{rot}}Z_{\text{vib}}Z_{\text{tr}}\text{AB},$$

where

$$\gamma = \exp[(\theta'/T)^{1/3}\hbar\omega/2D],$$

$$Z_{\text{vib}} = \tfrac{1}{2}[\cot^2 \beta_{\text{ABC}} + \cot^2 \beta_{\text{ACB}}]2\pi^2\theta/\theta', \tag{3.11}$$

$$Z_{\text{tr}} = \left(\frac{\theta'}{\pi\theta}\right)^2\left(\frac{2\pi}{3}\right)^{1/2}\left(\frac{\theta'}{T}\right)^{1/6}\exp\left[-\frac{3}{2}\left(\frac{\theta'}{T}\right)^{1/3}\right],$$

$\theta = \hbar\omega/\varkappa$ and $\theta' = (4\pi^2\omega_0^2\mu/\alpha^2\varkappa)$, while A and B are the above-mentioned corrections for attraction and vibrational frequency shift; explicit expressions for the latter can be found in the author's book (Nikitin, 1970b). The probability of deactivation is given by an analogous expression with $-(\Delta E_{n,n+1}/2\varkappa T)$ replaced by $(\Delta E_{n,n-1}/2\varkappa T)$. Such terms ensure that the detailed balance condition,

$$\frac{\langle P_{n,n+1} \rangle}{\langle P_{n+1,n} \rangle} = \exp\left(-\frac{\Delta E_{n,n+1}}{\varkappa T}\right), \tag{3.12}$$

is satisfied.

The most important condition which limits the applicability of Eq. (3.11), is that $\langle P_{n,n+1} \rangle$ remain small compared to unity. Whenever this condition is not satisfied, for example, for large values of $n$ or at high temperatures, multiple quantum transitions compete strongly with single quantum transitions, and it becomes necessary to go beyond perturbation theory.

C. Transitions between Highly Excited Molecular Vibrational
   States

Let us consider a multiple quantum vibrational excitation of the diatomic molecule BC within the framework of the model described earlier. If the elastic collision of atom A and of molecule BC in its unexcited state is taken as the zero-order approximation, and if the molecule is treated like a harmonic oscillator, the corresponding classical problem reduces to the forced vibrations of such an oscillator,

$$M\ddot{x} + M\omega_0^2 x = V_1(R)/l, \qquad (3.13)$$

under the influence of an external force determined by the perturbation $V_1(r)$ which is implicitly time-dependent as a result of the relative motion of A and BC. Integrating Eq. (3.13) starting with initial conditions corresponding to given values of the total vibrational energy $E_{\text{vib}}$ and of the oscillator phase $\phi$, one obtains the following expression for the change in vibrational energy in such a collision:

$$\Delta E_{\text{vib}} = E'_{\text{vib}} - E_{\text{vib}} = \Delta E_0 + 2(E_{\text{vib}} \Delta E_0)^{1/2} \cos \phi. \qquad (3.14)$$

Here $\Delta E_0$ is the energy transferred in a single collision to an oscillator initially at rest. Since the phase $\phi$ is randomly distributed over the allowed interval $0 \leq \phi < 2\pi$, the classical differential probability $f(E_{\text{vib}}, E'_{\text{vib}}) \times dE'_{\text{vib}}$ is simply proportional to $d\phi/2\pi$. It is important to note that, to a given final energy $E'_{\text{vib}}$, there correspond two different values $\phi_1$ and $\phi_2$ of the phase within the above-mentioned interval. Since both values give rise to equal contributions in our approximation, one obtains

$$f(E'_{\text{vib}}, E_{\text{vib}}) \, dE'_{\text{vib}} = \frac{dE'_{\text{vib}}}{\pi[4E_{\text{vib}} \Delta E_0 - (E'_{\text{vib}} - E_{\text{vib}} - \Delta E_0)^2]^{1/2}}. \qquad (3.15)$$

The corresponding transition probability is obtained by replacing $E'_{\text{vib}}$, $E_{\text{vib}}$, and $\Delta E_0$ by $(n' + \frac{1}{2})\hbar\omega$, $(n + \frac{1}{2})\hbar\omega$, and $\Delta n_0 \hbar\omega$, respectively:

$$P_{n,n'} = \frac{1}{\pi[4(n + \frac{1}{2}) \Delta n_0 - (n' - n - \Delta n_0)^2]^{1/2}}. \qquad (3.16)$$

This treatment of energy transfer is valid as long as $n'$ is such that the expression under the square root is positive, that is, $n'$ is in the classically allowed region.

The quantity $\Delta E_0$ depends on the details of the model. The solution of the classical problem corresponding to potentials of the form given in Eq. (3.7) yields

$$\frac{\Delta E_0}{E_{tr}} = 4 \cot^2 \beta_{ABC} f(\xi),  \qquad (3.17)$$

$f(\xi)$ being the function defined in Eqs. (3.8). One can easily check that the energy transfer $\Delta E_0$ computed classically actually coincides with its appropriate quantum counterpart. The latter is defined as the product of the probability of single quantum excitation and of the vibrational energy quantum $\hbar\omega$. For a harmonic oscillator one thus has

$$\Delta E_0 = \hbar\omega P_{01}.  \qquad (3.18)$$

This relation is often assumed to hold for more general models, and enables one to reduce the quantum mechanical calculation of $P_{01}$ to a classical one.

In the high velocity limit ($\xi \ll 1$) Eq. (3.11) reduces to

$$\Delta E_0/E_{tr} = 4 \cot^2\beta_{ABC}.  \qquad (3.19)$$

Thus the external force approximation imposes no upper bound on the ratio $\Delta E_0/E_{tr}$, so that Eq. (3.19) would violate energy conservation if $4 \cot^2\beta_{ABC} > 1$. This failure of the approximation is similar to that encountered in Section II when evaluating $\Delta j$. In order to avoid this defect Mahan (1970) proposed an improved impulse approximation in which the scattering of atom A by atom B rather than by the whole molecule BC is considered in zero order. In this modified theory the quantity $E_{tr}$ must be interpreted as the kinetic energy of A relative to B rather than BC. Effecting this change and transforming back to quantities describing the motion of A relative to BC, one finds that Eq. (3.19) is replaced by

$$\frac{\Delta E_0}{E_{tr}} = 4 \cos^2 \beta_{ABC} \sin^2 \beta_{ABC}.  \qquad (3.20)$$

This expression at least does not lead to physically absurd answers: the energy transfer always remains smaller or equal (in the special case where $\cot \beta = 1$) than the initial kinetic energy. Nevertheless, Eq. (3.20) is without firm foundations in the case where $\cot \beta > 1$, corresponding to a collision between heavy atom A with light atom B bound to heavy atom C, since so-called multiple collisions are neglected in the theory (Secrest, 1969).

Consider now the full quantum mechanical treatment of the problem.

Modifications to the classical result (3.16) will occur both in the classically allowed as well as the classically forbidden ranges of $n'$.

In the classically allowed range the main improvement is related to the description of *interference effects*. The simple addition of probabilities assumed in deriving Eq. (3.15) must, in a quantum description, be replaced by summing the appropriate probability amplitudes and then squaring the modulus of the total amplitude. Thus, in addition to simple probabilities, one obtains terms involving phase differences between different probability amplitudes. The simplest, semiclassical calculation which takes these terms into account for high quantum numbers $(n, n' \gg 1)$ (Miller, 1970) gives

$$P_{nn'} = \frac{2 \sin^2(\varphi + \pi/4)}{\pi [4n \, \Delta n_0 - (n' - n - \Delta n_0)^2]^{1/2}}, \qquad (3.21)$$

where

$$\varphi = 2(n \, \Delta n_0)^{1/2} [(1 - x)^{1/2} - x \cos^{-1} x]$$

and $x = |n' - n|/2(n \, \Delta n_0)^{1/2}$. The only difference between this expression and the classical result, Eq. (3.16), comes through the factor $2 \sin^2(\varphi + \pi/4)$; it can be replaced by its average value unity if it oscillates sufficiently fast so that an average over initial states $n$ effectively smooths them out.

In the classically forbidden range, quantum mechanics gives rise to a finite, though small transition probability. Thus Eq. (3.18), in particular, gives the probability of transitions for $\Delta E_0 < \hbar\omega$, which are forbidden in the classical approximation.

In order to illustrate the preceding discussion, consider the vibrational excitation of a hydrogen molecule by an He atom in a collinear collision. An exact quantum mechanical calculation of transition probabilities for this system was performed by Secrest and Johnson (1966), while the corresponding classical calculation has been done by Miller (1970); he also took interference effects into account (Miller, 1971). Results of the classical (dashed curve) and quantum (dotted curve) treatments are shown on Fig. 3. The semiclassical calculation including interference effects cannot be distinguished from the exact quantum mechanical results on the scale of the figure. The classical function $P_{nn'}$ computed for the forced oscillator model from Eq. (3.16) (full line), exhibits a U-shaped character for $2 \to n'$ transitions in the classically allowed range $0 \leq n' \leq 5$. Interference effects lead to a nonmonotonic variation of $P_{2n'}$ with $n'$, very small values of $P_{2n'}$ being obtained for some values of $n'$ even within the classically allowed range. The transition probabilities

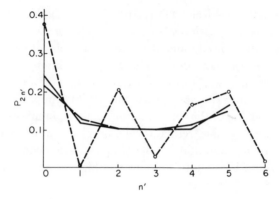

FIG. 3.    Dependence of the probability $P_{2n'}$ of $2 \to n'$ vibrational transitions on the quantum number $n'$ of the final state for a collinear collision of $H_2$ and He. Full curve computed according to Eq. (3.16) with $\Delta n = 0.9$. Dashed curve: exact classical solution (Miller, 1970). Circles connected by dotted lines: exact quantum and semiclassical calculations taking interference effects into account (Miller, 1971).

decrease monotonically for $n' > 5$, that is, in the classically forbidden range.

The difference between the classical and quantum predictions manifests itself most strongly for $0 \to n'$ transitions. The quantum solution of the forced oscillator problem (Nikitin, 1970b; Rapp and Kassal, 1969; Takayanagi, 1965) gives

$$P_{0n'} = (\Delta n_0)^{n'} e^{-\Delta n_0}/n'!, \tag{3.22}$$

while according to the classical Eq. (3.16)

$$P_{0n'} \simeq \frac{1}{\pi[2\Delta n_0 - (n' - \Delta n_0)^2]^{1/2}}. \tag{3.23}$$

Although these two expressions look very different, it is possible to establish a connection between them within the context of the general theory of the semiclassical approximation (Miller, 1971).

The close connection between results obtained in a semiclassical treatment of the forced harmonic oscillator, and the exact solution for that model, enables one to construct an approximate analytic formula for multiple quantum transitions in the quantum regime. Such a formula gives good results for harmonic (Heidrich et al., 1971) and even anharmonic (Morse and LaBrecque, 1971) oscillator models.

The theory outlined in this section, which completely neglects the possible transformation of the vibrational energy of a molecule into rotational energy of that same molecule or of its partner in a collision, is at its best for processes involving molecules with a weakly anisotropic interaction. By this we do not only mean that the coefficients in the expansion (2.2) for the anisotropic part of the interaction are small, but that they rapidly decrease with increasing $k$. Indeed, if vibrational as well as rotational transitions are taken into account in perturbation theory, then the $k$th term in the expansion (2.2) induces transitions with rotational quantum numbers differing by $\pm k$. The corresponding change in molecular rotational kinetic energy is $\Delta E_{\text{rot}} = (\hbar^2 jk/I)$, so that part of the translational kinetic energy which is converted into internal energy of the molecule is $\hbar\omega - \Delta E_{\text{rot}}$ for a single quantum transition. Replacing $\omega$ by $\omega - \Delta E_{\text{rot}}/\hbar$ in Eq. (3.5), one finds that taking rotational transitions into account changes the argument of the exponential by an amount $2(l/v)(\Delta E_{\text{rot}}/\hbar)$. Since, on the average, $\Delta E_{\text{rot}} \sim \hbar k(\varkappa T/2I)^{1/2}$, $v \sim (\varkappa T/\mu)^{1/2}$, a change in rotational angular momentum by $k$ can increase the transition probability by a factor $\exp[2(\mu/M)^{1/2}kl/r_e]$. Since $l/r_e \ll 1$ usually, such a correction can be ignored provided that $k$ is not too large, that is, if higher terms in the expansion (2.2) are small, and that the reduced mass $\mu$ of the colliding partners is not much larger than the reduced mass $M$ of molecule BC. These conditions are well satisfied in collisions of symmetric or nearly symmetric diatomic molecules with atoms or similar molecules. This justifies the validity of the breathing sphere model in describing the vibrational relaxation of molecules like $N_2$, CO, $O_2$, etc., in a broad temperature range.

One should not think that, even in such molecules, vibrational transitions are not accompanied by rotational transitions. However, these rotational transitions have little influence on the probability of vibrational transitions and can therefore be effectively taken into account when a semiempirical choice of interaction parameters is made.

In order to make a real check of the theory of translational-vibrational energy transfer, a proper vibrational excitation experiment must be designed in such a way that collisions involving large orbital angular momenta make a small contribution to the excitation process. This can be achieved in collision investigations using molecular beams in which one measures the translational energy loss of molecules which are backwards scattered in the center-of-mass reference frame, that is, the differential cross section for scattering through 180°. Such experiments generally confirm the validity of the models discussed previously in explaining the mechanism of translational-vibrational energy transfer (Held et al., 1970; Cheng et al., 1970; Cosby and Moran, 1970).

## IV. Transformation of Rotational and Translational Energy into Vibrational Energy (RV and TRV Processes)

Experimental investigations of the vibrational excitation and deactivation of molecules by means of various relaxation measurements, as well as studies of the population kinetics of individual vibrational levels under laser excitation (Yardley and Moore, 1968) have provided examples of many cases in which the breathing sphere model is completely inadequate. If one attempts to describe transition probabilities for such processes by means of a formula like Eq. (3.11), it is necessary to assume such small value of $l$ that would correspond to an unusually steep repulsive potential. Such anomalies manifest themselves for strongly asymmetric molecules with small moments of inertia, but large reduced masses, for example, hydrohalogenides (Chen and Moore, 1971), methane (Yardley et al., 1970) and others.

The estimates given at the end of Section III show that a strong influence of molecular rotation on the probabilities of vibrational transitions is expected under such conditions. However, this effect cannot be correctly accounted for within the framework of perturbation theory.

In the simplest generalization of the theory described in Section III, which takes this strong influence of rotation into account, the relative translational velocity $v$ is replaced by the relative orbital velocity of the partners at their distance of closest approach (Moore, 1965; Stevens, 1967). Such an approximation is equivalent to assuming that a quantum of vibrational energy is completely converted into rotational energy; the translational motion enters only insofar as it brings the molecules into contact with each other. One can easily see the analogy between this model for RV processes and the rough sphere model for TR processes (see Section II).

More refined models must involve details of the intermolecular potentials. The following generalized breathing sphere model (Kapralova et al., 1969) can serve as an illustration of the simplest approach incorporating such features. Equation (3.5) is assumed to hold at every point of a given equipotential surface, $v$ being interpreted as the component $v_\perp$ of the relative velocity normal to that surface. This component can be expressed in terms of the velocity $v$ of A relative to BC, the angular velocity $\omega$ of BC and the coordinates $R, \gamma$ of the appropriate point on the equipotential surface. Thus $P_{n,n+1}$ depends on $v$, $\omega$, $R$, and $\gamma$. The rate constant $K_{n,n+1}$ for a particular vibrational transition is then computed as the flux of representative points with different transition probabilities through a given equipotential surface, in accordance with the activated state concept.

Upon averaging over equilibrium distributions for $v$ and $\omega$ one finds that to every point $(R, \gamma)$ on the equipotential surface corresponds a transition probability $P_{n,n+1}$ of the same form as Eq. (3.11), except that $\mu$ is replaced by an effective mass depending on $R$ and $\gamma$. If the equation for the equipotential surface in polar coordinates is $R = R(\gamma)$, the variation of $\mu_{\mathrm{eff}}(\gamma)$ is given by the expression

$$\mu_{\mathrm{eff}}(\gamma) = \mu \, \frac{M r_e^2 (R^2 + R_\gamma^2)}{M r_e^2 (R^2 + R_\gamma^2) + \mu R^2 R_\gamma^2}, \qquad R_\gamma = \frac{dR}{d\gamma}. \qquad (4.1)$$

A study of the typical behaviour of $\mu_{\mathrm{eff}}(\gamma)$ shows that this quantity goes through a minimum value $\mu^*$ for a definite angle $\gamma^*$ (Kapralova et al., 1969). This means that the probability for a vibrational transition is maximum in a particular configuration corresponding to an activated complex that can be associated with the transformation of vibrational energy into rotational and translational energy.

The final expression for the averaged transition probability per collision is given by Eq. (3.11) with $\mu$ replaced by $\mu^*$ and an extra steric factor $Z_{\mathrm{rot}} < 1$ which takes into account the fraction of favorable configurations,

$$Z_{\mathrm{rot}} = (\pi \mu^* / \mu'')^{1/2} (\theta'/T)^{-1/6}. \qquad (4.2)$$

Here $\mu''$ is the second derivative of $\mu_{\mathrm{eff}}$ at its minimum.

Expression (4.1) for the effective mass has two interesting limits, corresponding to the breathing sphere and rough sphere models, respectively. In the first case $R_\gamma = 0$, since the equipotential surfaces are spherical, while in the second case $R_\gamma \gg R$ since the molecules are assumed to "stick" together when they come into contact. The effective masses in these two limiting cases are equal to $\mu$ and $M(r_e/R_0)^2$, respectively; the vibrational energy is then completely transformed into translational or into rotational energy.

In the general case $\mu^*$ can appreciably deviate from these limiting values, and the vibrational energy released in the deactivation process gets redistributed among translational and rotational degrees of freedom.

The activated state picture does not enable one to derive the form of this distribution, however, because the latter is determined by details of the intermolecular interaction not only close to the equipotential surface under consideration, but also far from it. This feature prevents one from extending the theory to situations where translational and rotational degrees of freedom are described by different distribution functions, thereby violating one of the basic assumptions of the activated state picture.

Such an extension can be simply achieved only if the anisotropic part of the interaction, $V_a$, can be treated as a perturbation in calculating the trajectory describing the relative motion of the colliding molecules. This approach was used by Shin (1971) in considering the vibrational deactivation of hydrogen halogenides. The molecule undergoing deactivation was modeled as a breathing sphere, and the interaction potential was assumed to depend on the intermolecular separation and on the angle between the collision axis and the rotation axis of the deactivated molecule. Such a model does in fact give a satisfactory description of the magnitude and temperature dependence of vibrational relaxation times of HCl, DCl, HBr, and HI molecules.

If the anisotropic part of the interaction is large, the energy transfer must be calculated from a numerical solution of the equations of motion. Results obtained to date in either classical (Benson and Berend, 1966; Kelley and Wolfsberg, 1967, 1970; Bergeron and Chapuisat, 1971) or semiclassical (Wartell and Cross, 1971) treatments all show the strong influence of TR energy transfer on TV processes.

## V. Quasi-resonant Transfer of Vibrational Energy (VV Processes)

In addition to processes involving the transformation of vibrational into translational and rotational energy, a direct transfer of vibrational energy between the two partners is in fact possible in collisions between diatomic or polyatomic molecules. If the resultant change in vibrational energy of both colliding molecules is small, one speaks of a quasi-resonant transfer of vibrational energy.

The simplest model describing this process envisages a collision between two collinear diatomic molecules represented by harmonic oscillators. In such a configuration the system can be specified by means of three coordinates: the deviation $x$ of the internuclear separation in molecule AB from its equilibrium value, the analogous quantity $y$ for molecule CD, and the distance $R$ between their respective centers of mass. If one considers transitions between the lowest vibrational levels and relies on the arguments used in our previous description of the interaction between an atom A and a molecule BC (see Section III,A), the interaction leading to vibrational transitions

$$AB(n) + CD(m) \rightarrow AB(n') + CD(m') \tag{5.1}$$

can be written as

$$V(x, y) = V_1'(x/l) + V_1''(y/l) + V_2(xy/l^2). \tag{5.2}$$

Terms in $x^2$ and $y^2$ have been neglected as being small compared to the linear terms which are responsible for TV processes. The cross term proportional to $xy$ has been retained; although it is *smaller* in magnitude than the first two, it is the leading one which gives rise to vibrational energy transfer. Besides the probability of such processes can be *higher* than that for vibrational-translational energy transfers if the latter occur under nearly adiabatic conditions.

According to the selection rules for matrix elements of the displacement of a harmonic oscillator, $n \rightarrow n \pm 1$ transitions of one oscillator must be accompanied by $m \rightarrow m \mp 1$ or $m \rightarrow m \pm 1$ transitions of the other oscillator under the influence of an interaction proportional to $xy$. In the first case the total change in vibrational energy is $\hbar(\omega_{AB} - \omega_{CD})$, while in the second one it is $\hbar(\omega_{AB} + \omega_{CD})$. Assuming nearly adiabatic conditions ($\omega\tau \gg 1$), one need only consider processes of the first kind, in which the transfer of a vibrational quantum is accompanied by the transformation of a small amount of vibrational energy into translational energy. First-order perturbation theory gives

$$P_{n,n+1;\,m,m-1} = (n+1)m \frac{|x_{01}|^2 |y_{01}|^2}{l^4}$$
$$\times \left| \int \frac{V_2(R)}{\hbar} \exp\left(\frac{i}{\hbar} \Delta E_{n,n+1}^{m,m-1} t\right) dt \right|^2. \tag{5.3}$$

Assuming an exponential interaction potential between atoms B and C of molecules AB and CD, Eq. (5.3) can be reduced to the following form:

$$P_{n,n+1;\,m,m-1} = (n+1)m Z_{\text{vib}}^{AB} Z_{\text{vib}}^{CD} Z_{\text{tr}},$$

where

$$Z_{\text{tr}} = \frac{4E_{\text{tr}}}{\varepsilon_0} f(\Delta\xi), \tag{5.4}$$

and

$$\Delta\xi = \pi \Delta\omega/av, \qquad \varepsilon_0 = (\hbar^2 a^2/2\mu).$$

The above expression for vibrational energy transfer should be compared with Eq. (3.8) for the probability of vibrational to translational energy conversion. For transitions between the lowest vibrational levels one obtains

$$\frac{P_{01,10}}{P_{01}} = \frac{\varepsilon_0}{\hbar\omega}\frac{f(\varDelta\xi)}{f(\xi)}.$$                                    (5.5)

if the masses of all constituent atoms are assumed nearly equal. The ratio $\varepsilon_0/\hbar\omega$ is of the same order as $\hbar\omega/D$; however, $f(\varDelta\xi)/f(\xi)$ is always larger than unity, actually much larger if $\varDelta\xi$ is sufficiently smaller than $\xi$. As $\xi$ increases the ratio $P_{01,10}/P_{01}$ exceeds unity, so that vibrational energy transfer becomes more effective than the transformation of vibrational into translational energy.

If the resonance condition is nearly satisfied, that is, $\varDelta\xi \ll 1$, the probability of a single vibrational quantum transfer is given by

$$P_{n,n+1;m,m-1} = (n+1)m\left(\frac{\varepsilon_0}{\hbar\omega}\right)^2 \cot^2\beta_{\text{AB(CD)}}\cot^2\beta_{\text{(AB)CD}}\frac{4E_{\text{tr}}}{\varepsilon_0}.$$        (5.6)

Under such conditions the transition probability depends only weakly on the parameter $l$ which characterizes the steepness of the interaction potential; we must therefore reconsider our previous argument (see Section III,A) that only the short-range part of the intermolecular potential plays a significant role in determining the amount of energy transfer.

As a matter of fact, general estimates show that, right on resonance, multipole interactions between molecules can lead to transition probabilities which exceed in magnitude those computed using only the short-range part of the intermolecular interaction (Mahan, 1967). Qualitatively speaking, the two parts of that interaction play different roles, for example, the short-range potential causes transitions, as well as changes in the classical trajectories describing the relative motion of the molecules, while the long-range potential essentially gives rise to transitions alone and has little influence on the relative motion. The energy dependence of the corresponding factors $Z_{\text{tr}}$ is therefore different for these two kinds of interactions. The maximum value of $V_2$ is proportional to the relative kinetic energy $E_{\text{tr}}$ for a short-range potential; this is the origin of the factor $E_{\text{tr}}$ in front of $f(\varDelta\xi)$ in Eq. (5.4). Both factors increase with $E_{\text{tr}}$, leading to a monotically increasing transition probability. For a long-range potential, however, the maximum value of $V_2$ is essentially independent of energy, being determined by the distance of closest approach between the molecules. Upon performing the integration in

Eq. (5.2) one obtains

$$Z_{tr} \approx \frac{|V_{2max}|^2}{\varepsilon_0 E_{tr}} f(\Delta\xi).$$ (5.7)

For a given value of $\Delta\omega$ this expression goes through a maximum with increasing $E_{tr}$ and decreases as soon as the condition $\Delta\xi \leq 1$ is satisfied. Thus, close to resonance, the probability for a $n \to n + 1$, $m \to m - 1$ transition is either proportional to the temperature $T$ if short-range forces are dominant, or inversely proportional to $T$ if transitions are mainly due to long-range forces. Since both types of interaction are present in a real situation, the net transition probability can be approximated by a sum of such contributions,

$$P_{n,n+1; m,m-1} \sim C_1 T + C_2 T^{-1}.$$ (5.8)

This result predicts a nonmonotic dependence of the transition probability $P(T)$ exhibiting a minimum.

If the condition for resonant scattering is not well satisfied, the contribution from long-range forces to vibrational energy transfer rapidly becomes small. The resonance condition can be assisted to a certain extent by accompanying rotational transitions, but the short-range eventually wins out.

As an example, one may consider the transition probability $P_{n,n-1; 0,1}$ for two colliding CO molecules. The appropriate $VV$ process becomes less and less resonant as $n$ increases. At 300°K the main contribution to the transition probability $P_{n,n-1; 0,1}$ comes from the long-range dipole-dipole interaction for $n < 7$, while for $n > 7$ the short-range exchange interaction dominates (Jeffers and Kelley, 1971).

## VI. Transformation of Translational, Rotational, and Vibrational Energy into Electronic Energy

### A. GENERAL REMARKS ABOUT NONADIABATIC TRANSITIONS

The basic assumption that enables one to introduce the concept of potential energy for a system of atoms is the adiabatic approximation. According to the basic idea of this approximation, the allowed energy levels of electrons $U_{el}(\mathbf{R})$ are first determined for each fixed configuration $\mathbf{R}$ of the nuclear coordinates. If these adiabatic electronic levels are well separated from each other, that is, if the parameter $\omega_{el}(\mathbf{R})\tau$ is sufficiently large for each relevant pair of levels, each such level can be considered as the potential energy of the nuclei or atoms belonging to the system in a given electronic state. In the adiabatic approximation one assumes that the motion of atoms does not cause transitions between different electronic levels. The problem of collisional energy transfer is then described in terms of the motion (classical or quantum mechanical) of atoms on a particular potential energy surface. Transitions between different electronic states can only be accounted for by going beyond the adiabatic approximation. The main goal of the theory of nonadiabatic processes is to calculate the probabilities of such transitions.

In looking for an interpretation of the mechanism for a particular elementary process, the choice of the best approximation depends on the nature of the process and on the conditions under which it occurs. For sufficiently small kinetic energies of the atoms in the system, the adiabatic approximation often provides a satisfactory picture of the physics, and nonadiabatic effects represent a small correction only. Nevertheless, there are quite a lot of processes in which nonadiabatic transitions do play a fundamental role, and which cannot be interpreted in terms of motion along a single potential energy surface. However, one finds that transitions between electronic levels are localized within rather small regions. In the remainder of configuration space adiabatic electronic terms can therefore still be thought of as potential energy surfaces. If this is the case, nonadiabatic transitions can be viewed in terms of atoms which move on portions of several different potential energy surfaces, and suddenly hop from one such surface to another one in regions where the nonadiabatic interactions are strong. Such a picture consisting of adiabatic motion interrupted by hopping becomes less accurate with increasing kinetic energy. For sufficiently high velocities of the atoms, regions where the adiabatic approximation is valid shrink or disappear altogether; adiabatic electronic levels then completely loose their meaning of effective potential energy. Such a situation obtains at rather high energies (above 10 to/100 eV, depending on the process under consideration), so that the picture involving sudden hops is actually useful for a wide class of elementary nonadiabatic processes.

The criterion for the validity of the adiabatic approximation in describing the motion of atoms in the vicinity of $\mathbf{R}$ is that the parameter $\omega_{el}(\mathbf{R})\tau$ be large. In order to determine the regions where hopping can take place, it is therefore important to investigate whether two potential energy surfaces do in fact intersect or come close together. Qualitative considerations concerning the possible arrangement of two such surfaces, describing a system with $s$ degrees of freedom, relative to each other, lead to the following possibilities (Landau and Lifshitz, 1963; Herzberg, 1966; Nikitin, 1970b).

1.  If these two $s$-dimensional surfaces correspond to electronic states of different symmetries, they can intersect along a $(s - 1)$-dimensional line. For a system with only one dimension, for example, two atoms with an interatomic distance as a coordinate, this means that terms with different symmetries can intersect at a point, whereas for a system with two degrees of freedom, for example, a system of three atoms with one coordinate fixed, the constant potential energy surfaces can intersect along a certain curve.

2.  If the two $s$-dimensional surfaces correspond to electronic levels of the same symmetry, they can intersect along a $(s - 2)$-dimensional line, as long as spin-orbit coupling is ignored. For a system with one degree of freedom this means that levels of the same symmetry cannot intersect, while for a system with two degrees of freedom the appropriate surfaces can only touch at a point.

3.  If the two $s$-dimensional surfaces correspond to electronic levels of the same symmetry in the presence of spin-orbit coupling, they can only intersect along a $(s - 3)$-dimensional line. For systems with both one or two degrees of freedom no intersection is then possible.

Whenever two electronic levels intersect or come close to each other (pseudocrossing), the Massey parameter becomes small for at least some possible trajectories; this signals the breakdown of the adiabatic approximation, that is, nonadiabatic transitions become possible. The corresponding probabilities depend on matrix elements of the nonadiabatic interaction $C_{ik}$ which is responsible for these transitions, as well as on the Massey parameter itself. Selection rules for $C_{ik}$ which establish general connections between different types of nonadiabatic interactions, and the symmetry properties of states $i$ and $k$ between which transitions take place, therefore play an important role in the theory.

## B. Classification of Nonadiabatic Transitions

In the semiclassical approximation the operator responsible for nonadiabatic transitions is simply represented by the time derivative $-i\hbar\, \partial/\partial t$, acting on adiabatic electronic wavefunctions. The latter depend on time because the nuclear coordinates, which enter into these wave functions as parameters, do in fact change as the nuclei move around (Nikitin, 1967).

It is natural to classify adiabatic wave functions according to their transformation properties under different symmetry operations of the Hamiltonian for fixed configurations of the nuclei. The transition operator can therefore be conveniently written in a form which reflects nuclear motions preserving particular symmetries. In order to clarify this question, consider the simplest case of two atoms. For fixed positions of the nuclei the electronic Hamiltonian exhibits axial symmetry, so that adiabatic electronic wave functions can be characterized by a quantum number $\Omega$ that determines the component of the total electronic angular momentum along the axis of the quasi molecule (Herzberg, 1950). The adiabatic levels of such a system depend on a single parameter, the interatomic separation $R$. Two adiabatic levels have the same symmetry if they correspond to the same value of $\Omega$; otherwise they have different symmetries. In the first case only pseudocrossing is possible, while in the second one a genuine crossing can occur.

When considering the motion of the nuclei, it is important to note that an arbitrary displacement can be represented as a linear combination of a radial motion that leaves the molecular axis invariant, and of a rotation which leaves the internuclear separation invariant. The operator $-i\hbar\, \partial/\partial t$ can accordingly be represented as a sum of operators, each describing one of the above-mentioned kinds of motion,

$$-i\hbar\, \partial/\partial t = -i\hbar \dot{R}\, \partial/\partial R + \omega J_\omega. \tag{6.1}$$

Here $\dot{R}$ and $\omega$ are the radial and angular velocities describing the relative motion of the nuclei, and $J_\omega$ is the operator corresponding to the component of orbital angular momentum along the angular velocity vector of the molecule. Equation (6.1) implies that matrix elements of the operator $-i\hbar\, \partial/\partial t$ can be expressed in terms of matrix elements of the more conventional operators $\partial/\partial R$ and $J_\omega$ which no longer depend on the relative velocity of the nuclei and obey well-known selection rules. Thus matrix elements of the operator $\partial/\partial R$ vanish unless both initial and final states have the same symmetry, while matrix elements of $J_\omega$ vanish unless the quantum numbers of the initial and final states differ by unity. The radial motion can therefore only give rise to nonadiabatic transitions between electronic levels of the same symmetry, while rotational motion can only cause transitions between levels of different symmetries such that the corresponding components of orbital angular momentum along the internuclear axis differ by $\pm 1$.

In addition to axial symmetry a system of two atoms can also have additional symmetries that lead to extra selection rules for nonadiabatic transitions (Nikitin, 1967). These selection rules are analogous to those governing the pre-dissociation of diatomic molecules (Herzberg, 1950).

The nonadiabatic transition operator for systems of three or more atoms can also be represented as a linear combination of operators, each of which describes a particular motion of the nuclei. Selection rules for a three-atom system are discussed in a review article by the author (Nikitin, 1967).

Such a classification of different allowed types of nonadiabatic transitions enables one to achieve considerable simplification in analyzing general features of the interactions between electronic and nuclear motions, in particular, the time-dependent equations that apply in regions of strong nonadiabatic coupling, characterized by the criterion $\omega_{el}(R)\tau \leq 1$. As long as nuclei move sufficiently slow, the characteristic extent of these regions is small; this enables one to approximate adiabatic electronic wavefunctions and matrix elements of the nonadiabatic interaction by means of simple functional forms that can easily be determined from the equations governing nondiabatic transitions. The corresponding probabilities can then be explicitly calculated.

## C. Probabilities of Nonadiabatic Transitions

A number of models in which the probabilities of nonadiabatic transitions can be determined in closed form exists at present (Nikitin, 1968, 1970a). We shall examine only two such models, pertaining to crossing and pseudocrossing electronic levels, respectively. For the sake of simplicity, we explicitly consider two colliding atoms, although many of our results can in fact be adapted to more complex systems.

If two adiabatic levels $U_1$ and $U_2$ cross, the corresponding wave functions must have different axial symmetry properties. Nonadiabatic coupling between these levels becomes important close to their point of intersection where the Massey parameter goes to zero.

The corresponding matrix element $C_{12}$, which is equal to $\omega\langle 2 \mid J_\omega \mid 1\rangle$ according to the selection rules examined above, can be treated as a constant in the relevant range, while the intersecting electronic levels can be approximately by linear functions of the internuclear separation $R$. One thus arrives at the model first considered by Landau (1932a):

$$U_1 = -F_1(R - R_0) + E_0, \qquad U_2 = -F_2(R - R_0) + E_0, \qquad (6.2)$$

where $R_0$ is the coordinate of the point of intersection, and $-F_1$, $-F_2$ the derivatives of the electronic energies $U_1$, $U_2$ at that point (see Fig. 4). Finally, the equation of a trajectory passing close to the point of intersection is approximated by a linear function of time in the vicinity of that point, that is,

$$R - R_0 = v_R t, \tag{6.3}$$

where $v_R$ is the relative velocity describing radial motion.

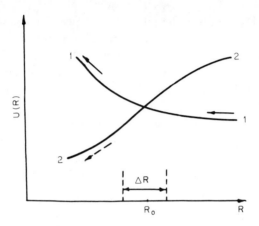

FIG. 4. Crossing between adiabatic electronic levels for two-atom system. The full arrow on the right indicates the direction of motion before the nondiabatic region of width $\Delta R$ is reached. Those on the left mark the alternative adiabatic (full arrow) and nonadiabatic (dashed arrow) paths which the system can follow.

First-order perturbation theory then gives for the probability $P_{12}$ of a nonadiabatic transition

$$
\begin{aligned}
P_{12} &= \left| \int \frac{C_{12}}{i\hbar} \exp\left( \frac{i}{\hbar} \int_0^t [U_1(t') - U_2(t')] \, dt' \right) dt \right|^2 \\
&= \frac{2\pi\omega^2 \, | \langle 2 \, | \, J_\omega \, | \, 1 \rangle |^2}{\hbar v_R \, | \, F_1 - F_2 \, |}.
\end{aligned} \tag{6.4}
$$

The quantities $\omega$ and $v_R$ depend on the impact parameter $b$ and the relative velocity $v$ of the atoms before the collision. This dependence is determined by the conservation laws for angular momentum and energy, namely,

$$\omega = vb/R_0^2, \qquad v_R = v[1 - (b/R_0)^2 - E_0/E]^{1/2}, \tag{6.5}$$

$E_{\mathrm{tr}} = v^2/2$ being the relative kinetic energy. Equation (6.4) for the transition probability is valid provided $P_{12} \ll 1$. This condition is always satisfied if the linear approximation (6.2) is valid in the range where the interaction is appreciable. In the model described by Eqs. (6.2) the two-atom system therefore tends to stay in its original adiabatic state with a probability $P_{11} = 1 - P_{12} \simeq 1$ (see Fig. 4).

Upon substituting Eq. (6.5) into Eq. (6.4), the transition probability can be expressed in terms of the impact parameter, and the average cross section and rate constant for the nonadiabatic process can then be calculated. It is important to realize that the intersection point must be crossed twice in atomic collisions: once when the atoms approach each other, and then when they fly apart. Thus, in evaluating the appropriate cross section, one must use a modified transition probability $\mathscr{P}_{12}$ which is related to be former one through the expression

$$\mathscr{P}_{12} = 2P_{12}(1 - P_{12}). \tag{6.6}$$

Since $P_{12} \ll 1$ in the case under consideration, $\mathscr{P}_{12} \simeq 2P_{12}$ to a good approximation.

Further calculations yield the following expression for the rate constant for the nonadiabatic process under consideration,

$$K_{12} = \left(\frac{8\varkappa T}{\pi\mu}\right)^{1/2} \pi R_0{}^2 \langle \mathscr{P}_{12} \rangle \exp\left(-\frac{E_0}{\varkappa T}\right), \tag{6.7}$$

where

$$\langle \mathscr{P}_{12} \rangle = \frac{2\pi^{3/2}(2\varkappa T/\mu)^{1/2}C_{12}^2}{\hbar R_0{}^2 \, |\, F_1 - F_2 \,|}. \tag{6.8}$$

The first factor in Eq. (6.7) is the number of collisions corresponding to a cross section of radius $R_0$, computed according to kinetic theory, the second one is the average transition probability, and the third one is a typical Arrhenius factor. The latter appears because the two atoms must come to a distance $R_0$ between each other, overcoming an energy of repulsion $E_0$ in the process, for the nonadiabatic transition to occur. The quantity $E_0$ therefore plays the role of an energy barrier.

Consider now the case of pseudocrossing electronic levels (Nikitin, 1970b). In the range where they are close together, the latter look like hyperbolas (see Fig. 5). If the corresponding asymptotes are given by $U_1{}' = -F_1(R - R_0)$, $U_2{}' = -F_2(R - R_0)$ and if the smallest separation of the levels is $2a$, these adiabatic levels can be well approximated as follows:

$$U_1 = -\frac{F_1 + F_2}{2}(R - R_0) + \left[\left(\frac{F_1 - F_2}{2}\right)^2 (R - R_0)^2 + a^2\right]^{1/2},$$

$$U_2 = -\frac{F_1 + F_2}{2}(R - R_0) - \left[\left(\frac{F_1 - F_2}{2}\right)^2 (R - R_0)^2 + a^2\right]^{1/2}.$$

(6.9)

The probability of a nonadiabatic transition in such a model using Eq. (6.3) as an approximation for the trajectory, was first found by Landau (1932b) and Zener (1932),

$$P_{12} = \exp[-2\pi a^2/\hbar v_R \mid F_1 - F_2 \mid].$$

(6.10)

According to this result, the transition probability is small at low velocities, that is, $\hbar v_R \mid F_1 - F_2 \mid \ll 2\pi a^2$; the system remains in the initial adiabatic state in this case. For sufficiently high velocities, $\hbar v_R \mid F_1 - F_2 \mid \gg 2\pi a^2$, the transition probability approaches unity and the system prefers to hop between the quasi-intersecting adiabatic levels. The latter condition involves the minimum separation $2a$ between these levels, as well as the velocity itself. For sufficiently small values of $a$ the system undergoes nonadiabatic transitions with a probability close to unity over a wide range of velocities $v_R$. In such a situation it is convenient to introduce the concept of *diabatic* levels that the system follows with high probability for sufficiently large velocities. In the particular model described by Eqs. (6.9) the appropriate diabatic levels are represented by the asymptotes of the hyperbola.

Such diabatic levels can usually be obtained in a natural way when potential energy surfaces are derived in an approximation that neglects some small part of the total interaction. One example is provided by spin-orbit coupling; it is indeed small compared to the Coulomb interaction of nuclei and electrons for light atoms and even atoms of intermediate mass. Conservation of electron spin is satisfied on potential energy surfaces obtained without taking spin-orbit coupling into account; such surfaces are associated with diabatic levels which do, in general, cross each other.

Far from their point of intersection diabatic levels essentially coincide with their adiabatic counterparts. A simple connection can therefore be established between transition probabilities between adiabatic and diabatic levels. If the latter are denoted by $P_{12}$ and $P'_{12}$, respectively, one has in fact (see Fig. 5)

$$P'_{12} = 1 - P_{12}.$$

(6.11)

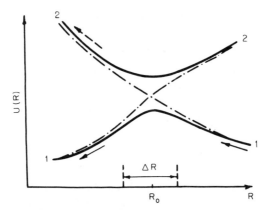

Fig. 5. Pseudo crossing adiabatic levels for two-atom system. The full arrow on the right indicates the direction of motion before the nonadiabatic region of width $\Delta R$ is reached. Those on the left mark the alternative adiabatic (full arrow) and nonadiabatic (dashed arrow) paths which the system can follow. The dot-dashed curves represent the appropriate crossing diabatic levels.

When $P_{12}$ is large, $P'_{12}$ must be small; expanding the exponential in Eq. (6.10), one finds

$$P'_{12} \simeq (2\pi a^2/\hbar v_R \mid F_1 - F_2 \mid). \tag{6.12}$$

This expression coincides with Eq. (6.4) if the parameter $a$ is identified with the off-diagonal matrix element $C_{12}$; this is as expected since in both cases one deals with transition probabilities between intersecting levels.

If the region where the levels nearly cross is traversed twice, the net transition probability is given by

$$\mathscr{P}_{12} = 2 \exp(-2\pi a^2/\hbar v_R \mid F_1 - F_2 \mid)$$
$$\times [1 - \exp(-2\pi a^2/\hbar v_R \mid F_1 - F_2 \mid)] \tag{6.13}$$

according to Eq. (6.6). In the literature this result is known as the Landau–Zener formula.

Going over to collisions between molecules, we note that the theory of nonadiabatic transitions must be modified in two respects. First, the trajectory describing the relative motion of the nuclei in the range of significant nonadiabatic coupling can, in general, be arbitrarily oriented with respect to the line along which adiabatic surfaces cross or pseudo-cross each other. Second, even in the case of a single collision, the representative point in configuration space traverses the region of non-adiabatic coupling more than twice, the latter being the case for a collision between two atoms. Moreover, the trajectory has a different orientation with respect to the line of intersection each time the former passes close to the latter. As a result the probability of a nonadiabatic transition $\mathscr{P}$ in a single collision cannot be expressed in a simple way in terms of the analogous quantity $P$ corresponding to a single passage through the region of nonadiabatic coupling.

In the case of pseudocrossing levels, Eq. (6.10) still turns out to be useful as far as the probability $P$ is concerned, provided that $2a$ is interpreted as the minimum separation between the adiabatic energy levels and that $F_1$, $F_2$ are the slopes of the associated diabatic levels computed on their line of intersection in a plane normal to the latter. Similarly $v_R$ must be identified with the velocity component normal to the same line.

If one adapts such a description of the transition probability corresponding to a single passage through the nonadiabatic region, the dynamics of two colliding molecules can be described as follows. Initially the representative point in configuration space moves on a particular potential energy surface, along a certain trajectory which may pass through a region where the surface in question nearly crosses another one. If this happens, then the representative point can hop onto the latter surface with a certain probability $P_{12}$. Thus, when the representative point emerges from the region of nonadiabatic coupling, it can follow two trajectories, one on the initial potential energy surface and another one on the neighboring surface. These two trajectories move apart, and the system can be again described in terms of adiabatic motion on either potential energy surface, until one of the trajectories brings the representative point once more into a nonadiabatic region, thus resulting in a new branching of trajectories. The successive occurrence of such cycles describing the nonadiabatic process leads to a redistribution of energy between electronic and nuclear degrees of freedom. Such an approach enables one to make maximum use of the theory of nonadiabatic transitions developed for atomic collisions and of the theory of inelastic collisions between molecules constructed within the framework of the adiabatic approximation.

There exist at present very many articles devoted to applications of the theory of nonadiabatic transitions to calculations of the cross sections and rate constants of various processes occuring in inelastic atomic collisions. The study of nonadiabatic processes in molecular collisions is only beginning. As an example we wish to mention investigations of the dynamics of electronic deactivation for alkali metal atoms colliding with diatomic molecules (Bjerre and Nikitin, 1967, Bauer *et al.*, 1971) and at the charge transfer and rearrangement in $H^+ + D_2$ collisions (Tully and Preston, 1971).

## VII. Influence of Nonadiabatic Effects on the Translational to Vibrational Energy Transfer

The theory of translational-vibrational energy transfer presented in Section III was based on the adiabatic approximation for the electronic states of the colliding molecules. The validity of the adiabatic approximation requires that the electronic levels of the colliding molecules be well separated at all times. If one of colliding molecules is in a degenerate electronic state, the adiabatic approximation is clearly inapplicable. The intermolecular interaction lifts this electronic degeneracy, so that a whole series of closely-lying potential energy surfaces, between which nonadiabatic transitions are possible, appear as the molecules approach each other. Quasiresonant transfer of vibrational energy into electronic energy is, in particular, possible near intermolecular separations such that the energy separation between split-up electronic levels becomes equal to that of a molecular vibrational quantum. The transferred electronic energy is transformed into relative kinetic energy as the molecules move apart, so that the net result of one collision is a transfer of molecular vibrational energy into translational energy with a nonadiabatic electronic transitions in the intermediate state. Such processes compete with the usual transfer processes within given electronic states; and actually become more effective if the condition $\omega\tau \gg 1$ is satisfied.

In order to discuss the relative importance of these two kinds of processes, let us analyze them from the point of view of nonadiabatic transitions between adiabatic "vibronic" states of the interacting system. Considering first a collision between atom A and molecule BC, both in nondegenerate electronic states, we assume that their relative motion is adiabatic with respect to vibrations of the molecule in zero order. An intermolecular potential can then be assigned to each vibrational level. In the simple case of a harmonic oscillator with a linear interaction such as in Eq. (3.3), these adiabatic potentials are obtained from the interaction potential between atom A and molecule BC in the absence of vibrations by shifting it by the appropriate amounts $(n + \frac{1}{2})\hbar\omega$. Collision-induced

changes in the vibrational state can be viewed as nonadiabatic transitions
between such levels. Such an interpretation of the single-quantum
deactivation process is illustrated by Fig. 6. One sees that the negligible
transition probability expected for $\omega\tau \gg 1$ can be thought of as resulting
from a tunneling transition between nonintersecting adiabatic levels.

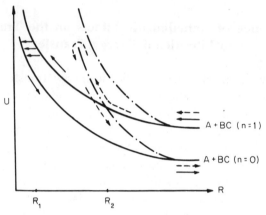

FIG. 6. Schematic representation of pure vibrational (full arrows near $R \sim R_1$)
and vibronic (dashed arrows near $R \sim R_2$) mechanisms for a $1 \to 0$ transition in a molecule BC colliding with an atom A. The full and dot-dashed curves represent different
vibronic levels which arise when the degeneracy of either partner in its free state is
lifted by their interaction.

Consider now the same collision, assuming now that either A or BC
are in a degenerate electronic state. Appropriate adiabatic vibronic levels
must be constructed in zero order already. For a given value of the vibrational quantum number $n$, the intermolecular interaction leads to a set
of levels which split apart as the intermolecular separation decreases.
Shifting this set of levels by successive amounts $(n + \frac{1}{2})\hbar\omega$, one obtains
a full set of vibronic levels exhibiting many intersections. If two levels
that cross are of the same symmetry one should treat them as nearly
crossing. Nonadiabatic transitions occur close to the points where
vibronic levels cross or nearly do so; they are accompanied by changes
in the vibrational and electronic states. Since such transitions are not
really tunneling processes, the corresponding probability decays much
more slowly with increasing values of the parameter $\omega\tau$ than that for
transitions between adjacent vibrational levels derived from the same
electronic state. In the simplest cases the transition probability between
vibronic levels can be computed according to the Landau–Zener formula.

The total transition probability can be written as a sum of contributions from two mechanisms associated with a vibrational transition with and without change in electronic state, respectively. The probability of the first process is given by the Landau–Zener formula, and that of the second one by the Landau–Teller formula. In the first case nonadiabatic transitions are due to spin-orbit coupling or to the Coriolis interaction (Nikitin, 1970b).

A detailed analysis of the competing contribution of the two above-mentioned mechanisms to the total probability of a vibrational transition shows that vibronic transitions are more effective for large values of $\omega\tau$, while pure vibrational transitions are favored in the opposite limit. The whole picture of vibrational-translational energy transfer thus changes significantly if the temperature varies over a wide interval. One example of such a competition is provided by the vibrational relaxation of $NO(^2\Pi)$; in this case vibronic transitions dominate pure vibrational transitions for $T < 3500°K$. As other examples, involving an atom rather a molecule in a degenerate state, one can cite the vibrational relaxation of $N_2$ and $O_2$ via collisions with O atoms in a $^3P$ electronic state (Nikitin and Umanski, 1971).

## REFERENCES

ALLISON, A. C., and DALGARNO, A. (1967). Proc. Phys. Soc. (London) 90, 609.
BAUER, E., FISHER, E. R., and GILMORE, F. R. (1969). J. Chem. Phys. 51, 4173.
BENSON, S. W., and BEREND, G. C. (1966). J. Chem. Phys. 44, 4247.
BJERRE, A., and NIKITIN, E. E. (1967). Chem. Phys. Lett. 1, 179.
BERGERON, G., and CHAPUISAT, X. (1971). Chem. Phys. Lett. 11, 334.
CHEN, H. L., and MOORE, C. B. (1971). J. Chem. Phys. 54, 4072.
CHENG, M. H., CHIANG, M. H., GISLASON, E. A., MAHAN, B. H., TSAO, G. W., and WERNER, A. S. (1970). J. Chem. Phys. 52, 6150.
COHEN, A. O., and MARCUS, R. A. (1970). J. Chem. Phys. 52, 3140.
COSBY, P. C., and MORAN, T. F. (1970). J. Chem. Phys. 52, 6157.
GORDON, R. G., KLEMPERER, W., and STEINFELD, J. I. (1968). Ann. Rev. Phys. Chem. 19, 215.
HEIDRICH, F. E., WILSON, K. R., and RAPP, D. (1971). J. Chem. Phys. 54, 3885.
HELD, W. D., SCHÖTTLER, J., and TOENNIES, J. P. (1970). Chem. Phys. Lett. 6, 304.
HERZBERG, G. (1950). "Molecular Spectra and Molecular Structure," 2nd ed., Vol. I, Spectra of Diatomic Molecules. Van Nostrand Reinhold, Princeton, New Jersey.
HERZBERG, G. (1966). "Molecular Spectra and Molecular Structure," Vol. III, Electronic Spectra and Electronic Structure of Polyatomic Molecules. Van Nostrand Reinhold, Princeton, New Jersey.
HERZFELD, K. F., and LITOVITZ, T. A. (1959). "Absorption and Dispersion of Ultrasonic Waves." Academic Press, New York.

HIRSCHFELDER, J. O., CURTISS, CH. F., and BIRD, R. B. (1954). "Molecular Theory of Gases and Liquids." Wiley, New York.

JEFFERS, W. Q., and KELLEY, J. D. (1971). *J. Chem. Phys.* **55**, 4433.

KAPRALOVA, G. A., NIKITIN, E. E., and CHAIKIN, A. M. (1969). *Kinet. Kataliz* **10**, 974.

KELLEY, J. D., and WOLFSBERG, M. (1967). *J. Phys. Chem.* **71**, 2373.

KELLEY, J. D., and WOLFSBERG, M. (1970). *J. Chem. Phys.* **53**, 2967.

KRENOS, J., PRESTON, R., and WOLFGANG, R. (1971). *Chem. Phys. Lett.* **10**, 17.

LANDAU, L. (1932a). *Phys. Z. Sow.* **1**, 88.

LANDAU, L. (1932b). *Phys. Z. Sow.* **2**, 46.

LANDAU, L., and TELLER, E. (1936). *Phys. Z. Sow.* **10**, 34.

LANDAU, L. D., and LIFSHITZ, E. M. (1958). "Mekhanika." Fizmatgiz, Moscow.

LANDAU, L. D., and LIFSHITZ, E. M. (1963). "Kvantovaya mekhanika." Fizmatgiz, Moscow.

LOWLEY, K. P., and ROSS, J. (1965). *J. Chem. Phys.* **43**, 2930.

MAHAN, B. H. (1967). *J. Chem. Phys.* **48**, 98.

MAHAN, B. H. (1970). *J. Chem. Phys.* **52**, 5221.

MILLER, W. H. (1970). *J. Chem. Phys.* **53**, 3578.

MILLER, W. H. (1971). *Accounts Chem. Res.* **4**, 161.

MOORE, C. B. (1965). *J. Chem. Phys.* **43**, 2979.

MORSE, R. I., and LaBRECQUE, R. J. (1971). *J. Chem. Phys.* **55**, 1522.

NIKITIN, E. E. (1967). *In* "Fast Reactions and Primary Processes in Chemical Kinetics" (S. Glaesson, ed.), p. 165. Almqvist and Wiksell, Stockholm.

NIKITIN, E. E. (1968). *In* "Chemische Elementarprozesse," p. 43. Springer-Verlag, Berlin and New York.

NIKITIN, E. E. (1970a). *Advan. in Quant. Chem.* **5**, 135.

NIKITIN, E. E. (1970b). "Teoriya Elementarnykh Atomno-molekularnykh Protsessov v Gasakh." Khimiya, Moscow.

NIKITIN, E. E., and UMANSKI, S. YA. (1971). *Dokl. Akad. Nauk SSSR* **196**, 145.

RAPP, D., and KASSAL, T. (1969). *Chem. Rev.* **69**, 61.

ROBERTS, C. S. (1963). *Phys. Rev.* **131**, 209.

SECREST, D., and JOHNSON, B. R. (1966). *J. Chem. Phys.* **45**, 4556.

SECREST, D. (1969). *J. Chem. Phys.* **51**, 421.

SHIN, H. K. (1971). *Chem. Phys. Lett.* **10**, 81.

SMITH, F. T. (1959). *J. Chem. Phys.* **31**, 1352.

STEVENS, B. (1967). "Collisional Activation in Gases." Pergamon, Oxford.

STUPOCHENKO, E. V., LOSEV, S. A., and OSIPOV, A. I. (1965). "Relaksatzionnyye protzessy v udarnykh volnakh." Nauka, Moscow.

TAKAYANAGI, K. (1965). *Advan. At. Mol. Phys.* **1**, 149.

TULLY, J. C., and PRESTON, R. K. (1971). *J. Chem. Phys.* **55**, 562.

WARTELL, M. A., and CROSS, R. J. (1971). *J. Chem. Phys.* **55**, 4983.

WONG, W. H., and MARCUS, R. A. (1971). *J. Chem. Phys.* **55**, 5663.

YARDLEY, J. T., and MOORE, C. B. (1968). *J. Chem. Phys.* **49**, 1111.

YARDLEY, J. T., FERTIG, M. N., and MOORE, C. B. (1970). *J. Chem. Phys.* **52**, 1450.

ZENER, C. (1932). *Proc. Roy. Soc. (London).* **A137**, 696.

Chapter 5

# Molecular Beam Scattering Experiments on Elastic, Inelastic, and Reactive Collisions

J. PETER TOENNIES

# I. Introduction

Molecular beam scattering experiments provide the most direct method for studying the intermolecular potentials between those molecular systems that do not form a stable compound under ordinary conditions. For studying the intramolecular potentials of stable system the relatively new method of beam scattering cannot yet compete with optical spectroscopy which, however, provides to a large extent only information on the attractive portion of the potential. The beam scattering method is, in principle, more universal than spectroscopy and covers the entire energy range.

Intermolecular potentials are of fundamental importance for an understanding of many of the macroscopic properties of matter. For instance, the potential is at the basis of all theories on the equation of state of gases, liquids, and solids. Furthermore, the two-body potential is the starting point for the theoretical description of all gas-kinetic processes. Thus once the potential curves (or hypersurfaces) are available, nonequilibrium statistical mechanics (Boltzmann equation), or in many cases the simpler equilibrium statistical mechanics can be used to calculate the transport coefficients (diffusion, viscosity, and heat conductivity), or when molecules are involved, relaxation times for rotational and vibrational degrees of freedom. Moreover, with further improvements in scattering theory it will soon be possible to start from a given potential hypersurface and calculate chemical reaction rates.

In the past, information on the intermolecular potential has been obtained from measurements of these and other macroscopic properties. These experimental methods have the principal disadvantage that since the observed values are averages over the behavior of many molecular interactions the data are frequently not sensitive to important details of the potential.

Quantum chemical theory provides another method for obtaining information on intermolecular potentials. Although quite successful in describing accurately the bond energies of simple stable diatomic systems and in a more approximate way the bonding in larger systems, quantum chemical calculations have only recently been able to predict the weak van der Waal's attraction for the simple system He–He. Such methods are still far too time consuming to calculate accurate potential hypersurfaces for even the simplest *open shell* atom-molecule system (e.g., $H$–$H_2$). At the present time good potential hypersurfaces covering a large range of internuclear distances exist for the nonreactive *closed shell* atom–molecule systems He–$H_2$ and $Li^+$–$H_2$. With only a few exceptions no reliable surfaces are available for systems with more electrons.

The significance of the molecular beam scattering experiments lies in the fact that in these experiments single collisions between species with defined velocities and in some cases in specified quantum states can be directly investigated. This was already realized in the early 1920's (see, e.g., Stern, 1926) when the techniques used in modern day experiments were first introduced. The fact that most of the important developments have occurred in the last 10 to 15 years is probably most largely due to the introduction of high speed computers which has made possible the lengthy calculations of quantum mechanical cross sections. Thus it is now possible to evaluate the scattering cross sections in terms of intermolecular potentials by a trial and error method in which the cross sections are calculated over and over using different models until a good fit has been achieved.

Figure 1 shows the important position of molecular beam experiments among the various methods used in studying nonequilibrium kinetic gas processes. In the theoretical flow diagram shown on the left the arrows indicate the "direction" in which the calculations can be performed. A reversal of the individual theoretical steps is usually mathematically extremely difficult and is referred to as inversion. As indicated in the diagram the only step that can be effectively inverted at the present time is the one leading from the potential to the differential cross section. In the case of elastic collisions of heavy atomic partners it is possible to obtain the potential curves directly from the scattering measurements (direct inversion of scattering data) without recourse to the trial and error method mentioned above. Thus the beam method provides the most direct "route" to the intermolecular potential.

The article starts with a brief review of basic scattering laws and the experimental techniques used in the experiments. Elastic scattering experiments on atom–atom systems, which provide very detailed information on the range dependence of the spherical symmetric potential, are then discussed in considerable detail. In this field the techniques are so well developed that the scattering experiment has become almost a routine measurement. Rotationally and vibrationally inelastic collisions, which provide information on the potential hypersurface, are discussed next. Finally, the results of reactive scattering experiments are surveyed. These experiments have provided deep insight into the dynamics of reactive collisions. Rough features of the potential hypersurface can be

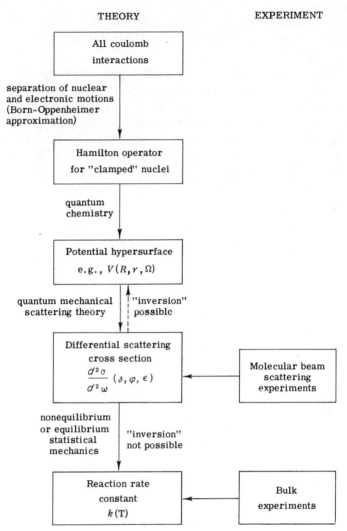

THEORY                                    EXPERIMENT

All coulomb
interactions

separation of nuclear
and electronic motions
(Born-Oppenheimer
approximation)

Hamilton operator
for "clamped" nuclei

quantum
chemistry

Potential hypersurface
e.g., $V(R, \gamma, \Omega)$

quantum mechanical        "inversion"
scattering theory          possible

Differential scattering
cross section
$$\frac{d^2\sigma}{d^2\omega} (\vartheta, \varphi, \epsilon)$$                    Molecular beam
                                          scattering
                                          experiments

nonequilibrium
or equilibrium
statistical          "inversion"
mechanics            not possible

Reaction rate
constant                                  Bulk
$k(T)$                                    experiments

FIG. 1.   Schematic flow diagram showing relationships between the various steps in gas kinetic theory and the contributions from experiments.

inferred from the dynamics, but at the present time the beam experiments do not yet provide enough information to obtain accurate values on potential parameters. Throughout the chapter the main emphasis will be on the scattering phenomena observed and the information that they provide on the intermolecular potential.

## II. Experimental Techniques Used in Molecular Beam
## Scattering Experiments

### A. Basic Beam Scattering Apparatus and Formula Used in Evaluating Experiments*

Figure 2 shows a schematic diagram of the typical experimental set up used in all molecular beam scattering experiments. Molecules or atoms leaving the two source chambers (commonly called ovens) designated in Fig. 2 by 1 and 2 are admitted into a highly evacuated ($p \simeq 10^{-6}$ Torr) experimental chamber. Since the mean free path at $10^{-6}$ Torr is of the order of 50 m and considerably larger than the dimensions of the apparatus, collisions of the admitted molecules with the rest gas are highly improbable. Under these conditions the molecules

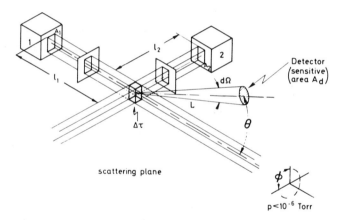

Fig. 2.   Schematic diagram showing the geometry of a typical crossed molecular beam apparatus.

form a molecular beam. Since the pressure in the beams is only $10^{-8}$ Torr or less collisions among beam molecules can also be neglected. Thus once they have left the source the beam molecules move along straight line trajectories without suffering a change in velocity or in internal states. For this reason stationary slits may be used to collimate the beams and "pulsed" slits as in a mechanical velocity selector may be used to select out a specific range of velocities.

* For a more detailed discussion see Pauly and Toennies (1965, 1968).

Collisions do occur in the intersection volume (see Fig. 2) and as a result of these collisions molecules are scattered in all directions. A detecting system having an entrance area $A_d$ (solid angle, $d\Omega = A_d/L^2$) at a distance $L$ from $\Delta\tau$ is used to measure the scattered intensity as a function of the angles $\theta$ and $\phi$. As will be discussed in more detail below the intensity distribution can be normalized to take account of the beam densities and geometry to obtain the *differential scattering cross section* $d^2\sigma(\vartheta, \varphi, g)/d^2\omega$ in the center-of-mass (c.m.) system in which the scattering angles corresponding to $\theta$, $\phi$, and $d^2\Omega$ are $\vartheta$, $\varphi$, and $d^2\omega$, and $g$ is the relative velocity ($\mathbf{g} = \mathbf{v}_1 - \mathbf{v}_2$). The differential cross section is proportional to the probability that in a collision of two particles with relative velocities $g$ one of them is scattered in the solid angle $d^2\omega$ at angles $\vartheta$, $\varphi$ with respect to its initial direction. The other important quantity which can be measured in a beam scattering apparatus is the *integral cross section* $\sigma(\theta_a, g)$, which is measured by placing the detector in the direction of one of the beams, corresponding to $\theta = 0$ and observing the attenuation of beam 1 by the collisions with beam 2. $\sigma(\theta_a, g)$ is the analogous quantity to an absorption coefficient in optical spectroscopy. $\sigma(\theta_a, g)$ is related to $d^2\sigma/d^2\omega$ by

$$\sigma(\theta_a, g) = \int_{\theta_a(\theta_a)}^{\pi} \int_{\varphi=0}^{2\pi} \frac{d^2\sigma(\vartheta, \varphi, g)}{d^2\omega} \sin\vartheta \, d\vartheta \, d\varphi,$$

where $\theta_a$ is the acceptance angle of the detector ($\theta_a^2 \simeq A_d/\pi L^2$) in the laboratory system.*

The formulas needed to interpret measurements of beam intensities are summarized in Table I. Expressions are given for the beam intensities (flux on to the detector area in particles/sec) expected when working with a simple molecular flow effusion source and with beams of specified velocities in a range between $v$ and $v + \Delta v$. The first two formulas for the beam intensities expected in the primary and secondary beams when no scattering can occur, show that all beam paths should be as short as possible.

---

* The definition of the integral cross section given here applies to the experimentally observed quantity. The integral cross section as formally defined in Eq. (3.21) is not a function of $\theta_a$. For a laboratory angular resolution $\theta_a < \theta_0$, where $\theta_0$ is given by the uncertainty principle [see Eq. (3.5)] the two are related by

$$\lim_{\theta_a \to 0} \sigma(\theta_a, g) = \sigma(g).$$

For $\theta_a > \theta_0$ the integral cross section is referred to as the incomplete cross section. It is an explicit function of $\theta_a$ as given by formula I in Table V.

TABLE I

OPERATIONAL FORMULAS[a]

| Detector position | Beams on | Formula for beam intensities measured at the detector[b] | |
|---|---|---|---|
| $\theta = 0°,\ \phi = 0°$ | 1 (2 off) | $I_{1_0} = N_1(v_1)A_1v_1\,\dfrac{A_d}{(L+l_1)^2}$ | (I) |
| $\theta = 90°,\ \phi = 0°$ | 2 (1 off) | $I_{2_0} = N_2(v_2)A_2v_2\,\dfrac{A_d}{(L+l_2)^2}$ | (II) |
| $\theta, \phi$ | 1 and 2 | $I_{1_0} = n_1(v_1)n_2(v_2)\,\lvert\,\mathbf{g}\,\rvert\,\Delta\tau\,\dfrac{d^2\sigma}{d^2\Omega}\,(\theta,\phi,v_1,v_2)\,\dfrac{A_d}{L^2}$ | (III) |
| $\theta = 0°,\ \phi = 0°$ | 1 and 2 | $I_1 = I_{1_0}\exp\{-\sigma(\theta_a,g)n_2(v_2)\,\Delta l\}$ | (IV) |

[a] Operational formulas relating measured beam intensities ($I$ in particles/sec) with and without scattering to the experimental geometry, beam densities, and cross sections. Idealized conditions of narrowly collimated primary (1) and secondary (2) beams of sharp velocities $v_1$ and $v_2$ ($\pm\frac{1}{2}\Delta v$) obeying Knudsen flow, an ideal detector and no scattering outside the scattering volume are assumed. The geometry is shown in Fig. 2.

[b] Definitions:

$N_1(v_1)$ = density of particles (particles/cm³) with velocity between $v_1$ and $v_1 + \Delta v$ in the beam source;

$A_1$ = beam source area;

$A_d$ = detector area (e.g., $A_{\text{det}}/L^2 \simeq d^2\Omega$);

$I$ = scattered beam intensity at angle $\theta, \phi$;

$n_1(v_1)$ = density of particles (particles/cm³) with velocity between $v_1$ and $v_1 + \Delta v_1$ in the scattering volume $\Delta\tau$. Note that $n_1(v_1) = N_1(v_1)/l_1^2$;

$\Delta l$ = beam path in beam 2 ($\Delta l \simeq \Delta\tau/A_1$, where $A_1$ is the area of beam 1 in the scattering region).

The third and fourth formulas are used in deriving cross sections from measurements of beam intensities. The evaluation of differential cross sections is based on the third formula which follows directly from simple kinetic gas theory, if only single collisions are assumed (neglecting successive collisions) to occur in the scattering volume. The differential cross section is of course measured in the laboratory system as a function of $\theta$ and $\phi$ and velocities $v_1$ and $v_2$. Unfortunately, these measured cross sections depend on the angles between $\mathbf{v}_1$ and $\mathbf{v}_2$ and on changes in the ratios ($\lvert\,\mathbf{v}_1\,\rvert/\lvert\,\mathbf{v}_2\,\rvert$), whereas the collision dynamics depend only on the relative velocity $g$. To eliminate this redundant information and to facilitate a comparison with scattering theory, which predicts cross sections in the center-of-mass system, it is customary to transform the measured results to the center-of-mass system. The techniques used in the transformation are discussed in the next section where it is shown that there exists a unique relationship between the angles $\vartheta, \varphi$ and $\theta, \phi$ and the corresponding solid angle elements $d^2\omega$ and $d^2\Omega$ if the velocities of the scattered particles are measured. Thus at least in principle there is no difficulty in relating the measured differential cross sections to the desired center-of-mass differential cross sections. In practice because of the velocity and angular spreads in the two beams, Eq. (III) (Table I) has to be averaged over the velocity and angular smearing and for this reason a trial and error method starting with an assumed differential cross section is usually found to be most expedient.

Equation (III) (Table I) is perfectly general and can be used for determining elastic, inelastic, and reactive cross sections provided that the apparatus is capable of distinguishing between these various types of collisions. Table II summarizes the different processes possible in an atom–molecule collision and how they' may be individually studied.

The fourth equation is just Beer's law applied to a beam experiment. This formula simply implies that the total loss of particles, due to differential scattering in all directions, leads to an attenuation of the beam. The beam attenuation is dependent on the product of the integral cross section, the target gas density $n_2$, and the beam path $\Delta l$ through the target gas.

## B. The Transformation, Center-of-Mass to Laboratory System

Let $R_1$ and $R_2$ denote the laboratory coordinates of particles 1 and 2.* Furthermore let $\mathbf{r} = \mathbf{R}_1 - \mathbf{R}_2$ denote the vector connecting the two particles and $R_{\text{c.m.}}$ the location of the center of mass. The particle coordinates $r_1$ and $r_2$ with respect to the center of mass are simply given by

$$\mathbf{r}_1 = \frac{m_2}{M}\,\mathbf{r}, \qquad \mathbf{r}_2 = -\frac{m_1}{M}\,\mathbf{r}, \tag{2.1}$$

where $M = m_1 + m_2$. Vector addition yields

$$\mathbf{R}_1 = \mathbf{R}_{\text{c.m.}} + \mathbf{r}_1, \qquad \mathbf{R}_2 = \mathbf{R}_{\text{c.m.}} + \mathbf{r}_2. \tag{2.2}$$

---

* Coordinates and velocities in upper case letters refer to the laboratory system and in lower case letters to the center-of-mass system.

TABLE II

Various Atom–Molecule Collision Processes and Observables Which Must Be
Specified to Make Their Identification Possible

| Collision process | Observables to be specified | Center-of-mass cross section designation |
|---|---|---|
| (a) elastic scattering $A+BC(i) \rightarrow A+BC(i)^a$ | change in direction of $\mathbf{v}_A$ or $\mathbf{v}_{BCj}$, e.g., scattering angles $\theta$ and $\phi$ | $\dfrac{d^2\sigma_{el}}{d^2\omega}(\vartheta, \varphi, g)$ |
| (b) inelastic scattering $A+BC(i) \rightarrow A+BC(f)$ | change in direction of $\mathbf{v}_A$ or $\mathbf{v}_{BC}$ and either change in quantum state (e.g., $j$, $m$, or $n$) or change in velocity magnitude[b] | $\dfrac{d^2\sigma_{inel}^{(i)\rightarrow(f)}}{d^2\omega}(\vartheta, \varphi, g)$ |
| (c) reactive scattering without identification of final states $A+BC \rightarrow AB+C$ | change in identity, e.g., AB in place of A and BC[c] | $\dfrac{d^2\sigma_{react}}{d^2\omega}(\vartheta, \varphi, g)$ |
| (d) reactive scattering with identification of final states $A+BC(i) \rightarrow AB(f)+C$ | change in identity and change in quantum state or change in velocity | $\dfrac{d^2\sigma_{react}^{(i)\rightarrow(f)}}{d^2\omega}(\vartheta, \varphi, g)$ or $\dfrac{d^2\sigma_{react}}{d^2\omega\, du}(\vartheta, \varphi, g, u)^d$ |

[a] $(i)$ and $(f)$ refer to the rotational $(j, m)$ and vibrational $(n)$ quantum states.

[b] A velocity change yields almost the same information as changes in quantum states by conservation of energy.

[c] In this case the cross section is the integral over final states and velocities. In actual practice it is necessary to know the laboratory velocity distribution of the products in order to transform the results into the center-of-mass system.

[d] $u$ is the velocity of one of the products in the center-of-mass system. If $d^3\sigma/d^2\omega\, du$ is measured, Eq. (III) (Table I) must be modified.

Time differentiation of Eq. (2.2) yields then the basic velocity transformation equations:

$$\mathbf{V}_1 = \mathbf{C} + \mathbf{u}_1, \qquad \mathbf{V}_2 = \mathbf{C} + \mathbf{u}_2, \qquad (2.3)$$

where $\mathbf{u}_1$ and $\mathbf{u}_2$ are the velocities with which the particles approach the center of mass and $\mathbf{C}$ is the laboratory velocity of the center of mass.

Since only forces between the particles need be considered, $C$ is a collisional invariant. Finally, differentiation of Eq. (2.1) yields

$$\mathbf{u}_1 = \frac{m_2}{M}\,\mathbf{g}, \qquad \mathbf{u}_2 = -\frac{m_1}{M}\,\mathbf{g}. \tag{2.4}$$

From these last equations it follows that the total linear momentum $(m_1\mathbf{u}_1 + m_2\mathbf{u}_2)$ in the center-of-mass system is zero.

Conservation of energy in the center-of-mass system requires for an elastic collision that the relative energy $E_{\rm rel} = E_{\rm c.m.} = \frac{1}{2}\mu g^2$ remains unchanged or that $|\,\mathbf{g}_f\,| = |\,\mathbf{g}_i\,|$. For a reaction of the type $A + BC(i) \rightarrow AB(f) + C$ conservation of energy requires

$$\tfrac{1}{2}\mu_i g_i^2 + E_{\rm int(i)} + \Delta D_0 = \tfrac{1}{2}\mu_f g_f^2 + E_{\rm int(f)}, \tag{2.5}$$

where the indices $i$ and $f$ refer to the velocities and reduced masses $(1/\mu_i = 1/m_A + 1/m_{\rm BC};\ 1/\mu_f = 1/m_{\rm AB} + 1/m_C)$ before and after collision, respectively. For electronic ground state molecules $E_{\rm int}$ is the sum of the rotational and vibrational energies and $\Delta D_0$ is the difference in the dissociation energies of the molecules AB and BC (positive for exothermic reactions). For an inelastic nonreactive collisions $\Delta D_0 = 0$ and $\mu_i = \mu_f$.

The Eqs. (2.3)–(2.5) are sufficient for constructing simple velocity diagrams for illustrating the relationships between the velocities and angles in the center-of-mass and laboratory coordinates. Figure 3a shows such a diagram without scattering while Fig. 3b shows a diagram with an example of a construction of the velocities and vectors after an elastic collision.

Although the diagram in Fig. 3a is two dimensional, the plane being defined by the incident velocities, the diagram at the right is three dimensional since all scattering directions $\vartheta, \varphi$ are possible after a collision. Diagrams of the type shown in Fig. 3b are especially useful for describing the results of inelastic and reactive scattering experiments. They are usually referred to as Newton diagrams or occasionally because of their three-dimensional nature as "onion-shell" diagrams.

The diagrams in Fig. 3 illustrate the transformation of velocities and angles. In transforming differential cross sections two cases are distinguished: (1) discrete final velocities (e.g., as in elastic scattering or in the excitation of rotational and vibrational degrees of freedom by observing changes in velocities) and (2) continuous final velocities (e.g., as in reactive scattering; see Table II). The observed laboratory differential cross section $d^3\sigma/d^2\Omega\, dV$ [case (2) above] is related to the center-

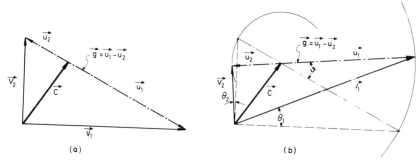

FIG. 3. Newton velocity diagrams for relating velocities in the laboratory (—) and center-of-mass (–·–·–) systems. In (a) the transformation of the laboratory velocities $\mathbf{V}_1$ and $\mathbf{V}_2$ before scattering into a collisional invariant center-of-mass velocity $\mathbf{C}$ and velocities $\mathbf{u}_1$ and $\mathbf{u}_2$ in the center of mass is shown. In (b) the new center-of-mass velocities resulting from elastic scattering ($\vartheta, \varphi$ in the plane) and the resulting new laboratory velocities $V_1$ and $V_2$ are shown. The indices $i$ and $f$ for initial and final state, respectively, have been omitted. Similar diagrams may be drawn for inelastic and reactive scattering. In this case the relative velocity $g$ and the reduced mass after scattering may be changed. (Letters with overhead arrows in figures are equivalent to boldface letters in text.)

of-mass differential cross section $d^3\sigma/d^2\omega\,du$ by

$$\frac{d^3\sigma}{d^2\Omega\,dV} = J(\text{c.m.} \to \text{lab})\,\frac{d^3\sigma}{d^2\omega\,du}, \qquad (2.6)$$

where the Jacobian $J$ is a function of the angles and of velocities in both systems (Helbing, 1968; Warnock and Bernstein, 1968a).

In case (1) the differential cross section is independent of $V$ or $u$, and $J$ is simply equal to $d^2\omega/d^2\Omega$, which follows directly from Eq. (2.6) since the probability of scattering expressed by $d^2\sigma$ is the same in both systems. An expression for $J$ can be obtained by noting that $d^2\omega = da/u_f^2$, where $da$ is a surface area segment on a sphere similar to the one illustrated in Fig. 3b and $\mathbf{u}_f$ is the velocity of the observed particle after scattering in the center-of-mass system. The solid angle in the laboratory system corresponding to $da$ is given by

$$d^2\Omega = \frac{\cos(\mathbf{u}_f, \mathbf{V}_f)}{|\mathbf{V}_f|^2}\,da.$$

Thus

$$J = \frac{d^2\omega}{d^2\Omega} = \frac{V_f^2}{u_f^2\cos(\mathbf{u}_f, \mathbf{V}_f)}. \qquad (2.7)$$

In case (2), the spread in velocities is accounted for by replacing $da$ by a volume element $d\tau$ in velocity space. Since the particles must be conserved in both velocity coordinate systems, it follows that

$$d\tau_{\text{c.m.}} = u_f^2 \, du_f \, d^2\omega = d\tau_{\text{lab}} = V_f^2 \, dV_f \, d^2\Omega.$$

Thus

$$J = \frac{d^2\omega \, du_f}{d^2\Omega \, dV_f} = \frac{V_f^2}{u_f^2}. \tag{2.8}$$

## C. Experimental Techniques

Although the crossed beam method appears simple, in concept the extremely small scattered beam intensities (less than $10^{-12}$ A, which corresponds to less than $10^7$ particles/sec) require a considerable amount of technical refinement. Thus extreme care must be taken in designing an apparatus, especially if very narrow velocity or angular distributions and quantum state selection are desired. Since the source intensities at the desired beam energies and selector transmission properties directly determine the scattered beam intensities and the sensitivity of a given experiment, these technical properties are briefly discussed below. For more details, the reader is referred to several recent reviews (Pauly and Toennies, 1965, 1968; Anderson et al., 1965; Toennies, 1968a).

### 1. Beam Sources

The commonly used method for producing a molecular beam is to allow the beam molecules to effuse through a small thin-walled orifice of an otherwise closed container. Beams of condensable substances are usually produced by heating the container, whence the name oven. If operated at pressures at which the mean free path $\Lambda$ in the oven is greater than the orifice diameter $d$ or slit width the velocity distribution is essentially Maxwellian. The curves for $M = 0$ in Fig. 4 illustrate the velocity and angular distributions of such a source.

Typical intensities which can be achieved with such a source are on the order of $5 \cdot 10^{16}$ [molecules/sr sec]. For a beam with a velocity of $5 \cdot 10^4$ cm/sec this corresponds to a particle density of $10^{10}$ [molecules/cm$^3$] at a distance of 10 cm from the source.

This source has the advantage that it can be adapted for use with any substance and that its behavior is easily predictable. For example, beams of atoms can be produced in discharges or by thermal dissociation. Even

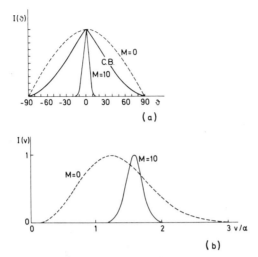

FIG. 4. Comparison of the properties of a molecular beam and a hydrodynamic beam source. (a) Angular distributions for an oven ($M = 0$), nozzle ($M = 10$), and channel beam (CB). $M$ is the flow mach number. (b) Velocity distributions for an oven and a nozzle beam. The curves are normalized to the same maximum intensity.

fairly pure hydrogen atom beams ($>85\%$ depending on the pressure) have been produced by heating a tungsten oven to over $2500°K$. Recently alkyl radical beams have been produced in a modified oven by pyrolysis of metal alkyls (Kalos and Grosser, 1969).

Narrow primary beams are usually required, especially when a velocity selector with a high velocity resolution is used. The requirements on the secondary beam are different. It should be arranged to make $\Delta\tau$, the scattering volume, as large as possible. High beam directivity then becomes important to reduce the amount of excess gas which has to be pumped out of the system and to assure that the beam intersection angle is as uniform as possible. An oven satisfying these requirements is made up of many parallel channels each with a length $l$ greater than the diameter $d$. When operated at pressures at which $\Lambda > l$ the directivity shown in Fig. 4a can be achieved.

The intensity of a simple effusive source can be increased by several orders of magnitude if the source pressure is increased beyond that required by the condition $\Lambda < d$. Under these conditions a supersonic nozzle beam is produced. To accommodate the greatly increased gas flows, large diffusion pumps ($\gtrsim6000$ liters/sec) and at least two pumping stages are required. In order to remove as much of the unused gas as possible and to keep the beam path in the region of high gas pressure as

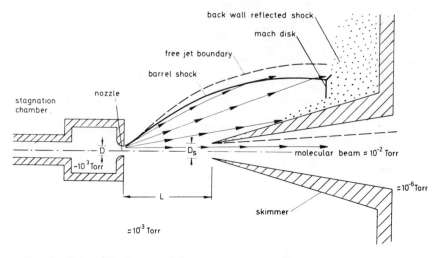

FIG. 5. Schematic diagram of the geometry of a modern nozzle beam source. The relative dimensions, geometry, and pressures are characteristic of a typical nozzle beam source. The heavy solid lines represent the approximate location of shock waves, which at the low prevailing pressures are much more diffuse than indicated by the lines.

short as possible, a specially designed skimmer shown in Fig. 5 is used between the first two pumping stages (Bossel *et al.*, 1969).

The properties of such nozzle beams can be easily understood in terms of conservation of enthalpy (Ashkenas and Sherman, 1966). Since at the high densities the molecules in the flow are in constant collisional contact, the increase in directed translational energy is drawn from the random thermal motion and the internal degrees of freedom. The beam energy $E$ can be estimated by assuming that the total enthalpy is converted into directed translational motion. Thus $E = C_p T_0$, where $C_p$ is the heat capacity and $T_0$ the source temperature. The translational temperature in the expanded gas and to a lesser extent the temperature of the internal degrees of freedom can be reduced to about 1% of the source temperature resulting in greatly narrowed velocity and angular distributions (see Fig. 4). This, together with the higher gas densities, accounts for beam intensities increased by more than a factor of 100. For many experiments additional state and velocity selection may not be needed, resulting in a further intensity gain over the conventional source used together with selectors.

The beam energy in a nozzle source can be varied in the following two ways: By simply changing the source temperature the beam energy can be changed proportionally without changing the relative velocity spread $\Delta v/v$. The second method involves the use of a mixture of a heavy and a light molecular weight gas. At the high beam densities, easily achieved with a nozzle beam apparatus, the velocities of both components will be the same but because of the different molecular weights the beam energies of the two components will be quite different. For such a so-called seeded beam the energy of one component $i$ is given simply by

$$E_i = (m_i/\bar{m})\bar{C}_p T_0,\qquad(2.9)$$

where $\bar{m}$ $(= \sum X_i m_i)$ is the average molecular weight ($X_i$ is the mole fraction) and $\bar{C}_p$ $(= \sum_i X_i C_{pi})$ is the average molar heat capacity. Thus depending on whether an excess (typically 90%) of a heavier or a lighter component is added, the solute beam energy is greatly decreased or increased respectively. By a combination of heating and seeding, the energy range of nozzle beams has been varied between $4 \cdot 10^{-3}$ eV to 5 eV (Subbarao and Miller, 1969; Anderson, 1967a,b).

At the present time the nozzle source appears to be by far the best molecular beam source for scattering experiments in the thermal energy range. By using an air heated seeded beam nozzle energies as high as 21 eV have been achieved (Young and Kunth, 1969). Special beam sources based on ion neutralization, sputtering, and other techniques have also been developed (Fenn, 1967).

## 2. Velocity Selectors

Velocity selectors are used to pick out a narrow band of velocities from the Maxwell–Boltzmann distribution of an effusive source or occasionally with nozzle beams to produce even narrower distributions. They are also employed to measure the velocity distributions of inelastically or reactively scattered atoms and molecules.

The most common velocity selector is the mechanical velocity selector similar to the one first used by Fizeau (see for example Fig. 6). The selector consists of a series of staggered toothed disks. The beam is chopped by the first disk. Those particles that traverse the distance to the following disks such that they arrive in time to pass through each of the following disks are transmitted. The disks can be arranged in such a way that virtually all molecules of undesired velocities can be removed from the beam.

The slit width is usually equal to the tooth width so that 50% of the molecules with the desired velocity are transmitted ($T = 50\%$). The

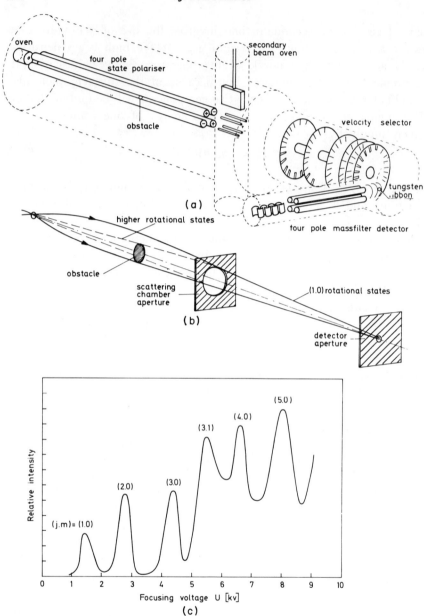

FIG. 6.   Molecular beam trajectories and apparatus used for performing experiments with state selected and oriented molecular beams. (a) The apparatus in a perspective view (the overall length of the four pole field is 1 meter). (b) The beam trajectories of a beam of state selected molecules obtained with an applied voltage on the four pole field. (c) The detector current as a function of the focusing voltage measured for CsF at $v_1 = 673$ m/sec.

transmission, velocity resolving power $A$ [given by $v_0/\Delta v_{1/2}$, where $\Delta v_{1/2}$ is the velocity spread at half of the maximum intensity (FWHM)], and the maximum velocity $v_{max}$ that can be selected, are related to the mechanical properties by the simple formula

$$TAv_{max} = ZLf_{max},$$

where $Z$ is the number of slits on the circumference of the rotor ($Z \gtrsim 2000$ for a 20-cm-diam disk), $L$ is the length of the rotor (typically $L \sim 5$–$10$ cm since for scattering experiments $L$ should be as short as possible), and finally $f_{max}$ is the maximum frequency of rotation (limited by the strength of the disk material to about 500–800 Hz depending on the disk diameter). With a velocity resolving power of $A \simeq 20$ the intensity of an effusive source beam is reduced by a factor $5 \cdot 10^{-2}$ at the most probable velocity. Velocities as high as 24,000 m/sec ($A \simeq 4$) corresponding to 3 eV $H_2$ molecules or 140 eV potassium atoms can be selected.

Velocity selection can also be achieved by a time-of-flight technique. The beam is usually pulsed mechanically and the distribution of arrival times at the detector is measured. The low response time ($\simeq 10^{-3}$ sec) of most neutral beam detectors can be a problem in applying this technique. On the other hand it offers the important advantage over the Fizeau selector that the entire velocity distribution is sampled by each pulse and a correction for apparatus drift is not needed. By using a sophisticated chopper design and electronic deconvolution techniques a much higher overall transmission can be achieved (Sköld, 1968). Time-of-flight measurements may also be made by using a pulsed electron beam to produce metastable atoms or molecules which can be much more easily detected than those in the ground state (French and Locke, 1967).

### 3. Quantum State Selectors

The selection and analysis of beam molecules according to their internal rotational and/or vibrational states is one of the most formidable experimental problems in molecular beam scattering experiments. Identification of the quantum states by absorption spectroscopy is not feasible because of the low beam densities. This applies to a lesser degree to emission spectroscopy, which has been used with some success as discussed in Section V,C,4. Another related technique, electron bombardment induced emission has been used to study internal states in nozzle beams (Scott and Mincer, 1969) but the interpretation of the results in terms of the ground state internal state distributions for most molecules is problematic.

The most successful techniques rely on the direct interaction of induced or permanent electric dipole moments (the magnetic interactions of most molecules are too small to be easily utilized) of the beam atoms or molecules with inhomogeneous electric fields (e.g., Stern–Gerlach experiment). In this way it can be arranged that only molecules in the desired quantum states pass through the fields, whereas molecules in other quantum states are deflected out of the beams.

Figure 6 shows an apparatus utilizing electrostatic quadrupole fields for focusing polar diatomic molecules (usually alkali halides) in low lying rotational states (Bennewitz et al., 1964). Molecules with small $j$ ($j$ is the rotational angular momentum quantum number) and $m = 0$ (e.g., $(j, m) = (1, 0)$, $(2, 0)$, and $(3, 0)$) leaving the source at small angles ($\lesssim 1°$) are deflected toward the axis and have sinusoidal paths in the quadrupole. Molecules in other states are either defocused or not deflected and cannot strike the detector. By varying the voltage successive rotational states are brought into focus on the detector. Because of the high acceptance of the focusing field, the intensity in one $(j, m)$ state with a relative population of $10^{-4}$ in the oven is about 10% of the total intensity measured without the quadrupole turned on. State and velocity selected beam intensities of $10^{-14}$ A have been achieved in this way. This technique has been successfully used to study rotational inelastic scattering (Section IV,C,1) and the rotational state distributions of molecules produced in a crossed beam chemical reaction (Section V,C,4).

Related focusing fields have been developed to focus $(0, 0)$, $(1, \pm 1)$, $(2, \pm 2)$ molecules (Waech et al., 1968). With an arrangement otherwise similar to Fig. 6 but employing electric six pole fields, it is possible to focus symmetric top molecules (Kramer and Bernstein, 1965; Brooks et al., 1969). In this case the focusing action depends only on the product $Km/j(j + 1)$ ($K$ is the projection of $j$ along the molecular symmetry axis) which is equal to the expectation value $\langle \cos \vartheta \rangle$, where $\vartheta$ is the angle between the field direction and the molecular axis. Thus the focusing action depends only on the orientation and not on the rotational states of the molecules. The focused symmetric top molecules when passed through a homogeneous field are oriented with their molecular axis lined up in the electric field. Reactive scattering experiments made on molecules oriented in this way are discussed in Section V,C,3.

Figure 7 shows an apparatus used to measure the vibrational state distribution of molecules in the $j = 1$ state (Bennewitz et al., 1971a;

Freund *et al.*, 1971). As in the apparatus shown in Fig. 6 molecules in the (1,0) state are deflected into a homogeneous field, where they interact with high frequency ($\sim$50 MHz) electromagnetic radiation. At resonance molecules undergo a change in their $m$ state ($m = 0 \to m = \pm 1$) and are defocused in the second half of the quadrupole. Thus at resonance a

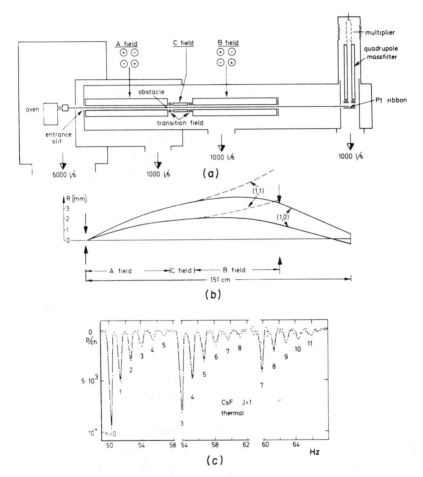

FIG. 7. Molecular beam trajectories and apparatus used for analyzing a beam for its vibrational state distribution. (a) The apparatus which contains two four-pole fields similar to those shown in Fig. 6. (b) Some typical trajectories in profile. When the resonance frequency is applied (1, 0) molecules (solid line) entering the $C$-field region are converted to (1, ±1) molecules which are defocused (dashed line) and cannot strike the detector. (c) The decrease in detector intensity as a function of the frequency for the individual vibrational states. The spectra are shown for three different accumulation times.

decrease in intensity proportional to the relative number of molecules affected by the radiation is observed. Since the resonance frequency depends on the vibrational state of the molecules, the vibrational state distribution shown for a thermal beam in Fig. 7c is measured. This technique has been used to study the vibrational excitation of reactively formed CsF molecules with vibrational quantum numbers $n = 0$ to $n = 8$ (see Section V,C,4).

### 4. *Beam Detectors*

The detection of molecular beams provides the most severe limitation on the types of experiments which can be successfully performed. The basic difficulty is that the particle density in the beam is of the same order of magnitude as that of the residual gas that, in a typical apparatus, is present at a pressure of $10^{-7}$ Torr. Although a large number of detection schemes have been proposed and tried, the most sensitive and universal methods involve conversion of the neutral beam atoms or molecules into ions that can then be measured as a current or counted individually.

To discriminate against the residual gas two schemes are used. In the first method, used with the Langmuir–Taylor detector, the atoms are permitted to strike a hot platinum or tungsten filament, both of which have a high work function. If the beam atoms striking the filament have an ionization potential lower than the work function, they are ionized by tunneling of the electron from the atom into the surface. The ions evaporate subsequently because of the high filament temperature. If equilibrium on the surface is assumed, the ionization efficiency can be calculated (Langmuir–Saha equation) and approaches 100% for most of the alkalis and molecules containing them. Since the residual gas molecules have much greater ionization potentials they are not ionized. This sensitive detector has made possible many of the scattering experiments discussed here. A similar technique involving a wire of low work function has been used (Persky *et al.*, 1968) to convert beams containing molecules with a high electron affinity into negative ions.

A special technique was required to facilitate the study of chemical reactions such as $M + X_2 \rightarrow MX + X$, where M and X are an alkali and a halogen atom, respectively, since the simple detector does not distinguish between products and reactants (one is and the other contains an alkali atom). The problem was solved by Taylor and Datz (1955) who discovered that, whereas alkali halide (MX) molecules and alkali (M) atoms are detected with nearly equal efficiency on tungsten filaments, only the alkali atoms are detected on platinum filaments. Thus the difference in ion currents ([MX + M] − M) coming from both wires alternately exposed at the scattering angle is a measure of the alkali halide intensity. More recent work indicates that selective detection can be attributed to contamination of the surface by carbon films (Holmlid, 1971) which can be achieved by heating the wires in a hydrocarbon atmosphere (Touw and Trischka, 1963).

Selective detection may also be achieved by passing the neutral molecular beam through an inhomogeneous magnetic (Stern–Gerlach) field prior to surface ionization (Parrish and Herm, 1971). The method relies on the fact that alkali atoms have magnetic moments and are, therefore, deflected, whereas the molecules which do not have magnetic moments are not deflected. This method is more reliable than selective ionization, which may give erroneous results because of filament contamination by the halogen reactants. A considerable loss in intensity has to be taken into account, however, since the product beam has to be narrowly collimated.

The detection of beams not containing an alkali is a much more difficult technical problem. In the most widely applicable method with the highest sensitivity the beam is ionized by electron bombardment; selection and discrimination are achieved by subsequent mass selection of the ion beam. Typically only one in a thousand beam atoms are ionized. Depending on the mass of the beam particle to be detected the background current from ionization of the residual gas may be a serious problem. For this reason ultrahigh vacuum techniques are used to produce overall pressures of $10^{-10}$ Torr and even smaller partial pressures at the beam mass in the detector chamber (Lee et al., 1970; Bickes and Bernstein, 1970). See Section V,B,1.

A further improvement in signal–to–noise ratio can be achieved with the modulated beams method. The method relies on the fact that the frequency spectrum of the noise in a typical apparatus is strongly peaked at low frequencies. By modulating the beam at high frequencies and amplifying the detector signal with a narrow band-pass amplifier a large part of the noise is filtered out. The ac signal is then rectified at the same frequency but with a phase shift corresponding to the beam transit time. An order of magnitude improvement in the signal–to–noise ratio is possible in this way. The remaining noise is usually determined by the statistical (random) fluctuations of the background. Despite the gain made possible by the modulated beam technique, the signal–to–noise ratio with a universal beam detector is many orders of magnitude worse than it is with a surface ionization detector.

A considerable improvement in the signal–to–noise ratio is always possible by increasing the overall measuring time. Generally, the gain is proportional to the square root of the measuring time. Such measurements are easily possible with counting techniques. Since a direct current signal can be converted to a frequency, long time measurements are possible even if a simple electrometer amplifier is used. In recent years small on-line computers have proved to be very useful in handling the large amounts of data collected in long time measurements.

## 5. *Some Typical Values Needed for Estimating Scattered Particle Intensities*

Below are summarized some typical values of quantities which are useful for estimating available product intensities. The values are rough lower estimates. The indicated beam densities can be exceeded in most cases by 1 or 2 orders of magnitude by using nozzle beams:

$n_1 \simeq 10^{10}$ [molecules/cm$^3$]     (for a molecular flow source),

$n_2 \simeq 10^{11}$ [molecules/cm$^3$]     (for a molecular flow source),

$g \simeq 5 \cdot 10^4$ cm/sec,

$\Delta\tau \simeq 4 \cdot 10^{-2}$ cm$^3$,

$d\Omega \simeq 2 \cdot 10^{-4} – 2 \cdot 10^{-5}$ sr.

The nonideality of the detectors and the velocity and state selectors leads to a loss in intensity. For a thermal beam the attenuation factors for some typical components are the following:

| | |
|---|---|
| Langmuir–Taylor detector | (0.1–1), |
| electron bombardment detector | ($10^{-2}$–$10^{-3}$), |
| velocity selector at most probable velocity | ($5 \cdot 10^{-2}$), |
| rotational state selector ($j = 1$) including focusing | ($10^{-3}$–$10^{-4}$). |

For a chemical reaction with $d^2\sigma_{\text{react}}/d^2\omega = 5$ Å$^2$/sr, and if an alkali halide product is formed in an experiment without state but with velocity selection the numbers above predict a signal intensity of $10^4$ mol/sec or $10^{-15}$ A. Signals down to $10^{-17}$ A corresponding to $10^2$ mol/sec with a background current several times this value can be detected using digital counting techniques and long integration times ($\sim\frac{1}{2}$ hour).

## III. Elastic Scattering Experiments

A. Introduction

Of the three types of scattering to be discussed (elastic, inelastic, and reactive) the experiments on elastic scattering are probably the least difficult to carry out and the simplest to interpret in terms of a potential. In the usual case of scattering of atoms in $^1S$ states the potential is spherically symmetric and depends only on the distance between the nuclei.

The field of atom–atom scattering has been extensively developed within the last few years and most of the important phenomena have been observed and understood. As a result of these advances elastic scattering has emerged as an almost routine laboratory tool (albeit a complicated one) for measuring potential curves. In the author's opinion this recent work has demonstrated that beam scattering experiments now provide the most accurate and most universal technique for studying the radial dependence of spherical symmetric potentials.

A typical intermolecular potential in the radial region most effective at thermal energies is shown in Fig. 8. Scattering experiments indicate that this potential shape is typical for collision partners of which at least one has a closed shell. For such systems the potential minima are located between 3.0 and 6.0 Å, while the depths lie between $1 \cdot 10^{-3}$ and $60 \cdot 10^{-3}$ eV. The attraction at long distances can be attributed to the long range Coulomb coupling between the electrons in the two systems (London dispersion forces). Thus the electron motions are "correlated" in such a way as to reduce the potential energy. Theoretical calculations predict for ground state atom–atom interactions an $R^{-6}$ behavior. The strong repulsion at short distances can be largely attributed to a repulsion of the electron clouds, due to the Pauli principle mutual exclusion of electrons, and to the electrostatic repulsion of the nuclei.

Although the origin of these effects is well understood the accurate quantum chemical calculation of potential curves and especially of the well location and depth is still not possible for most systems. Accurate calculations have only been carried out for a few simple systems such as H–H, H–He (Das and Wahl, 1971), Li–He (Das and Wahl, 1971), and He–He (Bertoncini and Wahl, 1970; Schaefer III et al., 1970). In view of these difficulties most of the theoretical understanding is based on approximate methods. At long ranges beyond the minimum ($R \gtrsim 2R_m$) reliable semiempirical methods are available for obtaining the constant $C$ in the expression $V(R) = -C/R^6$ (Langhoff and Karplus, 1970; Dal-

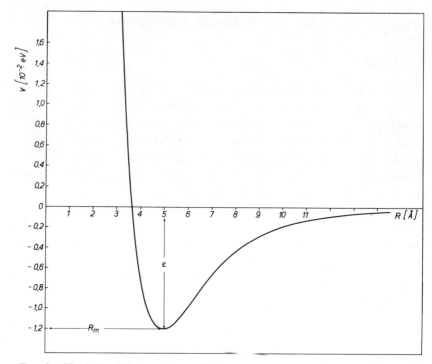

FIG. 8. Typical radial dependence of the atom-atom potential. The curve is based on the Lennard-Jones $(n, 6)$ model potential, shown in the insert, with $n = 8$. The parameter values correspond to the system Na–Xe, which has been carefully measured by the molecular beam method. $V(R) = 6\epsilon/(n - 6)[(R_m/R)^n - (n/6)(R_m/R)^6]$.

garno, 1967). Unfortunately, reliable methods are not available for estimating $\epsilon$ and $R_m$ (see Fig. 8). At very short ranges ($\sim$2 Å) the Thomas–Fermi–Dirac method has been shown to give reliable results (Abrahamson, 1969).

The interpretation of elastic scattering experiments in terms of the intermolecular potential has been carried out in two distinct ways. In the most common and general method some measured cross section property is compared with the results of exact quantum mechanical calculations based on an assumed potential model. The parameters in the potential model are varied until a best fit is achieved. Although somewhat time consuming the method is straightforward and gives results of sufficient accuracy for most purposes. For very accurate potential determination it suffers from the drawback that the parameters determined in this way are dependent on the potential model assumed at the outset. The other method, which has only recently been developed, involves a direct inversion of the scattering data to produce a model independent potential curve. This technique, discussed in Section III,E,1 and more extensively in the chapter by Pauly (see Volume VI,B), requires very accurate data and can only be applied to certain systems.

In this section the application of both methods will be discussed. After a brief survey of some potential models the classical and semi-classical theory of elastic scattering is reviewed. The advantage of the classical and semiclassical theories is that they provide a conceptual link between experimental observables and the collisional dynamics producing them. Then the various experimentally measured cross section features providing information on the long range attractive potential are discussed. Finally, cross section properties providing information on the short range repulsive potential are surveyed.

## B. Potential Models

Some commonly used potential models and the number of the parameters are in order of complexity:

(1)  the Lennard-Jones $(n, 6)$-potential (3 parameters);
(2)  the Slater and Buckingham potentials (3 parameters);
(3)  the Born–Mayer–Morse–Lennard-Jones potential (5 parameters);
(4)  a modified Lennard-Jones potential (5 parameters);
(5)  a two piece Lennard-Jones potential (5 parameters).

The formulas for theses potential models are listed in Table III. The special features of the various models and references to the literature are also given in the table. Figure 24 shows a comparison of attractive potentials of type (4) and (5) which have been fitted to cross section data for Na–Xe. Figure 28 shows a similar comparison of repulsive potentials of type (3) and (5) which have been fitted to experimental cross section data for He–$H_2$. The small spread in the best-fit potentials in both cases shows the accuracy of potential determination possible with these model potentials.

## C. Classical Scattering Theory*

Classical mechanics provides a reasonably good approximation for the dynamics of atomic collisions. The reason is that except for light atoms

---

* For a more extensive discussion of classical scattering theory see Hirschfelder et al. (1954), p. 43; Goldstein (1951), p. 58; Beck (1970).

TABLE III

| Designation | Potential formula | Meaning of potential parameters | Comments and special references |
|---|---|---|---|
| Lennard-Jones $(n, 6)$ potential (3 parameters) | $V(R) = \dfrac{6\epsilon}{n-6}\left[\left(\dfrac{R_m}{R}\right)^n - \dfrac{n}{6}\left(\dfrac{R_m}{R}\right)^6\right]$ | $\epsilon$   well depth <br> $R_m$   radius of well minimum <br><br> $n$   radial power of repulsive part | Most commonly used potential model <br> Easy to use in cross section calculations (Hirschfelder *et al.*, 1954; Pauly and Toennies, 1965) |
| Slater (3 parameters) | $V(R) = A\exp(-\alpha R) - \dfrac{C}{R^6}$ | $A$   potential at $R = 0$ ($C = 0$) <br> $\alpha$   Born–Mayer parameter <br> $C$   van der Waals constant | Provides more realistic description of repulsive region <br> Both models restricted to $R > 0$ since $V(R) = -\infty$ for $R = 0$ (Hirschfelder *et al.*, 1954; Pauly and Toennies, 1965) |
| Buckingham (3 parameters) | $V(R) = \dfrac{\epsilon}{1 - 6/\alpha'}\left[\dfrac{6}{\alpha'}\exp\left(\alpha'\left(1 - \dfrac{R}{R_m}\right)\right) - \left(\dfrac{R_m}{R}\right)^6\right]$ | $\alpha'$   Buckingham parameter $\alpha' = 13.772$ corresponds to a Lennard-Jones $(12,6)$ potential | |

| Potential | Equation | Parameters | Comments |
|---|---|---|---|
| Born–Mayer–Morse–Lennard-Jones (5 parameters) | $V(R) = A \exp(-\alpha R); \quad R < R_e$ <br> $\quad = 4B\left[\exp\left(2\gamma\left(1 - \frac{R}{R_0}\right)\right) - \exp\left(\gamma\left(1 - \frac{R}{R_0}\right)\right)\right];$ <br> $\quad R_e \leq R \leq R_0$ <br> $\quad = 4\epsilon\left[\left(\frac{R_0}{R}\right)^{12} - \left(\frac{R_0}{R}\right)^6\right]; \quad R_0 < R$ | $B$ equivalent well depth of the Morse part of the potential <br> $\gamma$ Morse exponent <br> $R_0$ point of zero potential <br> $R_e$ point at which Born–Mayer and Morse potential have same value and gradient | Provides more realistic description of intermediate region between $R_0$ and $R_e$ than Slater potential (Gengenbach et al., 1970) |
| Modified Lennard-Jones potential (5 parameters) | $\dfrac{V(\varrho)}{\epsilon} = V_0(\varrho) - \{V_0(\varrho) + 1\}\Gamma_1 \exp\left(-\left(\dfrac{\varrho - \varrho_1}{\gamma_1}\right)^2\right)$ | $V_0(\varrho)$ Lennard-Jones (12,6) potential <br> $\varrho$  $R/R_m$ <br> $\Gamma_1$ amplitude of additive Gauss modification <br> $\varrho_1$ location of modification <br> $\gamma_1$ width of modification | Lennard-Jones (12,6) potential can be modified at any arbitrary region without disturbing its asymptotic behavior <br> Usually $\varrho_1 = 1$ and modification is used to widen well (Düren et al., 1968) |
| Two piece Lennard-Jones potential (5 parameters) | $\dfrac{V(\varrho)}{\epsilon} = \dfrac{\varkappa_1}{n^2 - \varkappa_1}\left[\varrho^{-n} - \dfrac{n^2}{\varkappa_1}\varrho^{-\varkappa_1/n}\right], \quad \varrho \leq 1 \ (n^2 > \varkappa_1)$ <br> $\dfrac{V(\varrho)}{\epsilon} = \dfrac{36}{\varkappa_2 - 36}\left[\varrho^{-\varkappa_2/6} - \dfrac{\varkappa_2}{36}\varrho^{-6}\right], \quad \varrho \geq 1 \ (\varkappa_2 > 36)$ | $\varkappa_1$ curvature of potential at minimum for $\varrho \leq 1$ <br> $\varkappa_2$ curvature of potential at minimum for $\varrho \geq 1$ | The attractive and repulsive regions of the Lennard-Jones-type potentials are decoupled and asymmetric wells are possible (Buck and Pauly, 1968) |

(e.g., H and He) at low temperatures ($T < 300°K$), both the de Broglie wavelength and the quantum mechanical uncertainty in the position of the particle are small compared to the dimensions of the potential (Pauly and Toennies, 1965, p. 266).

Figure 9 shows the classical trajectories for particles interacting by way of a Lennard-Jones potential. The trajectories were calculated for an assumed stationary target shown in the left central portion of the diagram. The potential curve used in the calculations is shown (in profile) at the top of the diagram. As in the actual scattering the impact parameters $\beta$ [$\beta$ is the shortest distance of approach if there were no interaction potential (in reduced units; see Table IV) and is plotted at the left] are uniformly distributed. Only those trajectories in the plane of the drawing are shown. The polar plot at the right shows the differential cross section (weighted by $\sin \vartheta$ to reduce the forward scattering) as a function of angle. As is apparent from the figure the differential cross section is simply the normalized probability distribution function for scattering of particles with a homogeneous three-dimensional distribution of impact parameters.

From Fig. 9 it is further apparent that for a given relative translational energy, particles with small impact parameters are scattered into large

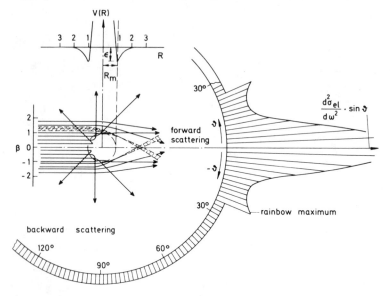

F$_{\text{IG}}$. 9.  Schematic diagram showing classical trajectories and the classical differential cross section for scattering from a Lennard-Jones potential. The potential is shown in profile at the top. The angular distribution is shown in a polar plot at the right.

angles. Since the effect of the attractive forces is felt as the particles move in and out of the potential they have little net effect on the scattering. With increasing impact parameter the angle of deflection decreases monotonically and for reduced impact parameter $\beta \simeq 1$ the repulsive and attractive forces just compensate each other and no net deflection is observed. This is called *glory scattering*. For still larger impact parameters, deflection angles to the opposite side are produced by the attractive forces. Then at a reduced impact parameter between 1 and 1.5 (depending on the energy) an interesting phenomenon is observed. For a small but finite range of impact parameters all the particles are scattered into one scattering angle. This "funneling" effect produces a large spike in the differential cross section, which is referred to as *rainbow scattering*. The angle at which the spike occurs is called the rainbow angle $\vartheta_R$. At larger impact parameters the particles no longer "feel" the repulsive forces and are deflected towards the scattering center by the long range attractive forces. At very large impact parameters the attraction diminishes rapidly until a deflection is no longer observed.

Thus on the basis of the classical model the differential cross sections at the different angular regions can be expected to provide information on the following potential regions:

(1)  small angle region $\vartheta < \vartheta_R$: mostly attractive potential;
(2)  intermediate angle region $\vartheta \sim \vartheta_R$: attractive and repulsive potential;
(3)  large angle region $\vartheta > \vartheta_R$: repulsive potential.

Of course in a scattering experiment the trajectories are not observed directly but only the differential cross section. To obtain the differential cross section the following expression relating scattering angles to the initial impact parameter is required:

$$\vartheta(K, \beta) = \pi - 2\beta \int_{\varrho_{min}}^{\infty} \frac{d\varrho}{\varrho^2 [1 - u(\varrho)/K - \beta^2/\varrho^2]^{1/2}}. \qquad (3.1)$$

The reduced parameters used here and elsewhere in this article are listed in Table IV. In addition $\varrho_{min}$ is the distance of closest approach during the collision. Equation (3.1) is usually referred to as the classical deflection function. Its typical form is shown in Fig. 10a.

The connection between the classical deflection function and the potential is more directly evident if the product $E\vartheta$ is expanded in energy (Smith, 1969),

$$E\vartheta(E, \beta) = \tau(E, \beta) = \tau_0(\beta) + E^{-1}\tau_1(\beta) + \cdots, \qquad (3.2)$$

## TABLE IV

### REDUCED PARAMETERS USED IN ELASTIC SCATTERING[a]

| | | |
|---|---|---|
| $U(\varrho)$ | $= \dfrac{V(\varrho)}{\epsilon}$ | reduced potential energy |
| $\varrho$ | $= R/R_m$ | reduced internuclear distance |
| $\beta$ | $= b/R_m$ | reduced impact parameter |
| $K$ | $= E/\epsilon$ | reduced kinetic energy |
| $A$ | $= kR_m$ | reduced wave number, where $k = \mu g/\hbar$ is the wave number ($\mu =$ reduced mass, $g =$ relative velocity) |
| $C_s{}^*$ | $= \dfrac{C_s}{\epsilon R_m{}^s}$ | reduced van der Waals constant |
| $B$ | $= \dfrac{2\mu\epsilon R_m{}^2}{\hbar^2} = \dfrac{A^2}{K}$ | quantum parameter: $B = (2\pi R_m/\lambda_0)^2$, where $\lambda_0$ is the de Broglie wave length at $K = 0$. Quantum effects are important for small $B$ |
| $g^*$ | $= \dfrac{\hbar g}{2\epsilon R_m} = \dfrac{A}{B} = \dfrac{K}{A} = \left(\dfrac{K}{B}\right)^{1/2}$ | reduced relative velocity $1/g^*$ is proportional to the ratio of the linear dimension of the potential to the quantum mechanical uncertainty of the particle |
| $\dfrac{d^2{}^*\sigma}{d^2\omega}$ | $= \dfrac{d^2\sigma}{d^2\omega}\dfrac{1}{R_m{}^2}$ | reduced differential cross section |
| $f^*$ | $= f/R_m$ | reduced scattering amplitude |
| $\sigma^*$ | $= \dfrac{\sigma}{R_m{}^2}$ | reduced integral cross section |

[a] $\epsilon$ and $R_m$ are the depth and location of the potential well, respectively.

where $\tau_0(\beta)$ does not depend on the energy but only on $\beta$ and the form of the potential. $\tau_0(\beta)$ is a kind of transform of the potential $V(R)$ and usually has a similar shape as $V(R)$.* As we shall see below $\tau$ is a con-

* The physical meaning of $\tau_0(\beta)$ can be seen by noting that in first order $\vartheta \cong P_\perp/P_\parallel$, where $P_\perp$, the perpendicular momentum, is given by an integral along a straight line path through the potential:

$$P_\perp = \int_{-\infty}^{+\infty} \operatorname{grad} V \, dt \simeq \frac{V(\beta)}{\varDelta R} \frac{\varDelta R}{g}$$

($\varDelta R$ is proportional to the range of the potential). Thus since $P_\parallel = \mu \cdot g$, $E \cdot \vartheta \simeq \tau_0(\beta) \simeq \tfrac{1}{2}V(\beta)$).

venient parameter for a reduced representation of differential cross section data.

The classical differential cross section is defined by

$$\frac{d^2\sigma^*}{d^2\omega}(E, \vartheta) = \sum_{i=1}^{3} \frac{d^2\sigma_i^*}{d^2\omega} = \frac{1}{\sin \vartheta} \sum_{i}^{3} \left| \beta_i \frac{d\beta_i}{d\vartheta} \right|, \tag{3.3}$$

where the sum takes account of the fact that particles with several impact parameters can lead to scattering at the observed angle (see Figs. 9 and 10a). Note however that for $\vartheta > \vartheta_R$ only one impact parameter contributes to the differential cross section.

By introducing a new quantity

$$P(E, \tau) = \vartheta \sin \vartheta \frac{d^2\sigma}{d^2\omega}(E, \vartheta),$$

which depends only on measurable quantities, the following convenient

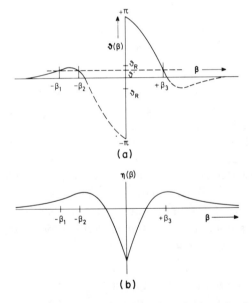

FIG. 10. Typical behavior of the classical deflection function (a) and quantum mechanical phase shift (b) for a Lennard–Jones $(n, 6)$ type of potential. Positive and negative values of the impact parameter correspond to scattering from different sides of the potential (see Fig. 9). Diagram (a) shows that for angles $\vartheta < \vartheta_R$ three impact parameters $\beta_1, \beta_2$, and $\beta_3$ contribute to the classical scattering observed at an angle $\vartheta'$. Diagram (b) shows that the semiclassical phase shift is a continuous function of $\beta$ and has a similar shape as the classical deflection function. The sign of $\eta$ is given by convention.

expansion in $E$ (or $\tau/\vartheta$) is obtained:

$$P(E, \tau) = P_0(\tau) + E^{-1}P_1(\tau) + E^{-2}P_2(\tau) + \cdots . \qquad (3.4)$$

This expansion also holds when several impact parameters contribute to the differential cross section. At small angles or high energies $P(E, \tau)$ is a function of $\tau$ only. In this way measurements over a large range of angles and energies can be reduced to a common curve by plotting $P$ as a function of $\tau$.

The results of classical scattering theory can be expected to give a qualitative picture of the scattering properties for heavy particles and not too low energies. At $\vartheta = 0$ and $\vartheta = \vartheta_R$ the classical differential cross section goes to infinity. As a result of the pole at $\vartheta = 0$ the classical integral cross section also diverges. This divergence is removed in quantum mechanics by way of the uncertainty principle. For small angles the uncertainty principle provides the following formula for the smallest angle in the laboratory system for which classical mechanics can be expected to be roughly valid:

$$\theta_0 = \frac{\hbar}{2m_1 v_1} \left(\frac{\pi}{\sigma}\right)^{1/2}, \qquad (3.5)$$

where $\sigma$ is the finite quantum mechanical integral cross section.

Some of the important results of classical scattering theory for integral and differential cross sections are summarized in Table V. From the classical formula it is apparent that the magnitude and energy dependence of the classical integral cross section and the small angle differential cross section provide information on $s$ and $C$ in the power law potential model. The location of the rainbow angle provides information on $\epsilon$. Since $C = 2\epsilon R_m^6$ for the Lennard-Jones (12,6) model, $R_m$ can be obtained from a knowledge of $C$ and $\epsilon$. Finally $C$ and $n$ of the repulsive potential can be obtained from the magnitude and energy dependence of the backward scattering.

## D. Semiclassical Scattering Theory

Semiclassical theory* provides a convenient way to introduce quantum effects without losing sight of the physical picture of scattering. Semi-

---

* For a more extensive review of semiclassical scattering theory see Pauly and Toennies (1965), Bernstein (1966b), Pauly in Chap. 8, Vol. VI,B of this series, and Ford and Wheeler (1959).

TABLE V

FORMULAS DESCRIBING CROSS SECTION DEPENDENCE ON POTENTIAL PARAMETERS DERIVED FROM CLASSICAL MECHANICS

| Formula | Angular region | Potential model | Classical formula | Reference |
|---|---|---|---|---|
| I[a,b] | $\vartheta_a > \vartheta_0$ | $V(R) = \pm \dfrac{C_s}{R^s}$ | $\sigma(\tau_a) = \pi\left(\dfrac{(s-1)f(s)C_s}{\tau_a}\right)^{2/s}$  $(\tau_a = E\vartheta_a)$ | Pauly and Toennies (1965) |
| II | $0 < \vartheta < \pi$ | $V(R) = \pm \dfrac{C_s}{R^s}$ | $\left\{\begin{array}{l}\dfrac{d^2\sigma}{d^2\omega}(E, \vartheta) = \dfrac{1}{s}\left(\dfrac{(s-1)f(s)C_s}{E}\right)^{2/s}\vartheta - \dfrac{(2s+2)}{s} \\[2ex] P(\tau) = \dfrac{1}{s}[(s-1)f(s)]^{2/s}\left(\dfrac{C}{\tau}\right)^{2/5}\end{array}\right.$ | Bernstein (1966b) <br> Pauly and Toennies (1965) <br> Kennard (1938) |
| III | $\vartheta = \vartheta_R$ | Lennard-Jones $(n, 6)$ | $\tau_R = E\vartheta_R = G(n)\epsilon$ <br> where $1.79(n=7) < G(n) < 2.10(n=14)$ | Hundhausen and Pauly (1965) |
| IV[c] | $\vartheta \simeq \pi$ | $V(R) = +\dfrac{C_n}{R^n}$ | $\dfrac{d^2\sigma}{d^2\omega}(E, \vartheta) = \dfrac{C_n^{2/n}}{E}[g(n)]^2$ | Kihara (1943) <br> Smith et al. (1966) |

[a] $\vartheta_0$ is the center-of-mass system angle corresponding to $\theta_0$ defined in Eq. (3.5).

[b] $f(s) = \dfrac{\sqrt{\pi}}{2}\dfrac{\Gamma(\frac{1}{2}[s-1])}{\Gamma(\frac{1}{2}s)}$.

[c] $g(n) = \dfrac{1}{2\sqrt{\pi}}\dfrac{\Gamma(1/n + \frac{1}{2})}{\Gamma(1/n + 1)}$.

classical theory is valid if the de Broglie wavelength ($\lambda = 1/k = \hbar/p$, $k$ is the wave number and $p$ is the linear momentum) is small compared to the scale of variation of the potential. In semiclassical theory the classical particles are replaced by wave packets which follow the classical trajectories shown in Fig. 9. As a result of the wave nature of the particles interferences occur. These interference patterns provide precise information on certain potential parameters and for this reason semiclassical theory is frequently used in interpreting elastic scattering measurements.

The basic equation for the differential cross section [corresponding to Eq. (3.3) in classical theory] is

$$\frac{d^2\sigma^*}{d^2\omega} = \left| \frac{f(\vartheta)}{R_m} \right|^2 = |f^*(\vartheta)|^2, \tag{3.6}$$

where $f^*(\vartheta) = f(\vartheta)/R_m$ is the reduced amplitude of the scattered wave at angle $\vartheta$. In exact quantum mechanical theory $f^*(\vartheta)$ is related to the quantum mechanical phase shift $\eta_l$ by

$$f^*(\vartheta) = -\frac{i}{2A} \sum_{l=0}^{\infty} (2l + 1)[\exp(2i\eta_l) - 1]P_l(\cos\vartheta), \tag{3.7}$$

where the sum extends over all partial waves of orbital angular momentum $l$ ($l\hbar = \mu g b$). $\eta_l$ contains all the information on the potential and in this sense corresponds to the classical deflection function in classical scattering theory.

In semiclassical theory (Ford and Wheeler, 1959) the trajectory concept is introduced by replacing $l$ by $\beta$ using the expression

$$l + \tfrac{1}{2} = kb = A\beta, \tag{3.8}$$

where $\beta$ is considered to be a continuous parameter. Thus $\eta$ becomes a continuous function of $\beta$ as shown in Fig. 10b. This substitution and an approximation for $P_l(\cos\vartheta)$ valid for $\sin\vartheta \geq 1/l$ leads to the following semiclassical expression for the scattering amplitude, which in the modification first suggested by Pritchard (1970)—whose treatment is followed closely in the present discussion—is given by

$$f^*(\vartheta) = A^{1/2}(2\pi \sin\vartheta)^{-1/2}$$
$$\times \int_{-\infty}^{+\infty} d\beta\, \beta^{1/2} \exp\{i[2\eta(\beta) - \vartheta\beta A - \tfrac{1}{4}\pi]\}, \tag{3.9}$$

where the integral extends over the whole range of negative and positive impact parameters. By introducing the classical action (Smith, 1965)

$$\mathscr{A}(\vartheta, \beta) = 2\hbar\eta(\beta) - \hbar\vartheta\beta A, \tag{3.10}$$

the integral simplifies to

$$f^*(\vartheta) = A^{1/2}(2\pi \sin \vartheta)^{-1/2} \exp(-i\pi/4) \int_{-\infty}^{+\infty} d\beta \, \beta^{1/2} \exp(i\mathscr{A}/\hbar), \tag{3.11}$$

where if $\beta < 0$, $\beta^{1/2}$ must be interpreted as $\exp(-i\pi/2) \mid \beta \mid^{1/2}$.

The integral in Eq. (3.11) can be approximated using the stationary phase technique. This approximation leads directly to an important semiclassical relationship between the phase shift and classical deflection function

$$\frac{d\eta(\beta_i)}{d\beta} = \frac{A\vartheta(\beta_i)}{2}, \tag{3.12}$$

which shows once more that $\vartheta(\beta)$ in classical theory corresponds to $\eta(l)$ in quantum mechanical theory. From (3.12) it follows that $\eta(\beta)$ is at maximum when $\vartheta = 0$ and for this reason the maximum value of $\eta$ is designated by $\eta_0$.

The final result for the semiclassical scattering amplitude is

$$f^*(\vartheta) = \sum_i \left[ \mid \beta_i \mid \sin^{-1} \vartheta \, \frac{d\beta_i}{d\vartheta} \right]^{1/2} \exp\left(\frac{i\mathscr{A}(\vartheta, \beta_i)}{\hbar}\right) \tag{3.13}$$

in which all quantities must be treated as complex numbers. For this reason a factor $\exp(-i\pi/2)$ appears (outside the square root) if either $\beta_i$ or $d\beta_i/d\vartheta$ are negative. Equation (3.13) can also be written as

$$f^*(\vartheta) = \sum_i \left[ \left(\frac{d^2\sigma}{d^2\omega}\right)_{\text{class}} (\vartheta) \right]^{1/2} \exp(i\alpha), \tag{3.14}$$

where $\alpha = \mathscr{A}/\hbar$. Because of the singularities of the classical cross section at $\vartheta = 0$ and $\vartheta = \vartheta_R$, this expression is not valid at these angles.

The close connection to classical theory becomes clear when Eq. (3.14) is substituted into Eq. (3.6) to obtain the semiclassical expression for the differential cross section:

$$\begin{aligned}
\frac{d^2\sigma^*}{d^2\omega}(\vartheta)_{\text{sclass}} &= \mid f^*(\vartheta) \mid^2 \\
&= \mid \{f_1^*(\vartheta) \mid^2 + \mid f_2^*(\vartheta) \mid^2 + \mid f_3(\vartheta) \mid^2\} \\
&\quad + 2f_1^* f_3^* \cos(\alpha_1 - \alpha_3) + 2f_1^* f_2^* \cos(\alpha_1 - \alpha_2) \\
&\quad + 2f_2^* f_3^* \cos(\alpha_2 - \alpha_3),
\end{aligned} \tag{3.15}$$

where the indices 1, 2, 3 refer to the three contributing branches of the classical deflection function (Fig. 10a). Thus the first three terms in the bracket are equal to the classical differential scattering cross section and are equivalent to Eq. (3.3). Because of the additional terms in Eq. (3.15) the semiclassical differential cross section shows an oscillatory behavior which is roughly centered about the classical curve. Figure 11, which is the result of an exact quantum mechanical calculation, confirms the oscillatory behavior of the differential cross section. The semiclassical approximation gives similar results to the exact calculations in the angular region $0 < \vartheta < \vartheta_R$. For $\vartheta > \vartheta_R$ the oscillations gradually disappear since only one impact parameter contributes at each angle.

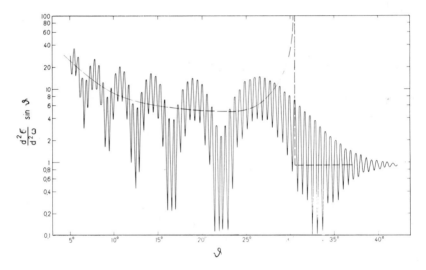

Fig. 11.   The quantum mechanical differential Cross Section calculated for a Lennard-Jones (12, 6) potential (Hundhausen and Pauly, 1965). Two main types of oscillations are observed. The slow oscillations are designated supernumerary rainbows and the other oscillations simply as "fast" oscillations. The dotted line shows the classical differential cross section. The classical differential cross section agrees well with the average quantum mechanical cross section except in the vicinity of the classical rainbow at 30°. $n = 12$, $A = 300$, $K = 4$.

As mentioned previously the oscillations in the differential cross section are an important source of information on potential parameters. To determine their angular spacing it is noted that

$$\frac{d}{d\vartheta}\,\alpha(\vartheta, \beta_i(\vartheta)) = \frac{\partial\alpha}{\partial\vartheta}\bigg|_{\beta_i} + \frac{\partial\alpha}{\partial\beta}\bigg|_{\beta_i}\frac{d\beta}{d\vartheta} = -\beta_i A, \qquad (3.16)$$

where the second step follows from Eq. (3.10) and because the second term on the right disappears since $(d\mathscr{A}/d\beta)\mid_{\beta_i} = 0$ (method of stationary phases). The spacing of successive maxima or minima is given by

$$\frac{d}{d\vartheta}(\alpha_i - \alpha_j)\,\Delta\vartheta = 2\pi. \qquad (3.17)$$

Substituting Eq. (3.16) we get finally

$$\Delta\vartheta = \frac{2\pi}{A[\beta_j(\vartheta) - \beta_i(\vartheta)]}. \qquad (3.18)$$

Since $A \sim g$ the interference oscillations are expected to become closer with increasing relative velocity.

On the basis of Eqs. (3.15) and (3.18) we expect two main types of oscillations: (1) widely spaced oscillations with an angular spacing inversely proportional to $\beta_2 - \beta_1$ and (2) rapid oscillations with an angular spacing proportional to $\beta_3 + \beta_2$ and $\beta_3 + \beta_1$. The former are referred to as *supernumerary rainbows* and the latter simply as "rapid" or *secondary oscillations*. The angular spacing and shape of the supernumerary rainbows obviously depend on the shape of the potential well since this is reflected directly in the shape of the classical deflection function. The angular spacing of the secondary oscillations provides direct information on $R_m$. This can be explained by noting that over a large range of angles $(<\vartheta_R)$, $\beta_3 + \beta_2 \sim 2\beta_0$ (see Fig. 10), where $\beta_0$ is the impact parameter corresponding to $\vartheta = 0$, which is equal to about unity. Thus $\Delta\vartheta \simeq \pi/A$ from which $R_m$ can be determined directly. Exact quantum calculations in which the potential parameters of the two piece Lennard-Jones potential (Table III) were varied over a large range, confirm the results of this simple estimate and show that $\Delta\vartheta$ is extremely invariant with respect to changes in the potential shape (Buck and Pauly, 1968) and $K$ and thus independent of $\epsilon$.

The angular location of the supernumerary rainbows as a function of relative velocity can also be easily estimated from semiclassical theory. The condition for a supernumerary rainbow extrema is

$$\Delta\alpha = 2\{\eta(\beta_1) - \eta(\beta_2)\} + \vartheta A(\beta_1 - \beta_2)$$

$$= n2\pi, \quad \text{where } n = 1, 2, 3, \ldots \text{ condition for maximum,}$$

$$n = \tfrac{1}{2}, \tfrac{3}{2}, \ldots \text{ condition for minimum.} \qquad (3.19)$$

The positive sign of the second factor on the right results from the fact that according to the convention of Fig. 10, $\beta_2$ and $\beta_1$ are negative quantities. $\pi/2$ enters because of the sign convention discussed in connection with Eq. (3.13). From Eq. (3.19) the angular location of an extremum with number $n$ is thus

$$\vartheta_n(g) = \frac{2}{A\,\varDelta\beta}\,\{n\pi + [\eta(\beta_2) - \eta(\beta_1)]\}. \tag{3.20}$$

Quantum mechanical approximations (high-energy approximations) for the phase shift show that for $K > 5$, $\eta \propto 1/g$. Furthermore, since $A \propto g$ the angular location of the oscillations is inversely proportional to the relative energy, $\vartheta_n(g) \propto 1/E$. The same energy dependence of the rainbow maximum ($n = 1$) is found in classical scattering theory (see Table V).

In contrast to the pure classical theory the location of the rainbow and the existence of supernumerary rainbows and their dependence on the potential are correctly predicted by semiclassical theory. At small angles the simple semiclassical theory discussed here is no longer valid. A more elaborate semiclassical approximation (uniform approximation) is however capable of describing the differential cross section over a much larger range of angles (Berry, 1966).

The quantum mechanical expression for the integral elastic cross section is

$$\sigma^*(g) = \int_{\vartheta=0}^{\pi} \int_{\varphi=0}^{2\pi} \frac{d^2\sigma^*}{d^2\omega}\,(g,\,\vartheta,\,\varphi)\,\sin\vartheta\,d\vartheta\,d\varphi \tag{3.21}$$

$$= \frac{4\pi}{A^2}\,\sum\,(2l + 1)\,\sin^2\eta_l. \tag{3.22}$$

In contrast to the classical integral cross section (see Table V) the quantum mechanical integral cross section is finite and virtually independent of the angular resolving power provided that $\theta_a < \theta_0$ of Eq. (3.5).

The calculated velocity dependence of the integral cross section is shown in Fig. 12. At velocities corresponding to $\hbar g/2\epsilon R_m < 1$ the attractive term dominates the long–range interaction. For a Lennard-Jones $(n, s)$ potential a semiclassical calculation based on the optical theorem (Bernstein, 1963; Pauly and Toennies, 1965) leads to the following result:

$$\sigma^*(g) = \pi\left(\frac{2s - 3}{s - 2}\right)\left(\frac{C_s^* f(s)A}{K}\right)^{2/s-1} + \varDelta\sigma^* \cos(2\eta_0 - \pi/4), \tag{3.23}$$

where $C_s^*$ and $f(s)$ are defined in Tables IV and V, respectively.

The repulsive potential term influences the scattering only indirectly by way of the glory undulations of amplitude $\Delta\sigma^*$. Physically these can be attributed to forward glory scattering (see Fig. 4) with impact parameters of about $\beta = 1$, which interfere with the unscattered wave. Since the phase shift corresponding to $\beta \simeq 1$ is $\eta_0$, which is proportional to $\epsilon R_m/g$, the spacing of the glory undulations contains information on the product $\epsilon R_m$. The interpretation of glory undulations is discussed in detail in Greene and Mason (1972) and Bernstein and LaBudde (1973).

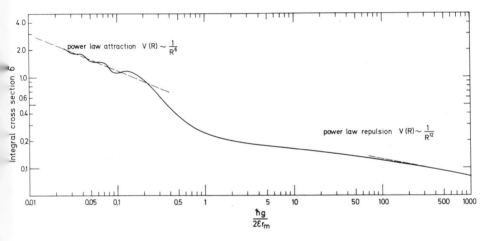

FIG. 12. Calculated integral scattering cross section for an assumed Lennard-Jones (12, 6) potential as a function of the reduced relative velocity. $g_c$ ($g_c = \epsilon R_m/\hbar$) indicates the critical velocity dividing the regions affected by the attractive and repulsive potentials. For not too small $\epsilon \cdot R_m$ and $\hbar g/2\epsilon R_m$ $\sigma(g)$ in nearly independent of the reduced mass.

At high velocities corresponding to $\hbar g/2\epsilon R_m > 1$ the attractive part of the potential no longer has a noticeable influence on the observed scattering and the scattering is produced entirely by the repulsive potential. The first term in Eq. (3.23) is still valid, but, of course, $n$ has to be inserted in place of $s$.

In concluding this theoretical discussion of semiclassical scattering theory the relation between the oscillations in the differential cross section and those in the velocity dependence of the integral cross section will be briefly discussed. At the small c.m. angles $\vartheta_0$, corresponding to $\theta_0$, $\eta(\beta_1)$ in Eq. (3.19) goes to 0, whereas $\eta(\beta_2)$ remains finite. Thus Eq. (3.19) reduces to

$$\alpha_1 - \alpha_2 = -2\eta_0, \qquad \alpha_1 - \alpha_3 = -2\eta_0 + \pi/2. \qquad (3.24)$$

Furthermore since $\alpha_3 - \alpha_2 \simeq \pi/2$, the differential cross section at $\vartheta_0$ simplifies to

$$\frac{d^2\sigma^*}{d^2\omega}(\vartheta_0) \simeq \left(\frac{d^2\sigma^*}{d^2\omega}\right)_{\text{class}}(\vartheta_0) + 2f_1{}^*f_2{}^*\cos 2\eta_0$$

$$+ 2f_1{}^*f_3{}^*\cos(2\eta_0 - \pi/2). \qquad (3.25)$$

Furthermore since $f_3{}^* \simeq f_2{}^*$ a further simplification is possible:

$$\frac{d^2\sigma^*}{d^2\omega}(\vartheta_0) \simeq \left(\frac{d^2\sigma^*}{d^2\omega}\right)_{\text{class}}(\vartheta_0) + 2f_1{}^*f_3{}^*\{\cos 2\eta_0 + \cos(2\eta_0 - \pi/2)\}, \quad (3.26)$$

which can be rewritten to give

$$\frac{d^2\sigma^*}{d^2\omega}(\vartheta_0) \simeq \left(\frac{d^2\sigma^*}{d^2\omega}\right)_{\text{class}}(\vartheta_0) + \frac{4}{\sqrt{2}}f_1{}^*f_3{}^*\cos(2\eta_0 - \pi/4). \quad (3.27)$$

Thus when $2\eta_0 - \pi/4 = n2\pi$ the $n$th supernumerary rainbow has a maximum at $\vartheta_0$ and because of the uncertainty principle is no longer resolvable in the differential cross section.

Since the differential cross section at $\vartheta < \vartheta_0$ contributes only little to the integral cross section, the latter is given to a good approximation by

$$\sigma^*(\vartheta_0) \simeq \int_{\vartheta_0}^{\pi}\int_0^{2\pi}\frac{d^2\sigma^*}{d^2\omega}(\vartheta, \varphi)\sin\vartheta\,d\vartheta\,d\varphi. \qquad (3.28)$$

Thus as a supernumerary rainbow maximum shifts to an angle $\vartheta_0$ it no longer makes a significant contribution to the integral cross section. At the velocity at which this occurs the integral cross section can be expected to decrease. Starting from low velocities the rainbows disappear one by one as the velocity is increased. As each rainbow disappears the integral cross section goes through a maximum. After the last maximum corresponding to the main rainbow ($n = 1$) has disappeared the integral cross section falls off monotonically since the repulsive part of the potential dominates the scattering behavior. Thus the number of supernumerary rainbows observed at one velocity equals the total number of glory maxima which can be observed in the integral cross section at higher velocities (Pritchard, 1972). This intimate relationship between the integral cross section and differential cross section is illustrated schematically in Fig. 13.

In summary, then, the interference phenomena contain the following

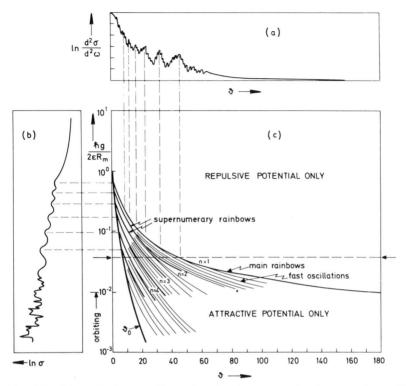

FIG. 13. Schematic diagram illustrating the close connection between the oscillations in the differential elastic cross sections and the velocity undulations in the integral elastic cross section. In the central portion (c) the various scattering features observed in differential cross sections are shown in the $g$, $\vartheta$ plane. The location of the supernumerary rainbows and the critical angle are shown by solid lines. The location of the rapid secondary oscillations are indicated by the thin dotted lines. At the top (a) a typical differential cross section at one velocity (indicated by arrows), corresponding to a cut through (c) at constant $g$, is shown. At the left the integral cross section, corresponding approximately to a cut along $\vartheta_0$ through (c), is shown. After each supernumerary rainbow reaches $\vartheta_0$ the integral cross section decreases. After the main rainbow has merged with $\vartheta_0$ the integral cross section falls off monotonically and is dominantly influenced by the repulsive potential.

additional information on the spherical symmetric potential: (1) angular spacing and shape of the supernumerary rainbows: shape of the potential well; (2) angular spacing of secondary oscillations: $R_m$; (3) velocity spacing of the glory undulations: the product $\epsilon R_m$; (4) the absolute value of the integral cross section: $C$. In the next section the sensitivity of the various cross section features to potential parameters will be discussed further.

E. Survey of Experimental Results

In the preceding theoretical introduction to elastic scattering it was shown that the important scattering features can be conveniently classified depending on whether the attractive forces are dominant or not. This depends on the quantity $g^* = \hbar g/2\epsilon R_m$. If $g^* < 1$ the attractive forces are dominant and if $g^* > 1$, repulsive forces are dominant. The relative velocities in an experiment are roughly related to the source temperatures by $g \simeq (2kT/m)^{1/2}$, where $T$ is in the range of $\sim$100 to $\sim$1000 °K. Since in general the well depth $\epsilon$ of the van der Waals interaction and with it the strength of the attractive potential are roughly proportional to the particle masses, it is found that the condition $g^* < 1$ is usually achieved in scattering experiments in which both partners have a mass greater than about 20 and that $g^* > 1$ is usually achieved for experiments in which one or both of the partners is lighter than about 10–20.

Since the scattering features and the methods of data analysis are distinctly different for $g^* > 1$ and $g^* < 1$ the experiments are classified accordingly. In choosing experiments for discussion preference was given to those which, at the present time, appear to exemplify techniques which hold the most promise for the future. For a more comprehensive survey of the older work the reader is referred to several reviews (Pauly and Toennies, 1965, 1968; Bernstein and Muckermann, 1967; Beck, 1970).

1. *Experimental Studies of the Long Range Attractive Potential* ($g^* < 1$)

   *a. Measurements of Differential Cross Sections; Supernumerary Rainbows.* Differential cross section measurements provide the most direct source of information on the intermolecular potential. Figure 14 shows the result of a measurement of the differential cross section for Cs–Hg over the entire range of angles. The large forward glory at 0° is clearly discernible. To the left of the main rainbow at about 30° two or three supernumerary rainbows are seen. Beyond the rainbow the differential cross section is almost constant (the drop off at large angles is due to the sin $\vartheta$ factor) as expected from the discussion of the previous section.

   As indicated by the classical formulas shown in Table V a considerable amount of information on the attractive potential can be obtained from measurements over a limited range of angles $\vartheta < \vartheta_R$. Thus the constant $C$ and the parameter $s$ can and have been measured from the small angle ($\vartheta \approx 1°$) shape of the differential cross section. Also the location of the main rainbow itself has been used to determine the potential well depth $\epsilon$. The related experiments and their interpretation will not be

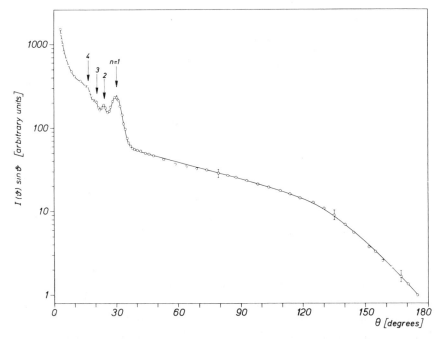

FIG. 14.   Measured differential cross section (weighted by sin $\vartheta$) for Cs–Hg (Buck *et al.*, 1972) at $E_{\text{c.m.}} = 0.19$ eV. $n = 1, 2, 3, 4$ designate the location of the main rainbow and adjacent supernumerary rainbows. The rapid secondary oscillations have not been resolved in this experiment.

discussed in detail here since these techniques have been largely replaced by the methods discussed below. They are also adequately discussed in the reviews listed at the beginning of this section. By far the most powerful experimental method for studying the long range attractive potential involves the analysis of supernumerary rainbows. Such data can be inverted directly within the framework of the semiclassical approximation permitting a determination of the shape of the potential without recourse to a potential model.

Sufficiently accurate data for direct inversion has recently been obtained for the systems Na–Hg, K–Hg, Cs–Hg (Buck and Pauly, 1971; Buck *et al.*, 1972). The apparatus used in these experiments is shown in Fig. 15. The alkali metal primary beam is produced in a supersonic nozzle source (1) and is velocity selected by the velocity selector (2), which has a velocity resolution of $\Delta v_1/v_1 \simeq 1.3\%$. The Hg secondary beam is also produced in a supersonic nozzle source (3). Since Hg is heavier and slower than the primary beam atoms, its velocity spread does not

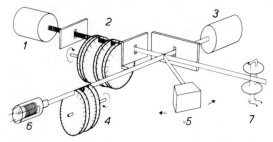

FIG. 15. Perspective view of the crossed molecular beam apparatus used to measure oscillations in the differential elastic cross section for Na–Hg, K–Hg, and Cs–Hg.

have as direct an influence on the spread in relative velocities as the primary beam. Thus the nozzle expansion velocity narrowing of $\Delta v_2/v_2 = 9.5\%$ is sufficient to produce a $\Delta g/g = 2\%$. In this way a velocity selector is not needed in the secondary beam and its path is kept as short as possible to provide a beam attenuation of 20%. The velocity spread of the Hg beam is monitored continuously during a run and this is done by the velocity selector (4) and the ionization gauge (6). The scattered beam detector (5) subtends an angle of only $\Delta\theta \simeq \Delta\vartheta \simeq 0.35°$. For the lighter primary beam atoms $\Delta\vartheta$ is only slightly smaller. The detector (7) is used to monitor the primary beam and also for measurements of the integral cross section, which can be performed with the same apparatus.

Figure 16 shows a measured differential cross section over a range of relative velocities for the system Na–Hg. The observation of supernumerary rainbows of order up to 7 or more can be attributed to the large number of bound states of the strong attractive van der Waals well. Superimposed on the supernumerary rainbows the secondary or rapid interferences are clearly visible especially in the measurements at $E = 0.19$ eV and at $E = 0.25$ eV.

Figure 17 shows a direct comparison of the measured integral elastic cross section and the differential cross section at three different closely spaced relative velocities (Buck *et al.*, 1971). The integral cross section has been corrected for the monotonic decrease produced by the attractive $R^{-6}$ potential by multiplying by a factor $g^{2/5}$ [see Eq. (3.23)] so that only the glory amplitudes are shown as a function of $g$. The differential cross sections shown at the bottom have also been corrected for the small angle drop off of the monotonic part of the cross section due to the $1/R^6$ term by multiplying by $\vartheta^{7/3}$ (see formula II, Table V).

The measured curves confirm the close relationship between the glory undulations and supernumerary rainbows (see Fig. 13). In the example shown the merging of the $n = 8$ supernumerary rainbow into the region of the critical angle is associated with the disappearance of the $n = 8$ glory undulation at 1300 m/sec.

These data have been inverted by a semiclassical modification of the classical inversion techniques of Firsov, etc. (Buck, 1971). For a more extensive discussion of the inversion techniques the reader is referred to Chapter 8 by Pauly in volume VI B of this series. We summarize here only briefly the assumptions involved.

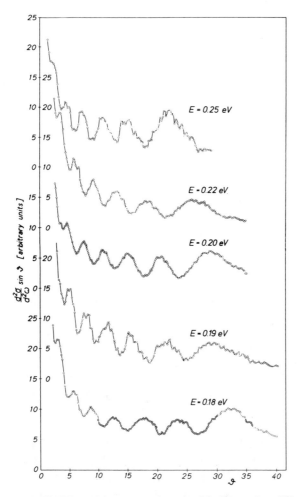

FIG. 16. Measured differential cross sections for Na–Hg at five different energies (Buck and Pauly, 1971). With increasing energy the rainbows shift to smaller angles and the higher order supernumerary rainbows disappear.

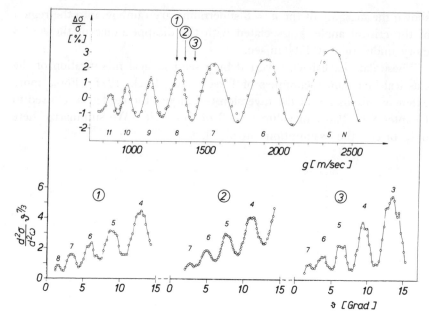

FIG. 17.   The undulations in the measured integral cross section are shown over a large range of relative velocities. The integral cross section has been corrected for the monotonic drop off due to the attractive $R^{-6}$ term. Differential cross sections, also corrected to account for the monotonic decrease due to the $R^{-6}$ term, are shown for three closely spaced relative velocities.

Analytic expressions are assumed for the classical deflection function in the following three regions: (1) $\vartheta \simeq \pi$, $\beta = 0$; (2) $\vartheta \simeq \vartheta_R$, $\beta = \beta_R$; (3) $\vartheta_R < \vartheta < 0$, $\beta > \beta_R$. The analytic expressions contain nine coefficients which have to be determined. Five of these, $\vartheta_R$, $(d^2\vartheta/d\beta^2)\,|_{\beta=\beta_R}$, $\beta_R$, $\eta_0$, $C$ are self-evident and have already been discussed. In addition four other constants that describe the shape of the classical deflection function are needed. The number of coefficients is reduced by taking account of (1) the condition of continuity of the deflection function, (2) an independent determination of $\eta_0$ from the glory scattering, and finally, (3) an independent determination of $C$ (either from the absolute integral cross section or from theory). The remaining five coefficients are then determined by a least squares fit of the measured supernumerary rainbow structure. As is to be expected the calculations show that at least five extrema (maxima or minima) are needed. Once determined in this way the potential is derived from the classical deflection function by an inversion technique similar to that used by Firsov.

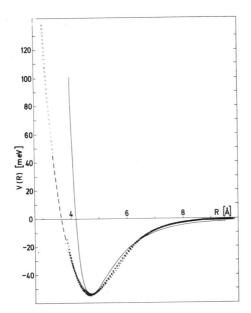

FIG. 18. The potential for Na–Hg obtained from the inversion of supernumerary data at five different energies [$E = 0.18$ eV ($\square$), $0.19$ eV ($\diamond$), $0.20$ eV ($\bigcirc$), $0.22$ eV ($*$), $0.25$ eV ($+$)]. The solid line shows a Lennard–Jones (12.6) potential, which is fitted at the minimum.

Figure 18 shows the potential curve obtained by a direct inversion of the data at five different energies (Buck and Pauly, 1971). The points in the repulsive force region starting at $-30$ meV and extending to 120 meV were obtained from a conventional Firsov inversion at wide angle scattering data. The solid line curve in Fig. 18 is a Lennard–Jones (12,6) potential that has been fitted at the minimum. Although a reasonable approximation to the right of the minimum, the (12,6) potential is clearly too steep in the repulsive region.

Figure 18 shows that the supernumerary rainbow structure provides information on the potential from the region slightly to the left of the minimum out to fairly large distances corresponding to $V/\epsilon \simeq -5 \cdot 10^{-2}$. The good agreement of the data obtained at different energies supports the internal consistency of the inversion techniques used.

The reduced potential curves for the systems Na–Hg, K–Hg, and Cs–Hg show very similar shapes which agree to within better than a few percent in the attractive region. In all cases the potential wells are found to be wider than that of the Lennard-Jones (12,6) potential. In the repulsive region more significant differences are observed. Thus the potential for Cs–Hg is twice as steep as for Na–Hg. In the framework of the Thomas–Fermi statistical model this difference can be attributed to the greater electron density in Cs compared to Na. The potential parameters for the three systems are shown in Table VI.

TABLE VI

COMPARISON OF POTENTIAL PARAMETERS OBTAINED BY A DIRECT INVERSION OF
SUPERNUMERARY RAINBOWS

|         | $R_0$ (Å) | $R_m$ (Å) | $\epsilon$ ($10^{-2}$ eV) |
|---------|-----------|-----------|---------------------------|
| Na–Hg   | 3.82      | 4.72      | 5.49                      |
| K–Hg    | —         | 4.91      | 5.24                      |
| Cs–Hg   | 4.26      | 5.09      | 5.00                      |

At the present time the direct inversion of supernumerary rainbows provides the best available technique for studying the attractive potential. The advantage of the technique is that the measured potential shape and potential parameters of the attractive potential are model independent and determined only for that range which is probed by the measurements. The disadvantages and limitations are: (1) The potential must have a deep well and the partners must be relatively heavy in order that a sufficient number of extrema be observed; this requires that $B > 500$ ($B$ is defined in Table IV). (2) A sufficient number of rainbows must lie in the easily accessible thermal beam range, which requires that $A/B \leq 0.04$. (3) A high angular and velocity resolution is required.

*b. Measurements of Differential Cross Sections; Secondary (rapid) Interferences.* Secondary interferences have been observed in the following alkali atom–rare gas atom or molecule systems: Li–Ar, Li–N$_2$ (Wharton, etc.), K–Ar (Beck, 1970), Na–Kr, Na–Xe (Barwig et al., 1966), and in Na–Hg, K–Hg (Buck and Pauly, 1971, Buck et al., 1972). For the last named systems the rapid secondary interferences can be seen in the Figs. 16 and 17.

As discussed in Section III,D the spacing of these undulations is given to a good approximation by

$$\Delta\vartheta \simeq \frac{2\pi}{A(\beta_3 + \beta_{1,2})} \simeq \frac{\hbar\pi}{\mu g R_m}. \qquad (3.29)$$

TABLE VII

$R_m$ in Å Determined Only from the Spacing of Secondary Interferences Using a Lennard–Jones $(8, 6)$ Potential Compared with $R_m$ Values Obtained from a More Flexible Potential Model and Taking Account of Other Experimental Data (Buck and Pauly, 1968)

| System | $R_m$ | |
|--------|-------------------------------|-----------------------------|
|        | From secondary interferences  | From all available data     |
| Na–Kr  | $4.95 \pm 2.5\%$              | $4.96 \pm 3\%$              |
| Na–Xe  | $4.93 \pm 2.5\%$              | $5.06 \pm 2\%$              |

The value of $R_m$ determined from Eq. (3.29) has been found to be quite independent of the assumed potential model and of $\epsilon$. This is illustrated by the data in Table VII where values of $R_m$ obtained from Eq. (3.29) are compared with more accurate values obtained by an exact quantum mechanical trial and error fit of all available cross section data. The agreement between the two sets of data is within the indicated error.

Secondary interferences are of particular interest for determining the potential parameters of light systems with $B < 500$ for which they are widely spaced and for which the supernumerary rainbows cannot be observed. In the case of the heavier systems the supernumerary rainbows are more easily resolved than the secondary interferences so that these are mainly of interest to check the results of a direct inversion.

c. *Measurements of Differential Scattering; Spin Exchange Cross Sections.* In the scattering of two open shelled atoms, two or more potential curves may be involved in the scattering depending on the total electron spin of the interacting atoms. For example in the scattering of two non-polarized alkali atoms (each with electronic state, $^2S_{1/2}$) the atoms will interact either by way of a singlet potential (total spin $S = 0$; $M_s = 0$) or by a triplet potential (total spin $S = 1$; $M_s = -1, 0, +1$). Thus because of the different spin degeneracies there is a 25% probability of a singlet interaction and a 75% probability of a triplet interaction. The singlet potentials in the alkali–alkali systems have deep minima $\frac{1}{2}$ eV $< \epsilon < 1$ eV; $R_m \simeq 3$ Å). The well depths and in some cases the potential shapes may be obtained from spectroscopic data for the corresponding molecules. The observed glory undulations of the integral cross sections of these systems is dominated by the stronger singlet potential and thus it is possible to determine the product $\epsilon R_m$ for this potential rather easily from the glory undulation (Neumann and Pauly, 1970). The antibonding triplet potential has, on the other hand, only a small van der Waals minimum ($\varepsilon \simeq 0.03$ eV, $R_m \simeq 5$ Å) and its contribution to the glory undulations is only noticeable at very low velocities. Furthermore, since the triplet van der Waals molecules have not been observed in spectra, little is known about their potential curves.

Scattering experiments with polarized primary atom beams provide a method for studying the triplet potential (Pritchard *et al.*, 1970; Höh

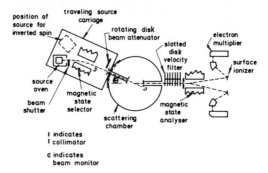

Fig. 19. Schematic view of an apparatus for studying scattering of polarized beams. The unpolarized secondary beam in the center of the scattering chamber is directed vertically upward (Pritchard *et al.*, 1970).

*et al.*, 1970). The apparatus used in such experiments is shown in Fig. 19. With this apparatus the three different differential cross sections summarized in Table VIII can be measured. Since

$$\left.\frac{d^2\sigma}{d^2\omega}\right|_{\text{sum}} = \left.\frac{d^2\sigma}{d^2\omega}\right|_d + \left.\frac{d^2\sigma}{d^2\omega}\right|_{\text{ex}},$$

only two of the three types of differential cross sections summarized in Table VIII need to be considered.

Figures 20a and 20b show data for

$$\left.\frac{d^2\sigma}{d^2\omega}\right|_{\text{sum}} \quad \text{and} \quad P_{\text{ex}} = \frac{(d^2\sigma/d^2\omega)|_{\text{ex}}}{(d^2\sigma/d^2\omega)|_{\text{sum}}}$$

for the system K–Cs (Pritchard *et al.*, 1970), respectively. These data are in essential agreement with measurements of another group (Höh *et al.*, 1970). In Fig. 20a the observed differential cross section $(d^2\sigma/d^2\omega)|_{\text{sum}} \sin \vartheta$ is compared with the $\vartheta^{4/3}$ law behavior expected for a long-range

TABLE VIII

DIFFERENTIAL CROSS SECTIONS WHICH CAN BE MEASURED IN THE APPARATUS OF FIG. 19
AND THE THEORETICAL EXPRESSIONS FOR THE OBSERVED SCATTERING AMPLITUDES. IN ALL
CASES THE SECONDARY BEAM IS UNPOLARIZED. THE INDICES $i$ AND $f$ REFER TO THE SPIN
ORIENTATION QUANTUM NUMBER $(m_s)$ BEFORE AND AFTER SCATTERING, RESPECTIVELY.
$f_1$ AND $f_3$ ARE THE SCATTERING AMPLITUDES FOR THE SINGLET AND TRIPLET STATES,
RESPECTIVELY.

| Primary beam | Scattered primary beam | Differential cross section |
|---|---|---|
| unpolarized | unpolarized | $\left.\dfrac{d^2\sigma}{d^2\omega}\right\|_{\text{sum}} = \frac{1}{4}\,\|f_1(\vartheta)\|^2 + \frac{3}{4}\,\|f_3(\vartheta)\|^2$ |
| polarized $(m_s{}^i)$ | polarized $m_s{}^f = m_s{}^i$ | $\left.\dfrac{d^2\sigma}{d^2\omega}\right\|_{d} = \frac{1}{8}\,\|f_1(\vartheta) + f_3(\vartheta)\|^2 + \frac{1}{2}\,\|f_3(\vartheta)\|^2$ |
| polarized $(m_s{}^i)$ | polarized $m_s{}^f = -m_s{}^i$ | $\left.\dfrac{d^2\sigma}{d^2\omega}\right\|_{\text{ex}} = \frac{1}{8}\,\|f_1(\vartheta) - f_3(\vartheta)\|^2$ |

$1/R^6$ potential (see Table V). Superimposed on this monotonic drop off several supernumerary rainbows are observable. The exchange cross section shows two maxima that roughly coincide with the $n = 2$ and $n = 1$ rainbow maxima.

Spin exchange scattering experiments are considerably more difficult to interpret than experiments involving only one potential curve. The reason is that at least three impact parameters contribute to both the singlet and triplet scattering, whereas only the interference between the two potentials is observed. A preliminary interpretation based on the semiclassical approximation (Pritchard and Chu, 1970; Höh et al., 1970) suggests the following conclusions:

(1) $(d^2\sigma/d^2\omega)|_{\text{sum}}$ and $(d^2\sigma/d^2\omega)|_{d}$ are dominated by the triplet interaction. For the triplet potential of K–Cs the data yield the following values for an assumed Lennard-Jones (8, 6) potential: $\epsilon = 32.4 \pm 1.2$ meV and $R_m = 6.3 \pm 0.8$ Å.

(2) $(d^2\sigma/d^2\omega)|_{\text{ex}}$ is not easy to interpret since it depends on the difference between the two scattering amplitudes. As is to be expected $(d^2\sigma/d^2\omega)|_{\text{ex}}$ depends to a large extent on $\Delta V = V_1(R) - V_0(R)$. In addition, however, especially for angles smaller than the main triplet rainbow angle $(d^2\sigma/d^2\omega)|_{\text{ex}}$ appears to be very sensitive to the long range attractive parts of the two potentials. To extract this information, addi-

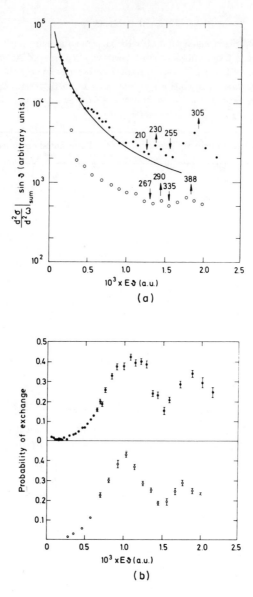

FIG. 20. Differential cross section for spin exchange scattering plotted as a function of $\tau = E\vartheta$ (Pritchard *et al.*, 1970). Diagram (a) shows the sum differential cross section for K–Cs at two different energies: $E_{rel} = 0.125$ eV ($4.6 \cdot 10^{-3}$ a.u.), $\Delta v_1/v_1 = 10\%$ ($\bigcirc$); $E_{rel} = 0.166$ eV ($6.1 \cdot 10^{-3}$ a.u.), $\Delta v_1/v_1 = 5\%$ ($\bullet$). Diagram (b) shows the probability of exchange $P_{ex}$ for the same two center-of-mass energies. Note that the second maximum in $P_{ex}$ corresponds to the main rainbow in both cases.

tional experiments involving polarized secondary beams or reliable theoretical estimates of $\Delta V$ are required.

*d. Measurements of Integral Cross Sections; Velocity Dependence.* In general integral cross sections provide less detailed potential information than differential cross sections. As mentioned previously integral cross sections cannot be directly inverted and consequently the derived potential parameters are always model dependent to a certain extent. However, since intensity limitations often prevent a high resolution measurement of differential cross sections, integral cross sections are frequently the first and only source of information on a particular system. Both the relative velocity dependence and the absolute value of the integral cross section provide nearly complementary sources of information on the potential.

At velocities corresponding to $g^* < 1$ the velocity dependence of the integral cross section is expected to be given by Eq. (3.23) and to exhibit the overall behavior shown in Fig. 12. Neglecting for the moment the small second term in Eq. (3.23) it is apparent that the slope of $\ln \sigma$ versus $\ln g$ ($A \sim g$) is a measure of $s$, the $R$ power of the attractive potential term. Furthermore as mentioned in connection with Eq. (3.23) the spacing of the velocity undulations provides information on the product $\epsilon R_m$.

A typical apparatus used in measurements with atoms of molecules not containing an alkali atom is shown in Fig. 21. All the conventional

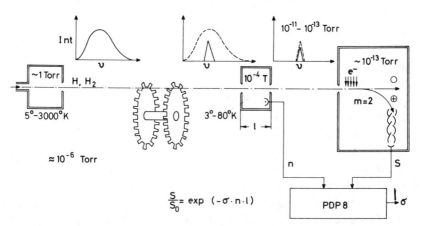

FIG. 21.   Diagram of an apparatus for measuring integral cross sections. The primary beam is first velocity selected before passing through a gas filled scattering chamber. In the apparatus shown, a universal electron-bombardment detector is used. At the top the velocity distributions in the beam at various stages in the apparatus are shown.

components described in Section II,C can be used in such measurements. The relative integral cross section is obtained from Beer's law (formula IV, Table I). In order to make a comparison with theory possible the measured integral cross sections have to be carefully corrected to account (1) for the small but nevertheless significant velocity dependent errors produced by the finite angular aperture of the detector, and (2) for the smearing produced by the distribution of velocities of the target gas (Pauly and Toennies, 1968). For these reasons most measurements are performed with a scattering chamber containing the target gas for which the velocity distribution is well known instead of with a secondary beam. However, if the velocity of the target gas is comparable to that of the primary beam then the use of a secondary beam is required to resolve the undulations and a crossed beam apparatus similar to the one shown in Fig. 15 will be required.

Figure 22 shows some results on the velocity dependence of integral cross sections for three different systems measured in an apparatus with a secondary beam (Beck and Loesch, 1966). The data have been corrected for the velocity distribution of the target gas. All curves show an average slope given by values of $d \ln \sigma / d \ln g$ between $-0.36$ and $-0.40 \pm 0.05$ (or less). It is recalled that a slope of $-2/5 = -0.40$ is expected for an $s = 6$ long range attractive potential [Eq. (3.23)]. Düren et al. (1968) have however pointed out that the small deviations from the $s = 6$ behavior can be explained in terms of the actual shape of the potential in the vicinity of the well. Thus for a realistic potential the overall slope is not entirely determined by the power law in the asymptotic long range potential as predicted by Eq. (3.23) for a Lennard-Jones potential.

To bring out the glory extrema more clearly, the data of Fig. 22a have been corrected to allow for the $-0.40$ slope of the curves. The reduced data for the systems K–Xe, K–Kr, and K–Ar are shown in Fig. 22b.

In order to extract information on the product of the well parameters $\epsilon R_m$ the index number of the extrema are plotted versus the reciprocal velocity. This is illustrated in Fig. 23, where the extrema data for K–Kr from three different laboratories has been plotted. As mentioned in Section III,D the slope of the plot shown in Fig. 23 provides a fairly model-independent determination of the product $\epsilon R_m$. This is illustrated in Table IX, where values for $\epsilon R_m$ for 3 different Lennard-Jones $(n, 6)$ potentials derived from the data in Fig. 23 are listed.

The deviations from the straight line plot for large $N$ (Fig. 23) have occasionally been interpreted as providing a measure of $\epsilon$. Recent analysis

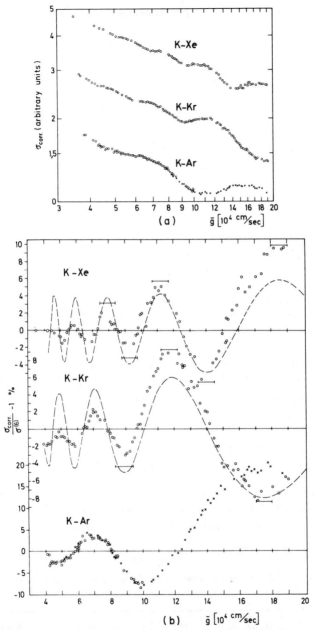

Fig. 22. Measured velocity dependence of the integral cross section of K with Ar, Kr, and Xe. Diagram (a) shows the log of the integral cross section corrected for the target beam velocity distribution as a function of the log of the relative velocity. Diagram (b) shows the glory undulations relative to a monotonic velocity dependence obtained from the same data. The dotted line shows the calculated curve for K–Xe using a Lennard–Jones (8,6) potential ($\epsilon R_m = 66.8 \cdot 10^{-3}$ eV Å; $\epsilon = 19 \cdot 10^{-3}$ eV) and for K–Kr using a Lennard–Jones (12.6) potential ($\epsilon R_m = 47.4 \cdot 10^{-3}$ eV Å; $\epsilon = 8.1 \cdot 10^{-3}$ eV) (Beck and Loesch, 1966).

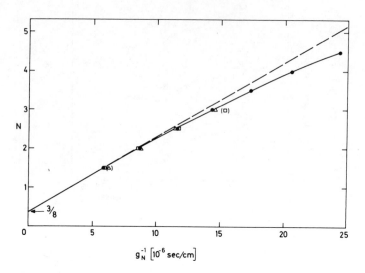

$$g_N^{-1}\ \left[10^{-6}\ \text{sec/cm}\right]$$

Fig. 23.   Glory extrema indexing plot for the K–Kr system, comparing results of experiments carried out in three laboratories. △ Rothe *et al.*, 1963; □ Beck and Loesch, 1967; ● Von Busch, Strunck, and Schlier, 1966; ( ) observation uncertain.

of glory undulations for the system Na–Hg for which the potentials are available from the direct inversion of differential cross section data seems to suggest that such an interpretation may not always be justified (Buck, 1972). The amplitudes of the glory undulations also contain information on the width of the potential well or in other words on the curvature of the potential in the region of the minimum. However, so far it has been difficult to extract this information from the data.

*e. Measurements of Integral Cross Sections; Absolute Values.*   Absolute values of integral cross sections measured at high angular resolving power provide a direct measure of the van der Waals constant $C$ by way

TABLE IX

$\epsilon R_m$ Values (meV Å) Obtained from Glory Undulations Using Three Different Lennard-Jones $(n, 6)$ Potentials (Beck and Loesch, 1966)

| System | (8, 6) | (12, 6) | (16, 6) | Error (%) |
|--------|--------|---------|---------|-----------|
| K–Xe   | 66.8   | 74.2    | 78.7    | ±2        |
| K–Kr   | 42.4   | 47.4    | 50.6    | ±2        |
| K–Ar   | 25.0   | 27.5    | 29.3    | ±3        |

of Eq. (3.23). Since the glory undulations to be discussed previously make only a small contribution to the cross section they can usually be averaged out of the data. Neglecting the second term in Eq. (3.23) the first term yields $C_s$ as a function of $\sigma$:

$$C_s = \frac{\hbar g}{2f(s)} \left( \frac{1}{\pi} \frac{s-2}{2s-3} \right)^{(s-1)/2} \sigma^{(s-1)/2}. \tag{3.30}$$

For the important case of $s = 6$ a slightly more accurate formula yields

$$C_6 = \hbar g \left( \frac{\sigma}{8.083} \right)^{5/2}. \tag{3.31}$$

Thus if $s$ is known from a measurement of the velocity dependence the absolute value of $\sigma$ provides a measure of $C_s$, which may however not be entirely model independent, as mentioned above. In general absolute values of integral cross sections provide a direct measure of the absolute value of the potential at some $R'$ but virtually no information on the $R$ dependence. For $g^* < 1$ the value of $R'$ corresponds roughly to a range given by the uncertainty principle and is approximated by $(\sigma/\pi)^{1/2}$.

Absolute integral cross sections, which are obtained from the ratio of measured intensities using Beer's law (formula IV, Table I) are among the most difficult quantities to measure. The difficulties arise from the fact that the precision in the determination of the density in the scattering chamber determines directly the precision in the absolute cross section. Ordinary pressure measuring techniques (McLeod manometer, ionization gauge, etc.) have absolute errors of the order of 10 to 30% and cannot therefore be used. Of the special techniques developed for absolute density determinations, the dynamical expansion method is probably the most reliable. At the present time this method is capable of a precision of $\pm 1\%$ (Bennewitz and Dohmann, 1965b).

Table X summarizes some results of absolute integral cross section measurements from various groups using different methods.* Since for all collision partners an $s = 6$ $R$-dependence was either measured directly or felt to be established from theory, a calculation of $C_6$ was possible. In the case of the rare gases the results for $C_6$ can be compared directly with semiempirical estimates as shown in Table XI. The agreement between experiment and theory is considered satisfactory in view of the large experimental errors.

---

* For a recent review of alkali atom integral cross sections see Croucher and Clark (1969).

TABLE X

SOME RECENTLY MEASURED ABSOLUTE INTEGRAL CROSS SECTIONS (corrected for target motion and insufficient angular resolution) FOR VELOCITIES AT WHICH THE ATTRACTIVE FORCES DETERMINE THE SIZE OF THE CROSS SECTION ($\hbar g/2\epsilon R_m < 1$)

| System | Velocity in meters per second | Absolute integral cross section in Å² | Reference |
|--------|------------------|------------------|-----------|
| He–He | $v_1 = 137.7$ | $98.9 \pm 1.29$ | Bennewitz et al. (1972) |
| K–He | $v_1 = 498$ | 296.5 | Politiek et al. (1970) |
| K–Ne | $v_1 = 465$ | 377.9 | Politiek et al. (1970) |
| K–Ar | $v_1 = 486.4$ | 635.9 | Politiek et al. (1970) |
| K–Kr | $v_1 = 473$ | 735 | Politiek et al. (1970) |
| K–Xe | $v_1 = 474$ | 852 | Politiek et al. (1970) |
| Ar–Ne | $g = 865$ | $188.6 \pm 3.9$ | Swedenburg et al. (1970) |
| Ar–Ar | $g = 670$ | $300 \pm 6.1$ | Swedenburg et al. (1970) |
| Ar–Kr | $g = 611$ | $355 \pm 7.5$ | Swedenburg et al. (1970) |
| CsF–Ar | $v_1 = 503$ | $579.6 \pm 18$ | Müller (1967) |
| LiF–Ar | $v_1 = 500$ | $447 \pm 6$ | Richman and Wharton (1970) |
| LiF–Kr | $v_1 = 500$ | $521 \pm 6$ | Richman and Wharton (1970) |

TABLE XI

COMPARISON BETWEEN EXPERIMENTAL AND THEORETICAL $C_6$ VALUES IN ATOMIC UNITS

| System | Measured $C_6$ | Theoretical $C_6{}^c$ |
|--------|-----------|---------------|
| Ar–Ar | 73.8[a] | 65 |
| Ar–Kr | 97.1[a] | 91 |
| Kr–Kr | 118.4[a] | 130 |
| K–Ar | 292[b] | 270 |
| K–Kr | 421[b] | 400 |
| K–Xe | 623[b] | 630 |

[a] Swedenburg et al. (1970).
[b] Politiek et al. (1970).
[c] Dalgarno (1967).

*f. Summary of Methods for Determining the Negative Part of the Potential.* The experimental methods discussed above can be divided into two groups: (1) direct inversion of supernumerary rainbows or (2) matching of a variety of experimental cross section data to a best fit potential model of sufficient flexibility.

The latter method appears necessary when $B < 500$ or when supernumerary rainbows have not been measured. The following data are useful for determining the parameters indicated in parentheses: rainbow angles ($\epsilon$), secondary rainbows ($R_m$), absolute integral cross sections ($C$, where $C = 2\epsilon R_m{}^6$ for a Lennard-Jones 12, 6 potential), spacing of glory undulations ($\epsilon R_m$), and finally amplitudes of glory undulations ($[d^2V/dR^2]\,|_{R=R_m}$).

This method of fitting several types of data has been carried out by two groups using different methods and different model potentials but essentially the same experimental data for alkali atom–rare gas systems. The results are summarized in Table XII. In Fig. 24 the potential shapes

TABLE XII

COMPARISON OF VALUES OF $R_m$ (Å) (top number) AND $\epsilon$ ($10^{-3}$ eV) (bottom number) OBTAINED BY THREE DIFFERENT FITTING PROCEDURES. THE BRACKETED VALUES ARE BASED ONLY ON MEASUREMENTS OF INTEGRAL CROSS SECTION

| | Ar | | | Kr | | | Xe | | |
|---|---|---|---|---|---|---|---|---|---|
| | I[a] | II[b] | III[c] | I | II | III | I | II | |
| Li | | [4.95 / 5.32] | | [4.65 / 7.93] | [4.87 / 8.55] | | | [4.90 / 13.18] | |
| | | | | | | | | | (IV)[d] |
| Na | [4.80 / 5.12] | 5.01 / 5.56 | | 4.73 / 8.55 | 4.96 / 8.68 | | 4.91 / 12.4 | 5.06 / 13.0 | 4.95 / 12.6 |
| | | | | | | | | | (III) |
| K | 5.05 / 5.37 | [5.34 / 5.24] | 5.05 / 5.18 | [4.84 / 9.05] | 5.24 / 8.86 | 5.36 / 8.49 | | 5.25 / 13.7 | 5.20 / 12.7 |
| Rb | | | | | [5.29 / 9.05] | | | | |
| Cs | | [5.50 / 5.62] | | | [5.44 / 9.18] | | | [5.47 / 13.6] | |

[a] Düren *et al.* (1968). The potential model used is given in Table III.

[b] Buck and Pauly (1968). The potential model used is given in Table III.

[c] Krämer (1967). A modified exponential potential was used.

[d] Okel and van de Ree (1971). A Buckingham–Corner potential was used.

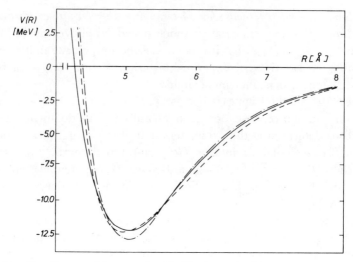

FIG. 24. Best fit potential curves for Na–Xe determined from several sets of beam scattering data using different potential models. —, based on a modified two piece 6 parameter Lennard–Jones potential (Buck and Pauly, 1968). —·—·—, based on a two piece 5 parameter Lennard–Jones potential (Buck and Pauly, 1968). - - -, based on a locally modified Lennard–Jones (12.6) potential (Düren, Raabe, and Schlier, 1968).

determined by the three different groups for Na–Xe are compared with each other. Except in the repulsive region the three potentials agree within better than 10% with each other.

Recently bulk data such as second virial coefficients and transport coefficients have also been found to be useful in providing additional

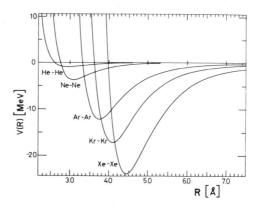

FIG. 25. Potential energy wells for the rare gas dimers determined by fitting a flexible model potential to experimental data from beam scattering experiments, as well as from spectroscopic, virial coefficient and solid state experiments (Farrar et al., 1973).

experimental information on the potentials. By adjusting a sufficiently flexible potential model to match all available experimental data, very accurate potential curves have been obtained. Figure 25 shows the results for the rare gas dimers obtained in this way (Siska *et al.*, 1971; Parson *et al.*, 1972; Schafer *et al.*, 1971).

## 2. Studies of the Short Range Repulsive Potential ($g^* > 1$)

*a. Measurements of Differential Cross Sections; Nonidentical Partners.* At angles greater than the rainbow angle the scattering is determined largely by the repulsive forces. As shown in Fig. 13 the repulsive potential is dominant at $g^* > 1$ and for angles greater than the rainbow angle. A measurement of the differential cross section (weighted with sin $\vartheta$) over the entire angular region from $0°$ to $180°$ can be seen in Fig. 14. At angles greater than the rainbow angle $(d^2\sigma/d^2\omega)$ sin $\vartheta$ decreases monotonically with increasing scattering angle as is to be expected from the classical description of the differential cross section

$$\frac{d^2\sigma}{d^2\omega}(\vartheta) \sin \vartheta = \beta \frac{d\beta}{d\vartheta},\tag{3.32}$$

since $\beta \to 0$ with $\vartheta \to \pi$ while $d\beta/d\vartheta$ remains nearly constant.

Since there is no interference from the attractive region, the classical deflection function can be determined directly from the measured differential cross section. The inversion formula used may be easily obtained by integrating Eq. (3.32) to get

$$\beta^2(\vartheta) = 2 \int_\vartheta^\pi \frac{d^2\sigma}{d^2\omega} \sin \vartheta \, d\vartheta.\tag{3.33}$$

Once the deflection function is known, the potential may be obtained directly using the procedures described in the previous section. The points marked by ($\square$) at positive energies in Fig. 18 show the repulsive potential obtained from such an inversion. This technique assumes the validity of the classical expression Eq. (3.1) and, where this expression can be expected to hold, the direct inversion of large angle differential cross sections provides the most accurate method for determining the repulsive potential. Of course the potential is only determined up to an energy equal to that of the relative energy in the collision.

*b. Measurements of Differential Cross Sections: Identical Particles.* In the case of identical particles symmetry effects must be taken into account in the calculations of the differential cross section. These symmetry effects lead to additional observable undulations which provide an independent method for determining the range of the repulsive potential.

Since the detector cannot distinguish between particles initially in the primary beam and those that were initially in the target beam (or gas) the scattering amplitudes of both these waves contribute to the observed cross section

$$\frac{d^2\sigma}{d^2\omega} = |f(\vartheta) \pm f(n - \vartheta)|^2, \tag{3.34}$$

where the positive sign applies for bosons and the negative sign for fermions (Mott and Massey, 1965; Hirschfelder et al., 1954, p. 74). As a result of destructive interference between the two scattering amplitudes only odd or even terms in the partial wave expansion of the differential and integral cross sections remain:

$$\frac{d^2\sigma}{d^2\omega} = \frac{1}{k^2} \left| \sum_l \omega_l (2l + 1) \exp(2i\eta_l - 1) P_l(\cos\vartheta) \right|^2 \tag{3.35}$$

and

$$\sigma = \frac{8\pi}{k^2} \sum_l \omega_l (2l + 1) \sin^2 \eta_l, \tag{3.36}$$

where for bosons without spin

$$\omega_l = 2 \quad \text{for even } l, \qquad \omega_l = 0 \quad \text{for odd } l$$

and for fermions without spin*

$$\omega_l = 0 \quad \text{for even } l, \qquad \omega_l = 2 \quad \text{for odd } l.$$

In the case of bosons the exclusion of odd Legendre functions in Eq. (3.36) leads to oscillations in the wide angle differential cross section. These oscillations have been observed in $^4$He–$^4$He and in $^{20}$Ne–$^{20}$Ne (Siska et al., 1971).

In Fig. 26 the experimental results for $^{20}$Ne–$^{20}$Ne are compared with a calculated curve in which the smearing effects in the apparatus have been

---

* Since spinless fermions do not exist a more realistic case is a fermion of spin $\frac{1}{2}$, where, however, the spin degeneracy leads to additional complications. For this case $\omega_l = \frac{1}{2}$ for $l = 0, 2, 4, \ldots$ and $\omega_l = \frac{3}{2}$ for $l = 1, 3, 5, \ldots$ .

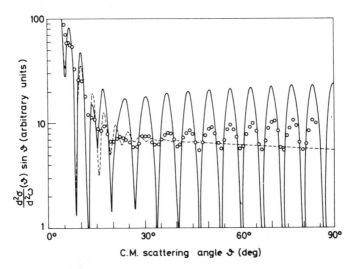

FIG. 26. Measured differential cross section for $^{20}$Ne–$^{20}$Ne at $E_{\text{c.m.}} = 62.0 \cdot 10^{-3}$ eV (Siska *et al.*, 1970). The solid line shows a curve calculated for a Lennard–Jones (12.6) potential ($\epsilon = 3.08 \cdot 10^{-3}$ eV; $R_m = 3.09$ Å) with account taken of the symmetry of the wave function. The dotted line is calculated for the same potential but neglecting symmetry.

neglected. An analysis of the results shows that the spacing of the undulations provides direct information on the potential radius at the energies corresponding to the minimum distance of approach.

*c. Measurements of Integral Cross Sections, Nonidentical Particles.* Because of the smallness of the large angle differential cross section especially at high energies, most of the present information on the repulsive potential comes from measurements of integral cross sections. Of course, in order to be sensitive to the repulsive potential, the relative velocities must be above the region, where the attractive potential is strong enough to produce glory undulations as expressed by the condition $g^* > 1$. On the other hand, in order to measure a quantum mechanical integral cross section, the critical angle must not be too small. Both of these conditions can be met at thermal beam velocities for light neutral particles because of their low masses and small $\epsilon$ values.

High precision measurements of this type have recently been carried out on the systems H–He, H–H$_2$, He–H$_2$, He–He, as well as for scattering of H and H$_2$ on the rare gases (Gengenbach and Hahn, 1972; Gengenbach *et al.*, 1973; Bickes *et al.*, 1973). The results for He–H$_2$ are shown in Fig. 27. At high velocities a small correction ($\sim 10\%$) for the insufficient an-

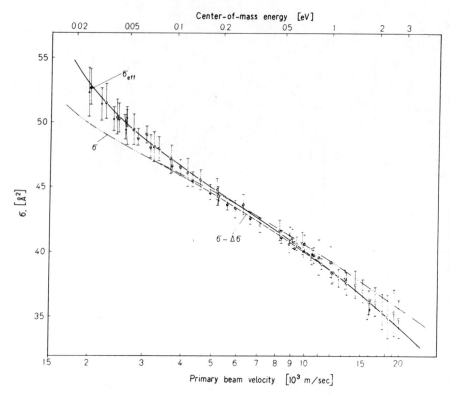

Fig. 27. Measured integral cross sections for $H_2$–He (points with an error of 1 standard deviation) and calculated integral cross sections for the best fit potential model (BMMLJ, see Table III) (–····–), with allowance for the angular resolving power ($\sigma - \Delta\sigma$, - - -), and finally after averaging over the distribution in relative velocity ($\sigma_{eff}$, —). The experimental points from five separate experiments are shown.

gular resolving power has to be applied. This can be accurately calculated by weighting the theoretical differential cross section with a quantity which gives the effective probability that a particle which has been deflected by a laboratory angle $\theta$ still strikes the detector. At small velocities this correction is negligible but another correction has to be applied to take account of the distribution of relative velocities. The error in the corrections is estimated to be less than 5% so that the corrected cross sections are reliable to better than 0.5%. In addition to the velocity dependence, the absolute cross sections were also measured with an accuracy $\Delta\sigma/\sigma \simeq 1\%$.

The results for the closed shell system He–$H_2$ and He–He are especially interesting since they can be compared with the spherical symmetric part* of the *a priori* potential hypersurfaces from quantum chemical self-consistent field (SCF) and configuration interaction (CI) calculations.

The calculations for He–H$_2$ (Krauss and Mies, 1965; Gordon and Secrest, 1970) do not show any evidence of the expected attractive dispersion potential. Thus in order to fit the experiments, a potential model had to be assumed, which included the theoretical $R^{-6}$ attractive term. It was found that whereas the Lennard-Jones potential would not fit the data, the Slater and Born–Mayer–Morse–Lennard-Jones (BMMLJ) potential models gave a satisfactory fit. Table XIII shows a comparison between theoretical potential parameters for He–H$_2$ and those obtained from the experiment by a least squares fit to measured corrected cross sections. The experimental best-fit and theoretical potential curves are shown in Fig. 28.

TABLE XIII

COMPARISON OF EXPERIMENTAL AND THEORETICAL POTENTIAL PARAMETERS FOR He–H$_2$
ASSUMING A BORN–MAYER REPULSIVE POTENTIAL $[(V(R) = A \exp(-\alpha R)]$

| Potential parameter | Experiment[a] | Theory |
|---|---|---|
| $A$ (eV) | 271 ($\pm 7\%$)[b] | 218,[c] 300[d] |
| $\alpha$ (a.u.$^{-1}$) | 1.944 ($\pm 1.5\%$)[b] | 1.862,[c] 1.94[d] |

[a] Evaluated using a BMMLJ potential model.
[b] Gengenbach *et al.* (1971a).
[c] Krauss and Mies (1965).
[d] Gordon and Secrest (1970).

*d. Measurements of Integral Cross Sections: Identical Particles.* Undulations corresponding to those observed in the differential cross section have also been observed in the integral cross section. Depending on the type of particle (boson or fermion) either odd or even partial waves only will make a contribution to the cross section [see Eq. (3.36)]. The

---

* Exact quantum mechanical calculations (Eastes and Secrest, 1972; Fremerey and Toennies, 1972) show that the measured integral cross sections in the case of some atom–molecule partners provides information only on the spherical symmetric part of the hypersurface.

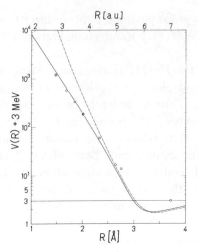

FIG. 28. Comparison between best fit potentials based on two different potential models for He–H$_2$. The potential models have been fitted to integral cross section measurements over a large range of velocities (150–15,000 m/sec). The dotted line is the best fit obtained with a two piece Lennard-Jones potential (see Table III). The solid line is the best fit, with a much smaller $\chi^2$, for a BMMLJ potential (see Table III) and represents the true potential to within a few percent. The points refer to the angle-averaged calculated potential obtained by Krauss and Mies (1965) ($\Diamond$) and Gordon and Secrest (1970) ($\bigcirc$).

appearance of undulations in the case of boson scattering, for example, $^4$He–$^4$He, can be easily understood if a hard sphere interaction (radius $= R_0$) is assumed (Dohmann, 1969). For this case (Mott and Massey, 1965)

$$\eta_l = kR_0 - \tfrac{1}{2}l\pi, \qquad (3.37)$$

and since only even $l$ contribute, it follows from Eq. (3.37) that the difference in phases is given by

$$\eta_{l+2} - \eta_l = \pi. \qquad (3.38)$$

According to Eq. (3.36) the largest contribution from a given partial wave will occur when $\eta_l = \pi/2$, $3\pi/2$, etc. Thus at velocities for which

$$kR_0 = n\pi/2, \qquad (3.39)$$

where $n$ is an integer, many partial waves will make a maximum contribution and the integral cross section will go through a maximum. The spacing in the relative velocity between two such maxima (or minima) corresponding to $\Delta n = 2$ is therefore given by

$$\Delta g = \frac{h}{2R_0\mu}. \tag{3.40}$$

According to this formula, $\Delta g = 380$ m/sec for $^4\text{He}-^4\text{He}$. Deviations from the hard sphere behavior and experimental smearing effects lead to a shift in the spacing and a reduction in the observed amplitude of undulations.

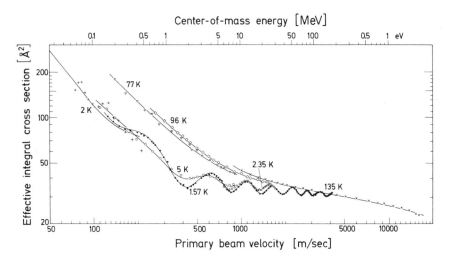

FIG. 29.    Effective integral cross section for $^4\text{He}-^4\text{He}$ as a function of the primary beam velocity. The points are measurements from five different experimental groups with scattering chamber targets at the indicated temperatures. The solid curve is calculated from a potential which was determined by a best fit of all the data (Gengenbach, 1972).

Figure 29 shows the results of the measured velocity dependence in the integral cross section for $^4\text{He}-^4\text{He}$ obtained by five groups (Cantini *et al.*, 1972; Bennewitz *et al.*, 1972; Gengenbach *et. al.*, 1971b; Farrar and Lee, 1972; Butz *et al.*, 1971 and Feltgen *et al.*, 1973). The symmetry undulations are well resolved in the experiments with low target temperatures.

*e. Measurements of Integral Cross Sections at High Energies.*    In order to probe the repulsive potential at interaction energies greater than $\sim 0.1$ eV, beam energies greater than those used ($\sim 3$ eV) in the measurements of integral cross sections described previously are required. At these high energies it is practically impossible to produce a narrow enough beam such that the acceptance angle is less than the critical angle.

If the c.m. acceptance angle $\vartheta_a$ is greater than the c.m. critical angle $\vartheta_0$, the classical formula for the integral cross section (formula I, Table V) is valid (provided $\vartheta$ is small):

$$\sigma(\vartheta_a E) = \pi\left(\frac{(s-1)f(s)C_s}{E\vartheta_a}\right)^{2/s}, \qquad (3.41)$$

where $C_s$ and $s$ refer to a repulsive potential $V(R) = C_s/R^s$. Since this cross section depends on $\vartheta_a$, it is commonly called an incomplete integral cross section. Thus just as in the case of the quantum mechanical cross section, the slope of log $\sigma(E\vartheta_a)$ versus log $E$ is a measure of $s$ and the absolute value of $\sigma(E\vartheta_a)$ provides information on $C_s$. In determining $C_s$, this method has one serious drawback as compared to using the quantum mechanical cross section which arises because of the necessity of absolutely determining $\vartheta_a$, which enters directly; $\vartheta_a$ depends on the geometry and the actual trajectories and cannot be easily calculated.

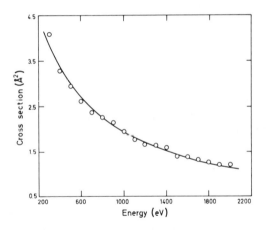

FIG. 30.  Measured incomplete integral cross section for He–He as a function of energy (Jordan and Amdur, 1967).

Figure 30 shows some typical results for the incomplete integral cross section measured for He–He at high energies. As is to be expected, the incomplete cross section is considerably smaller than the complete integral cross section measured at lower energies.

Figure 31 summarizes the potential data obtained from several different techniques for He–He. The high-energy data are based on incomplete

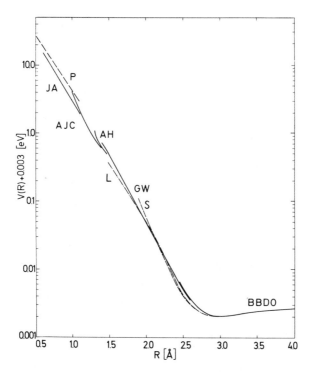

FIG. 31. Experimentally determined potential curves of He–He over 4 orders of magnitude. The curves JA, AJC, and AH stem from high-energy incomplete integral cross section measurements by Amdur and co-workers. JA refers to Jordan and Amdur (1967) where references to the earlier work can be found. The curve GW (Gengenbach *et al.*, 1971b) and BBDO (Bennewitz *et al.*, 1972) are from measurements of complete integral cross sections. These agree well with recent CI calculations. P refers to a theoretical calculation by Phillipson, 1962. The curves L (Farrar and Lee, 1972) and S (Cantini *et al.*, 1972) are from measurements of differential cross sections.

cross section measurements by Jordan and Amdur (1967). The potential at intermediate energies is derived from the measured velocity dependence of the complete cross section, and the potential curve at low energies is obtained by a best fit to the interference undulations in the integral cross section discussed in the previous section. Of the results presented in Fig. 31 those at high energies are probably the least reliable. Possibly the greatest source of error comes from the averaging over the actual beam geometry to obtain the effective average acceptance angle of the apparatus. Another source of uncertainty is the assumption of classical scattering for the smallest scattering angles, which occur in some of the possible beam trajectories.

## IV. Inelastic Scattering Experiments

### A. INTRODUCTION

The experimental study of the following processes will be discussed in this section:

(1) rotational excitation: $\quad A + BC(j, m) \rightarrow A + BC(j', m')$
(2) vibrational excitation: $\quad A + BC(n) \rightarrow A + BC(n')$
(3) dissociation: $\quad A + BC \rightarrow A + B + C$
(4) electronic excitation, chemionization, and ionization, e.g.:

$$A + B(^2P_{3/2}) \rightarrow A + B(^2P_{1/2}) \quad \text{or}$$
$$A + BC \rightarrow A^+ + BC^-$$

Much less experimental data is available on inelastic scattering than elastic or reactive scattering. Very likely this can be attributed to the fact that these processes are usually the most difficult to identify experimentally. Before discussing the experiments some recent theoretical developments are summarized.

In the case of rotational and vibrational excitation of $^1\Sigma$ molecules the collision dynamics are determined by the ground state potential hypersurface. Using recently developed quantum chemical computational techniques, potential surfaces have been calculated for systems with as many as 11 electrons. For example self-consistent field (SCF) and configuration interaction (CI) calculations are now available for the atom–diatomic–molecule systems He + $H_2$(SCF + CI), $Li^+$ + $H_2$(SCF+CI), Li + HF(SCF), and F + $H_2$(SCF + some CI). For a given hypersurface a nearly exact quantum mechanical calculation of the inelastic cross sections using recently improved computational techniques (Secrest and Johnson, 1966; Gordon, 1969) is now possible. Unfortunately, the required accuracy of the hypersurface calculations needed to obtain reliable theoretical cross sections is not yet known.

The hypersurface for He + $H_2$ has been studied more extensively both theoretically and experimentally (see Section III,E,2) than that for any other nonreactive system. Krauss and Mies (1965), who did the first SCF calculation for many different relative orientations of the three atoms, were able to fit their results to the following relatively simple 7-parameter formula:

$$V_{KM}(R, x, \Omega) = A \exp[-(\alpha_0 + \alpha_1 x)R]$$
$$\times \{a + bP_2(\cos \Omega) + [c + dP_2(\cos \Omega)]x\}, \qquad (4.1a)$$

where the coordinates are defined in Fig. 32. This calculation and a more recent configuration interaction calculation (Gordon and Secrest, 1970), however, failed to show the expected attractive potential from the long range dispersion force. The strength and the anisotropy of the long range potential are, however, known both from experiments and perturbation calculations (Victor and Dalgarno, 1970). As suggested by beam measurements of total integral cross sections (see Section III,E,2,c), a good approximation to the actual potential hypersurface at energies up to about 1 eV is given by adding an attractive dispersion term to Eq. (4.1),

$$V(R, x, \Omega) = V_{\mathrm{KM}}(R, x, \Omega) - \frac{C}{R^6}\,[1 + q_{2,6}P_2(\cos \Omega)], \qquad (4.1b)$$

where all of the altogether 9 $(7 + 2)$ parameters are known from theory. Figure 33 shows the equipotential curves for this potential model with the best available theoretical potential parameters.

FIG. 32. Coordinates used to describe the atom-diatom potential hypersurface, illustrated for He–H$_2$. $x = r - r_e$; $r_e$ = equilibrium H$_2$ bond length.

With this potential model, quantum mechanical calculations of the inelastic differential cross sections have been carried out (Fremerey and Toennies, 1972). Figure 34 shows the results of a calculation for 1.09 eV, where vibrational excitation can occur. In the calculations the simultaneous occurrence of rotational and vibrational transitions has been accounted for. The number of rotational and vibrational states making up the basis set has been restricted to two each (e.g., $n = 0, 1$, and $j = 0, 2, 4, 6$) so that the results are only approximate. The results show that for angles greater than 50° the differential cross section for rotational excitation is of the same order of magnitude as the elastic differential cross sections. Furthermore, vibrational excitation is less probable by 4 orders of magnitude and is strongly peaked in the backward direction. With increasing energy the cross sections for vibrational excitation increase drastically and the maxima tend to shift to smaller angles. The vibrationally inelastic cross section for rotationally excited $(j = 2)$ molecules is also shown in

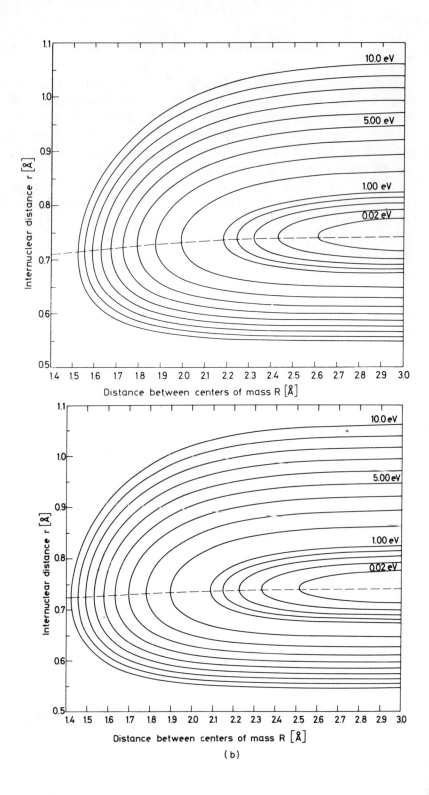

(b)

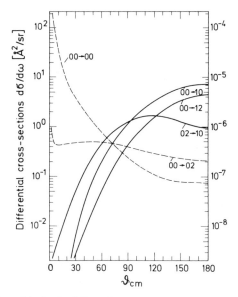

FIG. 34. Elastic and inelastic differential cross sections for rotational and vibrational excitation calculated by quantum mechanics for scattering of He on para-$H_2$ at $E_{c.m.} = 1.09$ eV. The dashed line is drawn to the scale at the left, whereas the solid line is drawn to the scale at the right. The results are based on the hypersurface given in Eq. (4.2) but with the potential parameters obtained by Gordon and Secrest (1970).

Fig. 34. Other calculations indicate that the differential cross sections depend sensitively on the shape of the hypersurface. Thus there is evidence from this and other computational studies that precise measurements of inelastic cross sections will eventually be useful in determining the shape of at least certain regions of the potential hypersurface. These nearly exact computational studies also suggest that many of the generalizations based on one-dimensional collisional models with approximate potentials are very likely incorrect.

Of course for most collision partners the hypersurfaces are not known and quantum mechanical calculations cannot be performed. In this case the Massey criterium (Mott and Massey, 1965, p. 353) is useful to obtain an order-of-magnitude estimate of the transition probability $P$ for an

---

← FIG. 33. The potential hypersurface for He–$H_2$ for two relative orientations of $r$ to $R$. (a) $\Omega = 0°$, (b) $\Omega = 90°$. The hypersurface was calculated by adding Eq. (4.2) (with, however, $q_{2,6} = 0$) to the Morse potential for the $H_2$ molecule. The dashed line shows the reaction coordinate.

inelastic transition,

$$P \simeq \exp(-2t/\tau), \qquad (4.2)$$

where $t$ is the time of the collision ($t \simeq R_0/g$), $R_0$ is the potential range, and $\tau$ is the period of the excited degree of freedom ($\tau \simeq \hbar/\Delta E$, $\Delta E$ is the change in internal energy). For $t/\tau > 1$, $P \simeq 0$ and the collision is adiabatic; otherwise, for $t/\tau \lesssim 1$, $P \simeq 1$ and the collision is nonadiabatic. At $T = 300°$K, $t/\tau_{\text{rot}}$ values of some typical diatomic molecules lie in the range 2–13 and $t/\tau_{\text{vib}}$ values lie in the range 10–80. Thus rotational transitions are, as shown also by the exact calculations (Fig. 34), considerably more probable than vibrational transitions.

The theories of inelastic collisions leading to dissociation and electronic excitation are not nearly as well developed. In the case of dissociation several approximate techniques have been tried. These include a first-order solution of the quantum mechanical Fadeev equations (Krüger, 1972) and classical trajectory calculations. The theory of electronic excitation is discussed briefly in connection with the experiments in Section IV,E.

## B. Experimental Methods

Two basic experimental methods are used. These are called the *state change* and the *velocity change* method. In the former the occurrence of a quantum transition is determined by the accompanying change in some observable property of the atom or molecule such as a change in the effective magnetic or electric dipole moment. A necessary requirement for using this method is that the atoms or molecules have permanent moments and that these change in the transition. This is the case, for example, in rotational transitions of polar molecules or in some electronic transitions of atoms. In these situations the electrostatic or analogous

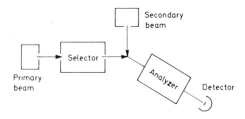

FIG. 35. Basic arrangement used in scattering experiments to study inelastic processes of the type A + BC($j, n, v$) → A + BC($j', n', v'$).

magnetic state selectors discussed in Section I can be used in the arrangement common to both methods and shown schematically in Fig. 35.

In the velocity change method the change in the velocity accompanying the internal energy change is used to observe and identify the transition. The change in the center-of-mass velocity of the collision partners follows from Eq. (2.4) and (2.5) (with $\Delta D_0 = 0$):

$$\frac{\mathbf{u}_1^{f}}{\mathbf{u}_1^{i}} = \frac{\mathbf{u}_2^{f}}{\mathbf{u}_2^{i}} = \left(1 \mp \frac{\Delta E_{\text{c.m.}}}{E_{\text{c.m.}}^{i}}\right)^{1/2}, \qquad (4.3)$$

where $\Delta E_{\text{c.m.}}$ is the relative change in translational energy accompanying the transition, and the minus sign is for excitation and the plus sign for deexcitation. Thus for each quantum transition (discrete value of $\Delta E$) the scattered particles have a discrete velocity in the center-of-mass

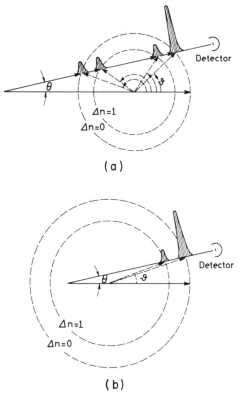

(a)

(b)

FIG. 36.   Newton velocity diagrams for inelastic (nonreactive) scattering on a stationary target. In (a) the projectile is heavier than the target $(m_1 > m_2)$, $\Delta E_{\text{lab}}/E_{\text{lab}}$ $< \Delta E_{\text{c.m.}}/E_{\text{c.m.}}$, whereas in (b) the projectile is lighter than the target $(m_1 < m_2)$, $\Delta E_{\text{lab}}/E_{\text{lab}} \sim \Delta E_{\text{c.m.}}/E_{\text{c.m.}}$.

system (see Fig. 36). The velocity change method has the advantage that it can in principle be applied to study all inelastic processes without any restriction on the collision partners. The resolving power of the velocity change method is however usually severely limited by the angular spread and velocity distribution of the target beam. This is not as serious a factor in the state change method. Largely for this reason it has so far only been possible to resolve rotational transitions clearly with the state change method.

The amount of smearing of the ideal velocity spectra can be reduced by a careful choice of the measuring plane to which, for experimental simplicity, the motion of the detector is usually restricted. Two measuring planes are used. The in-plane arrangement is shown in Fig. 1 if $\phi = 0$ and only $\theta$ is varied. In the other arrangement the plane is perpendicular to the secondary beam direction ($\phi = 90°$ in Fig. 1). In the latter arrangement the velocity spread of the secondary beam does not contribute in first order to the velocity spread of the scattered particles (Greene et al., 1969b). This arrangement usually has the disadvantage, however, that not all center-of-mass scattering angles $\vartheta$ are sampled by the detector.

In many of the experiments the velocity of the target molecule is much lower than that of the primary beam molecules. This is particularly the case in vibrational excitation experiments where in order to get appreciable excitation fast beams (several eV) are required. The kinematics are considerably simplified if a stationary target is assumed. For this simplifying case the relative energy loss in the laboratory system, $\Delta E_{\text{lab}}/E_{\text{lab}} = \epsilon$, is given in terms of the relative energy loss in the center-of-mass system, $\Delta E_{\text{c.m.}}/E_{\text{c.m.}} = \varepsilon$, by

$$\epsilon = \mu^2 \varepsilon \pm 2(1 - \mu) \cos \theta \{ f^{1/2} \mp (f - \mu^2 \varepsilon)^{1/2} \}, \qquad (4.4)$$

where $\mu = m_2/(m_1 + m_2)$, and $f = [\mu^2 - (1 - \mu)^2 \sin^2 \theta]$ and $\theta$ is the laboratory scattering angle. The upper signs refer to scattering in the forward hemisphere ($\vartheta \leq 90°$) and the lower signs to scattering in the backward hemisphere ($\vartheta \geq 90°$). The best resolution is obtained in the laboratory system when $m_1 < m_2$ and in this case Eq. (4.4) has the limiting form

$$\epsilon/\varepsilon \to 1 \quad \text{as} \quad m_2/m_1 \to \infty. \qquad (4.5)$$

Aside from the fact that $m_1 < m_2$ imposes restrictions on the choice of scattering partners this case has the experimental disadvantage that particles that have undergone central collisions ($\vartheta \sim 180°$) are scattered into large laboratory angles which are usually obstructed by the primary beam source and selectors (see Fig. 36).

In the other limiting case of $m_1 > m_2$ particles scattered in both the forward and backward directions in the center-of-mass system appear in the laboratory system within a forward cone with an angle given by $\sin \theta_{max} = m_2/m_1$ and can be easily observed. The kinematic smearing is largest near $\theta_{max}$ (see Fig. 36) and thus measurements are usually restricted to $\theta \simeq 0$. Equation (4.4) reduces in this case to

$$\frac{\epsilon}{\varepsilon} \simeq \frac{m_2(m_2 \pm m_1)}{(m_1 + m_2)^2} \quad \text{for} \quad \left(\frac{m_2}{m_1} < 1, \quad \theta \simeq 0, \quad \varepsilon \ll 1\right). \quad (4.6)$$

As follows from Eq. (4.4) the relative resolving power is least for backward scattering. Large angle inelastic scattering where the vibrational excitation usually has the highest probability (see Fig. 34), is therefore difficult to observe experimentally.* The Newton diagrams for the two extreme cases mentioned above are shown in Fig. 35.

## C. Experiments on Rotational Excitation

### 1. *Rotational Excitation of Alkali Halide Molecules Measured by the State Change Method*

The following collision process has been studied using a state selection apparatus (Toennies, 1965):

$$MX(j, 0) + A \text{ or } BC \rightarrow MX(j', 0) + A \text{ or } BC, \quad (4.7)$$

where MX is an alkali halide molecule, $j$ and $j' = 1, 2$, or 3, A is a rare gas atom and BC is a diatomic or polyatomic molecule.

Figure 37 shows the operating principle of the apparatus. MX molecules leave the oven with the rotational, vibrational, and velocity distributions corresponding to the equilibrium conditions in the oven ($T \cong 1000°K$). The beam then passes through an electric four-pole field rotational state selector (see Section II,C,3) which serves as a polarizer, and only molecules in one of the rotational states $(j, m) = (1, 0), (2, 0)$, or $(3, 0)$ are focused on the center of the scattering chamber. Since most

---

* If, however, velocities or flight times are measured the relative resolving power is greatest in the backward direction.

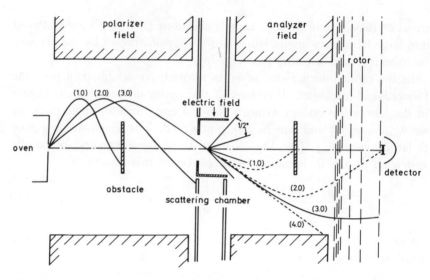

Fig. 37. Molecular trajectories and side view of the apparatus used for measuring inelastic cross sections. In the example shown, only molecules in the (3, 0) state can enter the scattering chamber, whereas only (2, 0) molecules can arrive at the detector. The transverse dimensions have been expanded by about a factor 100 compared with the longitudinal dimensions.

(70%) of the molecules are in the ground vibrational state, the quantum states of the molecules before collisions are almost entirely specified. After scattering in a gas filled scattering chamber, that part of the beam which has been scattered through small angles is analyzed for its rotational state with a second rotational state selector (analyzer) and then allowed to strike the detector. A homogeneous electric field is present in the scattering chamber to prevent a randomization of $m$ states (depolarization). Finally, a velocity selector ($\Delta v/v \sim 10\%$), necessary for the operation of the four-pole field, is introduced between analyzer and the detector.*

Sample beam trajectories for the transition from the rotational state $(j, m) = (3, 0)$ to $(2, 0)$ are shown in Fig. 37. As pointed out previously (see Section II,C,3) the rotational states (1, 0), (2, 0), and (3, 0) are most easily selected by the inhomogeneous electric four-pole fields. It is a fortunate circumstance that the inelastic cross sections for transitions among these states are particularly large since the rotational period of the

---

* Since the change in velocity accompanying transitions $\Delta v/v \simeq 10^{-3}$ is small compared to the velocity resolution of the rotor ($\Delta v/v \simeq 10^{-1}$) the actual location along the beam path of the selector is not important.

heavy MX molecules is of the order of the collision time [see Eq. (4.2)]. Actually, this connection between focusing and inelastic excitation can be traced back to the fact that both are the result of similar electrical interactions.

The inelastic cross sections are determined by measuring the dependence of the intensity transmitted by the analyzer field on the pressure of the target gas. The intensity is observed to first increase with pressure, reach a maximum, and then decrease at higher pressures. This behavior indicates that molecules that have been inelastically scattered through small angles may be subsequently scattered and removed from the beam. On the basis of this mechanism, the following formula for the pressure dependence can be derived:

$$\frac{I(j_i m_i \to j_f m_f)}{I_0(j_i m_i \to j_i m_i)} = \sigma_{\text{inel}}^{(j_i m_i) \to (j_f m_f)} nL \, \exp(-\sigma_{\text{tot}}^{(j_i m_i)} nL), \qquad (4.8)$$

where $I(j_i m_i \to j_f m_f)$ is the intensity measured at a scattering gas density $n$ with the polarizer and analyzer set for the states $(j_i, m_i)$ and $(j_f, m_f)$, respectively. $I_0(j_i m_i \to j_i m_i)$ is measured with the analyzer set for the same state as the polarizer and without gas in the scattering chamber. $L$ is the length of the scattering chamber, and $\sigma_{\text{tot}}^{(j_i m_i)}$ is the total integral cross section that is measured when both state selectors pass the same state. The pressure dependence predicted by Eq. (4.8) agrees well with the observed behavior. From the fit, the inelastic cross sections are determined.

Since the measured cross section is an integral over the small angle inelastic differential cross section it depends on the average laboratory acceptance angle $(\bar{\alpha})$ of the second four-pole field:

$$\sigma_{\text{inel}}(\alpha) = \int_0^{2\pi} \int_0^{\vartheta_\alpha} \frac{d^2 \sigma_{\text{inel}}}{d^2 \omega} \sin \vartheta \, d\vartheta \, d\varphi, \qquad (4.9)$$

where $\vartheta_\alpha$ is the center-of-mass angle is given approximately by

$$\vartheta_\alpha \simeq \frac{m_1 + m_2}{m_2} \bar{\alpha}$$

and $m_1$ and $m_2$ are the masses of primary and secondary beam particles.

In Table XIV the measured results are compared with cross sections calculated in the high-energy approximation (Toennies, 1966) using the dominant induction and electrostatic terms in the long range attractive potential. For comparison the total integral cross section measured

TABLE XIV

A Comparison between Measured and Calculated Inelastic Cross Sections for
TlF in Collisions with Various Gases[a]

| Type of scattering gas | Gas | Measured $(20) \to (30)$ $\sigma_{1nel}$[b] | Calculated $(20) \to (30)$ $\sigma_{1nel}$ | Measured $\sigma_{tot}^{jmp}$ |
|---|---|---|---|---|
| Atoms and spherical tops | He | 3.7 | — | — |
| | Ne | 4.6 | 0.5 | 407 |
| | Ar | 6.1 | 0.5 | 674 |
| | Kr | 6.4 | 0.2 | 825 |
| | $CH_4$ | 6.3 | 0.08 | 702 |
| | $SF_6$ | 6.8 | 0.04 | 955 |
| Fast-rotating molecules | $H_2$ | 19.4 | — | — |
| | $O_2$ | 7.8 | 6.8 | 461 |
| | Air($N_2$) | 24 | 124 | 571 |
| | $N_2O$ | 80 | 145 | 890 |
| | $H_2O$ | 70 | 81 | 862 |
| Symmetric tops | $NH_3$ | 580 | 800 | 940 |
| | $NH_3$   $50[(1, 0) \to (3, 0)]$ | | 150 | — |
| Slowly rotating polar molecule (resonance) | $CF_2Cl_2$ | 115 | — | 750 |

[a] The measured total integral cross sections for stationary scattering gas but without state selection are shown in the last column. The velocity of the TlF beam (305 m/sec) was always less than the average velocity of the scattering gas. All values are in square angstroms.

[b] The estimated experimental error is of the order of 40% for the small cross sections and about 10% for the larger values.

without state selection is shown in the last column. The integral cross section which depends mainly on the orientation averaged potential is the same (within a factor of 2) for all scattering gases. The large differences in the inelastic cross sections come about since they depend in first order on the square of the anisotropy potential parameters. Thus the inelastic cross sections provide a sensitive method for measuring the potential anisotropy.

From these results the differential cross section for small angle ($\vartheta < 4°$) inelastic scattering on atoms and spherical tops is estimated to be roughly $d^2\sigma/d^2\omega \sim 10^2$–$10^4$ Å²/sr.

## 2. Rotational Excitation Measured by the Velocity Change Method

Beck and Förster (1970) have recently carried out a careful study of rotational excitation in the system

$$K + CO_2(\bar{j}) \rightarrow K + CO_2(\bar{j} + \varDelta j), \qquad (4.10)$$

where $\bar{j}$ ($\simeq 20$) is the average rotational state of the thermal $CO_2$ beam. Because of the close spacing of the rotational levels these could not be resolved in the velocity change experiment. Energy transfers corresponding to $\varDelta j = 6$–$22$ were observed.

Figure 38a shows the apparatus used. Velocity selectors with a velocity resolution of 4.5% were used to specify the velocity of the K beam before and after scattering. The $CO_2$ secondary beam is directed downward and perpendicular to the measuring plane. The perpendicular-plane geometry was used because of the advantages discussed earlier (Section IV,B). To measure the angular distribution of the inelastically scattered particles the analyzer selector is rotated about the secondary beam in a plane containing the primary beam and perpendicular to the secondary beam. A conventional Langmuir–Taylor detector was used.

Figure 38b shows velocity spectra measured with an Ar and $CO_2$ secondary beam. The difference between the two spectra at the low velocity side of the maximum is attributed to rotational excitation of the $CO_2$. To obtain the center-of-mass differential cross sections for various amounts of energy transfer the $CO_2$ spectrum was then fitted to a calculated spectrum. Figure 39 shows the angular dependence of the differential cross sections (multiplied by $\sin \vartheta$) and also that of the elastic cross section. The elastic differential cross section shows the expected rainbow and the sharp fall off with increasing angle expected for scattering from a spherically symmetric potential. The inelastic cross sections, however, appear to be inversely proportional to $\sin \vartheta$. At center-of-mass angles greater than about 20–25° the inelastic cross sections become equal to the elastic cross sections. These large inelastic cross sections are unexpected since if direct collisions occur $t_{coll}/\tau_{rot}$ is estimated to be 10–50 implying small probability for energy transfer [see Eq. (4.2)].

To explain this apparently anomalous behavior a mechanism is proposed in which two types of collisions occur with vastly different time scales. In the one case adiabatic direct collisions occur that are largely elastic and therefore show the expected rainbow maximum and sharp drop off with increasing angle in the differential cross section. The $\sin^{-1} \vartheta$ angular dependence of the inelastic differential cross section,

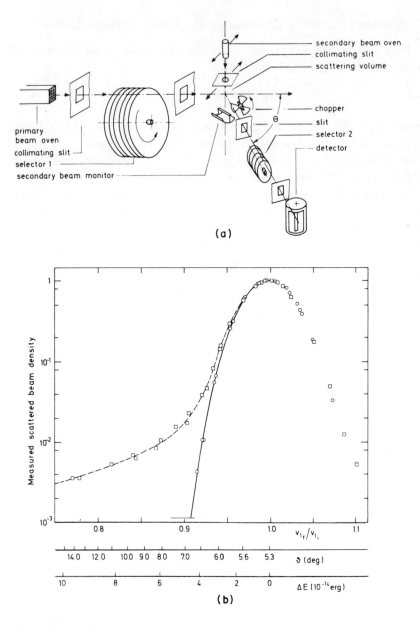

(a)

(b)

FIG. 38.   (a) Schematic diagram of the crossed beam apparatus used to study rotational excitation by the velocity change method. In (b) the measured velocity distributions of scattered K from $CO_2$ and Ar are shown. (○ K–Ar; □ K–$CO_2$). The difference at small velocities is attributed to rotational excitation of $CO_2$. The experimental conditions are $\theta = 3°$ and $v_{1_i} = 9.03 \cdot 10^4$ cm/sec (Beck and Förster, 1970).

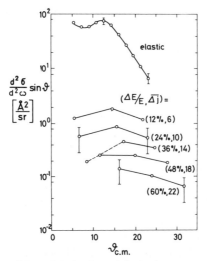

FIG. 39. Measured differential elastic and inelastic cross sections (weighted with $\sin \vartheta$) for $K + CO_2(\bar{j} = 20) \rightarrow K + CO_2(\bar{j} = 20 - \overline{\Delta j})$. The inelastic differential cross sections for several different values of the relative amount of energy transferred in the center-of-mass system, $\Delta E/E$, and the corresponding $\overline{\Delta j}$ values are shown.

on the other hand, suggests that a long-lived complex with probable geometry $(K^{(+)}\underset{O}{\overset{O}{\diagdown}}C^{(-)})$ is formed in some collisions. The complex is assumed to live long enough so that the total energy can be distributed among all available degrees of freedom. Thus these collisions have a high probability of being inelastic and are, therefore, predominantly observed in the inelastic channels. Additional evidence for complex formation in this system is provided by large angle scattering experiments on the same system (Ham and Kinsey, 1970).

In an earlier experiment Blythe *et al.* (1964), using a similar technique, investigated the deexcitation of ortho-$D_2$ in collisions with K atoms,

$$K + \text{ortho-}D_2(j = 2) \rightarrow K + \text{ortho-}D_2(j = 0). \qquad (4.11)$$

From a small bump in the velocity spectrum a differential cross section was estimated,

$$\left(\frac{d^2\sigma}{d^2\omega}\right)_{\text{inel}}^{2\rightarrow0}(\vartheta = 180^0, E_{\text{c.m.}} = 2.4 \cdot 10^{-2} \text{ eV}) = 0.05 - 0.15 \text{ Å}^2/\text{sr}.$$

Very recently small angle differential cross sections for the $j = 0 \rightarrow j = 2$ and $j = 1 \rightarrow j = 3$ inelastic transitions in Li$^+$–H$_2$ col-

lision at $E_{c.m.} = 0.6$ eV have been measured at small scattering angles
$(\vartheta_{c.m.} < 32°)$ (Van den Bergh et al., 1973). A time-of-flight technique
similar to that discussed in the next section was used.

### D. VIBRATIONAL EXCITATION AND DISSOCIATION

Vibrational excitation is more difficult to study than rotational excitation since the cross sections are many orders of magnitude smaller (see
Fig. 34) at thermal beam energies. For this reason it is necessary to go to
higher energies in order to get measurable inelastic cross sections, especially if molecules with widely spaced vibrational levels are to be excited.
Thus the best results on vibrational excitation have been obtained by
studying the scattering of atomic and molecular ions on neutral particles.
The results of recent experiments at center-of-mass energies less than
50 eV in which the velocity change method has been used are summarized
in Table XV.

TABLE XV

SURVEY OF VIBRATIONAL INELASTIC SCATTERING AT LOW BEAM ENERGIES

| Collision partners[a] | $E_{c.m.}$ (eV) | Authors |
|---|---|---|
| * $Li^+–H_2, D_2$ | 2–10 | Schöttler and Toennies (1968) <br> Held et al. (1970) <br> David et al. (1972) |
| $K^+, K, Na^+, Na–H_2, D_2$ | 3–35 | Dittner and Datz (1968) <br> Dittner and Datz (1969) |
| $Ar^+–D_2$ | 11–17 | Moran and Cosby (1969) |
| $H_3{}^+–Ne$ | — | Petty and Moran (1970) |
| $O^+–O_2$ <br> * $O_2{}^+–Ar$ | 6–12 | Cosby and Moran (1970) |
| $NO^+–He$ <br> $O_2{}^+–He$ | 4–25 | Cheng et al. (1970) |
| $K^+–H_2, D_2$ | 5–60 | Van Dop et al. (1971) |
| * $H^+–H_2, D_2$ | 3–10 | Udseth et al. (1971) |
| * $CsI + Ar$ | $\approx 10^{-1}$ | Creaser et al. (1971) |
| $CsI + Ar$ | 0.35–1.1 | Loesch and Herschbach (1972) |

[a] A star (*) denotes that the excitation of individual vibrational quantum states has
been observed.

With ions the energy range is limited only at the low end ($E_{lab} \gtrsim 5$ eV) and because ions can be directly measured, beam intensity is a less serious problem than with neutral atoms and molecules, which have to be ionized before they can be detected. In the case of scattering of closed shell alkali metal ions, which have a large ionization potential but a small electronic affinity, on simple molecules (e.g., $H_2$, $N_2$, $CH_4$) charge transfer and electronic excitation are energetically forbidden over a large range of energies ($E_{c.m.} \leq 6$ eV). Since experiment and theory suggest that the short range potentials are very similar to that of the isoelectronic neutral species these appear to be excellent prototype systems for studying energy transfer. In this section investigations on the system $Li^+ + H_2$ and $H^+ + H_2$ will be discussed in detail.

The inelastic collision process

$$Li^+ + H_2(n = 0) \rightarrow Li^+ + H_2 \qquad (n = 0, 1, 2, 3) \qquad (4.12)$$

has been extensively studied using a time-of-flight technique (David et al., 1971, 1972). This system is of particular interest since only four electrons are involved and the potential hypersurface is well known from quantum chemical calculations (Lester, 1970, 1971; Kutzelniss et al., 1973). The apparatus used is shown in Fig. 40. The lithium ion beam from a surface ionization source is energy selected in a 127° electrostatic sector field ($\Delta E/E \simeq 0.4\%$). The energy selected beam is the focused into a deflection plate system which produces short ($\sim$50 nsec at 15 eV) bursts of ions at a repetition rate of 10 kHz. These pass into a scattering chamber where they are crossed with a highly expanded skimmered nozzle beam of $H_2$ with an angular width of 3–4° (FWHM). The flight times of individual ions are measured using standard electronic techniques and stored in a pulse height analyzer or small computer.

Since the lithium ions are heavier than the target molecules the kinematics are unfavorable (see Fig. 36 and accompanying text), however, the ions inelastically scattered at $\sim$180° in the center-of-mass system, which probably provide most information on the hypersurface, can be observed as a slow component in the forward direction in the laboratory system. Figure 41 shows a typical time-of-flight spectrum measured at $\theta_{lab} = 3°$. The larger peak at small flight times, which is $10^{-3}$ of the total intensity, is attributed to scattering at small angles ($\vartheta \simeq 15°$) in the center-of-mass system. The small peak ($10^{-6}$ of the total intensity) at large flight times is attributed to large angle scattering ($\vartheta \simeq 167°$) in the center-of-mass system. From an absolute measurement of the flight

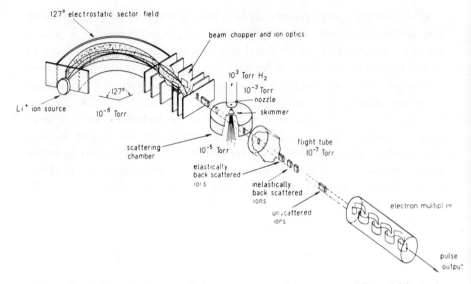

FIG. 40. Schematic diagram of the apparatus used to measure differential inelastic cross sections for vibrational excitation of $H_2$ in collisions with $Li^+$. The $Li^+$ ions are produced in a Kunsman anode, energy selected in a $127°$ energy analyzer and pulsed before being crossed with a highly expanded $H_2$-nozzle beam. The time of flight spectrum of the scattered ions is measured (David *et al.*, 1972).

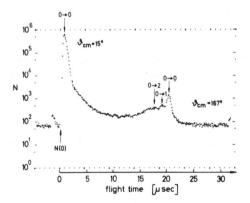

FIG. 41. Typical time-of-flight spectrum obtained with the apparatus shown in Fig. 40. The total number of ions registered over the measuring time of 16.5 hours are plotted as a function of the flight time. $N(O)$ indicates the arrival time of the unscattered incident $^7Li$ ions. The small precursor maximum is attributed to $^6Li$ ions. Apparatus parameters are: $E_{lab} = 16.3$ eV corresponding to $E_{c.m.} = 3.63$ eV and $\Theta = 3°$. Of the $1.6 \cdot 10^9$ incident ions $\sim 10^6$ have been scattered into small angles ($\vartheta \simeq 15°$ and only $\sim 2 \cdot 10^3$ have been scattered into large angles ($\vartheta \simeq 167°$). The small peaks with about $5 \cdot 10^2$ ions per channel correspond to vibrational excitation in large angle scattering.

times this small peak agrees exactly with that expected for elastic scattering. The even smaller peaks to the left of the backward peak which have been resolved up to $\Delta n = 4$ correspond to vibrational inelastic scattering. The excitation of individual rotational quantum state transitions has not yet been resolved but the narrowness of the peaks suggests that rotational transitions with $\Delta j > 4$ are improbable.

The area under each maximum can be used as a measure of the differential cross section for the corresponding vibrational transition including the $\Delta j = 0$ and $\Delta j = 2$ transitions. These were then transformed into the center-of-mass system by taking account of the appropriate Jacobian factor to obtain relative center-of-mass differential cross sections. These are shown in Fig. 42 for three different energies. In the energy and angular range studied the elastic cross section is always larger than the inelastic cross sections. These decrease in magnitude with increasing final vibrational quantum state. As expected from the quantum mechanical calculations for He–$H_2$ (Section IV,A) the inelastic cross sections increase with collision energy. The change from predominantly backward scattering to more forward scattering with increasing energy is also in agreement with the calculations.

The experimental value for the $0 \to 0$ cross section at $E_{\text{c.m.}} = 3.64$ eV and $\vartheta \simeq 160°$ is estimated to be about 0.65 $\text{Å}^2/\text{sr}$. Thus the $0 \to 1$ differential cross section at larger angles is 0.13 $\text{Å}^2/\text{sr}$.

Similar experiments have been reported with $Na^0$ (neutral atoms), $Na^+$, $K^0$, and $K^+$ on $H_2$ and $D_2$ over a large energy range (2 eV $< E_{\text{c.m.}}$ $<$ 44 eV) (Datz and Dittner, 1971). At center-of-mass energies below $\sim 15$ eV for Na and $\sim 20$ eV for K the most probable energy transfer (final vibrational states were not resolved) is less than the dissociation energy so that only rotational and vibrational energy transfer can occur. At higher energies the energy transfer was greater than the dissociation energy. With increasing energy the energy transfer increased nearly monotonically and in much the same way as below the dissociation threshold, and remained less than 30% of the collision energy.

In $Li^+$–$H_2$ at high energies even larger relative energy transfers have been observed (Schöttler and Toennies, 1972). At $E_{\text{lab}} > 150$ eV the observed energy transfer is greater than that possible in a binary collision with an $H_2$ molecule. This anomalous behavior has been explained by postulating that only one of the H atoms is struck and that the other H atom is a spectator. The detailed interpretation of these high-energy scattering results is complicated by the fact that the dissociation probably proceeds via electronically excited intermediate states.

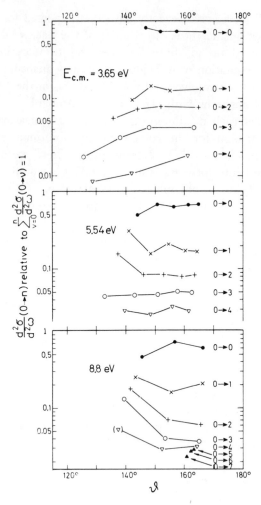

FIG. 42. Measured relative vibrationally inelastic differential cross sections at three energies for Li⁺–H₂. Note that at the lowest energies the cross sections are largest at $\vartheta \sim 180°$. At higher energies the maximum appears to shift to smaller angles.

In another recent study of dissociation Tully *et al.* (1971) used a high-energy Xe atom beam to produce dissociation to ions of CsI, CsBr, and RbI. A seeded nozzle beam technique (see Section II,C,1) was used to achieve laboratory energies up to 6 eV. The occurrence of dissociative ionization was determined by collecting the ions in the scattering chamber. The threshold for ion production agreed well with the accepted dissociation energies for the ionic bond.

The differential cross sections for the process

$$H^+ + H_2 \, (n = 0) \to H^+ + H_2 \qquad (n = 0, 1, 2) \qquad (4.13)$$

have also been studied using two 127° energy analyzers (velocity change method). Because of the kinematic advantages of this system (see Fig. 36) sufficient resolution to observe the excitation of individual final vibrational states was possible despite the use of a $H_2$ scattering chamber instead of a secondary beam.

Figure 43a shows the measured center-of-mass energy spectrum for forward scattering corresponding to $\vartheta = 22°$ and for $E_{lab} = 15$ eV. To obtain the center-of-mass energy profile directly the apparatus was programmed to vary the laboratory scattering angle synchronously with the energy. The $0 \to 0$, $0 \to 1$, $0 \to 2$, and $0 \to 3$ maxima are clearly observable. Figure 43b shows the measured angular distribution for elastic and inelastic scattering at small angles. A rainbow maximum is

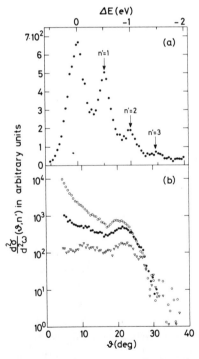

FIG. 43. Measured energy loss and angular distributions for $H^+ + H_2$ at $E_{lab} = 15$ eV. In (a) the measured energy loss spectrum at constant $\vartheta = 22°$ is shown. In (b) the center-of-mass differential cross section at three different values of $\Delta E_{c.m.}$ are shown: ○ $\Delta E = 0$ eV, ● $\Delta E = -0.516$ eV, ▽ $\Delta E = -1.003$ eV.

observed in all three collision channels. As expected from the calculations on He + $H_2$ (see Fig. 34) the inelastic cross section increases relative to the elastic cross section with increasing scattering angle. In the scattering of $H^+$ on $D_2$ the $0 \rightarrow 1$ cross section at $22°$ is greatly enhanced and is found to be even larger than the elastic cross section which can at least in part be attributed to the closer spacing of the vibrational levels in $D_2$.

The very large inelastic cross sections observed here in the forward direction and the differences from $Li^+ + H_2$ can in part be attributed to electron exchange, which leads to a deep attractive minimum in the reactive system $H^+ + H_2$. Furthermore, since the ionization potentials of H and $H_2$ are nearly the same the potential hypersurface for the charge transfer states, $(H_2^+ + H)$ and $(H^+ + H_2)$ lie close together and cross each other when the $H_2$ bond is somewhat extended (Csizmadia et al., 1970). Thus the interpretation of these results is considerably more complicated than in, say, the case of $Li^+ + H_2$ since charge transfer has to be taken into account (Tully and Preston, 1971).

### E. ELECTRONIC EXCITATION AND CHEMIONIZATION

At the present time relatively little is known about the detailed dynamics of collisions in which translational energy is transferred to electronic excitation of one or both of the collision partners. Present theories go back to the early work of Landau, Zener, and Stückelberg on atom–atom collisions (Nikitin, 1968). In these theories the assumption is made that the collision dynamics over most of the range of relative distances is governed by one of the potential curves corresponding to the ground or excited states of the partners. Only in well-located regions where a pseudocrossing of two potential curves occurs is there a finite probability that the colliding system (transient molecule) jumps from one curve to the other. These transitions may be thought of as resulting from a local break down of the Born–Oppenheimer principle. Experience has shown that under most circumstances the transition probability is well approximated by a simple formula first proposed by Landau and Zener.

For lack of a more detailed treatment these concepts have been adopted to explain the analogous process occuring in atom–molecule collisions. In this case the potential curves are replaced by families of curves corresponding to the individual vibrational sublevels (Bauer et al., 1969) and the possibility of jumps among these many curves is allowed for using the Landau–Zener theory at each intersection.

Prior to the beam experiments discussed below most of the data came from measurements of fluorescence quenching. These processes have been studied most extensively with the alkali atoms because of their large optical transition probabilities.

In the beam experiments the inverse process is usually observed. This is done by colliding a fast (1–60 eV) alkali atom beam with an atom or molecule. The fast atom beam is produced at the higher energies by charge exchange (see Fenn, 1967) or at lower energies by sputtering. The occurrence of a curve crossing to an electronically excited state is determined by detecting in the scattering chamber either light emission from the electronically excited alkali atom or in some cases from the excited target molecule. A crossing from the ground state potential surface of the composite system to an electronically excited state involving electron transfer can lead to ionization of the alkali atom and, if the target is sufficiently electronegative, to negative attachment on the target atom or molecule. For atomic targets the following processes involving primary alkali atom or ion beams have been studied (Anderson et al., 1969; Aquilanti et al., 1971; Moutinho et al., 1971b),

$$M + X \rightarrow M^+ + X^-, \tag{4.14a}$$

$$M + X \rightarrow M^* + X, \tag{4.14b}$$

$$M^+ + M' \rightarrow M^+ + M'^*, \tag{4.14c}$$

$$M + A \rightarrow M^* + A, \tag{4.14d}$$

where M and M' are alkali atoms, X is a halogen, and A rare gas atom.

These studies have shown that the threshold energies (AP) for charge transfer Eq. (4.14a) are well given by $AP = IP - EA$, where IP is the ionization potential and EA is the electron affinity. In an analogous fashion the measured curves of light-yield against energy for the other processes provide information on the energies at which curve crossing can occur. The curves have been well fitted by the Landau–Zener formula, but because of the approximations made in deriving this formula it is usually not possible to deduce potential parameters from it. Recently, however, the nondiagonal matrix element $H_{12}(R)$ determined by such a fit (Moutinho et al., 1971b) was found to be in satisfactory agreement with a theoretical calculation (Ewing et al., 1971).

In a very very recent study it has been possible to measure the differential cross section of $Na^+$ produced in collisions of Na atoms on I atoms at 13 eV with a very high angular resolution (Delvigne and Los, 1973). As shown in Fig. 44 the observed interference structure was in excellent agreement with that calculated from the known covalent and

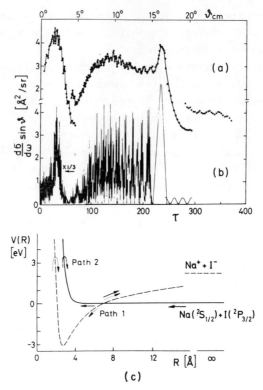

FIG. 44. Differential cross section measurements of Na⁺ ions, produced in the scattering of Na + I at 13.1 eV. The measured angular distribution in (a) is compared with the calculated distribution in (b). $\tau$ in the abscissa (bottom) is equal to the product $\vartheta_{c.m.} \cdot E_{c.m.}$ (in units of degrees × eV). In (c) the two different potential curves as well as the different "interaction" paths leading to ions in the exit channel are shown.

ionic potential curves with the crossing probability given by the Landau–Zener formula.

Processes corresponding to those listed in Eq. (4.14) have also been studied with target molecules. The following collision processes have been observed (Helbing and Rothe, 1969; Baede et al., 1969; Kempter et al., 1970a,b, 1971; Lacmann and Herschbach, 1970; Moutinho et al., 1971a; Baede and Los, 1971):

$$M + XY \rightarrow M^+ + XY^- \qquad (4.15a)$$
$$\rightarrow M^+ + X + Y^- \qquad (4.15b)$$
$$\rightarrow M^+ + XY \qquad (4.15c)$$
$$\rightarrow M^* + XY. \qquad (4.15d)$$

For the triatomic targets $NO_2$ and $SO_2$, similar processes and electronic excitation of the targets has been observed (Compton et al., 1971; Le Breton et al., 1971).

From these studies it appears that the energy thresholds for the process Eq. (4.15a) agree within the experimental error ($\Delta E \simeq 0.05$ eV) with the asymptotic ($R \sim \infty$) estimates given by $AP = IP - EA(XY)$, where EA(XY) is the adiabatic electron affinity of the negative molecule formed in the collision. The vertical electron affinity, it is recalled, is measured at constant internuclear distance and corresponds to the Franck–Condon approximation; whereas, the larger adiabatic electron affinity is measured between the ground vibrational state of $X_2$ and the ground vibrational state of $X_2^-$. In order to get good agreement between experiment and theory the probability distribution in the individual vibrational states and the thermal population distribution of vibrational states must be taken into account. These experiments are of considerable interest in connection with simple theories to explain the large cross section observed in beam studies of reactions of the type $M + X_2 \rightarrow MX + X$ (see Section V,B,2,a).

In the case of the more complicated processes of the type Eq. (4.15b) the thresholds are well reproduced by the formula $AP = D_0 + IP - EA(Y)$, where $D_0$ is the dissociation energy of the target molecule.

Considerable effort has gone into interpreting the light yield versus beam energy curves. Recently Lacman and Herschbach (1970) have been able to explain observed differences in the light yield curves at energies below the ionization threshold in terms of the electronic structure of the intermediate XY molecule. In this way they were able to explain the large differences observed between, say, $K + N_2$ and CO on the one hand and $K + NO$ and $O_2$ on the other hand.

## V. Reactive Scattering Experiments

### A. Introduction

The study of chemical reaction by beam techniques was initiated in 1955 by Taylor and Datz's (1955) now famous study of the exothermic bimolecular reaction

$$K + HBr \rightarrow KBr + H(\Delta D_0 = 3.8 \text{ kcal/mole}). \qquad (5.1)$$

In a crossed beam experiment they detected for the first time the angular distribution of one of the products (KBr) and in this way demonstrated the feasibility of beam scattering as a means for studying reactive collisions. Their choice of an alkali atom reaction was motivated by the fact that these had been carefully investigated in the 1930's using the sodium flame method. From these earlier studies it was known that these reactions have a number of features which make them more easily accessible for study in a beam scattering experiment than most other reactions. They are: large integral reactive cross sections of $\sigma_{react} \gtrsim 20$ Å, low activation energies, and easy detectability of the alkali halide product using a Langmuir–Taylor detector. Since 1955 several hundred reactions involving at least one alkali atom have been studied. Further technical developments in the last few years have made possible measurements of the product angular distribution for a considerable number of reactions not involving the alkali atoms. Much more work on nonalkali reaction can now be expected in the near future.

Nevertheless, the alkali reactions because of their special features have been examined in the greatest detail. In addition to product angular distributions the following reaction cross section properties have each been examined for one or more of the alkali atom reactions:

(1) chemical dependence: dependence of angular distribution on the chemical nature of the reactants,
(2) velocity distributions of the products,
(3) rotational energy distributions of the products,
(4) vibrational energy distributions of the products,
(5) absolute integral cross sections (also using nonbeam techniques)
(6) energy dependence of the reactive cross section from threshold up to several electron volts,
(7) dependence of the reactive cross section on vibrational excitation of a reactant,
(8) dependence of the reactive cross section on the relative orientation of the reactant molecule to the approaching atom.

The main purpose of this section is to review the results from detailed beam studies of chemical reactions. Since most of the experimental and associated theoretical work has concentrated on simple bimolecular atom–diatom reactions of the type

$$A + BC(j_i, m_i; n_i) \rightarrow AB(j_f, m_f; n_f) + C.$$

These will be discussed mostly here. The closely related ion–molecule reaction will not be discussed here since these are dealt with in Chap. 7, Vol. VI,B of this series.

The detailed results coming from beam studies have stimulated a considerable amount of theoretical work. Since quantum effects are small for heavy atoms at thermal energies, classical mechanics appears to provide a good approximation for calculating collision properties. For a given potential hypersurface the three-body classical equations are numerically integrated and the starting conditions occurring in the experiment are averaged over by a Monte Carlo method. For certain types of reactions it appears to be possible to get reasonable agreement with experiments by using a simpler approach in which only two-body interactions are taken into account (spectator stripping reactions; see Section V,B,2,a). In other cases there is evidence that a statistical phase space model can explain the results (Light, 1968). Unfortunately, however, it has not yet been possible to test the validity of these approximations by comparing with a three-dimensional nearly exact quantum mechanical calculation. Even for $H + H_2$ the three-dimensional quantum scattering problem is extremely difficult to solve rigorously and only recently have calculations been attempted (Wolken and Karplus, 1972). Only in the very special case of a colinear collision have the classical results been shown to be in agreement with an approximate quantum calculation (Diestler and Karplus, 1971; Bowman and Kupperman, 1971).

In appraising the beam scattering technique as a general means for studying chemical reactions it should be borne in mind that at its present stage of development it is still rather insensitive. The detailed studies mentioned above require integral cross sections greater than about $1 \text{ Å}^2$. These correspond to rate constants $k \simeq 10^9$ liters/mole sec, whereas most gas phase reactions have $k \simeq 10^5$–$10^6$ liters/mole sec. Thus several orders of magnitudes in sensitivity are still lacking before beam scattering can be used as a universal method for studying chemical reactions.

Finally we would like to call attention to several reviews of reactive scattering (Herschbach, 1966; Greene et al., 1966; Blythe et al., 1966; Toennies, 1968a,b; Greene and Ross, 1968; Steinfeld and Kinsey, 1970; Kinsey, 1972). The most important of these is the 1966 review by Herschbach, which has been recently updated by Kinsey (1972). A more elementary introduction to the field can be found in Toennies (1968b).

B. MEASUREMENTS OF DIFFERENTIAL AND INTEGRAL REACTIVE CROSS SECTIONS

Angular product distributions represent the most important type of measurement. As is discussed below the angular distribution contains

TABLE XVI

SURVEY OF REACTIONS STUDIED BY MOLECULAR BEAM SCATTERING

| Reactions (classified according to atom reactant) | | Latest references |
|---|---|---|
| **Hydrogen atom reactions** | | |
| $H + D_2 \rightarrow HD + H$ | | Fite and Brackmann (1964) |
| $D + H_2 \rightarrow HD + H$ | | Datz and Taylor (1963) |
| | | Geddes et al. (1970) |
| $D + HX \rightarrow DX + H$ | (HX = HCl, HBr, HI) | McDonald (1971) |
| $H + M_2 \rightarrow HM + M$ | ($M_2 = K_2$, $Rb_2$, $Cs_2$) | Lee et al. (1971) |
| $H + MX \rightarrow HX + M$ | (MX = KF, CsF, KCl, CsCl, KBr) | Siska (1970) |
| $H + XY \rightarrow HX + Y$ | (XY = $Cl_2$, $Br_2$, $I_2$, ICl, IBr) | Grosser and Haberland (1970) |
| | | McDonald et al. (1972) |
| **Alkali atom (M) reactions** | | |
| $K + HX \rightarrow KX + H$ | (HX = HCl, HCl†, HBr, DBr, TBr) | Airey et al. (1967a) |
| | | Martin and Kinsey (1967) |
| | | Gillen et al. (1969) |
| | | Odiorne et al. (1971) |
| $M + M'X \rightarrow MX + M'$ | (M, M' = Na, K, Rb, Cs, Tl; X = Cl, I) | Maltz et al. (1972) |
| | | Miller et al. (1967a) |
| $M + M'X \rightarrow MX + M'$ | (M = Li, M' = K, X = Br, F) | McDonald (1971) |
| | | Kwei et al. (1971) |

$M + XY \rightarrow MX + Y$    (M = Li, Na, K, Rb, Cs; XY = $Cl_2$, ICl, $Br_2$, $I_2$, IBr)

Birely et al. (1967)
Warnock et al. (1967)
Gordon et al. (1968)
Grice and Empedocles (1968)
Parrish and Herm (1968)
Birely et al. (1969)
Greene et al. (1969a)
Kwei and Herschbach (1969)
Parrish and Herm (1969)
Grice et al. (1970)
Kempter et al. (1970a)
Gillen et al. (1971)
Maltz et al. (1972)

$M + RI \rightarrow MI + R$    (M = Li, Na, K, Rb, Cs)
(R = $CH_3$, $C_2H_5$, etc.)

Buehler and Bernstein (1966, 1969)
Brooks and Jones (1966)
Airey et al. (1967b)
Gordon et al. (1968)
Birely et al. (1969)
Brooks (1969, 1971)
Kwei et al. (1970)
Harris and Wilson (1971)
Parrish and Herm (1971)
Gersh and Bernstein (1972)
Ottinger et al. (1972)
Maltz et al. (1972)

$M + NO_2(CH_3NO_2) \rightarrow MO + NO(CH_3NO)$    (M = Li, Na)

Herm and Herschbach (1970)
Parrish and Herm (1971)

TABLE XVI (continued)

| Reactions (classified according to atom reactant) | Latest references |
|---|---|
| $M + XCN \rightarrow MX + CN$     $(M = K, Cs; X = Br, I)$ | Grice et al. (1968) |
| $M + NOCl(SCl_2) \rightarrow MCl + NO(SCl)$ | |
| $M + poly - X_n \rightarrow MX + poly - X_{n-1}$    $(M = Li, K, Rb, Cs)$ <br> $(poly - X_n = PBr_3, PCl_3, CCl_4, CBr_4, SiCl_4, CHCl_3, SnCl_4, SF_6, \ldots$ etc.$)$ | Airey et al. (1967b) <br> Gordon et al. (1968) <br> Wilson and Herschbach (1968) <br> Greene et al. (1969a) <br> Parrish and Herm (1969, 1971) <br> Kempter et al. (1970a) <br> Kwei et al. (1970) <br> Freund et al. (1971) <br> Bennewitz et al. (1971b) <br> Siska (1970) <br> Maltz et al. (1972) <br> Riley and Herschbach (1973) |
| $Cs + C_nH_{2n}X_2 \rightarrow CsX + C_nH_{2n}X$     $(X = Cl, Br, I)$ | Entemann (1971) |
| $M + C_nH_{2n-m}X \rightarrow MX + C_nH_{2n-m}$     $(M = K, Cs; X = Cl, Br, I)$ | Entemann and Kwei (1971) |

**Alkaline–earth atom reactions**

| | |
|---|---|
| $A + XY \rightarrow AX(AY) + Y(X)$     $(A = Ba, Sr, Ca, Mg)$ | Mims et al. (1973) |
| $Ba + BrCN \overset{\rightarrow BaBr}{\underset{\rightarrow BaCN}{\phantom{\rightarrow}}}$ | Mims et al. (1973) |
| $A + X_2 \rightarrow AX + X$     $(A = Ba, Sr, Ca$ and $Mg)$ | Habermann et al. (1972) <br> Lin et al. (1973) |

| Reaction | Reference |
|---|---|
| $A + HI \rightarrow AI + H$  $(A = Ba, Ca, and Sr)$ | Mims et al. (1972) |
| $Ba + O_2 \rightarrow BaO^* + O$ | Cosmovici and Michel (1971) |
| | Fricke et al., (1971) |
| | Schultz et al. (1972) |
| | Loesch and Herschbach (1973) |
| $Ba + NO_2 \rightarrow BaO^* + NO$ | Ottinger and Zare (1970) |
| $A + Cl_2 \nearrow MCl_2^* \searrow MCl^* + C$   $(A = Ba, Sr)$ | Jonah and Zare (1971) |

Halogen atom (X) reactions

| Reaction | Reference |
|---|---|
| $F + D_2 \rightarrow FD + D$ | Schafer et al. (1970) |
| $X + YZ \rightarrow XY(XZ) + Z(Y)$   $(X = F, Cl, Br, I; YZ = F_2, Cl_2, Br_2, I_2, ClI, BrI)$ | Beck et al. (1968) |
| | Lee et al. (1968, 1969a) |
| | Cross and Blais (1970) |
| | Loesch and Beck (1971) |
| $X + M_2 \rightarrow MX + M$   $(X = Cl; M_2 = Na_2, K_2)$ | Struve et al. (1971) |
| $I + CH_3Br \rightarrow HI + CH_2Br (\rightarrow BrI + CH_3)$ | Wong and Lee (1972) |
| $F + C_nH_{2n} \rightarrow C_nH_{2n-1}F + H$ $C_{n-1}H_{2n-3}F + CH_3$ | Parson and Lee (1972) |
| $Cl + HI \rightarrow HCl + I$ | McDonald (1971) |

Other reactions

| Reaction | Reference |
|---|---|
| $K_2 + XY \rightarrow KX + K + Y$   $(XY = Br_2, ICl, IBr, BrCN)$ | Foreman et al. (1972) |
| $K_2 + poly - X_n \rightarrow 2KX + poly - X_{n-2}$ $(poly - X_n = PBr_3, PCl_3, BBr_3, CCl_4, SiCl_4, SnCl_4, CH_2Br_2, CH_3I, etc.)$ | Foreman (1971) |
| $HI + DI \rightarrow HD + I_2$ | Jaffe and Anderson (1969) |
| $O + CS_2 \rightarrow SO + CS$ | Moore et al. (1972) |
| $MX + M'X' \rightarrow MX' + M'X$   $(MX' = CsCl; M'X' = KCl, KI)$ | Miller et al. (1972) |
| $R + X_2(XY) \rightarrow RX + X(Y)$   $(R = CH_3, C_2H_5; X = Cl, Br, I; XY = ICl)$ | McFadden et al. (1972) |

information on the range and duration of the reactive collision. Moreover, in the process of measuring the angular distribution information
on the product velocity distribution is also obtained. Furthermore, in
the case of reactive scattering, as opposed to elastic scattering, the angular
distribution provides the most direct method for ascertaining the reactive
integral cross section.

Table XVI lists the neutral–neutral reactions that have been studied in
crossed beam experiments. Work reported on up to the summer of 1971
has been included. No attempt has been made to make an exhaustive
search of the literature. A similar table with more detailed information
can be found in Kinsey (1972).

The product angular distributions observed in most of these studies
can be classified into one of the following categories depending on the
location of the maximum of the center-of-mass distribution with respect
to the direction of the incident atom in the center-of-mass system:

(1)   forward scattering,
(2)   backward scattering,
(3)   symmetric forward-backward scattering,
(4)   sideways scattering (intermediate between 1 and 2),
(5)   mixed forward and forward-backward scattering (osculating
       complex).

A classification of reactions according to their angular distributions is to
a certain extent arbitrary since frequently the observed angular distributions show properties characteristic of several of the above categories.
For example, it is found that a large amount ($\approx 40\%$) of backward scattering occurs even in reactions which are classified as forward scattering
reactions.

After a brief discussion of the apparatus some reactions representing
the various angular distributions are discussed in the above order.

## 1. Typical Apparatus

In principle the apparatus used in reactive measurements is similar
to that used in elastic and inelastic scattering. Because of the possible
wide spread of the product velocity, especially in strongly exothermic
reactions, at least one velocity selector between scattering chamber and
detector is highly desirable in order to facilitate a reliable transformation
of the angular distributions into the center-of-mass system (see Section
I,B). In most experiments the in-plane arrangement, in which the angular

distribution is measured in the plane of the primary and secondary beams, has been preferred. This arrangement has the advantage that in principle all center-of-mass angles can be scanned, which is only possible in the alternative vertical plane arrangement if $m_1v_1 \gg m_2v_2$.

Figure 45 shows a typical apparatus used in measurements involving alkali atoms. Since the products and reactants are condensable, provision is made for large areas of cold shields to provide increased pumping speeds in the vicinity of the scattering volume. The detector is a Langmuir–Taylor detector (see Section II,C,4) that is specially pretreated to detect either the sum of the M + MX (M and MX refer to the alkali atom and alkali halide, respectively) or just the alkali atom M. The difference in signals is then proportional to the MX intensity.

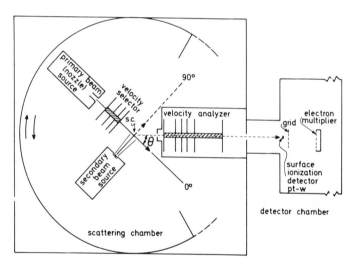

FIG. 45.   Schematic diagram of a typical crossed beam apparatus for studying chemical reactions of alkali atoms. In most experiments the velocity selector in the M atom primary beam is left out.

If a Langmuir–Taylor detector cannot be used, the apparatus becomes much larger and more complicated. In general at least one nozzle beam with the associated large pumps ($\sim$5000 liters/sec) is required to provide increased intensity (more than a factor 100 greater than from an effusive source) in order to compensate for the low efficiency of the electron-bombardment detector (typically 1 in $10^3$ particles are ionized). On the other hand this detector also requires elaborate ultra-high vacuum pumping (see Section II,C,4) to reduce the partial pressure of the prod-

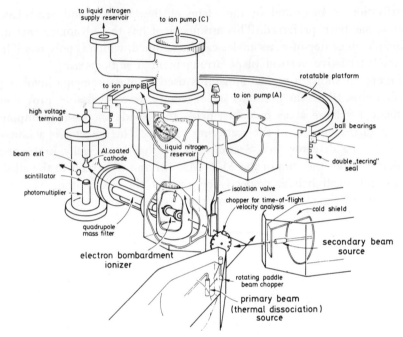

FIG. 46. Perspective cut away diagram of a typical crossed beam apparatus for studying chemical reactions in which alkali atoms are not involved. The two beam sources mounted on the walls of the main chamber (not shown) are seen in the foreground. In the background the electron bombardment ionization detector, mass filter, and pumping stages are shown. The entire detector assembly is mounted on the rotating lid of the main chamber (McDonald et al., 1972).

uct in the vicinity of the electron beam ionizer. Figure 46 shows a typical apparatus (McDonald, 1971). Three differentially pumped ultra-high vacuum stages with ion-getter pumps (A, B, and C) are provided to evacuate the detector. In this way the total pressure in the ionization chamber has been reduced to $\simeq 10^{-9}$ Torr and the partial pressure can be, depending on the product studied, as low as $10^{-12}$ to $10^{-15}$ Torr (Lee et al., 1969b; Bickes and Bernstein, 1970). In general, the background at low masses ($M < 40$) is greatest and in particular for $H_2$, special additional refinements are needed. Nevertheless, it has recently been possible to reduce the partial pressure of $H_2$ to below $10^{-12}$ Torr (Brokes et al., 1973). A further important background reduction is achieved by allowing the un-ionized beam to pass through the ionizing region in the detector without striking any walls inside the detector. For this reason an exit hole is provided at the far side of the detector (see Fig. 46). Instead of using a rotating disk velocity selector (see Fig. 45) product velocity distributions are measured by a time-of-flight technique in the machine shown in Fig. 46. The scattered beam is chopped by the rotating toothed disk and the arrival times of the ions are measured to give a flight time distribution.

Despite the use of a nozzle beam target the product intensities in reported studies of reactions between halogen or hydrogen atoms and halogen molecules and hydrogen halide molecules can be quite low—of the order of 100 counts/sec or even less (Lee *et al.*, 1969b).

Seeded beams (see Section II,C,1) have already been applied successfully to study chemical reactions over a large range of energies and hold great promise for future studies of chemical reactions.

## 2. *Product Angular and Velocity Distributions and Their Interpretation*

*a. Forward Scattering.* $M + X_2 \rightarrow MX + X$. The reactions of the alkali atoms with the halogen molecules, which were first studied in 1964, show a very distinct forward scattering (Datz and Minturn, 1964; Wilson *et al.*, 1964). Reactions of this type are characterized by a large exothermicity since a covalent bond is replaced by a much more stable ionic bond. As will be discussed later, the high exothermicity is largely responsible for the forward scattering of products.

Recently one of these reactions, $K + I_2 \rightarrow KI + I$ $(\Delta D_0 = 40.5$ kcal/mole), has been studied in more detail than previously possible using an apparatus in which both the primary and the scattered product beam were velocity selected (Gillen *et al.*, 1971). With this apparatus it was also possible to study the reaction over a small range of initial relative energies ($E_{trans} = 1.5$ to $3.6$ kcal/mole). From measurements of velocity distributions at various scattering angles the laboratory flux contour maps shown in Fig. 47, for three different relative energies were constructed. The corresponding Newton diagrams are also shown in Fig. 47. The angular distributions obtained by integrating the flux at one angle over all velocities agreed well with earlier results obtained without velocity selectors.

Using standard computational techniques the flux contour maps were transformed into the c.m. system and were found to be essentially the same at all three energies. A composite center-of-mass flux contour map for all three energies is shown in Fig. 48. Although the flux maximum in the laboratory system appears at about $20°$ with respect to the potassium laboratory velocity vector in the center-of-mass system, the maximum of

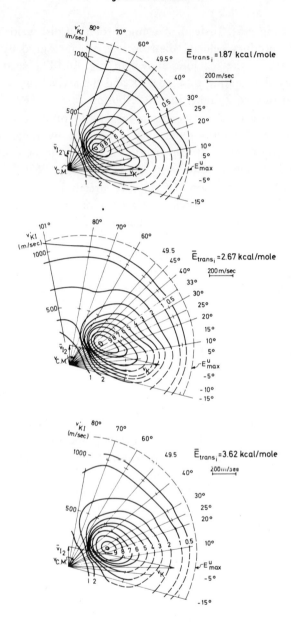

FIG. 47.  KI laboratory polar (velocity-angle) flux contour maps for three average center-of-mass energies ($E_{\text{trans}_i}$). Each distribution is normalized to 10 in the peak region. The dashed contours represent interpolations of the data. The dashed circle, designated by $E_{\text{max}}^u$, shows the thermodynamic energy limit for the KI product velocity.

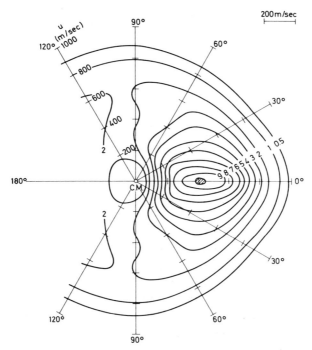

FIG. 48.   KI c.m. polar flux contour map obtained from the data shown in Fig. 47
for the reaction K + I₂ → KI + I. The assumption has been made that the c.m. differential cross sections are energy independent and that the contours are symmetric
about the 0°–180° line. The fluxes have been normalized to 10 at the maximum. The
contour map is typical of a reaction showing predominantly forward scattering.

the transformed flux distribution is at 0° (see Fig. 47). This shift in
maximum was brought about by the velocity dependent Jacobian factors
(see Section II,B). This example illustrates the type of error which could
occur in earlier work in which the product velocities needed for estimating
the Jacobian could not be measured.

In interpreting Fig. 48 it is important to recall that in the center-of-
mass system the K atom before reaction approaches from the 180°
direction and I₂ molecule from the 0° direction. The collision occurs at
the origin (where the imaginary center of mass resides). The flux contour
map thus provides a picture of where one of the products is distributed
in angle-velocity space. The distribution of the other product, in this
case an I atom, is specified by conservation of momentum. Its distribution is the same except that it is reflected through the origin. From the
flux map a considerable amount of information concerning the detailed
dynamics of the reaction can be derived. In particular, the symmetry

of the flux map, the most probable scattering angles and velocities, and the integral over the flux contour map (proportional to the integral reactive cross section) are usually sufficient to make a dynamic model. In the case of $K + I_2$ these properties are interpreted in the following way:

(1) The angular distribution KI is asymmetric with respect to inversion through the 90° axis, with a maximum in the forward direction. As is shown below a symmetric distribution implies that the collision time $t_{col}$ is long compared to the rotational period $\tau_{rot}$ of a possible intermediate complex. Thus an asymmetric distribution implies $t_{col} \lesssim 5 \cdot 10^{-12}$ sec and a single pass trajectory of the atoms involved in the collision (direct collision).

(2) The peaking at 0° and small product velocity ($\sim$400 m/sec) imply furthermore that most of the K atoms were not appreciably deflected in the process of picking up an I atom. The small final velocity implies that the most probable relative energy after reaction is small and roughly equal to the most probable relative energy of the reactants. Thus by conservation of energy it appears that almost all of the exothermicity has gone into internal degrees of freedom.

(3) The integral reactive cross section is given in principle by integrating the flux contour map over all velocities and angles*:

$$\sigma_{react} = \int_0^\infty du \int_0^{2\pi} d\varphi \int_0^\pi d\vartheta \, \frac{d^3\sigma(\vartheta, u, \bar{E}_i)}{d^2\omega \, du} \sin \vartheta. \qquad (5.2)$$

For $K + I_2$ the results of several independent determinations of $\sigma_{react}$ lie in the range between 125 to 236 Å², where the lower value appears to be the most reliable one (see Table XVII). From $\sigma_{react}$ a lower limit for the largest distance leading to reaction can be estimated by setting $\sigma_{react} \simeq \pi b_{max}^2 \simeq \pi R_{max}^2$.[†] In the present case then $R_{max} \simeq 6$ Å.

The dynamical model resulting from these conclusions, which were based on the flux contour map, is shown in Fig. 49. The radii of the atoms

---

* Absolute values of the differential reactive cross section over the entire range of angles are needed to determine $\sigma_{react}$ absolutely by Eq. (5.2). Measurements of this type are extremely difficult and usually rely on indirect methods to calibrate the apparatus. For a detailed discussion see Kinsey (1972).

† A more precise estimate can be made by setting $\sigma_{react} = 2\pi \int_0^\infty P(b)b \, db$, where $P(b)$ is the probability of reaction for a given impact parameter. The formula used in the text assumes $P(b) = 1$ for $b \leq b_{max}$ and $P(b) = 0$ elsewhere. If, however, $P(b) < 1$ for $b \leq b_{max}$, then $b_{max}$ will be larger and $R_{max}$ is thus a lower limit.

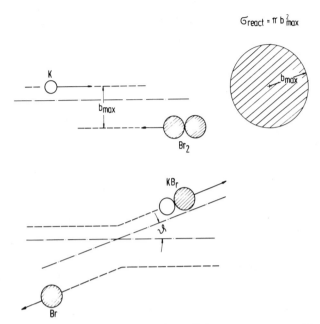

$$\sigma_{react} = \pi \, b^2_{max}$$

FIG. 49. Schematic diagram showing the collision partners represented as hard spheres before (top) and after (bottom) a reactive collision. The circles are drawn to scale to the atomic and ionic radii. At the upper right the area corresponding to the reactive cross section (assuming a reaction probability of one for all $b \leq b_{max}$) is shown.

and ionic species have been drawn roughly to scale. Also shown in the upper right is the area corresponding to the integral reactive cross section. The collision model shows clearly that the observed large cross section is consistent with the predominant forward scattering. The collision mechanism shown in Fig. 49 is called a stripping mechanism. If, furthermore, the assumption is made that the linear momentum of the remaining X atom is the same after the collision as before the collision, then the mechanism is referred to as a spectator-stripping mechanism.

All of the reactions of the type $M + X_2$ studied so far show the characteristic forward scattering and other properties found for $K + I_2$. The most striking differences are found in the measured values for the integral cross sections. Table XVII compares the values of integral cross sections obtained from several different beam scattering techniques with values obtained from nonbeam experiments. Because of the uncertainties in the absolute calibration of differential reactive cross sections the integral cross sections obtained from them are uncertain by about $\pm 30\%$ (Birely et al., 1967). The nonbeam photo dissociation method is more reliable

TABLE XVII

MEASURED AND CALCULATED INTEGRAL REACTIVE CROSS SECTIONS IN Å² FOR REACTIONS
OF THE TYPE $M + X_2 \rightarrow MX + X$[a]

| Reaction | Experimental method | | | Theory[b] | |
| | Reactive differential cross sections | Nonreactive differential cross sections | Gas photo-dissociation | Simple harpooning model | |
| | | | | Vertical e.a. | Adiabatic e.a. |
| --- | --- | --- | --- | --- | --- |
| Li + Br₂ | 130[c] ±30% | — | — | 30–48 | 64–97 |
| Na + Br₂ | 100[d] | — | — | 32–55 | 76–120 |
| K + Br₂ | 227[e] | 200–260[f] | — | 49–94 | 143–276 |
| Rb + Br₂ | 367[e] | — | — | 54–106 | 167–345 |
| Cs + Br₂ | 353[e] | — | — | 65–137 | 228–547 |
| Na + I₂ | — | — | 97[h] ±15% | 42–75 | 66–101 |
| K + I₂ | 236[e] | 125–140[g] | 127[h] | 66–143 | 119–216 |
| Rb + I₂ | — | — | 167[h] | 74–166 | 138–263 |
| Cs + I₂ | 246[e] | — | 195[h] | 90–229 | 182–391 |

[a] All the measurements are at thermal ($\gtrsim 1000°K$) energies. Since the energy dependence for these reactions is smaller than the experimental error, the actual energies are not listed.

[b] From Eqs. (5.4) and (5.5) with $E_v(X_2)$ and $E_a(X_2)$. The two values are based on the estimated upper and lower bounds on the electron affinities taken from Person (1963).

[c] Parrish and Herm (1969).

[d] Birely et al. (1969).

[e] Birely et al. (1967).

[f] Greene et al. (1969a).

[g] Gillen et al. (1971).

[h] Edelstein and Davidovits (1971).

and the absolute errors are estimated to be less than ±15% (Edelstein and Davidovits, 1971). Both sets of data do show that the cross section increases as one goes to the heavier alkali atoms in agreement with the simple harpooning model (last column in Table XVII) discussed below.

As mentioned earlier reactions of this type were first studied in the 1930's by Polanyi and co-workers using the sodium diffusion flame method. The measured rate constants indicated exceptionally large cross sections. Observation of other reactions with the MX products showed, furthermore, that these were highly vibrationally excited. To explain these results, Magee (Magee, 1940; Polanyi, 1949) proposed an electron transfer mechanism in accordance with the strong ionic bonding of the MX molecule. In this picture the neutral reactants approach on a covalent potential curve which is crossed* by the ionic curve at large distances. At the crossing point electron transfer is energetically possible, and if it occurs, then the strongly attractive Coulomb forces determine the further course of the reaction,

$$M + X_2 \rightarrow M^+ + X_2^- \rightarrow M^{(+)}X^{(-)} + X. \tag{5.3}$$

This mechanism has also been called harpooning: The alkali atom tosses out the electron (the harpoon) and the Coulomb force (rope) pulls in the halogen atom (whale).

Since the van der Waals interaction of the covalent curve is very weak at large separations, the crossing radius $R_c$ is given approximately (neglecting ion-induced dipole forces) by

$$e^2/R_c = I(M) - E(X_2), \tag{5.4}$$

where $I(M)$ is the ionization potential and $E(X_2)$ is the electron affinity of the $X_2$ molecule. There has in the past been some question as to whether the vertical or adiabatic electron affinity should be used.

According to this simple model and assuming $b_{\max} \simeq R_c$ the reactive cross section is given by

$$\sigma_{\text{react}} = \pi R_c^2. \tag{5.5}$$

For the $Br_2$ reactions calculated cross sections using estimated values for $E_v(Br_2)$ are substantially lower than experimental values obtained by integrating differential reactive cross sections (see Table XVII). The best overall agreement is achieved with cross sections based on the adiabatic electron affinities. This result suggests, in agreement with experiments discussed in Section VI,E, that the electron jumps adiabatically in processes of this type.

Further evidence in support of the harpooning mechanism is provided by the good agreement of Monte Carlo calculations based on a hypersurface with Coulomb attraction for $R < R_c$ with experimentally measured differential cross section features (Blais, 1968; Godfrey and Karplus,

---

* In an adiabatic interaction the curves do not in fact cross and the ground state covalent curve goes over into the ionic state implying electron transfer at the crossing point. The collisional situation is more complicated (see Fig. 44). In an atom-molecule interaction the corresponding hypersurfaces may cross depending on the geometrical configuration (Longuet–Higgins, 1963).

1968; Kuntz *et al.*, 1969). Evidence of another type comes from the striking correspondence between the rate constants from the sodium flame studies and capture coefficients for thermal electrons (Wilson and Herschbach, 1968).

A number of improvements of the simple harpooning model have been proposed. Herschbach (1966) has suggested that the vertical electron affinities and the cross sections are larger than estimated for the free molecules due to the perturbation of the $X_2$ molecule by the $M^+$ ion. Grice (1967) has shown that interaction between the zero-order covalent and ionic states extends the range of the potential and thus also leads to a larger cross section. Other dynamical improvements have been suggested by Anderson (1968) and Edelstein and Davidovits (1971).

A number of other reactions have also been found to give predominantly forward scattering. These are the reactions $Cl + HI \rightarrow HCl + I$ ($\Delta D_0$ = 31.7 kcal/mole) and the reactions involving halogen atoms and molecules: $X + YZ \rightarrow XY(XZ) + Z(Y)$ ($\Delta D_0$ = 3–14 kcal/mole).

Beam studies of the reaction $Cl + HI$ (McDonald, 1971) show it to have properties reminescent of the $M + X_2$ reactions, the only significant difference being considerably smaller integral cross sections (10 to 50 $Å^2$). Although the observed forward scattering would seem to suggest an attractive potential, these and other results for this reaction have been shown to be consistent with Monte Carlo trajectories on a highly repulsive energy surface (Parr *et al.*, 1973). The forward scattering in this reaction can be attributed to the small momentum transfer accompanying the transfer of the light H atom which may bounce back and forth between the two heavy atoms in the course of the collision.

The $X + YZ$ reactions have been studied by three independent beam groups with essentially similar results (Lee *et al.*, 1969a; Cross and Blais, 1970; Loesch and Beck, 1971). Depending on the reaction partners these reactions show product angular distributions that come under several of the categories listed on p. 326. The reactions of Cl atoms leading to formation of ClBr or ClI show predominate forward scattering. For some of the other reactions, especially for $Br + I_2$, the angular distributions show some evidence for the formation of an intermediate complex, with lifetimes comparable to or shorter than the collision time. In all cases the integral reactive cross sections are small and in the range 1 to 10 $Å^2$.

Of considerable interest is a comparative study of the two reactions $Cl + BrI \rightarrow ClBr + I$ and $Br + ClI \rightarrow BrCl + I$, both leading to the same products, but proceeding by way of different intermediates (e.g.,

ClBrI and BrClI, respectively) (Lee et al., 1969a). The cross section for the first reaction ($\approx 6$ Å$^2$) is found to be much larger than that for the second ($\approx 1$ Å$^2$). Whereas the first reaction shows forward peaking the second shows a predominantly sideways scattering and has therefore characteristics more typical of the rebound reactions to be discussed in the next section. This difference in behavior correlates with that expected on the basis of quantum chemical calculations which show that the most stable (and nearly linear) complexes have the least electronegative atom in the central position.

The overall behavior of the halogen substitution reactions is also explained by a short range attractive potential. The different types of distributions (forward, sideways, and short-lived complex) observed for these reactions can be attributed to large differences in the surfaces resulting from the competition between the short range repulsive and attractive forces.

Recently, Monte Carlo calculations have been performed in order to explore the possibilities of determining the potential well depth for the intermediate complex from the beam observations (Borne and Bunker, 1971). The authors conclude however that all the observed scattering features are "remarkably insensitive to the presence and properties of the potential well."

### b. Backward Scattering.

1. M + RX → MX + R. The most widely studied reaction of this type, the reaction K + CH$_3$I → KI + CH$_3$ ($\Delta D_0 = 22$ kcal/mole), was the second reaction to be studied in beam scattering experiments (Herschbach et al., 1961). Because the products have roughly equal masses they are more widely distributed in the laboratory system than in the case of the first studied reaction, K + HBr (see Section V,B,2,d). In the M + RX reactions the molecular reactant has a covalent-ionic bond that is broken to form a more strongly ionically bonded molecule. The exothermicities of these reactions are therefore somewhat less than for M + X$_2$.

The maximum in the angular distribution for K + CH$_3$I is observed at about 80° with respect to the initial K-beam direction or roughly in the initial direction of the CH$_3$I beam. A c.m. contour flux map for another reaction in this family, the reaction Cs + CH$_3$I (Ottinger et al., 1972), is shown in Fig. 50. The important features of the c.m. contour flux map are:

(1)   The angular distribution is asymmetric about 90° and as discussed previously this implies $t_{col} < 5 \cdot 10^{-12}$ sec and therefore a single pass trajectory of the atoms involved in the collision.

(2)   The distribution is peaked at large angles ($>120°$) and the final velocity of the CsI is only about 200 m/sec. Since the $CH_3$ is considerably

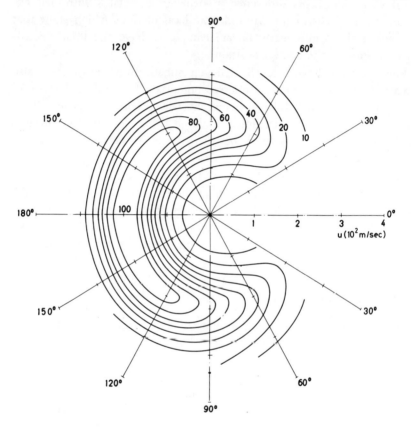

FIG. 50.   CsI c.m. polar flux contour map obtained from laboratory distributions for the reaction $Cs + CH_3I \rightarrow CsI + CH_3$. The fluxes have been normalized to 10 at the maximum. The contour map is typical of a reaction showing predominantly backward scattering.

lighter than CsI, most of the final translational energy, which is more than 75% of the exothermicity, is carried off by the $CH_3$, which is not shown on the flux map. As indicated by a related study of $Na + CH_3I$ about 70% of the products are scattered in the backward hemisphere (Birely et al., 1969) in reactions of this type.

(3) The integral cross section obtained by estimating the integral over the flux contour map is about 60 Å² for Cs + CH$_3$I and 34 Å² for K + CH$_3$I. This means that $b_{max}$ is 4.3 and 3.4, respectively.

For much the same reasons as in the case of the M + X$_2$ the simple collision model shown in Fig. 51 can be constructed for these reactions. The figure shows how the short reaction time and backward scattering is consistent with a rebound mechanism in which the maximum impact parameter is comparable with the atomic and ionic radii. Indeed the small integral cross section confirms this interpretation. Classical Monte Carlo calculations for this system (Raff and Karplus, 1966) also lead to the same conclusions.

Further confirmation that the reaction occurs at small impact parameters is provided by an entirely different technique involving measurements of the angular distribution of the nonreactively scattered alkali atom (Greene *et al.*, 1966). The angular distributions of K, Rb, and Cs after scattering from CH$_3$I for a range of energies are shown in Fig. 52 (Harris and Wilson, 1971). The differential cross section has been multiplied by $\vartheta^{4/3}$ to remove the rapidly falling differential cross section caused by the long range $R^{-6}$ potential and is plotted versus $\tau = E\vartheta$. The dashed curves show the behavior expected if no reaction occurs and corresponds to the angular distribution found for Cs–Hg (see Fig. 14).

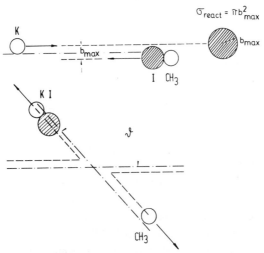

FIG. 51. Schematic diagram showing the collision partners represented as hard spheres before (top) and after (bottom) a reactive collision. The circles are drawn to scale to the atomic and ionic radii. At the upper right the area corresponding to the reactive cross section (assuming a reaction probability of one for all $b \leq b_{max}$) is shown.

The elastic scattering distribution was estimated by taking account of
the potential anisotropy (but not inelastic processes) and fitting the measurements to the left of the maximum where reaction is thought to have
no influence. The large difference between the estimated pure elastic
distribution (dashed line) and the measured distribution (points) observed in Fig. 52 is attributed to removal of the atoms from the scattered
beam by the reaction. From the point at which the two curves begin to
depart from each other the onset of reaction appears to occur at a value
of about $E\vartheta \simeq 10^2$ for all three reactions independent of the energy.
This corresponds to about $\vartheta = 35°$ at 3.1 kcal/mole and in the case of
$K + CH_3I$ to an impact parameter of about 4 Å.

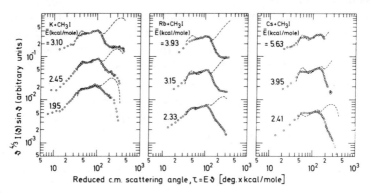

FIG. 52. Measured angular distributions of alkali atoms nonreactively scattered
from $CH_3I$ at several different c.m. energies $\bar{E}$. The differential cross section is weighted
by $\vartheta^{4/3}$ to remove the sharp drop off caused by the $R^{-6}$ attractive potential and is plotted
versus the reduced scattering angle $\tau = E\vartheta$. The first hump in the curves at about
$\tau = 50°$ kcal/mole corresponds to the main rainbow maximum. The dashed line shows
the angular distribution to be expected if only elastic scattering were to occur from an
anisotropic molecular target. The difference between the dashed line and the measured
distribution at $\tau \gtrsim 100°$ kcal/mole is a measure of the amount of alkali atoms removed
by the reaction.

Integral cross sections for these reactions are shown in Table XVIII.
Just as with the $M + X_2$ reactions the integral cross section increases
with increasing mass of the alkali atom. Furthermore, the cross sections
appear to be independent of the size or branching of the attached alkyl
group. This result is consistent with the collision model shown in Fig. 51
and the assumption that the reaction occurs preferentially for favorable
orientations of the RX molecule.

The observations made on the $M + RX$ reactions can all be explained
in terms of the harpooning model (Wilson and Herschbach, 1965;

TABLE XVIII

Measured Integral Cross Sections in Å² for Reactions of the Type M + RI → MI + R. The Mean Relative Collision Energies in kcal/mole Are Listed in Brackets Next to the Cross Section Values

| Reaction | From reactive differential cross sections | From nonreactive differential cross sections |
|---|---|---|
| Li + $CH_3I$ | 27 [2.67][a] | — |
| Na + $CH_3I$ | 5 [1.61][b] | — |
| K + $CH_3I$ | 34 [1.44][c] | 36.5 [3.10];[d] 50 [4.17][e] |
| Rb + $CH_3I$ | — | 38 [3.93][d] |
| Cs + $CH_3I$ | — | 45 [5.63][d] |
| K + $C_2H_5I$ | — | 22 [1.40][c] |
| K + $n-C_3H_7I$ | — | 19 [1.47][c] |
| K + $n-C_4H_9I$ | — | 30 [1.52][c] |
| K + $n-C_5H_{11}I$ | — | 28 [1.51][c] |
| K + $n-C_7H_{15}I$ | — | 22 [1.55][d] |

[a] Parrish and Herm (1971).
[b] Birely et al. (1969).
[c] Kwei et al. (1970).
[d] Harris and Wilson (1971).
[e] Airey et al. (1967b).

Toennies, 1968a). Unfortunately the electron affinities of the polyatomic molecules are only very roughly known so that a quantitative comparison with measured integral cross sections is not possible.

2. $D + H_2 \rightarrow HD + H$ and other H(D)-atom reactions. The experimental study of this reaction is of special interest since it provides a crucial test of the theoretical methods used in calculating cross sections and rate constants. Since only three electrons are involved, the hypersurface is the easiest to calculate by quantum chemical methods. Furthermore, because of the wide spacing of the vibrational and rotational levels it is the easiest to treat in a quantum mechanical scattering calculation. Nevertheless, a completely reliable *a priori* calculation has not yet been reported.

Because of the high activation energy, small reactive cross section, poor detectability of $H_2$ molecules, and other complications this is experimentally one of the most difficult reactions to study. Nevertheless,

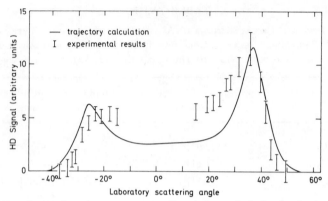

FIG. 53. Comparison between measured and theoretical distributions of HD produced by the reaction $D + H_2 \rightarrow HD + H$. The experimental distribution was measured in the plane of the reactants without velocity selection ($T_D \simeq 3000°K$, $T_{H_2} \simeq 77°K$). The theoretical distribution was obtained from a classical trajectory calculation based on a semiempirical hypersurface. The distributions were arbitrarily normalized at $\theta = 36°$.

the first crude beam experiments on this reaction and its isotopic variant $H + D_2 \rightarrow HD + D$ were carried out almost ten years ago (Fite and Brackman, 1965; Datz and Taylor, 1963). Recently considerably more accurate angular distributions were obtained for $D + H_2 \rightarrow HD + H$ (Geddes et al., 1970). The velocity of the scattered product HD needed for the transformation into the c.m. system was determined by a low resolution time-of-flight measurement. The experimental results are compared with the distributions obtained from classical trajectories on a semiempirical hypersurface in Fig. 53. Considering the approximate nature of the classical calculation and hypersurface the agreement is quite satisfactory.

A number of other H-atom reactions show predominantly backward scattering. These include $H + XY \rightarrow HX + Y$ for X, Y = Cl, Br, and I (Grosser and Haberland, 1970; McDonald, 1971) as well as some of the reactions $H + MX \rightarrow M + HX$ (Siska, 1970).

3. $F + D_2 \rightarrow FD + D$.   In the first reported beam investigation of this reaction Schafer et al. (1970) crossed a nozzle beam of $D_2$ ($\Delta v/v \simeq 8\%$) with a velocity selected F-atom beam ($\Delta v/v \simeq 20\%$). The relative rate constants for formation of vibrationally excited products had previously been extensively studied in an HF chemical laser as well as in infrared chemiluminescence experiments. In this and other experiments, at initial relative kinetic energies in the range 0.8 to 2.57 kcal/mole,

a structure in the laboratory angular distributions has been observed for the first time (see Fig. 54a).

The sharply peaked backward scattering and the structure in the laboratory distribution permits a reliable transformation of the laboratory angular distribution into the center of mass (Fig. 54b) without measuring a product velocity distribution. Because of the special features of the reaction listed below only a small amount of the exothermicity of 31.9 kcal/mole can be taken up by the rotational degrees of freedom of the reactively formed FD. Thus conservation of energy requires that the available energy has to be shared between vibrational excitation and translational motion. Consequently, the maximum with the largest center-of-mass velocity (largest positive laboratory angle) corresponds to molecules in the ground vibrational state. With decreasing velocity the maxima correspond to increasing vibrational excitation.

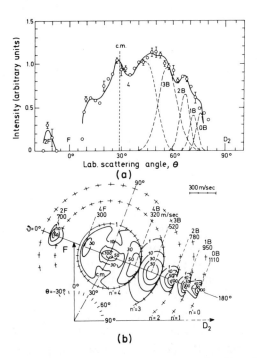

FIG. 54.   (a) Laboratory angular distribution of DF intensity (from $F + D_2 \rightarrow DF + D$) in arbitrary units: ○, experimental points; —, calculated total intensity for the c.m. distribution shown in (b); – – – –, intensity of DF in a particular vibrational state scattered forward (F) or backward (B) in c.m. system; $v_F = 909$ m/sec, $v_{D_2} = 2375$ m/sec, $E_{c.m.} = 2.57$ kcal/mole, $\Delta D_0 = 31.9$ kcal/mole. (b) Contour flux map obtained from (a). The dashed circles show the largest DF velocities allowed by energy conservation.

Rotational excitation is inhibited because the reaction is known from hypersurface calculations to be constrained to a colinear collision of small impact parameter ($<1$ Å). Furthermore, the rotationally cold $D_2$ ($T_{rot} \leq 100°K$) is mostly in the ground state and cannot contribute rotational angular momentum. Thus orbital angular momentum in the nearly central collision can contribute at most about 3 kcal/mole of rotational energy which is less than the vibrational spacing of 8 kcal/mole (see Section V,C,4,c).

*c. Forward-Backward Scattering.*   In all the reactions discussed so far evidence was found for a direct mechanism with a short collision time. This behavior, which was observed in all beam reactions until 1968, seems to contradict the generally accepted concept of a long-lived reaction complex, which is known from the study of unimolecular reaction to play an important role even in collisions involving only a few atoms. As already mentioned in Section V,B,2,a this "abnormal" behavior can, in the case of the alkali atom reactions discussed so far, be attributed to charge transfer (harpooning) and the resulting strong Coulomb attraction of the reactants. In 1967 the reactions of $M + M'X \rightarrow MX + M'$ which can be either slightly exo- or endothermic ($\Delta D_0 \leq \pm 10$ kcal/mole), were found to show a forward-backward symmetric scattering profile (Miller *et al.*, 1967a). As discussed below and mentioned previously, such an angular distribution can only be interpreted by assuming that the reaction proceeds via a long-lived complex having a lifetime large compared to the collision time.

The apparatus used in these experiments is similar to those used in other experiments on the alkali atoms (see Fig. 45). The only important difference is that a mass spectrometer is used to analyze the ions formed on the hot ribbon of the Langmuir–Taylor detector. This modification together with the wire preparation techniques discussed in Section II,C,4 made it possible to measure the angular distribution of both reactants and both products.

Figure 55 shows the measured laboratory angular distributions (without a velocity selector in front of the detector) for the exothermic reaction $Cs + RbCl \rightarrow CsCl + Rb$ ($\Delta D_0 \simeq 5.4$ kcal/mole). Both products, Rb and CsCl, show a laboratory angular distribution with two maxima, immediately suggesting a difference to the behavior observed in the previously discussed reactions. Another difference is also apparent in that the angular distribution of the Cs-atom reactant beam is much the same as that of the products. The large maximum at $0°$ is due largely

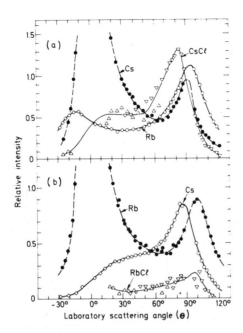

FIG. 55. Measured laboratory angular distributions of reactive $(\bigcirc, \diamondsuit, \triangle, \triangledown)$ and nonreactive $(\bullet)$ scattering of Cs + RbCl → CsCl + Rb (a) and the reverse reaction reaction Rb + CsCl → RbCl + Cs (b). Angular distributions of this type are characteristic of forward-backward scattering.

to the unreacted part of the incident beam. However, the smaller distinct maximum at 90° can only be explained by assuming that the scattered Cs atoms were tossed out of a long-lived complex which did not lead to a reaction. This interpretation is further supported by the observation of a similar double peaked structure in the reactant RbCl distribution (not shown in Fig. 55).

Measurements of product (and reactant) velocity distributions were also performed and the results were used to transform the data into the center-of-mass system. The flux contour map shown in Fig. 56 displays a definite forward-backward symmetry in both the angular and velocity distributions.

This characteristic symmetry can be simply explained by assuming that an intermediate complex is formed having a lifetime long compared to the collision time, and that the lifetime of the complex is randomly distributed. Under these circumstances the angular distribution is completely determined by conservation of angular momentum (Miller *et al.*, 1967). This is illustrated in Fig. 57 for the case in which the reactant

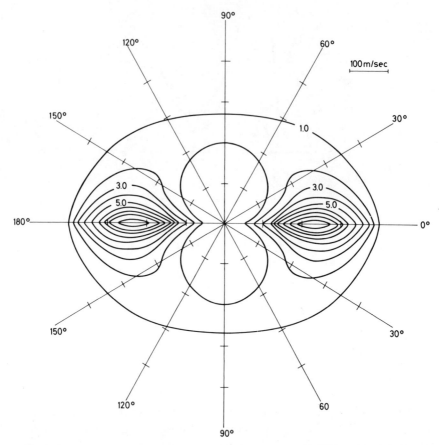

Fig. 56. CsCl c.m. polar flux contour map obtained from laboratory angular and velocity distributions for the reaction Cs + RbCl → CsCl + Rb at thermal energies. The fluxes have been normalized to 10 at the maximum. The contour map is typical of a reaction showing predominantly forward-backward scattering.

molecule has negligible rotational angular momentum compared to the orbital angular momentum (see Section V,C,4,c).

In Fig. 57 the two reactants are shown approaching the center of mass with impact parameter $b$. Since the integral reactive cross section for M + M'X is large ($\sigma \approx 150$ Å$^2$), most of the impact parameters leading to complex formation are quite large and of the order of 7 Å.*

---

* The most probable (and largest) orbital angular momentum ($|l| = \mu g b$) is typically $\geq 300\hbar$ and thus larger than the most probable rotational angular momentum ($<100\hbar$). Therefore, the assumption made in Fig. 57 that rotational angular momentum is small compared to the orbital angular momentum is justified.

In the "sticky" collision the orbital angular momentum is converted into angular momentum of the intermediate complex which rotates in a manner shown in Fig. 57b. Depending on the chemical forces among the atoms, these form either a linear or a bent activated complex. For the case of a linear activated complex, the angular momentum vector is

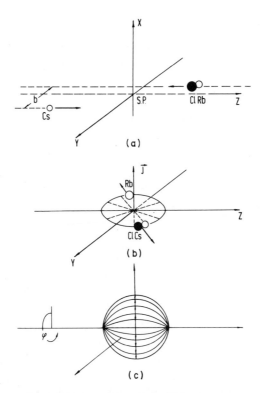

FIG. 57.   Schematic drawings showing the collision partners represented as hard spheres before (a) and after (b) a long-lived reactive collision. The upper two drawings show a collision in the yz plane. In (b) the rotating products are distributed uniformly as indicated by the circle. Averaging over $\varphi$ (about $z$) gives the three-dimensional distribution, shown schematically in (c) and the observed peaking in the forward and backward directions.

directed perpendicular to the symmetry axis. Thus when the activated complex decomposes after a random interval of time, the products fly off in some direction perpendicular to $l$ as indicated by the "spokes" (dotted lines) on the "flywheel" shown in Fig. 57b. For the linear complex the product molecules are not rotationally excited.

In order to obtain the angular distribution observed in the experiment, it is necessary to average the isotropic distribution of Fig. 57b over all azimuthal angles with respect to **g**. For each angle $\varphi$ a similar distribution holds, so that the overall distribution appears as in Fig. 57c. As seen in the figure the products are evenly distributed by the averaging process in directions perpendicular to the initial relative velocity **g**. In the forward or backward direction along **g**, on the other hand, the product intensity is enhanced. In other words, since the $\pm$**g** directions are common to all "flywheels" the intensity along this direction is largest.

This purely classical model leads to an angular distribution $P(\vartheta)$ $\alpha \sin^{-1} \vartheta$, which is also confirmed by a quantal calculation except that the singularities at $\vartheta = 0$ and $\pi$ are removed. If reactant rotation is accounted for the resulting distributions are much the same. For a bent intermediate complex the distributions depart slightly from the $\sin^{-1} \vartheta$ when $\vartheta$ is not too small. Thus aside from implying a potential hypersurface that favors a long-lived complex the angular distribution contains, in principle, also information on the geometry of the intermediate complex. In order to extract this information, however, much more highly resolved experimental data are required. Model calculations taking account of some bending of the complex give satisfactory agreement with the available experimental data (Miller *et al.*, 1967a; Safron, 1969) for the reactions with $M = M' = Na$, K, Rb, Cs, and $X = Cl$, I.

Reliable values of the integral reactive cross sections have not yet been determined for this reaction. Related information is, however, available from the measured ratios of reactive to nonreactive scattering yields, which were found to lie between 0.5 and 4.5 for the 16 reactions studied (Safron, 1969). These ratios are considerably smaller than values calculated from RRKM and phase space theory (Light, 1967) assuming a "loose" complex, in which products interact only weakly at the critical point. Although the discrepancy has not been resolved, it implies that these ratios are sensitive to the potential and the assumptions made in these theories.

The product velocity distributions were all found to be similar to a Maxwell–Boltzmann distribution and the most probable product velocities to be dependent only on the available energy and very little on the chemical species involved (Safron, 1969). The observed distributions are in good agreement with the RRKM and phase space theories giving support to the fundamental assumption made in these theories of no interaction beyond the critical point. Good agreement is also obtained using a thermal distribution and assuming equipartition of energy.

According to this theory $T_{\text{trans}}$, $T_{\text{rot}}$, and $T_{\text{vib}}$ are nearly equal and the common temperature is given by ($k$ is the Boltzmann constant)

$$T^* = \frac{\varepsilon_{\text{tot}}}{(3N - 5\frac{1}{2})k}.$$ 

(5.6)

Here the assumption is made that the total available energy $\varepsilon_{\text{tot}}$ ($= E_{\text{trans}_i} + E_{\text{rot}_i} + E_{\text{vib}_i} + \Delta D_0{}^0$) is divided equally among $3N - 6$ vibrational modes and one rotation (counts $\frac{1}{2}$). The other two rotational modes are assumed fixed by angular momentum conservation.

The formation of a long-lived complex suggests that the $M - M'X$ potential hypersurface has a deep well that leads to snarled oscillating trajectories in the vicinity of the well. The deep potential well is produced at long ranges by the dipole-induced dipole forces which are particularly strong because of the large polarizability of the atoms and large dipole moments of the alkali halides. To describe the short range potential for the system $K + NaCl$, Roach and Child (1968) have used a pseudo-potential semiempirical approximation, in which the single valence electron from the incident atom moves in the fields of the ions $Na^+$, $K^+$, and $Cl^-$. The ground state surface has no activation energy and shows a triangular complex with a well depth of 12 kcal/mole with respect to the products.

A similar deep well is expected to hold for the exchange reactions $MX + M'X' \rightarrow MX' + M'X$, since the alkali halide dimers are known to have large bonding energies ($\sim$30–50 kcal/mole). These are due to the strong dipole–dipole interaction occurring as a result of their "head to tail" structure. Angular distribution for the systems $CsCl + KI$ and $CsCl + KCl$ show the expected symmetric forward-backward angular distributions (Safron, 1969). Other reactions showing complex formation are the reactions of K, Rb, and Cs with $SF_6$ and $SnCl_4$ (Riley, 1970), as well as for Cs reactions with $SF_4$ (see Section V,C,4,b).

Recently, complex formation has been found for reactions of F atoms with 30 different olefins, halogenated olefins, cyclic olefins, conjugated olefins, and aromatic heterocyclic hydrocarbons (Parson and Lee, 1972; Parson et al., 1973; and Shobotake et al., 1973). Both angular and product velocity distributions were measured and in this way complete contour maps in the c.m. system could be inferred. Although the angular distributions show the existence of a long-lived complex the velocity distributions indicate that the internal energy has not had time to randomize before the complex has decomposed. This result is not in accord with current statistical theories of complex formation (e.g., RRKM theory).

Evidence for complex behavior is also available from nonreactive scattering studies of alkali atoms on $CO_2$, $SO_2$, and $NO_2$ (Ham and Kinsey, 1968) as well as from inelastic studies on K + $CO_2$ (see Section IV,C,2). In all of these systems the formation of a long-lived complex can be explained by charge transfer leading to formation of a negative molecule ion. In contrast to the harpooning model (see Section V,B,2,a) the molecule ion formed in these reactions is stable and, therefore, does not decompose readily into the products.

At the present time the important question as to the detailed features of a hypersurface which favor the formation of a complex is still largely unanswered (Kinsey, 1970a). The studies of the M + MX reactions do suggest that in order for a reaction to proceed via an intermediate complex not only must there be a well present but the reaction cannot be too strongly exothermic. Or as seen from the intermediate complex, the barrier for decomposition into products must not be much less than the barrier leading back into reactants. This follows from the observation that the ratio of reactive collision yield to nonreactive collision yield is largest for those reactions with the largest total available energy $\varepsilon_{tot}$ (Safron, 1969). It seems likely that the nonreactive decomposition of the reactants is less probable with increasing available energy simply because the number of oscillations of the trajectories in the well is reduced by the preferred "leakage" into the reaction channel.

Additional more direct evidence is provided by studies of the reactions of the alkali atoms (K, Rb, Cs) with TlCl and TlI (McDonald, 1971) and of Li atoms with KBr and KF (Kwei et al., 1971). For all but the reaction Li + KF a complex with a lifetime of the same order of magnitude as its rotational period $\tau_r$ ($= 2\pi I/l$, where $I$ is the moment of inertia of the complex and $l$ the orbital angular momentum) are formed. This correlates well with the larger exothermicities for these reactions. For the thallium halide reactions the exothermicities are in the range of 7 to 17 kcal/mole, while in the Li atom reactions they are 9 and 20 kcal/mole, respectively, and are therefore at least twice as large as for M + M'X reactions.

In the case of these reactions the average complex lifetime can be estimated (McDonald, 1971) from the angular distribution if the lifetimes $t$ are distributed according to

$$P(t) = e^{-t/\tau}/\tau, \qquad (5.7)$$

where $\tau$ is the mean lifetime. If $t$ is of the order of magnitude of $\tau$ such complexes are called osculating complexes. In simple RRK theory $\tau$ is given by

$$\tau = 10^{-13}\left(\frac{E - E_{\text{act}}}{E}\right)^{1-s} \text{sec}, \tag{5.8}$$

where $E_{\text{act}}$ is the activation energy for complex decomposition and $E$ is the total energy; $s$ is the total number of active degrees of freedom. The corresponding distribution in $\vartheta$ (measured from the direction of the incoming atom) is given by

$$P(\vartheta) = \exp(-\vartheta/\bar{\vartheta})/\vartheta, \tag{5.9}$$

where $\bar{\vartheta} = 2\pi\tau/\tau_r$ is the angular displacement (in radians) corresponding to the mean lifetime. Properly averaged this expression leads to a fall-off function which, depending on the ratio $\tau/\tau_r$, reduces the relative intensity of the backward peak. For $\tau/\tau_r \sim \frac{1}{2}$ the backward peak is about one half of the forward peak and for $\tau/\tau_r \sim 10^{-1}$ disappears altogether. In this way lifetimes of 3 to $8 \cdot 10^{-12}$ sec are found for the thallium reactions from the angular distributions. In the case of the most strongly exothermic reaction Li + KF no evidence for complex formation is found and the reaction appears to proceed by a spectator-stripping reaction.

This change in behavior with exothermicity is reminiscent of that observed in ion–molecule reactions where a transition from complex mechanism to direct mechanism is observed with increasing collision energy. Unfortunately because of the more severe technical difficulties in neutral–neutral scattering such a change over has not yet been observed.

*d. Intermediate Reactions.* Although the vast majority of all reactions studied so far fit into one of the above three categories, some reactions appear to show an intermediate behavior. An example of such a reaction is the reaction of the alkali atoms with $CCl_4$ ($\Delta D_0$ estimated at roughly 35 kcal/mole) (Wilson and Herschbach, 1968; Siska, 1970). In contrast to the other reaction types there appears to be a strong coupling between the product velocity distributions and their angular distribution. The observed behavior can be partially explained by assuming a direct mechanism and a type of spectator model in which the "spectator" is deflected but not slowed down.

The first reaction studied by beam scattering techniques K + HBr (Taylor and Datz, 1955) also appears to fall into this category. Because of the unfavorable mass ratios of the products, which means that the

KBr product recoils only little in the c.m. system, the angular distributions in the c.m. system are hard to measure. For K + HBr these show an almost isotropic distribution with a factor of 2 peaking in the backward direction (Gillen et al., 1969). For K + DBr the distribution is almost independent of angle (Gillen et al., 1969) and for K + TBr a pronounced backward peaking (Martin and Kinsey, 1967) is found. This apparent discrepancy has recently been attributed to an isotope effect entering in by way of the mass-dependent zero-point vibrational energy of the reactant molecule (Roach, 1970). It can also be explained by a statistical phase space theory (Truhlar, 1971).

In conclusion therefore there is no reason to expect in the future that the angular distributions of all reactions will fall neatly into one of the categories, forward, backward, or forward-backward. Indeed, as increasing complex reactions are studied in which harpooning is not an important factor, there is a good possibility that different reaction paths for the same reactants will follow different mechanisms.

C. MORE DETAILED STUDIES

1. Energy Dependence of Cross Sections and Activation Energies

The temperature dependence of the macroscopic bimolecular rate constant is a direct function of the energy dependence of the integral reactive cross section:

$$k(T) \simeq \int_0^\infty \sigma_{\text{react}}(E)E \exp(-E/kT)\, dE, \qquad (5.10)$$

where $\sigma_{\text{react}}(E)$ is the integral reactive cross section averaged over all initial and final quantum states (Shuler et al., 1969). In deriving Eq. (5.10) the assumption of Maxwell–Boltzmann velocities distributions has been made. Thus the integral reactive cross section provides the most direct link between beam experiments and the more conventional gas kinetic data. Unfortunately integral reactive cross sections cannot be easily measured directly and as mentioned previously (see Section V,B,2,a) this beam quantity is always derived from either measured reactive or nonreactive angular distributions.*

---

* In the case of ion–molecule reactions the experimental situation is more favorable. Recently it has been possible to measure directly the integral reactive cross section by trapping and collecting all the product ions using a specially designed radio frequency ion "funnel" (Teloy, 1971).

In the past most of the work on the energy dependence of integral cross sections has been based on measurements of nonreactive angular distributions (see Section V,B,2,b). For direct reactions with small reactive cross sections involving nearly spherically symmetric molecules the technique appears to provide a sensitive method for observing the maximum impact parameters leading to reaction and provides an upper limit to the integral reactive cross section. As discussed elsewhere (Toennies, 1968a; Kinsey, 1972) the quantitative interpretation of the data involves assumption concerning the role of inelastic processes. Figure 58 shows the energy

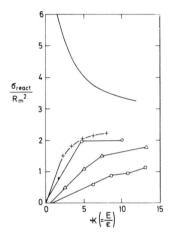

FIG. 58. Integral reactive cross section as a function of reduced energy for several reactions of alkali atoms on bromine compounds. The results were obtained indirectly from an analysis of nonreactive scattering. The measured systems and potential parameters are from top to bottom K + Br$_2$: $\varepsilon = 0.5$ kcal/mole, $R_m \simeq 8$ Å; Cs + HBr: $\varepsilon = 0.80 \pm 0.06$, $R_m = 2.3 \pm 0.4$; K + HBr: $\varepsilon = 0.57 \pm 0.01$, $R_m = 4.9 \pm 0.7$; K + CH$_3$Br: $\varepsilon = 0.38 \pm 0.01$, $R_m \simeq 4.4$; K + (CH$_3$)$_3$CBr: $\varepsilon = 0.45 \pm 0.03$, $R_m = 4.3 \pm 1.3$.

dependence and threshold behavior of several reactions measured in this way (Greene *et al.*, 1969). In all cases except K + Br$_2$ the cross section rises sharply in the vicinity of the threshold energy and approaches a constant value at high energies corresponding to K = $E/\varepsilon$ = 10–15. The K + Br$_2$ data show a different trend, which is similar to that of elastic scattering. This appears reasonable since at low energies the weak dispersion forces can serve to pull the partners together to where curve crossing (harpooning) can occur. The experiments for this and related systems are however more difficult to interpret since a rainbow maximum as shown in Fig. 52 is not observed and since the sharp drop off in the nonreactive differential cross section may be caused by non-reactive collisions involving curve crossing from the initial covalent state into the ionic state and back again (Fluendy *et al.*, 1970). On the other hand the integral reactive cross section determined by this method for K + $I_2$ (Gillen *et al.*, 1971) agrees well with the more reliable photo-dissociation data (see Table XVII).

In this connection similar experiments at higher energies are of interest. Using a fast K beam produced by sputtering, Kempter *et al.* (1970a) have measured nonreactive angular distributions for a number of non-reactive (K + $C_6H_{12}$, $SiCl_4$) and reactive (K + $Cl_2$, $Br_2$, $CCl_4$, and $SnCl_4$) systems. In contrast to the sharp cut off which is observed to wipe out the rainbow maximum at thermal energies these authors not only see a rainbow angle but at larger angles an actual increase in the reduced differential cross section. Presumably at the high energies (1 to 6 eV) curve crossing becomes less probable and the particles react more frequently by way of the covalent curves.

Recently Gersch and Bernstein (1971) have measured the reactive angular distributions for K + $CH_3I \rightarrow KI + CH_3$ in the energy range 0.1 to 1 eV. The large energy range was achieved by seeding the $CH_3I$ beam with different light gases. The KI product was detected by a two-wire detector on a goniometer which allowed measurements over a large range of angles ($\theta$ and $\phi$ in- and out-of-plane) in the laboratory system.

In this way the transformed distributions covered the entire range of $\vartheta$ in the center-of-mass system and could be directly integrated to yield relative integral cross sections. These were normalized to those from nonreactive angular distributions. The results of both types of experiments for this system are shown in Fig. 59. In contrast to the earlier work these more direct experiments show a maximum of about 40 Å$^2$ at 0.18 eV and a fall off to a constant value of about 10 Å$^2$ at higher energies. A final interpretation of these results has not yet been presented.

Finally, it should be pointed out that in general the understanding of high-energy scattering experiments is more difficult than at lower energies. For one, additional inelastic channels such as vibrational excitation or charge transfer are opened up and must be taken into account. Thus as discussed in Section IV,E most of the alkali atom reactions are also accompanied by charge transfer processes leading to ionic products. Another complication at high energies is introduced by the increased possibility of excited electronic states being involved in the reactions.

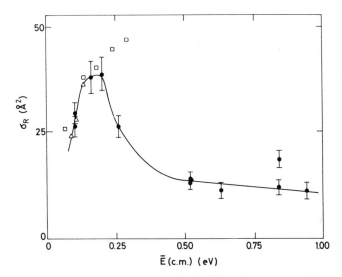

FIG. 59. Measured integral reactive cross sections for the reaction K + CH$_3$I → KI + CH$_3$ as a function of energy. The results (●) from a direct integration of the measured reactive differential cross section (Gersh and Bernstein, 1971) are compared with values obtained indirectly from angular distributions of nonreactively scattered K measured by Airey *et al.* (1967b) and Greene and Ross (1968) (□) and Harris and Wilson (1971). (△).

## 2. *Role of Reactant Vibrational Excitation in Activating Reactions*

In all of the studies of chemical reactions discussed so far the reactant beams had thermal internal energy distributions. Of considerable interest in connection with the kinetics of gas reactions, especially in fast flow situations as occur, for example, in shock fronts, is the role of internal degrees of freedom in activating reactions.

An indirect way of studying internal activation is to use microscopic reversibility to estimate rate constants for the reverse reaction rates of exothermic reactions from measured forward rate constants (Anlauf *et al.*, 1969). The method can only be applied if the forward rate constant is known for specified initial as well as final internal states and translational energies. Using data from nonbeam infrared chemiluminescence experiments the dependence of the rate constants on the reactant internal states and initial translational energy has been estimated for the endothermic reactions (Anlauf *et al.*, 1969; Polanyi and Tardy, 1969):

$$HCl(n', j') + I \to HI + Cl \quad (\Delta D_0 = -31.7 \text{ kcal/mole}), \quad (5.11a)$$

$$HCl(n, j) + Cl \to H + Cl_2 \quad (\Delta D_0 = -45.2 \text{ kcal/mole}), \quad (5.11b)$$

and

$$HF(n, j) + H \rightarrow F + H_2 \qquad (\Delta D_0 = -32 \text{ kcal/mole}). \qquad (5.11c)$$

This study shows that the detailed rate constant increases by orders of magnitude as the vibrational energy in the reactant molecule is increased and that vibrational energy is much more effective than translational energy in bringing about endothermic reactions. In the case of the second reaction producing H atoms the effect is modified somewhat because of a "light-atom anomaly" (Parr et al., 1973).

A direct beam study of the role of vibrational excitation has recently been carried out for the slightly endothermic reaction $K + HCl \rightarrow KCl + H$ ($\Delta D_0 = -1.4 \pm 1.2$ kcal/mole) by exciting the $n = 1$ state of HCl using a HCl chemical laser (Odiorne et al., 1971). This reaction had been previously studied using thermal beams and found by integration of the product angular distribution to have a reactive cross section of only 0.15 $\text{Å}^2$ (Odiorne and Brooks, 1969; Greene et al., 1966).

The laser emission was so intense that roughly 25% of the HCl beam was excited. The reactive cross section estimated for a 100% vibrationally excited beam was of the order of 20 $\text{Å}^2$. The observed cross section enhancement is similar to that observed for $He + H_2^+ \rightarrow HeH^+ + H$ (Chupka et al., 1969). In this case it was found that vibrational excitation had a much greater effect than translational activation.

A similar result comes from another neutral beam experiment (Jaffe and Anderson, 1969) on the much studied reaction $HI + HI \rightarrow H_2 + I_2$. A molecular beam of HI was accelerated to laboratory energies of 40–215 kcal/mole by using seeded beams (Section II,C,1). The primary beam was passed through a scattering chamber containing DI gas. The gas effusing from the scattering chamber was then analyzed for the reaction product HD with a mass spectrometer. The sensitivity of this arrangement was much higher than that of a crossed beam experiment and it was estimated that a reactive cross section of about $2 \cdot 10^{-2} \text{Å}^2$ could be detected.

Despite the fact that the relative translational energy was up to $2\frac{1}{2}$ times greater than the activation energy of 44 kcal/mole, no reaction products could be detected, indicating that $\sigma_{\text{react}} < 2–4 \cdot 10^{-2} \text{Å}^2$. This result has been compared with cross sections estimated from the measured reaction rate constants for an assumed activation mechanism. The observed upper limit on the reactive cross section is only in agreement with the kinetic data if activation by internal degrees of freedom is assumed.

Other beam experiments indicate that highly vibrationally excited molecules may open up new reaction channels. This is illustrated by a remarkable crossed beam study on $KBr^\dagger + Na$ (Moulton and Herschbach, 1966), in which the crossed beam reaction $K + Br_2 \rightarrow KBr^\dagger + Br$ was used to produce $KBr^\dagger$ molecules, which are known to contain more than 90% of the reaction energy of 44.5 kcal/mole in the form of vibrational excitation. The $KBr^\dagger$ was then passed into a second scattering chamber and was crossed with an Na beam. Intense emission of the potassium resonance line ($\Delta E = 37.2$ kcal/mole) was observed and attributed to the reactions

$$KBr^\dagger + Na \rightarrow NaBr + K^*, \qquad K^* \rightarrow K + h\nu. \qquad (5.12)$$

At thermal internal energies the same reaction is expected to proceed by a complex mechanism to ground state atoms (see Section V,B,2,c).

## 3. *Experiments with Oriented Molecules*

In order to measure the orientation dependence (steric factor) of a chemical reaction the target molecule has to be oriented with respect to the direction of relative velocity. Diatomic polar molecules are difficult to orient in an electric field because the interaction with the dipole moment is averaged out in first order by the rotational motion. In symmetric top molecules, on the other hand, the dipole moment remains largely oriented in laboratory space for those angular momentum states in which the rotation is about the symmetry axis. Because of the resulting strong interaction with the field, symmetric top molecules are easily deflected in an inhomogeneous electric field and once selected can be oriented in an homogeneous field (Brooks *et al.*, 1969).

This technique has been used to study the orientation dependence of the reactions $K + CH_3I$ (Brooks and Jones, 1966) and $Rb + CH_3I$ (Beuhler and Bernstein, 1966, 1969). The apparatus used in these experiments is shown in Fig. 60. An electric six pole field focuses the velocity selected $CH_3I$ beam molecules with large negative values of the product of the angular momentum quantum numbers K and M. These molecules are subsequently aligned in an electric field in which they are crossed with the atom beam. Depending on the electric field direction the molecules are oriented parallel to or antiparallel to the on-coming atom as shown in the bottom left-hand corner of Fig. 60. The product intensity was measured at the detector for a range of scattering angles. The extent of alignment could be varied by changing the

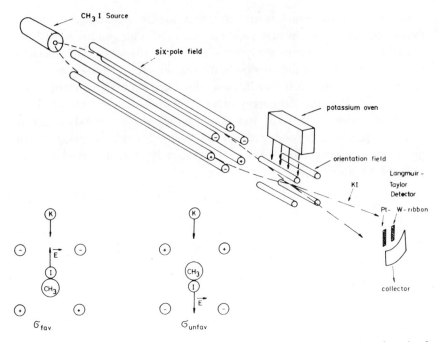

FIG. 60. Apparatus for measuring the orientation dependence (steric factor) of the reactive cross section $K + CH_3I \rightarrow KI + CH_3$. The $CH_3I$ beam is state selected by the six-pole field and oriented in the scattering region by a four-pole field. The insert at the bottom left shows the two relative orientations of the $CH_3I$ molecule with respect to the K-atom direction.

field strength and the results could therefore be extrapolated to 100% alignment.

The data show that the reaction probability is greater for the favorable orientation $(M \rightarrow ICH_3)$ than for the unfavorable orientation $(M \rightarrow CH_3I)$. The ratio of the differential reactive cross sections for backward $(180°)$ scattering in the c.m. system is more than four. In addition to providing further confirmation of the collision model proposed in Fig. 51, these results suggest that most of the anisotropy can be explained by a simple model in which reaction occurs only for collisions on the favorable hemisphere of the $CH_3I$ molecule which is considered to be spherical (Beuhler and Bernstein, 1969).

In a more recent experiment Brooks (1969, 1971) has found preliminary evidence that the reaction $K + CF_3I \rightarrow KI + CF_3$ can occur for alkali atom attack from both ends, for example, from the "unfavorable" $F_3C$ end as well as from the I end. Unfortunately there is only indirect evidence that the product of the observed reaction is indeed KI. Nevertheless, the result is interesting since it suggests that a "harpooning" to the more electronegative side of the molecule can initiate the reaction.

4. *Measurements of the Internal Excitation of Products (Partitioning of the Reaction Energy)*

Monte Carlo calculations show that the partitioning of the reaction energy among the three possible degrees of freedom of the products translations, rotations, and vibrations, is sensitively dependent on the shape of the potential hypersurface.* For example, in a recent Monte Carlo study of the $M + X_2$ reaction, Kuntz *et al.* (1969a) using 12 different hypersurfaces found large differences in the rotational and vibrational distributions whereas the angular distributions all had about the same shape and showed the expected forward scattering.

Some restrictions on the energy distribution come from the equations of conservation of energy and angular momentum. The former require that

$$E_{tot} = E_{trans_f} + E_{rot_f} + E_{vib_f} = E_{trans_i} + E_{rot_i} + E_{vib_i} + \Delta D_0, \quad (5.13)$$

where the index $f$ refers to the products and the index $i$ to the reactants and $\Delta D_0$ in the difference in the bond dissociation energies (relative to zero point vibrational levels). For the more highly exothermic reactions such as $M + X_2$ the energies of the reactants are small ($\sim 4\%$ compared to $\Delta D_0$ and can usually be neglected.

A variety of experimental techniques have been used to determine the excitation of the products of chemical reaction. These are discussed according to the degree of freedom observed.

*a. Translational Energy of the Products.* As pointed out earlier the flux contour maps contain information on the c.m. product velocity distributions at each scattering angle. Thus the product velocity distributions are usually a by-product of angular measurements. In some cases a crude determination of the c.m. velocity distribution is also possible from angular distributions measured over a range of $\phi$ as well as $\theta$ (Kwei *et al.*, 1970). In exceptional cases (see Fig. 54) the product translational energy distribution is projected on to the laboratory angular distribution and can be seen directly.

---

* Electronic excitation has not been considered since there is little evidence that electronic excitation occurs for most of the alkali atom reactions studied to date. For a possible exception see Gillen *et al.*, 1971).

## TABLE XIX

Some Typical Values of Product Translational Energy. All Energies Are in kcal/mole

| Reactions | $E_{trans_i}$ | $E_{int_i}^k$ | $\Delta D_0$ | $E_{tot}$ | $E_{trans_f}$ | $f_{trans}$ | Reference |
|---|---|---|---|---|---|---|---|
| Hydrogen atom reactions | | | | | | | |
| $D + Cl_2 \rightarrow DCl + Cl$ | 9.0 | 0.7 | 45 | 55 | 24 | 0.44 | a |
| $D + Br_2 \rightarrow DBr + Br$ | 9.0 | 0.85 | 41 | 51 | 15 | 0.3 | a |
| $D + I_2 \rightarrow DI + I$ | 9.0 | 0.94 | 34 | 44 | 12 | 0.27 | a |
| Alkali atom reactions | | | | | | | |
| $Li + Br_2 \rightarrow LiBr + Br$ | 2.0 | 0.85 | 54 | 57 | 6.6 | 0.12 | b |
| $Na + Br_2 \rightarrow NaBr + Br$ | 1.3 | 0.85 | 41 | 43 | 1.0–5.2 | 0.023–0.12 | c |
| $K + Br_2 \rightarrow KBr + Br$ | 1.2 | 0.85 | 45 | 47 | 1.2–3.7 | 0.026–0.079 | d |
| $Rb + Br_2 \rightarrow RbBr + Br$ | 1.0 | 0.85 | 44 | 46 | 1.1–2.8 | 0.024–0.061 | d |
| $Cs + Br_2 \rightarrow CsBr + Br$ | 1.1 | 0.85 | 50 | 52 | 1.1–1.8 | 0.021–0.035 | d |
| $Li + CH_3I \rightarrow LiI + CH_3$ | 2.0 | 1.11 | $30 \pm 2$ | 31–35 | 12–20 | 0.34–0.65 | e |
| $Na + CH_3I \rightarrow NaI + CH_3$ | 1.3 | 1.11 | 17 | 19 | 4–15.4 | 0.2–0.8 | c |

| | | | | | | | |
|---|---|---|---|---|---|---|---|
| K + CH$_3$I → KI + CH$_3$ | 1.0 | 1.11 | 23 | 25 | 2.0–11.0 | 0.08–0.44 | f |
| Cs + CH$_3$I → CsI + CH$_3$ | 1.0 | 1.11 | 27 | 28 | ~11.0 | 0.39 | g |
| Li + NO$_2$ → LiO + NO | 1.9 | 1.00 | 10 ± 4 | 9–17 | 2–3 | 0.12–0.34 | e |
| Halogen atom reactions | | | | | | | |
| Cl + Br$_2$ → ClBr + Br | 2.5 | 0.85 | 6.7 | 10.1 | 1.5–2.8 | 0.15–0.28 | h, i, j |
| Cl + I$_2$ → ClI + I | — | — | 14.1 | — | — | 0.5 | j |
| Br + I$_2$ → BrI + I | 2.7 | 0.94 | 7.0 | 10.6 | 1.7 | 0.16 | i |

[a] McDonald (1971).
[b] Parrish and Herm (1969).
[c] Birely et al. (1969).
[d] Birely et al. (1967).
[e] Parrish and Herm (1971).
[f] Kwei et al. (1970).
[g] Entemann (1967).
[h] Loesch and Beck (1971).
[i] Lee et al. (1968).
[j] Cross and Blais (1970).
[k] Value estimated by author.

From the c.m. velocity distribution of one of the products the final relative kinetic energy of the products can be easily calculated (see Section II,B). The results are usually summarized in terms of the ratio of either the most probable or average final kinetic energy $E_{\text{trans}_f}$ $(= \frac{1}{2}\mu_f g_f^2)$ to the total energy $E_{\text{tot}}$

$$f_{\text{trans}_f} = \frac{E_{\text{trans}_f}}{E_{\text{tot}}}. \tag{5.14}$$

Some representative results for $f_{\text{trans}_f}$ are shown in Table XIX. From the table it appears that for most reactions more than half of the total energy is converted into internal excitation (for diatomic products $f_{\text{int}} = 1 - f_{\text{trans}}$) of the product molecule.

A comparison of the $f_{\text{trans}}$ values with the angular distributions discussed previously suggests that there is a correlation between $f_{\text{trans}}$ and the angle of peak intensity $\vartheta_{\text{mp}}$. For small c.m. angles $f_{\text{trans}}$ is generally small and for large c.m. angles $f_{\text{trans}}$ is large. Riley (1970) has found a very definite correlation of this type for the halomethanes. For the reactions K and Cs on $CBr_4$, $CH_2I_2$, $ClBr_3$, $CCl_4$, $CH_2Br_2$, and $CH_3I$, $\vartheta_{\text{mp}}$ increases nearly linearly from 0 to $180°$ while $f_{\text{trans}}$ goes from 0.05 to 0.3 to 0.5. Such correlations must be treated with caution as shown by the fact that for a given target molecules the trend with changing M may go in a different direction.

A trend of the type discussed above is in accord with what is expected from the harpooning model. If harpooning occurs at large distances (forward scattering) the reactants attract each other strongly. Such a surface is termed an "early downhill" surface, and according to the rule of Evans and Polanyi (1939), which has been confirmed by a large number of recent Monte Carlo calculations, leads to high vibrational excitation of the products. If harpooning occurs at small distances (backward scattering) the attraction is weakened by the competing repulsive potential and may even carry over into the product channel where it can lead to a repulsion between the products. In this case classical mechanics predicts that there will be less vibrational excitation.

*b. Vibrational Energy of the Products.* The vibrational energy distribution of product molecules is one of the most difficult reaction properties to measure. In recent years however two well-established spectroscopic techniques have been improved to such an extent that they now provide information on vibrational energies of polar molecules. These are infrared chemiluminescence and molecular beam electric resonance (radiofrequency) spectroscopy.

Since infrared chemiluminescence is discussed elsewhere in this book only brief mention will be made of this technique here. Two uncollimated nozzle beams are crossed in a large reaction vessel, the walls of which are cooled to liquid nitrogen temperature or below to condense as much of the products as possible. The infrared light emitted in the reaction vessel is collected and analyzed in a sensitive Fourier transform infrared spectrometer. Because of the long radiative lifetime of the vibrationally excited molecules ($\approx$ milliseconds) and high residual pressure in the reaction vessel deexcitation collisions with the background gas molecules compete with the emission process. Thus in earlier work with a more simple apparatus the observed distributions were distorted by secondary collisions and provided only a lower limit on the vibrational excitation. Recently the technique has been improved by lowering the residual gas pressure and increasing the spectrometer efficiency so that the initial product distributions are now believed to be measured (Anlauf et al., 1967, Charters et al., 1971). Thus the technique now has all the special advantages of a crossed molecular beam apparatus. Using this technique the vibrational and rotational distribution of a large number of reactions involving H, O, N, and the halogen atoms have been studied (Carrington and Polanyi, 1972). Very recently, further improvements have made it possible to measure the collision energy dependence of the final-state distribution of Cl + HI $\rightarrow$ HCl $(n, j)$ + I (Cowley et al., 1971) and the dependence on reagent vibration energy for F + HCl $(n = 0, 1) \rightarrow$ HF $(n, j)$ + Cl (Kirsch and Polanyi, 1972).

The related technique of laser induced fluorescence has also recently been applied to the study of internal state distributions of the reaction Ba + $O_2 \rightarrow$ BaO $(n, j)$ + O (Schultz et al., 1972). A pulsed tunable dyelaser is used to scan the reaction zone. At certain wavelengths molecules are excited to the first electronic state of the BaO molecule. From the fluorescence intensity the rotational and vibrational population of the electronic ground state can be inferred. Although capable of providing detailed information on the quantum states of product molecules these techniques are relatively insensitive. Thus so far it has not been possible to measure the product distributions for different scattering angles.

A more direct measurement of vibrational energy distribution is only possible using the molecular beam electric resonance method (see Section II,C,3). The method was first applied by Freund et al. (1971) to the reaction Cs + $SF_6 \rightarrow$ CsF + $SF_5$. The vibrational energy distribution of the CsF product molecules among the lowest four or five vibrational levels for $j = 0 - 4$ was measured. The observed distribution was found to be nearly Boltzmann with a temperature of about 1200°K. This result is consistent with a reaction via a long-lived collision complex that is also indicated by the observed forward-backward peaking of the angular distribution observed in an independent study (Riley, 1970). The translational temperature of 1200°K which was taken from the flux contour map is almost the same as the vibrational temperature and thus in agreement with equipartitioning of energy (Safron, 1969) among all the available degrees of freedom (Freund *et al.*, 1971). See also Section V,B,2,c.

Using an improved apparatus described in Section II,C,3 Bennewitz *et al.* (1971b) have been able to extend the range of vibrational states to $v \cong 10$. Their results for Cs + SF$_6$ (see Fig. 61) agree well with those of Freund *et al.* (1971). They also studied the reaction Cs + SF$_4 \rightarrow$ CsF + SF$_3$ and found for this system a superposition of two distributions

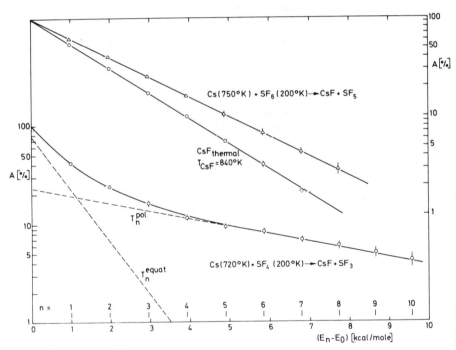

FIG. 61.   Vibrational energy distributions for CsF from two different reactions as measured by the molecular beam electric resonance method (Bennewitz *et al.*, 1971b). The relative populations are plotted as a function of the vibrational quantum number $n$. The results are for CsF molecules in the $j = 1$ rotational state. The laboratory scattering angle for both reactions is $\theta = 21°$. Also shown is the vibrational energy distribution obtained directly with a thermal beam of CsF.

characterized by two temperatures of $T \simeq 420°K$ and $T \simeq 2800°K$ as shown in the lower part of Fig. 61. This surprising result can be explained by the structure of the $SF_4$ molecule, which has two nonequivalent SF bonds with widely different bond strengths. Thus two channels with different amounts of exothermicity are possible and apparently observed.

The molecular beam electric resonance method has the drawback that the spectra become extremely complicated unless molecules with low nuclear spin are used. For this reason CsF is preferred. For similar reasons the technique can only be applied to a certain class of collisions leading to low lying rotational states with $j \leq 4$. Thus the results may not always be characteristic of the average or most probable distributions.

As mentioned previously (Section V,C,2) the amount of product vibrational energy has in one case ($K + Br_2 \rightarrow KBr^\dagger + Br$) been established by using the product beam to activate a second reaction ($KBr^\dagger + Na \rightarrow NaBr + K^*$) of known threshold.

Finally, it should be pointed out that if $E_{tot}$ [see Eq. (5.13)] and the mean product translational energy are known, an upper limit to $E_{vib_f}$ with an error roughly equal to $\pm E_{trans_i}$ is established. As discussed in the next section this can be attributed to the fact that $E_{rot_f}$ is limited by conservation of angular momentum to roughly $E_{trans_i}$. The reaction $F + D_2(n = 0) \rightarrow DF(n = n') + D$, discussed earlier (see Section V,B,2,b) is an extreme example of a reaction in which $E_{rot_f}$ is limited to small values. Table XX compares values for the relative population of different final vibrational states for the reaction $F + D_2$ coming from several different experiments and from classical trajectory studies. The agreement is reasonably good if account is made of the differences in energies and techniques (Lee, 1972).

*c. Rotational Energy of the Products.* Whereas the product vibrational energy distribution depends on forces along the product bond axis the product rotational energy distribution depends sensitively on forces producing torques during the reaction.

Before discussing the experiments the restrictions on the rotational energy imposed by conservation of angular momentum are summarized. In atom–molecule reactions the total angular momentum is composed of orbital angular momentum $|\boldsymbol{l}| = l = \mu bg$ and rotational angular momentum of the molecule $|\mathbf{j}| = j = I\omega$ (where $I$ is the moment of inertia and $\omega$ is the angular velocity of rotation). Since $\boldsymbol{l} = \mathbf{p} \times \mathbf{R}$ ($\mathbf{p}$ is the linear relative momentum and $\mathbf{R}$ the vector connecting the centers of mass) $\boldsymbol{l}$ is always perpendicular to $\mathbf{p}$ or the direction of relative motion $\mathbf{g}$. To

TABLE XX

Comparison of Relative Product Vibrational State Distributions Normalized at $n' = 3$ (Lee, 1972)

| Study | Method | $E_{trans}$ | $n' = 4$ | $n' = 3$ | $n' = 2$ | $n' = 1$ | $n' = 0$ |
|---|---|---|---|---|---|---|---|
| | | | | Relative population | | | |
| Parker and Pimentel (1969) | Laser | $T_F \sim 300°K$ | — | 1.00 | 0.63 | — | — |
| Anlauf et al. (1970) | Chemiluminescence | $T_F \sim 300°K$ | 0.7 | 1.00 | 0.5 | 0.1 | — |
| Schafer et al. | Angular distributions | 2.57 kcal/mole | 3.0 | 1.00 | 0.16 | 0.06 | 0.03 |
| Muckermann (1972) | Monte Carlo calculation | — | 2.2 | 1.00 | — | — | — |

obtain the initial total angular momentum, the two vectors must be added to yield.

$$\mathbf{J}_i = \mathbf{l}_i + \mathbf{j}_i \tag{5.15a}$$

or

$$J_i^2 = l_i^2 + j_i^2 + 2l_ij_i \cos \alpha_i , \tag{5.15b}$$

where $\alpha$ the angle between $l$ and $j$ takes on all values between 0 and $\pi$. For many of the alkali atom reactions observed so far the angular momenta in most of the collisions satisfy the inequality $l_i > j_i$ and since the probability distribution $p(l)$ is proportional to $l$ (the area in a ring of radius $b$ of width $db$ is proportional to $b$), it follows that $l_{i(mp)} \gg j_i$, where $l_{i(mp)}$ is the most probable orbital angular momentum of the reactants.

Conservation of angular momentum requires that the product angular momentum be given by

$$l_i^2 \simeq J_i^2 = J_f^2 = l_f^2 + j_f^2 + 2l_fj_f \cos \alpha_f , \tag{5.16}$$

where $\alpha_f$ may also have a range of values. For $\alpha_f = 0$, $\mathbf{j}_f$, $\mathbf{l}_f$, and $\mathbf{J}_i$ are parallel and in this case the scattering is said to occur in the plane of the reactants (two-dimensional scattering). There is some evidence from Monte Carlo calculations that $\mathbf{j}_f$ and $\mathbf{l}_f$ are nearly parallel. At any rate it is extremely improbable that $\mathbf{j}_f$ and $\mathbf{l}_f$ are larger in magnitude than $J_i$, which would be possible if they were oppositely directed. Thus as a rule the product molecule angular momentum is always less than that of the maximum initial orbital angular momentum or $\mathbf{j}_f \gtrsim \mathbf{l}_{i\,max}$, where $l_{i\,max} = \mu b_{max}g$ and $b_{max}$ is the maximum impact parameter leading to reaction. For reactions such as K + HBr, where one of the products is much lighter than the other, the greatly diminished reduced mass of products leads to the inequality $|\mathbf{l}_f| \ll |\mathbf{j}_f|$. Moreover, since $j_i \simeq 3\hbar$ for HBr, angular momentum conservation predicts for K + HBr that $\mathbf{j}_f \simeq \mathbf{l}_i$.

The resulting restrictions on the rotational energy can now be easily estimated. For the reaction A + BC $\rightarrow$ AB + C classical mechanics gives

$$E_{rot_f} = \tfrac{1}{2}(j_f^2/I_{AB}) \quad \text{where} \quad I_{AB} = \mu_{AB}R_{A-B}^2 .$$

From the discussion above

$$E_{rot_f} \leq \tfrac{1}{2}(l_{i\,max}^2/I_{AB}),$$

which on substituting $l_{i\,max} = \mu_i g b_{max}$ leads finally to the inequality

$$E_{rot_f} \leq E_{trans_i} \frac{\mu_{A-BC}}{\mu_{AB}} \frac{b_{max}^2}{R_{A-B}^2} \tag{5.17}$$

since $b_{max} \simeq R_{A-B}$ and $\mu_{A-BC} \simeq \mu_{AB}$, $E_{rot_f}$ and $E_{trans_i}$ are roughly equal. If as in K + HBr $\mathbf{j}_f = \mathbf{l}_i$, then the distribution $P(E_{rot_f})$ is a direct measure of the reaction probability $P(b_i)$ as a function of impact parameter.

The application of infrared chemiluminescence to rotational energy distributions is much more difficult than in the measurement of vibrational distributions. This has to do with the fact that the inelastic cross section for rotational deexcitation is much larger than for vibrational deexcitation so that even a few collisions with the background gas lead to a distortion of the original distribution. However, recently, in a number of instances measurements of initial rotational distributions have been obtained in infrared chemiluminescent experiments (Maylotte et al., 1972; Anlauf et al., 1972; Polanyi and Woodall, 1972; Polanyi and Sloane, 1972). The related technique of laser induced fluorescence has also been used to study the rotational level distribution of BaO from the reaction Ba + $O_2$ (Schultz et al., 1972).

The beam techniques are also restricted to polar product molecules since inhomogeneous electric fields are used to deflect the polar molecules. As mentioned in Section II,C,3, the deflection of polar molecules is dependent on the $(j, m)$ state of the molecules. The deflection also depends on the dipole moment, which in turn depends weakly on the vibrational state of the molecule. The deflection method has therefore the minor disadvantage that the measured distribution depends slightly on the vibrational energy distribution.

In the technique first applied by Maltz and Herschbach (1967) an electric Stern–Gerlach two-pole field is placed between the reaction zone and the Langmuir–Taylor detector. The apparatus can be used in two ways. Either the deflection pattern is measured by moving the detector in a plane perpendicular to the primary beam or the attenuation of the beam produced by varying the rod voltage is observed. The method is indirect in that the probability distribution $P(E_{rot_f})$ is first assumed* and a quantity such as the temperature, characterizing the mean energy is determined by matching measured and calculated attenuation curves. Since a velocity selector is not used the analysis of the data requires a knowledge of the laboratory product velocity distribution. Using this technique, Maltz has studied a large number of alkali atom reactions for which the average rotational energy $\overline{E_{rot_f}}$ was measured at one angle.

---

* Calculations by Maltz (1969) show that distributions of different shapes give very similar attenuation curves so that the method is not sensitive to the assumed distribution.

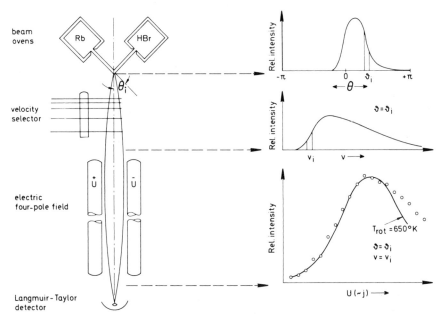

FIG. 62. Schematic diagram showing the apparatus used to measure rotational energy distributions at different scattering angles and product velocities. At the right typical measured distributions for the reaction Rb + HBr are shown.

Using an electric four-pole field Grice *et al.* (1970) and Mosch *et al.* (1972) have measured the rotational energy distribution for the reactions Rb + $Br_2$ and Rb + HBr. The apparatus is shown in Fig. 62. The reaction products leaving the reaction volume at a given angle with respect to the primary beam are first velocity selected and then focused in a long (2 m) electric four-pole field. The measured curve of focused intensity versus focusing voltage (see Fig. 62) is related more directly to the rotational energy distribution than in the previous experiment. Unfortunately, depending on the laboratory velocity, the four pole field analyzer used in these experiments, is limited in the range of states which can be focused. However, for small velocities the measuring range goes beyond the maximum of the distribution. As shown in Fig. 62 it is possible with this apparatus to study the rotational energy distribution over a range of scattering angles and product velocities and determine the rotational energy distribution at almost any point on the flux contour map. Since the product velocity is also specified, conservation of energy can be used to determine the vibrational energy distributions from the measured rotational energy distributions and the reactant beam energies.

## TABLE XXI

Energy Partitioning for Some Typical Alkali Atom Reactions. All Energies Are in kcal/mole and Are Only Approximate ($\pm \sim 0.5$ kcal/mole) Because of Experimental Uncertainties. Furthermore, the Product Energy Distributions Are Assumed Separable and Independent of Scattering Angle[a]

| Reaction | $\bar{E}_{\text{trans}_i}$ | $\bar{E}_{\text{int}_i}$ | $\Delta D_0$ | $\bar{E}_{\text{trans}_f}$ | $\bar{E}_{\text{rot}_f}$ | $f_{\text{trans}}$ | $f_{\text{rot}}$ | $f_{\text{vib}}{}^b$ |
|---|---|---|---|---|---|---|---|---|
| K + HBr → KBr + H | 1.5 | 0.6 | 4.2 | $\approx$1.5 | 1.32 | $\approx$0.3 | 0.31[c] | 0.3 |
| Rb + HBr → RbBr + H | 1.5 | 0.6 | 4.2 | — | 1.30 | — | 0.20[d] | — |
| Cs + HBr → CsBr + H | 1.5 | 0.6 | 8.6 | — | 0.95 | — | 0.11[c] | — |
| K + Br$_2$ → KBr + H | 1.23 | 0.75 | 45 | 1.2–3.7 | 4.9 | 0.03–0.08 | 0.11[c] | 0.81–0.86 |
| Rb + Br$_2$ → RbBr + H | 1.01 | 0.75 | 44 | 1.1–2.8 | 5.0 | 0.02–0.06 | 0.11[e] | 0.83–0.87 |
| Cs + Br$_2$ → CsBr + H | 1.06 | 0.75 | 50 | 1.1–1.8 | 3.9 | 0.02–0.04 | 0.078[c] | 0.88–0.90 |
| Cs + CH$_3$I → CsI + CH$_3$ | 1.5 | 0.7 | 30 | ~1.1 | 2.25 | 0.30 | 0.075[c] | — |
| Cs + CCl$_4$ → CsCl + CCl$_3$ | 1.5 | 0.6 | $\approx$37 | 4.0 | 4.9 | $\approx$0.10 | $\approx$0.13[c] | — |

[a] For Cs + CCl$_4$ the product translational energy is strongly dependent on the scattering angle.

[b] Calculated from conservation of energy: $f_{\text{vib}} = 1 - (f_{\text{trans}} + f_{\text{rot}})$.

[c] Maltz (1969).

[d] Mosch et al. (1972).

[e] Grice et al. (1970).

The measured rotational energy distributions (see Fig. 62) for both reactions are Boltzmann-like with $T_{rot} = 2500 \pm 300°K$ for Rb + Br$_2$ and $T_{rot} = 650° \pm 50°K$ for Rb + HBr in essential agreement with the results of Maltz. Furthermore, the distributions are independent of scattering angle and within the restrictions discussed above independent of velocity.

As pointed out previously in the case of Rb + HBr the rotational energy distribution is a direct measure of the probability of reaction as a function of initial impact parameter $P(b_i)$. This is confirmed by the experimentally measured distributions, which indicate furthermore that within the experimental error all collisions with impact parameter less than 3.5 Å lead to reaction.

Table XXI summarizes the values for the mean rotational energies $\overline{E_{rot}}$ and $f_{rot}$ obtained from these methods. Where possible the values of $f_{vib}$ obtained by conservation of energy are also shown. It is interesting to note a trend to smaller $f_{rot}$ with increasing mass of M. Since $\mu_{A-BC}/\mu_{AB} \sim 1$ for these reactions this implies a decreasing cross section for this series of reactions. Furthermore, the values of $E_{rot}$ are roughly the same as $E_{trans_i}$ as anticipated from the discussion at the beginning of this section.

## Acknowledgments

Many colleagues helped prepare this review. In particular I would like to thank R. Böttner, U. Buck, R. David, R. Gengenbach, G. Kendall, and Ch. Ottinger for their critical reading of various sections. Thanks are also due to G. Wolken and R. Koch for their help in preparing Fig. 33. I am also grateful to A. P. M. Baede, H. G. Bennewitz, R. B. Bernstein, E. F. Greene, J. C. Polanyi, D. Pritchard, and D. Truhlar for critical comments on the sections pertaining to their work. Finally I would like to thank Ch. Bertram and E. Rohrmoser for their help in organizing and typing the manuscript.

## References

ABRAHAMSON, A. A. (1969). *Phys. Rev.* **178**, 76.

AIREY, J. R., GREENE, E. F., KODERA, K., RECK, G. P., and ROSS, J. (1967a). *J. Chem. Phys.* **46**, 3287.

AIREY, J. R., GREENE, E. F., RECK, G. P., and ROSS, J. (1967b). *J. Chem. Phys.* **46**, 3295.

ANDERSON, J. B. (1967a). *AIChE J.* **13**, 1188.

ANDERSON, J. B. (1967b). *Entropie* **18**, 33.

ANDERSON, J. B., and JAFFE, S. B. (1968). *J. Chem. Phys.* **49**, 2859.

ANDERSON, J. B., ANDRES, R. P., and FENN, J. B. (1965). *Advan. At. Mol. Phys.* **1**, 345.

ANDERSON, J. B., ANDRES, R. P., and FENN, J. B. (1966). *Adv. Chem. Phys.* **3**, 275.

ANDERSON, R. W. (1968). Dissertation, Harvard Univ.

ANDERSON, R. W., AQUILANTI, V., and HERSCHBACH, D. R. (1969). *Chem. Phys. Lett.* **4**, 5.

ANLAUF, K. G., KUNTZ, P. J., MAYLOTTE, D. H., PACEY, P. D., and POLANYI, J. C. (1967). *Discuss. Faraday Soc.* **44**, 183.

ANLAUF, K. G., MAYLOTTE, D. H., POLANYI, J. C., and BERNSTEIN, R. B. (1969). *J. Chem. Phys.* **51**, 5716.

ANLAUF, K. G. *et al.* (1970). *J. Chem. Phys.* **53**, 4091.

ANLAUF, K. G., HORNE, D. S., MACDONALD, R. G., POLANYI, J. C., and WOODALL, K. B. (1972). *J. Chem. Phys.* **57**, 1561.

AQUILANTI, V., LIUTI, G., and VOLPI, J. G. (1971). *Abstr. Int. Conf. Phys. Electron. At. Collisions, 7th, Amsterdam 1971* p. 600. North-Holland Publ., Amsterdam.

ARMSTRONG, W. D., CONLEY, R. J., CREASER, R. P., GREENE, E. F. (1973). To be published.

ASHKENAS, H., and SHERMAN, F. S. (1966). *In* "Rarefied Gas Dynamics" (J. H. de Leeuw, ed.), Vol. 2. Academic Press, New York.

ATEN, J. A., LOS, J., and MOUTINHO, A. M. C. (1971). *Physica* **53**, 471.

ATEN, J. A., LOS, J., and MOUTINHO, A. M. C. (1971). *Abstr. Int. Conf. Phys. Electron. At. Collisions, 7th, Amsterdam 1971* p. 280. North-Holland Publ., Amsterdam.

AUERBACH, D., BAEDE, A. P. M., and LOS, J. (1971). *Abstr. Int. Conf. Phys. Electron. At. Collisions, 7th Amsterdam 1971* p. 283. North-Holland Publ., Amsterdam.

BAEDE, A. P. M., and LOS, J. (1971). *Physica* **52**, 422.

BAEDE, A. P. M., MOUTINHO, A. M. C., DE VRIES, A. E., and LOS, J. (1969). *Chem. Phys. Lett.* **3**, 530.

BAEDE, A. P. M., LOS, J., and MOUTINHO, A. M. C. (1971). *Physica* **51**, 432.

BARWIG, P., BUCK, U., HUNDHAUSEN, E., and PAULY, H. (1966). *Z. Phys.* **196**, 343.

BATALLI-COSMOVICI, CH., and MICHEL, K. W. (1971). *Chem. Phys. Lett.* **11**, 245.

BAUER, E., FISHER, E. R., and GILMORE, F. R. (1969). *J. Chem. Phys.* **51**, 4173.

BECK, D. (1970). *In* "Molecular Beams and Reaction Kinetics" (Ch. Schlier, ed.). Academic Press, New York.

BECK, D., and FÖRSTER, H. (1970). *Z. Phys.* **240**, 136.

BECK, D., and LOESCH, H. J. (1966). *Z. Phys.* **195**, 444.

BECK, D., ENGELKE, F., and LOESCH, H. J. (1968). *Ber. Bunsenges.* **72**, 1105.

BENDER, C. F., and SCHAEFER, H. F. (1970). *J. Am. Chem. Soc.* **92**, 4984.

BENNEWITZ, H. G., and DOHMANN, H. D. (1965a). *Z. Phys.* **182**, 524.

BENNEWITZ, H. G., and DOHMANN, H. D. (1965b). *Vakuum-Tech.* **14**, 8.

BENNEWITZ, H. G., KRAMER, K. H., PAUL, W., and TOENNIES, J. P. (1964). *Z. Phys.* **177**, 84.

BENNEWITZ, H. G., HAERTEN, R., KLAIS, O., and Müller, G. (1971a). *Z. Phys.* **249**, 168.

BENNEWITZ, H. G., HAERTEN, R., and MÜLLER, G. (1971b). *Chem. Phys. Lett.* **12**, 335.

BENNEWITZ, H. G., BUSSE, H., DOHMANN, H. D., OATES, D. E., and SCHRADER, W. (1972a). *Z. Phys.* **253**, 435.

BENNEWITZ, H. G., BUSSE, H., DOHMANN, H. D., OATES, D. E., and SCHRADER, W. (1972b). *Phys. Rev. Lett.* **29**, 533.

BERNSTEIN, R. B. (1966a). *Phys. Rev. Lett.* **16**, 385.

BERNSTEIN, R. B. (1966b). *Advan. Chem. Phys.* **10**, 75.

BERNSTEIN, R. B., and LaBUDDE, R. A. (1973). *J. Chem. Phys.* **58**, 1109.

BERNSTEIN, R. B., and MUCKERMANN, J. T. (1967). *Advan. Chem. Phys.* **12**, 389.

BERNSTEIN, R. B., and O'BRIEN, T. J. P. (1965). *Discuss. Faraday Soc.* **40**, 35.

BERNSTEIN, R. B., and O'BRIEN, T. J. P. (1967). *J. Chem. Phys.* **46**, 1208.

BERNSTEIN, R. B., GERSH, M. E., and RULIS, A. M. (1971). *Abstr. Int. Conf. Phys. Electron. At. Collisions, 7th, Amsterdam, 1971* p. 34. North-Holland Publ., Amsterdam.

BERRY, M. V. (1966). *Proc. Phys. Soc.* **89**, 479.

BERRY, R. S., LEE, Y. T., and TULLY, F. P. (1971). *Chem. Phys. Lett.* **9**, 80.

BERSOHN, R. (1971). *Comments At. Mol. Phys.* **2**, 156.

BERTONCINI, P., and WAHL, A. C. (1970). *Phys. Rev. Lett.* **25**, 991.

BEUHLER, R. J., and BERNSTEIN, R. B. (1968). *Chem. Phys. Lett.* **2**, 166.

BEUHLER, R. J., and BERNSTEIN, R. B. (1969). *J. Chem. Phys.* **51**, 5305.

BEUHLER, R. J., BERNSTEIN, R. B., and KRAMER, K. H. (1966). *J. Amer. Chem. Soc.* **88**, 5331.

BICKES, R. W., and BERNSTEIN, R. B. (1970). *Rev. Sci. Instrum.* **41**, 759.

BICKES, R. W., LANTZSCH, B., TOENNIES, J. P., and WALASCHEWSKI, K. (1973). *Faraday Disc. Chem. Soc.* **55**, 1967.

BIRELY, J. H., and HERSCHBACH, D. R. (1966). *J. Chem. Phys.* **44**, 1690.

BIRELY, J. H., ENTEMANN, E. A., HERM, R. R., and WILSON, K. R. (1969). *J. Chem. Phys.* **51**, 5461.

BIRELY, J. H., HERM, R. R., WILSON, K. R., and HERSCHBACH, D. H. (1967). *J. Chem. Phys.* **47**, 993.

BLAIS, N. C. (1968), *J. Chem. Phys.* **49**, 9.

BLAIS, N. C. (1969), *J. Chem. Phys.* **51**, 856.

BLYTHE, A. R., FLUENDY, M. A. D., and LAWLEY, K. P. (1966). *Quart. Rev.* **20**, 465.

BLYTHE, A. R., GROSSER, A. E., and BERNSTEIN, R. B. (1964). *J. Chem. Phys.* **41**, 1917.

BORNE, T. B., and BUNKER, D. L. (1971). *J. Chem. Phys.* **55**, 4861.

BOSSEL, U., HURLBUT, F. C., and SHERMAN, F. S. (1969). *Advan. Appl. Mech. Suppl.* 5 **2**, 945.

BOWMAN, J. M., and KUPPERMANN, A. (1971). *Chem. Phys. Lett.* **12**, 1.

BREDEWOUT, J. W., BOSMAN, N. J., VISSER, A. G., KORVING, J., and VAN DEN MEIJDENBERG, C. J. N. (1971). *Chem. Phys. Lett.* **11**, 127.

BRODHEAD, D. C., DAVIDOVITS, D., and EDELSTEIN, S. A. (1969). *J. Chem. Phys.* **51**, 3601.

BROOKS, P. R. (1969). *J. Chem. Phys.* **50**, 5031.

BROOKS, P. R. (1971), Private communication.

BROOKS, P. R., and JONES, E. M. (1966). *J. Chem. Phys.* **45**, 3449.

BROOKS, P. R., JONES, E. M., and SMITH, K. (1969). *J. Chem. Phys.* **51**, 3073.

BRUMER, P., and KARPLUS, M. (1971). *J. Chem. Phys.* **54**, 4955.

BRUS, L. E. (1970). *J. Chem. Phys.* **52**, 1716.

BUCK, U. (1971). *J. Chem. Phys.* **54**, 1923.

BUCK, U., and PAULY, H. (1968). *Z. Phys.* **208**, 390.

BUCK, U., and PAULY, H. (1971). *J. Chem. Phys.* **54**, 1929.

BUCK, U., KÖHLER, K. A., and PAULY, H. (1971). *Z. Phys.* **244**, 180.

BUCK, U., KICK, M., and PAULY, H. (1972). *J. Chem. Phys.* **56**, 3391.

BUTZ, H. P., FELTGEN, R., PAULY, H., and VEHMEYER, H. (1971). *Z. Phys.* **247**, 70.

BUTZ, H. P., FELTGEN, R., PAULY, H., VEHMEYER, H., and YEALLAND, R. M. (1971). *Z. Phys.* **247**, 60.

BYRNE, M. A., RICHARDS, W. G., and HORSLEY, J. A. (1967). *Mol. Phys.* **12**, 273.

CANTINI, P., DONDI, M. G., SCOLES, G., and TORELLO, F. (1972). *J. Chem. Phys.* **56**, 1946.

CARDILLO, M. J., CHOU, M. S., GREENE, E. F., and SHEEN, D. B. (1971). *J. Chem. Phys.* **54**, 3054.

CARRINGTON, T., and POLANYI, J. C. (1972). *In* "Chemical Kinetics" (Physical Chemistry, Series 1), Vol. 9, p. 135. (J. C. Polanyi, ed.), MTP International Review of Science. Butterworths Co., London.

CAVALLINI, M., MEGHETTI, L., SCOLES, G., and YEALLAND, M. (1970). *Phys. Rev. Lett.* **24**, 1469.

CHANG, TAI YUP (1967). *Mol. Phys.* **13**, 487.

CHARTERS, P. E., McDONALD, R. G., and POLANYI, J. C. (1971). *Appl. Opt.* **10**, No. 8, 1747.

CHENG, M. H., CHIANG, M. H., GISLASON, E. A., MAHAN, B. H., TSAO, C. W., and WERNER, A. S. (1970). *J. Chem. Phys.* **52**, 6150.

CHUPKA, W. A., BERKOWITZ, J., and RUSSELL, M. E. (1969). *Proc. Int. Conf. Phys. Electron. At. Collisions, 6th*, p. 71. M.I.T., Cambridge, Massachusetts.

COMPTON, R. N., NALLEY, S. J., SCHWEINLER, H. C., and ANDERSON, V. E. (1971). *Proc. Int. Conf. Phys. Electron. Collisions, 7th, Amsterdam* p. 288. North-Holland, Amsterdam.

COSBY, P. C., and MORAN, T. F. (1970). *J. Chem. Phys.* **52**, 6157.

COSMOVICI, J. B., and MICHEL, K.-W. (1971). *Chem. Phys. Lett.* **11**, 245.

COWLEY, L. T., HORNE, D. S., and POLANYI, J. C. (1971). *Chem. Phys. Lett.* **12**, 144.

CROSS, J. B., and BLAIS, N. C. (1969). *J. Chem. Phys.* **50**, 4108.

CROSS, J. B., and BLAIS, N. C. (1970). *J. Chem. Phys.* **52**, 3580.

CROSS, R. J., Jr., and GORDON, R. G. (1966). *J. Chem. Phys.* **45**, 3571.

CROUCHER, D. J., and CLARK, J. L. (1969). *J. Phys. B* **2**, 603.

CSIZMADIA, I. G., KARI, R. E., POLANYI, J. C., ROACH, A. C., and ROBB, M. A. (1970). *J. Chem. Phys.* **52**, 6205.

DALGARNO, A. (1967). *Advan. Chem. Phys.* **12**, 143.

DAS, G., and WAHL, A. C. (1971). *Phys. Rev. A* **4**, 825.

DATZ, S., and MINTURN, R. E. (1964). *J. Chem. Phys.* **41**, 1153.

DATZ, S., and TAYLOR, E. H. (1963). *J. Chem. Phys.* **39**, 1896.

DAVID, R., FAUBEL, M., MARCHAND, P., and TOENNIES, J. P. (1971). *Abstr. Conf. Phys. Electron At. Collisions, 7th, Amsterdam, 1971* p. 252.

DAVID, R., FAUBEL, M., and TOENNIES, J. P. (1973). *Chem. Phys. Lett.* **18**, 87.

DELVIGNE, G. A. L., and LOS, J. (1971). *Abstr. Int. Conf. Phys. Electron. At. Collisions, 7th, Amsterdam, 1971* p. 277. North-Holland Publ., Amsterdam.

DICKINSON, A. S. (1970). *Mol. Phys.* **18**, 305.

DIESTLER, D. J., and KARPLUS, M. (1971). *J. Chem. Phys.* **55**, 5832.

DITTNER, P. F., and DATZ, S. (1971). *J. Chem. Phys.* **54**, 4228.

DOHMANN, H. D. (1969). *Z. Phys.* **220**, 229.

DONDI, M. G., SCOLES, G., TORELLO, F., and PAULY, H. (1969). *J. Chem. Phys.* **51**, 392.

DOP, H. VAN, BOERBOOM, A. J. H., and LOS, J. (1971). *Physica* **54**, 223.

DÜREN, R., RAABE, G. P., and SCHLIER, CH. (1968). *Z. Phys.* **214**, 410; Sitzungsberichte der Heidelberger Akademie der Wissenschaften, Math.-Nat. Klasse, Jgg. 1968, 3. Abhandlung.

EASTES, W., and SECREST, D. (1972). *J. Chem. Phys.* **56**, 640.

ECKELT, W. R., SCHIMPKE, B., and SCHÜGERL, K. (1969). *Z. Phys. Chem.* **68**, 266.

EDELSTEIN, S. A., and DAVIDOVITS, P. (1971). *J. Chem. Phys.* **55**, 5164.

ENTEMANN, E. A. (1967). Dissertation, Harvard Univ.

ENTEMANN, E. A. (1971). *J. Chem. Phys.* **55**, 4872.

ENTEMANN, E. A., and HERSCHBACH, D. R. (1967). *Discuss. Faraday Soc.* **44**, 289.

ENTEMANN, E. A., and KWEI, G. H. (1971). *J. Chem. Phys.* **55**, 4879.

EVANS, M. G., and POLANYI, M. (1939). *Trans. Faraday Soc.* **35**, 178.

EWING, J. J., MILSTEIN, R., and BERRY, R. S. (1971). *J. Chem. Phys.* **54**, 1752.

FARRAR, J. M., and LEE, Y. T. (1972). *J. Chem. Phys.* **56**, 5801.

FARRAR, J. M., SCHAFER, T. P., and LEE, Y. T. (1973). *AIP Conf. Proc. (USA)* **11**, 279 (1973).

FELTGEN, R. (1970). Dissertation, Bonn.

FELTGEN, R., PAULY, H., TORELLO, F., and VEHMEYER, H. (1973). Phys. Rev. Lett. To be published.

FENN, J. B. (1967). *Entropie* **18**, 11.

FENSTERMAKER, R. W., JACKSON, W. M., LEFFERT, C. B., and ROTHE, E. W. (1971). *Abstr. Int. Conf. Phys. Electron. At. Collisions, 7th, Amsterdam, 1971* p. 285. North-Holland Publ., Amsterdam.

FISK, G. A., HERSCHBACH, D. R., and McDONALD, J. D. (1967). *Discuss. Faraday Soc.* **44**, 228.

FITE, W. L., and BRACKMANN, R. T. (1964). "Atomic Collision Processes" (M. R. C. McDowell, ed.), p. 955. North-Holland Publ., Amsterdam.

FLUENDY, M. A., Horne, D. S., LAWLEY, K. P., and MORRIS, A. W. (1970). *Mol. Phys.* **19**, 659.

FORD, K. W., and WHEELER, J. A. (1959). *Ann. Phys. (N.Y.)* **7**, 259.

FOREMAN, P. B. (1971). Thesis, Cambridge Univ.

FOREMAN, P. B., KENDALL, G. M., and GRICE, R. (1972). *Mol. Phys.* **23**, 127.

FREMEREY, H., and TOENNIES, J. P. (1971). *Abstr. Int. Conf. Phys. Electron. At. Collisions, 7th, Amsterdam, 1971* p. 249. North-Holland Publ., Amsterdam.

FREMEREY, H., and TOENNIES, J. P. (1972). To be published.

FRENCH, J. B., and LOCKE, J. W. (1967). *In* "Rarefied Gas Dynamics" *Proc. 5th Int. Symp.* **2**, 1461. Academic Press, New York.

FREUND, S. M., FISK, G. A., HERSCHBACH, D. R., and KLEMPERER, W. (1971). *J. Chem. Phys.* **54**, 2510.

FRICKE, J., KIM, B., and FITE, W. L. (1971). *Abstr. Int. Conf. Phys. Electron. At. Collisions, 7th, Amsterdam, 1971* p. 37. North-Holland Publ., Amsterdam.

GEDDES, J., KRAUSE, H. F., and FITE, W. L. (1970). *J. Chem. Phys.* **52**, 3296.

GENGENBACH, R. (1972). (Unpublished).

GENGENBACH, R., STRUNCK, J., and TOENNIES, J. P. (1971a). *J. Chem. Phys.* **54**, 1830.

GENGENBACH, R., HAHN, CH., TOENNIES, J. P., and WELZ, W. (1971b). *Abstr. Int. Conf. Phys. Electron. At. Collisions, 7th, Amsterdam, 1971* p. 653. North-Holland Publ., Amsterdam.

GENGENBACH, R., and HAHN, CH. (1972). *Chem. Phys. Lett.* **15**, 604.

GENGENBACH, R., HAHN, CH., and TOENNIES, J. P. (1973). *Phys. Rev.* **A. 7**, 98.

GERSH, M. E., and BERNSTEIN, R. B. (1971). *J. Chem. Phys.* **55**, 4661.

GILLEN, K. T., and BERNSTEIN, R. B. (1970). *Chem. Phys. Lett.* **5**, 275.

GILLEN, K. T., Riley, C., and BERNSTEIN, R. B. (1969). *J. Chem. Phys.* **50**, 4019.

GILLEN, K. T., RULIS, A. M., and BERNSTEIN, R. B. (1971). *J. Chem. Phys.* **54**, 2831.

GODFREY, M., and KARPLUS, M. (1968). *J. Chem. Phys.* **49**, 3602.

GOLDSTEIN, H. (1951). "Classical Mechanics." Addison-Wesley, Reading, Massachusetts.

GORDON, M. D., and SECREST, D. (1970). *J. Chem. Phys.* **52**, 120.

GORDON, R. G. (1969). *J. Chem. Phys.* **51**, 41.

GORDON, R. J., HERM, R. R., and HERSCHBACH, D. R. (1968). *J. Chem. Phys.* **49**, 2684.

GORDON, R. J., LEE, Y. T., and HERSCHBACH, D. R. (1971). *J. Chem. Phys.* **54**, 2393.

GREENE, E. F., and MASON, E. A. (1972). *J. Chem. Phys.* **57**, 2065.

GREENE, E. F., and ROSS, J. (1968). *Science* **159**, 587.

GREENE, E. F., MOURSUND, A. L., and ROSS, J. (1966). *Advan. Chem. Phys.* **10**, 135.

GREENE, E. F., HOFFMAN, L. F., LEE, M. W., ROSS, J., and YOUNG, C. E. (1969a). *J. Chem. Phys.* **50**, 3450.

GREENE, E. F., LAU, M. H., and ROSS, J. (1969b). *J. Chem. Phys.* **50**, 3122.

GRICE, R. (1967). Dissertation, Harvard Univ.

GRICE, R. (1970). *Mol. Phys.* **19**, 501.

GRICE, R., and EMPEDOCLES, P. B. (1968). *J. Chem. Phys.* **48**, 5352.

GRICE, R., COSANDEY, M. R., and HERSCHBACH, D. R. (1968). *Ber. Bunsenges. Phys. Chem.* **72**, 975.

GRICE, R., MOSCH, J. E., SAFRON, S. A., and TOENNIES, J. P. (1970). *J. Chem. Phys.* **53**, 3376.

GROSSER, J., and HABERLAND, H. (1970). *Chem. Phys. Lett.* **7**, 442.

GROVER, J. R., KIELY, F. M., LEBOWITZ, E., and BAKER, E. (1971). *Rev. Sci. Instrum.* **42**, 293.

HABERMANN, J. A., ANLAUF, K. G., BERNSTEIN, R. B., and VAN ITALIE, F. J. (1972). *Chem. Phys. Lett.* **16**, 442.

HAM, D. O., and KINSEY, J. L. (1968). *J. Chem. Phys.* **48**, 939.

HAM, D. O., and KINSEY, J. L. (1970). *J. Chem. Phys.* **53**, 285.

HAM, D. O., KINSEY, J. L., and KLEIN, F. S. (1967). *Discuss. Faraday Soc.* **44**, 174.

HARRIS, R. M., and WILSON, J. F. (1971). *J. Chem. Phys.* **54**, 2088.

HELBING, R. K. B. (1968). *J. Chem. Phys.* **48**, 472.

HELBING, R. K. B., and ROTHE, E. W. (1969). *J. Chem. Phys.* **51**, 1607.

HELD, W. D., SCHÖTTLER, J., and TOENNIES, J. P. (1970). *Chem. Phys. Lett.* **6**, 304.

HERM, R. R. (1967). *J. Chem. Phys.* **47**, 4290.

HERM, R. R., and HERSCHBACH, D. R. (1970). *J. Chem. Phys.* **52**, 5783.

HERSCHBACH, D. R. (1966). *Advan. Chem. Phys.* **10**, 319.

HERSCHBACH, D. R. (1970). *Proc. Conf. Pot. Energy Surfaces Chem.*, August, 1970, *Santa Cruz, California* IBM Res. Lab., San Jose, California.

HERSCHBACH, D. R., KWEI, G. H., and NORRIS, J. A. (1961). *J. Chem. Phys.* **34**, 1842.

HERZBERG, G., and LONGUET-HIGGINS, H. C. (1963). *Discuss. Faraday Soc.* **35**, 77.

HIRSCHFELDER, J. O., CURTIS, C. F., and BIRD, R. B. (1954). "Molecular Theory of Gases and Liquids." Wiley, New York.

HÖH, A., OERTEL, H., and SCHULTZ, A. (1970). *Z. Phys.* **235**, 20.

KUTZELNIGG, W., STAEMMLER, V., and HOHEISEL, K. (1973). *Chem. Phys.* **1**, 27.

HOLMLID, L. (1971). Private communication.

HUNDHAUSEN, E., and PAULY, H. (1965). *Z. Phys.* **187**, 305.

IOUP, G. E., and THOMAS, B. S. (1969). *J. Chem. Phys.* **50**, 5009.

JAFFE, S. B., and ANDERSON, J. B. (1969). *J. Chem. Phys.* **51**, 1057.

JAFFE, R. L., and ANDERSON, J. B. (1971). *J. Chem. Phys.* **54**, 2224.

JONAH, C. D., and ZARE, R. N. (1971). *Chem. Phys. Lett.* **9**, 65.

JONES, E. M., and BROOKS, P. R. (1970). *J. Chem. Phys.* **53**, 55.

JORDAN, J. E., and AMDUR, I. (1967). *J. Chem. Phys.* **46**, 165.

KALOS, F., and GROSSER, A. E. (1969). *Rev. Sci. Instrum.* **40**, 804.
KEMPTER, V., KNESER, TH., and SCHLIER, CH. (1970a). *J. Chem. Phys.* **52**, 5851.
KEMPTER, V., MECKLENBRAUCK, W., MENZINGER, M., SCHULLER, G., HERSCHBACH, D. R., and SCHLIER, CH. (1970b). *Chem. Phys. Lett.* **6**, 97.
KEMPTER, V., MECKLENBRAUCK, W., MENZINGER, M., and SCHLIER, CH. (1971). *Chem. Phys. Lett.* **11**, 353.
KENDALL, G. M., FOREMAN, P. B., and GRICE, R. (1971). *Abstr. Int. Conf. Phys. Electron At. Collisions, 7th, Amsterdam, 1971* p. 23. North-Holland Publ., Amsterdam.
KENNARD, E. H. (1938). "Kinetic Theory of Gases." McGraw-Hill, New York.
KIHARA, T. (1943). *Proc. Phys. Math. Soc. Japan* **25**, 73.
KINSEY, J. L. (1971a). *Chem. Phys. Lett.* **8**, 349.
KINSEY, J. L. (1971b). *J. Chem. Phys.* **54**, 1206.
KINSEY, J. L. (1972). In "Chemical Kinetics" (Physical Chemistry, Series 1), Vol. 9, p. 173 (J. C. Polanyi, ed.), MTP International Rewiev of Science. Butterworths, London.
KIRSCH, L. J., and POLANYI, J. C. (1972). *J. Chem. Phys.* **57**, 4498.
KONG, P., MASON, E. A., and MUNN, R. J. (1970). *Amer. J. Phys.* **38**, 294.
KRAMER, K. H., and BERNSTEIN, R. B. (1965). *J. Chem. Phys.* **42**, 767.
KRÄMER, R. (1967). Diplomthesis, Freiburg.
KRAUSS, M., and MIES, F. M. (1965). *J. Chem. Phys.* **42**, 2703.
KRÜGER, H. (1972). To be published.
KUNTZ, P. J., MOK, M. H., and POLANYI, J. C. (1969a). *J. Chem. Phys.* **50**, 4623.
KUNTZ, P. J., NEMETH, E. M., and POLANYI, J. C. (1969b). *J. Chem. Phys.* **50**, 4607.
KWEI, G. H., and HERSCHBACH, D. R. (1969). *J. Chem. Phys.* **51**, 1742.
KWEI, G. H., NORRIS, J. A., and HERSCHBACH, D. R. (1970). *J. Chem. Phys.* **52**, 1317.
KWEI, G. H., LEES, A. B., and SILVER, J. A. (1971). *J. Chem. Phys.* **55**, 456.
LACMANN, K., and HERSCHBACH, D. R. (1970). *Chem. Phys. Lett.* **6**, 106.
LANGHOFF, P. W., and KARPLUS, M. (1970). "The Pade Approximant in Theoretical Physics." Academic Press, New York.
LEBRETON, P. R., MECKLENBRAUCK, W., SCHULTZ, A., and SCHLIER, CH. (1971). *Abstr. Int. Conf. Phys. Electron. At. Collisions, 7th, Amsterdam* p. 291. North-Holland Publ., Amsterdam.
LEE, Y. T. (1971). Collection of Invited Papers presented at the *Int. Conf. Phys. Electron. At. Collisions, 7th, Amsterdam* p. 546. North-Holland Publ., Amsterdam.
LEE, Y. T. (1972). Private communication.
LEE, Y. T., McDONALD, J. D., LEBRETON, P. R., and HERSCHBACH, D. R. (1968). *J. Chem. Phys.* **49**, 2447.
LEE, Y. T., LEBRETON, P. R., McDONALD, J. D., and HERSCHBACH, D. R. (1969a). *J. Chem. Phys.* **51**, 455.
LEE, Y. T., McDONALD, J. D., LEBRETON, P. R., and HERSCHBACH, D. R. (1969b). *Rev. Sci. Instrum.* **40**, 1402.
LEE, Y. T., GORDON, R. J., and HERSCHBACH, D. R. (1971). *J. Chem. Phys.* **54**, 2410.
LESTER, W. A., Jr. (1970). *J. Chem. Phys.* **53**, 1511.
LESTER, W. A., Jr. (1971). *J. Chem. Phys.* **54**, 3171.
LIGHT, J. C. (1967). *Discuss. Faraday Soc.* **44**, 14.
LIN, S.-M., MIMS, C. A., and HERM, R. M. (1973). *J. Chem. Phys.* **58**, 327.
LOESCH, H. J., and BECK, D. (1971). *Ber. Bunsenges.* **75**, 736.
LOESCH, H. J., and HERSCHBACH, D. R. (1972). *J. Chem. Phys.* **57**, 2038.

MAGEE, J. C. (1940). *J. Chem. Phys.* **8**, 687.
MALTZ, C. (1969). Dissertation, Harvard Univ.
MALTZ, C., and HERSCHBACH, D. R. (1967). *Discuss. Faraday Soc.* **44**, 176.
MALTZ, C., WEINSTEIN, N. D., and HERSCHBACH, D. R. (1972). *Mol. Phys.* **24**, 133.
MARRIOT, R., and MICHA, D. A. (1969). *Phys. Rev.* **180**, 120.
MARTIN, L. R., and KINSEY, J. L. (1967). *J. Chem. Phys.* **46**, 4834.
MAYLOTTE, D. H., POLANYI, J. C., and WOODALL, K. B. (1972). *J. Chem. Phys.* **57**, 1547.
McCULLOUGH, E. A., and WYATT, R. E. (1969). *J. Chem. Phys.* **51**, 1253.
McCULLOUGH, E. A., and WYATT, R. E. (1971). *J. Chem. Phys.* **54**, 3592.
McCULLOUGH, E. A., and WYATT, R. E. (1971). *J. Chem. Phys.* **54**, 3578.
McDONALD, J. D. (1971). Dissertation, Harvard Univ.
McDONALD, J. D., LeBRETON, P. R., LEE, Y. T., and HERSCHBACH, D. R. (1972). *J. Chem. Phys.* **56**, 769.
MILLER, G., and LIGHT, J. C. (1971). *J. Chem. Phys.* **54**, 1643.
MILLER, W. B., SAFRON, S. A., and HERSCHBACH, D. R. (1967a). *Discuss. Faraday Soc.* **44**, 108.
MILLER, W. B., SAFRON, S. A., and HERSCHBACH, D. R. (1967b). *Discuss. Faraday Soc.* **44**, 292.
MIMS, C. A., LIN, S.-M., and HERM, R. R. (1972). *J. Chem. Phys.* **57**, 3099.
MIMS, C. A., LIN, S.-M., and HERM, R. R. (1973). *J. Chem. Phys.* **58**, 1983.
MOORE, P. L., CLOUGH, P. N., and GEDDES, J. (1972). *Chem. Phys. Lett.* **17**, 608.
MORAN, T. F., and COSBY, P. C. (1969). *J. Chem. Phys.* **51**, 5724.
MOSCH, J. E., SAFRON, S. A., and TOENNIES, J. P. (1972). To be published.
MOTT, N. F., and MASSEY, M. S. W. (1965). "The Theory of Atomic Collisions." Oxford Univ. Press, London and New York.
MOULTON, M. G., and HERSCHBACH, D. R. (1966). *J. Chem. Phys.* **44**, 3010.
MOUTINHO, A. M. C., BAEDE, A. P. M., and LOS, J. (1971a). *Physica* **51**, 432.
MOUTINHO, A. M. C., ATEN, J. A., and LOS, J. (1971b). *Physica* **53**, 471.
MUCKERMANN, J. T. (1971). *J. Chem. Phys.* **54**, 1155.
MÜLLER, G. (1967). Diplomthesis, Bonn.
NEUMANN, W., and PAULY, H. (1970). *J. Chem. Phys.* **52**, 2548.
NIKITIN, E. E. (1968). In "Chemische Elementarprozesse" (H. Hartmann, J. Heidberg, H. Heydtmann, and G. H. Kohlmaier, eds.). Springer, New York and Berlin.
OATES, D. E., and KING, J. G. (1971). *Phys. Rev. Lett.* **26**, 735.
ODIORNE, T. J., and BROOKS, P. R. (1969). *J. Chem. Phys.* **51**, 4676.
ODIORNE, T. J., BROOKS, P. R., and KASPER, J. V. V. (1971). *J. Chem. Phys.* **55**, 1980.
OKEL, J. G. R., and VAN DE REE, J. (1971). *J. Chem. Phys.* **54**, 4259.
OTTINGER, CH., and ZARE, R. N. (1972). *Chem. Phys. Lett.* **5**, 243.
OTTINGER, CH., STRUDLER, P., and HERSCHBACH, D. R. (1972). To be published.
PARKER, J. H., and PIMENTEL, J. C. (1969). *J. Chem. Phys.* **51**, 91.
PARR, C. A., POLANYI, J. C., and WONG, W. H. (1973). *J. Chem. Phys.* **58**, 5.
PARRISH, D. D., and HERM, R. R. (1968). *J. Chem. Phys.* **49**, 5544.
PARRISH, D. D., and HERM, R. R. (1969). *J. Chem. Phys.* **51**, 5467.
PARRISH, D. D., and HERM, R. R. (1970). *J. Chem. Phys.* **53**, 2431.
PARRISH, D. D., and HERM, R. R. (1971). *J. Chem. Phys.* **54**, 2518.
PARSON, J. M., and LEE, J. T. (1972). *J. Chem. Phys.* **56**, 4658.
PARSON, J. M., SCHAFER, T. P., TULLY, F. P., SISKA, P. E., WONG, Y. C., and LEE, Y. T. (1970). *J. Chem. Phys.* **53**, 2123.

PARSON, J. M., SISKA, P. E., and LEE, Y. T. (1972). *J. Chem. Phys.* **56**, 1511.
PAULY, H., and TOENNIES, J. P. (1965). *Advan. At. Mol. Phys.* **1**, 195.
PAULY, H., and TOENNIES, J. P. (1968). *Methods Exp. Phys.* **7A**, 227.
PERSKY, A., GREENE, E. F., and KUPPERMANN, A. (1968). *J. Chem. Phys.* **49**, 2347.
PERSON, W. B. (1963). *J. Chem. Phys.* **38**, 109.
PETTY, F., and MORAN, T. F. (1970). *Chem. Phys. Lett.* **5**, 64.
PHILIPSON, P. E. (1962). *Phys. Rev.* **125**, 1981.
PHIPPS, J. A., and SCOTT, J. E., Jr. (1969). *Entropie* **30**, 148.
POLANYI, M. (1949). *Endeavour* **8**, 3.
POLANYI, J. C., and TARDY, D. C. (1969). *J. Chem. Phys.* **51**, 5717.
POLANYI, J. C., and SLOAN, J. J. (1972). *J. Chem. Phys.* **57**, 4988.
POLANYI, J. C., and WOODALL, K. B. (1972). *J. Chem. Phys.* **57**, 1574.
POLITIEK, J., LOS, J., SCHIPPER, J. J. M., and Baede, A. P. M. (1967). *Entropie* **18**, 82.
POLITIEK, J., ROL, P. K., LOS, J., and IKELAAR, P. G. (1968). *Rev. Sci. Instrum.* **39**, 1147.
POLITIEK, J., SCHIPPER, J. J. M., and LOS, J. (1970). *Physica* **49**, 165.
PRITCHARD, D. E., and CHU, F. Y. (1970). *Phys. Rev. A* **2**, 1932.
PRITCHARD, D. E., CARTER, G. M., CHU, F. Y., and KLEPPNER, D. (1970). *Phys. Rev. B* **2**, 1922.
RAFF, L. M., and KARPLUS, M. (1966). *J. Chem. Phys.* **44**, 1212.
RICHMAN, E., and WHARTON, L. (1970). *J. Chem. Phys.* **53**, 945.
RILEY, C., GILLEN, K. T., and BERNSTEIN, R. B. (1967). *J. Chem. Phys.* **47**, 3672.
RILEY, S. J. (1970). Dissertation, Harvard Univ.
RILEY, S. J., and HERSCHBACH, D. R. (1973). *J. Chem. Phys.* **58**, 27.
ROACH, A. C. (1970). *Chem. Phys. Lett.* **6**, 389.
ROACH, A. C., and CHILD, M. S. (1968). *Mol. Phys.* **14**, 1–15.
ROTHE, E. W., and FENSTERMAKER, R. W. (1971). *J. Chem. Phys.* **54**, 4520.
ROTHE, E. W., and NEYNABER, R. H. (1965). *J. Chem. Phys.* **42**, 3306.
ROTHE, E. W., and NEYNABER, R. H. (1965). *J. Chem. Phys.* **43**, 4177.
ROTHE, E. W., NEYNABER, R. H., SCOTT, B. W., TRUJILLO, S. M., and ROL, P. K. (1963). *J. Chem. Phys.* **39**, 493.
SAFRON, S. A. (1969). Dissertation, Harvard Univ.
SCHAEFER III, H. F., MCLAUGHLIN, D. R., HARRIS, F. E., and ALDER, B. J. (1970). *Phys. Rev. Lett.* **25**, 988.
SCHAFER, T. P., SISKA, P. E., PARSON, J. M., TULLY, F. P., WONG, Y. C., and LEE, Y. T. (1970). *J. Chem. Phys.* **53**, 3385.
SCHAFER, T. P., SISKA, P. E., and LEE, Y. T. (1971). *Abstr. Int. Conf. Electron. At. Collisions, 7th, Amsterdam, 1971* p. 546. North-Holland Publ., Amsterdam.
SCHEER, M. D., and FINE, J. (1969). *Advan. Appl. Mech.* **5, 2**, 1469.
SCHLIER, CH. (1969). *Ann. Rev. Phys. Chem.* **20**, 191.
SCHÖTTLER, J., and TOENNIES, J. P. (1968). *Z. Phys.* **214**, 472.
SCHÖTTLER, J., and TOENNIES, J. P. (1972). *Chem. Phys. Lett.* **12**, 615.
SCHULTZ, A., CRUSE, H. W., and ZARE, R. N. (1972). *J. Chem. Phys.* **57**, 1354.
SCOTT, P. B., and MINCER, T. (1969). *Entropie* **30**, 170.
SECREST, D., and JOHNSON, B. R. (1966). *J. Chem. Phys.* **45**, 4556.
SHULER, K., ROSS, J., and LIGHT, J. (1969). *In* "Kinetic Processes in Gases and Plasmas" (A. R. Hochstim, ed.). Academic Press, New York.

SISKA, P. E. (1970). Dissertation, Harvard Univ.

SISKA, P. E., PARSON, J. M., SCHAFER, T. P., TULLY, F. P., WONG, Y. C., and LEE, Y. T. (1970). *Phys. Rev. Lett.* **25**, 271.

SISKA, P. E., PARSON, J. M., SCHAFER, T. P., and LEE, Y. T. (1971). *J. Chem. Phys.* **55**, 5672.

SKÖLD, K. (1968). *Nucl. Instrum. Methods* **63**, 347.

SMITH, F. T. (1965). *J. Chem. Phys.* **42**, 2419.

SMITH, F. T. (1969). *Lectures Theor. Phys.* **11-C**, 95.

SMITH, F. T., MARCHI, R. P., and DEDRICK, K. G. (1966). *Phys. Rev.* **150**, 79.

STEINFELD, J. I. (1972). *In* "Chemical Kinetics" (Physical Chemistry, Series 1), Vol. 9, p. 247 (J. C. Polanyi, ed.), MTP International Review of Science. Butterworths, London.

STEINFELD, J. I., and KINSEY, J. L. (1970). *Progr. Reaction Kinet.* **5**, 1.

STERN, O. (1926). *Z. Phys.* **39**, 751.

STRUVE, W. S., KITAGAWA, T., and HERSCHBACH, D. R. (1971). *J. Chem. Phys.* **54**, 2759.

STWALLEY, W. C. (1968). *Bull. Amer. Phys. Soc.* **13**, 1655.

SUBBARAO, R. B., and MILLER, D. R. (1969). *Chem. Phys.* **51**, 4679.

SWEDENBURG, R. L., PHIPPS, J. A., and SCOTT, J. E., Jr. (1970). Interim Tech. Rep. Aerospace Res. Lab. Wright-Patterson AFB, Ohio, 45433.

TANAKA, Y., and YOSHINO, K. (1970). *J. Chem. Phys.* **53**, 2012.

TAYLOR, E. H., and DATZ, S. (1955). *J. Chem. Phys.* **23**, 1711.

TELOY, E. (1971). Private communication.

TOENNIES, J. P. (1965). *Z. Phys.* **182**, 257.

TOENNIES, J. P. (1966). *Z. Phys.* **193**, 76.

TOENNIES, J. P. (1968a). *In* "Chemische Elementarprozesse" (H. Hartmann, J. Heidberg, H. Heydtmann, and G. H. Kohlmaier, eds.). Springer, Berlin and New York.

TOENNIES, J. P. (1968b). *Ber. Bunsenges.* **72**, 927.

TOUW, T. R., and TRISCHKA, J. W. (1963). *J. Appl. Phys.* **34**, 3635.

TRUHLAR, D. G. (1971). *J. Chem. Phys.* **54**, 2635.

TULLY, F. P., LEE, Y. T., and BERRY, R. S. (1971). *Chem. Phys. Lett.* **9**, 80.

TULLY, J. C., and PRESTON, R. K. (1971). *J. Chem. Phys.* **55**, 562.

UDSETH, H., GIESE, CL. F., and GENTRY, W. R. (1971). *J. Chem. Phys.* **54**, 3642.

VAN DEN BERGH, H. E., FAUBEL, M., and TOENNIES, J. P. (1973). *Faraday Disc. Chem. Soc.* **55**, 203.

VAN DOP, BOERBOOM, A. J. H., and LOS, J. (1971). *Physica* **54**, 223.

VICTOR, G. A., and DALGARNO, A. (1970). *J. Chem. Phys.* **53**, 1316.

VON BUSCH, F., STRUNCK, H. J., and SCHLIER, CH. (1967). *Z. Phys.* **199**, 518.

WAECH, T. G., and BERNSTEIN, R. B. (1967). *J. Chem. Phys.* **46**, 4905.

WAECH, T. G., and BERNSTEIN, R. B. (1968). *Chem. Phys. Lett.* **2**, 477.

WAECH, T. G., KRAMER, K. H., and BERNSTEIN, R. B. (1968). *J. Chem. Phys.* **48**, 3978.

WARNOCK, T. T., and BERNSTEIN, R. B. (1968a). *J. Chem. Phys.* **49**, 1878.

WARNOCK, T. T., and BERNSTEIN, R. B. (1968b). *J. Chem. Phys.* **51**, 4682.

WARNOCK, T. T., BERNSTEIN, R. B., and GROSSER, A. E. (1967). *J. Chem. Phys.* **46**, 1685.

WHITE, R. A., and LIGHT, J. C. (1971). *J. Chem. Phys.* **55**, 379.

WILSON, K. R., and HERSCHBACH, D. R. (1965). *Nature (London)* **203**, 182.

WILSON, K. R., and HERSCHBACH, D. R. (1968). *J. Chem. Phys.* **49**, 2676.

WILSON, K. R., KWEI, G. H., NORRIS, J. A., HERM, R. R., BIRELY, J. H., and HERSCH-
BACH, D. R. (1964). *J. Chem. Phys.* **41**, 1154.
WOLKEN, G., MILLER, W. H , and KARPLUS, M. (1972). *J. Chem. Phys.* **56**, 4930.
WON, Y. C., and LEE, Y. T. (1972). To be published.
YOUNG, W. S., and KNUTH, E. L. (1969). *Entropie* **30**, 25.

Chapter 6

# The Dynamics of Bimolecular Reactions

J. C. POLANYI AND J. L. SCHREIBER

## I. The Microscopic and the Macroscopic

In recent years attention has turned away from the study of the properties of chemical reactions in bulk (i.e., reaction rates as a function of concentration, temperature, etc.) to the study of the same phenomena at the molecular level (reactive cross sections as a function of collision parameters, such as molecular energies and orientations). The details of the reactive event at the molecular level are referred to as the "reaction dynamics." Since such bulk properties as the rate coefficient continue to be of great interest, it is important to establish the connection between these macroscopic properties, and the microscopic details on which they depend. This will be the subject of Section I. The definitive work on this topic is that of Light *et al.* (1969) and Shuler (1968), where the material of Sections I,A and I,B can be found in fuller detail. Further references will be cited in the text.

## A. SIGNIFICANCE OF THE RATE CONSTANT

In the classical chemical kinetic experiment, for an elementary bimolecular reaction

$$A + B \rightleftharpoons C + D,$$

concentrations of reactants and/or products are monitored as functions of time, and are fitted to the empirical second-order rate law

$$-dn_A/dt = k_f n_A n_B - k_r n_C n_D. \tag{1.1}$$

The form of the rate law (1.1) presumes that only two-body encounters are of importance. The rate coefficients, more often termed rate constants, $k_f$ and $k_r$, can under many circumstances be considered to be independent of concentrations $(n_A, n_B, \ldots)$ and time. They should, in this case, be completely characterized by the temperature of the system. In the realm of pressures (concentrations) and temperatures in which rates have traditionally been studied, these assumptions are well founded. As chemistry moves into new domains (reactions in lasers, in the upper atmosphere, interstellar space and so on) it becomes a matter of more than pedantic interest to examine the foundations for these assumptions.

The temperature dependence of phenomenological rate constants can usually be described by the Arrhenius equation

$$k(T) = A \exp(-E_{\exp}/k_B T), \tag{1.2}$$

where $k_B$ is Boltzmann's constant. $E_{\exp}$ is called the activation energy, and $A$ is the frequency factor. Simple collision models of reaction suggest that $E_{\exp}$ is related to the threshold for reaction, i.e., the minimum energy required to produce reaction between any pair of reactant molecules. The exponential term in the Arrhenius equation is a measure of the probability that a pair of reactant molecules *will* have at least this minimum energy. The frequency factor $A$ is the rate at which reactant collisions, successful or otherwise, occur. This simple rationalization is intended to give some idea of the information summarized by the rate constant $k$. Thus we do not press such points as why is $A$ temperature independent in Eq. (1.2). In fact, if it is understood as being a collision frequency, one would expect it to be temperature dependent.

It is clear that not much of the detail of the molecular encounters is described by macroscopic rate constant measurements. This has led modern kineticists to resort to nonclassical experimental techniques; molecular beams, chemiluminescence experiments and others, to examine chemical reactions on the more nearly microscopic level.

To gain a fuller understanding of all that is encompassed in the macroscopic rate constant, we must consider the details of the microscopic encounters which occur. These are well characterized by their cross sections.

## B. SIGNIFICANCE OF THE CROSS SECTIONS

In the study of transport properties, it is useful to think of molecules as being spheres of well-defined radius. Despite the artificiality of this picture, we can usefully ascribe an effective size to the molecule so that geometrical arguments can be used to determine its transport properties. This effective size is called the cross section for the phenomenon under study, and has the dimensions of area.

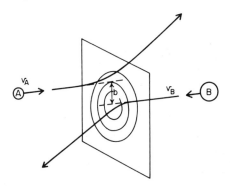

FIG. 1.   The scattering of particles A and B, with impact parameter $b$, as seen in the center-of-mass reference frame.

In the simplest classical model, a collision may be characterized by its impact parameter $b$. The impact parameter is the distance of-closest-approach in the absence of inter-particle forces (Fig. 1). The reaction probability would be some function of $b$, $P(b)$ decreasing to zero for large $b$, and which can be regarded as negligible for $b > b_{max}$. The total area in which reaction may occur would be $\pi b_{max}^2$. This quantity over-estimates the *average* size of the interaction range. We should instead weight each annulus of the target by its reaction probability, rather than giving all annuli the same weight. Then the reaction cross section $\sigma$, is given by

$$\sigma = 2\pi \int_0^{b_{\max}} P(b)b \, db. \tag{1.3}$$

This is the sum of the areas of the annuli (area $2\pi b \, db$) weighted by $P(b)$. Thus $\sigma$ is the effective area of the target.

In order to talk about collision phenomena in more quantitative terms let us consider an idealized scattering experiment, where molecules A are incident in a beam of well-defined speed, $v$ $[= (| \mathbf{v}_A - \mathbf{v}_B |)]$ upon a scattering zone of volume $V$, containing the molecules B. The two reactants have number densities $n_A$ and $n_B$, respectively. If a detector of the product C is placed at an orientation in space $\Omega$ with respect to the incoming direction, and has an angular acceptance of $d\Omega$, the rate at which the product is detected is given by

$$dN_C(\Omega)/dt = (n_B V)(n_A v)\sigma(v, \Omega) \, d\Omega. \tag{1.4}$$

The terms on the right-hand side of Eq. (1.4) are, respectively, the number of particles of type B in the scattering zone, the number of type A entering the zone per unit time, and the probability of scattering particle C into an angle in the range $\Omega$ to $\Omega + d\Omega$. Simple dimensional analysis shows that $\sigma$ has the dimensions area/particle, and hence may be looked upon as the effective "target area" for the transformation of A + B into C + D.

The quantity defined above, $\sigma(v, \Omega)$, is the differential cross section. If we are not interested in angular distribution, but are only concerned with the net production of C, we can integrate over the angular dependence to get the total cross section $S(v)$,

$$S(v) = \int \sigma(v, \Omega) \, d\Omega. \tag{1.5}$$

When products and reactants have internal states, as is most often the case, more information must be supplied to specify the process, and hence the cross section, completely. For the reaction

$$A(i) + B(j) \rightarrow C(l) + D(n),$$

where $ijln$ are, each, sets of indices completely specifying the internal state of the molecule to which they refer, the differential scattering cross section would be written as

$$\sigma(ln \mid ij; v, \Omega).$$

We must note that for reactants with internal states, we have not one but many reactive cross sections—one for each set of product- and reactant-state indices. In general the choice of the particular internal states will influence the values of the cross section. For any pair of reactant states, there are generally a large number of inelastic processes as well as reactive processes, each with their own cross section.

It is instructive to examine some properties of cross sections that arise from the invariance of the Schroedinger equation, or the classical equations of motion, under time reversal. We shall see that there is a connection between the cross section for a given process and the cross section for the reverse process.

The transition probability, if fully specified, refers to a transition between an initial and a final element of phase space $(dx\,dp$ and $dx'\,dp')$. The following transition probability is fully specified, in this sense. Such a probability per unit time is independent of the direction in which time is chosen to move:

$$P(ln\Omega \leftarrow ijv) = P(ij\Omega \leftarrow lnv'). \tag{1.6}$$

[This equation must be modified for reactants with internal angular momenta; see Eq. (1.10) below]. Here $v'$ is the final relative velocity determined by conservation of total energy. If in Eq. (1.4) we take the number of particles of type B in the scattering zone as unity, and number density of particle A to be $V^{-1}$, then the rate can be written as a total probability,

$$dP_{\text{tot}} = (v/V)\sigma(ln \mid ij; v\Omega)\,d\Omega\,\delta(E' - E)\,dE'.$$

The probability as defined here refers to the formation of product in an interval of space $d\Omega$ and product total energy, $dE'$. The delta function ensures that the probability is zero unless the initial and final total energies are the same. This total probability can also be expressed as the transition probability per phase space cell, times the total number of phase space cells in the increment:

$$dP_{\text{tot}} = P(ln\Omega \leftarrow ijv)(Vp'^2\,dp'\,d\Omega/h^3),$$

where we use the volume of available phase space as $V\,d\mathbf{p}' = Vp'^2\,dp'\,d\Omega$, and the volume of a phase space cell as $(dp^3 \cdot dx^3) = h^3$. Equating both expressions we find

$$\frac{\sigma(ln \mid ij; v\Omega)(v/V)\, \delta(E' - E)\, dE'}{Vp'^2\, dp'/h^3} = P(ln\Omega \leftarrow ijv). \qquad (1.7)$$

Similarly,

$$\frac{\sigma(ij \mid ln; v'\Omega)(v'/V)\, \delta(E - E')\, dE}{Vp^2\, dp/h^3} = P(ij\Omega \leftarrow lnv'). \qquad (1.8)$$

Using Eq. (1.6), we get

$$p^2\sigma(ln \mid ij; v\Omega)v\, dp = p'^2\sigma(ij \mid ln; v'\Omega)v'\, dp'.$$

Now make use of conservation of total energy, writing $\Delta E_{\text{int}} = E(l, n) - E(i, j)$, $p'^2/2\mu' = p^2/2\mu - \Delta E_{\text{int}}$. Differentiation gives

$$p'\, dp'/\mu' = p\, dp/\mu.$$

Substituting $p'/\mu' = v'$, and $p/\mu = v$, we get $v\, dp = v'\, dp'$, so that

$$p^2\sigma(ln \mid ij; v\Omega) = p'^2\sigma(ij \mid ln, v'\Omega). \qquad (1.9)$$

This is the equation of microscopic reversibility for systems with no internal angular momenta.

Since angular momentum is a pseudovector (i.e., its direction is determined only by convention) the quantum number corresponding to projection along a chosen axis (usually written as $m_j$ for angular momentum associated with the index $j$) changes sign on time reversal. This alters the Eq. (1.6) so that

$$P(lm_lnm_n\Omega \leftarrow im_ijm_jv) = P(i - m_ij - m_j\Omega \leftarrow l - m_ln - m_nv'). \qquad (1.10)$$

We may use these relations to derive an expression similar to Eq. (1.9). First we define the overall cross section $\bar{\sigma}$ as

$$\bar{\sigma}(ln \mid ij; v, \Omega) = (g_ig_j)^{-1} \sum_{\substack{m_im_j \\ m_lm_n}} \sigma(lm_lnm_n \mid im_ijm_j; v\Omega).$$

This is the total cross section into all the final $m$ levels, averaged over the initial $m$ levels. The degeneracies of the angular momentum states are symbolized $g_i$ and $g_j$ and are given by the number of different $m_i$ or $m_j$ levels. Since in the absence of fields all the $m_l$ and $m_n$ are degenerate,

$p'$ is independent of $m_l, m_n$, and on doing the sum over all $m_i, m_j, m_l$, and $m_n$ in Eqs. (1.7) and (1.8), we get

$$p'^2 g_l g_n \bar{\sigma}(ij \mid ln; v'\Omega) = p^2 g_i g_j \bar{\sigma}(ln \mid ij; v\Omega). \tag{1.11}$$

We will use this expression later in our discussion of the relationship between forward and reverse rate constants (Eq. (1.22)).

C. Relationship between Cross Sections and Rate Constants

As already noted, the rate constant averages over all of the microscopic processes. Each type of encounter has associated with it a cross section for each possible outcome. We shall now describe the averaging process required in order to reconstruct the rate constant.

In a real reaction situation, we do not have the ideal experiment to which Eq. (1.4) applies, but rather a multitude of such binary collision pairs. We can generalize Eq. (1.4) (integrated over $\Omega$ and divided by the scattering volume) for distributions of reactant states and velocities to yield an expression for the rate of formation of species C in state $l$,

$$\frac{dn_C(l)}{dt}\bigg|_{ijn} = [n_B(j)f_{Bj}(\mathbf{v}_B)\, d\mathbf{v}_B][n_A(i)f_{Ai}(\mathbf{v}_A)\, d\mathbf{v}_A \mid \mathbf{v}_B - \mathbf{v}_A \mid]$$
$$\times S(l, n \mid ij; \mid \mathbf{v}_B - \mathbf{v}_A \mid), \tag{1.12}$$

where $n_A(i)$ and $n_B(j)$ are the number densities of the species A and B in the states $i$ and $j$. The probability density distributions for the velocity of species $A(i)$ and $B(j)$, normalized to unity, are $f_{Ai}(\mathbf{v}_A)$ and $f_{Bj}(\mathbf{v}_B)$. $S$ is the total cross section for the reaction of

$$A(i) + B(j) \to C(l) + D(n)$$

when the reagents meet with the specified relative velocity. It should be noted that the rate on the left-hand side of Eq. (1.12) is that for the detection of $C(l)$, when $C(l)$ and $D(n)$ are produced; another rate (another $S$) would be appropriate if $C(l)$ and $D(n')$ were produced.

In general, we do not resolve the reactant velocities, hence we must integrate over the velocity distributions,

$$\frac{dn_{Cl}}{dt}\bigg|_{ijn} = n_B(j)n_A(i) \int d\mathbf{v}_A\, d\mathbf{v}_B\, f_{Ai}(\mathbf{v}_A)\, f_{Bj}(\mathbf{v}_B)$$
$$\times \mid \mathbf{v}_A - \mathbf{v}_B \mid S(ln \mid ij; \mid \mathbf{v}_A - \mathbf{v}_B \mid).$$

If we define the detailed rate coefficient

$$k_{ij}^{ln} = \int d\mathbf{v}_A \, d\mathbf{v}_B \, f_{Ai}(\mathbf{v}_A) \, f_{Bj}(\mathbf{v}_B) v S(ln \mid ij; v), \qquad (1.13)$$

where $v = \mid \mathbf{v}_A - \mathbf{v}_B \mid$. The "detailed rate equation" is then

$$\frac{dn_C(l)}{dt}\bigg|_{ijn} = k_{ij}^{ln} n_A(i) n_B(j), \qquad (1.14)$$

which closely resembles the phenomenological Eq. (1.1). We do not, in classical kinetic experiments, resolve either product or reactant states; thus the overall rate equation is

$$dn_C/dt = \left\{ \sum_{ijln} k_{ij}^{ln} x_A(i) x_B(j) \right\} n_A n_B, \qquad (1.15)$$

where $x_A(i) = n_A(i)/n_A$, $n_A = \sum_i n_A(i)$. The term in braces is the rate coefficient, $k$. It is evident that there are circumstances under which $k$ will vary with time, namely, a situation in which the distribution over internal energy states or velocities is changing. The only instance where the rate coefficient is clearly time independent is when the system has achieved full equilibrium.

For equilibrium velocity distributions, the detailed rate coefficients take a simple form. The normalized equilibrium velocity distribution for the species A is given by the Maxwellian expression

$$f(\mathbf{v}_A) = (m_A/2\pi k_B T)^{3/2} \exp(-m_A v_A^2/2k_B T). \qquad (1.16)$$

The same velocity distribution applies irrespective of the particular internal state of A. With this, and a similar expression for $f(\mathbf{v}_B)$, Eq. (1.13) becomes

$$k_{ij}^{ln}(T) = (m_A m_B/(2\pi k_B T)^2)^{3/2}$$

$$\times \int\int d\mathbf{v}_A \, d\mathbf{v}_B \, \exp[-(m_A v_A^2 + m_B v_B^2)/2k_B T] \mid \mathbf{v}_A - \mathbf{v}_B \mid$$

$$\times S(ln \mid ij; \mid \mathbf{v}_A - \mathbf{v}_B \mid).$$

Since the total cross section does not depend on the individual velocities, but only on the relative velocity $v$, it is convenient to transform from $\mathbf{v}_A$ and $\mathbf{v}_B$ to the coordinates

$$\mathbf{v} = \mathbf{v}_A - \mathbf{v}_B, \qquad \mathbf{V} = (m_A \mathbf{v}_A + m_B \mathbf{v}_B)/m_{AB},$$

where $m_{AB} = m_A + m_B$. We can rearrange the integrand to give

$$k_{ij}^{ln} = \left(\frac{\mu}{2\pi kT}\right)^{3/2} \left(\frac{m_{AB}}{2\pi kT}\right)^{3/2}$$

$$\times \iint d\mathbf{v} \, d\mathbf{V} \exp[-(\mu v^2 + m_{AB}V^2)/2k_B T]vS(v)$$

where $\mu = (m_A m_B)/m_{AB}$. The terms with $\mathbf{V}$ and $m_{AB}$ dependence may be integrated out to give unity, since it is of the same form as the normalized velocity distribution [Eq. (1.16)]. The remainder of the integrand depends only on the magnitude of $v$, so that integration over the angular dependence of $\mathbf{v}$ yields a factor of $4\pi$. Thus

$$k_{ij}^{ln} = 4\pi \left(\frac{\mu}{2\pi k_B T}\right)^{3/2} \int_0^\infty v^2 \, dv \, \exp(-\mu v^2/2kT)vS(ln \mid ij; v).$$

In terms of relative translational energy $E_T = \mu v^2/2$, the detailed rate coefficient is proportional to the Laplace transform of $E_T S(E_T)$; the transform variable being $\beta = (k_B T)^{-1}$, where $k_B$ is Boltzmann's constant.

$$k_{ij}^{ln}(T) = \left(\frac{2}{k_B T}\right)^{3/2} \frac{1}{(\pi\mu)^{1/2}}$$

$$\times \int_0^\infty E_T S(ln \mid ij, E_T) \exp(-E_T/k_B T) \, dE_T. \qquad (1.17)$$

Equation (1.17) clarifies the connection between the cross section $S$ and the equilibrium detailed rate coefficient $k$ (Eliason and Hirschfelder, 1959). Later we shall make use of this relationship in order to investigate the dependence of $k$ on $S$.

When the system of interest is at thermal equilibrium, we may use the equilibrium partition function expressions for the relative populations in the internal states of reactants and products to obtain an expression for the overall equilibrium rate constant. If the energy of state $i$ of particle A, relative to the ground state of A is $\varepsilon_{iA}$, then the fraction of A in state $i$ is given by

$$x_A(i) = g_i \frac{\exp(-\varepsilon_{iA}/k_B T)}{Q_A},$$

where $g_i$ is the degeneracy of the state $i$, and $Q_A$ is the equilibrium partition function for A,

$$Q_A = \sum_i g_i \exp(-\varepsilon_{iA}/k_B T).$$

The expression for the overall rate constant is then

$$k(T) = \sum_{ijln} \frac{g_i g_j \exp(-\{\varepsilon_{iA} + \varepsilon_{jB}\}/k_B T)}{Q_A Q_B} k_{ij}^{ln}(T). \qquad (1.18)$$

Using Eq. (1.17) we can examine the temperature dependence of the rate constant, as determined for various assumed forms of the cross section. Several very general forms have been integrated analytically by LeRoy (1969). Consideration of Eq. (1.2) would lead us to expect that a plot of $\ln k(T)$ versus $T^{-1}$ would yield a straight line of slope $-E_{\exp}/k_B$. In fact, the quantity

$$E_{\exp}(T) = -k_B \frac{d \ln k(T)}{d(T^{-1})} \qquad (1.19)$$

is observed, in general, to be weakly temperature dependent. If we differentiate Eq. (1.17), we obtain (Menzinger and Wolfgang, 1969)

$$E_{\exp} = \frac{\int_0^\infty E_T [E_T S(E_T) \exp(-E_T/k_B T)] \, dE_T}{\int_0^\infty E_T S(E_T) \exp(-E_T/k_B T) \, dE_T} - \tfrac{3}{2} k_B T. \qquad (1.20)$$

The ratio of integrals in Eq. (1.20) may be regarded as the average translational energy for reactive collisions, if we regard $E_T S(E_T) \exp(-E_T/k_B T)$ as the distribution function for reactive collisions, often referred to as the "reaction function." The quantity $\tfrac{3}{2}(k_B T)$ is the average relative translational energy for all pairs of molecules. Thus, $E_{\exp}$ as defined by Eq. (1.19) is the *average* excess energy of a reactive collision over a thermal collision:

$$\bar{E}_T = E_{\exp} + \tfrac{3}{2} k_B T, \qquad (1.21)$$

where $\bar{E}_T$ is the average reactive collision energy.*

As a particular example of $S(E_T)$ we consider the line-of-centers model of reactive collisions. We suppose that spherical molecules A and B with radii $r_A$ and $r_B$ will react only if the component of relative velocity along the line between the centers of A and B corresponds to a kinetic energy

---

* This is actually the experimental activation energy $E_{\exp}$ interpreted in terms of the temperature dependence of an individual detailed rate coefficient, $k_{ij}^{ln}(T)$. A similar treatment of the overall rate constant $k(T)$, which includes a weighted summation over the internal energy states of the colliding species [Eq. (1.18)], leads to a somewhat different expression for $E_{\exp}$. It is found that $E_{\exp}$ is the mean translational *plus internal* energy of reactive pairs of molecules, less the mean translational *plus internal* energy of all pairs of molecules.

greater than the threshold value $E_0$. If A and B meet with impact parameter $b$, the translational energy along the line of centers $E_{LC}$ is given by

$$E_{LC} = E_T(1 - b^2/(r_A + r_B)^2),$$

where $E_T$ is the total relative kinetic energy. We suppose that the reaction probability $P(b) = 1$ for all $b$ such that $E_0 \leq E_{LC}$. This defines a maximum reactive impact parameter $b_{max}(E_T)$:

$$b_{max}(E_T) = (r_A + r_B)(1 - E_0/E_T)^{1/2}.$$

Integrating Eq. (1.3) we obtain for the line-of-centers cross section $S_{LC}(E_T)$

$$\begin{aligned} S_{LC}(E_T) &= \pi(r_A + r_B)^2(1 - (E_0/E_T)), & E_T \geq E_0 \\ &= 0, & E_T < E_0. \end{aligned}$$

For this cross section one obtains by Eq. (1.20)

$$E_{exp} = E_0 + (k_B T/2).$$

If, as is the case in many reactions, $E_{exp} \gg k_B T$ over the energy range in which it is determined, then the line-of-centers model suggests that $E_{exp}$ is very near the threshold above which reaction starts to occur.

From consideration of other forms for $S(E_T)$ (LeRoy, 1969; Menzinger and Wolfgang, 1969) it has been shown that this conclusion need not be valid in general. For cross sections which rise monotonically, $E_{exp}$ tends to increase steadily with temperature, as reaction at high collision energy becomes more likely. For cross sections which pass through a maximum and then decrease, $E_{exp}$ may well become negative as the temperature increases, since at high temperature the average relative translational energy may exceed the average reactive energy. The dependence of $E_{exp}$ on temperature is illustrated in Fig. 2 for some hypothetical cross section functions, $S(E_T)$.

From experimentally or theoretically known cross sections one can construct rate constants with a high degree of accuracy. This follows from the fact that the overall temperature dependence of rate constants is dominated by the Boltzmann factor in the temperature ranges which are conventionally studied (Hochstim and Shuler, 1967). The observed cross section data can either be fitted to analytic forms, such as those suggested by LeRoy (1969), or a numerical quadrature can be performed

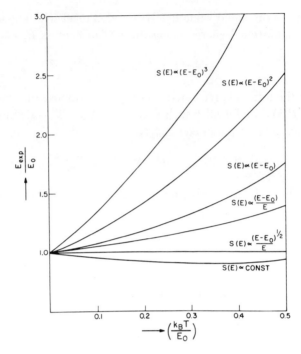

F‍IG. 2.   Dependence of the reduced activation energy $E_{exp}/E_0$ on the reduced temperature $k_B T/E_0$ for various forms of the onset of the cross section function. Relative translational energies are symbolized $E$ ($E_T$ in the text) (Menzinger and Wolfgang, 1969).

in place of the integral in Eq. (1.17) (Hochstim and Shuler, 1967; Kinsey, 1971b). Either technique should give good results for rate constants, provided the thermal equilibrium assumption implicit in Eq. (1.17) is not violated.

The reverse process, which would derive cross sections from rate data, is a much more difficult procedure. Since the form of the cross section affects the rate constant only relatively weakly, a large variation in the cross section may produce only minor, experimentally undetectable changes in the rate constants. In attempting to extract cross sections from rate data, a number of approaches may be taken. The rate constant can be fitted to a form which assumes some parametrized cross sections, such as those suggested by LeRoy (1969) or Menzinger and Wolfgang (1969). If enough data are available to determine the rate of change of activation energy with temperature, $\partial^2 \ln k/\partial(1/T)^2$ (which is not generally the case) the steepest-descent method could be employed to make an approximate inversion of the Laplace transform (Lin and Eyring, 1971). Malerich and Davis (1971) have applied this technique to a number of reactions to calculate threshold behavior of reactive cross sections. It is difficult to obtain any estimate of the accuracy of $S(E_T)$ obtained by either of these approaches. What is needed is some method of obtaining bounds on the cross section.

Melton and Gordon (1969) have given a method for calculating bounds to the "fractional extent of reaction below energy $E$," $G_E(T)$, defined by

$$G_E(T) = \frac{\int_0^E P(E_T) \exp(-E_T/k_B T) \, dE_T}{\int_0^\infty P(E_T) \exp(-E_T/k_B T) \, dE_T},$$

where $P(E_T) = E_T S(E_T)$. They showed that the maximum and minimum values of $G_E(T)$ are achieved when $S(E_T)$ is of the form

$$S(E_T) = \sum_{k=0}^{N} \varrho_k \delta(\xi_k - E_T).$$

The $\varrho_k$ and $\xi_k$ are weights and positions of Dirac $\delta$ functions. These quantities are chosen to reproduce as closely as possible the experimentally observed rate constants. This can be done by nonlinear least squares fit to $C_i$ (related to the rate constant at temperature $T_i$),

$$C_i = \int_0^\infty E_T S(E_T) \exp(-E_T/k_B T_i) \, dE_T = \sum_{k=0}^{N} \varrho_k \xi_k \exp(-\xi_k/k_B T_i).$$

If one has the rate constant at $n$ temperatures, one can determine $N$ pairs of $(\varrho_k, \xi_k)$, where $N$ is the greatest integer less than or equal to $n/2$. Melton and Gordon applied their technique to the experimental rate data of Westenberg and de Haas (1967) for the reaction of $D + H_2 \rightarrow HD + H$.

Information about cross sections may be obtained with greater certainty from nonequilibrium data. The recent photolytic hot-atom work of Gann and co-workers (1971) exemplifies this. Although in this type of experiment there are uncertainties in the appropriate form for the nonequilibrium distribution functions, the approach gives a good idea of the overall shape of the reactive cross section for the abstraction reaction

$$H + n\text{-}C_4D_{10} \rightarrow HD + sec\text{-}C_4D_9.$$

By assuming a cross section of the form

$$S(E_T) \propto [1 - (E_0/E_T)^P][1 - A(E_T/E_0)^Q]$$

with $P$ and $Q$ adjustable parameters, they were able to reproduce the trend of the experimentally determined reaction yield with initial energy of the hot H atom. This cross section rises from a threshold of $E_0$, with an initial behavior determined by $P$, passes through a maximum and falls to zero with a high-energy behavior determined by $Q$. The best fit is shown by the middle curve in Fig. 3.

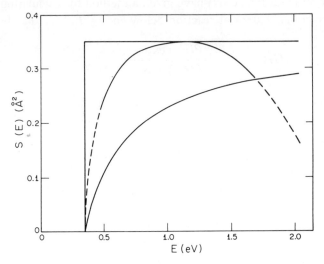

FIG. 3. Comparison of the step function for $S(E)$ (top curve) and line-of-centers function (bottom curve) with the measured excitation function (middle curve) obtained in a photolytic recoil experiment on $H + n\text{—}C_4D_{10} \rightarrow HD + sec\text{—}C_4D_9$. Note that $E$ is the relative translational energy, symbolized $E_T$ in the text. The values of the constants in the equation for $S(E)$ were $A = 3.2 \times 10^{-5}$, $P = 3$, $Q = 5$ (Gann et al., 1971).

Direct determination of (relative) total reactive cross sections as a function of collision energy are beginning to be possible. Gersh and Bernstein (1972) have used a seeded supersonic beam of $CH_3I$ to obtain $S(E_T)$ for $K + CH_3 \rightarrow KI + CH_3$ over a range of $E_T$ extending from thermal energies up to $\sim$20 kcal mole$^{-1}$. The cross section rises steeply to a maximum at $E_T \approx 4$ kcal mole$^{-1}$, and thereafter declines monotonically. The maximum in $S(E_T)$ at such a low $E_T$ may perhaps be connected with the tendency for this particular system at higher collision energies to make abortive trips onto an upper (covalent) surface, from which it returns to the reagents (see Sections II,C,1 and III,A,1). For further discussion see Bernstein and Rulis 1973, Bunker and Goring-Simpson 1973, La Budde et al. 1973, and Harris and Herschbach 1973. See also section III,A,1,c.

There has been considerable speculation regarding the extent of deviation of rate constants from their equilibrium values, as a consequence of thermal disequilibrium. A reaction may selectively depopulate certain internal states (particularly vibrational states, see Fig. 4, and Section II) or ranges of translational energy of the reactant. If this is the case, the rate at which these "reactive" states are refilled by relaxation

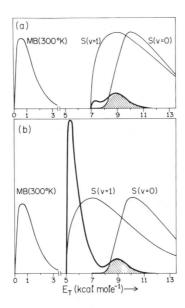

FIG. 4. Illustration of the working of equations (1.17) and (1.18). For simplicity it is assumed that one of the reagents has only a single internal energy state ($i$A) and the other has two internal energy states ($j$B), $v = 0$ and $v = 1$, where $v$ is the reagent vibrational quantum number. The difference in vibrational energy $E(v = 1) - E(v = 0)$ = 2 kcal mole$^{-1}$. In (a) and (b) we make two different (plausible) assumptions regarding the forms of $S(v = 0)$ and $S(v = 1)$ as a function of the collision energy $E_T$. In (a) the threshold energy $E_0$ for reaction is assumed to be the same for $v = 0$ and $v = 1$; the effect of vibrational excitation is to enhance the initial rate of increase of $S$ with $E_T$. In (b) reagent vibration assists the system in crossing the energy barrier, consequently, $E_0$ drops from 7 kcal mole$^{-1}$ to 5 kcal mole$^{-1}$ when $v = 1$. These two types of behavior correspond qualitatively to the dynamics on surfaces I and II of Figs. 15 and 16, below. The curve labeled MB is the Maxwell–Boltzmann distribution of translational energy for 300°K. The "reaction function" $[E_T \cdot S(v = 0; E_T) \times \exp(-E_T/k_BT)] + [E_T \cdot S(v = 1; E_T) \exp(-E_T/k_BT)]$ is indicated by a heavy curve. The area under the reaction function is proportional to the rate constant $k(T = 300°K) = [k_{v=0}(T)] + [k_{v=1}(T)]$. The area corresponding to $k_{v=0}(T)$ has been shaded. Figure 4b illustrates that for a reaction governed by a potential energy surface of "type II" (see below), a small fraction of the reagent in $v > 0$ can make the major contribution to $k(T)$. [In the case illustrated $n(v = 1)/n(v = 0) \approx 0.04$.]

processes can have a marked, and as yet not fully explored, effect on the observed reaction rate. Recent theoretical calculations (Shizgal and Karplus, 1970, 1971) on realistic systems indicate that deviations from translational equilibrium can decrease reaction rates by $\lesssim 10\%$. More striking is the effect which a lag in internal relaxation may have on reaction rates, when the reaction cross section for a particular internal state is of comparable magnitude to the inelastic cross section. Widom (1971) showed that such effects can cause a factor of 2 or more errors in the calculated equilibrium rate constant, as compared with the experimentally determined quantity. It appears, however, that most reactions that have been studied till now have been investigated under conditions for which the reaction rate is small compared with the rate of relaxation. Consequently, internal relaxation can be regarded as being complete, and the rate coefficient of Eq. (1.15) can properly be termed a rate constant.

## D. Properties of Detailed Rate Constants

The properties of cross sections discussed in the previous sections are directly reflected in the properties of the detailed rate constants obtained from those cross sections by Eq. (1.17). Rearranging (1.17) somewhat, we may write

$$k_f(T) = \frac{4\pi}{(2\pi\mu_f k_B T)^{3/2}} \int v_f S_f(v_f) \exp(-p_f^2/2\mu_f k_B T) p_f^2 \, dp_f$$

and

$$k_r(T) = \frac{4\pi}{(2\pi\mu_r k_B T)^{3/2}} \int v_r S_r(v_r) \exp(-p_r^2/2\mu_r k_B T) p_r^2 \, dp_r,$$

where $f$ and $r$ refer to the forward and reverse reaction, and the $p$'s are momenta. Using conservation of energy and the microscopic reversibility expression, Eq. (1.11), we can obtain

$$k_f/k_r = (\mu_r/\mu_f)^{3/2}(g_r/g_f) \exp(-\Delta E_{\rm int}/k_B T). \tag{1.22}$$

Here we have denoted the degeneracies of the reagents in the forward and reverse directions by $g_f$ and $g_r$. We can now rearrange Eq. (1.18) for the overall rate constant, and its analog for the reverse reaction, to obtain

$$k_f(T)/k_r(T) = (\mu_r/\mu_f)^{3/2}(Q_r/Q_f) \exp(-\Delta E^0/k_B T) = K(T),$$

where $Q_f$ and $Q_r$ are the reactant and product internal state partition functions, $(\mu_r/\mu_f)^{3/2}$ is the ratio of translational partition functions, and $\Delta E^0$ is the energy difference between the product and reactant ground states. We thus identify the ratio of equilibrium thermal rate constants with the well-known expression for the equilibrium constant $K(T)$.

In infrared chemiluminescence experiments (see Section I,E below) relative rates are obtained into specified quantum states, from a thermal distribution of reactant states. Since the spread of product total energies due to the distribution of reagent energies is small compared to the total product energy, we can reasonably regard these reactions as occurring at some mean reagent energy. This approach, first developed by Anlauf et al. (1970) and since examined in more detail by Kinsey (1971) and Marcus (1970), leads to a simplification of Eq. (1.22).

Classical trajectory calculations indicate that the product energy distribution (that is, relative rates into different $v'J'$ levels) is insensitive to the value of the initial $v$ and $J$ quantum numbers for a small variation in $v, J$ corresponding to room temperature reagents. Thus we can, for a particular $v'J'$, assume that

$$S_f(v'J' \mid vJE_T) \cong S_f(v'J' \mid \hat{v}\hat{J}E_T),$$

where $\hat{v}$ and $\hat{J}$ are representative values of the quantum numbers. Similarly, consideration of the shape of reaction functions for reactions with thresholds greater than $k_BT$ suggests that the range of reactive $E_T$ is quite narrow (see, for example, Fig. 4). We will assume that

$$k_f(v'J') = \bar{v}_f S_f(v'J' \mid \hat{v}\hat{J}\bar{E}_T)$$

[cf. Eq. (1.4)], where $\bar{E}_T$ is the mean reactive kinetic energy [cf. (1.21)], and $\bar{v}_f = (2\bar{E}_T/\mu_f)^{1/2}$.

Since, as noted above, the total energy of the products is quite well defined, we can ask how best to distribute this energy among vibration, rotation, and relative translation in order to increase the rate of the reverse (endothermic) reaction. We define a reverse rate constant at fixed total energy by

$$k_r(v', J') = \bar{v}_r S_r(\hat{v}\hat{J} \mid v'J'E_{T'}), \tag{1.23}$$

where $E_{T'}$ is the translational energy of the reaction products for the forward (exothermic) reaction implied by the values of $v'$ and $J'$ in conjunction with the total energy available to the products, $E'_{tot}$:

$$E_{T'} = E'_{tot} - E(v', J') \tag{1.24}$$

in which

$$E'_{\text{tot}} = E_{\text{exp}} + \tfrac{3}{2}k_{\text{B}}T + k_{\text{B}}T - \Delta H_0^0. \tag{1.25}$$

The first two terms of (1.25) give the mean reagent translation $\bar{E}_T$ [see Eq. (1.22)], the additional $k_{\text{B}}T$ approximates the mean reagent rotational energy, and $-\Delta H_0^0$ is the energy released by the reaction. (This expression for $E'_{\text{tot}}$ has been checked experimentally for some exothermic reactions.) The mean relative speed of the products, required for (1.23), is $\bar{v}_r = (2\bar{E}_{T'}/\mu_r)^{1/2}$.

From the microscopic reversibility relation (1.11) between the forward and the reverse cross sections, it follows that the forward and reverse rate constants at fixed total energy obey the equation

$$\frac{k_r}{k_f} = \frac{2J+1}{2J'+1}\left(\frac{\mu_f}{\mu_r}\right)^{3/2}\left(\frac{\bar{E}_T}{E_{T'}}\right)^{1/2}.$$

Using this relation one can calculate the detailed rate constants of the endothermic reaction $k_r(v'J'E_{T'})$ as a function of the distribution of the (fixed total) reagent energy over vibration, rotation, and translation, from the detailed rate constants of exothermic reaction $k_f(v'J'E_{T'})$ obtained experimentally (Anlauf *et al.*, 1969; Polanyi and Tardy, 1969). The results of such a calculation are referred to in Section II. The method of calculation has been validated in a 3D trajectory study (Perry *et al.*, 1974a).

E. EXPERIMENTAL

In view of the integrations over microscopic parameters that enter into the evaluation of macroscopic quantities, it is to be expected that it will be very difficult indeed to obtain dependable data concerning the microscopic event from experiments which measure heavily averaged macroscopic quantities, such as overall reaction rate.

The ion–molecule reaction $Ar^+ + D_2 \rightarrow ArD^+ + D$ will serve as an example. The success of the Langevin–Stevenson–Gioumousis theory in explaining the approximate overall reaction rate (Section III) led to a picture of the reaction as occurring under the influence of the attractive ion + induced-dipole interaction. This made it appear plausible that the reagents might be held together in a sticky complex which eventually, through the random accumulation of energy in a degree of freedom, underwent unimolecular dissociation. The relative rates of reaction paths differing only in the hydrogen isotope ($Ar^+ + HD \rightarrow ArH^+ + D$, or $ArD^+ + H$; Moran and Friedman, 1965) appeared to substantiate the long-lived complex model. However, crossed ion + molecule beam experiments on $Ar^+ + D_2$ (Herman et al., 1967) revealed, even at center-of-mass collision energies as low as a few kcal mole$^{-1}$ ($\sim 0.1$ eV), that the angular distribution was peaked in the forward direction (along the continuation of the direction of approach of $Ar^+$, as viewed in the center-of-mass frame). It followed that there could be no long-lived complex. A complex which persisted for several rotational periods would "forget" the direction from which $Ar^+$ had approached, and would spray product in all directions leading to a symmetric distribution in the center-of-mass. In other reactions molecular beam experiments have provided examples of scattering which must be ascribed to the formation of long-lived complexes (e.g., $Cs + RbCl \rightarrow CsCl + Rb$; Miller et al., 1967).

The experimental techniques which measure quantities relating more directly to the microscopic event are quite far from the level of sophistication where they measure, directly, fully specified reactive cross sections. Averaging over reagent states, product states, and instrumental factors occurs to a greater or lesser degree in all the experimental techniques that are currently available. The most elegant approach, because it is ultimately capable of development to the point where it measures fully specified cross sections, is the crossed molecular beam method. The present status of the molecular beam technique has been reviewed recently (Kinsey, 1972; Herschbach, 1973). The *prime* measurables are the product angular distribution and translational energy distribution. A complementary approach is the infrared chemiluminescence method which exploits the excellent energy resolution provided by spectroscopic measurements, in order to obtain the product energy distribution over vibrational and rotational states (for a review see Carrington and Polanyi, 1972). Product translational energy distributions can be derived from infrared chemiluminescence results for comparison with the corresponding distributions obtained in the beam experiments (for the former see Anlauf et al., 1970; for the latter see Schafer et al., 1970, who have obtained evidence of vibrational structure in the translational distribution). The chemiluminescence data offer superior energy resolution; the beam data, on the other hand, are able to allocate angular directions to the components of the translational distribution. Since the chemiluminescence method operates at low pressures with crude uncollimated reagent beams, it will, as infrared detectors improve, incorporate an increasing number of the features that distinguish the molecular beam method. Both techniques, for example, have yielded information with regard to the effect on the reaction dynamics of changing reagent collision energy (e.g., Gillen *et al.*, 1971; Cowley *et al.*, 1971; McDonald *et al.*, 1972; Ding *et al.*, 1973).

It should be evident from the discussion of the following two sections that the interpretation of these experiments which bear more directly upon the microscopic reactive event is *also* fraught with ambiguities. However, it does not appear too much to hope that with the accumulation of detailed, nonequilibrium, experimental data of this sort, at first the broad features and later some of the finer points regarding the reaction dynamics will emerge.

## II. Detailed Models

In this section we give a brief account of the methods employed and the findings obtained from computations which treat reaction dynamics at the microscopic level in full detail. The numerical solution of the classical equations of motion for $n$ bodies moving in three dimensions is now a commonplace. For reactive collisions this type of investigation began with the work of Wall *et al.* (1958, 1961) which in turn stemmed from the precomputer trajectory studies of the 1930's (see Glasstone *et al.*, 1941). The world championship at the time of writing is held by Bunker and Pattengill (1970) who performed a $3D$ classical trajectory calculation on a six-atom reactive system ($T + CH_4$; also $K + ICH_3$, Bunker and Goring-Simpson, 1973).

The corresponding quantum calculations are, at present, a great deal more difficult, though they are becoming more tractable with the development of "natural" coordinate systems well adapted to reactive and inelastic encounters (Marcus, 1968; Shipsey, 1969, 1972; Wyatt, 1972; Harms and Wyatt, 1972). At the same time an approximate numerical method of solving the scattering problem, which involves representation of successive intervals of the potential function in terms of polynomial expansions, can greatly speed up the process of computation (Gordon, 1971). Progress with quantum calculations has been reviewed recently by Levine (1969), Ross (1970), Karplus (1970c), Light (1971), Marcus (1973) and Gordon (1973). There is evidence, from the quantum calculations themselves and from comparison of classical theory with experiment (see for example, introduction to II,C below), that the classical trajectory method may provide a sufficiently dependable guide to the nature of the reaction dynamics for the present. The prospects for prolonging this convenient state of affairs have improved with the development of a procedure for extracting quantum transition probabilities from classical dynamics (see independent studies by Marcus and by Miller referenced in Marcus, 1973). Quantum effects are, in fact, quite difficult to observe, since they are blurred by averaging over the $3D$ range of collision parameters, and over even a small range of reagent and product energies. It is the existence of this averaging in *nature* that makes classical mechanics an acceptable tool for the exploration of the detailed dynamics of even such an unpromising system as $H + H_2$.

## A. The Classical Trajectory Method

While quantum mechanics requires a "global" solution of the scattering problem, classical mechanics allows a trajectory by trajectory piecewise construction of the dynamical picture. By running large numbers of classical trajectories one seeks to sample the entire range of initial conditions, and thus compute the distribution of final results associated with a particular "potential energy surface," that is, a particular interaction potential. The method has been the subject of recent reviews (Bunker, 1970, 1971).

The calculation of an individual trajectory conveniently falls into three parts: selection of initial conditions, integration of the equations of motion, and analysis of results.

### 1. *Selection of Initial Conditions*

In order to embark on the integration of the equations of motion it is necessary to stipulate the initial values of the coordinates and momenta of the atoms. It is most convenient to select these on the basis of a set of coordinates which reflect the molecular picture of the reacting species. Consider the case of an atom colliding with a diatomic molecule (we shall confine our attention to the three-atom case, unless otherwise stated). A useful coordinate system is shown in Fig. 5.

The three atoms, labeled A, B, and C, may be taken to lie in the xy plane at the instant that the trajectory begins. Atom A is a distance R from the center of mass of BC, which is placed at the origin of the coordinates. The BC internuclear distance $r$ makes an angle $\alpha$ with the x axis. This completely specifies the instantaneous positions of the three atoms. The molecule BC has some vibrational energy $E_V$, which along with sign ($+$ or $-$) fixes the momentum of B and C along the line $r$. The molecule may also have nonzero angular momentum $\mathbf{J}$. This vector

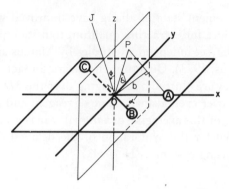

FIG. 5. An example of a coordinate system used in selecting initial conditions for a $3D$ trajectory calculation involving atoms A, B, and C. The atoms lie initially in the xy plane (heavy lines). The angle $\alpha$ is measured in the xy plane. The initial velocity of A is directed at point $P$ in the yz plane; the out-of-plane angle $\delta$ is measured in the yz plane. (Based on Kuntz *et al.*, 1969, with the difference that the rotational vector direction $J$ is permitted in the present representation to make an angle $\phi$ with the z axis.)

lies perpendicular to $r$, and makes an angle $\phi$ with the z axis. The direction and magnitude of **J** fix the momentum of B and C perpendicular to $r$. Finally, the atom A and molecule BC have some relative kinetic energy $E_T$. This fixes the magnitude of the relative velocity vector **v**. The direction of **v** is determined by $b$, the impact parameter, and $\delta$, the angle which the projection of **v** onto the yz plane makes with the y axis. Once these quantities are specified, the integration coordinates and momenta may be calculated (see II,A,2 below).

The choice of initial values for these parameters deserves comment. All of the quantities defined in the previous paragraph may be taken as independent random variables. They have known ranges, and known distribution functions. The initial separation $R$ is in general fixed at some value so large that the interaction between A and BC is negligible, but not so large as to unnecessarily prolong the calculation. The value of $r$ is distributed in proportion to the time spent by the oscillator at a given value of $r$, and hence is proportional to the inverse of the velocity of the oscillating particle. If the oscillator potential (with A removed to infinity) is $U(r)$, and the vibrational energy is $E_V$, the probability distribution function for $r$ is

$$P(r) \propto [E_V - U(r)]^{-1/2}.$$

This distribution is singular at the turning points (where the velocity is zero), and is taken to be zero beyond those points.

The angle $\alpha$ is a polar angle, consequently,

$$P(\alpha) \propto \sin \alpha$$

over the range 0 to $\pi$. The angles $\delta$ and $\phi$ are azimuthal angles, and are distributed uniformly over the range 0 to $2\pi$,

$$P(\delta) = P(\phi) = 1/2\pi.$$

The impact parameter $b$, as we see from Eq. (1.4), has a distribution function

$$P(b) \propto b,$$

i.e., $P(b^2) = $ constant, so that equal increments in $b^2$ (corresponding to equal area annuli at the target) get equal weight.

The energetic variables may either be fixed or chosen from a distribution appropriate to the experimental conditions which are being simulated. For example, one might choose $E_T$ from

$$P(E_T) \propto E_T \exp(-E_T/k_\mathrm{B}T)$$

so that the resulting average of the cross section over $E_T$ corresponds to Eq. (1.17) for the rate constant. Vibrational and rotational energies may be selected from continuous distributions or from quantized distributions.

Given the distribution function, a procedure is required for the selection of successive values of the variable in question. Three techniques are standardly used, as well as variants and combinations of these: systematic selection, inversion, and rejection. The last two are Monte Carlo methods; that is to say, they involve weighted-random sampling (Halton, 1970). We illustrate each by its application to the selection of the impact parameter, $b$.

By some prior calculation or by direct testing, a value $b_{\max}$ is chosen, beyond which no reaction occurs. In the systematic technique, values of $b$ are preselected from the range $[0, b_{\max}]$, and only these values are used. For example we could select $n$ values $b_i$ in such a way that each $b_i$ represents an interval $\Delta b_i$, and each $\Delta b_i$ interval has equal integrated weight. We require that, for $S_i = \sum_{i'=1}^{i} \Delta b_{i'}$, $S_0 = 0$,

$$\int_{S_i}^{S_{i+1}} P(b)\,db = (1/n) \int_0^{b_{\max}} P(b)\,db, \qquad i = 0, n-1$$

(this gives equal weight to each $\Delta b_i$ interval); then we choose a $b_i$ in the range $[S_{i-1}, S_i]$ such that

$$\int_{S_{i-1}}^{b_i} P(b)\,db = \int_{b_i}^{S_i} P(b)\,db.$$

This puts $b_i$ at the point of equal weight within the interval $\Delta b_i$. For our known $P(b)$ we have

$$S_i = \left(\frac{i}{n}\right)^{1/2} b_{\max}, \qquad b_i = \left(\frac{i - \frac{1}{2}}{n}\right)^{1/2} b_{\max}.$$

If the probability distribution function is not too complicated, the inversion technique can be applied so that values of the variable may be selected at random, in accordance with the known probability distribution. We define the cumulative probability

$$C(b) = \int_0^b P(b)\,db \bigg/ \int_0^{b_{\max}} P(b)\,db = b^2/b_{\max}^2.$$

$C(b)$ takes values from 0 to 1, as $b$ goes from 0 to $b_{\max}$. It can be shown (Shreider, 1966) that the values of $C(b)$ are a uniformly distributed random variable. Thus if we generate a random number $\xi$ in $[0, 1]$, and let $\xi = C(b)$, the resulting $b$

$$b = b_{\max}(\xi)^{1/2}$$

obeys the distribution

$$P(b) = \frac{dC(b)}{db}.$$

In the case of distributions for which the function $C$ is not calculable, or for which $\xi = C(x)$ is not invertable to obtain $x = C^{-1}(\xi)$, the von Neumann rejection technique is of value. We suppose that $P_{\max}$, some number greater than or equal to the maximum $P(b)$ within the range of selection of $b$, is known. In our example $P_{\max} = b_{\max}$. We select a value of $b$ uniformly from the range of selection, using

$$b = \xi_1 b_{\max},$$

but we reject this value if

$$\xi_2 > \frac{P(b)}{P_{\max}} = \xi_1,$$

where $\xi_1$ and $\xi_2$ are independent values selected uniformly from $[0, 1]$.

A combination of the systematic, the inversion, and the rejection techniques can be used to select initial values for the variables in accordance with any desired distribution function.

## 2. Integration of Equations of Motion

Once the geometric and energy parameters are selected, the Cartesian coordinates and momenta may be calculated. The overall motion of the center of mass of the system is of no importance, and can be eliminated. If we require that the center of mass be at the origin of the coordinate system,

$$m_A \mathbf{r}_A + m_B \mathbf{r}_B + m_C \mathbf{r}_C = 0,$$

and if we further require that it be at rest,

$$\mathbf{p}_A + \mathbf{p}_B + \mathbf{p}_C = 0,$$

where $\mathbf{r}_A, \mathbf{r}_B, \mathbf{r}_C$ are position vectors and $\mathbf{p}_A, \mathbf{p}_B, \mathbf{p}_C$ are the conjugate momentum vectors. We can write the Hamiltonian for the system in terms of only two of the three sets of vectors,

$$H = \frac{(m_A + m_C)}{2m_A m_C} \mathbf{p}_A{}^2 + \frac{(m_B + m_C)}{2m_B m_C} \mathbf{p}_B{}^2 + \frac{1}{m_C} \mathbf{p}_A \cdot \mathbf{p}_B + U(\mathbf{q}_A, \mathbf{q}_B),$$

where $\mathbf{q}_A = \mathbf{r}_A - \mathbf{r}_C$, $\mathbf{q}_B = \mathbf{r}_B - \mathbf{r}_C$. Hence for three atoms we have six independent coordinates and six independent momenta. Further reduction of the Hamiltonian, although possible (Whittaker, 1961), introduces unnecessary complications.

The equations of motion of the system can be expressed in terms of the Hamiltonian,

$$\partial H / \partial p_i = \dot{q}_i, \qquad \partial H / \partial q_i = -\dot{p}_i, \qquad i = 1, \ldots, 6. \qquad (2.1)$$

Equation (2.1) comprises 12 coupled first-order ordinary differential equations. With the initial values of $p_i, q_i$ specified, one can proceed with the integration. Several numerical techniques are available. These are discussed very thoroughly by Gear (1971) and Hull et al. (1971). The two principal types are the single-step procedures and the multistep (predictor corrector).

The single-step methods, the best known of which is the Runge–Kutta method, uses the values of $p_i, q_i$ and their derivatives at time $t$ to estimate the values at time $t + h$, $h$ being the step size. It evaluates the derivatives at a number of intermediate points in time to do a quadrature over the interval. The error in the estimates of $q_i(t + h)$ and $p_i(t + h)$ decreases, as $h$ decreases, proportional to $h^{r+1}$, where $r$ is the order of the method. Unfortunately, the total number of steps, and hence the total amount of computing, increases at the same time.

The single-step methods have the advantage that they allow variation in the step size at each step. The error incurred at each step can, therefore, be kept below some chosen value. In easily integrated regions, where the forces are small, the step size may be increased, thus speeding up computation. On the other hand, the single-step methods require evaluation of the derivative at each step at least once for each order. When the derivative is a complicated function, this may add seriously to the computation time.

In contrast to the single-step methods, multistep methods of arbitrary order can proceed with as few as two evaluations of derivatives per step. (Recently Smith and Wood, 1973, have shown how this can be reduced effectively to a single evaluation). This is accomplished through the use of a table of earlier values of the derivatives at equally spaced intervals of time $h$. The multistep method in effect fits polynomials to this table of values of derivatives, and then integrates the polynomials from $t$ to $t + h$ to obtain (for example)

$$p_i(t + h) = p_i(t) + \int_t^{t+h} \dot{p}_i(t') \, dt'.$$

This gives the "predicted" value of $p_i$, $q_i$. With this approximation to $p_i$, $q_i$, $\dot{p}_i(t + h)$ can be evaluated and an improved estimate can be obtained for the integral over $\dot{p}_i$ (the "corrected" value). Longer tables of derivatives give higher-order methods, each requiring only two derivative evaluations. Higher-order methods require somewhat more time per step, and tend to be somewhat more sensitive to error buildup. The principal drawback of the multistep method is the fixed step size. If the integration maintains a constant level of difficulty, this causes no problem. Multistep methods such as the Adams–Moulton and Nordsieck methods have been used widely in trajectory calculations (Bunker, 1970, 1971, outlines and illustrates the fourth-order Runge–Kutta method as well as the fourth-order Adams–Moulton predictor-corrector procedure). The method and order best suited for a particular case can be determined only by competitive trials.

The required accuracy of trajectories depends on the accuracy desired in product attributes. Serious nonconservation of total energy or total angular momentum act as warnings to indicate poor integration; however, conservation of "conservables" is not a sufficient condition for good integration. An overall check of integration accuracy is accomplished by "back integration." Taking the final $p_i$, $q_i$ values as initial values for an integration with step size $-h$, that is, backwards in time, the initial $p_i$, $q_i$ should be regenerated (usually to three or four decimal places). The best (as well as the most expensive) test is to repeat a given trajectory at decreasing values of step size until the calculated results are stable to the desired number of decimal places. Fortunately, since no conclusions are drawn from individual trajectories, we have some leeway in the error allowable in each trajectory.

## 3. Interpretation of Data

Once the trajectory has been integrated to some cutoff point chosen so that the products are no longer interacting, the integration coordinates and momenta may be analyzed to yield the product attributes. From the integration variables the following two vectors and their corresponding momenta can be constructed. Let $\mathbf{r}'$ be the vector between the atoms of the product molecule, $\mathbf{p}_r'$ the relative momentum of these atoms, $\mathbf{R}'$ the position of the free atom relative to the center of mass of the molecule, and $\mathbf{p}_R'$ the relative momentum of the atom with respect to the molecule. Then the relative translational energy is

$$E_T' = \mathbf{p}_R'^2/2\mu_R',$$

where $\mu_R'$ is the reduced mass of the product atom–molecule pair.

The internal energy is

$$E_{\text{int}}' = \mathbf{p}_r'^2/2\mu_r' + U(|\,r'\,|)$$

and $\mu_r'$ is the reduced mass of the diatomic product molecule. The internal energy $E_{\text{int}}'$ is made up of $E_V'$, the vibrational energy, and $E_R'$, the rotational energy. Unfortunately, there is no unique separation of these latter quantities. One method (analogous to the experimental procedure for defining $E_V'$ and $E_R'$) is to extract from $E_{\text{int}}'$ and $\mathbf{J}'$,

$$\mathbf{J}' = \mathbf{r}' \times \mathbf{p}_r',$$

a semiclassical quantum number $n'$, by the WKB quantization formula,

$$(n' + \tfrac{1}{2})\pi\hbar = \int_{r_<}^{r_>} \{2\mu_r'[E_{\text{int}}' - U(r')] - |\,\mathbf{J}'\,|^2/r'^2\}^{1/2}\,dr',$$

where $r_<$ and $r_>$ are the zeros of the integrand. This may be substituted into $E_{V'}(n)$, the formula for the quantized energy levels. Then

$$E_{V'} = E_{V'}(n'),$$
$$E_{R'} = E'_{\text{int}} - E_{V'}.$$

It should be noted that the $n'$ will not be integer valued, as it is the outcome of a classical calculation.

The molecular scattering angle $\theta$ is given by

$$\cos \theta = \frac{-\mathbf{p}_R(\text{final}) \cdot \mathbf{p}_R(\text{initial})}{|\,\mathbf{p}_R(\text{final})\,|\,|\,\mathbf{p}_R(\text{initial})\,|}.$$

The initial relative momentum defines the direction of forward scattering. The vector $-\mathbf{p}_R$ (final) therefore gives the direction of scattering of the molecular product. Thus if $-\mathbf{p}_R$ (final) is parallel to the initial atomic direction, $\theta = 0$; this is termed "forward molecular scattering," or, more often, simply "forward scattering."

Once a batch of trajectories have been run and the individual trajectory results analyzed, the products are characterized by computing averages, and, when the statistics merit it, distributions of product attributes. Suppose that a particular product attribute $A$ has a distribution function $P(A)$. The computed product attributes should be randomly distributed over this distribution. The true average of the $A$ values is

$$\bar{A} = \int AP(A)\, dA,$$

which we approximate by

$$\bar{A} \simeq \sum_{\substack{\text{reactive} \\ \text{trajectories}}} A_j/N_r,$$

where the $A_j$ are the values of $A$ observed in the reactive trajectories. This is, of course, only an estimate of $\bar{A}$. The narrower the distribution $P(A)$, the more accurate the estimate of $\bar{A}$. Also, the more trajectories in the sample, the more accurate the estimate of the mean. The standard deviation of the estimate is given by

$$\overline{dA} = \left[\frac{\overline{A^2} - (\bar{A})^2}{N_r}\right]^{1/2}.$$

Here, again, one can only estimate $\overline{dA}$ using the estimates of $\overline{A^2}$ and $\bar{A}$. For small numbers of trajectories, $\overline{dA}$ must be treated with caution.

One aspect of the reactive system which is of primary interest is the overall reactivity. We can express this as the average of $\delta_r$

$$\delta_r = 1 \quad \text{if reaction occurs}$$
$$= 0 \quad \text{if no reaction occurs.}$$

We average $\delta_r$ over all the trajectories $N_{\text{tot}}$, reactive and unreactive, to obtain $P_r$, the average reaction probability,

$$P_r = N_r/N_{\text{tot}}.$$

Since $\delta_r^2 = \delta_r$, the standard deviation associated with $P_r$ is given by

$$dP = [P_r(1 - P_r)/N_{\text{tot}}]^{1/2}.$$

A more common expression for the average reaction probability is the total cross section $S$. If we have chosen $b_{\max}$ such that no reaction occurs beyond $b_{\max}$, then (Karplus $et\ al.$, 1965)

$$S = \pi b_{\max}^2 P_r.$$

Product attribute distribution functions are usually constructed in an approximate sense by histograms of probability versus value of the attribute. The area of a histogram bar is essentially the relative cross section into a particular range of values of the product attribute. We define $P_r(A, \varDelta A)$ to be the number of reactive events observed to have A in the range A to A $+ \varDelta A$, divided by $N_{\text{tot}}$ [this is essentially the average of a restricted $\delta_r(A, \varDelta A)$]. By increasing the width of histogram bars, the number of trajectories in each range is increased, thus decreasing the standard deviations of each histogram bar, but at the same time decreasing the resolution of the histogram (we are then saying less, more accurately).

The differential cross section, $dS/d\Omega$, is related to the angular distribution function by

$$\frac{dS(\theta)}{d\Omega} = \frac{\pi b_{\max}^2 P_r(\theta)}{2\pi \sin \theta}.$$

The corresponding histogram bar heights increase in uncertainty to either end of the angular scale, since the weighting factor, $\sin^{-1} \theta$ gives prominence to a few trajectories at very large and at very small $\theta$. The factor $\sin^{-1} \theta$ takes into account the fact that the classical trajectory method computes all the scattered product in an interval of $\theta$ and is not restricted to one scattering plane of observation, as required for $dS\,(\theta)/d\Omega$ the angular distribution normally obtained in scattering experiments.


## B. Potential Energy Surfaces

In the Born–Oppenheimer approximation the potential energy $U$ of the lowest electronic energy state is a function of the configuration of the nuclei, only. Within this approximation we can picture a reacting system as proceeding across a well defined "potential energy hypersurface." The central problem of reaction dynamics, for the present, is the empirical determination of the shape of this hypersurface. Experimental studies in the field of reaction dynamics, and theoretical trajectory studies, provide a means to this end. In the coming decade we should enter a new era in which *ab initio* potential energy surfaces are used as a basis for trajectory calculations. Such surfaces will be obtained directly from the Schroedinger equation by variational solution (Krauss, 1970, 1971; Karplus, 1970a; Conroy, 1970; Wahl and Das, 1971; McLean, 1971; Bender *et al.*, 1972; Liu, 1973). Despite great advances in the techniques of variational solution, it is, however, still difficult to obtain *ab initio* potential energy surfaces at a level of accuracy which would justify their use in trajectory studies. This level of accuracy has been achieved for $H_3^+$, for $H_3$ and perhaps for $FH_2$. In the first case a full potential energy surface has been computed to an accuracy of about 2 kcal mole$^{-1}$ in its important regions, and trajectory calculations have been performed (Csizmadia *et al.*, 1969, 1970).

We can distinguish three categories of *empirical* potential energy surface functions. The most used has been the "extended LEPS (London, Eyring, Polanyi, Sato) function" (Sato, 1955; Polanyi, 1963, and earlier references dating back to 1929 cited there):

$$
\begin{aligned}
U(r_1, r_2, r_3) = {} & \frac{Q_1}{1+S_1} + \frac{Q_2}{1+S_2} + \frac{Q_3}{1+S_3} \\
& - \left[ \frac{J_1^{2}}{(1+S_1)^2} + \frac{J_2^{2}}{(1+S_2)^2} + \frac{J_3^{2}}{(1+S_3)^2} \right. \\
& - \frac{J_1 J_2}{(1+S_1)(1+S_2)} - \frac{J_2 J_3}{(1+S_2)(1+S_3)} \\
& \left. - \frac{J_1 J_3}{(1+S_1)(1+S_3)} \right]^{1/2}
\end{aligned}
\tag{2.2}
$$

The coordinates $r_1, r_2, r_3$ refer to the internuclear separations between pairs of atoms AB, BC, and AC. The Coulombic and exchange integrals for each pair of atoms ($Q_1, J_1$ for AB, etc.) are obtained from the Morse function for that atomic pair and from the repulsive anti-Morse function proposed by Sato. The constants $S_1$, $S_2$, $S_3$ replace the single adjustable constant $S^2$ to be found in Sato's reformulation of the LEP equation; they therefore bear a formal resemblance (but no more than a formal resemblance) to the square of the overlap integrals between the various pairs of atoms. These $S$ parameters are in fact adjusted freely in order to obtain potential energy surfaces with desired properties. A similar function to that of Eq. (2.2) has been used for studies of four-atom reactions [Mok and Polanyi, 1970; the function is $U(r_1, r_2, \ldots, r_6)$]. These extended LEPS functions provide a smooth and flexible interpolation between the Morse functions for reagents and those for products.

A second type of function $U(r_1, r_2, r_3)$ was introduced by Blais and Bunker (1962). It is purely empirical in its origins, and has the virtue that its terms are clearly identifiable. There are four terms; the first two describe the Morse attraction in the reagent and the product molecules, BC and AB, the third term (called the "switching term") makes the reagent molecule attraction in BC diminish as $r_1$ decreases, and the fourth term ensures that reaction gives AB and not AC:

$$
\begin{aligned}
U(r_1, r_2, r_3) = &\; D_1[1 - e^{-\beta_1(r_1 - r_1^0)}]^2 \\
&+ D_2[1 - e^{-\beta_2(r_2 - r_2^0)}]^2 \\
&+ D_2[1 - \tanh(ar_1 + b)]\, e^{-\beta_2(r_2 - r_2^0)} \\
&+ D\, e^{-\beta(r_3 - r_0)}
\end{aligned}
\tag{2.3}
$$

The parameters $a$, $b$, $D$, $\beta$, and $r_0$ are adjustable; $D_1, D_2, \beta_1, \beta_2, r_1^0, r_2^0$, are the Morse parameters appropriate to the product and the reagent molecules. Equation (2.3) only illustrates the simplest possible form of "switching function" potential energy surface. Though the individual terms are identifiable as to their general purpose, the switching function, like the LEPS function, must be adjusted by trial and error. The basic reason for this is that the adjustments are being applied to terms which describe pairwise interaction, and not to a function that is designed to represent the shape of the resulting energy surface as directly as possible.

The third (and final) potential energy function to be noted here provides an elegant tool for fitting the potential energy map itself. The function is termed the "hyperbolic map function" (HMF: Bunker and Blais, 1964; Bunker and Parr, 1970). The map is constructed on a co-

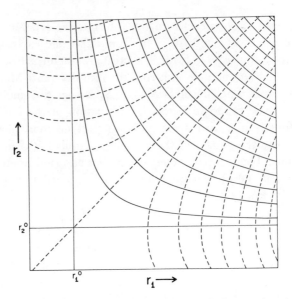

FIG. 6.  Coordinate grid for the HMF (hyperbolic map function).

ordinate grid consisting of conjugate hyperbolae; see Fig. 6. Loosely
speaking, the potential energy changes in a Morse-like fashion along the
broken lines of the grid, whereas the parameters ($D$ and $\beta$) governing
the shape of the Morse function vary along the orthogonally intersecting
solid lines of the grid. For further details the reader should refer to
Bunker's review (1971). This type of approach should become particularly important in the future as tabulations of *ab initio* potential energies
become available. Preparatory to performing trajectory computations it
will, in general, be necessary to fit the *ab initio* points to a smooth and
continuous "map." The HMF method will provide an excellent basis
for this "fitting" process.

## C. Some Characteristic Features of Potential Energy Surfaces

In this section we consider the characteristic features of potential
energy surfaces under four broad headings. If we are to identify categories
of potential energy surface with types of reaction dynamics observed in
the laboratory, it is essential that we reduce the number of variables
governing the form of the energy surface. The only way that we can do this
is to select from among the variables those that seem to play a particularly
significant role in determining the outcome of reaction. In Section II,B

we described several flexible functions that can be used to vary the form of the energy surface. In Section II,A we gave a terse account of the classical trajectory method, which can be used as a means to explore the properties of potential energy surfaces.

Once the properties of contrasting types of energy surface have been determined by full trajectory studies, one can, in many cases, improve one's understanding of these findings by means of a picturesque solution of the collinear equations of motion. It has been known for some time that the motion of a sliding point mass across a suitably skewed and scaled representation of the collinear potential energy surface gives the solution to the classical equations of motion for three masses moving under the influence of that potential (see Glasstone et al., 1941). The sliding mass representation is often very revealing. It should be stressed, however, that it is not a predictive tool, (a) since it is easy to be mistaken about the optimal path of the sliding mass if one relies on visual inspection of the skewed and scaled surface (and it is, today, as easy to integrate the equations of motion as it would be to compute the path of the sliding mass), and (b) the neglect of trajectories which proceed through bent configurations can falsify the outcome [for example, the effect of increased reagent translational energy on product vibrational excitation for surface I of Polanyi and Wong (1969), was qualitatively different for a collinear trajectory as compared with the mean of a representative batch of trajectories in $3D$].

The procedure for skewing and scaling the axes of a collinear potential energy surface so that the path of a sliding mass solves the classical equations of motion, depends on the fact that the kinetic energy of the three particles A, B, C is

$$T_{ABC} = (1/2m_{ABC})\{m_A m_{BC} \dot{r}_1{}^2 + 2m_A m_C \dot{r}_1 \dot{r}_2 + m_{AB} m_C \dot{r}_2{}^2\}, \qquad (2.4)$$

where $m_{ABC} = m_A + m_B + m_C$, $r_1 \equiv r_{AB}$, $r_2 \equiv r_{BC}$. By contrast, the sliding mass (of mass $M$) has

$$T_M = (1/2M)\{\dot{x}^2 + \dot{y}^2\}. \qquad (2.5)$$

If $T_M$ is to tell us $T_{ABC}$ we must transform the coordinates $r_1$ and $r_2$ in Eq. (2.4) so as to eliminate the term in $\dot{r}_1 \dot{r}_2$. (A general "diagonalization" procedure has been described for the $n$-atom case by Hirschfelder and Dahler, 1956, and Jepsen and Hirschfelder, 1959.) Diagonalization is accomplished in the present case by skewing the coordinate $r_2$ away from the Cartesian coordinate y toward x through an angle $\theta$ such that

$$\sin \theta = C_{A,C}^{1/2}, \tag{2.6}$$

where $C_{A,C} = (m_A/m_{AB})(m_C/m_{BC})$. In addition to eliminating the cross term in $\dot{r}_1\dot{r}_2$ from Eq. (2.4), it is necessary to make the coefficients of $\dot{r}_1$ and $\dot{r}_2$ equal. This is accomplished by applying a scaling factor of $c^{-1}$ to the exit valley $r_2$ of the energy surface, where

$$c = (m_A m_{BC}/m_{AB} m_C)^{1/2}. \tag{2.7}$$

If the mass of the particle is $M = \mu_{A,BC}$, then $T_M = T_{ABC}$.

It appears that the best empirical test we have, at present, of the validity of classical trajectory calculations as a solution to what is in reality a quantum mechanical problem, comes from the investigation of isotopically related pairs of reactions. The potential energy hypersurface $U(r_1, r_2, r_3)$ is the same for such pairs of reactions. A surface which has been chosen to be optimal for one member of a pair should also be optimal for the other. A 3D trajectory study has been made of the reaction Cl + HI → HCl + I (Anlauf et al., 1968; Parr et al., 1973). Monte Carlo methods were used for the selection of initial state parameters so that the trajectories simulated a thermal distribution over reagent translation, rotation, and vibration at 300°K. The potential energy function was of the LEPS type, adjusted to give the best fit with the product vibrational energy distribution obtained experimentally for Cl + HI → HCl + I. This LEPS surface (largely 'repulsive' in character; see II.C.1 below) predicted for Cl + DI → DCl + I a very similar energy distribution (Fig. 7b) and, consequently, a markedly different vibrational distribution (Fig. 7a). In the absence of the corresponding experimental data (also shown in Fig. 7) there would be serious question whether a redistribution over vibrational energy levels predicted by a theory that takes no account of the existence of discrete energy states, could be given any credence. The question would be particularly worrisome for a case, such as the one exemplified here, in which the vibrational energy spacing is large. It is reassuring, therefore, to find that the predicted shift is in good agreement with observation.

The discussion that follows will be restricted to the dynamics of reactions which can, with reasonable justice, be regarded as taking place across a single (effective) potential energy hypersurface. Tully and Preston (1971; also Tully, 1973) have taken the trajectory method into the nonadiabatic domain by treating $H^+ + D_2$ as a system that can "hop"

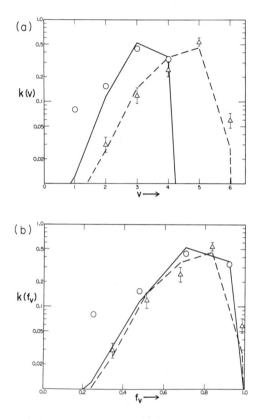

FIG. 7. (a) Semilog plot of $k(v)$, the relative probability of forming product in vibrational level $v$. The lines (solid for Cl + HI, broken for Cl + DI) are from trajectory calculations; the points ($\bigcirc$ Cl + HI, $\triangle$ Cl + DI) are from infrared chemiluminescence experiments. The curves are normalized to $\sum_v k(v) = 1$. (b) Semilog plot of $k(f_v)$, the relative probability of converting a fraction $f_v$ of the available energy (34 kcal mole$^{-1}$ for both the Cl + HI and the Cl + DI reactions) into product vibration. The curves are normalized to $\sum_{f_v} k(f_v) = 1$ (Anlauf et al., 1968).

to and fro between alternative potential energy surfaces. After a "hop" the classical trajectory resumes on the new potential energy surface.

In connection with the following part of Section II the reader may find it helpful to refer to a recent review (Polanyi, 1972) which gives a simplified account of some of these topics.* Sections 1 and 2 that follow, will be concerned with the dynamics of exothermic reactions. Thermo-

---

* A 35-minute film illustrating a number of the points made in Section II,C is available on loan (Charters et al., 1970).

neutral and endothermic reactions will be discussed in Section 3 (and Section 4).

## 1. *Attractive and Repulsive Energy Surfaces*

The concept of an "attractive" potential energy surface arose out of considerations of the dynamics of reactions between alkali metals and halogens. These were described in terms of an electron switch model (Ogg and Polanyi, 1935; Evans and Polanyi, 1938, 1939; Magee, 1940) in which the neutral species became ionic species while still far apart,

$$M + XY \rightarrow M^+ + XY^- \rightarrow M^+X^- + Y.$$

In terms of the energy surface the system has passed from a level plateau corresponding to the covalent surface $(M + X_2)$ at large $r_1$ to a descending hill on an ionic surface $(M^+ + X_2^-)$. Since this downward slope is situated to a large extent along the "approach coordinate" we characterize the energy surface as being of the "early downhill" or (more tersely) the "attractive" variety.

It is to be expected that a force which pulls the reactants together will give rise to internal excitation in the new bond. Evans and Polanyi (1939) argued that this would be the case on the grounds that a sliding mass which has been accelerated along the entry valley of a (skewed and scaled) energy surface will tend to oscillate to and fro across the exit valley, that is, will tend to channel reaction energy efficiently into vibration in the newly formed bond. Blais and Bunker (1962, 1963) put this generalization on a more solid footing by subjecting it to a test by the classical trajectory method in the course of the first trajectory study of a molecular beam reaction.

A more extensive study set out to examine a whole spectrum of potential energy surfaces ranging from highly "repulsive," with energy released predominantly as the products separate, to highly attractive. The early work on these lines was restricted to the mass combination in which a light atom attacks two heavy ones, **L + HH**. The effect of increasing attractive energy release for the **L + HH** case was qualitatively in accord with the expectations. (See Polanyi, 1962, for a "spectrum" of five surfaces, with product vibrational and translational energies recorded for mass combinations $H + Cl_2$ and $D + Cl_2$, for a range of initial conditions and collision energies.) Subsequently, an attempt was made to put this correlation on a quantitative footing by ascribing a numerical value to the percentage attractive and repulsive energy release

(Kuntz *et al.*, 1966). Three related methods of categorization were proposed. Only the first of these will be discussed in this section; the other two will be introduced in Section II,C,2. (For a detailed description of the three methods, see Perry *et al.*, 1974).

The simplest method of categorization, which turned out to be entirely adequate for the special case of **L + HH**, takes the attractive energy release $\mathscr{A}_\perp$ to be the energy released as A approaches BC (with BC "clamped" at its normal equilibrium separation, $r_2{}^0$) collinearly up to the normal AB bonding distance, $r_1{}^0$. The repulsive energy release $\mathscr{R}_\perp$ is the balance of the energy release. This will be referred to as the "perpendicular" method of assigning $\mathscr{A}$ and $\mathscr{R}$. Where there is an energy barrier the attractive energy release is (in all three methods of categorization) reckoned from the crest of the barrier, since the total energy available to the products includes the energy released in the trip down the far side of the barrier. If, as most commonly happens, atom A approaching a "clamped" BC in the perpendicular method of categorization encounters repulsion before reaching the equilibrium separation $r_1{}^0$, then $\mathscr{A}_\perp$ is taken to be the energy released up to that point (i.e., the point at which the onset of "core repulsion" puts an end to purely attractive energy release). This division of the energy release into two categories, $\mathscr{A}_\perp$ and $\mathscr{R}_\perp$, can only provide a crude index of the nature of the collinear energy surface. It should be noted, moreover, that this index (in common with the alternative indices described in Section II,C,2) is taken from a single cut through the potential energy hypersurface and can, therefore, only provide an approximate guide to the behaviour of *2D* or *3D* trajectories.

Figure 8 shows three collinear potential energy surfaces in ascending order of $\mathscr{A}_\perp$, increasing overall from $\mathscr{A}_\perp = 4\%$ to $72\%$ while $\mathscr{R}_\perp$ decreases from $96\%$ to $28\%$. (Whenever the energy release is expressed in percentages, the denominator is the classical barrier height $E_c$ plus the classical exothermicity, $-\Delta H_c$; the "classical" designation simply means that zero point energies have been neglected.) In Fig. 9 the mean vibrational energies in the products of *2D* classical trajectory computations are compared with the $\%\mathscr{A}_\perp$ for eight different LEPS potential energy surfaces. (These results, regarding product energy distribution, would be the same for calculation in *3D*; see, for example, Karplus and Raff, 1964; Bunker and Blais, 1964; Kuntz *et al.*, 1969a,b, in all of which *2D* and *3D* calculations are compared. Though the effect on the product energy distribution is, it appears, insignificant, the effect on the angular distribution is large enough to make *3D* computations mandatory for

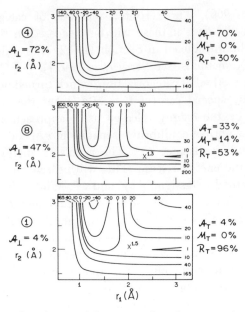

FIG. 8.   Three exothermic potential energy surfaces (reagents at lower right, products at upper left) for collinear reaction A + BC → AB + C. The energies are in kcal mole$^{-1}$ relative to the reagent energy as zero. The **X** marks the barrier crest (if any), and the number beside the **X** indicates the height of the barrier. The designations at the left of each surface give the percentage of the total energy release that is attractive, according to the "perpendicular" method of assessment. The designations at the right of each surface give the percentages attractive, mixed, and repulsive energy release for the **L + HH** mass combination based on the "trajectory" method (a single collinear trajectory). The surfaces represent cuts through corresponding hypersurfaces used in the trajectory calculations. The surfaces are arranged in sequence so that the most repulsive is at the bottom, the most attractive at the top. The spectroscopic constants were largely those appropriate to H + Cl$_2$ (the exception was surface 8, for which the force constant of the bond under attack was increased—this is evident from the narrower entry channel). The constants governing the extended LEPS equation were as follows: for surface ① $S_1 = S_3 = 0.10$, $S_2 = -0.25$; for ⑧ $S_1 = S_2 = S_3 = 0.05$; for ④ $S_1 = S_2 = S_3 = 0.20$. The numbering of the surfaces corresponds to Kuntz et al. (1966) from which these data were taken and to which the reader is referred for full details.

angular distribution studies.) The mean vibrational excitation is seen to increase systematically with increasing $\%\mathscr{A}_\perp$ (the batch of trajectories at very high $\%\mathscr{A}_\perp$ will be discussed later); $\%\langle E_V'\rangle \sim \%\mathscr{A}_\perp$ (but see caption to Fig. 9). Reactions of mass combination **L + HH** have been studied experimentally and are thought to span a significant range of the $\mathscr{A}_\perp$ scale in this graph. Thus H + F$_2$ → HF + F has $\mathscr{A}_\perp \sim 45\%$, H + Cl$_2$ → HCl + Cl has $\mathscr{A}_\perp \sim 25\%$,   H + Br$_2$ → HBr + Br   has

$\mathscr{A}_\perp \sim 45\%$ (Anlauf *et al.*, 1967; Polanyi and Sloan, 1972), $H + M_2$ $\rightarrow MH + M$ (where M is an alkali metal atom) is likely to have a substantially larger $\%\mathscr{A}_\perp$ (Lee *et al.*, 1971), as is $Li + Br_2 \rightarrow LiBr + Br$ (Parrish and Herm, 1969). In Section II,C,2 we shall note that the **L + HH** mass combination is anomalous (the so-called "light-atom anomaly" exhibited by reactions with a light attacking atom) in showing such a sensitivity to $\%\mathscr{A}_\perp$; the majority of mass combinations give efficient vibrational excitation even on potential energy surfaces with quite low $\%\mathscr{A}_\perp$. The existence of the "anomaly" has the effect of making the vibrational energy distribution for **L + HH** reactions particularly revealing regarding the nature of the interaction.

A second feature of attractive energy surfaces is their tendency to favor "forward scattering." Used without qualification this term means that the differential cross section for the molecular product AB of the reaction $A + BC \rightarrow AB + C$ has its maximum more or less along the continuation of the original direction of approach of the atomic reagent, A. That attractive interaction favors forward scattering and repulsive

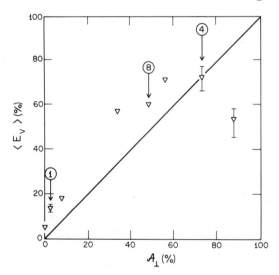

FIG. 9. The mean vibrational excitation in the molecular product of reaction **L + HH → LH + H** (where the mass of the light atom **L** corresponds to atomic hydrogen, and the heavy atom **H** to Br; $L = 1$ amu, $H = 80$ amu), plotted against the percentage attractive energy release determined by the perpendicular method. Surfaces ①, ⑧, and ④ are those shown in Fig. 8. The (approximate) mean product vibrational excitation was obtained from batches of $2D$ trajectories. The solid line was drawn to indicate $\%\langle E_V\rangle = \%\mathscr{A}_\perp$ for comparison. [Neglecting the two most attractive energy surfaces (see text) the best fit is $\%\langle E_V\rangle \approx 1.25 \ (\%\mathscr{A}_\perp)$.]

interaction tends to send the new molecule back along the direction from
which A came, appears (today) intuitively reasonable. For a single mass
combination the effect of increased repulsive energy release in shifting
the angular distribution from forward to backward has been clearly
documented on a number of potential energy surfaces (all of the $M + XY$
$\rightarrow M^+X^- + Y$ variety, but with widely different reactive cross sections
and exothermicities; Godfrey and Karplus, 1968; Kuntz et al., 1969b).
The effect of increasing attractive energy release on product angular
distribution for a range of mass combinations is illustrated in Fig. 10.

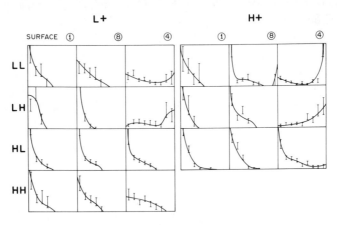

Fig. 10.   Curve drawn through histograms of the differential cross section for AB
formed from $A + BC \rightarrow AB + C$, as viewed in the center-of-mass frame of reference.
The collision energy is 1 kcal mole$^{-1}$ above the classical barrier height, corresponding to
approximately room temperature reaction. Directly "forward" scattering of the molecular
product is at the right of each box, backward scattering at the left. All seven mass combinations of two masses **L** and **H** (**L** = 1 amu, **H** = 80 amu) are represented on three
different energy surfaces ranging from the highly repulsive surface ①, through the
intermediate surface ⑧, to the attractive surface ④ (cf. Fig. 8). Scattering of AB can
be seen to be more forward on surface ④ than on surface ①, particularly when the mass of the
attacking atom is $m_A \geq m_B$ (Polanyi and Schreiber, 1972).

The results comprise 21 batches of $3D$ trajectories encompassing all
combinations of the masses L and H on the three LEPS potential
energy surfaces shown in Fig. 8. It is evident (scanning the trios of
graphs along each horizontal row) that there is a discernible shift toward
more forward scattering of the molecular product in going from surface ①
(repulsive) to ④ (attractive). This effect is particularly marked in cases
where the attacking atom A has a mass $m_A \geq m_B$, B being the atom under
attack. The initial momentum of $A$, $p_A = p_{BC}$. If $m_A \geq m_B$, then $p_A > p_B$

and the momentum of A is more likely to carry B along in the forward direction on an attractive surface (this argument assumes, for simplicity, that BC has no internal energy). On a repulsive surface which favors collinear approach of A to BC, the B · C repulsion adds to the initial backward directed $p_B$ so that the inequality can become $p_B > p_A$, and AB as a whole must move backward.

The potential energy surfaces used in trajectory studies of reactions $M + X_2$, for example, $K + Br_2 \rightarrow KBr + Br$, were substantially more attractive than the most attractive of the three surfaces pictured in Fig. 10 (Blais, 1968, 1969; Godfrey and Karplus, 1968; Kuntz et al., 1969a,b). They yielded, in agreement with the crude generalizations of the previous paragraphs, high product vibrational excitation and a significant amount of forward scattering. These results were in rough accord with the experimental findings (see Chapter 5 of this Volume). Equally noteworthy was the fact that by increasing the percentage repulsive energy release from $\sim 1\%$ for $M + X_2$ to $\sim 50\%$ (Kuntz et al., 1969b), it was possible to simulate, in a qualitative fashion, the marked diminution in mean vibrational excitation, coupled with the backward shift in the angular distribution, observed experimentally in going from $M + X_2$ (alkali metal plus halogen) to $M + XR$ (alkali metal plus alkali halide; see Chapter 5 of this Volume). Experiment and theory are in general accord in linking product energy distribution and angular distribution (see also Section III). The interconnection takes a particularly simple form if the reactions are chemically similar (in the present case both form MX as product), and the reacting masses are not widely different.

The mass combination **L + HH** (for example, $H + Cl_2 \rightarrow HCl + Cl$) has been referred to earlier in this section as being anomalous in regard to product energy distribution. The anomaly stemmed from the low mass of the attacking atom relative to the molecule under attack. It consisted in a marked diminution in vibrational excitation, with concurrent enhancement in product translational excitation, on repulsive energy surfaces. There is a related "light-atom anomaly" in regard to product *angular* distribution. Surface four in Fig. 8 is only 28% repulsive; this is a sufficiently low product repulsion to give significant forward scattering for all mass combinations with the exception of **L + HH** and **L + HL**. These are both mass combinations that tend to channel repulsive energy release into translational rather than internal excitation of the products. The tendency for backward scattering of the molecular product can be understood in terms of the **L + HH** trajectory pictured in Fig. 11. For thermal reaction the momentum of the attacking atom $p_A$

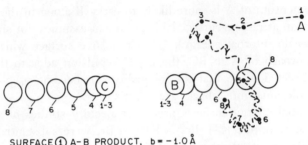

SURFACE ① A-B PRODUCT, b = -1.0 Å

FIG. 11. The mass combination **L** + **HH** reacting (in the center-of-mass frame) on a repulsive energy surface of the LEPS variety (surface ① of Fig. 8). The attacking atom A approaches roughly collinearly with a nonrotating BC. The initial line of approach of A defines the "forward" direction. The repulsion sends the ejected atom C forward, and consequently AB is sharply backward scattered. (Kuntz *et al.*, 1966).

is small. Once the repulsive energy release starts to occur, that is, shortly after stage three, atoms B and C recoil away from one another. Since A approached roughly along the BC axis (the preferred line of approach in reactive encounters on a normal LEPS surface), the direction of recoil of B is "backwards." The momentum $p_B$ greatly exceeds $p_A$; consequently, AB is sharply backward scattered.

Herschbach and co-workers (Herschbach, 1971; McDonald *et al.*, 1972) have pointed out that for the mass combination **L** + **HH** the peak of the angular distribution of the molecular product is likely to be governed by the preferred direction of approach of A to BC, since at normal BC rotational energies and normal A + BC collision energies BC will rotate little during the course of the encounter. Consequently, the observation by the same authors of a shift from backward to sideways peaked scattering in going from D + $Cl_2$ → DCl + Cl to D + $I_2$ → DI + I is indicative of a change in the preferred direction of approach of D to $X_2$ from collinear to lateral approach as $X_2$ is altered from $Cl_2$ to $I_2$ (McDonald, 1973; Polanyi and Schreiber, 1973). The stately progress of separation of the two heavy atoms in Fig. 11 is seen to be unaffected by the complicated antics of the light attacking atom. If A approaches collinearly and reacts with B it will be sharply backward scattered (as shown). The enhanced forward scattering for **L** + **HH** on the more attractive surface in Fig. 10 is likely to be due to a relaxation of the requirement for collinear approach on that surface.

This discussion has centered on the relative magnitudes of the attractive and repulsive components in the energy release. In addition to the magnitude of the potential drop, some importance attaches to the form of the drop. For collisions between atoms and stable molecules it is well known that a steep potential is much more effective in inducing vibrational excitation than a gradual one. The same consideration carries over, qualitatively, to reactive systems (see Section III). Smith (1967) has stressed the importance of the repulsive *force* in determining the extent of vibrational excitation in the "old" bond CD when a reaction A + BCD → AB + CD occurs on a repulsive surface [e.g., $O(^3P) + CS_2$ → SO + CS; the "old" bond is in CS]. The repulsive force is also an important variable in cases where the efficiency of vibrational excitation in a newly formed bond is low. Light and co-workers found a marked increase on the vibrational excitation from H + $Cl_2$ → HCl + Cl when the slope of the outrun was made steeper on a highly repulsive energy surface (these results were obtained in a series of quantum mechanical calculations for the collinear reaction; see Miller and Light, 1971a,b). A qualitatively similar effect was obtained by Kuntz *et al.* (1969a) for the **L** + **HH** mass combination in a comparison of surfaces with only ∼20% repulsive energy release.

If this additional variable were freely disposable the simple correlation between $\%\langle E_V'\rangle$ and $\%\mathscr{A}_\perp$ (Fig. 9) would disappear. Such correlations must be used with caution. They will be most instructive when applied to reactions differing widely in $\%\langle E_V'\rangle$ and consequently (provided the mass combinations are comparable) most likely differing in $\%\mathscr{A}_\perp$. Smaller changes in $\%\langle E_V'\rangle$ are most likely to correlate with $\%\mathscr{A}_\perp$ if the reactions being compared are members of a chemically "homologous series" (i.e., the same family of reactions).

Because product vibrational and angular distributions have tended to be the main experimental observables, they have been given the most attention by theorists. It is, however, now possible to obtain detailed product rotational distributions for a number of reactions (Carrington and Polanyi, 1972, and Toennies, Chapter 5, this volume). The amount of energy which is channeled into rotation in the reaction products is invariably a small fraction of that entering vibration and translation. Nonetheless, the magnitude of this fraction, its variation from one vibrational energy state of the products to the next, and its distribution over $J'$ states within the individual $v'$ states, provides a new set of clues as to the nature of the potential energy surface. More theoretical work needs to be done before it is possible to interpret these clues. One can speculate, with reasonable assurance, that there are two sources of rotational excitation among the products of exothermic reaction: (i) on attractive energy surfaces the most important source of product rotational excitation is likely to be the high impact parameter collisions which convert their large initial orbital angular momentum into product rotational excitation; (ii) on repulsive surfaces there may, in addition, be a significant contribution to the product rotational excitation arising from the release of $_AB \cdot C$ repulsion in a bent configuration, $\rightarrow AB(J' \gg 0) + C$.

Case (i), above, is exemplified in Figs. 12a and 12b. The masses are $K + Br_2$ reacting on a highly attractive surface. The rotation of product AB around its center of mass is evident in the product of (a) (the petal shape is due to concurrent vibration with rotation), and the rotation of product AC can be seen in (b): only 1% of the exothermicity ended up in rotation in case (a), 44% in case (b). The low rotation in the product of (a) was due entirely to the "clouting secondary encounter" (see below), as is evident from the trajectory. Case (ii), the channeling of repulsion into

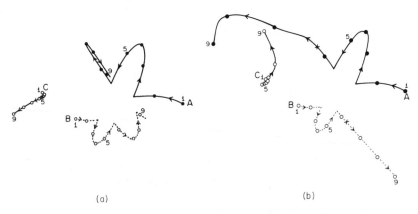

(a)                                              (b)

Fig. 12.   Two types of secondary encounter (a) clouting and (b) clutching, on an attractive surface, with Coulombic attraction. The three masses corresponded to $A \equiv K$ and $B \equiv C \equiv Br$. The trajectories are coplanar (i.e., 2D). They are pictured as they would appear to an observer whose frame of reference is locked onto the center of mass of the system. Initially he sees A approaching BC, and BC recoiling in the opposite direction. The time lapse between successive points is $0.9 \times 10^{-13}$ sec ($\sim 10^2$ steps of the Adams–Moulton integration). The initial conditions were chosen to be identical for both the trajectories pictured here. The energy surfaces were fundamentally the same, embodying the same long-range ionic attraction and small product repulsion. The surfaces differed in that for the clouting case only reaction of A with B was permitted, but for the clutching case A was attracted to C after passing through the isosceles configuration [indicated by $\times$ in (b)]. Up to the time corresponding to $\times$ (mid-way between points 6 and 7) the two trajectories are identical. The clouting in (a) causes a reversal of the direction of rotation, and backward scattering of AB (as is evident from the forward scattering of C). The clutching in (b) results in "migration," and forward scattering of the molecular product AC (Kuntz et al., 1969b).

rotation, is favored if atom B is light, since the torque exerted on AB by the primary release of repulsion, or by secondary encounters between AB and C, is maximized. The reactive trajectory for $Cl + HI \rightarrow HCl + I$ recorded in Fig. 13a exemplifies the case of an exchange reaction with light central atom occurring on a repulsive energy surface ($\mathscr{R}_\perp = 76\%$; Anlauf et al., 1968). The product molecule is highly rotationally excited, as is evident from the rapid circling of H around Cl (see the caption to Fig. 13 for details).

In the simple models of reactive encounters to be discussed in Section III, it will invariably be assumed that reactions are "direct." The most stringent criterion of directness (Polanyi, 1967) is to require that once the products start to separate they continue to do so, albeit at varying speed. If the separation between the products starts to decrease again, then the reactive encounter is labeled "indirect." (In practice, this could be too stringent a criterion, but it will serve as a basis for discussion.) The decreasing separation between the products, characteristic of an indirect reactive collision, can lead to a "secondary encounter" between them. Secondary encounters can occur with the colliding partners in many different orientations; their outcome is not easy to predict. Most often the effect of secondary encounters will be to broaden the product energy and angular distributions. Such encounters will occur (i) most frequently on highly attractive surfaces, where there is little repulsive energy to separate the products, and (ii) less commonly on repulsive surfaces, for those mass combinations which channel a very high proportion of the repulsion into internal excitation.

Category (i) is illustrated in Fig. 12 for two types of secondary encounter, both on highly attractive energy surfaces (see caption). The first type of secondary encounter (Fig. 12a), termed "clouting," involves a repulsive encounter between A and C. (The force of this encounter is such as to reverse the direction of rotation of AB, and greatly diminish its angular velocity.) The other type of secondary encounter (Fig. 12b) is favored if A can react with C. The approach of A to C gives rise to attraction, consequently, this is termed a "clutching" secondary encounter. In the case shown the clutching leads to AC being formed as product, rather than AB. Reactive collisions of this type could play a part, for example, in the dynamics of reactions in the families $M + X_2$ and $H + M_2$; attractive reactions in which both ends of the molecule under attack are reactive. Clutching secondary encounters in which A interacts strongly with B and thereafter reacts with C, have been termed "migratory" encounters. Their dynamics has been explored quite extensively (Kuntz et al., 1969a,b).

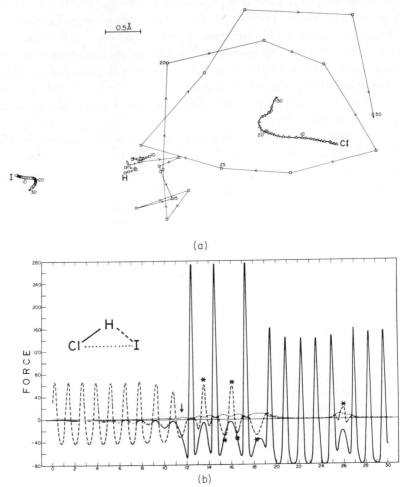

FIG. 13. (a) A center-of-mass trajectory for mixed energy release in the reaction
Cl + HI → HCl + I on a repulsive LEPS potential energy surface ($\mathscr{R}_\perp = 76\%$;
Anlauf $et~al.$, 1968). (b) The corresponding force plot. The dashed line is the force along
the HI coordinate, the solid line is the force along ClH. The units of force are kcal
mole$^{-1}$ Å$^{-1}$. Positive force is repulsive, negative attractive. At the time labeled with an
arrow in Fig. 13b the attraction in the new bond ClH for the first time exceeds the
repulsion in the old bond, HI. The force between the end atoms, which is low throughout, is recorded as a dotted line. The high vibrational excitation in the new bond is
evident from the large excursions in the solid line of (b). Following a succession of
alternating attractive and repulsive secondary encounters (late peaks in the HI force,
labeled *) the vibration in the new bond HCl has diminished. Inspection of (a) indicates
that the incipient vibration has become rotation in the same molecule; one-third of the
reaction energy became product rotation in this encounter (Wong, 1968; Parr $et~al.$, 1973).

It has yet to be established, however, in which cases migration plays a significant role. It has been argued (Kuntz *et al.*, 1969b) that migration could account for the forward scattered reaction product of K + ICl (i.e., KCl; the KI is scattered sideways and backwards; Moulton and Herschbach, 1966). Migration may also be indicated by the striking finding (Brooks, 1969, 1973) that forward scattered KI results from K + CF$_3$I when the K approaches from the CF$_3$ end.

Category (ii), in which secondary encounters occur on repulsive energy surfaces, is illustrated in Fig. 13. The mass combination for Cl + HI → HCl + I is such as to favor an exceptionally high degree of internal excitation on a repulsive energy surface (see Section II,C,2). The trajectory itself does not easily reveal the existence of secondary encounters. A clearer guide is obtained from the corresponding "force plot," shown in Fig. 13b. (Force plots record the partial derivatives of U with respect to $r_1$, $r_2$, and $r_3$ as a function of time; they are discussed by Kuntz *et al.*, 1970.) It is evident that at position 12 there is a strong attraction in the new bond, Cl–H, and a corresponding marked diminution in the force of the old bond, H–I. The large regular oscillations in the force of the new bond betoken a high initial vibrational energy. On an outward excursion away from Cl the light H atom has a repulsive secondary encounter with the slowly departing I atom (this is indicated by the first asterisk in Fig. 13b). A succession of attractive and repulsive secondary encounters (clutching and clouting) along the H–I coordinate ensue. These can be seen to have a marked effect on the oscillatory energy of the new bond Cl–H.

The trajectory and force plot of Fig. 14 have been included as an example of a direct interaction. In this abstraction reaction the product, tritium hydride, once it starts to separate from $R$, never returns. The forces go through a *single* maximum, at the time that the three particles make their closest approach.

As already remarked the gross effect of numerous secondary encounters is likely to be a broadening of the energy and angular distributions. If these distributions are broad even for direct encounters, then the net effect will be slight, and simple models (on the lines of those that will be examined in Section III) will have a good chance of predicting the outcome. If, on the other hand, the direct encounters give rise to a narrow distribution over $E_V'$, $E_R'$, $E_T'$, and $\theta'$, then the occurrence of secondary encounters will make the simple models less useful—except as a method for ascertaining the importance of secondary encounters in the reaction dynamics.

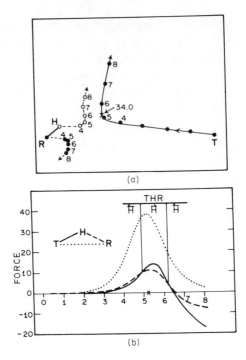

(a)

(b)

Fig. 14.   (a) Trajectory for the abstraction reaction T + HR → TH + R, where
T ≡ 3 amu, H ≡ 1 amu, and R ≡ 15 amu. The reagent translational energy is 2 eV,
$\alpha = 40°$, $b = 0.9$ Å. The × in (a) indicates the maximum potential energy relative to
the reagents as zero. The × in (b) indicates, on the same time scale as (a), the time at
which the total force reached its maximum. The symbols above the force curves in (b)
indicate whether there is a net force moving the central atom toward the attacking atom
T or away from it (Kuntz *et al.*, 1970).

In Fig. 9 it was observed that at very high $\%\mathscr{A}_\perp$ the $\%\langle E_V'\rangle$ obtained
from detailed trajectory calculations was significantly less than the value
of $\langle E_V'\rangle \sim 90\%$ predicted by the simple correlation. This discrepancy
was traced to a broadening of the product vibrational energy distribution
arising from the occurrence of secondary encounters on the most highly
attractive surface (Kuntz *et al.*, 1966).

### 2. *Mixed Energy Release*

The contrast in reaction dynamics on *highly* attractive and on *highly*
repulsive potential energy surfaces is valid for all reactant mass combinations. However, within a more probable range of variation, such as that
exemplified by the range of potential energy surfaces pictured in Fig. 8,

reactant mass combination can be as important a variable as $\%_{v}\mathscr{A}_{\perp}$ and $\%_{v}\mathscr{R}_{\perp}$.

Reference has been made to the fact that the masses **L + HH** occupy a special position among mass combinations. Figure 9, linking $\%\langle E_{V}'\rangle$ in a simple fashion to $\%_{v}\mathscr{A}_{\perp}$, was drawn only for the **L + HH** mass combination. The special feature has been identified with the fact that the attacking atom A is light. The consequence of this is that A can approach to something approximating the normal AB equilibrium separation before the B · C repulsion separates the heavy atoms B and C. The B · C repulsion will therefore be inefficient in channeling energy into AB vibration, for much the same reasons that translation-to-vibration transfer in collisions AB + C → AB · C is inefficient. The low efficiency of even quite strong interactions in inducing vibration in already existing bonds is illustrated by the low vibrational excitation in the "old" bond CD following reaction A + BCD → AB + CD (Carrington and Polanyi, 1972). Trajectory calculations on this system (Raff, 1966; Smith, 1967) predict only very moderate excitation of the "old bond" CD.

The dynamics of most chemical reactions differs markedly from that encountered in translation-to-vibration transfer. If A is of normal mass and energy it approaches B *while* the B · C repulsion is being released. So long as the A—B bond is extended, the repulsion A—B · C is in a favorable situation to give rise to recoil of B, and hence internal excitation of AB rather than recoil of AB as a whole. The release of B · C repulsion while the new bond A—B is extended has been termed "mixed energy release" (Polanyi, 1965). While mixed energy release is taking place the representative point on the energy surface is moving simultaneously toward smaller $r_1$ and large $r_2$, that is, it is "cutting the corner" of the energy surface. Considerations of the sliding mass make it clear why this "corner cutting" should enhance the product vibrational excitation. Even if the energy release is along the exit valley $r_2$ (as on a repulsive energy surface) corner cutting will bring the sliding mass into the exit valley from the side; an oscillatory motion will ensue.

The anomalous case of the very light attacking atom is represented by a sliding mass that travels down the entry valley to $r_1 \sim r_1^0$, and then enters the downward sloping exit valley (not at its side but) at its head. The repulsive energy release in this anomalous case largely accelerates the sliding mass along $r_2$, that is, gives rise to high translational energy in the products.

If the extent of mixed energy release is gauged by the likelihood that a sliding mass will cut the corner of the potential energy surface, it is easy to see that a favorable mass combination for mixed energy release will be $H + HL \rightarrow HH + L$. The scaling (and slight skewing) of the energy surface [Eqs. (2.6) and (2.7)] is such as to make the entry valley long (this simply ensures that the approach of $H$ to $HL$ shall be slow) and the exit valley short and broad ($HH$ and $L$ separate quickly). The thermoneutral energy surface scaled in this fashion will be pictured in Section II,C,3. We have, for this mass combination on a repulsive exothermic surface, a narrow level path that borders on a broad downward sloping valley. There are many diagonal paths a rolling ball could take down this broad valley.

The anomalous light atom case, by contrast, is exemplified in its most extreme form by the mass combination $L + HH \rightarrow LH + H$. The appropriate scaled surface will be illustrated, for thermoneutral reaction, in Section II,C,3. For a repulsive exothermic surface we have the converse of the $H + HL$ situation described above. A broad level meadow leads at one corner to a narrow slowly descending valley. If a rolling ball is to find its way into the narrow exit valley it must start at the head of that valley. Lateral entry into this slowly descending valley would, moreover, only lead to strong oscillatory motion of the rolling ball, if it occurred well down the valley (i.e., well along $r_2$). This, in turn, would require the crossing of a high-energy barrier. Consequently, at normal collision energies $L + HH$ will not exhibit mixed energy release.

The extension of the entry valley and compression of the exit valley that favors mixed energy release is purely a scaling effect. Inspection of Eq. (2.7) for the scaling factor $c$ shows that this effect will be greatest if $m_A > m_C$, with $m_B$ large. There is a second type of distortion of the potential energy surface that favors mixed energy release, and hence enhances vibrational excitation on repulsive energy surfaces. This is an acute skewing. From Eq. (2.6) it is evident that the skewing angle $\theta$ is maximized if $m_A \sim m_C \gg m_B$. This situation is realized for some hydrogen atom transfer reactions, such as the $X + HY \rightarrow XH + Y$ family (X and Y are halogen atoms). For sharply skewed axes the sliding mass is likely to bounce off the repulsive wall of the entry valley and enter the exit valley from the side, cutting the corner of the surface in the manner characteristic of mixed energy release. The high vibrational energy that it picks up in the process can return it to the entry valley one or more times; the oscillations of the sliding mass, trapped in the jaws of an extremely skewed surface, correspond to the secondary encounters recorded in Fig. 13 for Cl + HI. The sliding mass picture is, however, likely to exaggerate the frequency of secondary encounters, since it refers only to the case where the three atoms are constrained throughout to remain in a single straight line.

The significance of these purely kinematic effects is evident from a comparison of $\%\langle E_V'\rangle$ for two mass combinations, both on surface ①: (a) for **L + HH**, $\langle E_V'\rangle \approx 14\%$ (as indicated in Fig. 9), and (b) for **H + HL**, $\langle E_V'\rangle \approx 65\%$ (Kuntz et al., 1966). Figure 7b shows the large fraction of the available energy channeled into vibration by the reaction $Cl + HI \rightarrow HCl + I$, experimentally and theoretically. The "theory" was a 3D trajectory calculation on a strongly repulsive ($\mathscr{R}_\perp = 76\%$) LEPS energy surface (Anlauf et al., 1968). To test the importance of mass combination in bringing about this result, the same surface was used in a calculation of the **L + HH** system; a marked drop in mean vibrational excitation was observed. The computed angular distribution for the room temperature $Cl + HI$ reaction included significant forward scattering (Anlauf et al., 1968; Parr et al., 1973), whereas the $H + Cl_2$ system gave exclusively backward scattering (Anlauf et al., 1967). The sharp backward scattering for $H + Cl_2$ and substantial forward scattering for $Cl + HI$ have been observed in recent molecular beam studies (McDonald et al., 1972; McDonald and Herschbach, 1972). It appears a reasonable surmise that both the $H + Cl_2$ and the $Cl + HI$ reactions are occurring on predominantly repulsive potential energy surfaces. The difference in energy distribution and angular distribution between them is linked to the light atom anomaly in the $H + Cl_2$ case, and mixed energy release in the $Cl + HI$ case. There is reason to believe that the reaction $F + H_2$, which is known to channel its reaction energy efficiently into vibration (see, for example, Polanyi and Woodall, 1972), occurs on a very repulsive potential energy surface (Muckerman, 1971; Jaffe and Anderson, 1971). Here again the attacking atom is heavy, and mixed energy release is operative.

Though the operation of the light atom anomaly is most evident on predominantly repulsive energy surfaces, it may still be observable on attractive surfaces (see, however, Bunker and Blais, 1964; Bunker and Parr, 1970), since it affects the efficiency with which the relatively small repulsive fraction of the energy release is channeled into vibration in the new bond. Thus Kuntz et al. (1969a) found that, on a surface with $80\%$ attraction and only $20\%$ repulsion, a change in the mass combination from **H + LL** to **L + HH** decreased $\langle E_V'\rangle$ from 93 to $76\%$. Parrish and Herm (1969) have collected experimental data on the mean product translational excitation following the reaction $M + Br_2 \rightarrow MBr + Br$ as the mass of $M$ is increased from Li (7 amu) to Cs (133 amu). The results for $\langle E_T' \rangle$ in the sequence $M \equiv$ Li, Na, K, Rb, Cs, are: 6.6, 5.1, 3.7, 2.8, and 1.8 kcal mole$^{-1}$. They suggest that this may be due to the effect of increasingly mixed energy release, channeling the small repulsive energy more efficiently into *vibration* (the main repository for the reaction energy). This is at least a plausible explanation, in view of the fact that the atoms that are repelling one another are Br · Br in every case, and the most obvious variable is the mass combination.

Repulsive potential energy surfaces which are flatter in the region adjacent to the uplands of the exit valley will be more conducive to mixed energy release (Light, 1971). Such surfaces, with a minimum energy path that permits a sliding mass to cut the corner and enter the exit valley from the side, would be expected to favor mixed energy release. Even if the surfaces were indistinguishable according to the perpendicular method of categorization ($\mathscr{A}_\perp, \mathscr{R}_\perp$) they would give very different $\langle E_V' \rangle$ in the reaction products, for a given mass combination. A scheme of categorization is required which includes some measure of the extent to which the surface is conducive to mixed energy release. Two such methods of categorization have been employed (Kuntz *et al.*, 1966).

In the first method the minimum energy path on the collinear surface is divided into three parts: $\mathscr{A}_M$, $\mathscr{M}_M$, and $\mathscr{R}_M$ (the subscript refers to the minimum path). The path is regarded as having deviated significantly from the entry valley $r_1$ when $r_2$ exceeds the normal classical amplitude for BC with a vibrational energy of either $k_B T$ or $v = 0$, whichever is greater (this deviation is in the range 0.01–0.1 Å depending on BC). Energy released thereafter is no longer $\mathscr{A}_M$ but $\mathscr{M}_M$. A similar criterion can be used to determine when the minimum path is to be regarded as having joined the exit valley. Energy released after this is $\mathscr{R}_M$. For a single mass combination the minimum path categorization may provide a useful guide to the relative importance of $\mathscr{A}$, $\mathscr{M}$, and $\mathscr{R}$ on different potential energy surfaces (Muckerman, 1972). However, in the case that varying mass combinations are involved, the minimum path criterion will be inadequate, since different mass combinations take characteristic paths across the potential energy surface, that differ in varying degrees from the minimum energy path. In this case it is necessary to base $\mathscr{A}$, $\mathscr{M}$, and $\mathscr{R}$ either on the path that a sliding mass takes across the skewed and scaled energy surface or, more conveniently, on the computed path of a single collinear trajectory. The path taken by this trajectory can be divided up in a similar fashion to that used for aportioning the minimum energy path (see Kuntz *et al.*, 1966, Perry *et al.*, 1974, for details) so as to obtain $\mathscr{A}_T$, $\mathscr{M}_T$, and $\mathscr{R}_T$ for the particular surface. Since both attractive and mixed energy release are channeled efficiently into vibration, one can get a satisfactory measure of the mean vibrational excitation in the reaction product from $\langle E_{V'} \rangle \approx (\mathscr{A}_T + \mathscr{M}_T)$ (Kuntz et al., 1966; Smith, 1967; Muckerman, 1972).

### 3. Barrier Location

Sections II,A,1 and II,A,2, dealing with attractive, repulsive, and mixed energy release, have been concerned with exothermic reactions. (The discussion of 1 and 2 also has a definite bearing on the fate of energy released in thermoneutral or endothermic reactions, as the representative point moves down the far side of the energy barrier.) The present section has to do with the dynamical "problem" of barrier crossing—a question which is of importance for any energy surface, whether exothermic, thermoneutral, or endothermic, if it has a barrier of significant height located somewhere along the reaction coordinate.

The most detailed studies that exist in relation to any single potential energy surface come from the work of Karplus and co-workers on the exchange reaction $H + H_2 \rightarrow H_2 + H$. Their potential energy surface (Porter and Karplus, 1964) was based on a more complete formulation of the London equation for $H_3$ than is used in the LEPS approach. The equation is, nonetheless, very approximate. Some empiricism was introduced into the solution with the object of improving its accuracy. A smooth potential energy surface was obtained with a classical barrier height $E_c = 9.13$ kcal mole$^{-1}$ for collinear reaction. The collinear surface is necessarily symmetrical about $r_1 = r_2$. Provided there is only a single barrier, as was found to be the case, its crest must be located on this line of symmetry at a point half way along the reaction coordinate. The properties of this surface have been reviewed recently (Karplus, 1970). Insertion of theoretical cross sections into Eq. (1.18) permitted the rate constant $k$ to be calculated as a function of temperature. The dependence of $k$ on $T$ agreed well with the Arrhenius equation (1.2). The Arrhenius activation energy taken from Eq. (1.19) was found to be $E_{exp} = 7.44$ kcal mole$^{-1}$. The fact that this is in quite close accord with experiment (Ridley et al., 1966; Westenberg and de Haas, 1967; LeRoy et al., 1967) shows that the surface is an admissible one. It is noteworthy that $E_{exp}$ is significantly less than $E_c$.

Examination of the cross section functions which went into the calculation of $k(T)$ showed that both vibrational and translational energy in the reagents contributed efficiently to the energy required for barrier crossing (Karplus *et al.*, 1965). Reagent rotational energy did not contribute to barrier crossing; in fact, the presence of rotation slightly increased the threshold collision energy for reaction.

The reaction was almost invariably direct. Any reference to an "intermediate" or "activated complex" for this reaction is no more than a formal designation, in order to convey the idea that the totality of collisions produces something resembling an equilibrium distribution over the degrees of freedom available to a hypothetical intermediate. Energy analysis of a group of trajectories as it passed over the barrier crest revealed that, to a good approximation, both the reaction coordinate (asymmetric stretch) and the symmetric stretch coordinate corresponded to Boltzmann distributions, with a characteristic temperature close to that of the reagents. This is a condition for application of absolute rate theory (transition state theory), which is therefore obeyed to good accuracy by $H + H_2$ (Morokuma *et al.*, 1969; Morokuma and Karplus, 1971).

The dynamics alter markedly in the case that the barrier is displaced from the symmetric position characteristic of $H + H_2$. This has been shown in a model study in which batches of $3D$ trajectories were run on contrasting potential energy hypersurfaces of the LEPS type (Wong and Polanyi, 1969). Collinear cuts through these contrasting surfaces are shown in Fig. 15. In order to stress the fact that the computations do not restrict the reactions to these collinear surfaces, the surfaces are sometimes described as being "diagnostic" cuts through the hypersurface

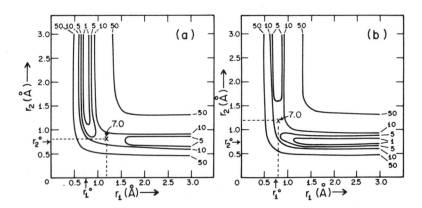

FIG. 15.   (a) Potential energy "surface I" for collinear reaction. (b) Potential energy "surface II" for collinear reaction. These surfaces are cuts through the corresponding hypersurfaces used in the $3D$ trajectory calculations described in the text. All energies are in kcal mole$^{-1}$, relative to the reagents as zero. Reaction proceeds from lower right to upper left so that I is an early barrier and II is a late one (Polanyi and Wong, 1969).

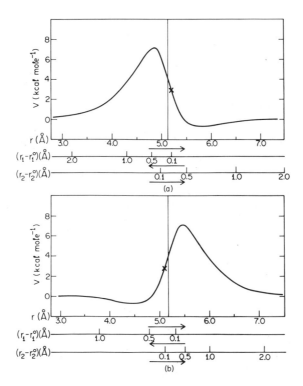

FIG. 16. Energy profiles showing the changes in potential energy along the minimum paths (a) of "surface I" and (b) of "surface II." Two methods were used to indicate the point along the reaction coordinate at which the entry valley gives way to the exit valley: (i) the vertical line indicates the point where $r_1 - r_1^0 = r_2 - r_2^0$ and (ii) the $\times$ indicates the point at which the tangent to the minimum path is perpendicular to the bisector of the 90° angle between the $r_1$ and $r_2$ axes of Fig. 15. These are comparable definitions of the "entry" and "exit" valleys (for the present case).

(similarly, the division of energy release for exothermic reactions in Sections II,C,1 and II,C,2 was based on a diagnostic collinear cut through the hypersurface). The surfaces used in this model calculation described a thermoneutral reaction. The shape of the 7 kcal mole$^{-1}$ barrier was identical on surfaces I and II, but the location of the crest was shifted from the entry valley (on I) to the exit valley (on II).

Figure 16 shows this shift in terms of the energy profile along the minimum energy path across each surface. The vertical line indicates the configuration for which the extension in the new bond relative to its normal equilibrium separation is equal to the extension in the old bond, i.e., $r_1 - r_1^0 = r_2 - r_2^0$. We can regard this, arbitrarily, as the point at which the entry valley gives way to the exit valley (or, expressed in different terms, the approach coordinate meets the retreat coordinate). The energy profile shows clearly that despite a shift in the barrier *crest* from the entry valley into the exit valley ($r_1 - r_1^0 = 0.03$ Å on surface I; $r_2 - r_2^0 = 0.03$ Å on surface II) the barrier itself is broad enough to extend into both the entry and the exit valley on surface I, and on surface II.

A shift in barrier location by this amount was sufficient to give rise to a fundamental change in reaction dynamics. This is illustrated for the equal mass case in Fig. 17. (The masses were **L + LL**, but any other equal mass combination would give precisely the same dynamics. Kuntz *et al.*, 1966). With the barrier in the approach coordinate (Fig. 17a;

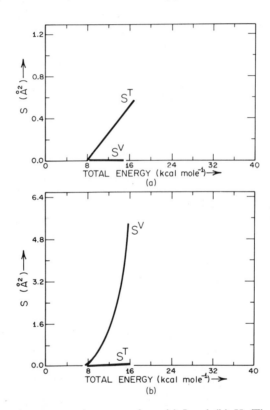

FIG. 17. Reactive cross sections on surfaces (a) I and (b) II. The curves labeled $S^T$ give the cross section as a function of the collision energy $E_T$. The curves labeled $S^V$ give the cross section as a function of reagent vibrational energy $E_V$ plus a constant translational energy $E_T = 1.5$ kcal mole$^{-1}$ (required to bring the reagents together). The reaction was **L + LL** (Polanyi and Wong, 1969).

surface I) a reagent translational energy only slightly in excess of the barrier height gave a calculable reaction cross section; by contrast a reagent vibrational energy *double* the barrier height gave a reactive cross section too small to be computed. The converse behavior was found for surface II (Fig. 17b); reagent vibrational energy (with a small admixture of translation to bring the reagents together) was highly effective in promoting reaction, whereas translation was ineffective.

Here again the sliding mass analog, applicable to collinear reactive encounters, is revealing. If the major part of the barrier (including its highest point) lies along $r_1$ ($r_2 \approx r_2^0$) then momentum of the sliding mass along $r_1$, i.e., reagent translation, will carry the mass over the barrier. If, by contrast, the crest of the barrier is in the exit valley, then a significant portion of the uphill slope lies along $r_2$ ($r_1 \approx r_1^0$). The sliding mass cannot efficiently convert momentum along $r_1$ into momentum along $r_2$. It is preferable in this case to give the sliding mass momentum perpendicular to the entrance valley (corresponding to reagent vibration). Provided the phase of the oscillation is right, the oscillating mass will convert lateral momentum across the entry valley into longitudinal momentum along the exit valley, thus successfully surmounting that part of the barrier which is located in the exit valley. These motions are illustrated in Figs. 18 and 19.

If barrier location is to be used as anything more than a crude qualitative index of the reaction dynamics, the location of the barrier should be considered as it appears on the surface skewed and scaled for the appropriate reagent mass combination [Eqs. (2.6) and (2.7)]. Figures 18 and 19 (Hodgson and Polanyi, 1971) show the shape of the same surfaces pictured in Fig. 15 as they appear when they have been skewed and scaled so that a sliding mass will solve the classical equations of motion for collinear **L + HH** (Fig. 18) and **H + HL** (Fig. 19). These two mass combinations have been chosen for purposes of illustration since they correspond to the two extreme forms of scaling. (The **L + HH** case was representative of the extreme light atom anomaly in Section II,C,2; **H+HL** represented an extreme of mixed energy release.) The generalization that $S^T > S^V$ (these being the reactive cross sections with the reagent energy in translation or predominantly in vibration) on surface I, whereas $S^V > S^T$ on surface II were still applicable to these extreme mass combinations. Some modifications in behavior were apparent. For **L + HH** (Fig. 18) the stretching of the exit valley had the effect of displacing the barrier to a later position. Consequently, the behavior which characterized surface I was less marked, that for surface II

more marked. The converse was true for **H + HL**: surface I behavior
($S^T > S^V$) was accentuated and surface II behavior ($S^V > S^T$) was
lessened. Clearly it would be advantageous to redefine barrier location
with respect to a datum line on the skewed and scaled surface. This
datum line (the point at which entry and exit valleys meet) could be
established in much the way that the locations labeled × were obtained
in Fig. 16; × would be the point at which the tangent to the minimum
energy path was perpendicular to the bisector of the angle between the
axes of the (skewed and scaled) surface.

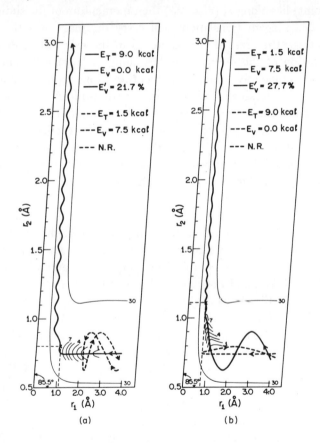

FIG. 18.   Collinear trajectories for the mass combination **L + HH** (L = 1 amu,
**H** = 80 amu) on scaled and skewed surfaces; (a) surface I, (b) surface II. The angle of
skewing is 4.5°, the $r_2$ axis is elongated by a factor of 6.84×. (a) Surface I; for the solid
line the reagents have exclusively $E_T$; for the broken line the reagents have almost
exclusively $E_V$. (b) Surface II; for the solid line the reagents have almost exclusively
$E_V$; for the broken line the reagents have exclusively $E_T$ (Hodgson and Polanyi, 1971).

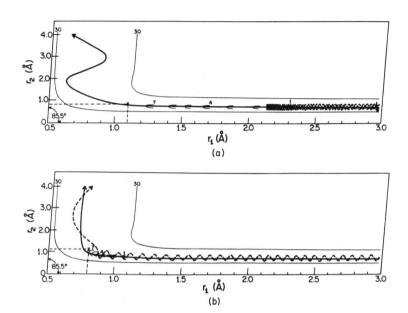

Fig. 19. Collinear trajectories for mass combination **H** + **HL** on scaled and skewed surfaces; (a) surface I, (b) surface II. For this mass combination the skewing angle was again 4.5°, but in this case the $r_1$ axis was elongated by 6.84×. (a) Surface I; for the solid line the reagents have exclusively $E_T$ ($E_T = 9.0$ kcal, $E_V = 0.0$ kcal, $E_V' = 87.7\%$); for the broken line the reagents have almost exclusively $E_V$ ($E_T = 1.5$ kcal, $E_V = 7.5$ kcal, no reaction). (b) Surface II; for the solid line the reagents have exclusively $E_T$ ($E_T = 9.0$ kcal, $E_V = 0.0$ kcal, $E_V' = 1.9\%$); for the broken line the reagents have almost exclusively $E_V$ ($E_T = 1.5$ kcal, $E_V = 7.5$ kcal, $E_V' = 36.9\%$). Primed quantities refer to the product (Hodgson and Polanyi, 1971).

It should be observed that the ordinate on Fig. 17b is on one quarter the scale of that for Fig. 17a: the absolute cross sections for $S^V$ on surface II greatly exceed those for $S^T$ on surface I. The large cross sections at high vibrational energy were due to reaction at large impact parameter at the moment that B–C was approaching maximum extension.

The reactive cross section was markedly less for **L** + **HH** than for **H** + **HL** both on surface I and II. This can most easily be understood from the skewed and scaled surfaces. (The form of these surfaces was commented on from the same standpoint, though in the context of product energy distribution, in Section II,C,2.) For **L** + **HH** the sliding mass must find its way from a broad valley into a narrow one; a less probable process than the converse, which characterizes **H** + **HL**.

It was found, for both surfaces and all mass combinations, that there was a tendency on these thermoneutral surfaces for reagent energy close to the threshold for reaction, to be transposed in the products: on surface I, $E_T \to E_V'$; on surface II, $E_V \to E_T'$. This transposition occurs as the system negotiates the corner of the surface. Since the barrier crest is beyond the corner on surface II, and since the reactive trajectories have a low $E_T$, the hypothetical "activated state" at the barrier crest will be lacking in vibration. Koeppl and Karplus (1971) have examined the energy distribution at the barrier crest, using the same surfaces as are pictured in Fig. 15, and have found a deviation from "equilibrium" in this sense. Nonetheless, the discrepancy between their trajectory and absolute rate theory "average cross sections" amounts to less than a factor of 2.

Reagent energy $\Delta E$ in excess of that required for barrier crossing, does *not* suffer transposition as reagents are converted to products. Instead $\Delta E_T \to \Delta E_T'$, and $\Delta E_V \to \Delta E_V'$ (Polanyi and Wong, 1969; Ding et al., 1973). This has been explained by a shift toward reaction through more-compressed configurations when $\Delta E_T \to \Delta E_T'$, and more-extended configurations when $\Delta E_V \to \Delta E_V'$. The former effect can be characterised as involving induced repulsive energy release, the latter as involving induced attractive energy-release (Ding et al., 1973; Polanyi, 1973).

For all the thermoneutral reactions referred to in this section—whether the barrier is symmetric, early, or late—reaction at energies in the region of the threshold energy for reaction leads to computed differential cross sections that are peaked in the backward direction, that is, the molecular product is thrown back along the direction from which the attacking atom came. This is true for all mass combinations. On surface I, for which the reagent energy takes the form of translation, the **L + HH** mass combination gives markedly sharper backward scattering than does **H + HL**. All this constitutes a close parallel to the behavior described earlier (Sections II,C,1 and II,C,2) for repulsive exothermic energy surfaces. The AB · C repulsion in the present, thermoneutral, case arises from that part of the energy barrier that lies along $r_2$ (see also Polanyi, 1967).

A study of reaction dynamics on surfaces with "early" and "late" energy barriers comparable to that described for $A + BC \to AB + C$ above, has been made for the four-center exchange reaction $AB + CD \to AC + BD$ (Mok and Polanyi, 1970). Barrier location was defined in terms of a diagnostic potential energy surface which considered only reaction by way of rectangular coplanar configurations. Judging by these cuts through the full hypersurfaces, surface I had a 34 kcal mole$^{-1}$ barrier with its crest displaced by about 0.3 Å into the entry valley, and surface

II had a similar barrier displaced 0.3 Å into the exit valley. Trajectory calculations with the atoms free to move in $3D$ yielded $S^T > S^V$ on surface I, $S^V > S^T$ on surface II—as before. On surface II (for **LL+LL**) it was found that an equal distribution of the vibration between the reacting molecules was somewhat more favorable to reaction than an unequal distribution. Figure 20 shows (a) a reactive trajectory on surface I with $70\,\text{kcal mole}^{-1}$ reagent translational energy, and (b) a reactive trajectory on surface II with $34\,\text{kcal mole}^{-1}$ of vibration in each of the reagent molecules. On surface I reagent translation $E_T$ at threshold was channeled into internal excitation of the products $(E_V{}' + E_R{}')$, and on surface II the tendency was for $E_V \to E_T{}'$; this behavior is evident in the specimen trajectories of Fig. 20. Here again there is evidence of a transposition of reagent energy at threshold into complementary degrees of freedom in the products of thermoneutral reaction.

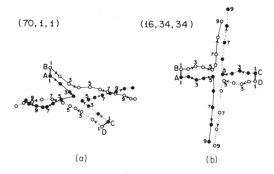

(a)                                   (b)

FIG. 20. Planar trajectories for the reaction AB + CD → AC + BD (a) on surface I (early barrier) and (b) on surface II (late barrier). (a) The reagent translational energy was $E_T = 70\,\text{kcal mole}^{-1}$, and the reagent vibrational energies in AB and CD were $(E_V)_{AB} = 1\,\text{kcal mole}^{-1}$ and $(E_V)_{CD} = 1\,\text{kcal mole}^{-1}$. (b) $E_T = 16\,\text{kcal mole}^{-1}$ $(E_V)_{AB} = (E_V)_{CD} = 34\,\text{kcal mole}^{-1}$. Translation gives rise to reaction on surface I; vibration on surface II (Mok and Polanyi, 1970).

An earlier computation on AB + CD → AC + BD by Morokuma *et al.* (1967) investigated the bimolecular reaction between hydrogen molecules in various states of initial vibrational excitation. The barrier crest on their rectangular coplanar potential energy surface was (as would be expected) symmetrically placed, corresponding to a square configuration. In this case both $E_T$ and $E_V$ were effective in promoting reaction.

The studies of the effect of barrier location on reaction dynamics, described above, stemmed from earlier work in which the location of the barrier crest was identified as being in the approach coordinate for exothermic reactions and in the retreat coordinate for endothermic reactions (Polanyi, 1959). This identification was made on the basis of a valence bond model employing similar assumptions to the LEP method. The location of the barrier for exothermic reaction in the approach coordinate, it was argued, would ensure that enough of the energy was released at extended $r_1$ (as attractive and mixed energy release, it would now be said) to result in efficient vibrational excitation of the new bond. Conversely, endothermic reaction, with the barrier crest in the retreat coordinate would require predominantly reagent vibrational excitation for reaction to occur.

The two essential components of this argument had to do with (i) correlation between barrier location and major changes in reaction energy (exothermic as distinct from endothermic reaction), and (ii) correlation between barrier location and reaction dynamics. Trajectory studies, as noted above, have been able to illuminate (ii). Item (i), since it requires a dependable method for calculating potential energy surfaces, is less tractable. The best we can do, for the moment, is to look for common features of surfaces calculated by different approximate methods. The Bond Energy Bond Order method (BEBO: Johnston, 1960, 1966; Johnston and Parr, 1963) provides a valuable check on the qualitative predictions of the LEPS approach, since each is based on a different type of empiricism. The BEBO method rests on Pauling's relationship between bond energy and bond order, together with the assumption that, in hydrogen atom transfer reactions (for which, according to Pauling's relationship the initial and final bond orders, $n_2^0$ and $n_1^0$, must be unity), the total bonding is such that $n_1 + n_2 = 1$ throughout. Maximization of bonding along the minimum energy path is to be expected, and conservation of bonding appears reasonable. That it is reasonable is confirmed by the success of the BEBO method in predicting energy barriers correctly for almost 130 H-atom transfer reactions to within 2 or 3 kcal mole$^{-1}$.

Figure 21 shows the potential-energy profile along the reaction coordinate for three different families of H-atom transfer reaction as obtained using the BEBO method (Mok and Polanyi, 1969). It is evident that as the barrier-height falls within a family of reactions, the location of the barrier crest shifts systematically to "earlier" positions along the reaction coordinate (lower $n_1$ corresponding to larger $r_1$). This same behavior was observed in the LEPS approximation. Within a family of exothermic reactions it was found that as the barrier height decreased and the barrier shifted to earlier positions, more of the reaction energy

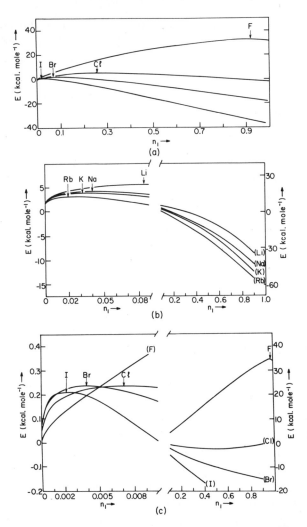

FIG. 21. Energy profiles along the reaction coordinate for the families of reaction (a) H + HX (X≡F, Cl, Br, I), (b) H + HM (M≡Li, Na, K, Rb), (c) Cl + HX (X≡F, Cl, Br, I); all calculated by the Bond Energy Bond Order method and plotted against the bond order of the single bond being formed. The arrows indicate the locations of the crests of the barriers (Mok and Polanyi, 1969).

was liberated along the approach coordinate, i.e., $\mathscr{A}_\perp$ increased. The relationship within families of reactions was

$$\Delta \log E_c = -(\beta_1^l/\gamma_1)\,\Delta(\mathscr{A}_\perp) \tag{2.8}$$

with $\beta_1^l/\gamma_1$ typically $\sim 1 \times 10^{-2}$ ($\beta_1^l$ governs the relationship between the barrier height and the extension of the new bond at the crest of the barrier, $r_1^{\ddagger,0}$; $\gamma_1$ governs the relationship between $r_1^{\ddagger,0}$ and $\mathscr{A}_\perp$). At the present stage of our knowledge, Eq. (2.8) deserves more credence as a qualitative relationship than as a quantitative one (Mok and Polanyi, 1969, were able to provide one experimental test). It forms part of the broader qualitative conclusion, based on 18 LEPS and 14 BEBO energy profiles, that the crest of the energy barrier for substantially exothermic reactions lies in the entry valley, and the crest of the energy barrier for endothermic reactions lies in the exit valley. [Organic chemists will recognize this as providing a rationale for Hammond's postulate (Hammond, 1955).] In the light of the studies of barriers of types I and II, this implies that the cross sections for exothermic reactions will rise most steeply with increasing translational energy in the reagents, whereas the cross sections for the endothermic reactions will rise most steeply with increasing vibrational energy in the bond under attack.

A trajectory study of the endothermic reaction $HF + H \rightarrow F + H_2$ (Anderson, 1970) exemplifies this. Trajectories were run in $1D$. The endothermic barrier was $E_c = 33.0 \text{ kcal mole}^{-1}$; a little less than the vibrational energy of the $v = 3$ state of HF. A negligible reaction cross section was found for HF in $v = 0$ and 1, but considerable reaction for $v \geq 2$. It was concluded that for the collinear system with a thermal energy distribution in the reagents, reaction must proceed almost exclusively as $H + HF$ ($v = 2$), that is, with $28 \text{ kcal mole}^{-1}$ present as vibration in the bond being broken. The findings for this system have been substantiated and extended in $3D$ by Wilkins (1973). A 3D trajectory calculation on another endothermic surface (embodying a considerable range of reagent energies and mass combinations) provides further confirmation for the view that the dynamics of endothermic reaction resemble those for reaction on "surface II" (Perry et al., 1974b).

Experimental evidence for the proposition that $S^V > S^T$ for substantially endothermic reactions, has been accumulating (Parker and Pimentel, 1969; Anlauf et al., 1969; Polanyi and Tardy, 1969). The most detailed experimental data at the present time come from application of microscopic reversibility to the "detailed rate constants" for exothermic reactions, obtained by the infrared chemiluminescence method (Carrington and Polanyi, 1972; see Section I of the present article for an account of the theory relating $k_f$ to $k_r$, where $k_r$ in the present case is the detailed endothermic rate constant. For confirmation of the validity of the procedure see Perry et al., 1974a). An example is given in Fig. 22. The contours in Fig. 22 are lines of equal detailed rate constant $k_r(E_V'$,

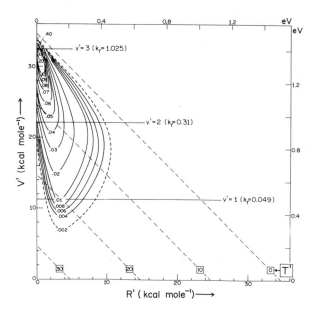

FIG. 22. Experimental data indicative of the high efficiency of reagent vibration in promoting an endothermic reaction. Contours join points of equal detailed rate constant $k_{endo}(V', R', T')$ for the endothermic reaction HF $(V', R')$ + H → F + H$_2$. The energies $V'$ (ordinate), $R'$ (abscissa), and $T'$ (increasing toward the $V' = 0$, $R' = 0$ corner of the figure, as recorded by the diagonal grid) refer to the *reagent* vibrational, rotational, and translational excitation for endothermic reaction. The contours describe a mountain with its peak at high $V'$, and low $R'$ and $T'$. Note that $k_{endo}(V', R', T')$ is given for a constant total reagent energy of $E'_{tot} = 34.7$ kcal mole$^{-1}$ (Polanyi and Tardy, 1969).

$E_R'$, $E_T'$) for the endothermic reaction HF + H → F + H$_2$ (in the figure $E_{V'}$, $E_{R'}$, $E_{T'}$, the reagent vibrational, rotational, and translational energies for endothermic reaction, are symbolized $V'$, $R'$, and $T'$. Primes were previously used to designate *products* of exothermic reaction; for consistency we use them now to designate *reagents* of endothermic reaction). The values of $E_V'$ and $E_R'$ are given along the ordinate and abscissa, respectively ($E_V'$ is measured relative to the energy of vibrational level $v' = 0$). The total energy available for distribution is fixed, consequently, a grid of diagonal lines gives the reagent translational energies $E_T'$ increasing from right to left. It should be noted that detailed rate constants $k_r(E_V', E_R', E_T')$ are closely related to the corresponding cross-section function. They differ in that the cross section would, additionally, be fully specified as to $E_V$, $E_R$ and $E_T$ (energies of the products of endothermic reaction) whereas $k_r(E_V', E_R', E_T')$ involves some averaging over these quantities; see section I, D., Eq. (1.23). Perry *et al.* (1974a) have shown that this averaging is unimportant provided that (as is the case here) the detailed rate constant refers to energies close to the threshold for endothermic reaction. Figure 22 shows that the detailed rate constants for endothermic reaction are low for low vibrational levels of the molecule under attack. From the contours it is apparent that the highest rate constant for vibrational level $v' = 0$ (corresponding to $E_V' \equiv V' = 0$) comes at a reagent translational energy of $E_T' \equiv T'$ $\approx 30$ kcal mole$^{-1}$, and a reagent rotational energy of $E_R' \equiv R' \approx 5$ kcal mole$^{-1}$. The magnitude of $k_r$ ($V' = 0$, $R' = 5$, $T' = 30$), judging by the downward slope of the $k_r$ "hill" from $v' = 3$ down to $v' = 1$, is $\ll 0.001$. If we take 28 kcal mole$^{-1}$ of the translational energy, and also the major part of the rotational energy, and put it into vibration, we obtain a detailed rate constant of 0.40 for the most reactive $J'$ level of $v' = 3$. By redistributing the reagent energy for this endothermic reaction so as to favor reagent vibration, we have increased the detailed rate constant by $\gtrsim 10^3$.

It should be stressed that the generalisations referred to above deal with reaction *cross sections* and not with thermal rates. The cross-section function $S^V$ must rise more steeply with reagent vibration than the Boltzmann function $P^V$ decreases, in order that the thermal *rate constant* shall be dominated by contributions from $v > 0$. In view of the steep rise in $S^V$ with $V$ (Fig. 17(b)) in substantially endothermic reactions, a preponderant contribution to the thermal rate from $v > 0$ is likely, though not inevitable. The exceptions will involve reagents with wide vibrational-spacing, and reaction at moderate temperatures. These points are exemplified in a $3D$ trajectory study of endothermic rate constants for the reactions $H_2(D_2, T_2) + X \rightarrow H + HX$ (X $\equiv$ Br, I), and $HCl + Cl \rightarrow H + Cl_2$, performed by Porter *et al.* (1973). The authors propose an empirical rule for determining whether $v > 0$ will make the dominant contribution to the thermal rate.

In the case of the endothermic ion–molecule reaction $H_2^+ + He \rightarrow H + HeH^+$ Chupka and co-workers have been able to compare, in remarkable detail, the relative efficiency of reagent vibration and reagent translation in promoting reaction (Chupka and Russell, 1968; Chupka, 1972; Dubrin and Henchman, 1972). This reaction is endothermic by 18 kcal mole$^{-1}$. The potential energy surface includes charge induced dipole interaction that gives rise to a $\sim$5 kcal mole$^{-1}$ potential well through which the reacting particles pass *en route* to the endothermic hill located in the exit valley (Brown and Hayes, 1971). This appears, there-

fore, to be a surface with a type II barrier. The experimental finding is
that near to the threshold energy for reaction, vibrational energy is more
than $10\times$ as effective in promoting reaction as is an equivalent amount
of reagent translational energy.

An elegant molecular beam study (Odiorne *et al.*, 1971; see Toennies,
Chapter 5, this volume) has provided evidence of the effect of reagent
vibrational excitation in promoting the slightly endothermic reaction
$HCl + K \rightarrow H + KCl$. The HCl was excited by crossing a laser beam
with the HCl beam; the consequent increase in reactive cross section
was $\sim100\times$. More recently the substantially endothermic reaction
$HCl(v') + Br \rightarrow Cl + HBr$ ($Q = -16.5$ kcal mole$^{-1}$) has been studied
by infrared chemiluminescence. The reagent $HCl(v' = 1 - 4)$ was
formed in a pre-reactor. For $v' = 4$ ($E_V' = 31$ kcal mole$^{-1}$) it was estimated that $S = 1 - 10$ Å$^2$. It follows that at collision energies $E_T'$ an
order-of-magnitude less than the barrier height this endothermic reaction proceeds with high probability if the molecule under attack is
vibrationally excited. High rotational excitation was found to reduce the
detailed rate constant for endothermic reaction (Douglas *et al.*, 1973).

The theoretical discussion which leads to $S^V > S^T$ for endothermic
reactions relates to processes $AB + C \rightarrow A + BC$ for which the preferred line of approach is collinear. No theoretical comparison has yet
been made of $S^V$ with $S^T$ for reactions that favor lateral approach. A
recent study of a polyatomic reaction with 3 endothermic reaction paths
serves as a reminder that we have much more to learn. Lee and co-
workers (Lee, 1972) find that the abstraction reactions of $I + CH_3Br$
to give IH or IBr (both with $Q \approx -25$ kcal mole$^{-1}$) proceed readily
with predominantly translational energy in the reagents. On the other
hand the endothermic Walden inversion reaction $I + CH_3Br \rightarrow ICH_3$
$+ Br$ ($Q \approx -12.5$ kcal mole$^{-1}$) fails to occur despite the presence of
ample translational energy in the reagents.

### 4. *Potential Hollows*

In Section II,C,1 it was remarked that very attractive surfaces favor
secondary encounters, since there is insufficient repulsion to separate the
products cleanly. The products may have a sufficient number of encounters before they separate, so that the time spent at close range
approaches a rotational period (see Figs. 12a and 12b; the same thing
can happen with an exceptional mass combination on a repulsive surface,
as pictured in Fig. 13). In the present section we consider the case where
there is a potential hollow (or "well") in which the interacting particles

may be trapped. The particles will remain trapped for a limited length of time, since the reagent potential and kinetic energy is greater than that required to escape from the potential well. The effect of a shallow potential well is, therefore, not very different from that of low product repulsion. In both cases we have what Herschbach and co-workers have called an "osculating" collision (Fisk *et al.*, 1967; Herschbach, 1971; the term was previously applied by Wigner to an analogous regime in nuclear reactions); this denotes an interaction which is indirect, but not so indirect as to give the symmetrical forward-backward scattering characteristic of a long-lived complex.

If the mean lifetime for the complex is $\bar{\tau}$ and its mean rotational period is $\bar{\tau}_{rot} = 2\pi(I^*/\bar{L})$ (where $I^*$ is the moment of inertia of the complex, and $\bar{L}$ is its mean orbital angular momentum) then for $\bar{\tau} \gtrsim 4\bar{\tau}_{rot}$ the intensity of forward and backward peaks in the differential cross section for the molecular product is nearly the same, whereas for $\bar{\tau} \approx 0.8\bar{\tau}_{rot}$ the backward peak is about half as great as the forward peak. This simple analysis, based, it should be stressed, on the assumption that the "complex" even for short $\tau$ is subject to decomposition with a random lifetime distribution, $\exp(-t/\tau)$, provides a very simple method of estimating the complexity of an encounter from the experimentally observed asymmetry in forward-backward scattering (Fisk *et al.*, 1967). Examples have been found experimentally of reactions with intermediates having lifetimes comparable to a rotational period (e.g., $Cs + TlX \rightarrow CsX + Tl$, $X \equiv Cl, I$), and also lifetimes of several rotational periods (e.g., K or Cs, $+RbCl \rightarrow KCl$ or $CsCl$, $+Rb$; also several nonreactive systems such as $K + SO_4$, $NO_2$, etc.); see Kinsey, 1972, and Toennies, Chapter 5, this volume. A particularly elegantly documented example of reaction through a long-lived intermediate is the reaction $Cs + SF_6 \rightarrow CsF + SF_5$ (Freund *et al.*, 1971). Four-atom exchange reactions, $CsCl + KX \rightarrow CsX + KCl$ ($X \equiv Cl$ or I), $CsI + Cl_2 \rightarrow CsCl + ICl$, which take place by way of collision complexes with lifetimes $\bar{\tau} \gtrsim \bar{\tau}_{rot}$, have been reported recently (Miller *et al.*, 1972; King and Herschbach, 1973).

It has also been suggested that the interhalogen reactions, of which the most famous is $Cl + Br_2 \rightarrow ClBr + Br$ (studied in recent years at Freiburg, Harvard, and Los Alamos; see Kinsey, 1972, and Toennies, Chapter 5, this volume) may be interpreted in terms of an osculating complex model (Lee *et al.*, 1969). This reaction shows points of resemblance to the $K + Br_2 \rightarrow KBr + Br$ reaction, with the difference that the total cross section is small. Figure 12b shows how a migratory collision at moderate impact parameter $b$, so long as it produced some rotation of A around B, could, following migration, scatter AC sharply forward; Kuntz et al. (1969) suggested this as a possible mechanism for the Cl + $Br_2$ reaction. Since atom B tends to be released on the outward excursion of an AB vibration, it carries considerable translational energy with it. As a result, forward scattered molecules have more than the mean translational energy—as may be the case for Cl + $Br_2$.

Some model studies have been made to ascertain the effect of shallow potential wells on the reaction dynamics. A study which, in effect, turned the two contrasting surfaces I and II of Fig. 15, and hence the energy profiles of Fig. 16, upside-down, examined the effect on a thermoneutral energy surface, without an energy barrier, of shifting the minimum of a 7 kcal $mole^{-1}$ potential well slightly (0.2 Å) from the entry valley into the exit valley* (Nomura, 1971; Polanyi, 1972; Nomura and Polanyi, 1974). The contrasting surfaces, both of the LEPS type, were called —I and —II. It was found that the reaction was indirect; consequently, there was a less clean-cut correlation between the type of reagent energy and the tendency for reaction to occur than there was on surfaces +I and +II. Nonetheless, it was evident that the rule applicable to surfaces +I and +II had been inverted: on surface —I $S^V > S^T$, on surface —II $S^T > S^V$ (significantly on —I, marginally on —II). Angular distributions were broad.

The LEPS surface also readily gives a hollow in the entry valley (7 kcal $mole^{-1}$) combined with a barrier in the exit (4 kcal $mole^{-1}$); this surface was symbolized —I + II. The dynamics on this surface were compared with that on an identical surface with the features reversed; +I — II. The former gave $S^V > S^T$, the latter $S^T > S^V$. This is reasonable since both features, hollow and barrier, are working in the same direction on —I + II and again on +I — II. The hollow after the barrier, +I — II, gave rise to markedly forward peaked scattering. Blais (1968, 1969) also found a shift toward forward scattering, on an attractive surface for K + $Br_2$, when he introduced a moderate attraction between the reaction products. One may surmise that attraction between reaction products can give an intermediate ABC a sufficiently long lifetime that A swings ~180° around BC and leaves, as AB, in the forward direction.

---

* The longer version of the film referred to on p. 417 (Charters, et al., 1970) includes, in addition to trajectories illustrative of secondary encounters on attractive surfaces, trajectories for reaction across surfaces —I and —II. The degree of complexity on surfaces —I and —II resembles that for the more intricate trajectories on the attractive surfaces. The effect of vibration in promoting reaction on —I and translation on —II is illustrated.

The amount of BC attraction required for forward scattering would be expected to depend on the other features of the surface, the reactant masses, and the collision energy. [It can happen that A swings right around BC, $\sim 360°$, and is released in the backward direction. This sort of behavior was described for an attractive surface by Kuntz et al. (1969b). It occurred commonly at large impact parameter on surface $-$I and sometimes on $-$II; this behavior is illustrated in the film (Charters et al., 1970).]

A much more extensive multivariant model study of surfaces with shallow potential hollows has been made by Borne and Bunker (1971) using the HMF potential (see Section II,B). Twenty-one different energy surfaces were examined in a study of the effect on the reaction dynamics of changes in well shape, well depth, well location, width of the approach channel, reagent energy, and particle masses (Br + $I_2$, Cl + $Br_2$, or Cl + $I_2$). The spectroscopic constants were those for the Br + $I_2$ reaction; consequently, all the surfaces were exothermic by 6.3 kcal mole$^{-1}$ and none had barriers. Migration was permitted, and took place in about a third of the trajectories. The overall conclusion from this study was that the dynamics, using the HMF, are rather insensitive to the presence and properties of a 0–10 kcal mole$^{-1}$ potential well. The angular distribution was approximately sideways peaked on all surfaces. The product internal energy ($E_V' + E_R'$) amounted to 50–100% of the 9 kcal mole$^{-1}$ available energy, depending on the extent of mixed energy release. The forward peaked scattering observed experimentally for Cl + $Br_2$ could not be reproduced. The authors surmised that if they could, by some adjustment of the *long-range* part of the interaction, have held the three particles together for long enough, then the osculating complex would have released the new molecule in a forward direction.

There is some cold comfort in the finding that multivariant potentials, which one might reasonably fear would explain anything, are sometimes at a loss to explain quite broad types of behavior. This strengthens the hope that when a potential with the correct properties is found (and as the types of observations requiring explanation are further refined—see Bunker and Goring-Simpson, 1973, for an instructive example) the ambiguities in interpretation will not be so great as to rob the undertaking of its value. Ultimately, of course, the choice between alternative energy surfaces will have to be made by recourse to *ab initio* calculation.

The *ab initio* potential energy surface for which we have trajectory data, namely, that for $H_3^+$, involves a deep potential well. In its most stable triangular configuration $H_3^+$ has 108 kcal mole$^{-1}$ of binding with respect to $H^+ + H_2$. The trajectories (Csizmadia *et al.*, 1969) were run in $3D$ for the reactant masses $D^+ + H_2 \rightarrow DH + H^+$. Three collision energies were examined; $E_T = 3$ eV, 4.5 eV, and (in a smaller sample) 6 eV. Particularly at the two higher energies these trajectories were unrealistic so far as the $D^+ + H_2$ reaction was concerned, since no attempt was made to include the effect of transfer to and from the energy surface correlating with $DH^+ + H$ (Preston and Tully, 1971; Tully and Preston, 1971). This surface hopping occurs as the products separate, and does not effect the following observations. The reagents were found to spiral in toward one another from maximum impact parameters, $b_{max}$, significantly in excess of the Gioumosis and Stevenson polarization limit, $b_{max}^p$ (see Wagner and Hoyerman, Chapter 12, Volume VIB, and also Section III). It was found that $b_{max} > 2.4$ Å at both 3 and 4.5 eV, whereas $b_{max}^p$ is 1.66 Å at 3 eV and 1.5 Å at 4.5 eV. This discrepancy can be explained qualitatively by the effect of the valence forces in the neighborhood of $b_{max}^p$ in increasing the *attraction* and hence decreasing the height of the rotational barrier on the effective potential. It does not follow that the polarization model cross sections will be smaller than the computed ones, since the trajectories, as a result of complex interaction, often lead to reformation of the reagents. The reaction probability was $\leq 0.2$–0.3 for $b \leq 2.4$ Å (the reaction probability is stated as an upper limit since nonadiabaticity in the exit valley could cause a further reduction). The polarization theory assumes unit probability for reaction.

The trajectories were far more "snarled" (i.e., indirect) than was the case in the two studies of shallow potential wells referred to above. At a collision energy of 3 eV (i.e., 3 eV in excess of the energy required to dissociate the "complex") the complex had a lifetime which was typically $\sim 1 \times 10^{-13}$ sec. The great majority ($>90\%$) of the trajectories took from $(0.4$–$3.0) \times 10^{-13}$ sec. The shorter of these times corresponds to the time required for one rotation of the complex. The longer time, for which $\tau/\tau_{rot} \sim 10$, corresponded to collisions of large impact parameter. The product distributions may not be correct for $DH + H^+$ (because of the failure to include nonadiabaticity) but they shed light on the dynamics of reaction on a surface with a deep hollow. The angular distribution was found to be almost symmetrical, forward and backward, as would be expected for random break up of a long-lived complex. The product *energy* distribution, however, was not random (when compared with random distributions calculated by Light and Lin, 1965; Pechukas *et al.*, 1966). A statistical distribution of angles is achieved, it appears, more easily than a statistical distribution over energy states. For a statistical distribution over angles the particles must have scrambled their momenta to the point that the initial direction of approach of $D^+$ has been "forgotten." A statistical distribution over energies involves the more stringent requirement that there be no preferred paths (of differing $\mathscr{A}$, $\mathscr{M}$ and $\mathscr{R}$) through phase-space, for the separation of the products.

Another type of deviation from statistical behavior has been noted for reactions which proceed through long-lived complexes, namely the alkali halide four-atom exchange reactions (e.g., $CsCl + KI$, p. 450). The experimental finding is that the product angular and energy distributions are consistent with the predictions of a simple statistical model resembling the RRKM (Rice, Ramsperger, Kassel, Marcus) theory of unimolecular decay. However, the ratio of non-reactive to reactive decay—the property most directly obtained from RRKM theory—is found to be 2–3 times larger than the statistical prediction. An extensive trajectory study of a similar exchange reaction (NaBr + KCl; Brumer and Karplus, 1973— with further work in progress) indicates that preferred atomic arrangements for the 4-atom intermediates $MXM'X'$ can account for the non-statistical yield of products, while perhaps retaining a statistical outcome with respect to angle and energy.

There is evidence to suggest that isotope effects may provide a useful tool in probing the shape of potential energy surfaces embodying quite deep wells. Chapman and Suplinskas (1974) have run trajectories using masses appropriate to the exothermic ion–molecule reaction $Ar^+ + HD$, across LEPS surfaces having potential wells of 40–90 kcal mole$^{-1}$ depth, below the reactant energy. The preliminary results indicate a lengthening of the life of the complex as the well becomes deeper, and also a significant decrease in the ratio of the alternative isotopic products, $ArH^+/ArD^+$ as the location of the well is made "later" along the reaction coordinate.

## III. Simple Models

Treatments of the full three- (or $n$-) body problem using, so far as possible, realistic interaction potentials (as discussed in the previous section) are valuable since they reveal effects which simple models rule out in advance. A drawback to the "full" treatments is that the salient features may be obscured by a host of minor features to such an extent that there is little real improvement in understanding. For understanding it is necessary to formulate generalizations, that is to say, simple models. The efforts that have been made, and continue to be made, to isolate the most important features of potential energy surfaces (some of these have been described in the previous section) should assist in bridging the gap between the calculations using elaborate potential energy hypersurfaces, and the simple models required for understanding. In this section, as in Section II, we restrict ourselves to the consideration of models based on classical mechanics.

Since the two-body problem is the most complex that can be handled analytically, the quest for simple models is, in essence, an attempt to represent the many-body phenomenon in terms of a two-body event, or a succession of such events. In the course of a chemical reaction

$$A + B—C \rightarrow A—B + C,$$

there is (in general) initially an attraction between B and C which becomes a repulsion, and an initial repulsion between A and B which becomes an attraction. There appear to be two distinguishable types of simple models; in the first type the interesting part of the interaction is regarded as occurring largely before or largely after the bond has switched from B—C to A—B, that is, *either* as the reagents approach *or* as the products separate. This type of model we shall refer to as a "single-coordinate model"; it may be either an "approach coordinate" or a "retreat coordinate" model. A second type of simple model takes explicit account of interactions that occur *both* as the reagents approach *and* as the products separate. In order that this may remain a simple model it is a common practice to separate the two types of motion. This is achieved by what may be regarded as a switching of the bond from the molecule under attack, B—C, to the new molecule, A—B; we shall, therefore, term this type of model a "switching model." This scheme of categorisation is far from all-embracing. It may, nonetheless, prove helpful.

As aids to understanding, the single-coordinate models are not necessarily inferior to the switching models. In constructing simple models we are concerned with achieving the maximum physical insight (a model which works, and works for the right reasons) combined with the maximum simplicity (a model which is clear in concept, and mathematically tractable).

## A. Single-Coordinate Models

### 1. *Approach Coordinate*

There are at present no dynamical models of the entire reactive event that focus attention exclusively on the approach coordinate. Since forces that are operative in the approach coordinate are most likely to govern the probability of reaction, there are, however, models which try to account for the magnitude of the reactive cross section, and its energy dependence, in terms of changes in potential along the coordinate of approach. The hard-sphere collision theory model, which makes use of collision diameters obtained from gas-phase transport phenomena, comes under this heading. So also do the cross section models for three special families of reaction that will now be discussed.

*a. Alkali Metal Atom Plus Halogen Reactions.*    Magee (1940) proposed a method for calculating the reactive cross sections of reactions involving alkali metal atoms and halogens,

$$M + XY \rightarrow M^+X^- + Y.$$

He took the same view of these reactions as had Ogg and Polanyi (1935), and also Evans and Polanyi (1938), namely, that these were electron jump or "harpooning" reactions. On this picture an electron was regarded as having been transferred from M to XY ($\rightarrow M^+ + XY^-$) while the reagents were still several angstroms apart. The ·electron jump was regarded (in all the references cited) as occurring when the point of degeneracy was reached,

$$E(M + XY) = E(M^+ + XY^-).$$

The symbols represent the energies of the designated electronic configurations. Magee calculated the separation $r^{\ddagger}_{MX}$ in the degenerate configuration, and showed that, because of the low ionization potential of M and high electron affinity of XY, the electron jump would occur at $r^{\ddagger}_{MX} \sim 5\text{--}10$ Å. Since the corresponding cross sections would be in the region of approximately $100\text{--}300$ Å², this accounted for the remarkably large cross sections that had been measured for these reactions (Polanyi, 1932).

The region of degeneracy between the covalent and ionic states occurs in the neighborhood of the MX separation given by

$$e^2/r^{\ddagger}_{MX} = I(M) - E^v(XY),$$

where $I$ and $E^v$ are ionization potentials and vertical electron affinities. The model has been examined by Herschbach (1966) and, still more recently, by Edelstein and Davidovits (1971). In its simplest form the model is not fully accurate, but it can safely be said that it succeeds in giving a genuine insight into the nature of the first stage of this reaction.

Once the electronic state $M^+ + XY^-$ has been achieved, the likelihood of reaction is very high (the model takes it to be unity). However, the interaction has barely begun. These reactions are highly exothermic, substantial energy ($\sim 2$ eV) being released as $M^+$ and $XY^-$ approach, and $M^+X^-$ separates from Y. The electron jump model suggests that a major portion of the energy release occurs as attraction between $M^+$ and $XY^-$ (Evans and Polanyi, 1939). This is in accord with the high vibrational excitation in the reaction products. The dynamics of these reactions is now known in great detail (for a review see Herschbach, 1966). The literature does not seem to contain any single-coordinate models of type A,1 which attempt to account for the major features of the $M + XY$ reaction dynamics. Instead, a good deal of work has been done on single-coordinate models of type A,2 (Kuntz et al., 1969b) and on simple bond switch models (Minturn et al., 1966; Herschbach, 1966) as they apply to these reactions.

b. Ion–Molecule reactions. A further example of a model of type A,1 (an approach-coordinate model) which appears to have achieved an important physical insight, is the Langevin (1905) and Gioumousis–Stevenson (1958) polarization model of ion–molecule reaction. The model considers only the attractive force between the attacking ion $A^+$ and the neutral molecule under attack BC. Despite this restricted view of the reaction, which considers only the forces operating during the first part of the approach coordinate (repulsive forces are certain to be important when $A^+$ approaches BC closely), the model has had substantial success in predicting reactive cross sections, and also in a number of cases accounting for the dependence of reactive cross section on the relative velocity, $S \propto v^{-1}$.

The attraction between an ion and the dipole that it induces in a neutral molecule is given by $U(r) = -\alpha e^2/2r^4$. If an ion and a molecule approach with a relative kinetic energy $T$ then they will behave as if they were moving in a potential,[*]

$$U_{\text{eff}} = U(r) + T(b^2/r^2)$$

(Herzberg, 1950, p. 426). This function passes through a maximum, with $U_{\text{eff}} = U_{\text{eff}}^*$ and internuclear separation $r^*$. By differentiation the maximum can be shown to lie at $r^* = (\alpha e^2/Tb^2)^{1/2}$. Substituting into the

---

[*] In Section III translational, vibrational, and rotational energies are symbolized $T$, $V$, and $R$ (in place of $E_T$, $E_V$, and $E_R$), to allow for further subscripts.

expression for $U_{\text{eff}}$; $U_{\text{eff}}^* = T^2 b^4 / 2\alpha e^2$. The model assumes that all collisions with $T \geq U_{\text{eff}}^*$ result in ion and molecule spiralling into one another to give reaction. Writing $U_{\text{eff}}^* \equiv T$ one obtains $b_{\text{max}}^4 = 2\alpha e^2 / T$, as the expression for the largest impact parameter that can lead to reaction. It follows from $S = \pi b_{\text{max}}^2$ that

$$S(T) = \pi (2\alpha e^2 / T)^{1/2}$$

so that $S \propto v^{-1}$. The model also gives useful absolute values for $S$, providing that the collision energy is not so high that the maximum in $U_{\text{eff}}$ ceases to exist, and the notion of $A^+$ spiraling in to BC to form the reaction products no longer has meaning. This upper limit in the useful energy range for the theory is reached at $T \sim 1$ eV, an energy approximately equal to the depth of the minimum in the $-\alpha e^2 / 2r^4$ ion induced dipole attractive potential.

We shall encounter this model again as a component in bond switch models of ion–molecule reaction.

*c. Alkali metal atom plus alkyl halide reaction.* Gersh and Bernstein (1971, 1972) have found that the total reactive cross-section for K + $ICH_3$ → KI + $CH_3$ passes through a peak at 4 kcal mole⁻¹. The peak is an intriguing feature since it is located at an unexpectedly low energy, and is surprisingly sharp (see also section I,C).

Harris and Herschbach (1973) have devised an approach-coordinate model that provides an instructive analysis of this peak. They postulate the existence of an energy barrier (taken for simplicity to be a step function) along the approach coordinate, followed by a region of attraction. At low collision energy the cross section rises, as would be expected from the line-of-centers model cross-section function $S_{\text{LC}}(E_T)$ in Section I,C. At higher collision energies the cross section falls because of the increasing height of the centrifugal barrier—as illustrated above (III,A,1,b) for ion–molecule reaction.

## 2. Retreat Coordinate

The approach-coordinate models discussed above focused attention on various types of attractive force that may be responsible for bringing the reagents together. Retreat coordinate models have, so far, stressed the repulsive force which must be responsible for separating the products. For some reactions of a less specialized type than the M + $X_2$ and ion–molecule reactions just examined, there is evidence to indicate that a major proportion of the energy release may be "repulsive" (see Section II), i.e., it occurs along the coordinate of separation as AB · C, where the dot represents the location of the repulsion. This is the case, for example, for the M + XR family of reactions referred to under III,A,1,c above.

The effectiveness of AB · C repulsion in producing vibration in AB has been extensively explored through experimental and theoretical studies of translation-to-vibration, T–V, energy transfer (Herzfeld and Litovitz, 1959; Cottrell and McCoubrey, 1961). In general T–V transfer is a very inefficient process. It is easy to see from classical mechanical considerations why this should be so (Landau and Teller, 1936; Landau and Lifschitz, 1960). For thermal collisions the time $t_F$ (which we need not define precisely) during which the AB · C force is significant, is long compared to the time $t_V$ of an oscillatory period of AB ($t_V = \omega^{-1}$, where $\omega$ is the classical vibrational frequency of AB). The force therefore produces a relative motion of B with respect to A that averages, over several AB oscillations, to give no more than a small net change in internal motion of AB.

It is a corollary of this simple analysis that a force of significant magnitude that operates over a brief period $t_F \ll t_V$ will be efficient in T–V transfer. The limiting case of this is a "sudden" or "impulsive" force, for which $F(t)$ is a delta function. This type of interaction is a poor approximation to the normal case of T–V transfer. Something approaching it will be observed in hot atom collisions, and also in cases where the molecule AB has an exceptionally long vibrational period, as is the case for highly vibrationally excited molecular iodine (Brown and Klemperer, 1964; Steinfeld and Schweid, 1970) and for highly vibrationally excited dissociating molecules (Shuler and Zwanzig, 1960). The sudden approximation is clearly appropriate for the calculation of the extent of internal excitation in AB recoiling from the effect of $\gamma$ photon emission by atom B. It was with this application in mind that Suess (1940) considered the classical mechanical effect of an impulse applied to B, collinearly with AB. Subsequently, Steinwedel and Jensen (1947) extended Suess' model of radioactive recoil to include the effect of $\gamma$ photon emission at an angle to the AB axis, using both classical and quantum mechanical treatments to compute the effect of the impulse.

More recently the impulsive model has been used in attempts to describe the vibrational excitation in AB released by the photodissociation of ABC (Basco and Norrish, 1962) and vibrational excitation in AB which has quenched electronic excitation in an atom C* (Karl *ei al.*, 1967). In these cases the event that leads to the onset of AB · C repulsion is sudden, and the initial force can be large, so that the sudden approximation may be successful. Electronic quenching parallels the second half of certain reactive collisions (Polanyi, 1965). For example, if the quenching process is Hg*(6 $^3P_{1,0}$) + CO → Hg(6 $^1S_0$) + CO$_{v\geq0}$ the triplet excited atom may use one of its valencies to form a complex Hg$^{II}$CO which by intersystem crossing becomes Hg$^0$ · CO → Hg + CO$_{v\geq0}$ (the roman numeral indicates the valency). The intersystem crossing gives rise to the sudden application of a repulsive force. A comparable reaction would be O + ClHg$^{II}$ → (OClHg$^{II}$ → OCl · Hg$^0$ →)OCl$_{v\geq0}$ + Hg; or, in general, A + BC$^m$ → AB + C$^n$. The impulsive approximation may, therefore, have application to a restricted class of chemical reactions. As a limiting case it is likely to be instructive for a considerable range of reactions.

*a. Impulsive Force.* Though we shall only discuss the case of an impulsive repulsion, AB · C, the same model could be applied to a case in which an impulsive attraction suddenly came into existence. The general form of the potential and force for the repulsive case are indicated in Fig. 23a.

Since the force between AB and C is instantaneous it operates initially between atoms B and C only. The center of mass of BC remains at rest, so that $p_B^0 = -p_C^0 = p$ (the superscripts 0 indicate quantities which are applicable immediately following the impulse). The translational energy of the recoiling system is $E'_{tot} = (p^2/2m_B) + (p^2/2m_C)$. As B recoils it strikes A and produces an overall motion in AB. Conservation of momentum requires that $p_{AB} = p_B^0$. The translational energy of AB will be less than that of B since $T'_{AB}/T_B^{'0} = m_B/(m_A + m_B)$. The balance of $T_B^{'0}$ must go into internal excitation of AB. If AB · C recoils in a linear configuration the internal excitation is vibration, $V'$:

$$V'_{imp} = T_B^{'0} - T'_{AB} = \frac{p^2}{2m_B} - \frac{p^2}{2(m_A + m_B)}.$$

Using the expression for $E_{tot}$ given above,

$$V'_{imp} = E'_{tot} \frac{m_A}{(m_A + m_B)} \frac{m_C}{(m_B + m_C)}. \tag{3.1}$$

The ratio $m_C/(m_B + m_C)$ is the fraction of $E'_{tot}$ that is transferred to A+B, and $m_A/(m_A + m_B)$ is the fraction of this that becomes vibration. Later we symbolize the product of these factors as $C_{A,C}$.

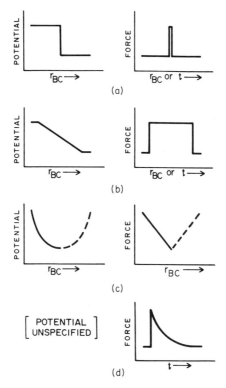

FIG. 23. Four types of simple "retreat-coordinate model." (a) Impulsive force, (b) constant force, (c) simple harmonic force, (d) DIPR model. In all four the force (pictured here as repulsive) is assumed to be located between the separating particles AB · C. These models attempt to account for the reaction dynamics in terms of forces operative in the exit valley of the potential energy surface. The potential slope along the exit valley is pictured at the left (except in the case of the DIPR model, for which only $F(t)$ is specified) and the corresponding force as a function of internuclear separation and/or time is shown at the right.

Equation (3.1) predicts that in the limit $m_B \rightarrow 0$, $V'_{imp} = E'_{tot}$. In this limit $m_A$ and $m_C$ are very large compared with $m_B$, consequently, the impulsive release of repulsion between B and C (in collinear AB · C) causes at first a very small recoil in C sufficient to conserve momentum, and a large velocity in B. Thereafter, only a very small fraction of this $v_B^0$ need be transferred into $v_{AB}$ in order that the momentum shall be conserved in the system A + B. The central particle B is like a bullet bouncing off a floating steel block C against another floating block A: It will ricochet many times before the two steel blocks float apart. It is evident that these predictions bear some resemblance to the observations made for the reactive system $Cl + HI \rightarrow ClH + I$, for which the mass combination is $m_A, m_C \gg m_B$. For this reaction the efficiency of conversion of what is believed to be predominantly repulsive energy release into vibration is high, as might be expected. It is also to be expected on the basis of this or more sophisticated models that secondary encounters between the reagents, as they separate, will be numerous. Evidently even an extremely simple single-coordinate model may reveal some, at least, of the essential features of a chemical reaction.

Herschbach and co-workers (Herschbach, 1970; McDonald et al., 1972; Herschbach, 1973) have been able to explain the product translational energy distribution in a number of reactions, particularly $H + X_2$, on the basis of a simple model which assumes (in accord with trajectory results) that a substantial repulsive energy release of magnitude $\mathscr{R}$ is released between the $X_2$ atoms. Instead, however, of merely inferring $\mathscr{R}$ from the dynamics, they obtain $\mathscr{R}$ on the assumption that $X_2$ is transferred from its ground electronic state, in which it is presumed to have retained its normal distribution of internuclear separations, to its lowest repulsive electronic state. The model predicts a parallelism between the product $(HX + X)$ translational energy distribution from the reactions $H + X_2$, and the translational energy distribution in $X + X$ coming from the photolysis of thermal $X_2$. The parallelism is observed. This infusion of chemistry into what was hitherto a wholly empirical model, represents a most desirable trend (see also DIPR-DIP and FOTO, p. 471–472).

It is a simple matter to raise the restriction that $AB \cdot C$ shall be linear at the moment of impulsive energy release. The energy entering vibration for a configuration bent by an angle $\alpha$ ($\alpha$ being defined so that $\alpha = 0$ for collinearity) is

$$V'_{imp}(\alpha) = V'_{imp}(\alpha = 0) \cos^2 \alpha.$$

For the case of electronic-to-vibrational energy transfer an unrestricted $\alpha$ ($\alpha = 0$–$90°$) broadens $V'$ so that the calculated vibrational distribution agrees more nearly with experiment (Karl et al., 1967).

*b. Gradual Force.* If the impulsive force along the retreat coordinate, that is, between atoms B and C, is replaced by a gradual force (Fig. 23b), it becomes necessary to make some explicit assumption regarding the nature of the A–B interaction. This is because in any finite time some of the B · C force will be transmitted to A while B and C are still interacting. The problem is well known in mechanics as that of "forced oscillation" (see, for example, Landau and Lifschitz, 1960; Cottrell and McCoubrey, 1961; Holdy et al., 1970). For harmonic oscillatory motion—i.e., a particle of mass $\mu$ attracted toward the equilibrium position by a force $-kx$, having a frequency (radians sec$^{-1}$) $\omega = (k/\mu)^{1/2}$—the classical equation of motion is

$$\ddot{x} + \omega^2 x = \mu^{-1} F(t),$$

where $F(t)$ is the force as a function of time. This second-order differential equation can be solved to obtain $x(t)$. The expression for $x(t)$ can then be used to obtain an analytical expression for the energy of the oscillator after the force $F(t)$ has been applied [$F(t)$ can have any form so long as it is zero at $t = 0$ and zero once again after a finite time $t$]. After averaging over the initial phase of the oscillator, the mean vibrational excitation induced by the force is found to be

$$V' = (2\mu)^{-1} \left| \int_{-\infty}^{+\infty} F(t) e^{-i\omega t} \, dt \right|^2. \tag{3.2}$$

The vibrational excitation is seen to depend upon the square of the modulus of the Fourier component of the force $F(t)$, at the frequency $\omega$ characteristic of the harmonic oscillator.

The next level of sophistication in a retreat coordinate model, beyond the impulsive description of Section 2,a, is a model (Fig. 23b) which assumes that the new bond is a harmonic oscillator, and that the repulsion has a finite duration and a simple form $F(t)$. Since $F(t)$ is a consequence of some potential slope $\partial U/\partial r_{BC}$ along the outrun of the potential energy surface, as well as being dependent on the masses of the particles, one obtains more insight into the interaction by stipulating $U(r_{BC})$ and then deriving $F(t)$. Provided that $F(t)$ is not too complicated it can be made to yield the vibrational excitation $V'$.

In the case of a repulsive potential $U(r_{BC})$ that starts at $U_0$ for some $r_{BC}^0$ and then falls off linearly to $U(r_{BC}) = 0$ at $r_{BC} = a$, that is, $U(r_{BC}) = U_0[1 - (r_{BC} - r_{BC}^0)/a]$, the classical equations of motion yield for $m_C \sim \infty$ (Karl, 1964),

$$F = \frac{U_0}{a} \frac{m_A}{m_A + m_B}.$$

From Eq. (3.2), for a harmonic force between A and B,

$$V' = \mu^{-1}(U_0^2/a^2\omega^2)(m_A/m_A + m_B)^2(1 - \cos \omega t_c), \tag{3.3}$$

where $\mu = m_A m_B/(m_A + m_B)$, and $t_c$ is the duration of the collision, that is, the time taken for $r_{BC}$ to increase from $r_{BC}^0$ to $a$.

As expected, Eq. (3.3) resembles Eq. (3.1) in the impulsive limit. For very short $t_c$, $\omega t_c \ll 1$, and Eq. (3.3) reduces to $V' = U_0[m_A/(m_A+m_B)]$. The ratio $m_A/(m_A + m_B)$ has already been identified as the fraction of energy transferred impulsively to AB that becomes AB vibration.

For a slowly decaying potential, $\omega t_c \gg 1$, $V' \to 0$. Some intermediate cases are instructive. If, for example, $m_A = 16$ amu and $m_B = 12$ amu (i.e., AB $\equiv$ OC), $U_0 = 4.7$ eV (the energy released in quenching Hg*$6^3P_0$) and $t_V = 2.7 \cdot 10^{-15}$ sec (a vibrational period for CO), then $V'/V'_{imp}$, the ratio of the forced vibrational excitation to the impulsively induced vibration, decreases as shown in Table I with increase in the ratio $t_c/t_V$:

TABLE I

DIMINUTION IN THE EFFICIENCY OF VIBRATIONAL EXCITATION WITH INCREASED COLLISION TIME

| $t_c/t_V{}^a$ | 0.04 | 0.10 | 0.23 | 0.27 | 0.31 | 0.44 | 0.54 |
|---|---|---|---|---|---|---|---|
| $V'/V'_{imp}$ | 0.98 | 0.95 | 0.89 | 0.79 | 0.72 | 0.44 | 0.08 |

[a] The collision times $t_c$ ranged from $1 \cdot 10^{-15}$ sec up to $14.0 \cdot 10^{-15}$ sec from left to right in this table; corresponding to distances "$a$" ranging from 0.04 Å up to 0.40 Å.

It would appear from Table I that an impulsive model will give a reasonable approximation to the truth if the collision time is $<10^{-1}\times$ the vibrational period. (Harris and Herschbach, 1971, compared the impulsive model with exponential energy release and found the impulsive approximation to be surprisingly good.)

In considering the interaction distances "$a$" for the gradual force model just given, it must be borne in mind that a different form for $U(r_{BC})$, and hence $F(t)$, would lead to the same vibrational excitation if the interaction range were adjusted. Since one would like to compare the interaction range with characteristic distances obtained (for example) in scattering experiments, it is worth making an effort to choose a realistic potential. The linear $U(r_{BC})$ used in the preceding paragraphs is unrealistic. A more realistic form (Fig. 23c) would be $U(r_{BC})=\frac{1}{2}k(r_{BC}-r_{BC}^0)^2$, a simple harmonic function. In this case ABC is represented by three masses connected by a pair of simple harmonic springs. Linked harmonic oscillators have often been used to describe polyatomic molecules (Polanyi and Wigner, 1928; Slater, 1959). They can also be used to describe a reaction "intermediate" AB · C giving products AB + C, by regarding the BC spring as initially under compression (Kuntz et al., 1969a). As the expanding BC separation reaches the minimum in its potential, the BC spring is regarded as ceasing to exist; this allows the products to separate. A system of three harmonic springs has been used to describe the second half of a reaction A + BCD → (AB · CD →)AB + CD, making the same assumption regarding the compressed spring BC (Parrish and Herm, 1970). The objective in the four-atom study was to simulate the observed behavior for the reaction Cs + I—$CH_2$—R → CsI + $CH_2$—R ($CH_2$ and R being treated as single particles). It was found that, provided a large part of the exothermicity was released as nearly impulsive I · $CH_2$ repulsion, the experimental observation of substantial product translational energy could be matched. For many-atom systems this model has the virtue of simplicity, which need not be bought at the price of ignoring the possibility of internal excitation remote from the site of scission. In their calculations Parrish and Herm found significant vibrational excitation in both the diatomic and the quasi diatomic fragments.

The objective in the study of AB · C → AB + C using a harmonic AB oscillator and a harmonic B · C repulsion (Kuntz et al., 1969a) was to examine the nature of "mixed energy release" as it is evidenced under the simplest circumstances. It has been remarked that Eq. (3.3) predicts a maximum (mean) vibrational excitation in the AB bond for the case that $t_c → 0$, that is to say in the limit of impulsive energy release. On closer examination it is evident that $V'_{imp}$ is *only* an upper limit on the vibrational excitation if it is assumed that AB is equally likely to be extended or compressed during the period for which $F(t)$ operates. It is clear, however, that in cases where a trajectory "cuts-the-corner" of the potential energy surface—whether due to the nature of the surface or to the relative masses participating in the reaction—the trip along the coordinate of separation will begin with the new bond significantly extended (Polanyi, 1965). This phenomenon, termed mixed energy release, has already been discussed in Section II. It has its analog in the harmonic model if the products are required to separate from a configuration A—B · C in which A—B represents an extended spring of force constant $k_1$ and B · C a compressed spring of force constant $k_2$.

In the harmonic oscillator calculation on AB · C the system was regarded as comprising three equal masses restricted to collinearity. The initial extension of the AB bond, $x_0$ (initial value of $r_1 - r_1^0$), was treated as changing with time due to a relative translational energy of A with respect to BC; $T = m\dot{x}^2/3$. The product energies were

$$T' = 3/4(\dot{a}_3')^2, \qquad V' = E'_{tot} - T,$$

where $a_3$ is the distance of the departing atom C from the center of mass of ABC [hence $a_3 = -(r_1 + 2r_2)/3$] and $\dot{a}_3'$ is the final velocity of C in the center-of-mass system. The expression for $V'$ follows from the fact that in a collinear configuration there can be no product rotation. The equations of motion were solved to obtain $\dot{a}_3'$ for the case of three equal masses (see Kuntz, 1970, for the unequal mass case). The extent of vibrational excitation in AB, $V'$, was then compared with the energy, released as repulsion between B and C, $\mathscr{R}$. Note that this model allows for release of a chosen amount of the exothermicity as attraction along $r_1$; *simultaneous* decrease in $r_1$ and increase in $r_2$ is characteristic of mixed energy release.

The fraction $f$ of $\mathscr{R}$ that became product vibration was determined for a range of model parameters; the parameters varied were the reagent translation $T$, the ratio of the initial force between A and B to the initial force between B and C, symbolized $z$ (this was adjusted by changing the relative force constants), and the percentage of the energy release that occurred as repulsion, $\mathscr{R}/E'_{tot}$. It was found that over a very considerable range of settings of these three parameters, including $(\mathscr{R}/E'_{tot}) \times 100 \approx 0\text{--}70\%$, the fraction $f$ of the repulsion entering vibration exceeded the fraction (0.25) which would enter AB as a consequence of an impulsive release of $\mathscr{R}$ between B and C. This simple model sheds some light on the nature of mixed energy release (see Section II). The effect is seen to be fairly general. It consists in an enhancement of the efficiency of conversion of the repulsive energy into vibration above that calculated for an impulsive force, and hence markedly above that which would be obtained from a force of finite duration driving an oscillator at its equilibrium separation (or the average energy transferred to an oscillator, oscillating about equilibrium).

In the two models described above, involving a force of finite duration $F(t)$, the form of the repulsive potential $U(r_{BC})$ has been stipulated, and $F(t)$ has then been derived (Fig. 23b and c). More elaborate functions $U(r_{BC})$ will lead to more complicated $F(t)$. At some sacrifice in physical insight one can base a model directly on an $F(t)$ chosen to be flexible and mathematically tractable. If the $F(t)$ is sufficiently flexible, or if the model being used is realistic, it should be possible to fit the parameters governing $F(t)$ to the "true" $F(t)$ obtained by closer examination of the reactive event. In the DIPR ("direct interaction with product repulsion") model the force function applied to atom C was taken to be

$$F(t) = -m_C a^0 e^{-ct}, \qquad (3.4)$$

where $a^0$ and $c$ were constants (Kuntz et al., 1969b). The choice of adjustable parameters was justified by fitting this function to a numerical $F(t)$ obtained from a single collinear classical reactive trajectory across the potential energy hypersurface for the reaction in question. Later an alternative fitting procedure was employed which made use of the simple harmonic model described above (in which AB and BC are linked by harmonic forces) as an indication of the "real" behavior (Kuntz, 1970). It should be noted that the $F(t)$ described by Eq. (3.4) was chosen as a matter of mathematical convenience. In adjusting the constants of Eq. (3.4) we are simply adjusting the impulse ($\int F(t)\,dt$), which is the only quantity the model requires. Very different forms for $F(t)$ that had the same integral value would give precisely the same outcome according to this model. A more realistic force function for the generality of reactions would be one that increased from zero to a maximum and then fell again to zero, as pictured in Fig. 14 of Section II. This could be "fitted" to more detailed information for a wider range of reactions than can Eq. (3.4).

Figure 24 gives a pictorial representation in the center-of-mass frame of an initial ($t = 0$) and a later ($t > 0$) configuration of the system

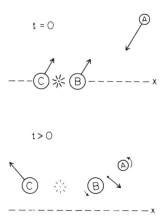

FIG. 24.  A schematic representation of reaction products AB + C shown in the course of separation under the influence of a repulsive force $F(t)$ operating parallel to the x axis throughout. This is illustrative of the DIPR model (based on Kuntz et al., 1969b).

AB · C, according to the DIPR model. The $x$ direction extends from atom C along the CB axis. The initial force on atom C, $F(0) = -m_C a^0$, being repulsive, is directed toward C. (The model has also been applied to the case of an attractive force.) The three atoms approach the center of mass with velocities $v_A$, $v_B$, $v_C$ in 3D. The model assumes (a) that the repulsive force acts throughout along the original CB axis, and (b) that it falls to zero with the passage of time [Eq. (3.4)]. Henglein (1970) has used a "recoil stripping" mechanism as a qualitative model for ion–molecule reaction. The concept is similar to the DIPR one.

The repulsive force deflects the original velocity vectors as pictured (schematically) in Fig. 24. From the deflection of atom C at $t = \infty$ the product scattering angle can be calculated for any given set of initial velocities. From the final velocity of atom C in the center of mass, the product translational energy can be calculated,

$$T' = m_C m_{ABC} v'^2 / [2(m_A + m_B)],$$

where $m_{ABC} = m_A + m_B + m_C$ and $v'$ is the final velocity of atom C. The relative velocity of A with respect to BC before the release of the repulsion defines an initial orbital angular momentum $(= \mu_{A,BC} v_{rel} b)$. The final relative velocity of C with respect to AB defines $L' = \mu_{AB,C} v'_{rel} b'$. Since the initial rotational angular momentum of BC was zero for the cases to which the model was applied,

$$J' = L - L'$$

From $J'$ the product molecule rotational excitation $R'$ could be calculated. Finally $V' = E'_{tot} - (T' + R')$, where $E'_{tot}$ was the experimental total product energy. It should be noted that the model only considers the effect on the *departing atom* C of an assumed $F(t)$. No attempt is made to calculate $V'$ forced upon the oscillator by the recoil, consequently, the nature of the coupling between atoms A and B need not be specified. The model yields $V'$ only through the use of the empirical $E'_{tot}$. If the absolute values of $a_0$ and $c$ are chosen outside a limited range, $V'$ will be negative, that is, nonphysical.

The change in velocity $g$ of atom C due to the operation of $F(t)$ is given by

$$v' = v_0 - a^0/c = v_0 - g.$$

A parameter which turns up in a number of contexts is the ratio of the initial velocity to the change in velocity; $v_0/g \equiv p$. An increase in $p$ implies either that the collision energy has increased or that $a^0/c$ has decreased (or both). A decreased $a^0/c$ may mean either a diminished initial force $(a^0)$ or an increase in the rate at which $F(t)$ falls off with $t$ (or both); in either case the impulse between the products will be less. It has already been remarked that it is only the impulse that figures in the DIPR model, since it is this that brings about the central event; the change in momentum of C by $-gm_c$ (for a recent discussion see Marron and Bernstein, 1972).

The solid lines in Fig. 25 show product angular and energy distributions calculated according to the DIPR model for values of $p$ ranging from 0.04 at the left up to 5.0 at the right. The distributions over product angles and energies arise from variation in the directions from which the reagents approach. The repulsion $F(t)$ was "switched on" in every case when the reagents were 5 Å apart. The masses corresponded to the reaction $K + Br_2 \to KBr + Br$. The dots, in the same figure, show the product angular and energy distributions from 3D classical trajectory calculations across potential energy hypersurfaces of a type designed for alkali metal plus halide reactions $M + XC \to M^+ + (X \cdot C)^-$ (see Kuntz et al., 1969a,b; surfaces without migration). Comparison of the DIPR model results with the 3D trajectories shows, for these cases, very good agreement.

The behavior of the model with variation in the parameter $p$ is instructive. As $p$ increases, (i) the angular scattering of the molecular product shifts from backward peaked, through sideways peaked, to forward peaked, (ii) the mean vibrational excitation in the products increases markedly, and (iii) the angular energy distributions become narrower. It is noteworthy not only that these effects correlate with $p$, but also that they correlate with one another.

Molecular beam experiments have provided substantial evidence for a correlation between (i) and (ii) (Herschbach, 1966). Reactions of alkali metal atoms with alkyl halides, $M + XR$, give markedly lower internal excitation and more backward peaked scattering than do reactions of alkali metal atoms with halogens, $M + XY$. The shift to forward scattering and high internal excitation, in the alkali metal atom reactions, also correlates with increased reactive cross section. It is tempting to suggest, therefore, that the forward scattering and high vibration are caused by the high impact parameter collisions, and this may be the case. (Trajectory calculations commonly show a correlation between increased impact parameter and increased forward scattering, but not necessarily increased vibration.) However, as more types of reaction of varying reactive cross sections are examined, it seems that the correlation between more forward scattering and enhanced internal excitation may prove to be more fundamental than the link between these quantities and the reactive cross section. The DIPR model results support this view since they show the angular distribution and energy distribution varying in concert over a wide range, though the reactive cross section is invariant. (The DIPR model, and the corresponding hypersurfaces for M + XC, make all approaches of M to within 5 Å of XC, reactive—so that $b_{max}$ = constant.)

The parameter that is varying widely in Fig. 25 is the parameter $p$ which, for approximately constant reagent collision energy, is to be interpreted as a change in the magnitude or the duration of the force (attractive or repulsive) between the reaction products. If we regard this force as repulsive (as in the previous paragraphs) then the *increasing* $p$ with increasing forward scattering and vibrational excitation in Fig. 25 should be interpreted as implying *decreasing* repulsive energy release. The DIPR model, therefore, shows forward scattering increasing with increasing attractive energy release, in a comparable though somewhat more striking fashion than do the trajectory calculations (see Fig. 10 of

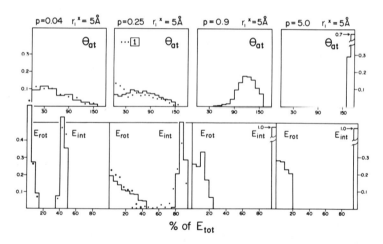

FIG. 25. The solid lines in the top row of figures are histograms of the differential cross section as predicted by the DIPR model for the values of $p$ indicated (note that backward molecular scattering is at the left of each box, forward scattering at the right). The solid lines in the bottom row are histograms of the percentage rotational and total internal energy, predicted by the DIPR model. The dots (open or closed) are located at the center of the horizontal bars on the histograms obtained by numerical integration of the 3D equations of motion for comparable potential energy hypersurfaces. Increasing $p$ from left to right in the figure corresponds to either increased reagent collision energy, or decreased duration of the product repulsion (based on Kuntz et al., 1969b).

Section II; equal-mass case $\mathbf{L} + \mathbf{LL}$). The effect is more striking here because the model, as its name implies, presupposes *direct* interaction. On very attractive surfaces, as already noted, secondary encounters can be expected to broaden the observed product distributions.

The parameter $p$ of the DIPR model will also increase if for a particular repulsive energy release (i.e., a particular chemical reaction) the collision energy is increased. This equivalence is intuitively reasonable since at an enhanced collision energy the products separate more rapidly, and the force between them (that has been shown above to be a cause of backward scattering and lowered vibrational excitation) has less time in which to affect the outcome; that is, the impulse will be less. The same thing can be expressed differently by saying that with increasing collision energy the dynamics approach the limit of "spectator stripping" (see Section III,B) in which limit the scattering is sharply forward, the major part of the product energy is in vibration, and both the angular and energy distributions are delta functions. The DIPR model shows that the more repulsive is the energy surface, and hence the larger is $a^0/c$, the higher will be the "stripping threshold energy" $T_s$, that is, the collision energy above which $>90\%$ of AB is scattered into the forward hemisphere. It had been proposed (Polanyi, 1967) that $T_s$ might constitute a useful index of the magnitude of the product interaction. The DIPR model provides a crude device for translating $T_s$ into quantitative information regarding the force between the products. Inspection of Fig. 25 shows that $T_s$ corresponds to $p^s \approx 1$. Since $p^s = v_0{}^s(c/a^0)$, a knowledge of $v^s$ leads to information concerning the constants governing $F(t)$ and hence the magnitude of the impulse applied to C.

In discussing simple impulsive models (2,a, above) it was noted that in certain cases the repulsive energy-release, $\mathscr{R}$, could be obtained from the experimental findings regarding product translational energy following photo-dissociation of the molecular reagent, BC. This approach has been combined with the DIPR model (by the same authors: Herschbach, 1973; Harris and Herschbach, 1974). The combination is termed DIPR–DIP, where DIP denotes "distributed as in photo-dissociation". Instead of having a single $\mathscr{R}$ (governed by the single parameter $p$) as in the normal DIPR formulation, a Gaussian distribution over $\mathscr{R}$ was obtained from the "reflection" of the thermal distribution of $r_{BC}$ separations in the bound state, onto the repulsive state from which photo-dissociation takes place. The DIPR model was used, in preference to the simple impulsive model, so that important effects arising from the initial collision energy and impact parameters would be included.

A serious weakness of the DIPR model is its failure to take account of the forces between A and B. The effect of attraction between A and B can be included in DIPR calculations in an approximate and nonphysical way by increasing the repulsion between B and C. It would be more satisfactory to use a model of the forced harmonic oscillator variety that takes account of the unique feature of the $T-V$ transfer problem as one meets it in chemistry. This unique feature would appear to be the fact that the oscillator has a characteristic frequency which is increasing to $\omega_{AB}$ and an equilibrium separation that is decreasing to $r^0_{AB}$ during the time that the repulsion $F(t)$ is operative. A model of this kind has been developed (Pattengill and Polanyi, 1974).

The model—termed FOTO, for Forced Oscillation of a Tightening Oscillator—assumes that reaction proceeds by the relaxation of a selected starting configuration A——B·C to give products AB + C. The extended A——B bond is treated as an harmonic oscillator of diminishing equilibrium separation and increasing force constant, being "forced" by a B·C repulsion of constant magnitude and finite duration. As the repulsion is released, A——B evolves from a fractional bond to a normal one. Pauling's bond-order relationships and Badger's rule suffice to parameterise the initial A——B·C configuration and the required time-dependences in terms of a single input parameter, namely the initial fractional bond-order of A——B. The model has been applied to 10 reactions for which some experimental data and trajectory results exist. The correspondence is encouraging. In contrast to the other simple models mentioned above, this model is sufficiently complete to embody recognisable analogues of "attractive," "mixed," and "repulsive" energy release. It is, therefore, no longer strictly a retreat-coordinate model.

## B. Switching Models

We include under this heading models which explicitly take account of forces operating in the approach coordinate and in the retreat coordinate. The first example, spectator stripping, is a model which applies in the limit of high reagent collision energy. Since all other models should reduce to this model it is somewhat arbitrary to include spectator stripping under a single heading (Sections III,A or III,B).

### 1. The Spectator Stripping Model

This model, which stems originally from nuclear physics (see Butler, 1957), was first applied to chemical reactions by Henglein and Muccini

(1962, 1963, 1965). Henglein and co-workers successfully employed the model for ion–molecule reactions occurring at high collision energies ($\gtrsim 5$ eV). The same model has been applied to the thermal reactions of alkali metal atoms with halogens (Datz and Minturn, 1964; Minturn *et al.*, 1966; Birely and Herschbach, 1966; Herschbach, 1966). The model has proved less satisfactory when applied to (even these exceptional) thermal reactions. This was to be expected since it postulates the existence of a limiting situation which is only likely to occur at high collision energy.

In its simplest form the spectator stripping model treats the molecule under attack, BC, as having no internal motion. Atom A approaches BC and "picks up" B while leaving C undisturbed. Viewed in the center of mass, C has an initial velocity and momentum opposed to that of the approaching atom; it retains that momentum after the encounter. The model implies a sudden "bond-switch," since it initially regards A as approaching BC, so that the momenta

$$p_A = -p_{BC}, \tag{3.5}$$

and then later (without any intervening regime), considers AB to be recoiling from C,

$$p'_{AB} = -p_C' \tag{3.6}$$

The sudden switch of the bond to A–B leaves atom C moving with the same center-of-mass velocity that it had in BC,

$$p_C' = m_C v_{BC}. \tag{3.7}$$

Atom C also retains its initial direction of motion, which was opposed to the direction of approach of A, that is, $\theta_C = 180°$. The spectator stripping model therefore predicts an angular distribution for the molecular reaction product that is pathologically forward scattered; a delta function centered on $\theta_{AB} = 0°$. The observation in molecular beam experiments of angular distributions with significant breadth does not automatically disqualify the spectator stripping model, since (apart from instrumental factors, such as variation in beam crossing angle and collision energy which produce breadth in the observed distribution) breadth in $\theta_C$ and hence $\theta_{AB}$ is introduced by the internal motion of BC prior to the collision (Herschbach, 1965; Birely, 1966). It is found, however, that these effects are not sufficient to account for the observed breadth in the center-of-mass product angular distribution.

The product energy distribution can also be calculated on the basis of the spectator stripping model. The model postulates that there is no energy transferred to C; any energy released in the course of the reaction must go, therefore, into internal excitation of AB. The other component in the product excitation is the energy arising from the collision. Some of the center-of-mass collision energy $T$ is carried away by particle C [cf., Eq. (3.7)]. Initially,

$$T = (p_A^2/2m_A) + (p_{BC}^2/2m_{BC}) = p_C^2(m_{ABC}m_{BC}/2m_A m_C^2), \qquad (3.8)$$

where $m_{ABC} = m_A + m_B + m_C$, $m_{BC} = m_B + m_C$. Finally

$$T' = p_C^2[(1/2m_{AB}) + (1/2m_C)]. \qquad (3.9)$$

Substituting (3.8) into (3.9),

$$T' = (m_A/m_{AB})(m_C/m_{BC})T = C_{A,C}T. \qquad (3.10)$$

[The factor $C_{A,C}$ appears in Eqs. (2.6), (3.1), and (3.19).] From Eq. (3.10) it is evident that $T' < T$. The balance of $T$ goes into internal excitation of the new molecule, AB.

It is to be expected that for some reactions it will be impossible to achieve the high collision energy at which the spectator stripping model can usefully be applied, since incipient AB will be dissociated by the energy $T-T'$. From Eq. (3.10) it appears that this is likely if $m_B$ is large. From the discussion of the DIPR model in Section III,A,2 it is evident that the stripping threshold energy $T_s$ (corresponding to 90% forward hemisphere scattering) is highest if the BC interaction is strong. For spectator stripping the collision energy must be substantially greater than this; $T_{ss} \gg T_s$ (Kuntz et al., 1969b), and the absolute magnitude of $T-T'$ may well be sufficiently great to dissociate AB. (Molecular beam experiments are particularly well suited to the measurement of $T' - T = Q$, which has therefore been given the name "translational exoergicity." In spectator stripping, $Q < 0$; at normal collision energies $Q$ may be large and positive due to energy liberated in the reaction being channeled into product translation.) It seems likely that there will be a substantial range of reactions for which the spectator stripping model is of little value at moderate collision energy, because of strong BC interaction, or at high collision energy, because of dissociation, $A+BC \rightarrow A+B+C$ (for an example of the latter behavior, see Doverspike et al., 1966). Nonetheless, for many ion–molecule reactions at high collision energies the model has achieved a considerable measure of success; in every case it has provided a valuable standard against which to measure the observed behavior.

It will be interesting, when information comes available concerning product rotational excitation for ion–molecule (and other) reactions at high collision energy, to compare the observed distributions with the predictions for spectator stripping (Kuntz, 1968). If $R$ is the distance between A and the center of mass of BC at the moment when C is uncoupled from B, and $\alpha$ is the angle between $R$ and the line joining B to C at this same moment, then (assuming that the motion is in the plane of the three atoms) the exit impact parameter is

$$b' = [m_A/(m_A + m_B)]b + (m_{ABC}m_B/m_{AB}m_{BC})\beta r_2^x, \qquad (3.11)$$

where $r_2^x$ is the BC separation at the time that the bond switch occurs and

$$\beta = b \cos \alpha/R - \sin \alpha(1 - (b/R)^2)^{1/2}.$$

If BC has no initial rotation then

$$J' = L - L' = \mu_{A,BC}v_{rel}b - \mu_{AB,C}v'_{rel}b'.$$

Since $v'_{rel} = (m_A/m_{AB})v_{rel}$, and $b'$ is given by Eq. (3.11),

$$J' = (m_A m_B/m_{AB})v_{rel}(b - m_C\beta r_2^x/m_{BC}). \qquad (3.12)$$

The product rotational energy is $(J')^2/2I_{AB}$, where $I_{AB}$ is the instantaneous moment of inertia of AB,

$$R' = (m_{ABC}m_B/m_{AB}m_{BC})[b - (m_C\beta r_2^0/m_{BC})]^2[T/(r_1^x)^2]. \qquad (3.13)$$

The internuclear separation $r_1^x$ is the AB distance at the moment that the bond switch occurs; $I = \mu_{AB} \cdot (r_1^x)^2$. The spectator stripping model predicts high values of $R'$ for collisions of large impact parameter $b$. Since these are the more probable impact parameters for reactions of large cross section, such as $M + XY$, the model predicts a rotational distribution peaked at high $J'$ for these reactions. An experimental study of the form of the RbBr rotational distribution, coming from the reaction $Rb + Br_2$, indicates by contrast that it peaks toward low $J'$, resembling a Boltzmann distribution (Grice et al., 1970).

## 2. Models with Repulsion

The limitations of the spectator stripping concept have led to various modified stripping models. The main objective has been to take some account of the forces on particle C—forces which are entirely neglected in the spectator stripping approach. Herschbach (1965) proposed an "elastic spectator" model in which particle C was presumed to bounce off AB. Henglein (1970) described a "recoil stripping" mechanism in which a B · C force is explicitly included (Section III,A,2). Since such models provide for large effects due to short-range forces, they represent a radical departure from spectator stripping.

Herschbach (1965) reformulated the dynamical problem in a way which allows inclusion of forces in the approach and in the retreat coordinates, by picturing the reactive event as a special type of elastic scattering: He called this the "optical potential" (one might term it quasi-elastic-scattering) model. The essence of the model was not the use of some particular form for the potential, but the use of the normal equations governing two-body elastic scattering in a central force field, to depict a reactive event.

When A approaches BC closely, some AB is regarded as coming into existence (a sudden "bond switch" has occurred). In the second half of the trajectory AB bounces off C; the potential energy that has been built up in the approach of A to BC becomes kinetic energy in the release of repulsion between AB and C. The product is scattered over a range of angles depending on initial impact parameter and the relative probability (determined by unspecified chemical forces) of the bond switch occurring in various A–B–C configurations. This latter consideration determines geometrically the relation between $b$ and $b'$. Obviously the outcome of an encounter is not fully determined unless the interaction potential prior to the bond switch (during the approach) and following it (during the retreat) is specified. If the interaction potential is characterized qualitatively as consisting of an outer zone of attraction and an inner zone of repulsion (Herschbach, 1966), then low impact parameter reactive collisions lead to backward scattering of molecular product, high impact parameter collisions to forward scattering. This broad generalization is not very sensitive to the relationship between $b$ and $b'$, that is, to the preferred A–B–C angle for reaction.

A more detailed model designed specifically for the case of ion–molecule reaction, but embodying a similar philosophy to the quasi-elastic-scattering model, has been developed by Wolfgang and co-workers

(Herman *et al.*, 1967; Hierl *et al.*, 1968; Wolfgang, 1969). The essential features of the model are a two-body interaction between A and BC in a field of force centered on BC, a sudden bond switch when $r_1$ (i.e., $r_{AB}$) reaches some critical value $r_1^x$ (called the "reaction radius"), followed by elastic rebound of the ejected atom C in a two-body trajectory governed by a field of force centered on AB. The model has been applied to ion–molecule reaction. The most studied example is shown in Fig. 26;

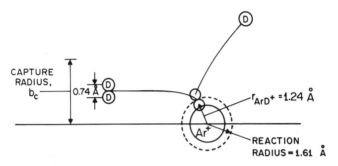

FIG. 26. A simple model of the ion–molecule reaction $Ar^+ + D_2 \rightarrow ArD^+ + D$. The collision is represented as a two-body interaction between $D_2$ and a fixed center-of-force at the center of $Ar^+$. A sudden bond switch occurs when $DDAr^+$ is collinear and the central D is a distance $r_1^x$ (called the "reaction radius") away from $Ar^+$. The central D remains attached to $Ar^+$. The outer D is elastically scattered and follows a two-body scattering trajectory under the influence of the same fixed center of force. This illustrates the "polarization stripping" model of Wolfgang and co-workers (Herman *et al.*, 1967).

$Ar^+ + D_2 \rightarrow ArD^+ + D$ (corresponding to $A + BC \rightarrow AB + C$). The central field of force is provided in the calculation exclusively by ion induced dipole attraction $U_{att}$ between A and BC during the approach, and a corresponding attraction $U'_{att}$ during the retreat. The dynamics can be followed through four stages: the initial condition of the reagents, not subscripted; the condition following application of $U_{att}$, subscripted 2; the condition following bond switching, subscripted 3; and the final state, superscripted with a prime. The translational energy at each stage can be calculated from that at the prior stage. The total translational energy at stage two is

$$T_2 = T + U_{att}. \tag{3.14}$$

By conservation of momentum,

$$T_{2,BC} = (m_A/m_{ABC})T_2. \tag{3.15}$$

After transfer, just as in spectator stripping, C continues with the same speed as it had in BC; $v_C = v_{BC}$, therefore,

$$T_{3,C} = (m_C/m_{BC})T_{2,BC} \tag{3.16}$$

and

$$T_{3,AB} = (m_C/m_{AB})T_{3,C}. \tag{3.17}$$

By analogy with Eq. (3.15),

$$T'_{AB} = (m_C/m_{ABC})T', \tag{3.18}$$

therefore,

$$v_{AB} = (2T'_{AB}/m_{AB})^{1/2}.$$

Combining equations,

$$T'_{AB} = (m_C/m_{ABC})[C_{A,C}(T + U_{att}) - U'_{att}], \tag{3.19}$$

where $C_{A,C} = (m_A/m_{AB})(m_C/m_{BC})$, as before. If $U_{att} = U'_{att} = 0$, or if $T$ is so large that these terms become negligibly small, Eq. (3.19) reduces to $T'_{AB} = (m_C/m_{ABC})C_{A,C}T$. Similarly $T_C'$ reduces to $T_C' = (m_A/m_{ABC}) \times C_{A,C}T$, so that $T'(= T'_{AB} + T_C') = C_{A,C}T$. This is the total product translational energy according to the spectator stripping model; see Eq. (3.10). It is the presence of $U_{att}$ and $U'_{att}$ that differentiates this model from the spectator stripping model.

The model has one adjustable parameter, the reaction radius $r_1^x$. This was adjusted to give the correct experimental $T'_{AB}$ for a single value of $T$ (chosen at low $T$ where the $T'_{AB}/T$ differs most markedly from the spectator stripping prediction). The model accounted very well for the manner in which $T'_{AB}/T$ approached the spectator stripping limit.

Isotopic effects provide a valuable testing ground for any model. Light and Chan (1969) extended the polarization stripping model so that it could be used to calculate the relative yield of $ArH^+/ArD^+$ from the reaction $Ar + HD^+$, as a function of collision energy. In place of the single reaction radius, they introduced the more general concept of a three-dimensional surface surrounding the molecule BC under attack. This surface was divided into three regions corresponding to reaction with B, reaction with C, and no reaction. In the case of $BC \equiv HD^+$ they noted that the distance from the center of force to the surface of reaction would be expected to be about the same for H and D. However, the solid angle within which D reaction can occur, measured from the center of mass of HD, will be significantly greater than the solid angle for H reaction. [A still more sophisticated treatment of the isotope problem, applied to $Ar^+ + HD$, which includes the torque that $Ar^+$ produces on HD, has been given by George and Suplinskas (1971b) in terms of their model, which is discussed below.]

The polarization stripping model makes an important further step in the gradual refinement of "simple models." When employed without further elaboration it is, nonetheless, subject to two criticisms. Applied to the ion–molecule reaction $Ar^+ + D_2$ it leads to an entirely reasonable reaction radius, $r_1^x = 1.61$ Å (compared with $r_1^0 = 1.24$ Å), but a rather large value for $U_{att}$ at this close approach of the ion to the molecule; $U_{att} \approx -0.5$ eV. An inherent limitation of the model is its failure to make provision for forces operative during the release of reaction energy consequent on the formation of a stronger bond from a weaker one (the reaction $Ar^+ + D_2 \rightarrow ArD^+ + D$ is probably about 34 kcal mole$^{-1}$ exothermic; this is too large to be due merely to the difference between $U_{att}$ and $U'_{att}$). One must suppose, as in the spectator stripping model, that all this energy somehow finds its way into internal excitation of the new bond, since there is no mechanism whereby it can become relative translation of the products. Chang and Light (1970) extended the polarization stripping model to the point where it could be used to predict product angular distributions. The intermediate ABC ($Ar^+D_2$) was taken to be linear at the moment that the bond switch occurred, and the products were treated as if they were separating initially under the influence of an AB · C impulse (this was termed the "impulsive reaction model"). It followed that

$$T_3 = C_{A,C}T_2,$$

where $T_2$ is the total relative translational energy of A + BC just before the bond switch, and $T_3$ just after. The energy that was being distributed impulsively between the products was the reagent collision energy plus energy accumulated in the approach to $r_1^x$ under the influence of $U_{att}$. The model made no provision for forces arising from the release of the "heat of reaction" (i.e., the reaction energy, referred to above).

Kuntz applied the DIPR model to the reaction $Ar^+ + D_2$ and found this model to be as successful in accounting for the dynamics as was the polarization stripping model. The DIPR model errs in the opposite direction to the polarization stripping model; in effect it takes $U_{att} = U'_{att} = 0$ and explains the dynamics exclusively in terms of the reagent velocities and the forces separating the products which the polarization stripping model ignores. The DIPR model postulates have the virtue that they permit inclusion of the effect (which can be substantial) os forces arising from the energy liberated by the reaction. A model that ie closer to reality would lie between the extremes exemplified by thf polarization stripping and the DIPR models.

Suplinskas and co-workers have explored a model which takes account of long-range attractive forces and also provides for a more detailed treatment of the short-range repulsions. The model evolved from a hard sphere treatment without long-range forces (Suplinskas, 1968). The billiard balls collided in pairs; the reactant atom, represented by a hard sphere, was incident on two hard spheres nearly in contact. Examination of the final velocities, as the billard balls separated, revealed whether or not one pair had a relative translational energy low enough to permit that pair to remain "bound," given the experimental binding energy for the pair in question. (The particles do not, of course, remain together in the calculation, since binding forces are absent.) A similar argument applied to the reagents permitted the inclusion of a requirement for "activation excitation"; it was required that the relative translational energy of the particles BC, struck by the attacking particle A, must exceed a critical value. As in the other simple models described above, vibration and rotation of the reactant molecule were neglected. The model was applied to the $Ar^+ + D_2$ reaction and its isotopic analogs. The effect of $U_{att}$ and $U'_{att}$ on the incoming and outgoing trajectories was included (George and Suplinskas, 1969, 1971a,b). The required activation excitation was taken to be 7.8 kcal mole$^{-1}$; this did not constitute a serious restriction on reaction probability, owing to the attraction between the reagents. The energy liberated by the reaction (beyond that arising from the difference between $U'_{att}$ and $U_{att}$) was assumed to go entirely into product translation. It was introduced by increasing the radial component of the relative velocity between the products, immediately following the bond switch, that is, at what corresponded to stage three of the polarization stripping model. A promising model for reactions between alkali metal atoms and alkyl iodides, $M + IR \rightarrow MI + R$, includes attractive and repulsive contributions in a comparable fashion (Grice and Hardin, 1971). In George and Suplinskas' hard sphere model the bond switch is regarded as occurring at the instant that BC attains an internal excitation (i.e., a relative translational energy) equal to the excitation energy required for reaction. This consideration barely arises for $M + IR$, since the energy barrier is approximately zero.

An interesting conclusion from this hard sphere model, known as the "kinematic model," is that the forward peaked distribution of $ArD^+$

observed experimentally (Chiang *et al.*, 1970) can only be reproduced if there is attraction $(U'_{\text{att}})$ between the reaction products. Since the DIPR model produces the forward scattering without inclusion of $U'_{\text{att}}$, a plausible interpretation of this finding is that the product attraction in the kinematic model is required in order to offset the effect of what would otherwise be an overwhelming tendency for the hard spheres to rebound under the influence of an impulsive B · C (or A · C) encounter.

The "kinematic model", like FOTO, is a fairly sophisticated type of simple model. It takes us a small part of the way back to the detailed models of Section II. Simple models are open to the criticism on the one hand that they embody unrealistic assumptions, and on the other that in an attempt to be realistic they fall short of the desired simplicity. Both types of criticism are valid, and neither need be a cause for despair. Simple models can only be expected to describe restricted types of chemical behavior; even then it is unlikely that they will reproduce the full details of so complex an event as a reactive encounter. The task ahead is to identify those simple models which depend for their simplicity on the retention of only the most important features of the real event.

## ACKNOWLEDGMENTS

We are grateful to Professor G. Karl for permission to use Table I, to Dr. W. H. Wong for permission to use Fig. 13, and to Dr. P. J. Kuntz for permission to use the DIPR model data at $p = 0.04$ embodied in Fig. 25. The data were taken from G. Karl, Ph.D. Thesis, University of Toronto (1964), W. H. Wong, Ph.D. Thesis, University of Toronto (1968), and P. J. Kuntz, Ph.D. Thesis, University of Toronto (1968). Financial support from the National Research Council of Canada, is gratefully acknowledged.

NOTE. A selection of recent references has been added in proof, but with only minor textual revisions.

## REFERENCES

ANDERSON, J. B. (1970). *J. Chem. Phys.* **52**, 3849.

ANLAUF, K. G., KUNTZ, P. J., MAYLOTTE, D. H., PACEY, P. D., and POLANYI, J. C. (1967). *Discuss. Faraday Soc.* **44**, 183.

ANLAUF, K. G., POLANYI, J. C., WONG, W. H., and WOODALL, K. B. (1968). *J. Chem. Phys.* **49**, 5189.

ANLAUF, K. G., MAYLOTTE, D. H., POLANYI, J. C., and BERNSTEIN, R. B. (1969). *J. Chem. Phys.* **51**, 5716.

ANLAUF, K. G., CHARTERS, P. E., HORNE, D. C., MACDONALD, R. G., MAYLOTTE, D. H., POLANYI, J. C., SKRLAC, W. J., TARDY, D. C., and WOODALL, K. B. (1970). *J. Chem. Phys.* **53**, 4091.

BASCO, N., and NORRISH, R. G. W. (1962). *Proc. Roy. Soc. (London)* **A268**, 291.

BENDER, C. F., O'NEIL, S. V., PEARSON, P. K., and SCHAEFER, H. F., III (1972). *Science* **176**, 1412.

BERNSTEIN, R. B., and RULIS, A. M. (1973). *Faraday Disc. Chem. Soc.* **55**, 293.

BIRELY, J. H. (1966). Ph.D. Thesis, Harvard Univ.

BIRELY, J. H., and HERSCHBACH, D. R. (1966). *J. Chem. Phys.* **44**, 1690.

BLAIS, N. (1968). *J. Chem. Phys.* **49**, 9.

BLAIS, N. (1969). *J. Chem. Phys.* **51**, 856.

BLAIS, N. C., and BUNKER, D. L. (1962). *J. Chem. Phys.* **37**, 2713.

BLAIS, N. C., and BUNKER, D. L. (1963). *J. Chem. Phys.* **39**, 315.

BORNE, T. B., and BUNKER, D. L. (1971). *J. Chem. Phys.* **55**, 4861.

BROOKS, P. R. (1969). *J. Chem. Phys.* **50**, 5031.

BROOKS, P. R. (1973). *Faraday Disc. Chem. Soc.* **55**, 299.

BROWN, P. J., and HAYES, E. F. (1971). *J. Chem. Phys.* **55**, 922.

BROWN, R., and KLEMPERER, W. (1964). *J. Chem. Phys.* **41**, 3072.

BUNKER, D. L. (1970). *In* "Molecular Beams and Reaction Kinetics" (Ch. Schlier, ed.), p. 355. Academic Press, New York.

BUNKER, D. L. (1971). *Methods Computational Phys.* **10**, 287.

BUNKER, D. L., and BLAIS, N. C. (1964). *J. Chem. Phys.* **41**, 2377.

BUNKER, D. L., and GORING-SIMPSON, E. A. (1973). *Faraday Disc. Chem. Soc.* **55**, 93.

BUNKER, D. L., and PARR, C. A. (1970). *J. Chem. Phys.* **52**, 5700.

BUNKER, D. L., and PATTENGILL, M. D. (1970). *J. Chem. Phys.* **53**, 3041.

BUTLER, S. T. (1957). *In* "Nuclear Stripping Reactions." Wiley, New York.

CARRINGTON, T., and POLANYI, J. C. (1972). *In* "Reaction Kinetics" (J. C. Polanyi, ed.) Chapter 5. MTP Int. Rev. of Sci., Med. and Tech. Publ. Co. Butterworths, London and Washington, D.C.

CHANG, D. T., and LIGHT, J. C. (1970). *J. Chem. Phys.* **52**, 5687.

CHAPMAN, S., and SUPLINSKAS, R. J. (1974). *J. Chem. Phys.* **60**, 248.

CHARTERS, P. E., PARR, C. A., and POLANYI, J. C. (1970). Some Concepts in Reaction Dynamics. A computer-animated film with sound commentary, available in 35 min. and 45 min. versions on loan from J.C.P. Shown at the *Conf. Potential-Energy Surfaces Chem.* Univ. of Calif., Santa Cruz, August 1970; see J. C. POLANYI (1971). IBM Publ. RA18, San Jose, California, p. 10.

CHIANG, M., GISLASON, E. A., MAHAN, B. H., TSAO, C. W., and WERNER, A. S. (1970). *J. Chem. Phys.* **52**, 2698.

CHUPKA, W. A. (1972). *In* "Ion-Molecule Reactions" (J. L. Franklin, ed.), Chapter 3. Plenum Press, New York.

CHUPKA, W. A., and RUSSELL, M. E. (1968). *J. Chem. Phys.* **49**, 5426.

CONROY, H. (1970). *In* "Molecular Beams and Reaction Kinetics" (Ch. Schlier, ed.), p. 349. Academic Press, New York.

COTTRELL, T. L., and McCOUBREY, J. C. (1961). *In* "Molecular Energy Transfer in Gases." Butterworths, London and Washington, D.C.

COWLEY, L. T., HORNE, D. S., and POLANYI, J. C. (1971). *Chem. Phys. Lett.* **12**, 144.

CSIZMADIA, I. G., POLANYI, J. C., ROACH, A. C., and WONG, W. H. (1969). *Can. J. Chem.* **47**, 4097.

CSIZMADIA, I. G., KARI, R. E., POLANYI, J. C., ROACH, A. C., and ROBB, M. A. (1970). *J. Chem. Phys.* **52**, 6205.

DATZ, S., and MINTURN, R. E. (1964). *J. Chem. Phys.* **41**, 1153.

DING, A. M. G., KIRSCH, L. J., PERRY, D. S., POLANYI, J. C., and SCHREIBER, J. L. (1973). *Faraday Disc. Chem. Soc.* **55**, 252.

DOUGLAS, D. J., POLANYI, J. C., and SLOAN, J. J. (1973). *J. Chem. Phys.* **59**, 6679.

DOVERSPIKE, L. D., CHAMPION, R. L., and BAILEY, T. L. (1966). *J. Chem. Phys.* **45**, 4385.

DUBRIN, J., and HENCHMAN, M. (1972). *In* "Reaction Kinetics" (J. C. Polanyi, ed.), Chapter 7. MTP Int. Rev. of Sci., Butterworths, London and Washington, D.C.

ELIASON, M. A., and HIRSCHFELDER, J. O. (1959). *J. Chem. Phys.* **30**, 1426.

EVANS, M. G., and POLANYI, M. (1938). *Trans. Faraday Soc.* **34**, 11.

EVANS, M. G., and POLANYI, M. (1939). *Trans. Faraday Soc.* **35**, 178.

FISK, G. A., MCDONALD, J. D., and HERSCHBACH, D. R. (1967). *Discuss. Faraday Soc.* **44**, 228.

FREUND, S. M., FISK, G. A., HERSCHBACH, D. R., and KLEMPERER, W. (1971). *J. Chem. Phys.* **54**, 2510.

GANN, R. G., OLLISON, W. M., and DUBRIN, J. (1971). *J. Chem. Phys.* **54**, 2304.

GEAR, C. W. (1971). *In* "Numerical Initial Value Problems in Ordinary Differential Equations." Prentice-Hall, Englewood Cliffs, New Jersey.

GEORGE, T. F., and SUPLINSKAS, R. J. (1969). *J. Chem. Phys.* **51**, 3666.

GEORGE, T. F., and SUPLINSKAS, R. J. (1971a). *J. Chem. Phys.* **54**, 1037.

GEORGE, T. F., and SUPLINSKAS, R. J. (1971b). *J. Chem. Phys.* **54**, 1046.

GERSH, M. E., and BERNSTEIN, R. B. (1971). *J. Chem. Phys.* **55**, 4661.

GERSH, M. E., and BERNSTEIN, R. B. (1972). *J. Chem. Phys.* **56**, 6131.

GILLEN, K. T., RULIS, A. M., and BERNSTEIN, R. B. (1971). *J. Chem. Phys.* **54**, 2831.

GIOUMOUSIS, G., and STEVENSON, D. P. (1958), *J. Chem. Phys.* **29**, 294.

GLASSTONE, S., LAIDLER, K. J., and EYRING, H. (1941). *In* "The Theory of Rate Processes." McGraw-Hill, New York.

GODFREY, M., and KARPLUS, M. (1968). *J. Chem. Phys.* **49**, 3602.

GORDON, R. (1971). *Methods Computational Phys.* **10**, 81.

GORDON, R. G. (1973). *Faraday Disc. Chem. Soc.* **55**, 22.

GRICE, R., and HARDIN, D. R. (1971). *Mol. Phys.* **21**, 805.

GRICE, R., MOSCH, J. E., SAFRON, S. A., and TOENNIES, J. P. (1970). *J. Chem. Phys.* **53**, 3376.

HALTON, J. H. (1970). A Retrospective and Prospective Survey of the Monte Carlo Method, *SIAM Rev.* **12**, 1.

HAMMOND, G. S. (1955). *J. Amer. Chem. Soc.* **77**, 334.

HARMS, S. H., and WYATT, R. E. (1972). *J. Chem. Phys.* **57**, 2722.

HARRIS, R. M., and HERSCHBACH, D. R. (1971). *J. Chem. Phys.* **54**, 3652.

HARRIS, R. M., and HERSCHBACH, D. R. (1973). *Faraday Disc. Chem. Soc.* **55**, 121.

HARRIS, R. M., and HERSCHBACH, D. R. (1974). *Chem. Revs.* (In preparation).

HENGLEIN, A. (1970). *In* "Molecular Beams and Reaction Kinetics" (Ch. Schlier, ed.), p. 139. Academic Press, New York.

HENGLEIN, A., and MUCCINI, G. A. (1962). *Z. Naturforsch.* **17a**, 452.

HENGLEIN, A., and MUCCINI, G. A. (1963). *Z. Naturforsch.* **18a**, 735.

HENGLEIN, A., and MUCCINI, G. A. (1965). *J. Chem. Phys.* **43**, 1048.

HERMAN, Z., KERSTETTER, J., ROSE, T., and WOLFGANG, R. (1967). *Discuss. Faraday Soc.* **44**, 123.

HERSCHBACH, D. R. (1965). *J. Appl. Opt. Suppl.* **2**, 128.

HERSCHBACH, D. R. (1966). *In* "Molecular Beams" (J. Ross, ed.), Chapter 9. Wiley (Interscience), New York.

HERSCHBACH, D. R. (1971). *Conf. Potential Energy Surfaces Chem.* (W. A. Lester, Jr., ed.), Publ. RA18, p. 44. IBM Res. Lab., San Jose, California.

HERSCHBACH, D. R. (1973). *Faraday Disc. Chem. Soc.* **55**, 233.

HERZBERG, G. (1950). *In* "Molecular Spectra and Molecular Structure," Vol. I, Spectra of Diatomic Molecules. Van Nostrand Reinhold, Princeton, New Jersey.

HERZFELD, K. F., and LITOVITZ, T. A. (1959). *In* "Absorption and Dispersion of Ultrasonic Waves." Academic Press, New York.

HIERL, P., HERMAN, Z., KERSTETTER, J., and WOLFGANG, R. (1968). *J. Chem. Phys.* **48**, 4319.

HIRSCHFELDER, J. O., and DAHLER, J. S. (1956). *Proc. Nat. Acad. Sci.* **42**, 363.

HOCHSTIM, A. R., and SHULER, K. E. (1967). *J. Chem. Phys.* **47**, 1894.

HODGSON, B. A., and POLANYI, J. C. (1971). *J. Chem. Phys.* **55**, 4745.

HOLDY, E. K., KLOTZ, L. C., and WILSON, K. R. (1970). *J. Chem. Phys.* **52**, 4588.

HULL, T. E., ENRIGHT, W. H., FELLEN, B. M., and SEDGWICK, A. E. (1971). Dept. of Computer Science Technical Report No. 29. University of Toronto.

JAFFE, R. L., and ANDERSON, J. B. (1971). *J. Chem. Phys.* **54**, 2224.

JEPSEN, D. W., and HIRSCHFELDER, J. O. (1959). *Proc. Nat. Acad. Sci.* **45**, 249.

JOHNSTON, H. S. (1960). *Advan. Chem. Phys.* **3**, 131.

JOHNSTON, H. S. (1966). *In* "Gas Phase Reaction Rate Theory," pp. 80, 209, 339. Ronald Press, New York.

JOHNSTON, H. S., and PARR, C. (1963). *J. Amer. Chem. Soc.* **85**, 2544.

KARL, G. (1964). Ph.D. Thesis, Univ. of Toronto.

KARL, G., KRUUS, P., and POLANYI, J. C. (1967). *J. Chem. Phys.* **46**, 224.

KARPLUS, M. (1970a). *In* "Molecular Beams and Reaction Kinetics" (Ch. Schlier, ed.), p. 320. Academic Press, New York.

KARPLUS, M. (1970b). *In* "Molecular Beams and Reaction Kinetics" (Ch. Schlier, ed.), p. 372. Academic Press, New York.

KARPLUS, M. (1970c). *In* "Molecular Beams and Reaction Kinetics" (Ch. Schlier, ed.), p. 407. Academic Press, New York.

KARPLUS, M., and RAFF, L. M. (1964). *J. Chem. Phys.* **41**, 1267.

KARPLUS, M., PORTER, R. N., and SHARMA, R. D. (1965). *J. Chem. Phys.* **43**, 3259.

KING, D. L., and HERSCHBACH, D. R. (1973). *Faraday Disc. Chem. Soc.* **55**, 331.

KINSEY, J. L. (1971a). *J. Chem. Phys.* **54**, 1206.

KINSEY, J. L. (1971b). *Math. Comput. Suppl.* **25**, C.

KINSEY, J. L. (1972). *In* "Reaction Kinetics" (J. C. Polanyi, ed.), Chapter 6. MTP Int. Rev. of Sci., Med. and Tech. Publ. Co. Butterworths, London and Washington, D.C.

KOEPPL, G. W., and KARPLUS, M. (1971). *J. Chem. Phys.* **55**, 4667.

KRAUSS, M. (1970). *Amer. Rev. Phys. Chem.* **21**, 39.

KRAUSS, M. (1971). *Conf. Potential Energy Surfaces* (W. A. Lester, Jr., ed.), Publ. RA18, p. 6. IBM Res. Lab., San Jose, California.

KUNTZ, P. J. (1968). Ph.D. Thesis, Univ. of Toronto.

KUNTZ, P. J. (1970). *Trans. Faraday Soc.* **66**, 2980.

KUNTZ, P. J., NEMETH, E. M., POLANYI, J. C., ROSNER, S. D., and YOUNG, C. E. (1966). *J. Chem. Phys.* **44**, 1168.

KUNTZ, P. J., NEMETH, E. M., and POLANYI, J. C. (1969a). *J. Chem. Phys.* **50**, 4607.

KUNTZ, P. J., MOK, M. H., and POLANYI, J. C. (1969b). *J. Chem. Phys.* **50**, 4623.

KUNTZ, P. J., NEMETH, E. M., POLANYI, J. C., and WONG, W. H. (1970). *J. Chem. Phys.* **52**, 4654.

LaBudde, R. A., Kuntz, P. J., Bernstein, R. B., and Levine, R. D. (1973). *Chem. Phys. Lett.* **19**, 7.

Landau, L. D., and Lifschitz, E. M. (1960). *In* "Mechanics," p. 61. Addison-Wesley, Reading, Massachusetts.

Landau, L. D., and Teller, E. (1936). *Phys. Z. Soujetunion* **10**, 34.

Langevin, P. (1905). *Ann. Chim. Phys.* **5**, 245.

Lee, Y. T. (1972). *In* "Physics of Electronic and Atomic Collisions" (T. R. Govers and F. J. deHeer, eds.) (VII ICPEAC). North Holland, Amsterdam, p. 357.

Lee, Y. T., Le Breton, P. E., McDonald, J. D., and Herschbach, D. R. (1969). *J. Chem. Phys.* **51**, 455.

Lee, Y. T., Gordon, R. J., and Herschbach, D. R. (1971). *J. Chem. Phys.* **54**, 2410.

LeRoy, R. L. (1969). *J. Phys. Chem.* **73**, 4338.

Le Roy, D. J., Ridley, B. A., and Quickert, K. A. (1967). *Discuss. Faraday Soc.* **44**, 92.

Levine, R. D. (1969). *In* "Quantum Mechanics of Molecular Rate Processes," Oxford Univ. Press (Clarendon), London and New York.

Light, J. C. (1971). *Methods Computational Phys.* **10**, 111.

Light, J. C., and Chan, S. (1969). *J. Chem. Phys.* **51**, 1008.

Light, J. C., and Lin, J. (1965). *J. Chem. Phys.* **43**, 3209.

Light, J. C., Ross, J., and Shuler, K. E. (1969). *In* "Kinetic Processes in Gases and Plasmas" (A. R. Hochstim, ed.), p. 281. Academic Press, New York.

Lin, S. H., and Eyring, H. (1971). *Proc. Nat. Acad. Sci. U.S.* **68**, 402.

Liu, B. (1973). *J. Chem. Phys.* **58**, 1925.

Magee, J. L. (1940). *J. Chem. Phys.* **8**, 687.

Mahan, B. H. (1970). *J. Chem. Phys.* **52**, 5221.

Malerich, C. J., and Davis, D. R. (1971). *J. Chem. Phys.* **55**, 4141.

Marcus, R. A. (1968). *J. Chem. Phys.* **49**, 2610.

Marcus, R. A. (1970). *J. Chem. Phys.* **53**, 604.

Marcus, R. A. (1973). *Faraday Disc. Chem. Soc.* **55**, 9.

Marron, M. T., and Bernstein, R. B. (1972). "Impulsive Model for Reactive Collisions," Univ. of Wisconsin Theoretical Chemistry Institute Report WIS-TCI-470, 25 February.

McDonald, J. D. (1973). *Faraday Disc. Chem. Soc.* **55**, 372.

McDonald, J. D. (1971). Ph.D. Thesis, Harvard Univ.

McDonald, J. D., and Herschbach, D. R. (1972). Private communication.

McDonald, J. D., Le Breton, P. R., Lee, Y. T., and Herschbach, D. R. (1972). *J. Chem. Phys.* **56**, 769.

McLean, A. D. (1971). *Conf. Potential Energy Surfaces* (W. A. Lester, Jr., ed.), Publ. RA18, p. 87. IBM Res. Lab., San Jose, California.

Melton, L. A., and Gordon, R. G. (1969). *J. Chem. Phys.* **51**, 5449.

Menzinger, M., and Wolfgang, R. (1969). *Angew. Chem. Int. Ed.* **8**, 438.

Messiah, A. (1968). *In* "Quantum Mechanics," Vol. I, p. 240. Wiley, New York.

Miller, G., and Light, J. (1971a). *J. Chem. Phys.* **54**, 1635.

Miller, G., and Light, J. (1971b). *J. Chem. Phys.* **54**, 1643.

Miller, W. B., Safron, S. A., and Herschbach, D. R. (1967). *Discuss. Faraday Soc.* **44**, 108.

Miller, W. B., Safron, S. A., and Herschbach, D. R. (1972). *J. Chem. Phys.* **56**, 3581.

Minturn, R. E., Datz, S., and Becker, R. L. (1966). *J. Chem. Phys.* **44**, 1149.

Mok, M. H., and Polanyi, J. C. (1969). *J. Chem. Phys.* **51**, 1451.

Mok, M. H., and Polanyi, J. C. (1970). *J. Chem. Phys.* **53**, 4588.
Moran, T. F., and Friedman, L. (1965). *J. Chem. Phys.* **42**, 2391.
Morokuma, K., and Karplus, M. (1971). *J. Chem. Phys.* **55**, 63.
Morokuma, K., Pedersen, L., and Karplus, M. (1967). *J. Amer. Chem. Soc.* **89**, 5064.
Morokuma, K., Eu, B. C., and Karplus, M. (1969). *J. Chem. Phys.* **51**, 5193.
Muckerman, J. T. (1971). *J. Chem. Phys.* **54**, 1155.
Muckerman, J. T. (1972). *J. Chem. Phys.* **56**, 2997; **57**, 3388.
Nomura, Y. (1971). M.Sc. Thesis, Univ. of Toronto, Toronto, Canada.
Nomura, Y., and Polanyi, J. C. (1974). *J. Chem. Phys.* (to be published).
Odiorne, T. J., Brooks, P. R., and Kasper, J. V. V. (1971). *J. Chem. Phys.* **55**, 1980.
Ogg, R. A., and Polanyi, M. (1935). *Trans. Faraday Soc.* **31**, 604.
Parker, J..H., and Pimentel, G. C. (1969). *J. Chem. Phys.* **51**, 91.
Parr, C. A., Polanyi, J. C., and Wong, W. H. (1973). *J. Chem. Phys.* **58**, 5.
Parrish, D. D., and Herm, R. R. (1969). *J. Chem. Phys.* **51**, 5467.
Parrish, D. D., and Herm, R. R. (1970). *J. Chem. Phys.* **53**, 2431.
Pattengill, M. D., and Polanyi, J. C. (1974). *J. Chem. Phys.* **3**, 1.
Pechukas, P., Light, J. C., and Rankin, C. (1966). *J. Chem. Phys.* **44**, 794.
Perry, D. S., Polanyi, J. C., and Wilson, C. W. (1974a). *Chem. Phys. Lett.* **24**, 484.
Perry, D. S., Polanyi, J. C., and Wilson, C. W. (1974b). *Chem. Phys.* **3**, 317.
Polanyi, J. C. (1959). *J. Chem. Phys.* **31**, 1338.
Polanyi, J. C. (1962). *In* "Transfert d'Energie dans les Gaz" (R. Stoops, ed.), pp. 177, 526. Wiley (Interscience), New York.
Polanyi, J. C. (1963). *J. Quant. Spectrosc. Radiat. Transfer* **3**, 471.
Polanyi, J. C. (1965). *J. Appl. Opt. Suppl.* **2**, 109.
Polanyi, J. C. (1967). *Discuss. Faraday Soc.* **44**, 293.
Polanyi, J. C. (1972). *Accounts Chem. Res.* **5**, 161.
Polanyi, J. C. (1973). *Faraday Disc. Chem. Soc.* **55**, 389.
Polanyi, J. C., and Schreiber, J. L. (1972). Unpublished work.
Polanyi, J. C., and Schreiber, J. L. (1973). *Faraday Disc. Chem. Soc.* **55**, 372.
Polanyi, J. C., and Sloan, J. J. (1972). *J. Chem. Phys.* **57**, 4988.
Polanyi, J. C., and Tardy, D. C. (1969). *J. Chem. Phys.* **51**, 5717.
Polanyi, J. C., and Wong, W. H. (1969). *J. Chem. Phys.* **51**, 1439.
Polanyi, J. C., and Woodall, K. B. (1972). *J. Chem. Phys.* **57**, 1574.
Polanyi, M. (1932). *In* "Atomic Reactions." Williams and Norgate, London.
Polanyi, M., and Wigner, E. (1928). *Z. Phys. Chem.* **A139**, 439.
Porter, R. N., and Karplus, M. (1964). *J. Chem. Phys.* **40**, 1105.
Porter, R. N., Sims, L. B., Thompson, D. L., and Raff, L. M. (1973). *J. Chem. Phys.* **58**, 2855.
Preston, R. K., and Tully, J. C. (1971). *J. Chem. Phys.* **54**, 4297.
Raff, L. M. (1966). *J. Chem. Phys.* **44**, 1202.
Ridley, B. A., Schultz, R. W., and Le Roy, D. J. (1966). *J. Chem. Phys.* **44**, 3344.
Ross, J. (1970). *In* "Molecular Beams and Reaction Kinetics" (Ch. Schlier, ed.), p. 392. Academic Press, New York.
Sato, S. (1955). *J. Chem. Phys.* **23**, 592, 2465.
Schafer, T. P., Siska, P. E., Parson, J. M., Tully, F. P., Wong, Y. C., and Lee, Y. T. (1970). *J. Chem. Phys.* **53**, 3385.
Shipsey, E. J. (1969). *J. Chem. Phys.* **50**, 2685.
Shipsey, E. J. (1972). *J. Chem. Phys.* **56**, 3843.

SHIZGAL, B., and KARPLUS, M. (1970). *J. Chem. Phys.* **52**, 4262.

SHIZGAL, B., and KARPLUS, M. (1971). *J. Chem. Phys.* **54**, 4345, 4357.

SHREIDER, Y. A. (1966). *In* "The Monte Carlo Method." Pergamon, Oxford.

SHULER, K. (1968). *In* "Chemische Elementarprozesse" (H. Hartmann, ed.), p. 1. Springer-Verlag, Berlin and New York.

SHULER, K. E., and ZWANZIG, R. (1960). *J. Chem. Phys.* **33**, 1778.

SLATER, N. B. (1959). *In* "Theory of Unimolecular Reactions." Methuen, London.

SMITH, I. W. M. (1967). *Discuss. Faraday Soc.* **44**, 194.

SMITH, I. W. M., and WOOD, P. M. (1973). *Mol. Phys.* **25**, 441.

STEINFELD, J., and SCHWEID, A. N. (1970). *J. Chem. Phys.* **53**, 3304.

STEINWEDEL, H., and JENSEN, J. H. D. (1947). *Z. Naturforsch.* **2a**, 125.

SUESS, H. (1940). *Z. Phys. Chem.* **B45**, 297, 312.

SUPLINSKAS, R. J. (1968). *J. Chem. Phys.* **49**, 5046.

TULLY, J. C. (1973). *Ber. Bunsen-Gesells. f. phys. Chem.* **77**, 557.

TULLY, J. C., and PRESTON, R. K. (1971). *J. Chem. Phys.* **55**, 562.

WAHL, A. C., and DAS, G. (1971). *Conf. Potential Energy Surfaces* (W. A. Lester, Jr., ed.), Publ. RA18, p. 83. IBM Res. Lab., San Jose, California.

WALL, F. T., HILLER, L. A., and MAZUR, J. (1958). *J. Chem. Phys.* **29**, 255.

WALL, F. T., HILLER, L. A., and MAZUR, J. (1961). *J. Chem. Phys.* **35**, 1284.

WESTENBERG, A. A., and DE HAAS, H. (1967). *J. Chem. Phys.* **47**, 1393.

WHITTAKER, E. T. (1961). *In* "A Treatise on the Analytical Dynamics of Particles and Rigid Bodies." Cambridge Univ. Press, London and New York.

WIDOM, B. (1971). *J. Chem. Phys.* **55**, 44.

WILKINS, R. L. (1973). *J. Chem. Phys.* **58**, 3038.

WOLFGANG, R. (1969). *Accounts Chem. Res.* **2**, 248.

WYATT, R. E. (1972). *J. Chem. Phys.* **56**, 390.

# Author Index

Numbers in italics refer to the pages on which the complete references are listed.

## A

Abrahamson, A. A., 250, *371*
Acrivos, A., 61, *72*
Airey, J. R., 322, 323, 324, 341, 355, *371*
Albrecht, A. C., 126, *185*
Alder, B. J., 249, *379*
Alfrey, T., 58, *72*
Allen, R. H., 58, *72*
Allison, A. C., 196, *225*
Amdur, I., 294, 295, *376*
Ames, W. F., 60, *72*
Amundson, N. R., 61, *72, 74*
Anderson, J. B., 238, 241, 325, 356, *371,*
   433, 446, *481, 484*
Anderson, R. W., 317, 336, *371, 372*
Anderson, V. E., 319, *374*
Andres, R. P., 238, *371*
Anlauf, K. G., 324, 355, 366, 368, *372, 376,*
   399, 400, 401, 416, 417, 421, 427, 428,
   433, 446, *481*
Aquilanti, V., 317, *372*
Arbesman, R. W., 61, *72*
Aris, R., 60, 61, *72, 73*
Armstrong, W. D., *372*
Ashkenas, H., 240, *372*
Aten, J. A., 317, 318, *372, 378*
Auerbach, D., *372*
Austin, B., 166, *185*
Averson, A. E., *75*

## B

Bader, R. F. W., 168, 169, 170, 171, 180,
   *185*
Baede, A. P. M., 284, 317, 318, *372, 378,*
   *379*
Bailey, T. L., 474, *483*
Bak, T. A., 15, 50, 61, *72*
Baker, E., *376*
Bankwitz, C., 54, *72*

Barwig, P., 275, *372*
Basco, N., 459, *482*
Basham, J. A., 47, *72*
Batalli-Cosmovici, Ch., *372*
Bauer, E., 223, *225,* 316, *372*
Beck, D,, 251, 268, 275, 282, 307, 308,
   325, 336, 361, *372, 378*
Becker, R. L., 457, 473, *485*
Bender, C. F., *372,* 412, *482*
Bennett, D. E., 120, *120*
Bennewitz, H. G., 244, 283, 284, 293, 295,
   324, 364, *372*
Benson, A. A., 47, *72*
Benson, S. W., 210, *225*
Berend, G. C., 210, *225*
Bergeron, G., 210, *225*
Berkowitz, J., 356, *374*
Bernstein, R. B., 119, *120, 120,* 237, 244, 247,
   258, 259, 264, 265, 268, 309, 321, 322,
   323, 324, 328, 329, 354, 355, 357, 358,
   *372, 373, 375, 376, 377, 379, 380,* 396,
   400, 402, 446, 458, 469, *481, 482, 483,*
   *485*
Berry, M. V., 264, *373*
Berry, R. S., 317, *375*
Bersohn, R., 126, *186, 373*
Bertoncini, P., 249, *373*
Beuhler, R. J., 357, 358, *373*
Bickes, R. W., 247, 290, 328, *373*
Bird, R. B., 115, 116, 117, *120,* 191, *226,*
   251, 252, 288, *376*
Birely, J. H., 323, 329, 333, 334, 338, 341,
   361, *373, 381,* 473, *482*
Bjerre, A., 223, *225*
Blais, N. C., 325, 335, 336, 361, *373, 374,*
   413, 418, 419, 423, 433, 451, *482*
Blythe, A. R., 309, 321, *373*
Boddington, F., 43, *72*
Bodenstein, M., 16, 21, *72*
Boerboom, A. J. H., 310, *380*

489

# Subject Index

## A

Activation energies, energy dependence of in reactive scattering, 352

Alkali atoms
  angular distributions of, 340
  energy partitioning for, 370
  nonreactive scattering studies of, 350

Alkali reactions, beam techniques in, 319-320

Alkalyl halide, reaction with alkali metal atom, 458, 469

Alkali metal atom, reaction with halogens, 456-457

Angular distributions, of reactive scattering, 344-346

Atom-atom potential, radial dependence in, 250

atom-atom scattering, research in, 249

Atom-molecule collision processes, 235

Attractive potential energy surface, 418-430

Automomous systems, in reaction kinetics, 69

## B

Backward scattering, 337-344

BBGKY (Bogolubov, Born-Green, Kirkwood, Yvon) equations
  Boltzmann equations and, 107-109
  in kinetic theory, 83-86, 88, 119
  quantum mechanical, 95-96

Beam detectors, in molecular beam scattering experiments, 246-248

Beam scattering, see Molecular beam scattering

Beer's law, 283

Bimolecular reactions, 171-179
  alkali metal atom plus halogen reactions in, 456-457
  attractive and repulsive energy surfaces in, 418-430
  barrier location in, 435-449

Bond Energy Bond Order Method in, 444-446

center-of-mass trajectory in, 428

classical trajectory method in, 403-412

cross sections, in, 385-389

cross sections vs. rate constants in, 389-398

data interpretation in, 409-412

detailed models in, 402-454

detailed rate constants in, 398-400

detailed rate equation in, 390

direct interaction with product repulsion, (DPR) model in, 420-422, 467-468

dynamics of, 383-481

entry and exit valleys in, 432

equations of motion in, 407-409

experimental microscopic and macroscopic results in, 400

Forced Oscillation of a Tightening Oscillator (FOTO) model in, 472, 481

gradual force in, 462-472

hyperbolic map function (HMF) in, 413 413-414

initial conditions in, 403-407

ion-molecule reactions and, 457-458

macroscopic vs. microscopic, 383-402

kinematic model of, 480-481

light atom anomaly in, 431-433

minimun energy path of collinear surface in, 434

mixed energy release in, 430-435

models with repulsion in, 476-481

potential energy surfaces in, 412-414

potential hollows in, 449-454

product attribute distribution functions in, 411

product energy distribution in, 474

rate constant in, 384-385

reduced activator energy in, 394

repulsive force in, 460-462

retreat coordinate in, 458-460

simple methods in, 454-481

500